Northern
California

ISBN 978-0-88150-832-1

Cover photo © Layne Kennedy
All interior photos by Michele Bigley unless otherwise noted
Book design by Bodenweber Design
Page composition by PerfecType, Nashville, TN
Maps by Mapping Specialists Ltd., Madison, WI © 2009 The Countryman Press

Published by The Countryman Press, P.O. Box 748, Woodstock, Vermont 05091

Distributed by W. W. Norton & Company, Inc., 500 Fifth Avenue, New York, NY
10110

Printed in the United States of America

10 9 8 7 6 5 4 3 2 1

DEDICATION

For Eddie, Kai, Mom, and Dad for always traveling with me . . .

And for Grumpy, who is not the first road-tripper in my clan, but is one of the best.

EXPLORE WITH US!

Welcome to the first edition of *Northern California: An Explorer's Guide.* Unlike most guidebooks, I have highlighted both tourist attractions and Northern California's diverse communities, including a number of locally favored (and by nature, under-the-tourist-radar) destinations. However, understanding that local townsfolk appreciate some level of sacredness to their secret spots, I have chosen to include only tried and true (and for the most part safe) adventures. In these pages you will be privy to heaps of less-traveled waterfall hikes and hidden restaurants (as well as the superstar sights to see), but you probably will have to make friends with some locals to learn about that little-known swimming hole on private property. However, I have included a few of my favorite Northern California hidden gems and up-to-date Nor Cal news and changes on my blog: michelebigleysnorcaladvice.blogspot.com.

Just so you know, we did not charge innkeepers, restaurants, or outfitters to be included in this book. In addition, I've included zillions of Web sites throughout these pages, which I know will be a great resource for you; however, the Internet has actually increased the need for opinionated guidebooks like this one. I can't tell you how many inns looked like the Queen's summer home online, but when I saw the property, there were stains on the sheets and curtains falling off their rods. I have spent the last six months on the road snooping around to find the best deals and unexplored gems for you. So sit back, grab a cup of coffee, and enjoy reading about the history, humorous tidbits, wealth of activities, lodging, and restaurants, from Big Sur to Yosemite, and all the way to the Oregon border.

WHAT'S WHERE

In the beginning of this book you'll find a list of special highlights, with important information and advice on everything from gold panning to weather. Think of it as a cheat sheet to what you'll find in this amazing and huge region.

PRICES

Please don't hold us (or the listed innkeepers) responsible for the rates listed as of press time in 2009. Changes are inevitable. California has a statewide lodging tax of 10 percent and an average sales tax of 7.5 percent (though each city decides on its own sales tax, with some as high as 8 percent).

SMOKING

California enforces a statewide ban on smoking in restaurants, bars, nightclubs, hotels, and within 10 to 15 feet of these establishments. There is even talk about banning smoking in some public places.

RESTAURANTS

Note the distinction between *Dining Out* and *Eating Out.* By nature, the restaurants listed in the *Eating Out* section are generally inexpensive, except in Napa and San Francisco.

KEY TO SYMBOLS

✐   The kid-friendly crayon symbol appears next to listings with special appeal to young people.

♿   The wheelchair symbol appears next to listings that are partially or fully handicap accessible.

🐾   The dog paw symbol appears next to lodgings that accept pets. In general, you can expect to pay a fee for letting Duke the dog or Luna the cat come along. Make sure to tell the owners upon your reservation that you plan to bring an animal.

Y   The martini glass symbol appears next to restaurants with bars or drinking establishments.

☘   The blue ribbon symbol appears next to lodging and restaurants that give you an exceptional deal for your money.

∞   The wedding ring symbol appears next to facilities that serve as venues for weddings and civil unions.

"1"   The Wi-Fi symbol indicates lodgings that offer wireless or data ports. In many cases, the more expensive hotels charge a fee for this while B&Bs and inns do not.

▼   The triangle symbol indicates lodgings that go out of their way to welcome LGBT travelers.

LODGING PRICES

The prices listed range from low season to high season rates. On summer weekends and holidays (especially on the coast), prices can double. I have not included tax in the prices.

$	under $100
$$	$101–200
$$$	$201–300
$$$$	over $300

DINING PRICES

The prices listed do not include drinks, tax, or gratuity (which is normally 15 percent of your total bill). Prices are generally for an entrée (except for the occasional prix fixe tasting menu). Note that San Francisco requires all businesses to offer health insurance to their workers; many restaurants tack on an extra few bucks to cover this cost.

$	Under $10
$$	$10–19
$$$	$20–29
$$$$	Over $30

We would appreciate your comments and corrections about places you visit or know well. Please email Michele at mishmell2@mac.com or write Explorer's Guide Editor, The Countryman Press, P.O. Box 748, Woodstock, Vermont 05091.

ACKNOWLEDGMENTS

This book would not be possible without the assistance of The Countryman Press crew: Kermit Hummel, Jennifer Thompson, Lisa Sacks, Douglas Yeager, Julie Nelson, and my mentor and often my mental savior, Kim Grant. Nor would you be able to read these words as easily but for the meticulous eye of Sandy Rodgers.

Here in Northern California, the following people helped direct me towards the best the state has to offer, and most times they were correct: Thanks to Michele Mandell, Diana Gil-Osorio, Dan McGuire, Kate Colby, Tanya Houseman, Jody Franklin, Lucy Steffens, Tara Melinchuk, Karen Whitaker, Charles Graver, Kelly Chamberlain, Jamie Law, Keri Hanson, Lisa Sesto, Trisha Clayton, Aphrodite Caserta, Circe Sher, Jamie Williams, Kellie James, Richard Stenger, Cynthia Traina, Lisa Rogovin, Greg Silva, John Hickock, Don Martine, Nina Laramore, Eden Umble, Jeanne Sullivan, Brian Larsen, Michael and Stephanie McCaffrey, Christina Glynn, Andy Troia, Katie Besmer, Emile Gourieux, Koleen Hamblin, Erin and Carl Schemmler, Britt Bowles, Autumn Cobb, Jennifer Boyd, Sarah Logan, Kris McMillan, Candy Apple Blossom, Emily Polsby, Kendrick Petty, Vikram Seshadri, Joan Caputi, Valeska Muromoto, Heidi Darling, Nyna Cox, Brenda Hughes, Kevin Kopjak, Mary Mancera, Richard Kannapell, Kenny Karst, Anna Davies, and Charlie Jonas (most especially for letting me steal Eddie on more days than you would have liked). There are many more people who offered sage advice on this edition, and if I spaced on including your name, I sincerely apologize. Know that you are appreciated.

Anne Mandler appeared, like a morning latte after a night of nursing a new baby, to contribute her favorite locations in Calaveras County, and for that I offer many thanks. Taylor Williams and Emily Bertolino made having only six months to write a first edition manageable by their blessed research skills. For all their hard work and slave labor, I owe them each heaps of gratitude.

For moral support I need to offer humble appreciation to Linda Lou, Coralissa and Ivan Delaforce, Ali Nachman, and Oliver Reyes; to Julie Young and Adrian Ordenana for many meals when I just couldn't manage; and of course my family— Mom and Dad, BJ, Shanna and Logan, Sam, Ron, Zach, Alec, Valentina and Efim, and Grumpy.

Kai, I want to thank you for being such a wonderful traveling companion. You are so filled with wonder, you allow me to see this state I grew up in with new eyes. In this first year of your life, you have traveled to every place listed in this book and if it made the final cut, chances are you liked it enough for me to explore it fully. Thank you for napping so I could write; playing with me when I needed a break; and being the joy of my day.

Eddie, there are no words to express the sincere thanks I owe you for sticking by me, by us, through this process. You tirelessly followed me to the ends of Northern California, doing more than your part, and rarely complained. You amaze me. You inspire me. And you are loved.

Michele Bigley
mishmell2@mac.com

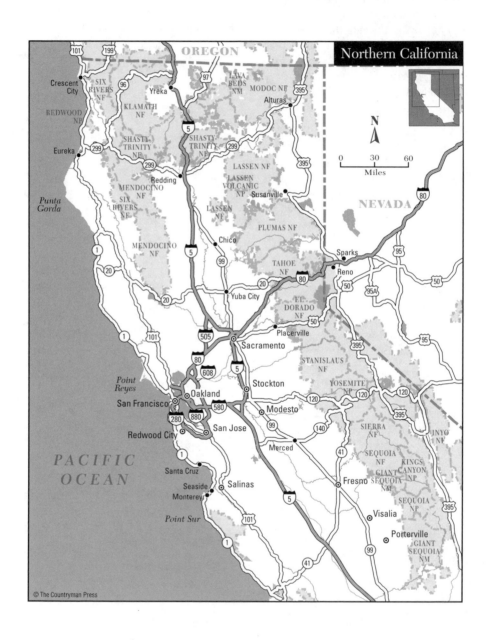

CONTENTS

LIST OF MAPS

INTRODUCTION

On a sunny morning, I sit in my San Francisco flat attempting to pay tribute to my affair with Northern California. From Big Sur to Yosemite, all the way north to the Oregon border, this region's unsurpassed natural and cultural beauty is as close to a heaven worth rhapsodizing as the United States is going to get. Consider the elements: Redwood trees guarding rugged coastal bluffs, Wild and Scenic Rivers winding past granite peaks and bubbling turquoise lava pools, vineyard-covered rolling hills that boast the finest haute cuisine in the state, and one of the most dynamic cities in the world. Add to that the finest wine in the United States (and some say the world—though don't say that in Burgundy), innovative museums and public art spaces, a food revolution that changed how Americans view their hamburgers and hot dogs, unprecedented technological and ecological advances, and kids splashing in rivers. On any given day you might hear someone speaking Hindi, Tagalog, Spanish, or German; smell eucalyptus, salty seas, and earthy fields; eat *posole*, *dosas*, Kobe beef burgers, or a tofu scramble; touch the silky bark of a madrone tree, smooth river rocks flecked with gold, and the fleshy skin of a peach; or see half-dressed people dancing in Golden Gate Park, surfers riding giant waves, and farmers relaxing on a porch.

Whenever I return home to this majestic region, I marvel at the synergy of nature and human creation. Here the diverse landscape mirrors her inhabitants. We are a blend of explorers, nesters, innovative technicians, and folks who major in celebrations (there's no party like one in San Francisco's Castro district). We hike Castle Crags and create computer languages. While eating at Chez Panisse, you might hear diners discussing where their next meal will be. Our kids play in city playgrounds and backcountry camps. We protest, plant trees, grow parsnips, and talk politics over breakfast, yet we take our libations seriously. In San Francisco, museums boast lines around the block, while even in peak summer season, you can still spot a bear in Yosemite. We snowboard Northstar, raft the American River, then soak in natural hot springs near Mono Lake. We kayak the Pacific, fish the Trinity, and visit the Big Foot Museum. And those are just some of the reasons to become smitten with Northern California.

From the first Indian settlers and Anglo explorers to the deluge of annual visitors and transplants, this region has countless enthusiasts, and, as you will soon learn, the feeling of fierce devotion to the land is deserved. Not only is the soil rich with agriculture and gold, but also with a year-round appeal. Summers bring everything from blistering inland temperatures that beg you to dive into the thousands of alpine lakes and rivers, to foggy fireplace-worthy mornings along the coast. Winters deliver a showy snowpack in the mountains and a mellow chill along the coast. Our springtime daffodils bloom in March and our rainbow of fall foliage lasts through January. You can't complain of not finding enough activities to keep you busy, regardless of the season.

And so, when writing this book, I had to imagine the panoply of readers who will use this guide. I aim to appeal to families who might spring for some wine country luxury or stay in a family-owned mountain cottage, couples looking for romance or adventure, girlfriends who camp in Big Sur and then get a spa treatment, grandparents willing to summit Mt. Shasta or be pampered in San Francisco, folks who want a Thomas Keller meal one night and tacos the next, people who pan for gold and shop for gold, wine snobs and beer drinkers, fishermen, bikers, hikers, sunbathers, kids, and even your dog. If I have done my job right, this book (and this region) will lure you back to explore deeper, further, and longer.

In these pages you'll read my love letter to Northern California, and it is my hope that this region can inspire a twinge of attraction, a spark of romance, a flutter in your heartbeat. I intend this book to be used as if an overly opinionated friend were traveling in your front seat, inviting you to share in the love fest as millions before you have done. I also hope that as you drive these scenic roads, your nose isn't buried so deep in these pages that you miss the joys that come up around each bend. The riches you'll find here will get inside you and linger like a malady that you never want to cure.

Happy Travels,
Michele Bigley

NOT TO BE MISSED—THE CHEAT SHEET TO NORTHERN CALIFORNIA

Sites to See

Yosemite National Park
Golden Gate Bridge
Lake Tahoe
CA 1 from Santa Cruz to Big Sur
Redwood State and National Park
Mt. Shasta
Lassen Volcanic National Park
Marshall Gold Discovery
   State Park
Historic Mendocino
Sundial Bridge

Family Adventures

Tour Safari West
Take a Whale-Watching Tour to
   Farallon Islands
Ski or Swim at Lake Tahoe
Pan for Gold in the Sierra Foothills
Take a Surf Lesson in Santa Cruz
Hike to Waterfalls in Yosemite
Kayak the Russian River
Visit San Francisco's California
   Academy of Sciences
Encounter Sea Mammals at
   Monterey Bay Aquarium
Swim in a Hot Spring

Towns that Inspire Romance

Mendocino
Point Reyes Station
Big Sur
Fair Play
St. Helena
Kenwood
Carmel
San Francisco
Olympic Village at Tahoe
Half Moon Bay

Worldly Resorts

Meadowood
Post Ranch Inn
Cavallo Point

Auberge Du Soleil
Plumpjack Inn
Carneros Inn
Huntington Hotel
Inn at Spanish Bay
Ahwahnee Hotel
Sea Ranch Lodge

Inns for Romantics

Inn at Victorian Gardens
Farmhouse Inn
Kenwood Inn
Hotel Boheme
Milliken Creek Inn
The Beach House
Treebones
Costanoa
Deerfield Lodge
Inn Above Tides

Striking Gold— the Best Lodging Deals

Costanoa
Asilomar
One Mesa
Rustic Cottages
Mar Vista Cottages
Inn 1890
Redwood Hostel
Landmark Winery Cottages
Golden Haven Hot Springs
Curry Village

Top Beaches

Ocean Beach
Limantour Beach
Camp Richardson Beach
Asilomar Beach
Carmel Beach
Pacifica Beach
Baker Beach
Stinson Beach
McClure's Beach
Lake Tenaya Beach

WHAT'S WHERE IN NORTHERN CALIFORNIA

AGRICULTURE Californians take their food very seriously, which is why the newest fad in Northern California travel is farm visits. Throughout Santa Cruz, Sonoma County, and El Dorado County you can visit working farms, learn about their farming practices, and even in some cases pick your own fruit and veggies. This isn't only the coveralls and tractors type of event you might envision; tours can be educational and fun. I've visited everything from alpaca farms to cheese farms to vineyards and rarely gotten dirty.

AIRPORTS Nearly every major national and international airline flies into **San Francisco International Airport**. You can also fly into Oakland, San Jose, and Sacramento Airports on many major airlines. Santa Rosa, Eureka, and Monterey have small airports. See *Getting There* in specific chapters.

ANTIQUES If you love poking through vintage shops to find that perfect dress or dish, you'll want to make time to explore the shops in Marin County's **San Anselmo,** as well as the small Sierra Foothills towns of **Placerville, Nevada City**, and **Amador**.

AQUARIUMS AND ZOOS The **Monterey Bay Aquarium** (mbayaq .org) and San Francisco's new **Califor-**nia **Academy of Sciences** (calacade my.org) are both well worth a visit. If you want to visit a zoo, head to **San Francisco Zoo** (sfzoo.org), **Oakland Zoo** (oaklandzoo.org), or **Sacramento Zoo** (saczoo.com). Other worthy stops on your animal viewing tour are to the privately owned **Safari West** (safari west.com), and Redding's **Turtle Bay** (turtlebay.org).

ART MUSEUMS You'll find art showcased all over Northern California—from museums to galleries to wineries to public spaces. Don't miss the **deYoung Museum** (famsf.org) and the **Museum of Modern Art** (sfmoma.org) in San Francisco. In Wine Country, head out to the **diRosa Preserve** (dirosapreserve.org), **Clos Pegase Winery** (clospegase.com), and **Cornerstone Gardens** (cornerstone gardens.com).

ATTIRE For the most part, Northern California is a casual region. I've dined at more than my fair share of restaurants in jeans and flip-flops. There are a few restaurants that require (or highly recommend) men to wear jackets—mostly in Wine Country and Yosemite. Also, if you are spending any time along the western edge of the state, carry a warm jacket, even in the height of summer.

BEACHES In general, you're going to be bummed with the beaches rather than bumming on them. Fog, wind, and icy water characterize our beaches. Throw in great white sharks and chances are you won't want to plan your vacation around lazy days on the sand. That being said, some of my favorite beaches in the world are right here in Northern California. Along the Central Coast, you can't miss **Asilomar Beach**, **Carmel Beach, Julia Pfeiffer Burns State Park**, and **Natural Bridges State Park**. In the Bay Area, you'll have to stop at **Pacifica Beach** and **Baker Beach**. In Marin, head to **McClure's Beach** and **Limantour Beach**. For desolate beaches, explore the **Lost Coast**. In Mendocino County, **Gualala Point Regional Park** and **Greenwood Cove** are great for oceanfront strolls.

BICYCLING Whenever biking is a highlight in a particular region, I have noted it under *To Do* and *Green Spaces*. Furthermore, mountain biking was invented in Marin County and perfected in Downieville, so those of you who are into off-road biking are in the right place.

BIRD-WATCHING Birders flock to Northern California, a major point of rest for migrating birds. The Mecca for bird-watchers is way up north in the **Klamath Basin National Wildlife Refuge**. In all of Northern California, there are 559 bird species recorded each year. For those of you who can't travel to the Shasta Cascade you can spot hundreds of shorebirds along the coast in the wetlands and marshes of **Watsonville, Moss Landing,** and **Point Reyes National Seashore**.

BOTANICAL GARDENS In San Francisco, you must visit the **Strybing Arboretum** (sfbotanicalgarden.org). University of California (UC) Berkeley's lovely **Botanical Garden** (botanicalgarden.berkeley.edu) is worth a stop as well.

CALIFORNIAN ARCHETYPE Though you may have heard the rumors that Californians are laid-back hippies with blond hair who exercise all day long and say, "Bra that was a gnarly, tubular wave," this is not always the case. Sure, people tend to be friendlier than in Manhattan, and yes, there are loads of beautiful blond surfers, but you'll also find the most diverse communities in the United States. Yuba City has a huge Indian population; San Jose is home to a large Vietnamese community; and just about every culture is represented in San Francisco, where you'll be able to eat at a taqueria for lunch and a Burmese restaurant for dinner, then return to your room by train, sitting between a woman wearing a burka and a scholar from Kenya.

CAMPING This book lists dozens of campgrounds in the *Green Spaces* section of each chapter. Campgrounds in National Parks like **Yosemite** and **Redwood State and National Park**

(800-365-2267; recreation.gov) usually require a fee. Campgrounds are either by reservation or by first-come, first-served, though in summer they all fill quickly. If you are lax in making plans (like me), you might check cancellations 10 days before your trip, otherwise, get to first-come, first-served sites early (before noon).

For National Forests and Wilderness Areas, contact the **U.S. Forest Service** (877-444-6777; reserveusa.com) to obtain a permit or reserve a site in the wealth of campgrounds dotting the forests.

✐ To camp in **State Parks** (800-777-0369; parks.ca.gov) you'll want to reserve early—you can do it up to eight months in advance. Campground fees range from $35, for fancy oceanfront campgrounds with everything from Wi-Fi to clean toilets, to free, for primitive hike-in sites.

✐ CHILDREN, ESPECIALLY FOR

Look for this symbol throughout the book to denote which activities, restaurants, and lodgings go out of their way to accommodate kids. In researching this book, I lugged my year-old son to pretty much every place listed. Most spots were welcoming, even when he screamed. Others weren't. Pay attention to those symbols.

Many big resorts offer babysitting services. But if you aren't staying at a resort, you might want to search through the listings on sittercity.com to find a good match. If you didn't want to schlep a stroller, car seat, or pack-n-play, you can rent one in Napa, Sonoma, and Solano Counties from **Travel'n Tots** (707-256-3555), in Lake Tahoe from **Away Wee Go Rentals** (800-305-1088), and in the Bay Area from **Little Luggage** (877-FLY-BABY).

My absolute must stops for families include the **California Academy of**

Sciences (calacademy.org), **Zeum** (zeum.org)**, The Bay Area Discovery Museum** (baykidsmuseum.org), and San Jose's **Children's Discovery Museum** (sdc.org) in the Bay Area. In Monterey, you visit the **Monterey Bay Aquarium** (mbayaq.org), and the **Dennis the Menace Playground**. In Sonoma County, don't miss **Safari West** (safariwest.com).

COMMITMENT CEREMONIES

San Francisco made history by allowing gays and lesbians the right to marry, making weddings an even bigger business in Northern California than they already were. Since this monumental step towards equality, hordes of people from around the state and country have traveled to San Francisco to exchange vows. Many people sojourn to City Hall in San Francisco to have a snappy ceremony then go

Edward Broitman

elsewhere to celebrate. Others organize fancy affairs at wineries, restaurants, parks, and beaches. If you are in the latter category, know that you need to get a wedding license at the **County Clerk's Office** before your ceremony to make it official.

Another notable detail: Most wineries in Napa County do not allow weddings on the property—except for the big wineries that were grandfathered in. If you dream of saying vows at a winery, head to Sonoma, Livermore, the Sierra Foothills, or Lodi, where you can say "I Do" in the vineyards.

CULTURE San Francisco is one of the most culturally rich cities in the United States. With more museums, galleries, worldly restaurants, and music events happening daily than occur annually in most towns, you won't be at a loss for ways to whet your cultural appetite. But you won't only find cultural riches in the City. From Redding's new **Sundial Bridge** to Albany's **Albany Bulb,** the wealth of places to visit extends throughout Northern California. In most cases, cultural sites are listed under *To See*.

DINING Throughout this book you'll notice that I separated *Dining Out* and *Eating Out*. Besides listings in Napa Valley and San Francisco, where restaurant prices often get jacked up, most entries listed under *Eating Out* are there because they are cheaper—but no less delicious. I've attempted to create listings of the best spots to eat, though food critics generally compile magazines full of the hundred best restaurants in just the Bay Area. I probably left out many wonderful restaurants, which will be remedied in later editions of this book. See also *Food*.

EARTHQUAKES The plates below Northern California shake all day every day. However, the chances of you feeling an earthquake during your visit are about the same as the chance of you being chomped on by a great white shark when you swim in the ocean. If you do start to feel some rocking and rolling, head straight for the doorway and duck your head under your arms. If it is a *BIG* one, wait until the shaking has subsided and take the stairs down to the middle of the street, don't stand under any trees, and begin to make friends with your neighbors.

EMERGENCIES Call 911. I have listed major hospitals in every chapter.

ENTERTAINMENT Northern Californians don't just like to hike and kayak, we love to play at night. Near the end of each chapter, I have included places to get a nightcap, hear live music, or see some good local theater, as well as the best place to scout for events. Most national and international musicians pass through the Bay Area, Sacramento, and even the small college towns of Santa Cruz and Arcata. In San Francisco and Berkeley, you will find some of the best theater in the country. For discount tickets, visit the kiosk in San Francisco's Union Square.

FARMERS' MARKETS From Weed to San Francisco (and in summer you might even find ones in the towns of Cool or Rough and Ready) many towns host a farmers' market. My favorites are the **San Rafael** and San Francisco's **Ferry Building**. I have listed many in the *To Do* sections of each chapter.

FERRIES AND BOAT TRIPS The **Blue and Gold Fleet** (blueandgoldfleet.com) and **Red and White Fleet** (redandwhite.com) ferry commuters throughout the Bay Area. For more

Shoplifters will be COMPOSTED. Pl... se ... sk for ... ance.

information, see *Getting There* and *Getting Around* in the Bay Area chapters.

If you want to get on the ocean, **Oceanic Society** and **Sanctuary Cruises** will take you to see wildlife beyond your dreams. For boat journeys, see *To Do*.

FISHING Fly-fishers as well as deep-sea anglers head to Northern California to search for salmon, trout, and bass. You need a fishing license in order to cast your line into rivers, streams, lakes, and the ocean. Contact the **Department of Fish and Game** (dfg.ca.gov) for details—though you can get a license at most tackle shops, listed throughout this book. The most popular fishing spots include **Bass Lake, Clearlake,** and in the **Shasta Cascade** rivers.

FOG Northern Californians have a love-hate relationship with the fog. Because of inland heat and cold air blasting in from the Arctic, the coast receives chilly temperatures all year-round. Coastal Nor Cal dwellers definitely don't get that summer of shorts and flip-flops from June through August (actually, it is from September through October, but we don't like to advertise that), but the fog is the reason we have redwood trees, lush forests, and gardens to brag about. Plus, there is nothing like the dramatic sight of the blanket of whiteness rolling over the mountains, through the bay, and seeming to swallow the coast.

FOOD Northern Californians are food snobs. We have the highest concentration of restaurants serving farm-to-table food in the country, not to mention a wealth of restaurants focusing on organic produce, humanely treated meats, and sustainable seafood. Here chefs are celebrities; farmers' markets are gathering spots; and you won't have to look far for delicious eateries—everything from taco trucks to five-star restaurants. In general, when we talk about California cuisine, we mean food that combines elements of French and Italian preparation with California ingredients. That gives you everything from grass-fed beef burgers to wild-caught arctic char with vanilla bean foam. Lately, restaurants interested in decreasing their carbon impact have also added locally grown produce to the menu.

▼ **GAY, LESBIAN, BISEXUAL, AND TRANSGENDER** Not only is the Castro district in San Francisco a mecca for LBGT travelers from around the world, but also so is the entire Bay Area, stretching into Wine Country, Mendocino, and even Sacramento. Overall, Northern California businesses welcome same-sex couples. I have used the triangle symbol when businesses go out of their way to welcome LBGT travelers, but don't let that sway you from visiting other businesses listed in this book.

GOLD PANNING If you're itching to get in the water and find your riches, head to the Sierra Foothills to try your luck. I have listed parks, museums, and outfitters that will set you up with equipment and teach you how to pan correctly in *To Do*.

GOLF In these pages, you'll find golf courses that are known nationally as competitive courses (often having astronomical greens fees) as well as municipal courses where you can tee off for a few bucks. For more detailed information, contact the **Northern California Golf Association** (ncga .org).

HIGH SEASON From Memorial Day to Labor Day travelers flock to California looking for summer sun, beaches, and great recreational activities. Hoteliers know this and inflate prices. The holiday season also gets booked—especially in Lake Tahoe and Yosemite. And in Wine Country, the harvest, from August to October, generates crowds.

HIKING I have listed a number of hikes throughout Northern California—including the Pacific Crest Trail to wheelchair accessible trails, and more. Look for these in the *Green Spaces* section of each chapter.

HISTORY Earthquakes, volcanic activity, and erosion created this volatile landscape of endless coastline, sharp mountainous peaks, and seas of trees. Yet today as the land continues to evolve, so does California's populace.

Though experts debate exactly how the first people arrived on North America, there is no question that they became commonly known as Native Americans, or Indians. They lived all over Northern California, near the

oceans, in the mountains, even in the Lava Beds region. From the 1500s through the 1700s Spanish explorers, the English pirate Sir Francis Drake, the Spanish explorer Gaspar de Portola, and finally the missionaries, all arrived and staked claims in the region. Soon Mexico claimed California as a territory, but that short-lived honeymoon was put to the test (and ultimately failed) when the Americans laid eyes on California and wanted her for themselves. The typical wars, disputes, and confusions ensued until July 7, 1848, when California raised the U.S. flag.

For years afterwards, California was known for her epic space as well as mythic gold. And when, in January 24, 1848, James Marshall struck gold in Coloma, his find caused the greatest human migration California has ever known. Stagecoaches packed with hungry folks from around the world descended on the Sierra Foothills, all the way through Napa County and into San Francisco (whose population swelled to 30 times its original size). Riding on the heels of the gold rush was the Pony Express, the Transcontinental Railroad, and a booming agricultural feast. The state had created the notion of the American Dream, attracting legal and illegal immigrants from around the world to come search for their metaphorical gold.

Throughout the 1900s, California became the biggest agricultural producer in the country, as well as home to the Silicon Valley technological gold rush. And though setbacks like earthquakes, fires, wars, Prohibition, protests, and overpopulation have stunted the region, somehow Northern California has always been able to bounce back.

HOT SPRINGS Northern California boasts a number of hot springs. Many resorts have tapped into the geothermal heat pulsing beneath the earth to create resorts. The majority of these resorts are in Napa Valley's town of Calistoga. Elsewhere you'll find hot springs in the Sierra Foothills, Mendocino County, Lake County, and Williams, for a fee, and in Mono County for free. You'll find these listed in the *To Do* and *Green Spaces* sections.

INFORMATION AND GUIDANCE
Prior to your visit, contact the **California Visitor Bureau** (visitcalifornia .com) for maps and information on visitor centers in the regions you plan to visit.

LAKES AND RIVERS Most visitors to the region know about our diva Lake Tahoe, but Northern California has hundreds of lakes and rivers to explore. From alpine hideaways to reservoirs, beer guzzling Spring Breakers, anglers, swimmers, boaters, and water sports enthusiasts will not be at a loss for waterways. The majority of lakes are listed in the Sierra Foothills, High Sierra, and Shasta Cascade chapters, with my favorites being **Mono Lake, Lake Alpine, Pinecrest Lake, Lake Siskiyou,** and **Bass Lake**.

LODGING Accommodations listed in this book range from primitive campgrounds to B&Bs to five-star resorts. Since locating franchise hotels is easy, I have chosen to include locally owned businesses—though there were a few times when the franchise was too much a part of the landscape to leave out.

I included most campgrounds in *Green Spaces*, since you should always contact ranger stations to obtain permits, maps, reservations, and information.

All lodging options listed accept credit cards unless otherwise noted.

Rates are quoted for two people sharing one room and are often what those in the travel industry call "rack rates," which are generally higher than what you will pay—especially if you do some hunting online. Don't forget to add tax of up to 18 percent to the bill. Many inns and B&Bs don't accept children. And it is always best to call the particular accommodation you want to stay at to check if the room can accommodate your needs. In high season, most inns and B&Bs require a minimum night stay on weekends, which because of space constraints I haven't listed. Also, note that fees listed are for one or two people in one room, if you are traveling with a third person, there is generally a fee.

As you know, prices change, hotels close and open. Feel free to let me know if I got a listing glaringly wrong. See also *Camping*.

MUST-SEE SITES If I only had a couple weeks to explore this heartbreakingly beautiful region, I would not want to miss **San Francisco** (more specifically **Golden Gate Park, Golden Gate Bridge,** and the many museums), **Santa Cruz's** beaches,

Monterey Bay Aquarium, Big Sur's rugged coastline, **Point Reyes National Seashore, Wine Country** (see *Wines*), the historic beachfront town of **Mendocino, Sacramento's Grid** neighborhood, **Redwood State and National Park, Lake Tahoe, Yosemite National Park,** a historic, small gold rush-era town in the **Sierra Foothills** (either Placerville, Nevada City, or Murphys), and **Lassen State Volcanic Park.** Of course, I could go on and on, which is why I wrote this book.

NEWSPAPERS The major newspaper for Northern California is the *San Francisco Chronicle*. Other notable papers include the *Sacramento Bee, Oakland Tribune,* and the *Press Democrat.*

☙ PETS I have noted lodging and restaurants that want your pet to visit too—in fact, many inns and restaurants offer doggie welcome baskets or doggie menus. In almost every case, the inns charge a fee for allowing your pooch to stay over, but the dog usually gets his own bed.

POPULATION As of December 2008, San Francisco's population topped 800,000, while the entire Bay Area houses 7.3 million. Sacramento's residents number over 2 million. Elsewhere you'll find 90,000 people in Redding, almost 500,000 in Sonoma County, and just over 400,000 in Monterey County.

RAILROADS First stop you should head to is the **California State Railroad Museum** (parks.ca.gov) in Sacramento. If you want to ride the rails, go to the **Roaring Camp Railroads** (roaringcamp.com) near Santa Cruz, Fort Bragg's **Skunk Train** (skunktrain.com), **Gold Country Railtown**

1897 (parks.ca.gov) in Jamestown, Sacramento's **Yolo County Railroad,** the **Yosemite Mount Sugar Pine Railroad** (ymsprr.com), Napa's **Wine Train** (winetrain.com) and Sonoma's **Traintown** (traintown.com) in Wine Country, **the McCloud Dinner Train** (shastasunset.com) and the **Yreka Western Railroad Blue Goose Steam Train** (yrekawesternrr.com) in the Shasta Cascade.

REDWOOD TREES The largest living trees in the world can reach taller than a 30-story skyscraper. Coastal redwoods (*sequoia sempervirens*) generally grow along the coastal mountains from Santa Cruz to the Oregon border. From a seed no bigger than an apple, these giants reach great heights (the tallest trees in the world are found in Humboldt County). These trees thrive in coastal fog and cool weather. Another sequoia (*sequoiadendron giganteum*) grows in the foothills of the Sierra Nevada mountains. These giants aren't as tall as their cousins are; rather

Edward Broitman

they grow so wide that nearly 50 people can fit standing side by side on a stump. Coastal redwoods grow near Santa Cruz, in Muir Woods, and from north Mendocino County to the Oregon border. In the Sierra Foothills head to **Big Trees State Park** (parks .ca.gov) in Calaveras County, and **Yosemite National Park's Mariposa Grove**.

SCENIC DRIVES AND BYWAYS
There are so many beautiful drives to take in Northern California. Start with the **49 Mile Scenic Drive** in San Francisco. My absolute favorite is the stretch of **CA 1** from Big Sur to Santa Cruz, with the section of **CA 1** stretching from San Francisco to the Lost Coast running a close second. Other amazing roads include the **Scenic Byways of the Shasta Cascade**, **Avenue of the Giants,** and **US 395**.

SCUBA
If you don't mind getting cold, head to Monterey County and dive the spectacular **Monterey Canyon**. I have listed a number of dive companies in Monterey who have come highly recommended by friends who scuba dive.

SHOPPING
Each section has a short list of Selective Shopping. Basically, I guide you to the areas where shops are concentrated—in most cases these are commercial areas rather than malls. Occasionally, I have listed shops that stand out from the masses.

SMOKING
Smoking is a major faux pas in California. It is outlawed in any restaurant, bar, hotel, or building, and in a few parks and beaches. It is also against the law to smoke within 15 feet of a business establishment. You'll get kinder looks dressing your dog in leather chaps than smoking in public.

SPAS
In San Francisco, head to **Sen-Spa** (senspa.com) or **Kabuki Hot Springs** (joiedevivre.com). In the Central Coast area, you shouldn't miss a visit to the famed **Bernardus Lodge Spa** (bernardus.com), or the **Ventana Inn Spa** (ventanainn.com). While visiting Wine Country you can't go wrong with a spa treatment at **Kenwood Inn** (kenwoodinn.com), **Osmosis** (osmosis.com), **Calistoga Spa Hot Springs** (707-942-6269), **Villagio Inn** (villagio.com), or the **Carneros Inn** (thecarnerosinn .com). You'll find more spas in *To Do*.

SPECIAL EVENTS
In these pages, you'll find a collection of seasonal event highlights, including everything from San Francisco's Folsom Street Fair (the biggest event to honor leather on earth) to the quaint Apple Fair of Sebastopol. If I had to attend a handful of seasonal events, I would not miss **Bay to Breakers** (see photo below), **SF Pride, Hardly Strictly Bluegrass, Reggae Rising, High Sierra Music Festival, Half Moon Bay's Pumpkin Festival, Kinetic Sculpture Race,** the **Calistoga Lighted Tractor Parade,** and the **Lake Tahoe Music Festival**.

SURFING
Santa Cruz, Santa Cruz, Santa Cruz. Did I mention Santa Cruz?

TIME ZONE California is on Pacific Time.

TO SEE AND TO DO Each chapter begins with a To See then a To Do section, generally listed in alphabetical order. Unless otherwise noted, I have organized towns within particular chapters so that the towns closest to San Francisco are listed first, ending with the regions farthest from the city.

TRAFFIC Bottlenecks, merging freeways, and too many people make the Bay Area one of the top regions for traffic. Other spots where you should expect some slow going include US 101 near San Rafael, US 101 and I-880 in San Jose, CA 17 to Santa Cruz, US 101 near Santa Rosa, and during rush hour on all highways in Sacramento. Visit transitinfo.org for more information.

VOLCANOES See Shasta Cascade.

WATERFALLS People are surprised to know that Northern California offers a wealth of waterfalls to explore. My favorites include **Yosemite Falls** and **McArthur-Burney Falls**.

WATER SPORTS To live in or visit Northern California you'll want to have a relationship with the water. From swelling surf to rushing rivers, you can pretty much indulge in about any water sports activity you choose. For surfing, you'll definitely want to head to Santa Cruz. My favorite places to kayak are **Elkhorn Slough** in the Central Coast, **the Russian River** in Sonoma County, and **Lake Tahoe**. Anglers head to **Clearlake** and **Bass Lake** to try their luck for salmon, bass, and trout (see *Fishing*). Swimmers will love the warm swimming holes in the **Sierra Foothills**, **Lake Tahoe**, and the chilly **Pacifica Beach**. If you want to go white-water rafting, there is nothing better than the American River—especially for beginners. Outfitters and guides that rent equipment, take you on tours, or help you locate the best ways to get wet are listed throughout this book in *To Do*.

WEATHER I have listed specific information about climate in the introduction sections of each chapter. For the most part, we have a Mediterranean climate of warm summers and cool winters in the valleys and foothills. Along the coast expect cool temperatures year-round, and in the mountains you can take advantage of warm summers, spectacular fall foliage, and blustery winter storms ideal for snow bunnies.

WHALE WATCHING California gray whales migrate past the coast from December through April, while humpbacks and orcas feed off the Monterey Coast in summer. You'll find whale-watching cruises along the Central Coast—my favorite there is **Sanctuary Cruises** (sanctuarycruises.com) from San Francisco—and in Fort Bragg. If you don't want to get on the water, head to the Lighthouse in Point Reyes in winter for a show.

WILDLIFE Many animals, birds, and fish call Northern California home. Probably the most popular inhabitant is the black bear (which is actually brown). You'll find them in the forests of the Sierra Mountains and foothills, throughout the Shasta Cascade, and in the redwood forests along the far north coast. Other land mammals you might encounter are deer, mountain lions, and tule elk (the best spot to see these guys is in Point Reyes).

As for sea life, you'll likely spot a sea lion or 20 at Fisherman's Wharf in San Francisco, off the Municipal Pier in Santa Cruz, along the coast at Monterey and Elkhorn Slough, and in Crescent City's harbor. To see elephant seals, head to Año Nuevo State Reserve.

Other critters you'll have to contend with on hikes and camping are rattlesnakes, ticks, garter snakes, butterflies, frogs, rabbits, and squirrels. See also *Bird-Watching, Whale Watching.*

WINE I recently heard the statistic that Napa Valley had the highest number of tourists in the state, second only to Disneyland. And though most people head to this granddaddy of wine regions (and you should, especially if you like Cabernet Sauvignon), there are a number of other wine regions worth your attention. Folks who enjoy Chardonnay and Pinot Noir should definitely mark Sonoma County on your itinerary. Mendocino County wineries are amongst the greenest in the nation and known for great Pinot Noir and sweet white wines. Other wine regions include Lake County and Lodi (which grows a number of grape varietals for wineries in Napa County). The up-and-coming regions in the Sierra Foothills, including Fair Play and Plymouth, have been getting lots of press for their wonderful Zinfandels. Finally, the Carmel Valley and Santa Cruz mountains have ideal conditions for Chardonnay. You'll find tasting

rooms listed in the *To Do* sections of each chapter.

WINTER SPORTS Snow playgrounds are in full effect in the northeast of California, with the highlight being Lake Tahoe. Winter sports enthusiasts might be surprised to learn there are a number of ski resorts in the Shasta Cascade as well as great family-friendly (and cheaper) spots to ski around Truckee.

San Francisco

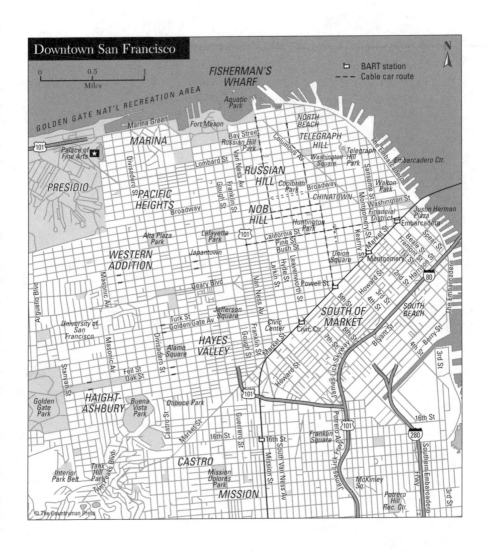

Downtown San Francisco

0   0.5   1
Miles

⊐ BART station
- - - Cable car route

N

FISHERMAN'S
WHARF

GOLDEN GATE NAT'L RECREATION AREA

Aquatic
Park

NORTH
BEACH

Marina Green   Fort Mason

101

Palace of
Fine Arts ★

MARINA

Bay Street
Russian Hill
Park

Columbus Av

TELEGRAPH
HILL

Telegraph
Hill
Park

Embarcadero Ctr.

Lombard St

Washington
Square

Divisadero St

Franklin St

RUSSIAN
HILL

Sansome St

Walton
Park

PRESIDIO

PACIFIC
HEIGHTS

Gough St

Coolbrith
Park

Broadway

Montgomery St

Washington St

Justin Herman
Plaza

Broadway

NOB
HILL

CHINATOWN

Financial
District

Embarcadero

Alta Plaza
Park

Lafayette
Park

Huntington
Park

California St

Kearny St

101

Pine St
Bush St

Speer St

Beale St

Union
Square

Fremont St

Japantown

Hyde St

Montgomery

WESTERN
ADDITION

Geary Blvd

Leavenworth St

Powell St

2nd St

Harrison

80

Masonic Av

Larkin St

Howard St

SOUTH
BEACH

Jefferson
Square

Turk St

Civic
Center

SOUTH OF
MARKET

3rd St

Arguello Blvd

University of
San
Francisco

Golden Gate Av

Franklin St

Civic Ctr.

7th St

4th St

Berry St

Masonic Av

HAYES
VALLEY

Alamo
Square

Divisadero St

Gough St

Market St

Bryant St

3rd St

Stanyan St

Fell St
Oak St

Howard St

Potrero Av

James Lick Skyway

Golden
Gate
Park

HAIGHT-
ASHBURY

Buena
Vista
Park

Duboce Park

101

16th St

Interior
Park Belt

Tank
Hill
Park

Castro St

Market St

Guerrero St

16th St

16th St

Franklin
Square

101

280

The Embarcadero

3rd St

CASTRO

Mission
Dolores
Park

Mission St

South Van Ness Av

McKinley
Sq.

Twin Peaks Blvd

MISSION

Potrero
Hill
Rec. Ctr.

Southern Embarcadero Fwy

© The Countryman Press

SAN FRANCISCO

My dad says that the Bay Area—and San Francisco more specifically—exists in a bubble. Once you are here, you forget that the world is different a mere 50 miles away. Suddenly the rolling hills, the rainbow-colored Edwardian homes, the bridges, the sparkling bay, and the wacky festivals start to seem normal. Here, Chihuahuas dress better than most people do; more bikes fill the streets than cars; chefs create more hype than movie stars do; that hot chick walking down the street is actually a dude; and it's illegal to give out a plastic bag at a grocery store, but smoking pot is often overlooked. At festivals nudists come out in droves, and whenever there is a protest it seems the whole town doesn't have to work. I've seen citywide pillow fights, bike protests stop traffic, and our mayor partying at the Gay Pride Parade. On the same street you might see old Chinese ladies hawk loogies after eating a pork bun, while society ladies lunch with views of the entire bay; one of the highest concentrations of rich folks live here, yet we have one of the largest populations of homeless people. And these dichotomies are nothing new.

We live on a fault line that is repeatedly shaken up. The city constantly reinvents itself. Starting with the accidental *finding* of San Francisco by Gaspar de Portola, who quickly stationed himself here (wouldn't you?) and constructed a mission, claiming the area for Mexico. That is, until the Anglos figured out what good real estate the Bay Area was, and conquered the Latinos, claiming the city for the United States.

Then along came the gold rush pioneers, who made this small town's population swell to 30 times its original size. The young, adventurous folks looking to strike it rich arrived like nobody's business, with prostitutes, gunslingers, and hangers-on following close behind. Similar to the Internet boom that would bring another gold rush to the Bay Area over 150 years later, the riches started to dwindle, causing a major economic depression. Add to that, six fires that burned the city to bits, and you start to see a pattern.

From those ashes rose the Transcontinental Railroad, funded by the Big Four railroad barons, whose massive project attracted American and international workers. Then, just when San Francisco was starting to find calm waters, on April 18, 1906, the city was rocked by a massive earth shaker. The 1906 earthquake led to a fire that destroyed the entire downtown area from the bay to Van Ness Street, leaving over half of the residents homeless.

As proof it had rebounded once more, the 1915 World's Fair and Panama-Pacific International Exposition decided to celebrate here, creating Treasure

Island as well as the Marina district. From there, the city traveled the ups and downs of the rest of the country—the Depression, the world wars, the Beat generation, the Vietnam War, the AIDS epidemic, the dot com era, and the more recent economic shake up.

Since its conception, San Francisco has been home to renegades, iconoclasts, leaders, and idealists, often creating the zeitgeist for the country before the rest of the U.S. knew what was coming. Today it is one of the greenest cities in the world, one of the most far left politically (there are more Green Party members than there are Republicans, at last count), and one of the most accepting of differences. San Francisco inhabitants appreciate the heart-stopping vistas around every new bend, work to make the city better, and take pride in being San Franciscan. Take a walk around the city and you will start to see why people who live here love it so fiercely that they will put up with natural disasters, foggy, cold summers, and exorbitant real estate prices. It's a bubble most of us can't bear to leave.

GUIDANCE San Francisco Visitor Bureau (415-391-2000; onlyinsanfrancisco .com) 900 Market Street, on the lower level of Hallidie Plaza, next to the cable car at Powell and Market Streets. Open daily from 9–5 on weekdays and 9–3 on weekends (closed on winter Sundays). Make sure to visit their Web site for information on travel deals and special events.

HELPFUL WEB SITES
Onlyinsanfrancisco.com
Sfstation.com
Sfgate.com
Sfgov.org
Transitinfo.org
Newspapers and Radio
San Francisco Chronicle
94.1 KPFA and KPFK
91.3 NPR

WEATHER You'll hear the Mark Twain saying, "The coldest winter I ever spent was a summer in San Francisco," time and time again. Though global warming is doing its part to grace San Francisco with the warm California sun, the truth is that San Francisco is often a cold, foggy, and windy place. So feel grateful if you have a day or two of warm sunny weather, because chances are, it won't last. Often we get four seasons—in one weekend. So here's how to manage the San Francisco weather. Pack layers. Always carry a hat and scarf in your day bag, and never (even though the sun is out) leave your hotel without a jacket—or you'll be buying one of those tacky San Francisco sweatshirts at Fisherman's Wharf.

MEDICAL EMERGENCIES Call 911.
CPMC (415-600-6000; cpmc.org) 3700 California Street.
SF General (415-206-8000) 1001 Potrero Ave.

GETTING THERE *By air:* **San Francisco International Airport** (SFO) S. McDonnell Road and S. Link Road. Nearly every national and international carrier serves this airport. You can rent cars here as well.

By BART: The easiest way to get into the city is to take the BART (Bay Area Rapid Transit). At SFO, take the airport monorail to the BART station. Make sure to save your ticket, as that is how you exit the station. BART goes to Oakland Airport as well. The main downtown exits are Powell Street, Montgomery, and Embarcadero.

By boat: Coming from Sausalito, Tiburon, or Larkspur take **Golden Gate Ferry** (baycrossings.com) and from Vallejo and Oakland in the East Bay, you can get to the city by **East Bay Ferry** (eastbayferry.org). Trips take about 30 minutes. Get a round trip ticket, because when you come back there are usually lines.

A number of cruise ships dock in San Francisco before heading to Alaska or Mexico, including **Carnival, Crystal,** and **World Explorer**. They dock near Fisherman's Wharf.

By bus: **Greyhound** (greyhound.com) serves the Bay Area, with a major stop in San Francisco at 425 Mission Street. If you are coming from the South Bay, you can get here using **Samtrans** (samtrans.com). From the East Bay, take **AC Transit** (actransit.org).

By car: From the airport, drive north on US 101 and you will see San Francisco rise like a phoenix before you. Usually there is traffic on US 101 between 8 AM–10 AM and again from 4 PM–7 PM.

From the north, take US 101 over the Golden Gate Bridge (at press time the city was talking about raising the bridge toll from $6 to a whopping $8) and voila, you are there. US 101 continues through the city along Lombard Street to Van Ness Avenue.

From the east, I-80, heading west, turns into the Bay Bridge ($4). Note that there is usually a backup at the bridge tollbooth. For both bridges, make sure to have cash with you.

If you are not renting a car, **Go Lorrie's Shuttle Service** (lorries-shuttles.com; 415-334-9000) takes you to San Francisco from the airport for $16 per person.

By train: **Amtrak** (Amtrak.com) has a station at 825 Market, but you have to take a bus from one of the East Bay stations. From the South Bay, take the plush **Caltrain** (caltrain.com), which travels from Gilroy to San Francisco approximately every 30 minutes throughout the day.

DRIVING TIMES AND DISTANCES		
SF-Humboldt County	5 hours	261.54 miles
SF-Mendocino	3 hours	155.19 miles
SF-Monterey	2 hours	112.14 miles
SF-Napa	1 hour	46.62 miles
SF-Sacramento	1.5 hours	86.58 miles
SF-Santa Rosa	1 hour	55.1 miles
SF-Shasta	3.5 hours	222.69 miles
SF-Sonoma	1 hour	45.34 miles
SF-Tahoe	3.5 hours	199.24 miles
SF-Yosemite	4 hours	188.68 miles

GETTING AROUND The best resource for getting around is 511.org. Here you can plot your trip, figure out public transportation, and even check traffic. Another fun option to check out is nextbus.com, which tells you, as the name implies, when the next bus or Muni is coming.

By BART: **BART** gets you from the East Bay through San Francisco and all the way to the San Francisco Airport. It runs all day (stopping around midnight) and ticket fares depend on which route you take (note: all train lines pass through the city). Make sure to save your ticket, as that is how you exit the train.

By boat: See *Getting There.*

By car: Though I drive a lot in the city, I dread it. Parking is worse than the mall on the day after Thanksgiving; kamikaze bike messengers come out of nowhere like dive bombers; traffic hardly moves, no matter what time of day; trucks block roads; and knowing that the city is only 7 miles across makes the 30-minute trek from the southern edge to Golden Gate Bridge pretty intolerable. So it is best to take public transportation whenever possible.

If you must drive, know that Market Street divides the city in half, pirouetting around Twin Peaks (that radio tunnel on the mountains), turning into Portola, and depositing you in the foggy West Portal neighborhood. Most streets are laid out in a grid, but they change names, weave, and suddenly start heading in another direction. Main thoroughfares include the east/west one-way streets of Fell and Oak, which take you from downtown to Golden Gate Park and the beach, and the north/south one-way streets of Franklin and Gough (pronounced like "cough").

As for parking, I wish you luck. Though it is nearly impossible to find parking downtown (if you try, bring rolls of quarters), in Haight Ashbury, the Mission District on a Friday night (see *Sidebar*), and the Marina, parking is to be had for the diligent. If you are headed to Fisherman's Wharf, know that if you eat at one of the restaurants around Boudin Bakery, you can park for free in the lot. In the Mission District and North Beach, there are a couple lots. Downtown, park at the Metreon.

By foot: My favorite way to see the city is to put on some sneakers and hit the pavement. You'll get your bootie in shape and discover some of the quirkiest San Francisco finds. Here are some of my favorite urban hikes.

WHAT'S THE DEAL WITH PARKING IN THE MEDIAN???

So it's a Friday afternoon in the Mission District, the sun is out, it seems everyone in the city is gathered at Dolores Park, and you notice that cars are lined in twos in the center median. You are tempted. You've been driving for 30 minutes trying to secure a spot. All I can say is, don't.

Officially the San Francisco rule is that if church is in session, people can park in the center median to attend services—and being San Francisco, some kind of church is always in session. And even if you poke your head into Mission Dolores, the traffic cops (especially on Friday and Saturday nights) don't care about your sob story—trust me, I've tried it.

So keep driving. At some point, you'll find a spot.

The Bay to Breakers Route: Start at the Ferry Building for breakfast. Walk west on Market Street, weaving through Union Square, Civic Center, Hayes Valley, the Haight, through Golden Gate Park to the beach. You can take the N-Judah trolley back to downtown.

The South of Market Tour: From the giant rainbow flag in the Castro, travel south on Castro. Walk east on 18th Street to see **Dolores Park, Mission Dolores,** and the **Women's Building.** Turn right on Valencia Street and walk to 24th Street (turn left). On your right, you'll find **Balmy Alley**. When you are done, catch BART at Mission and 24th Street

Golden Gate Park Stroll: There is so much to see in the park, you'll need days of exploring. Starting from the east, you'll notice the newly refurbished **Children's Playground** next to Hippie Hill. Wander through the **Strybing Arboretum, Japanese Tea Garden, Stow Lake, Shakespeare Garden, AIDS Memorial Grove,** and **Conservatory of Flowers. Don't miss** the herd of buffalo, a **Dutch windmill,** and the **Beach Chalet**. If you have time, you might also check out the **de Young Museum** and the **California Academy of Sciences**. Take the N-Judah trolley back to downtown.

By public transportation: By far the easiest way to get around the city, San Francisco has one of the best public transportation networks around. If you plan to be here for longer than a month without a car (that is from the 1st of the month through the 30th or 31st), it might be helpful to buy a Fast Pass, which gets you unlimited rides on all public transportation in the city, including cable cars, BART, and Muni. Inquire at the Visitor Center or Muni Stations for information.

It is also helpful to know that when riding Muni (the bus and streetcar), you must have a receipt (which you can use for more rides until the time it says it expires). Do not test the Muni cops. I once rode on an expired ticket and got a $100 ticket. Compared to the $1.50 fare, it isn't worth it. You need exact change to buy a ticket (and Downtown, you need coins), which lasts for two hours from your point of purchase. If you don't have coins, go to a BART ticket dispenser and press "H" for change.

If you want to ride the cable car (which costs $5), you might consider picking it up on California and Polk Street instead of waiting in the long lines between Powell Street and Fisherman's Wharf. Make sure to bring a jacket.

San Francisco just added the new 74X line, called the **Culture Bus,** which shuttles visitors to the major city sites including Golden Gate Park, the museums, and Fisherman's Wharf for $7 all day.

TOURS *By boat:* **Blue and Gold Fleet** (415-773-1188; blueandgoldfleet.com) Fisherman's Wharf, Pier 39. These guys go out on one-hour bay cruises and Alcatraz tours. They pretty much have the monopoly on ferry cruises, but they also provide tours in a variety of languages, styles, and fees. Their newest addition, the **Rocketboat**, takes you on a 40-mile per hour wind-whipping tour of the bay. Ferry: $11 adults; $6.75 kids. Tour: $22–43 adults; $11–31 kids.
Red and White Fleet (415-673-2900; redandwhite.com) Fisherman's Wharf, Pier 43½. Multilingual bay tours and cruises, including a sunset cruise, last two hours. There is a full bar and Boudin Bakery snacks. Sunset tours head out on Thursday through Saturday at 6 PM. $22–48 adults; $16–34 kids.

MUSTS FOR FIRST-TIME VISITORS

1. Bike the Golden Gate Bridge to Sausalito and take the ferry back.
2. Eat your way through Chinatown and North Beach.
3. Tour the Mission District's colorful murals.
4. Walk the windswept Ocean Beach, then have a drink at the Park Chalet.
5. Shop the Marina District boutiques.
6. Pamper yourself at SenSpa.
7. Explore the Saturday market at the Ferry Building.
8. Take in the views of the city from atop Twin Peaks.
9. Spend a day exploring Golden Gate Park.
10. Museum hop at the San Francisco Museum of Modern Art (SFMOMA), de Young Museum, Asian Art Museum, and the California Academy of Sciences.

MUSTS FOR REPEAT VISITORS

1. Spend an afternoon lounging in Dolores Park.
2. Visit the Musée Mecanique.
3. Hike Angel Island; or better yet, camp there.
4. Trek Lands End and visit the Sutro Baths.
5. Eat and drink your way through the Mission District.
6. Go to a music event at the Fillmore or Yoshi's.
7. Hang glide at Fort Funston.
8. Visit Alcatraz.
9. Watch either Teatro Zinzanni or Beach Blanket Babylon.
10. Kayak the bay.

By car: **49 Mile Scenic Drive** Follow the signs around the city to see all the beautiful parts of San Francisco. You can get a map of the drive from the Visitor Center.

Blue Heron (415-337-1874, blueherontours.com) 275 Staples Avenue. A wealth of knowledge, Rick takes folks on customized tours of the Bay Area, Wine Country, Central Coast, Mendocino, and even the Sierra Foothills. You tell him what you want, and he'll create the ideal trip. He knows more about wine and food than most.

Mr. Toad's (877-4MR-TOAD, mrtoadstours.com) Fisherman's Wharf at Mason and Jefferson. Old school hydrogen-powered cars from the 1920s take you on tours of the famed must-see San Francisco destinations like the Golden Gate Bridge, Chinatown, and Grace Cathedral. Cars are open air, so they provide you with blankets and heaters—but it does get chilly, so dress warm. The 90-minute tours are great if you have your own car to explore the rest of the city. Without your own car, go for the three-hour postcards tour: It is a great way to get pictures of all the sites without having to make a day of it. They also have night tours with tea tastings and stops at the Fortune Cookie Factory. $16–48.

By foot: **Barbary Coast Walking Tours** (barbarycoasttrail.com). You can find this self-guided tour of the historic Barbary Coast area at the Visitor Center; see *Guidance*. This is a great way to learn about the Financial District, Fisherman's Wharf, and the debauchery that took place in present-day Jackson Street Historic District.

Hobnob (415-771-9866; hobnobtours.com) 700 Geary Street. If you are interested in the history of the elite Nob Hill Silver Kings and Railroad Barons, Val's tour cannot be beat. She'll tell you everything you ever wanted to know and more about San Francisco's first hobnobbers. Tours are generally two hours. You can also arrange to lunch in the Huntington Hotel. $30.

In the Kitchen With Lisa (415-806-5970; inthekitchenwithlisa.com). Lisa Rogovin takes folks on the ideal Bay Area experience. She celebrates the rich culinary world, offering tours of San Francisco's Ferry Building, Berkeley's Gourmet Ghetto, Napa, and West Marin. Most tours are private, so you can arrange your own chocolate tours, farm visits, or shop with a chef and have them cook you lunch. Tours start at $70.

HEAD TO THE FARALLON ISLANDS

Oceanic Society Expeditions (415-474-3385; oceanic-society.org) 35 N. Fort Mason, San Francisco. Since 1972, the Oceanic Society has offered naturalist-led bird- and whale-watching cruises to the Farallon Islands. Located on the boundary zone between two of the Earth's major tectonic plates, you'll see granite peaks and learn about the underwater valleys reaching depths of 6000 feet.

Getting here is a trek. Cold, rough waters make the over two-hour boat trip (often accompanied by the sweet smell of vomit) unpleasant, but also allow for a rich feeding area for a variety of sea mammals including seals, elephant seals, sea lions, sharks, dolphins, and whales. Bird-watchers will be in heaven with 12 species of breeding seabirds, including common murres, Cassin's auklets, rhinoceros auklets, pigeon guillemots, and tufted puffins. Other seabirds migrate through here annually allowing up close views of cormorants, pelicans, and petrels. Year-round you'll see animals, with fall being the best time to view great white sharks and winter the time for gray whales.

Though people once lived on these islands, today the islands are a wildlife refuge and only researchers can wander the shores. You, on the other hand, get to motor out here on an eight-hour journey to the continental shelf. I can't tell you what a treat this journey is—as long as you take some Dramamine, bring a winter coat, and are okay leaving the kids at home (since they must be 10 years old to come along). Trips go out from May through November weekends, and some Friday and Mondays. The society also runs shorter (three-hour) trips from Half Moon Bay to view whales. $105.

THE TRANSAMERICA PYRAMID IN THE BACKGROUND AND CHINATOWN IN THE FOREGROUND.

Local Tastes of the City Tours (415-665-0480 or 888-358-8687; sffoodtour.com). Daily tours at 10 AM and 2 PM last two or three hours and lead you on an eating stroll through the historical North Beach and Chinatown areas. Created to show you the benefits of eating locally, to learn this, you get to eat some of the best food in town. These tours are perfect for families and folks who want to learn about local food finds. Adults: $59; Youth: $15–39; under 8 free.

San Francisco City Guides (415-557-4266; sfcityguides.com) SF Public Library, 100 Larkin Street. These free tours of almost every neighborhood and destination in the city last two hours. You can hit up Chinatown, Victorians, murals, or even learn the history of "working ladies" during the gold rush era. Check online or call for the schedule and then show up (unless you have more than eight people in your group, then you must make a reservation). Free.

By plane: **SF Helicopters** (650-635-4500; sfhelicoptertours.com). SF Helicopters offers 20–30 minute flights over the San Francisco skyline, Alcatraz Island, the bridges, the Marin Headlands, California's Pacific Coast, Angel Island, and Sausalito. Tours start at $150.

✈ **San Francisco Seaplane Tours** (415-332-4843; seaplane.com) 242 Redwood Highway, Mill Valley. Fly over the Golden Gate Bridge, Alcatraz Island, downtown San Francisco, Fisherman's Wharf, the Bay Bridge, Angel Island, Marin, and Muir Woods before splashing down in the bay. $139 per person.

✳ To See

Downtown
For the purposes of this book, Downtown is considered everything from the Embarcadero to Van Ness, and from Fisherman's Wharf to Pac Bell Park on the south. This includes the Financial District, Chinatown, North Beach, South of Market (SoMa), Union Square, Civic Center, Nob Hill, Russian Hill, and Mission Bay.

Financial District and the Embarcadero
Jackson Square Historic District (See Barbary Coast walking tour above).

Transamerica Pyramid (Montgomery and Washington). This was once the city's tallest building and now the spiky pyramid is a welcome reminder of San Francisco's oddities. You won't get to explore inside much, but outside the building is a

THE FERRY BUILDING—CONFESSIONS OF A FOOD WHORE

1 Ferry Building, at the end of Market Street, Open 10–5 daily (9–6 on Saturday).

Since the Ferry Building renovation, whenever locals and visitors enter this bright space you hear oohs and aahs at every turn. Where else can you find organic hot dogs, zillions of mushroom varieties, artisan chocolate, locally grown lavender and heirloom tomatoes, grass-fed beef and fresh-off-the-boat Dungeness crab, gigantic Italian coppa sandwiches, pumpkin milkshakes, rose-flavored gelato, flower bouquets, caviar, flights of wine, and Blue Bottle lattes all in one place? This is my number one spot to bring anyone from out of town. Especially on Saturday morning, when the Farmers' Market hugs the bay and the entire city comes out to play. Watch for the guys pushing carts around the market, chances are you are passing one of the city's famous chefs.

Be sure not to miss bayside oysters at **Hog Island Oyster**, a steamed bun at **Out the Door** (or Slanted Door—see *Dining Out*), a glass of wine at the **Wine Merchant**, a cheese tasting at **Cowgirl Creamery**, a cup of tea at **Imperial Tea Court**, a piece of chocolate (or three) at **Recchiuti**, and a gingerbread cupcake at **Miette**.

If you are still hungry, other favorites include quesadillas at **Mijita**, a bento box at **Delica rf1**, brunch at **Market Bar**, a tasting at **Tsai Nicoulai Caviar**, gelato at **Ciao Bella Gelato**, a burger at **Taylor's Refresher**, and an olive oil tasting at **McEvoy Ranch Olive Oil**.

I love browsing for books and looking at the bay at **Book Passage**, or wandering through **The Gardener** dreaming of growing my own food.

Finally, Tuesday and Saturday brings the Farmers' Market where you can find the most beautiful produce in the area. It is the Academy Awards for foodies, offering smoked salmon, artisan jam, salad mixes that are works of art, and the famed Blue Bottle coffee cart.

THE FERRY BUILDING AND COIT TOWER GUARD THE EASTERN EDGE OF THE CITY.

Edward Brotman

nice redwood park, where, if you are lucky, you might spot some of the local parrot residents.

SoMa

Because sections of SoMa (namely Sixth Street) are home to numerous residential hotels filled with addicts and homeless people, stick to the areas near South Park, the ballpark, and Yerba Buena gardens.

✦ **Cartoon Art Museum** (415-CAR-TOON; cartoonart.org) 655 Mission Street. Tuesday through Sunday, 11 AM–5 PM. Cartoon art for kids and adults make this a great stop for the whole family. They also have a fantastic gift shop. $6 adults; $2 kids.

Contemporary Jewish Museum (415-344-8800; thecjm.org) 736 Mission Street. Open Daily (except Wednesday) from 11 AM–5:30 PM and Thursday from 1 AM–8:30 PM. This new museum made a splash in the city with the unusual architecture. Inside, the contemporary art highlights the experience of being Jewish rather than focusing solely on the Holocaust. Innovative art in all mediums deserves a visit. $10 adults; $5 kids.

✦ **Metreon** (415-369-6000; westfield.com/metreon) 101 4th Street. Open Monday through Thursday from 10 AM–9 PM, and Friday through Saturday from 10 AM–10 PM. Most people come here to go to the movies or the IMAX theater or eat in the food court. This entertainment center also has a *Where the Wild Things Are* exhibit and a Chronicle Books bookstore. If the weather is nice, head out to the gardens, where there are often free live-music events. This is also the place to park your car if you must drive downtown. Expect to pay—a lot—but it is the cheapest lot in the area.

THE NEW CONTEMPORARY JEWISH MUSEUM IN DOWNTOWN.

Museum of the African Diaspora (415-358-7219; moadsf.org) 685 Mission Street. Open Wednesday through Saturday 11 AM–6 PM. Here you will find a tribute to African rituals, music, culinary traditions, and adornment. Plus there is an educational exhibit documenting the slavery passage. $10 adults, $5 kids.

San Francisco Modern Art Museum (415-357-4000; sfmoma.org) 151 3rd Street. Open 11 AM–5:45 PM. Closed Wednesday (Thursday until 8:45 PM). The city's premier modern art destination, world-renown collections constantly pass through, including most recently Frida Kahlo, Olafur Eliason, and Diane Arbus. The building itself, designed by Mario Botta in 1995, is a work of art. The gift shop is where I do all my holiday shopping. And at press time, the museum was turning the roof into a sculpture garden, which will surely be an added bonus to your visit. I put this museum high on my must-see list, though when big name artists have exhibitions here, the wait can be excruciating. If you visit on the monthly free day (see *Sidebar*), prepare for crowds. $12.50 adults; $7 kids.

Yerba Buena Center For the Arts (415-978-ARTS; ybca.org) 701 Mission Street. Open Tuesday through Sunday 12–5. See innovative music, film, and modern art. Since 1993, this Fumihiko Maki-designed building has brought out the most daring in the art world. Check local listings for events at this intimate setting.

♧ ♿ **Zeum** (415-820-3320; zeum.org) 221 4th Street. Open every day from 11 AM–6 PM, in summer on Tuesday through Sunday, from 11 AM–5 PM. Kids of all ages can create clay-mation

MODERN ART INSIDE AND OUT AT THE SAN FRANCISCO MOMA.

movies, dress up, sing karaoke, and make their own music. There is also a carousel, a bowling alley, and a theater attached. $10 adults; $8 kids.

North Beach and Telegraph Hill

City Lights Bookstore (415-362-8193; citylights.com) 261 Columbus Avenue. Open daily from 10 AM–12 AM. A San Francisco icon, Lawrence Ferlinghetti's bookshop and publishing house still attracts bohemians. Though you won't find many of the old beat writers hanging around as they used to in the 1950s, poets, philosophers, and mere book lovers flock to explore the stacks.

Coit Tower (415-362-0808) 1 Telegraph Hill Boulevard. Open daily from 10 AM–6:30 PM. It is worth the hike up the hill to see Lillie Hitchcock Coit's 1933 tribute to firemen. All the times I have been up here, I have never actually reached the top of the tower. I always end up in the lobby checking out the mural, then cuddling with whomever I am with to ward off the wind. Instead of parking up here, you might take the 39 bus. Free to view murals, $5 to go to the top of the tower.

Saints Peter and Paul Church (415-421-0809; stspeterpaul.san-francisco.ca.us/church) 666 Filbert Street.

ST. PETER AND PAUL CHURCH IN NORTH BEACH.

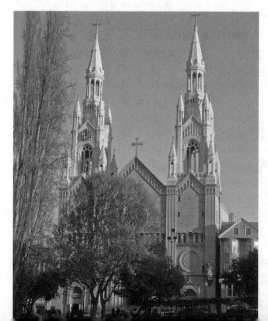

Open daily from 7–4. Marilyn Monroe and Joe DiMaggio took their wedding pictures here. Now this church is the centerpiece for North Beach happenings. Walking through the 1924 church always makes me feel like I am in Europe. Free.

Chinatown

Just a walk down Grant and Stockton is a tourist attraction in itself: Hordes of people push down the streets, shopping for everything from live chickens to jade statues. I prefer the real Chinatown in the Richmond district; however, a walk along Stockton Street (and maybe even Grant) will still afford you an entertaining experience.

Chinatown Gate Grant Avenue at Bush Street. The brightly colored pagoda-topped gate indicates that you have arrived in Chinatown. A gift from the Republic of China, the design represents peace, love, respect, and prosperity. It makes a good picture spot, but that's about it.

Chinese Historical Society of America (415-391-1188; chsa.org) 965 Clay Street. Open Tuesday through Friday 12 PM–5 PM, Saturday 11 AM–4 PM. If you are interested in the Chinese American experience, this museum not only offers a historical perspective, but also some great modern art. $1–3.

Golden Gate Fortune Cookie Factory (415-781-3956) 56 Ross Alley. Open daily from 9–8 PM. This working cookie factory will show you how these sugar cookies are made. You can even buy cookies with racy fortunes. Free.

Kong Chow Temple (415-788-1339) 855 Stockton Street. The temple was constructed by immigrants in 1851, but wasn't used as a site of worship until 1977. The god that this temple worships has been attributed to war, trust, and honesty . . . hmmm. Free.

&. **Pacific Heritage Museum** (415-399-1124; ibankunited.com) 608 Commercial Street. Open Tuesday through Saturday from 10 AM–4 PM. The building has been preserved and restored, and documents the history of the Branch Mint and Subtreasury buildings. You can see architectural plans, photographs, coins, and other artifacts integral to the early development of San Francisco. You can also see art by Bay Area Chinese artists.

EARLY MORNING, A MAN PRACTICES TAI CHI.

Union Square and the Tenderloin

Glide Memorial Church See *The Downtown Debacle.*

Union Square Geary and Powell Streets. Once the site of a sand dune, Mayor Geary ordered the land to become a public space in 1850. And now, after a recent renovation, Union Square acts as a central meeting ground, a stage for music and theater, and a gathering place to enjoy a cup of coffee while shopping.

THE DOWNTOWN DEBACLE

It is impossible to miss the high population of homeless people living on the streets of San Francisco. The majority of them stake claim at corners throughout Union Square, the Tenderloin, and Golden Gate Park begging for smiles, cash, and sometimes even beer. This has been a political and social issue since the gold rush era. People come here, can't afford the high rent, or lose themselves to drugs or mental illness, and never leave. I suppose it is a tribute to the wealth of services the city offers those down on their luck to see so many on the streets, but local activists work hard to help cure the problem rather than propagate it. To learn about services some of these amazing do-gooders offer the homeless, start with a visit to **Glide Memorial Church** (415-674-6175, glide.org) 330 Ellis Street. Open daily 9–5 PM.

As for your safety, wallets, and sense of obligation, I haven't heard many stories about aggressive panhandling (which is illegal here in San Francisco). If you don't want to give change, you might carry with you some candy or at least a kind smile—it goes a long way.

Nob Hill

Known as Snob Hill to locals, Nob Hill is renowned for its city landmarks, spectacular views, swanky hotels, and the odd sense of affluence and privacy you rarely get in the center of a city. The privileged aura of this neighborhood dates back to the gold rush era. The Big Four railroad barons constructed their mansions here, and one of them—Leland Stanford—built the California Cable Car line to connect his and his partners' mansions with Downtown. Now luxury hotels occupy those original palaces, which burned to the ground during the 1906 earthquake and fire—all but the **Flood Mansion** and **Fairmont Hotel,** which are striking reminders of the opulence cultivated in this hilltop nook.

🏛 **Cable Car Barn** (415-474-1887; sfcablecar.com) 1201 Mason Street. Open at least 10 AM–5 PM. Kids especially like to see the main electrical grid that works the cable cars. There is also a gift shop and some old cars to explore.

Flood Mansion/Pacific Union Club 10000 California. Once the home of the railroad baron James Flood, this mansion is one of the only places to survive the 1906 fire. Now owned by Pacific Union Club (the P.U. Club for short), this swanky men's club doesn't allow visitors, women, or Democrats to enter.

Grace Cathedral (415-749-6300; gracecathedral.org) 1051 Taylor Street. Open Sunday through Friday 7–6 PM and Saturday 8–6 PM. Worth the exhausting uphill hike (or a trip up the cable car) is Grace Cathedral, one of the largest neo-Gothic structures in the U.S. Not only can you visit the cathedral, but you can also attend concerts, services, view the Keith Haring sculpture, and walk the meditative labyrinth.

Russian Hill

Lombard Street Between 20th and 22nd Streets. Billed as the most crooked street in the world, picturesque Lombard Street is actually not—that honor goes to Vermont Street in Potrero Hill. But driving down this street still makes my knuckles turn white. Especially because of all the tourists standing at the bottom taking pictures.

Macondry Lane Between Leavenworth and Taylor Streets. The wealthy inhabitants of this quiet Russian Hill street also share their zip code with Armistead Maupin's *Tales of the City* residents. If you watched the show, you'll recognize the trellised walkways, the gorgeous houses, and plenty of flowers.

Fisherman's Wharf

What used to be a serious fishing port now has displaced its namesake for a more lucrative business venture. Fisherman's Wharf, the number one tourist destination in San Francisco, rarely sees any locals and only a few fishermen can actually afford mooring fees here. Instead, millions of tourists flock here to head to **Alcatraz**, sample clam chowder in sourdough bowls, taste Ghirardelli chocolate and fresh Dungeness crab, and take photos of the sea lions—who arrived eight years ago, and are now protected by the Marine Mammal Act to frolic and bark as long as they'd like. Cluttered with enough souvenir shops to make anyone sick of seeing the same tacky San Francisco sweatshirt or Alcatraz snow globe, the draw here is that unmistakable feeling of being on vacation.

If you plan to spend a lot of time around here, the best deal is to get a **Wharf Pass** (415-440-4474; wharfpass.com). You can choose between a tour, a bay cruise, and four of these six main attractions (**Ripley's Believe it or Not**, the **Wax Museum**, a submarine tour, the **Historic Ships at Hyde Street Pier**, the **Boudin Sourdough Bakery Museum**, or the **Aquarium**). The pass lasts for three days and costs $61 for adults and $38 for kids 5–11.

♪ ⚐ **Alcatraz** (415-981-7625; alcatrazcruises.com) Alcatraz Landing, Pier 33. Since 1853, this island has been a U.S. Army fort, a military prison, and most famously, the home of criminals, including Al Capone and Machine Gun Kelly. The million people who visit the Rock each year take multilingual audio tours. These tours sell out so book early. Go mid-afternoon as, if the fog is going to burn off, that is generally when it happens. Regardless, dress warm. Night Tours are fun as well. $56 adults; $24 kids.

Ghirardelli Square (415-775-5500; ghirardellisq.com) 900 N. Point Street. No longer a chocolate factory, instead a timeshare has gone up, a wine shop and a killer cupcake shop opened, and yet the tourists still keep coming. Avoid the lines at the Ghirardelli shop: The cupcake place is much better.

Hyde Street Pier (415-561-6662; nps.gov/safr) corner of Jefferson and Hyde Streets/499 Jefferson. Open daily from 9:30–5 PM. If historic ships float your boat, head over to the Hyde Street Pier Ships, where you can see cool old ships built from 1880–1915. Around here, you might also find folks willing to take you on bay cruises for super cheap. $5.

Musée Mecanique (415-346-2000, museemechanique.org) The Embarcadero and Taylor Street. Open Monday through Friday from 10 AM–7 PM and Saturday through Sunday from 10 AM–8 PM. Hands down my favorite spot on Fisherman's Wharf, this collection of antique carnival games and video games from the 1970s and 1980s will keep you entertained. Free.

National Maritime Museum of San Francisco (415-447-5000; maritime .org) 499 Jefferson Street. Open daily during the summer 9–8 PM. Worth a peek, if nautical history fascinates you. You'll view everything from exhibits that display the history of ferries and fishing boats to a re-creation of a radio room. $9 adults; $4 kids.

Pier 39 Beach Street and Embarcadero. Sea lions are the only reason to come here. They hang out on the end of the pier, barking and pushing each other around, staring at you. Otherwise, you'll see hordes of tourists, souvenir shops, and restaurants not worth your time, a carousel, and the **Aquarium of the Bay** (415-623-5300; aquariumofthebay.com), which costs $8–14.95.

SS *Jeremiah O'Brien* (415-544-0100; ssjeremiahobrien.org) 23 Pier Street. Open daily 9–4 PM. This 441-foot long ship is still powered by its original engines. Even after 11 Atlantic crossings. Now, you can tour the ship on land, or take one of the cruises that head out a few times a year. $10.

MUSEE MECANIQUE'S ANTIQUE WELCOME STATUE.

USS *Pampanito* (415-775-1943; maritime.org/pamphome.htm) 45 Pier. Open daily from 9–8 PM. This Balao-class World War II submarine enchants the maritime fans, who tour the ship and pretend to be lost at sea. $9 adults; $2 kids.

Civic Center

Just west of City Hall, you'll notice some modern buildings cluttered with society folks. This is the high art area. Visit the opera and ballet at the **War Memorial Opera House**, the symphony at the **Louise M. Davies Symphony Hall,** or attend a great arts lecture at **Herbst Theater**.

♿ **Asian Art Museum** (415-581-3500; asianart.org) 200 Larkin Street. Open Tuesday through Sunday 10 AM–5 PM, Thursday until 9 PM. Built in 2003, this is now the largest museum in the western world for Asian art, with over 16,000 works, spanning over 6000 years. This is a *must* experience in the city. $12 adults; $5 kids.

♿ ▼ **San Francisco City Hall** (415-554-4933; sfgov.org/cityhall) 1 Dr. Carlton B. Goodlett Place. Open Monday through Friday 8–8 PM. The gold-topped building, renovated after the 1989 earthquake, was a thorn in

FREE MUSEUM DAYS IN THE CITY
Though these days get packed, if your budget is tight, you might want to visit these museums when they are free. Go early.

Free First Sunday of the month
Asian Art Museum

Free First Tuesday of the month
Cartoon Art Museum, de Young Museum, Legion of Honor, San Francisco Museum of Modern Art.

Free First Wednesday of the month
Exploratorium

Free Third Wednesday of the month
California Academy of Sciences

former Mayor Willie Brown's side, then Mayor Gavin Newsom created history and allowed gays and lesbians to tie the knot. Take a free guided tour of the building, Monday through Friday at 10, 12, and 2.

✐ ♿ **San Francisco Main Library** (415-557-4400; SFPL.org) 100 Larkin Street. Open daily, Tuesday through Thursday 9–8 PM, Friday 12 PM–6 PM, Saturday and Monday 10 AM–6 PM, and Sunday 12 PM–5 PM. I've wasted hours here, roaming the stacks, surfing the Internet (for free), and listening to authors read. It's not much, but it's the best we have. And there is a great kids' section with story time.

Hayes Valley

Painted Ladies Steiner and Fulton Streets. Epitomized on postcards, in the TV series *Full House*, and paid homage to by flocks of tourists, the Painted Ladies draw herds of visitors each day. Architecture buffs will be especially enthralled by this cluster of six restored Victorians built in 1894 and painted shades of green, blue, and cream, as they are Italianate in style but have gables.

Other Neighborhoods

Mission

The highlight of the Mission District is the vibrancy. Walking the streets, you'll experience a world unlike anywhere else in the city: food stalls, hip boutiques, great thrift stores, piñata shops, Dolores Park, and murals galore. In *Getting Around*, I detailed some of the mural highlights in the Mission District. Below I have listed my two favorites. If you want a mural tour, contact the nonprofit **Precita Eyes** (415-285-2287; precitaeyes.org). From downtown take the #14 bus along Mission Street or take BART and get off on 16th or 24th Street.

Balmy Alley Between Treat Avenue and Harrison Street between 24th and 25th Streets. For a true San Francisco mural tour, you can't miss this colorful alley in the heart of the Mission District. Marvel at the detail, the messages, and the talent hidden in this alley.

Mission Dolores (415-621-8203; missiondolores.org) 3321 16th Street. Tourists dutifully stop at Junípero Serra's sixth mission. A highlight of your visit here is the oldest building in the city: **Mission San Francisco de Asis**, an adobe erected in 1791. Most people either tour the museum, the basilica, and the cemetery, or attend a service. $3–5.

Women's Building (415-431-1180; womensbuilding.org) 3543 18th Street #8. Open Monday through Sunday 9–9 PM. Though there's not much for visitors to do inside, you have to see the mural covering the entire building. You'll know it when you see it. It gets more resplendent every time I walk by.

Potrero Hill

Vermont Street Located between 20th and 22nd Streets. On Easter, the city hosts a big wheel race down the real curviest street in the city. Not as picturesque (or as crowded) as Lombard Street, this street is fun to drive down.

A BALMY ALLEY MURAL IN THE MISSION DISTRICT.

Castro

The Castro used to be dairy farms and dirt roads until Mexican and European home-steaders built the grand Victorians in what was then considered the suburb, Eureka Valley. After the war, when people started moving to the real suburbs, gay men bought and restored those Victorians and coined this neighborhood The Castro after its busiest street. Soon a community of political activists, thrust together to create a safe place to celebrate gay rights, claimed the Castro as their own. Since the assassina-tion of San Francisco openly gay Supervisor Harvey Milk and the rise of AIDS, this community has become a mecca for gay and lesbians from all over the world. For a great tour, check out **Cruisin the Castro** (415-255-1821, cruisinthecastro.com). All Muni street cars stop in the Castro. But the best way to get here is to take the F-line.

Castro Theater (415-621-6120; thecastrotheatre.com) 429 Castro Street. Built in 1922, this Art Deco theater still plays current and classic movies with the help of a live organ player. There are plenty of film festivals here and entering the building makes you feel like an old-time movie star.

♂ ♿ **Randall Museum** (415-554-9600; randallmuseum.org) 199 Museum Way. Open Tuesday through Saturday 10 AM–5 PM. Mostly a children's museum, this is a great place for kids (and curious adults) to explore the natural world. There are plenty of arts and crafts for kids and a wonderful toddler room. Free.

Haight Ashbury

The eight blocks of restored Victorians and Edwardians of the Haight-Ashbury dis-trict are home to one of the richest cultural histories of San Francisco. Until 1865, the Haight was sand dunes marked *Wasteland* on most maps; that was until City Supervisor Frank McCoppin marked the spot to be the site of Golden Gate Park. Victorian houses sprung up, a cable car line appeared, along with an amusement park (which is now long gone), and by the 1890s the Haight was a middle-class enclave. The Depression and World War II decreased the rents and by the 1950s, student activists began taking over the classic homes. The hippies arrived as an off-shoot to the Beats, and soon narcotics unified the masses, protesting against the Vietnam War, gathering in Golden Gate Park for music festivals and the famed Be-In. Kids from all over America arrived in droves, and by 1967 about 75,000 tran-sient residents made the Haight their home.

Today, though the corner of Haight and Ashbury bustles with tourists and chain stores, the allure of the 1960s counterculture movement that once resided here still begs to be relived. Here you'll notice neo-punk squatters begging for cash for drugs, street drummers in tie-dye, and drunken folks spilling onto the streets. If you are in town on the second Sunday in June, the Haight Street Fair rocks.

The best way to get here is to take bus # 7 or #71 up Haight from downtown or take the N-Judah street car, get off in Cole Valley and walk north to Haight Street. Parking teeters on impossible.

Grateful Dead House 710 Ashbury Street. In the 1960s the Grateful Dead, and their many followers, lived together in this 1890 building. You can't go in; don't even try it.

Red Vic Movie House (415-668-3994; redvicmoviehouse.com) 1727 Haight Street. Because the Red Vic shows indie art and cult films at reasonable prices, people line up for hours to sit on couches, munch organic popcorn with nutritional yeast, and sip tea from a real mug.

Pacific Heights and Japantown

Architecture fans head for Victorians on Laguna Street, between Pine and Bush Streets, and the Spreckels Mansion at Washington and Octavia Streets.

Franklin Street Historic District Between Washington and California Streets. A walk up this classic San Francisco street offers a glimpse of some wonderfully renovated Queen Anne Victorians, a Tuscan church, and the Golden Gate church's redwood-paneled stone facade. Another interesting stop is the **Haas Lilienthal House** (415-441-3004; sfheritage.org) at 2007 Franklin Street. You can tour the 1886 Queen Anne and view pictures from the pre-earthquake days. Open Wednesday, Saturday, and Sunday. $8.

Japan Center Geary and Fillmore Streets. An apologetic gesture from the city to the Japanese residents it incarcerated during World War II, here you'll find a three-block mall cluttered with Japanese restaurants, markets, shops, a state of the art cinema (that serves gourmet food and wine during the film), and flower stores. This is the best spot in the city to get any variety of Japanese food you can imagine or relax by the Peace Pagoda, designed in 1960 as a peace gesture from the Japanese people.

Marina

Originally a landfill, until the 1915 Panama-Pacific Exposition forced the city to reconsider wasting such a divine geographical location on mere rubble. Now, the Marina District's Victorian, Edwardian, and Mediterranean architecture are all the rage for cell-phone chatting, stroller-pushing, dog-walking young professionals. Even with the young crowd trading in their apple martinis for Baby Bjorns, there is still quite a singles scene here on weekends, centering on Chestnut Street's bars and restaurants. Take the #30 bus.

⚓ ♿ **Exploratorium** (415-EXPLORE; Exploratorium.edu) Inside the Palace of Fine Arts, 3601 Lyon. Open Tuesday through Sunday 10 AM–5 PM. This family science museum with over 650 exhibits is a great place to kill a few hours. Kids and adults will be fascinated with hands-on science and art exhibits, from how eggs fertilize to how bodies decompose to how water and air make fog. Though little guys will find plenty to entertain, this museum is better for kids over five. For a really tripped-out experience, head to the Tactile Dome, the Superstition Obstacle Course, or view the light display in the back. $14 adults; $9–11 kids.

Fort Mason (415-441-3400; fortmason.org) Buchanan Street and Marina Boulevard. Open daily 9–5 PM. Recently I wandered around here after a trip to Greens restaurant and was astounded by how much great stuff is packed into this old World War II depot. Head into the visitor center for a map, then cruise the aisles of art spaces (including the SFMOMA Artist's Gallery and the Museo Italo-Americano). Once you are done, head up the hill to the lovely green space that offers great Golden Gate Bridge views.

Palace of Fine Arts (415-563-6504, palaceoffinearts.org) 3301 Lyon Street. Built for the 1915 Pan-Pacific Exposition, this faux Roman palace takes you to another time and another place. One of the most peaceful spots in the city—when the hordes of tour buses aren't here: Go early or in the evening, so you can enjoy the swans, the lake, and the renovated dome.

Presidio

Golden Gate Bridge US 101. Nothing represents San Francisco more than the organic-orange painted suspension bridge. The 1.2-mile walk (or bike ride) across the bridge is a must. Be forewarned, it is windy and blustery, even when it is warm and sunny downtown. You might also consider parking on the Marin side and walking towards the city—you'll get better pictures this way. Below the bridge, you'll find **Fort Point**, a museum of military gear, and hopefully by the time you read this, a renovated Warming Hut

PALACE OF FINE ARTS INSPIRES ARTISTS AND ROMANTICS.

(their hot chocolate will sound good after a walk or bike ride around here).

Sunset/Richmond

Take the N streetcar or the #38, #5, #71, or the culture bus.

California Academy of Sciences (415-379-8000; calacademy.org) 55 Music Concourse Drive. Open Monday through Saturday 9:30–5 PM and Sunday 11 AM–5 PM; open late on Thursday evenings. It seems as if the entire city has been awaiting the opening of the new location—and the constant lines around the building prove it! Complete with a sustainable, weather-resistant living roof that cools the interior of the museum, it contains the Steinhart Aquarium, which houses a re-creation of a Philippine coral reef; a three-story glass dome rainforest; and an African hall that so replicates the original, folks who grew up visiting the academy will appreciate the authenticity of these over 100-year-old animal exhibits. Live animals outnumber people touring the academy, with highlights being the penguins, the zillions of fish, the albino alligator, the smallest living tortoises on earth, an anaconda, and jellyfish. The Planetarium show takes you from your seat in the academy to past the Milky Way and back; the whale and dinosaur bones humble most visitors; and don't get me started on the food. First off, Charles Phan and Loretta Keller, two of San Francisco's superstar chefs, teamed up to create the best cuisine any museum has ever seen. Upstairs enjoy a plethora of organic, local options including my vote for the best house-made almond butter and jelly sandwich ever—other highlights include the *pho*, chicken curry, and tacos. Downstairs, walk along a two-story wall of living moss to the **Moss Room** restaurant (see *Dining Out*). $24.95 adults; $19.95 youth and seniors; $14.95 kids 6–12; under 6 free.

THE GOLDEN GATE BRIDGE SANS FOG.

Conservatory of Flowers (415-666-7001, conservatoryofflowers.org) John F. Kennedy Drive. Open Tuesday through Saturday from 9–4:30 PM. After a wicked storm destroyed the

EXPLORING LOCAL NEIGHBORHOODS—GET OFF THE TOURIST RADAR

My favorite way to spend a day is wandering through San Francisco neighborhoods. Below are some of my favorite strolls and communities listed from south to north.

Glen Park

Take BART to Glen Park station.

Glen Park used to be known as Little Switzerland, with its steep eucalyptus-covered hills, and damp fog hugging the mountains. Now it has turned into one of San Francisco's *It* neighborhoods. With the new, gourmet **Canyon Market** (415-586-9999; 2815 Diamond Street), and the super-yummy upscale pizza restaurant **Gialina** (415-239-8500; 2842 Diamond Street) to add flavor to the strip along Chenery and Diamond—which already had bragging rights to the kid-friendly **Chenery Park Restaurant** (415-337-8537; 683 Chenery Street), and the fabulous **Bird and Beckett Books** (415-586-3733; 653 Chenery Street)—Glen Park is becoming a destination for people who live outside the neighborhood. But the star of this foggy patch of southern San Francisco is **Glen Canyon**, which is one of the best places to walk in San Francisco and pretend you aren't in a city.

Bernal Heights

Take #14 bus to Cortland Avenue.

The small hillside bungalows that used to house people displaced by the 1906 quake/fire now are home to a tight-knit community on the steep **Bernal Hill**. You'll also notice community gardens lining stairways that also connect streets, playgrounds, and the excellent **Holly Park**. The commercial district runs down a couple block stretch of Cortland Avenue, where locals enjoy coffee, pastries, and beer in the hidden back gardens of **Liberty Café** (415-695-8777; 410 Cortland Avenue), **Progressive Grounds** (415-282-6233, 400 Cortland Avenue), and the lesbian bar **Wild Side West** (415-647-3099, 424 Cortland Avenue). Or browse through books at **Red Hill Books** (415-648-5331, 401 Cortland Avenue).

Noe Valley

Take J Muni to 24th Street.

The main drag of 24th Street and Church Street houses a collection of upscale restaurants, including the delicious **Fresca** (415-447-2668,

2114 Fillmore Street), **La Ciccia** (415-550-8114, 291 30th Street) (don't miss La Ciccia!), and **Pomelo** (415-285-2257, 1793 Church Street), boutiques, and **Cover to Cover Bookstore** (415-282-8080, 1307 Castro Street). Recently, Noe Valley began spreading southward to include a food-lovers stretch along Church Street. You'll also find some of the city's best antique shops on this stretch.

Potrero Hill

Potrero Hill is home to some of the most beautiful houses as well as one of the biggest housing projects in the city. The commercial heart of Potrero Hill is on 18th Street, between Connecticut and Texas Streets, where you should try out **Chez Maman** (415-824-7166, 1453 18th Street) and **Baraka** (415-255-0370, 288 Connecticut Street) restaurants, **Farley's** coffee shop (415-648-1545, 18th Street), and **Goat Hill Pizza** (415-641-1440, 300 Connecticut Street).

Dogpatch

Take the 3rd Street rail.

This slice of working-class historic homes and buildings is located just east of Potrero Hill (and conveniently, walking distance to the Caltrain station). A slew of modern lofts have appeared to serve artists and commuters, and there's the not-to-be-missed **Flora Grubb/Ritual Coffee** (415-648-2670 or 415-694-6458, 1634 Jerrold Avenue), **Serpentine** (415-252-2000, 2495 3rd Street), and **Piccino** (415-824-4224, 801 22nd Street) restaurants.

Inner Richmond

Take the #38 bus to 3rd Street, walk to Clement.

If you are looking for the true Chinatown of San Francisco, head to the first 10 blocks of Clement Street, where markets hawk everything from chickens to plastic spatulas at low costs. Here you can also find baby stores, students studying in coffee shops, boba teahouses filled with Chinese playing mah-jongg, and a constant bustling energy. A little farther out into Central Richmond is the old **4 Star Theater** (415-666-3488; 2200 Clement Street) that residents fought (and fight still) to keep alive. This is one of the only places in San Francisco where you can view double features and Hong Kong action films on the big screen.

original white dome, the city re-created it, offering a fresh dollop of whiteness to complement the ever-changing gardens of green. I love to hang out in the tropical rooms on a cool day. Moms and Dads, note that you cannot take strollers inside. $1.50–5.

de Young Museum (415-863-3330; thinker.org) 50 Hagiwara Tea Garden Drive, Golden Gate Park. Open Tuesday through Sunday 9:30–5:15 PM, tower closes at 4:30. After years of hoopla, this copper museum reopened in 2005. Now it seems like it has always been a part of the Golden Gate Park landscape. If you are around in March, their Bouquets to Art flower event is sure to impress. The rest of the year, you'll appreciate the collection of American art, the Oceana and Africa exhibits, Andy Goldsworthy's piece in the front of the museum, and the highlight, the 144-foot tower that offers views of the entire park and beyond. The organic café and outdoor area make a welcome pit stop even if you aren't going inside the museum. $10 adults; $6 youth; under 12 free (with paid admission, you can also visit the Legion of Honor on the same day); visitors with a Fast Pass or a Culture Bus ticket get $2 off admission.

Legion of Honor (415-750-3600; thinker.org) Lincoln Park, 34th Avenue and Clement. Open Tuesday through Sunday 9:30–5:15 PM. I come here for the views: expansive Marin, the ocean and city spreading out for miles below you, with Rodin's statue of *The Thinker* behind you. This tribute to ancient European art makes a wonderful stop in conjunction with a visit to the de Young (since you get one-day admission to both). $10 adults; $6 youth; under 12 free.

SAN FRANCISCO VIEWS

Though the best vistas of San Francisco are found across the bay in Marin and Berkeley, you'll find some lovely places to get above the city and take it all in.

Bernal Hill Bernal Heights Boulevard, from the 24th Street BART station, take the 67 Bus. My favorite place to watch fireworks on Fourth of July, this dog park/walking trail offers views from the south of the fog traveling into the city.

Coit Tower See *To See.*

deYoung Tower See *To See*

Dolores Park See *Green Spaces.*

Tank Hill 1 Carmel Street. One of the best local view spots in San Francisco, atop the 600-foot-high hill named for an old water tank stationed there in the late 1800s.

Twin Peaks 100 Christmas Tree Point Road. Native American myth suggests that the Peaks were created when a married couple argued so much that the Great Spirit threw a bolt of thunder and separated them forever. Now families make their homes atop this granite rock, often shrouded by dense fog that dramatically blankets these hills, and tourists crowd the overlook, shivering in the cold.

Sutro Baths Point Lobos Avenue and Merrie Way. In 1881, Adolph Sutro bought most of the western headlands of San Francisco and opened the Sutro Baths, a bathhouse spreading over 3 acres. Glass enclosed with views of the ocean, the baths contained almost 2 million gallons of water and could entertain over 10,000 people. The baths were demolished to make room for a development that never happened. Today, you can walk through the ruins of the baths and get fabulous views of the sea and Seal Rock. Free.

✔ **San Francisco Zoo** (415-753-7080, sfzoo.org) 1 Zoo Road. Open daily from 10 AM–5 PM. After making international news with a tiger attack, the zoo has fought to revive its image. Aside from that event, the SF Zoo is actually a lovely place to spend the day. Here you'll find a great Africa exhibit, grizzly bears, penguins, and a wonderful play area for the little ones spread across acres of trees by the ocean. $11 adults; $5 kids; come with a SF resident for discounts.

✴ To Do

ATHLETIC EVENTS Golden State Warriors. See Oakland *To Do*.

San Francisco Giants 24 Willie Mays Plaza. In a recent *New York Times* article about baseball stadiums, the writer learned what we in San Francisco already knew: Our baseball stadium has the best food around. Plus there is a play structure for kids high in the bleachers, views of the bay, and spots where you can watch the game for free, down by the water. A visit to the park is an unbeatable experience.

San Francisco 49ers 4949 Centennial Boulevard. There is talk that the 49ers will move from their long-lived Candlestick Park location to the South Bay. For now, you can still see the big guys play in the fall at this chilly stadium by the bay.

CABLE CAR RIDES See *Getting Around*.

CYCLING One iconic San Francisco adventure is to cross the Golden Gate Bridge. Locals ride bikes everywhere, dodging traffic like stunt players. If you are like me (read: more cautious when it comes to biking), you will be pleased to know that Golden Gate Park is car-free on weekends. So a ride to the beach is a wonderful activity. If you want, attach your bike to a bus and head over to the park.

You can rent bikes at the outfitters below.

Bay City Bike Rentals and Tours (415-346-2456; baycitybike.com) 2661 Taylor Street, and 1325 Columbus. Opens at 8 AM daily. $25–60 for the day.

Blazing Saddles (415-202-8888; blazingsaddles.com) 1095 Columbus Avenue. Open daily at 8 AM. $7–8 per hour.

KIDS PLAY BASEBALL AT AT&T PARK DURING THE GAME.

Edward Broitman

A CABLE CAR MOTORS DOWN THE STREET.

FARMERS' MARKETS Alemany Farmers' Market, 100 Alemany Boulevard, Saturday, 7:30–5. **Ferry Building Market,** 1 Ferry Building, Tuesday 10 AM–2 PM, and Saturday 8AM– 2 PM PM. **Heart of the City Farmers' Market,** 1182 Market Street, Wednesday and Sunday, 8 AM–5 PM.

FISHING If you are interested in renting a charter boat, visit sfsportfishing.com. From land, the best places to fish are the **South Beach Marina Pier** (The Embarcadero at Pier 40) and the **Fort Baker Pier** (Take Alexander Avenue off US 101 to Danes Drive then turn right onto Bunker Road and follow it down to the pier).

GOLF Golden Gate Park Course (415-751-8987, goldengateparkgolf.com) 47th Avenue at Fulton Street. Open daily 30 minutes after sunrise and 30 minutes before dark. A great cheap course, though often foggy. $6–25.

Presidio Course (415-561-4653, presidiogolf.com) 300 Finley Road. Open daily 7–6 PM. The 17th hole offers views of the bridge to inspire. $15–145.

HANG GLIDING Fort Funston (1116 Wrigley Way) is one of the premier spots in Northern California to hang glide. If you are interested in renting gear or taking a lesson, contact **Mission Soaring Center** (408-262-1055; hang-gliding.com).

FIND GOODIES YOU NEVER IMAGINED AT THE FERRY BUILDING FARMERS' MARKET.

SPAS Kabuki Springs and Spa (415-922-6000, kabukisprings.com) 1750 Geary Boulevard. Open daily 10 AM–6 PM. When all else fails, I head here for a day in the communal baths. This Japanese-style bathhouse is the perfect place to relax after a day of walking. If you can spring for it, get the *Abhyanga* Massage with *Shirodhara* Treatment—talk about bliss, it feels like someone slides your scalp off and fills your brain with honey.

Nob Hill Spa (415-345-2888, huntingtonhotel.com) 1075 California Street. Open daily 7:30 AM–9 PM. Inside the Huntington Hotel, this spa offers views of the city from the infinity pool and Jacuzzi. A place to hang out to escape the chaos of downtown and enjoy the

Art at the Dump

SF Dump (415-330-1415; sfrecycling.com/AIR) 503 Tunnel Avenue. Since 1990, over 70 professional Bay Area artists have completed residencies in making art, not landfill. The program provides accomplished artists with unlimited access to waste materials at the company's 46-acre site, which includes the transfer station, public dump, and several recycling facilities.

Every three months, the dump holds a free public artist exhibition. Shows are held in the company's art studio and have been everything from a circus to a symphony. On a typical opening night, crowds of up to 700 people show up. Most shows have an extra bonus: the increasingly popular *give-away pile* in which artists discard items previously scavenged but unused in their artwork.

Every third Saturday of the month at 10:00 AM, you can tour the dump. The tour consists of a recycling and sustainability discussion, a trip to the art studio to meet the current artist-in-residence, a stop at the Household Hazard Waste Facility, an unforgettable visit to the transfer station, and finally a walk through the sculpture garden. Call for reservations.

eucalyptus steam room and sauna. Or, you can try out the decadent spa treatments, a champagne mani-pedi, or shop in the gift shop. This spa is a good spot for people who want a *Sex in the City* day with a couple friends.

SenSpa (415-441-1777, senspa.com) 1161 Gorgas Avenue. Open Tuesday through Friday 10 AM–9 PM and Saturday through Sunday 9 AM–7 PM. When the architects of this Zen-themed spa heard you couldn't make these old army medical barracks into a spa, they set out to prove the inspectors wrong. And what a job they did. Possibly the most relaxing spa in the city, fit with waterfalls, organic snacks, and stonework throughout, SenSpa gets it right. Even down to the inspirational quotes you receive at every turn.

TENNIS Most San Francisco parks offer free tennis courts at a first-come first-served basis. Go early (or prepare to wait) as they fill up fast, especially on weekends. None rent racquets.

Alamo Square 535 Scott Street.

Dolores Park 18th Street and Dolores Street.

Golden Gate Park 12th Avenue and Rockridge Drive.

Holly Park Bocana Street and Highland Avenue.

WATER SPORTS

Kayaking

City Kayak (415-357-1010; citykayak.com) 2 Townsend Street, #4-108. Open daily from 10 AM–5 PM. Head out on a kayak trip through the bay with these experienced guides. Make sure to dress warmly, especially if you take a full-moon tour.

Many people opt to rent a kayak during Giants' games to try to catch fly balls. Fees for trips: $49–69. Fees for rentals: $15–30.

Sailing

Captain Kirk's Sailing Adventures (650-492-0681; sfbaysail.com) 310 Harbor Drive. There is nothing like being on a sailboat on the bay on a sunny day. Some trips pass under the Golden Gate Bridge, while others tool around the Marina, offering unsurpassed views of the city. Fees for trips: $130–225.

Surfing, Kiteboarding, and Windsurfing

Yes, the water up here is cold, freezing, if you will. You might look at the surfers lining up for waves and call them hardcore, or stupid. But you won't find waves like this in many places. So get a good wetsuit and dare yourself. In winter, we get huge swells that attract surfers from around the world. The best surf spots in the city are under the Golden Gate Bridge and Ocean Beach. And the best place to windsurf and kiteboard is in the bay near Crissy Field.

Rentals and Lessons

Aqua Surf Shop (415-876-2782; www.aquasurfshop.com) 1742 Haight Street. Open daily 11 AM–7 PM. Rentals: $10–25.

Mollusk Surf Shop (415-564-6300; mollusksurfshop.com) 4500 Irving Street. Open daily from 10 AM–6:30 PM.

Sports Basement (800-869-6670; sportsbasement.com) 610 Mason Street. This is a great place to get gear for windsurfing.

WHALE WATCHING Oceanic Society Expeditions See *Head to the Farallons.*

✴ Green Spaces

SOMA South Park South Park Street, between 2nd and 3rd Streets, south of Harrison. Since San Francisco's first round of banking elite abandoned South Park, this neighborhood has managed to retain some of the 19th-century classiness; it is a civilized place to enjoy a sandwich on the grassy square, bordered by several good shops (including the discount designer store **Jeremy's**) and restaurants.

Yerba Buena Gardens Howard and Mission Streets, between 3rd and 4th Streets. This iconic green development added a lovely garden to the downtown area. Explore the dramatic fountain with a tribute to Martin Luther King Jr. and check out the weekly free arts events. This green space is a central gathering place for SoMa workers and students.

Chinatown

Portsmouth Square Kearny and Washington Streets. Saturday mornings this square bustles with old Chinese ladies gossiping and playing mah-jongg, men playing chess, kids running around the play structures—it actually feels like China (except the babies wear diapers instead of pants with the holes cut out in the bottom).

North Beach

Telegraph Hill Lombard and Kearny Streets. A hike up this steep green hill brings great views of the city, the Golden Gate Bridge, and the famed parrots of Telegraph Hill. Plus, you can visit Coit Tower (see *To See*).

Washington Square Park Columbus Avenue, between Filbert and Union Streets. Whenever I hang out in this park, either sipping a coffee or watching the old Chinese ladies do tai chi (get here early, it is a sight!), I feel like I am in another country. In the afternoon, the park fills with dogs, kids, and locals smoking who knows what while soaking up the sun.

Nob Hill

Huntington Park California and Cushman Streets. Worth the trek up the hill, this park, set before Grace Cathedral and next to the Flood Mansion, welcomes dogs, kids, people doing tai chi, and tons of tourists wanting to snap photos of the view.

Hayes Valley

Alamo Square 1235 McAllister Street. Literally, a square of green atop steep Hayes hill, you'll find some of the best views of downtown and the bay, plus a great area for morning coffee and pastries, a tennis court that fills quickly, and a hidden shoe garden at the top.

Hayes Green/Octavia Street's Median Hayes and Octavia Streets. Thanks to the 1989 earthquake, this old freeway off-ramp turned green space is now populated by picnickers and public art. I love to grab a Blue Bottle hot chocolate and sit in the square watching the hipsters and ballerinas pass.

Mission

✐ **Dolores Park** Between Dolores and Church Streets and 18th and 20th Streets. Second to Golden Gate Park, this is the best green space in the city. When the rest of the city is fogged in, Mission hipsters party it up in the sun. On weekends and warm evenings, this spot turns into a beach, filled with DJs (and sometimes live music like the symphony, SF Mime Troupe, or even movies in the park), dogs, plenty of people drinking, kids playing, guys wearing next to nothing, and food. On Easter, don't miss the drag queen Easter Bonnet competition.

Haight Ashbury

Buena Vista Park 498 Buena Vista Avenue at Haight. Buena Vista Park is a wooded green space where Spanish soldiers used to spend the night when traveling from the Mission to the Presidio. It acts as the unofficial barrier between Upper and Lower Haight and the Heights neighborhoods leading up to Twin Peaks. Sometimes you'll see groups of the homeless lounging on the hillside or crowds of kids drinking, but mostly, this park is known as a gay cruising spot.

Marina and the Presidio

Crissy Field Between Marina and Lincoln Park. Rain or shine, this green area, complete with a walking path across the northern edge of the city, soccer fields, a mellow beach, and the best spot in the city to windsurf, attracts stroller-pushing moms, dog walkers, joggers, and heaps of city folks who come to recall why they live in such a gorgeous city. The views of the Golden Gate Bridge, Alcatraz, Angel Island, and Marin are spectacular. This is where I bring my son to play in the water and watch barges pass under the bridge.

Lands End At the western end of Geary Street. A local gem, this sandy hiking path weaves around the northwest side of the city and offers spectacular views of the sea, Marin, the bridge, and the fancy houses in Seacliff. Though it gets windy, this is my favorite place for a city hike.

Presidio The northwest edge of the city, from Lombard to the ocean. With 1400 acres of woods, eucalyptus trees, beaches, rambling trails, a pet cemetery, a bowling alley, George Lucas's new offices, a summer Shakespeare festival, old military barracks, and views of the Pacific, this park begs to be explored. This area was a military post after the Americans forced the Mexicans out. Now the city-owned national park is reinventing itself with a number of high-end restaurants and the sublime SenSpa (see *Spas*).

Sunset and Richmond

Lake Merced 1 Harding Road. Just shy of the ocean, you'll find this large lake with a great running and walking path.

Stern Grove Junípero Serra and Sloat. Pine Lake Park and Stern Grove make up a 64-acre bio-diverse environment that has often been congratulated for providing a wildlife habitat and green space in a very residential neighborhood. Despite the fog that drapes these hills in summer, this park gets to boast one of San Francisco's best summer activities—the Sigmund Stern Grove Festival. Every Sunday, the city presents free live shows in an idyllic evergreen grove, attracting big name musicians, the San Francisco Opera and Symphony, and international music sensations.

Angel Island

Angel Island (415-435-3522; angelisland.org). You'll need to catch the ferry from Tiburon to get here. The largest island in the bay was once a Japanese internment camp. Now, locals ferry in and out all day to hike, photograph the city, and even camp. If you want to camp, book early, sites fill up. It can be very cold and there

---

GOLDEN GATE PARK

✂ ♿ ☀ **Golden Gate Park** (parks.sfgov.org) Between Fulton and Lincoln and Arguello and the ocean. William Hammond Hall made the park happen, but John McLaren, the one-time superintendent of the city, made the park into the tribute to wild space you see now. With so much to do packed into 1000 acres, you could spend days exploring this area—I still find new things. Other than the museums listed above (deYoung, Conservatory of Flowers, and the California Academy of Sciences), you will find the following highlights:

AIDS Memorial Grove Dogwood and redwood trees shade the trail and make this a perfect place to remember those you lost to AIDS. Even if you don't know anyone with AIDS, come to check out the only garden of its kind.

Bison On John F. Kennedy Drive and Chain of Lakes Drive, in the western part of the park. Yes, your eyes are not playing tricks on you, there are bison living in the park—a herd of them in fact.

Japanese Tea Garden (415-752-4227) 72 Tea Garden Drive and Martin Luther King Jr. Drive. Open daily from 10:30 AM–4:30 PM. This peaceful spot makes a lovely place to space out in, drink tea, or marvel in the gardens. Check out the large Buddha from 1790, the 9000-pound Lantern of Peace, and the *taiko hashi* drum bridge. $5.

Lindy in the Park (lindyinthepark.com). At 12:30 on Saturdays, you can

are no services here, so you have to bring everything. Contact **Golden Gate Ferry** (baycrossings.com) for ferry schedules and times.

BEACHES **Baker Beach** Gibson Road, Presidio. Locals flock here on warm days for views of the Golden Gate Bridge and Marin. Parking is fairly easy so people bring food to barbeque and plenty of beach gear to laze in the shadow of the bridge. For the adventurous, the eastern edge, just under the bridge, is a nude beach.

Crissy Field Beach 603 Mason Street. On warm days, bring the kids to this mellow beach on the bay. Views rock. And the kids and dogs will be entertained for hours. The beach just before the warming hut attracts families with little kids, while surfers drop in next to the Golden Gate Bridge.

&. ☀ **Fort Funston** 500 Skyline Boulevard. Another local favorite, especially with dog walkers, this beach offers a paved trail along the dunes and another very steep sandy path down to the ocean. This is a great place to hang glide. It gets windy on most days, so bring a warm jacket.

Ocean Beach Great Highway. Though the most crowded area is near Judah Street, where you can catch the N-Muni, San Francisco's busiest and most accessible beach stretches across the entire west end of the city. Dirty and crowded on warm days, this is the spot to come when the sun shows her face. There are artsy fire pits made by Burning Man artists, and bathrooms by the Judah Street path. This is also where the surfers head out on swell days.

partake in free Lindy dancing in the shadow of the de Young.

Rose Garden In summer, when the roses are in full bloom, your nose gets a luscious treat. Seventy beds of rose varietals live here.

♂ &. **Stow Lake and Strawberry Hill** Just east of 19th Avenue. I like to come here early in the morning and watch the birds. Others enjoy pedaling or rowing around this lovely man-made lake. You can hike to the top of Strawberry Hill as well. Check out the turtles that live on the north side of the lake. You can rent paddleboats on the western edge of the lake.

♂ &. **Strybing Arboretum and Botanical Gardens** (415-661-1316; sfbotanical garden.org) Ninth Avenue and Lincoln Way. Open Monday through Friday 8 AM–4:30 PM and Saturday through Sunday 10 AM–5 PM. With 70 acres of outdoor gardens, I never get sick of this space. In summer, the Golden Gate Park Band plays free weekend concerts. In the evenings look for the fox that lives here. Free.

Windmills There are two windmills in the far west edge of the park. The largest is the Dutch Windmill, in the northwest corner of park, designed by Alpheus Bull Jr. in 1903. It reaches 75 feet high and spins 102-foot-long spears. Surrounded by the Queen Wilhelmina's tulip garden (go in February through April when the 10,000 tulip bulbs—planted in October—bloom) and restored in 1981, this is a great place to picnic. The windmill produces no power. The other one is the Murphy windmill in the southwest corner of the park, which was built in 1905.

✳ Lodging

Aside from the famed Fairmont Hotel, I have decided not to include any major chain hotels. However, if none of the hotels listed suffice, there are a number of four-star chain hotels that might be more your speed. Here is a compilation of some of the more famous ones and their Web sites. Around the Moscone Convention Center in SoMa, you'll find the newly built **Intercontinental** (ichotelsgroup.com), the plush **Four Seasons** (fourseasons .com), the chic **W** (starwoodhotels .com), amazing views at the **St. Regis** (starwoodhotels.com), the **Palace** (starwoodhotels.com) and the nicely appointed **Marriott** (marriott.com). On Nob Hill, expect a lovely **Ritz Carlton** (ritzcarlton.com), as well as the renovated **Intercontinental Mark Hopkins** (ichotelsgroup.com). In and around Union Square are the **Grand Hyatt** (grandsanfrancisco.hyatt.com), Kimpton's **Hotel Monaco** (monaco-sf.com), the huge **Parc 55** (parc55 hotel.com), **Hotel Nikko** (hotel-nikkosf.com), and the renovated **Westin St Francis** (starwoodhotels.com). In the financial district are the **Omni Hotel** (omnihotels.com) and **Le Meridien** (starwoodhotels.com). Around Fisherman's Wharf, you'll find a **Sheraton** (starwoodhotels.com) and another **Marriott** (marriott.com). The local chain **Joie De Vivre** (jdvhotels.com) owns a numbers of San Francisco properties.

HOTELS AND RESORTS

Downtown

♦ & ⁞¶⁞ ♒ **Argonaut Hotel** (415-563-0800; argonauthotel.com) 495 Jefferson Street. Located in a 1908 warehouse overlooking Fisherman's Wharf, this nautical themed 252-room hotel is a great choice for families and business travelers who don't want to be in downtown. Exposed Douglas fir beams from the original structure, brick, and beds reminiscent of a boat make this a unique option. Interior rooms work for those of you on a budget, but the best option is to spring for a bay view room. Amenities include gym, Blue Mermaid Chowder House Restaurant, business center, concierge, wine hour, room service, parking (fee). $$$–$$$$.

♦ & ⁞¶⁞ **Fairmont** (415-772-5000; fairmont.com/sanfrancisco) 950 Mason Street. It's hard to think of San Francisco and imagine the city without the iconic Fairmont Hotel. The first of the luxurious franchise, located at the summit of Nob Hill, attracts businesspeople, dignitaries, and those looking for a glimpse at the high life . . . literally. Reagan and Gorbachev signed off on the end of the Cold War in the pricey President's Suite (a mere ten grand will get you a night there); the original UN pact began here (all the flags out front represent each country that attended). And make sure to check out the old Prohibition bar. Completed in 1906,

THE NAUTICAL-THEMED ARGONAUT HOTEL.

just before the earthquake, the original structure burnt to the ground; only a couple marble walls and mirrors (which you can see in the lobby) were salvaged. The 591 rooms and suites are as glorious as you would expect and the views can't be beat. Amenities include two restaurants, room service, Frette linens, spa, fitness center, business center, concierge, and parking (fee). $$$$.

ᵀ Hotel Boheme (415-433-9111; hotelboheme.com) 444 Columbus. Want to feel like a beat poet and stay where Ginsberg did? Hotel Boheme not only offers the bohemian experience similar to a Parisian hotel, but also celebrates the literary roots of the North Beach neighborhood. Here you'll get one of 15 small rooms with wrought iron beds, striped carpet, city views, a mosquito net, and city noise (but you don't stay in North Beach for the serene atmosphere). Try to get a room off Columbus Street (rooms 107, 207, and 208), which also have views of Coit Tower. $$.

& ᵀ Hotel Des Arts (415-956-3232; 800-956-4322; sfhoteldesarts.com) 447 Bush Street. When the owners took this 51-room hotel and renovated, they offered emerging global artists the opportunity to paint murals on the walls of each room. Aside from the colorful murals, expect simple rooms with wainscoting, flat screen TVs, low Japanese-style beds, and continental breakfasts. For my money, I would go for a Deluxe Queen room with a private bathroom. Located across from the Chinatown gate, this is a great spot for people who want to be in the center of downtown, but don't want the run-of-the-mill type of room. $–$$.

♂ & ❦ ᵀ Hotel Diva (415-885-0260, hoteldiva.com) 440 Geary Street. The sexiest kid-friendly hotel in the city offers 116 rooms and suites with cold-rolled steel headboards, a free condom in the safe, and four lounges created by local designers. The Kids' Suite is a work of art—with a bunk bed, karaoke machine, computer, toys, and dress-up clothes. Amenities include Colibri restaurant (room delivery for dinner), continental breakfast, gym, concierge, iPods for rent, and parking (fee). $$–$$$$.

& ᵀ Hotel Frank (415-986-2000; personalityhotels.com) 386 Geary Street. Thomas Schoos turned the 100-year-old Maxwell Hotel into a 153-room cutting-edge hotel fit with: a rotating flat screen TV and mirror; black, white, and emerald color schemes; urban photography; hand-blown smoked glass bubble lights; gilded frames; crocodile headboards; and Carrera marble baths. There is also a restaurant, concierge, business center, room service, and parking (fee). $$–$$$$.

♠ & ᵀ Hotel Mark Twain (415-673-2332; hotelmarktwain.com), 345 Taylor. This hotel pays tribute to its namesake with his quotes on the windows and a simple vibe. Exposed pipes, 118 rooms with subdued tones, flat screen TVs, plus continental breakfasts, room service from the excellent **Fish and Farm** restaurant, and parking (fee). Go for a deluxe king room, with high thread-count sheets, plush quilts, and free wireless. Lower rooms have triple-paned windows and higher-level rooms can be loud. $–$$.

♠ ♂ & ❦ ᵀ Hotel Metropolis (415-775-4600; hotelmetropolis.com) 25 Mason Street. If you can handle being on the fringe of the Tenderloin, this hotel offers the nicest rooms for the price. Its 105 Zen-themed rooms and suites honor the four elements of nature. Rooms on higher levels have balconies and upgraded amenities, while the kids' suite boasts toys, games, and a SpongeBob-themed bathroom. Check out the art by the Tenderloin Children's Center. The excellent **farmerbrown** restaurant, small gym, business center, weekend wine social, and parking (fee) are some of the amenities. $–$$$.

⚓ ♿ 🐾 ⁼ı⁼ **Hotel Triton** (415-394-0500; hoteltriton.com) 342 Grant Avenue. Arguably the hippest hotel in the city, Hotel Triton offers 140 rooms and suites plus 7 celebrity-designed suites (including one designed by Jerry Garcia), or you might opt for the new Premier King eco-suites. Centrally located, with views of the Chinatown gate, you'll be hard pressed to find another hotel as funky as this. Amenities include Café de la Presse restaurant (and room delivery service), Friday night DJ, fitness room, and parking (fee). $$–$$$$.

⚓ ♿ ⁼ı⁼ **Huntington Hotel** (415-474-5400 or 800-227-4683; huntingtonhotel .com) 1075 California Street. The only family-owned luxury hotel perched on top of Nob Hill. Guests get the royal treatment—from a hot towel on a silver platter when you arrive, to day-use of the spa and pool. These 136 large rooms and suites are romantic, with stellar views, gold mirrors, silky bedding, rich wood furniture, marble bathrooms, and even an oxygen machine to help curb jet lag. There is also a restaurant and parking (fee). $$$$.

⚓ ♿ ⁼ı⁼ 🐾 **Kensington Park Hotel** (415-788-6400; kensingtonparkhotel .com) 450 Post Street. After a million dollar renovation, this 92-room hotel offers custom made furniture that is both antique and modern, cherry blossom-textured carpet, gilded mirrors, and a mod desk; it would be tough to find another hotel as classy as this for the price. Get a corner room with a Union Square view. Amenities include the excellent **Farallon** restaurant, flat screen TV, and parking (fee). $$–$$$$.

⚓ ♿ ⁼ı⁼ **Orchard Garden Hotel** (415-399-9807; theorchardgardenhotel .com) 466 Bush Street. Built from the ground up in 2006, San Francisco's only 100 percent green boutique hotel caters to travelers who want to chill on a chemical-free mattress while watching a flat screen TV. Tan and green color schemes, an entryway fountain, and Asian antiques inspire calm in the heart of the city. Guests in 86 rooms have access to the business center and fitness room. The European-style Continental breakfast, room service from the organic restaurant, and parking all cost extra. $$–$$$$.

INNS AND B&BS

Downtown

⚓ ⁼ı⁼ 🐾 **Golden Gate Hotel** (415-392-3702; goldengatehotel.com) 775 Bush. This yellow Edwardian on the outskirts of Nob Hill offers frilly décor for reasonable prices. Most of the 25 rooms share a bathroom, offer plush

THE KIDS' SUITE AT HOTEL METROPOLIS.

hypoallergenic linens, breakfast, and claw-foot tubs. But it can get loud if you are in a street-facing room. $–$$.

ᵀ Washington Square Inn (415-981-4220, wsisf.com) 1660 Stockton. This North Beach bed-and-breakfast faces the park, and is close (but not too close) to the main drag of North Beach and Fisherman's Wharf. Victorian frilliness, fireplaces, and comfortable beds make this an ideal place for older travelers who want sophisticated accommodations. Maria and Daniel Levin go out of their way to create a peaceful environment. Guests in the 15 rooms get continental breakfasts. $$–$$$.

✐ White Swan Inn (415-775-1755; jdvhotels.com) 845 Bush. In the middle of downtown, this 26-room B&B offers a classic British experience complete with breakfast, parking (fee), and afternoon treats. A lovely respite from the masses, you'll feel like you entered a Jane Austen novel. I especially like sitting by the fireplace and enjoying the nightly wine and cheese. $$$.

Other Neighborhoods
Inns listed from east to west.

The Mission
❀ ✐ ▼ ᵀ The Inn San Francisco (415-641-0188 or 800-359-0913; innsf.com) 943 S. Van Ness. The antiques throughout the two houses, the black-and-white pictures, the library of San Francisco history books, and the mere fact that this has been an inn for the past century, hints that Marty knows how to offer an authentic experience. My favorite details about this 21-room B&B are the garden with the hot tub, the truffles in your room, expanded continental breakfast, Marty's dog Marshmellow, and the solar panels. $$–$$$$.

Hayes Valley
❀ ✐ ✤ ᵀ Hayes Valley Inn (415-431-9131; hayesvalleyinn.com)

417 Gough. Located on a busy street in the heart of chic Hayes Valley, this 28-room inn is one of the cheapest around. If you don't mind sharing a bathroom and having a tiny room, you'll dig the central location away from the hordes of tourists downtown, but close to public transportation. Continental breakfast is included in the price. $.

Haight Ashbury
✐ ᵀ Inn 1890 (415-386-0486 or 888-Inn-1890; inn1890.com) 1890 Page Street. If you are looking for an authentic San Francisco experience, look no further than this 17-room Victorian with lots of light, hardwood floors, skylights, and a lovely breakfast area. Expect wainscoting, plush bedding, some bathtubs, fireplaces or kitchens in-room, and Tempur-Pedic beds. Other perks include snacks available all day and night (including gummy bears), a library, games, communal kitchen, expanded continental breakfast, and comfy robes. I like rooms 11, 16, and 17 because they have tubs and tiled bathrooms. $–$$.

✐ ♿ ᵀ Stanyan Park Hotel (415-751-1000; stanyanpark.com) 751 Stanyan Street. Classic and classy, this is a wonderful choice for families wanting to be away from the hustle of downtown. Across the street from Golden Gate Park (though you are still across a busy street from the greenery), this Victorian offers 36 large and mellow accommodations and expanded continental breakfast. Spring for a corner room or the suites with kitchens. $$–$$$$.

Marina/Cow Hollow
ᵀ Union Street Inn (415-346-0424; unionstreetinn.com) 2229 Union Street. This 1903 Victorian sits on prim real estate: the fancy shopping area of Cow Hollow's Union Street. Five rooms offer royal-looking beds with

plush linens, bay windows, garden views, and a super good breakfast. Though public transportation is a bit trickier out here, this fancy inn and its gardens will make the trek home worth it. $$–$$$$.

The Richmond

🖉 ♿ 🐾 **Seal Rock Inn** (415-752-8000 or 888-732-5762; sealrockinn.com) 545 Point Lobos Avenue. Since the 1950s, Seal Rock Inn has capitalized on offering 27 reasonably priced rooms near the ocean. Large rooms with fireplaces and kitchens, queen beds, plus a pool, ping-pong tables, badminton, restaurant, and free parking make it the ideal spot for families. And when the fog lifts, you'll get priceless views of Seal Rock and the ocean. Third-floor rooms have better views. $$.

HOSTELS Hostelling International Fisherman's Wharf (415-771-7277; sfhostels.com) Fort Mason, Building 240. City dwellers pay big bucks for this view of the bay and Golden Gate Bridge and if you don't mind sacrificing luxury, you can enjoy the vistas for a steal. Spring for a three-person room, because doubles are in the basement. Or if you want to save heaps of cash, go for a dorm bed. All rooms come with access to the communal kitchen and a breakfast bagel or waffle. Set on national park land, this property is quiet, pretty isolated, and feels like summer camp. $–$$.

✳ Where to Eat

DINING OUT Without wanting to go overboard, I have decided to include my favorites that you might not find on your own. For a complete listing of local restaurants, you might want to visit sfstation.com or sfgate.com. The latter has a wonderful compilation of the Top 100 restaurants in the Bay Area as well as the best Bargain Bites.

Downtown

♿ ♟ **Acme Chophouse** (415-644-0240; acmechophouse.com) 24 Willie Mays Plaza. Open for lunch Tuesday through Friday and dinner Tuesday through Saturday (if there is a ballgame at the park, they serve dinner on Sunday). Located inside Pac Bell Park, this high-profile steakhouse delivers fresh meat and vegetables that live up to San Francisco standards. Here you'll find sustainable wood tables and TVs showing the baseball game, excellent steak tartare, and the mac and cheese side dish is the creamiest around. Reservations recommended. $$$–$$$$.

🖉 **Boulevard** (415-543-6084; boule vardrestaurant.com) 1 Mission Street. Open for lunch Monday through Friday and for dinner nightly. Nancy Oakes and Pamela Mazzola created this delicate tribute to California cuisine 15 years ago and it has endured the onslaught of their followers. An exposed brick ceiling, blown-glass lights, white-shirt-and-tie waiters, views of the bay, and the open kitchen offer sophistication in a friendly environment. Plus the building is a historical landmark: Rumor has it that it survived the 1906 earthquake and fire because the bartender bribed the firemen with whiskey and wine to protect it. The menu changes every couple of days, but the last time I was here, I had Dungeness crab, stuffed calamari, and *ah*-mazing cookies. Reservations required for dinner. Lunch: $$–$$$$. Dinner: $$$$.

♟ ♿ **Café Bastille** (415-986-5673; cafebastille.ypguides.net) 22 Belden Place. Open Monday through Friday 11:30 AM–3 PM and 5 PM–10 PM. An evening on Belden Place, with outside tables lining an alley strung with lights, is not about the food. We come here to feel like we are in Europe—that is, when the weather is warm enough to eat outdoors. You can pick from a number of restaurants (most of them decent enough), but I always come back to Café Bastille, where they serve up traditional French food like onion soup, lamb, and dessert crepes. Reservations recommended. $$$.

𝖸 & **Coco500** (415-543-2222; coco500 .com) 500 Brannan Street. Open for lunch Monday through Friday, and for dinner Monday through Saturday. Bamboo walls and a sea-glass mosaic bar underscore the single-minded attention Loretta Keller and her staff devote to their food. Highlights include the flatbreads, fried green beans, beef cheeks, and grilled seafood. Everything is affordable except the wine list: Peruse it; you'll notice a price tag on a bottle that might blow you away. Reservations required for dinner. $$–$$$$.

♪ & 𝖸 **farmerbrown** (415- 409-3276; farmerbrownsf.com) 25 Mason Street. Open from 5 PM–1 AM nightly; Sunday brunch. Entering this dimly lit bar/restaurant, you'll feel like you found the hippest spot in town: salvaged furniture, found art, silkscreen photo wall hangings, and the best restaurant music play-list in town— plus serious, Southern comfort food grown by African American organic farmers. You can't miss the Rocky Jr. fried chicken, served with smoky macaroni and cheese; and greens, pecan pie, and sweet potato fries the size of my kid's arm. Plates are gigantic; don't go crazy on the appetizers—though you might be tempted to. The Sunday gospel brunch buffet is worth a stop, as at-risk youth run the whole shebang. Reservations recommended. $$–$$$.

♪ 𝖸 **Millennium** (415-345-3900, millenniumrestaurant.com) 580 Geary Street. Open Sunday through Thursday from 5:30 PM–9:30 PM and Friday and Saturday from 5:30 PM–10 PM.

Eating at this vegan restaurant will convert most carnivores, at least for one meal. While I am deciding, I always start with fresh organic fruit cocktails. Since everything on the menu is seasonal and organic, imagine dishes like emerald-seared rice cake with curry, or charmoula-grilled portobello mushroom. If you can afford the chef's tasting menu ($65), it is worth it. Reservations recommended. $$$–$$$$.

♪ & 𝖸 **Moss Room** (415-876-6121; themossroom.com) 55 Music Concourse Drive, Golden Gate Park. Open for lunch and dinner daily. Superstar chef Loretta Keller has created one of the most anticipated new restaurants in San Francisco history, located in the California Academy of Sciences' new digs. Descend the stairs alongside a wall of living moss to enter a cavernous room dotted with hanging lights. Organic and seasonal dishes almost outshine the décor, with highlights being the grilled Monterey squid, smoked trout salad, lamb, albacore, and steak. To eat here at lunch, you need to pay admission to the Academy. For dinner, reservations are highly recommended. $$–$$$$.

𝖸 **Restaurant Gary Danko** (415-749-2060; garydanko.com) 800 N. Point Street. Open daily from 5:00 PM–12:00 AM. Classic, clean, and fresh—famed chef Gary Danko has been serving the San Francisco food scene the finest cuisine for years. Choose a la carte or go for the tasting menu. Specialties might include lemon-herb duck breast with duck hash, or branzini with fennel puree. Reservations required. $$$–$$$$.

& 𝖸 **Rose Pistola** ((415-399-0499; rosepistolasf.com) 532 Columbus Avenue. Open daily for lunch from 11 AM–4 PM, and for dinner Sunday through Thursday from 5:30 PM–11 PM and Friday through Saturday from 5:30

PM–12 AM. High-end California Italian fare in a spacious room, this North Beach spot is my choice in the area. Rustic cuisine of the highest quality, you can get everything from a pizza cooked in a wood burning oven to family-style pasta. This is the only restaurant I have ever ordered the same dessert twice in one sitting—pumpkin bread pudding with caramel gelato—yum! Reservations recommended. $$–$$$$.

Y **Slanted Door** (415-861-8032; slanteddoor.com) 1 Ferry Plaza. Open daily 11 AM–2:30 PM and 5:30 PM–10 PM. Charles Phan took a big chance when he relocated his popular Vietnamese restaurant from its low-key location in the Mission to the Ferry Building. And it paid off. Now not only locals fill this lofty wall-to–ceiling-windowed eatery, but also tourists wait at the bar, sipping fruity cocktails, staring wistfully at the bay. To say everything I have eaten here is good is an understatement. People come here for the Niman Ranch shaking beef, but I always end up with local organic vegetable dishes, steamed buns, and some soup. They also have a couple cafes around the city called Out the Door, which serve up cheaper Vietnamese street food with organic ingredients (see *Eating Out*). Reservations required. $$–$$$.

🍴 ♿ **Yank Sing** (415-957-9300; yanksing.com) 101 Spear Street. Open daily from 11 AM–3 PM during the week and 10 AM–4 PM on weekends. Every time visitors come to town, we go to Yank Sing. It is not the best dim sum in the world, but it might be the best in San Francisco. And the priciest. Pick what you like from rolling carts and gorge yourself until you can hardly breathe. Watch out for the specials, they are pricey. $–$$ (but you'll need to order at least four dishes per person to fill up).

Other Neighborhoods
Mission

♿ Y **Blue Plate** (415-282-6777; blueplatesf.com) 3218 Mission Street. Open daily at least 6–10 PM. Mellow, off the radar, and finger-licking comfort food served by hipper-than-rock-star servers. Think gourmet meatloaf, drunken mac and cheese, buttery apple crumble, the best dinner rolls in town, and a wine list that will make you have more than you should. Try to sit on the back patio on a nice evening. Reservations recommended. $$–$$$.

♿ Y **Delfina** (415-552-4055; delfinasf.com) 3621 18th Street. Open daily at least 5:30–10 PM. Delfina always turns me into a goofy kid out to her first nice meal: Everything on the California Italian seasonal menu makes me giggly and hungry for more. This famous spot even brings the Pacific Heights crowd to the Mission to eat the grilled calamari over white beans and Caesar salad. Reservations required. $$–$$$.

🍴 ♿ Y **Foreign Cinema** (415-648-7600; foreigncinema.com) 2534 Mission Street. Open Monday through Friday 6 PM–2 AM; Saturday through Sunday 11 AM–2 AM. Dining on an outside patio, while foreign films play on the building's outer wall, and you sip fruity cocktails, is my favorite way to spend a warm Mission evening. With a new menu every meal, you can't possibly get sick of the adventurous California cuisine. I have had everything from pea and prosciutto risotto to Madras curry-fried chicken, plus the intelligent kids' menu and a lovely oyster bar rounds out the experience. Reservations recommended. $$–$$$.

Mid-City

Y ♿ **NOPA** (415-864-8643; nopasf.com) 560 Hayes Street. Open daily 5 PM–1 AM. This lofty California cuisine restaurant made a splash when it opened a couple years ago. You'll wait for tables, even with reservations, but it is worth it, oh-so worth it. Organic wood-fired cuisine like flatbread, rotisserie chicken, and baked pasta populate the menu. Everything is good. Reservations highly recommended. $$–$$$.

𝒮 ⅃ ℽ **Poleng Lounge** (415-441-1751; polenglounge.com) 1751 Fulton Street. Open Tuesday through Sunday from 4 PM–2 AM. This hip Asian eatery blends small tastes from around Asia with California consciousness. Set in a small room with the four elements represented, electronic and hip hop music, live DJs, drink specials (Tuesday everything is half off), and plenty of beautiful people, this lounge is like nothing else in the city. Dishes like grilled edamame, garlic noodles with Dungeness crab, or lettuce cups are surefire bets. Since they serve small plates, expect to order two to three dishes per person. Reservations recommended. $–$$.

ℽ ⅃ **Zuni Café** (415-552-2522; zuni cafe.com) 1658 Market Street. Open Tuesday through Saturday 11:30 AM–12 AM. Iconic San Francisco dining: Big windows, a stellar wine list (and great Bloody Mary's), an oyster bar, and simple food that will make you want to return the next day. I'll say this: Their famous wood-fired chicken and bread salad stopped me from being a vegetarian. Reservations recommended. $$–$$$.

Marina

ℽ ⅃ **A16** (415-771-2216; a16sf.com) 2355 Chestnut Street. Open Wednesday through Friday, 11:30–2:30; Sunday through Thursday from 5 PM–10 PM; and on Friday and Saturday until 11 PM. Marina yuppies wait for hours for the wood-fired pizzas, pastas, and meats, while in-the-know folks make reservations to sit in the narrow dining room, watching the chefs sling food.

The dark bar area is a good spot for wine and pizza, but good luck getting a table. At press time, there was talk of opening another location in Dogpatch. The chef also just opened a new restaurant on Fillmore called **SPQR,** which is even busier than A16. Reservations required. $$–$$$.

𝒮 ⅃ **Greens** (415-771-6222; greens restaurant.com) Building A, Fort Mason Center. Open Tuesday through Saturday 12 PM–2:30 PM; Sunday 10:30 AM–2 PM; nightly for dinner 5:30 PM–9 PM. Even meat eaters love this organic vegetarian restaurant. Is it the views of the bay? The food grown by the monks at the Tassajara Zen Center? Or the wood and windows that make you feel like you are dining in the woods? I prefer brunch or the takeout stand. On Saturday evenings, you might try the prix fixe dinner. Reservations recommended. Brunch and lunch: $–$$. Dinner: $–$$$.

EATING OUT

Downtown

ℽ ⅃ **Bocadillos** (415-982-2622) 710 Montgomery Street. Open Monday through Friday from 7 AM–11 PM and Saturday 5 PM–11 PM. Basque small plates and sandwiches, wonderful wine, and mouth-watering desserts put this at the top of my list for lunch or an early dinner. Lunch is the best deal, where you choose any two small sandwiches. My favorites are the turkey Brie and the double cheese. And for dinner, I still dream of the warm octopus. For a real treat, visit Chef Hirigoyen's other restaurant, the swanky **Piperade,** for port and dessert. Reservations recommended for dinner. $–$$ (though you need to order at least three tapas plates to fill up).

Citizen Cake See *Sweet Tooth* sidebar.

Dim Sum Nice Food (415-397-2688)

900 block of Stockton Street. Open daily from at least 7 AM–6:30 PM. I wracked my brain for a funky Chinatown spot for you to try. I wanted you to have an authentic experience, complete with loud Chinese ladies pushing past you in line and super good dim sum for pennies. This is the place. $.

&️ ♪ **Dottie's True Blue Café** (415-885-2767) 522 Jones Street. Open Wednesday through Monday from 7:30 AM–3 PM. People line up here for breakfast almost every day. Is this small country diner worth it? Depends how much you like your eggs. If the line is long, try ordering the blueberry cornmeal pancakes to go. $–$$.

♪ & ♈ **Franciscan** (415-362-7733; Franciscanrestaurant.com) 43½ Pier. Open daily from at least 11:30 AM–10 PM. Finding a great spot to eat on Fisherman's Wharf is a drag. Most restaurants milk you for every hard-earned penny for food slightly better than dorm food. Franciscan, however, besides doling out validated parking *and* having one of the most cultivated views around, actually delivers on decent seafood. Go for anything you have to coax out of its shell. At the bar booths, they have binoculars on tables to gaze out at the bay. $$–$$$$.

♪ & **Henry's Hunan** (415-956-7727; henryshunanrestaurant.com) 924 Sansome Street. Open Monday through Friday 11:30 AM–6 PM. Forget the tourist trap Chinese places, this is the spot—if you don't mind the rush of financial district workers. Service can be crass and it isn't the nicest dining experience, but you come for the food. Favorites are Marty's Special, sizzling rice, house bean curd, and polish sausage Hunan style. $–$$.

Liguria Bakery (415-421-3786) 1700 Stockton Street. The Soccorro family has been serving up slabs of fresh focaccia since 1911. Note that they

have stayed in business serving only these slabs of bread. It's that good. North Beach residents know to come early, because when they sell out, that's it. The mushroom slab will make your mouth sing. Cash only. Dishes: $

♪ & **Mama's on the Square** (415-362-6421; mamas-sf.com) 1701 Stockton Street. Open daily from 8–3, closed Monday. You won't find a Mama here, instead hipsters and tourists line up to order at the counter and eat heaps of Grandma-like cooking without the Grandma. This country-style North Beach restaurant is a bit overrated, but you can get a decent breakfast. Just get here when it opens. It is not worth the wait. Cash only. $–$$.

& **Medicine East Station** (415-677-4405; medicinerestaurant.com) 161 Sutter Street. Open Monday through Friday 11:00–3:00 PM. A couple of newer fish items were added to the mostly organic vegetarian Japanese cuisine, and this spare lofty restaurant has re-established itself with the down-

IF SHE DOESN'T MAKE YOU WANT TO GO TO LIGURIA BAKERY, I DON'T KNOW WHAT WILL.

town work crowd. The vegetable curry is quite good, and many of the other dishes taste so healthy they can be considered medicine. $$.

✄ & **Mixt Greens** (415-433-6498; mixtgreens.com) 114 Sansome Street, #120. Open Monday through Friday, 10:30 AM–3 PM. The Financial District suits line up for lunches of organic salads with chicken, fish, and tofu. Salads are big enough for two meals and come with a slice of fresh bread. Currently I am enamored with the Madison. $–$$.

✄ & **Osha Thai** (415-278-9991; osha thai.com) 149 2nd Street. Open Monday through Saturday 11 AM–11 PM, Sunday 4 PM–11 PM. See Mission *Eating Out*.

Swan Oyster Depot (415-673-1101) 1517 Polk Street. Open Monday through Saturday 8–5:30 PM. For almost a century San Franciscans have lined up to sit on a bar stool and eat super-fresh fish. Oysters, clam chowder, and smoked fish will make your day. Don't let the lines throw you off, they move quickly. Cash only. $–$$.

✄ & **Tommaso's** (415-398-9696; tommasosnorthbeach.com) 1042 Kearny Street. Open Tuesday through Saturday 5 PM–11 PM; Sunday 4 PM–10 PM. This North Beach restaurant has been around for ages and still uses its original wood-burning oven for pizza. If you want an authentic North Beach experience without people hawking you to eat at their overpriced restaurant, this is the spot. I also like to get their pizzas to go and eat in Vesuvio bar. $$–$$$.

Turtle Tower (415-409-3333) 631 Larkin Street (between Eddy and Ellis). Breakfast, lunch, and early dinner Wednesday through Monday. On weekends, folks line up out the door for 10 types of pho, packed with noodles and every imaginable cut of beef

or chicken swimming in subtle broth. A solid selection of bun (vermicelli) and *com* (rice-based) platters, round out the menu. $.

Westfield Shopping Center Food Court (415-512 6776, westfield.com/sanfrancisco/dining) 865 Market Street. Open Monday through Saturday 9:30 AM–9 PM; Sunday 10 AM–7 PM. Chaotic, but cheap, this is not your ordinary mall food court. My favorite stop is Charles Phan's **Out the Door**. My husband swears by the Thai food at **Coriander**. Other worthy eateries are the local chains **San Francisco Soup Company, Beard Papa's,** and **Andale.** $.

The Mission/Outer Mission/Noe Valley/Bernal Heights

Avedanos (415-285-6328; avedanos .com) 235 Cortland Avenue. Open daily 11 AM–8 PM. This female-run butcher shop in the Bernal Heights neighborhood serves up excellent panis and nightly dinner specials. If you are around on a Sunday, they do a killer taco, and Friday is fried chicken night. They also have a nice collection of artisan pasta, sauces, and sweets. The only place to eat is. so head up o Holly Park or on the bench out front. $.

& **Bissap Baobab** (415-826-9287; bissapbaobab.com) 2323 Mission Street. Open Tuesday through Sunday 6 PM–10:30 PM. After two coconut-infused rums and a bowl of vegetable stew, I was dancing it up at their little location around the corner until way past my bedtime. Local musician Michael Franti frequents this place, as do the Mission locals looking for authentic African food. This popular restaurant will have you wanting to visit the tropics. $–$$.

✄ & 🐾 **Boogaloo's** (415-824-4088; boogaloossf.com) 3296 22nd Street. Open daily 8 AM–3 PM. It could have been their vegetarian biscuits and gravy that made me move to San Francisco; now I have graduated to the *Desayuno Tipico:* a plantain cake smothered in tamarind sauce, eggs, tortilla, and beans. Hipsters line up for hours to cure hangovers on weekends. Check out the local art by Creativity Explored (see Selective Shopping). $.

✂ ⚲ **Chaya** (415-252-7825) 762 Valencia Street. See Berkeley *Eating Out.*

⚲ ⚱ **Dosa** (415-642-3672; dosasf.com)

TAQUERIAS

Ask 10 locals about their favorite taqueria, you'll for sure hear 10 different answers. Tacos and burritos are as much a part of San Francisco culture as rainbow flags and fog. Below I have listed my favorites, and those of my friends and local food reviewers.

Carnivores love **La Corneta** (415-469-8757) 2834 Diamond Street. Open Monday through Saturday 10 AM–10 PM; Sunday 11 AM–9 PM. With long lines and fat burritos, this Glen Park eatery keeps the locals happy.

My vegetarian and vegan friends swear by **El Toro** (415-431-3351) 598 Valencia Street. Open Monday through Sunday 10 AM–10 PM. Here you get huge tacos with super spicy salsa (or mild if you prefer) and heaping burritos for cheap.

Nearly every Best of San Francisco list mentions the spicy burritos at **Taqueria Cancun** (415-252-9560) 2288 Mission Street. Open Monday through Thursday 9 AM–12:45 AM, Friday and Saturday 9 AM–1:45 AM. I prefer their quesadillas to the burritos.

Looking for healthy tacos made of free-range meats, organic veggies, and sustainable seafood? Try **Papalote** (415-970-8815; papalote-sf.com) 3409 24th Street. Open Monday through Saturday 11 AM–10 PM; Sunday 11 AM–9 PM.

La Taqueria (415-285-7117) 2889 Mission Street. Open daily 11 AM–9 PM. This place always makes the *San Francisco Chronicle's* best 100 restaurants list, and it's competing with places like Chez Panisse. The grilled burritos and quesadillas do it for me.

Try the tamales at the **Alemany Farmers' Market** (Saturday from 8 AM–1 PM) or the **Ferry Building Saturday Market.** See *Farmers' Markets.*

Though it is not officially a taqueria, I have to include the best deal in town: pupusas at **Balompie** (415-648-9199; balompie.net), 3349 18th Street. Open daily 8 AM–9:30 PM. If you are a soccer fan, World Cup is the time to eat here.

Mijita (415-399-0814; mijitasf.com) 1 Ferry Bldg. Open Monday through Thursday from 10 AM–7 PM; Saturday 9 AM–8 PM; Sunday 10 AM–4 PM. Traci Des Jardiniere and her crew serve up the best chilaquiles in the city. It's pricey, but foodies will find this taqueria fresh and delicious. And the views are hard to top.

995 Valencia Street. Open 5:30 PM–10 PM Sunday through Thursday; 5:30 PM –11 PM on Friday and Saturday, and on weekends for brunch from 11:30 AM– 3:30 PM. When I was pregnant, I ate a Dahi Rice and *masala* dosa weekly. Serving what one friend calls white-people-friendly Indian food, this hotspot is not to be missed. Go for the tasting menu to really get a feel for the South Indian cuisine that ranges from curries to *uttapam,* and of course the spectacular dosas. Reservations recommended. $$.

✍ 🍷 Ⴥ **Emmy's Spaghetti Shack** (415-206-2086) 3355 Mission Street. Open daily at least 5:30–11. Folks in Bernal Heights whisper the existence of this funky spaghetti shack and still people line up for tables on weekends when live DJs spin, kids run around, and the heaping plates of spaghetti keep on coming. The menu changes seasonally, but the spaghetti and meatballs are always on the menu. Unless you are a teenage boy, you might consider splitting your order. $–$$.

Ⴥ ✍ **Little Nepal** (415-643-3881; littlenepalsf.com) 925 Cortland Avenue. Open Tuesday through Sunday 5 PM–10 PM. I have two words to write: *Kukhurako Ledo.* That creamy chicken dish makes the most generous people I know hug their food close and refuse to share. The salmon, vegetarian curries, and noodle dishes are good, just not as good. Dishes come with rice and *naan.* $$.

✍ Ⴥ 🍷 **Little Star Pizza** (415-551-7827; littlestarpizza.com) 400 Valencia Street. Open Tuesday through Sunday at least 5 PM–10 PM. See NoPa *Eating Out.*

✍ Ⴥ **Mega Mouth Burgers** (415-821-4821) 3392 24th Street. Open daily 11 AM–10 PM. Whenever the craving for a burger hits, I head over to this little hole-in–the-wall for huge burgers (turkey, beef, vegetarian, or fish), fries, and a Mitchell's ice cream milkshake. It doesn't look like much, but all the food comes from sustainable sources. $.

Ⴥ **Minako Organic Japanese Food** (415-864-1888) 2154 Mission Street. Open Wednesday through Sunday 5:30 PM–9 PM. Located in a sketchy stretch of Mission Street, where crack addicts outnumber the rest of us, this small unpretentious restaurant offers some of the best Japanese food in town—but don't tell anybody. It is already tough to get a seat on weekends. A Mom and Daughter team has created a Japanese country kitchen, using all organic ingredients. Trust the daughter when she tells you what to order. My favorite is the Noopy Roll. $$.

✍ Ⴥ **Osha Thai** (415-826-7738; osha thai.com) 819 Valencia Street. Open daily 11 AM–12 AM. The number of this Thai restaurant is programmed into my cell phone and is the first place I call when I get back in town. And I am not alone in this. People leave the city and mourn abandoning Osha Thai more than their friends. Lately the owners have started creating an empire—yet each location is unique. The modern (and super busy) Valencia location specializes in curry, noodle dishes, and a creamy *pra ram.* Round out the meal with some coconut rice. $–$$.

✍ Ⴥ **Pizzeria Delfina** (415-437-6800; pizzeriadelfina.com) 3611 18th Street. Open daily for lunch and dinner (dinner only on Monday). Now that the gourmet pizza craze has struck San Francisco, it is not surprising that one of the best Italian restaurants in the city jumped in the game. On weekends, we wait ages for fresh thin-crust pizza and wine. Since there are only a couple tables, leave your name on the chalkboard, grab a pastry from Tartine, and be okay waiting it out. $$.

Rainbow Grocery (415-863-0620; rainbowgrocery.org) 1745 Folsom Street. Open daily from 8 AM–8 PM.

Though you can't get a sandwich made to order, you shouldn't come to San Francisco without a visit to this vegetarian organic co-op, where thunder showers water the produce, hip hop and punk music make people dance down the aisles, you get to taste unusual cheeses, and you can find pretty much any bulk item or supplement you can imagine.

Roxie Deli (415-587-2345) 1901 San Jose Avenue. Open 9 AM–7 PM daily. This two-aisle market has locals lining up out the door at lunch for heated deli sandwiches stuffed so full that it takes me two days to eat a *junior*-sized one. There are no tables, but Balboa Park across the street makes a nice place for a picnic. $.

✍ ⚅ **Savor** (415-282-0344) 3913 24th Street. Open Sunday through Thursday 8 AM–10 PM; Friday and Saturday 8 AM–11 PM. Noe Valley families hang out front of this eatery for weekend breakfasts that are too big for two people to share, huge salads, and crepes. I usually sit on the patio under the shady tree, but inside is festive, especially when the fire is going. The staff is amazingly kind. And their jalapeno cornbread sent me into labor with my son Kai. $–$$.

✍ ⚅ **Tartine** (415-487-2600; tartine bakery.com) 600 Guerrero Street. Open daily at least 8 AM–7 PM. People line up down the block for the savory pastries, the plump fruit tarts, the creamy chocolate cakes, the Mexican wedding cookies, and cheesy *tartines* on big slabs of French bread, cut in thirds and served with a side of pickled spicy carrots. $–$$.

✍ ⚅ ⚆ **Ti Couz** (415-252-7373) 3108 16th Street. Open for breakfast and lunch on Friday through Monday and nightly for dinner. Ti Couz is the place for crepes, fresh green salad, and a glass of wine. I can never eat here

without getting a savory crepe and a Nutella/banana crepe. Hopefully you have more luck than I do. $–$$.

Castro

✍ ⚅ **Chow** (415-552-2469; chowfood bar.com) 215 Church Street. Open Sunday through Thursday 8 AM–11 PM; Friday and Saturday 8 AM–12 AM. One of the city's best diners, Chow serves organic comfort food in a down-home environment. Breakfast scrambles and pancakes rule. Their eggplant parmesan and lasagna should be illegal and their chicken dishes, seasonal pies, and organic coffees are worth a try. Most dishes: $–$$.

⚅ **Samovar Tea House** (415-626-4700; samovartea.com) 498 Sanchez Street. Open Sunday through Thursday 10 AM–8 PM; Friday and Saturday 10 AM–9 PM. Zen-themed, this teahouse is where I come to mellow out and escape the bustle of the city. The food leans towards macrobiotic, but tastes pretty good. I prefer to come for their house-made Chai or the peppermint-lavender tea with a pastry. If you have the inclination, you can get a full Russian tea service complete with food. They have another location in Yerba Buena Gardens, but it isn't as quaint. $–$$.

✍ ⚅ **Sparky's Diner** (415-626-8666) 242 Church Street. Open all day, all night. At the end of a late night, this is where we come for burgers, fries, apple pie, and shakes. The food is greasy and the perfect antidote to a night of drinking, and every time I am here, they play music from Michael Jackson's *Thriller* or Prince's *Purple Rain*. Eat at the counter to really go back in time. $.

Haight Ashbury and Vicinity

⚅ **Citrus Club** (415-387-6366) 1790 Haight Street. Open daily from at least 11:30 AM–10 PM. Haight hipsters hang out in this noodle house that serves up

COFFEEHOUSES AND CAFES

With a coffee shop on almost every corner, San Francisco rivals Seattle for the coffee capital of the U.S. With gourmet coffee on the rise, you can bet you'll find the perfect cup somewhere in the city. Below are the best of the best.

Blue Bottle (415-252-7535; bluebottlecoffee.net) 315 Linden Street and 66 Mint Street. Mint Plaza, open Monday through Friday 7–7, Saturday 8–8, Sunday 8–4. These guys started in a small office in Oakland and now run the most popular coffee spots in the city. Their lattes are superb and the new Siphon machine (served after 10 AM at Mint Plaza) brews up a unique (and all organic) coffee experience. The Linden location forces hipsters to order lattes and sip them in a Hayes Valley alley. They recently opened a new location in the Ferry Building.

Café Roma (415-296-7942; cafferoma.com) 526 Columbus Avenue. Open daily from 6 AM–7 PM. Tony Azzolini takes his coffee seriously. After getting his law degree, he bailed and opened a coffee shop. He takes each cup as seriously as the bar. You can also get pastries here, watch soccer, and see some local celebrities hanging out at the coffee bar.

Café Trieste (415-392-6739) Vallejo at Grant. Open Monday through Friday 6:30 AM–7 PM; Saturday and Sunday 7 AM–11 PM. Over 20 years old, this old Beat hangout is where Coppola wrote the *The Godfather*. They roast their own coffee and don't even bother with soy milk, but the cappuccinos are just right.

Ritual Coffee Roasters (415-648-2670 or 415-641-1024; floragrubb.com) 1634 Jerrold or 1026 Valencia Street. Ritual took San Francisco by storm when it opened a couple years ago. The *uber* hip must-have-your-Mac-book Valencia Street location serves up the best lattes and vegan donuts in town. The Flora Grubb location is my favorite place to stroll through gardens on a Sunday afternoon.

dishes from across the Asian continent. Plates are huge, service is swift (which is good because you normally have to wait ages to sit), and your coolness factor will rise just by sipping a beer in this funky spot. $.

& **Kate's Kitchen** (415-626-3984) 471 Haight Street. Open daily from at least 9 AM–3 PM. This breakfast spot makes the hungover and tattooed young people wait for ages to gorge on giant plates of eggs, vegan biscuits and gravy, and pancakes. Not much to speak of in the décor, you can guarantee that you will need a nap after filling up on the country-style food. $.

& **Zazie** (415-564-5332; zaziesf.com) 941 Cole Street. Open for breakfast, lunch, and dinner daily. On weekend mornings, get here early. Locals line up to sit on the heated patio in the garden, where they offer knitted blankets to keep warm, bowls of coffee drinks, and the best gourmet breakfast around. The potatoes have chunks of roasted garlic in them and the lemon ricotta pancakes will blow your mind. I never come for dinner, but I am sure the French country cooking is just as good as brunch. $–$$.

North Panhandle (NoPa)

✐ ♿ **Little Star Pizza** (415-441-1188; littlestarpizza.com) 846 Divisadero Street. Open Tuesday through Sunday at least 5 AM–10 PM. Eating Chicago-style deep-dish pizza served in a dark bar-like setting, while drinking a microbrew or local wine and listening to Radiohead on the jukebox, is the perfect Sunday evening. Most people in the city agree, which is why you'll have to wait for your table. If you are really hungry, get a salad while you wait, because it takes 40 minutes to cook your pie. I can't live without a Little Star special at least once a month. $$.

Pacific Heights/Japantown

At press time both **Dosa** and **Pizzeria Delfina** were opening new locations on Fillmore Street. There is a wealth of great Japanese restaurants here, with my choices being **Mifune** (415-992-0337), **Isobune** (415-563-1030), or my favorite **Iroha** (415-922-0321).

Marina

✐ ♿ **Lettus Café** (415-931-2777; lettusorganic.com) 3352 Steiner Street. Open daily at least 11 AM–10 PM. San Francisco needed this organic café, bathed in natural light with earthy colors accompanying the food. Stand in line and order from a huge menu of organic options. The papaya enzyme smoothie, the Chinese chicken salad, the veggie burger, or the crab sandwich all make great choices. $–$$.

✐ ♿ ♟ **Mamacita** (415-346-8494; mamacitasf.com) 2317 Chestnut Street. Open daily 5:30 PM–10 PM. Right when they open, Marina families line up to get a table at this modern Mexican small-plates spot. The singles crowd hits the bar for strong margaritas. Favorite dishes include guacamole, *camaron al pastor,* and *callos de mula.* $–$$.

Pacific Catch Seafood (415-440-1950; pacificcatch.com) 2027 Chestnut Street. Open daily 11 AM–10 PM. See Sunset *Eating Out.*

Sunset/Richmond

Arizmendi See *Sweet Tooth* sidebar.

✐ ♿ ♟ **Beach Chalet/Park Chalet** (415-386-8439; beachchalet.com) 1000 Great Highway. Open daily at least 9 AM–10 PM. Originally built in 1900, rebuilt in 1925, and restored in 1981, this restaurant offers options: ocean view dining on the second floor, and the park view outdoor café and brewery on the first floor. I prefer the Park Chalet, where families sit on Adirondack chairs sipping beer and eating their decadent mac and cheese. The food options aren't the best (and get even slimmer once you sit outside), but it is all about the live music on weekend afternoons and the chance for mom and dad to drink beer while the little dudes playing in the trees. $$–$$$.

✐ ♿ **Burma Superstar** (415-387-2147; burmasuperstar.com) 309 Clement Street. Open daily from 11 AM–3:30 PM and 5 PM–9:30 PM, and until 10 PM on weekends. Get here right when they open or expect to wait over an hour to be packed in a table so close to your neighbor that you can share food. Try the rainbow salad, *samosa* soup, and anything with pumpkin. Burma Superstar will make you forget you liked Thai food so much. $–$$.

✐ ♿ **Ebisu** (415-566-1770; ebisusushi .com) 1283 9th Avenue. Open Monday through Friday 11:30 AM–2 PM and 5 PM–10 PM (no lunch on Friday), and Saturday 11:30 AM–11 PM. When the city of San Francisco was trying to woo Virgin Airlines into making SF their hub, they brought them here for the freshest sushi in town. This family-owned sushi spot gets crowded with people from all over the city. I come here for creative rolls, excellent *gyozas,* and the fact that the owner takes my son and walks him around the restaurant to give us a chance to dine. When the wait is too long, head across the street to their sister restaurant **Hotei** for noodle soup and the same sushi you get on Ebisu's menu. $–$$.

🍴 ♿ **Louis'** (415-387-6330) 902 Point Lobos Avenue. Open daily from 6:30 AM–4:30 PM, until 6 PM on weekends. Since 1937, the Hontalas family has served up greasy diner food with the best views in the city. From the minute you walk on the checkerboard floor, sit at the counter or one of the booths by the window, and see the expansive vistas of the Pacific and Sutro Baths, you'll know why you waited for buttery eggs, fluffy pancakes, and burgers. Vegetarians will go hungry here. Cash only. $–$$.

🍴 ♿ 🍸 **Pacific Catch Seafood** (415-504-6905; pacificcatch.com) 1200 9th Avenue. Open 11 AM–10 PM daily and until 11 PM on weekends—bar open later, with food service. When Pacific Catch took over the art/coffee shop space where Canvas used to be, no one was sure what to make of it. The new owners, a local family, set out to create a green dining experience using sustainable seafood: imagine sitting in a room with big windows, a skylight, and surrounded by sea-glass mosaic. Then throw in edamame and pretzel snacks, wasabi bowls, a killer crab salad and sushi rolls, a bar with park views and friendly servers, and you have a great neighborhood joint. $–$$.

🍴 ♿ 🍸 **Park Chow** (415-665-9912) 1240 9th Avenue Open daily from 11 AM–10 PM. See Castro *Eating Out.*

🍴 ♿ **San Tung** (415-242-0828) 1031 Irving Street. Open daily 11 AM–9:30 PM except Wednesday. This crowded, unassuming spot is the place to go for good Chinese food. The dumplings, mushu, and vegetables can't be beat. Plates are large and it seems every Chinese person in San Francisco knows about this place, so go with a bunch of people (to share with) and be prepared to wait. $–$$.

🍴 ♿ **Ton Kiang** (415-752-4440; tonkiang.net) 5821 Geary Boulevard. Open daily at least 10 AM–9 PM. For dim sum, this Richmond restaurant makes its voice heard around the Bay Area. You can eat for half the price of what you will at popular Yank Sing. They specialize in seafood, so don't miss the crab claw, shrimp dumplings, or scallop specials. On weekends this place fills up. $–$$.

✳ Entertainment

On any given night, there is so much going on in the city your head will spin. The best places to find local events are in the *Guardian, San Francisco Weekly, San Francisco Chronicle,* and sfstation.com.

For theater events, you might consider stopping by the **Theater Bay Area** ticket office in Union Square (Tixbay area.com) for discount last-minute tickets to major shows. The major theater houses are the **Curran** (curran -theater.com), **ODC** (odctheater.org), **Orpheum** (shnsf.com), **New Conservatory** (nctcsf.org), and **ACT** (act-sf .org) for world class theater and Broadway shows **Theater Rhinoceros** (therhino.org), **Yerba Buena** (ybca .org), and **Intersection for the Arts** (theintersection.org) specialize in innovative new works by local artists. **Magic Theater** (magictheater.org) is where the big names come to test new material. The **Marsh** (themarsh.org) and **Brava Theater** (brava.org) are great black-box theaters, perfect for finding next year's big star. You won't be disappointed with a show at the Marsh, ACT, and Magic Theaters.

For live music, check listings at the following: For rock and major recording artists check out the **Fillmore** (the fillmore.com)**, Warfield, Great American Music Hall** (music hallsf.com), and the **Independent** (theindependentsf.com). For indie rock bands in an "I saw them first" venue, head to **Bottom of the Hill** (bottomofthehill.com) and **Slims** (slims-sf.com). Big name electronic and hip-hop artists frequent the **Mez-zanine** (mezzaninesf.com).

Below are other spots to experience San Francisco nightlife at its finest.

Ψ **Asia SF** (415-255-2742; asiasf.com) 201 9th Street. Open Tuesday through Thursday 6:30 PM–10 PM; Friday 5:30 PM–10 PM; Sat 5 PM–10 PM; Sun 6:30 PM–10 PM. These gender illusionists will confuse the straightest of men and women. This is the place for a birthday party, great strong drinks, and doing a shot from between one of the server's legs. Enjoy lip-synching dancers while you dine on Asian fusion cuisine, served in a three-course deal called a ménage a trois. Reservations required. Dinner: $$$$.

Ψ **Beach Blanket Babylon** (415-421-4222; beachblanketbabylon.com) 678

SWEET TOOTH? THE REAL SAN FRANCISCO TREATS.
San Francisco serves up more sweets than should be legal. Below is a list of some of my favorite finds.

Arizmendi (415-566-3117; arizmendibakery.org) 1331 9th Avenue. Open Tuesday through Sunday at least 8 AM–7 PM (until 4 PM on Sunday). Cheese bread, focaccia, cookies, and the blueberry corn muffin are staples. Every day the pizza changes, but you can always guarantee it to be good.

Bi Rite Creamery (415-626-5600, biritecreamery.com) 3692 18th Street. Open daily at least 11 AM–10 PM. Since this organic ice cream shop opened around the corner from Dolores Park, locals have lined up for the decadence. Though flavors change with the seasons, the mint chip, the honey lavender, and the salted caramel are winners. Get the Recchiuti *fleur de sel* pieces on top. If the line is too long, you might pop into **Bi Rite Grocery** to get pints of the ice cream and sweets without the excruciating wait.

Bittersweet (415-346-8715; bittersweetcafe.com) 2123 Fillmore Street. Open daily at least 10 AM–8 PM (until 10 PM on Friday and Saturday). This coffee/chocolate shop in Pacific Heights will make the kid in you whine for more. In summer, the chocolate coconut cooler is as refreshing as it gets. Check out the incredible amount of chocolate bars for sale. And the house-made marshmallows . . . yum.

Citizen Cake (415-861-2228; citizencake.com) 399 Grove Street. Open Tuesday through Friday 8 AM–10 PM; Saturday 10 AM–10 PM; Sunday 10 AM–5 PM. Though this place also serves fantastic dinners, I had to highlight the

Green Street. Shows start Wednesday and Friday 8 PM; Friday and Saturday 6:30 PM and 9:30 PM; Sunday 2 PM and 5 PM. For over 20 years, this cabaret has been entertaining San Francisco audiences. Even if you have seen it before, the show changes as pop culture does. Singing, dancing, comedy, and drinks, what more could you ask for? And the wigs are out of sight. No one under 21 admitted.

Ᵽ **Bimbos 365** (415-474-0365; bimbos 365club.com) 1025 Columbus Avenue. This is my favorite venue for live shows. Big name musicians and comedians play here, the staff is super helpful, and it's in North Beach, which is always fun.

A GENDER ILLUSIONIST AT ASIA SF.

bakery. I come here for their ginger cookies, but the gelato, cakes, Mexican wedding cookies, and well, everything, is to die for. Don't miss the hot chocolate.

Italian French Baking Company of San Francisco (415-421-3796) 1501 Grant Avenue, North Beach. Open every day, except Christmas, from 6 AM–6 PM. A tour of this 130-year-old bakery is a must. Their heirloom yeast is as old as the bakery and the baking hearth has been in use since the spot opened. I come here for the coconut macaroon—which is the best in the city. Cash only.

Miette See *Ferry Building* Sidebar.

Mission Pie (415-282-1500, pieranch.org) 2901 Mission Street. Open Monday through Thursday 7 AM–9 PM; Saturday 8 AM–10 PM; Sunday 9 AM–9 PM. Local Mission District kids farm the fruit and bake the pies for this newly opened pie shop. Every pie I have had makes the last pale by comparison.

Mitchell's Ice Cream (415-648-2300; mitchellsicecream.com) 688 San Jose Avenue. Open daily 11 AM–10 PM. This ice cream shop has been around for decades. Still people line up on cold or warm days. Besides traditional favorites, try out some funky flavors like purple yam and pumpkin.

Recchiuti See *Ferry Building* Sidebar.

Tartine See Mission *Eating Out.*

Victoria Pastry Co (415-648-2300; victoriapastry.com) 1362 Stockton Street. Open daily 11 AM–11 PM. Since 1914, Susan Flaherty and Dino Belluomini have been serving up the best éclairs on the West Coast. They also specialize in cakes and other sweets.

Ｙ **Bourbon and Branch** (415-346-1735; bourbonandbranch.com) 501 Jones Street. Open Monday through Saturday 6 PM–2 AM. You have to make a reservation at this speakeasy and give a password to enter the main room, which turns cocktails into an art. I am not going to tell you what this place looks like; you need to see it for yourself. Know this, the drink menu is more like a book, and you get an appetizer drink; so make sure to eat in advance. If you can't get a reservation, head next door and give the password *books,* which gets you into the bar (but that isn't as cool).

San Francisco Ballet (415-865-2000; sfballet.org) 455 Franklin Street. The ballet's Nutcracker performance is legendary around these parts. But a trip to check out the regular season of this daring dance troupe is a must-see experience.

San Francisco Opera (415-861-4008; sfopera.com) 301 Van Ness Avenue. The opera not only performs in the War Memorial Opera House, but also does an amazing free opera in the park in the summer.

San Francisco Symphony (415-864-6000; sfsymphony.org) 201 Van Ness Avenue. Local conductor Michael Tilson Thomas brings world-class musicians together on the stage to wow audiences. Check local listings because the symphony often plays free shows at parks.

Ｙ **supperclub** (415-348-0900, supper club.com) 657 Harrison Street. Open Tuesday through Saturday 6:30 PM–2 AM; Sunday 6:30 PM–12 AM. While you wait for your three- to five-course dinner, you can recline on white leather beds, sip cocktails, get massages, and watch near-nude performance artists. Electronic music, low lights, and an international crowd make this feel like the international terminal of an airport—except for the drag queens staging cat fights. If you don't want the dinner experience (which can be pricey) you can just go to the bar. Reservations required. Dinner: $$$$.

Ｙ **Teatro ZinZanni** (415-438-2668; zinzanni.org) 29 Pier # 2. Take a trip back in time with a vaudeville cabaret theater and some great gourmet food. Most people wonder if they can afford this high-priced evening, but if you head out for a nice dinner and show, it ends up about the same cost. The actors interact with the audience, famous actors perform, and local performance artists will dazzle you with juggling and trapeze artistry. Sip a champagne cocktail, dress to the nines, and pretend you are in San Francisco circa 1920. $116–166, plus tax, tip, and drinks.

Ｙ **Top of the Mark** (415-616-6916, topofthemark.com) 999 California Street. Open daily. Classic San Francisco, this bar at the top of the Mark Hopkins Hotel offers stellar views of the city for big bucks.

Ｙ **Yoshi's** (415-655-5600, yoshis.com) 1330 Fillmore Street. This Oakland jazz club retained its authenticity and class when it added itself to the list of jazz clubs in Western Addition. Dining in the Japanese fusion lofty restaurant is a treat, but pricey. Instead, have a drink at the bar and enjoy the fantastic lineup of jazz musicians that pass through town.

✳ Selective Shopping

The main shopping area of the city is centered in **Union Square** (Powell and Geary). New boutiques open daily, designers sell their wares for big bucks, and chain stores hook up the rest of us. Worth a stop is **Maiden Lane,** an alley that is now the it-spot for brides-to-be. Here you'll find the famed **Gump's** (135 Post Street). Also around here are tons of galleries. One of the best places to find out about openings is in the Thursday 96 Hours section of the *San Francisco Chronicle* or at sf station.com. Some of my favorite galleries are 111 **Minna** (111 Minna Street) and the Frank Lloyd Wright-designed **Xanadu Gallery** (140 Maiden Lane.).

There are a couple great malls downtown, including the Financial District's **Embarcadero Center** (3 Embarcadero Center, #A), which also has one of the best cinemas for independent and foreign films. And in SOMA the new San Francisco Centre mall (865 Market Street), with a $380 million Bloomingdales and a movie theater lures shoppers.

In the Mission District, along Valencia Street, between 16th and 24th Streets, you can find a number of vintage shops and local designer boutiques. On 16th Street, check out **Creativity Explored,** a nonprofit that holds art classes for the mentally disabled, then sells their work. Another fun stop is the co-op sex shop **Good Vibrations.** Just a few blocks away, Hayes Valley, along Hayes Street (between Laguna and Octavia), has become the place for pricey boutiques.

Along Haight Street you can find Eastern-influenced smoke shops, plenty of tie-dye shirts, clothing boutiques, and high-end vintage-clothing shops. Pacific Heights attracts the nouveau riche who stroll up and down Fillmore Street (between Laguna and Steiner), with Blackberrys and well-dressed Chihuahuas, shopping for designer clothes and makeup. While others spend hours checking out *anime* in the Japan Mall (1737 Post Street).

Finally, in the Marina, along Union Street (between Franklin and Columbus) and Chestnut Street (between Avila Street and Pierce Street), the young, beautiful, and rich shop for everything from yoga gear to blue jeans, diamond-framed glasses to pet clothes.

BOOKSTORES We are lucky to have too many great independent bookstores in the city. Downtown has a number of places to find good reads, in the Ferry Building check out **Book Passage** (Ferry Plaza, Building 42). If you are in North Beach, you can't miss **City Lights Bookstore** (261 Columbus Avenue).

In the Mission, along Valencia Street you'll find a number of great used bookstores that specialize in everything from mystery to progressive topics. My favorites are **Dog Eared Books** and **Modern Times.** The Castro has a few good bookstores, including **Get Lost Travel Books** (1825 Market Street), **Books Inc** (601 Van Ness Avenue) and the LGBT **Different Light** (489 Castro Street). By far the best selection of new and used books, CDs and DVDs, and the best place to bide your time while waiting for a table at Burma Superstar, is **Green Apple Books** (506 Clement Street).

NEIGHBORHOOD PUB CRAWLS
Union Square Area

Start with a rye cocktail at **Bourbon and Branch** (see *Entertainment*) or **Rye** (415-474-4448; ryesf.com; 688 Geary Street) where mixologists make Jim Beam drinkers smile. You'll actually have to slide down a slide to get into **Slide** (415-421-1916; slidesf.com; 430 Mason Street). If you are interested in writers, head to **Edinburgh Castle Pub** (415-885-4074; castlenews.com; 950 Geary Street) where you might catch folks like Irvine Welsh sipping Guinness. For live music by local rock bands, **Hemlock Tavern** (415-923-0923; hemlocktavern.com; 1131 Polk Street) is the spot. Finally, head over to **Bambuddha Lounge** (415-885-5088; bambuddhalounge.com; 601 Eddy Street) where you might see some rock stars hanging by the pool.

North Beach

Start at the **Bubble Lounge** (415-434-4204; bubblelounge.com; 714 Montgomery Street) or **Bix** (415-433-6300; bixrestaurant.com; 56 Gold Street). Then head over to **Vesuvio** (415-362-3370; vesuvio.com; 255 Columbus Avenue) and top the night off at **Specs** (415-421-4112; 12 Adler Street).

Mission

Drinkers come from around the city to party in the Mission. On a nice day, you can't beat a Bloody Mary or microbrew at the biker-bar beer garden **Zeitgeist** (415-255-7505; 199 Valencia Street). On a foggy day, sip microbrews at **Amnesia** (415-970-0012; amnesiathebar.com; 853 Valencia Street), where they also have live music. Other spots to check out are **Little Baobab** (415-643-3558; bissap-baobab.com; 3388 19th Street) for African-themed cocktails and dancing. For jazz, I like **Bruno's** (415-550-7455; brunoslive.com; 2389 Mission Street) or **Savanna Jazz** (415-285-3369, savannajazz.com; 2937 Mission Street).

✳ Selective Seasonal Events

San Francisco likes to party. Every weekend there are events and festivals. Below are just some of the more noteworthy ones. For full listings check onlyinsanfrancisco.com. In summer every neighborhood has a street festival, which is a great way to buy local art.

January or February: **Chinese New Year** (415-391-9680, chineseparade.com) Market and Second Street to Kearny and Jackson. Usually it rains for this huge parade that runs through downtown. The floats are out of this world, the firecrackers are loud, and keep an eye out for the folks participating in the scavenger hunt.

February: **Valentine's Day Pillow Fight** (pillowfight.info) Justin Herman Plaza. If you are mad at your honey, or are on the hunt for one, head to the citywide pillow fight on Justin Herman Plaza.

April: **St. Stupid's Day Parade** (saintstupid.com) Embarcadero Plaza. Sometimes tourists know more than locals, which is the case when it came to this festival. A girl from Missouri told me this was a fun event, where everyone dresses funny and carries signs with silly sayings.

Cherry Blossom Festival (415-563-2313, nccbf.org) 1759 Sutter Street. Lately the cherry blossoms have

The gay and lesbian bars, **The Lexington Club** (415-863-2052; lexingtonclub.com; 3464 19th Street) and **Wild Side West** (415-647-3099, 424 Cortland Avenue) are popular with the ladies and pretty low key. Guys, head to **Truck** (415-252-0306; trucksf.com; 1900 Folsom Street); on rainy days it is two-for-one drinks, or to **El Rio** (415-282-3325, elriosf.com; 3158 Mission Street) in the Mission for outdoor salsa dancing.

Castro and Soma

In the Castro friends recommend **Lime** (415-621-5256; lime-sf.com; 2247 Market Street) and **Moby Dick** (415-861-1199; mobydicksf.com; 4049 18th Street). In SOMA, leather daddies like **Eagle Tavern** (415-626-0880; sfeagle.com; 398 12th Street) and if you are looking for after-hours dancing, you can't beat the **End Up** (415-896-1095; theendup.com; 401 6th Street).

Other Popular Bars

Though these might be impossible to hit all in one night, these bars and pubs are worth a visit. In lower Haight, if you are a beer drinker, head to the loud **Toronado** (415-863-2276; toronado.com; 547 Haight Street). Up the street **Mad Dog in the Fog** (415-626-7279; 530 Haight Street) has fun trivia nights at 9 PM on Tuesday and Thursday; this is also the spot to watch soccer. Richmond's **540 Club** (415-752-7276; 540 Clement Street) has one of the best jukeboxes around. In Fisherman's Wharf, the classic **Buena Vista Café** (415-474-5044; thebuenavista.com; 2765 Hyde Street) serves a popular Irish coffee. For wine check out **Cav** (415-437-1770; cavwinebar.com; 1666 Market Street) and **Hotel Biron** (415-703-0403; hotelbiron .com; 45 Rose Street)—at press time **The Press Room** was opening on Market Street near the Contemporary Jewish Museum.

bloomed before the festival, but that doesn't mean you shouldn't attend.

San Francisco International Film Festival (925-866-9559, sffs.org) Main venue 1881 Post Street. World-class films compete, famous actors and directors show up, and San Francisco turns into Hollywood for a couple weeks.

May: **Bay to Breakers** (415-359-2800, baytobreakers.com). I can't encourage you to come to this Only in San Francisco event enough. Early in the morning, the professional runners show their stuff and run from the bay to the beach in about 20 minutes. For the rest of the day it seems the entire city dresses in costume (or nothing at all), decorates floats (complete with kegs of beer), and dances (or stumbles) to the beach for a concert. It is nutty, fun, and not to be missed. Don't forget your camera.

Carnaval (carnavalsf.com) Mission District. On Memorial Day weekend the Mission District turns into Brazil, complete with drummers, samba dancers, and street parties.

June: **Haight Street Fair** (haightash burystreetfair.org). The granddaddy of SF street festivals, Haight Street turns into a sea of people, drinking, dancing, and hoping the fog burns off.

THE ANNUAL BAY TO BREAKERS RACE AND PARTY.

Pride Weekend (415-864-0831, sfpride.org) Market Street. The LGBT community knows how to throw a party. It lasts for a weekend and lures people from all over the world. Parades, politicians, musicians, and street festivals fill the packed streets.

STILTWALKERS ATTEND MANY SAN FRANCISCO EVENTS.

You'll see the best-dressed drag queens in the world.

July: **Stern Grove Festival** (415-252-6252, sterngrove.org) 19th Avenue and Sloat Boulevard. Every Sunday afternoon in summer (though it doesn't feel like summer—Brrrr) San Franciscans bring beer, wine, cheese, and blankets to this free music festival in a grove of eucalyptus trees. World-class musicians grace the stage. This festival lasts through August.

August: **Comedy in the Park** (comedyday.com) Sharon Meadow, Golden Gate Park. Sometimes local Robin Williams graces the stage, but mostly you'll see less famous—albeit local—comedians.

September: **Folsom Street Fair** (folsomstreetfair.org) Folsom Street. Leather, whips, chains, and free condoms are about what you expect from this wild festival. This is not for the prude or Granny.

Power to the Peaceful (415-865-2170, powertothepeaceful.org) Speedway Meadows, Golden Gate Park. Local musician Michael Franti organized this free music festival after September 11, 2001. Now you can hear local peace activists from Joan Baez to beat boxers.

October: **Fleet Week** (650-599-5057, military.com/fleetweek) You either love the loud Blue Angel planes zooming overhead, doing tricks, or you hate them. I am of the hate them camp, so I probably shouldn't go on. There are plenty of service folks in town, parades, and more.

Halloween After a bloody couple years at the Castro Halloween party, the city canceled the festivities, only to encounter some bummed-out folks. In 2008, the city moved the party to SoMa, but most people still headed to the Castro. If all else fails, the bars are hopping.

Hardly Strictly Bluegrass (hardly strictlybluegrass.com) 25th Avenue and Fulton Street. A local billionaire bluegrass fan sponsors this gigantic music festival in the park. You can see everyone from Los Lobos to Dolly Parton to Robert Plant to MC Hammer for free!

Litquake (415-750-1497, litquake.org) 3512 24th Street. Writers from around the world participate in this free tribute to the pen. My favorite event is the Mission LitCrawl, where you can bar- and bookshop-hop to hear hundreds of writers read their work.

SF Jazz Festival (415-398-5655, sfjazz.org) 3 Embarcadero Center. Big names from around the world and local musicians entertain jazz fans.

November: **Day of the Dead** 24th and Bryant. Begins at 7 PM. This Mission celebration to honor dead friends and family is a colorful, musical sight.

December: **New Year's Eve** (415-440-0732, sfnewyears.com) 1760 Union Street. The city sponsors fireworks on the Embarcadero on New Year's Eve.

The Bay Area

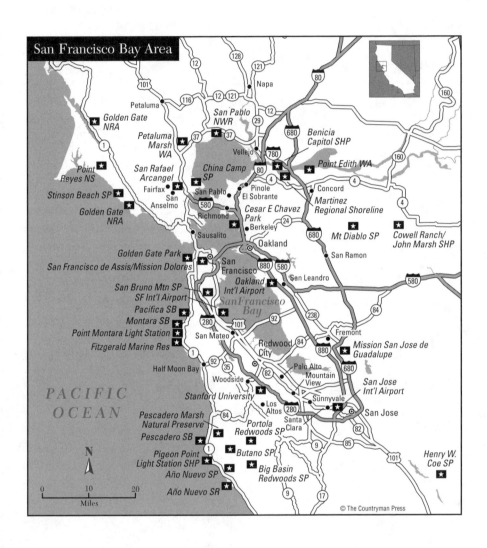

San Francisco Bay Area

128
12
121
101
Petaluma
116
Napa
80
Golden Gate NRA
Petaluma Marsh WA
San Pablo NWR
12
121
Vellejo
12
29
680
Benicia Capitol SHP
37
37
780
Point
Reyes NS
San Rafael
Arcangel
China Camp SP
80
Point Edith WA
160
Stinson Beach SP
Fairfax
San
Anselmo
San Pablo
Pinole
El Sobrante
4
4
Concord
Golden Gate NRA
580
Richmond
Cesar E Chavez Park
Martinez Regional Shoreline
4
Berkeley
24
Sausalito
680
Mt Diablo SP
Cowell Ranch/ John Marsh SHP
Golden Gate Park
Oakland
San Ramon
San Francisco de Assis/Mission Dolores
San Francisco
880
580
580
Oakland Int'l Airport
San Leandro
San Bruno Mtn SP
SF Int'l Airport
San Francisco Bay
Pacifica SB
92
238
84
Montara SB
Point Montara Light Station
280
Fremont
Fitzgerald Marine Res
San Mateo
101
84
880
Mission San Jose de Guadalupe
Half Moon Bay
92
35
Redwood City
680
1
Woodside
82
Palo Alto
Mountain View
San Jose Int'l Airport
PACIFIC OCEAN
Stanford University
Sunnyvale
San Jose
Los Altos
280
Pescadero Marsh Natural Preserve
84
Santa Clara
82
Pescadero SB
Portola Redwoods SP
9
85
N
Pigeon Point Light Station SHP
1
Butano SP
Henry W. Coe SP
Año Nuevo SP
Big Basin Redwoods SP
101
Año Nuevo SR
9
17
0   10   20
Miles
© The Countryman Press

THE EAST BAY

On one hand, you have Nobel Laureates lecturing on black holes, while on the other you'll find economically depressed neighborhoods planting community gardens. There's a nuclear power plant, a homeless salvaged art space, a tool-lending library, the Gourmet Ghetto, and a street filled with taquerias. Here you'll find the tallest mountain in the area—where you can see Yosemite on a clear day—complete with hiking trails to waterfalls, as well as an underage punk club. The East Bay has everyone covered.

It is tough to think of **Berkeley** without tagging on the moniker *Berzerkeley*. Known for its political outlandishness and its radical history, many people don't know the subtle sophistication Berkeley offers. Home to Chez Panisse, Alice Water's restaurant that spearheaded the slow food movement in the United States, you'll now find a slew of gourmet restaurants surrounding hers on Shattuck Avenue in North Berkeley. Central Berkeley, home to University of California Berkeley, attracts college students with ethnic eateries, thrift stores, and hiking trails in Tilden Park. South Berkeley has recently seen a renaissance, with a number of boutiques, restaurants, and cafés lining San Pablo Avenue, as well as a renovated Eastshore Park strung along the bay.

OAKLAND'S CHILDREN'S FAIRYLAND.

Between Berkeley and Oakland, the little town of **Emeryville** is starting to come up. With local superstar movie studio Pixar attracting creative types, new wine bars, cafes, and restaurants keep popping up.

Oakland, the biggest city in the East Bay, is beginning to shed its tough façade. Where once you probably couldn't walk down many streets without holding onto your wallet, gentrification (for good and bad) is changing the face of the inner city, especially around Lake Merritt. Recently the

Downtown area has been compared to Brooklyn, attracting San Franciscans looking to score on reasonably priced condos in an up-and-coming neighborhood. However, what most visitors don't know is that Oakland has family-friendly commercial areas teeming with strollers and iPhones in the Rockridge and Piedmont regions, as well as some of the Bay Area's most innovative museums and restaurants.

Spreading north and south along the bay are a number of bedroom communities (**Alameda, San Leandro, Hayward,** and **Fremont** to the south and **Albany, El Cerrito, Richmond,** and **San Pablo** to the north), which boast lively ethnic communities—and some of the best ethnic food in the Bay Area. Though tourists rarely make it out to these parts, a short BART trip gets you to the compact downtowns that feel as multicultural as a Benetton ad. Here you will also find excellent hiking opportunities, a decent beach, and even a silent movie theatre.

Just over the Oakland and Berkeley Hills, the fog lifts. The suburban towns (**Orinda, Lafayette, Walnut Creek**, and **Livermore**) are starting to come of age, offering excellent restaurants and bars, wineries, a wonderful Shakespeare Festival, and heaps of outdoor activities. Most people rarely make these towns a destination, but those who do find humble charm in the vineyard-covered hills.

GUIDANCE Berkeley Visitor Bureau (510-549-7040; visitberkeley.com) 2015 Center Street, Berkeley.

Oakland Visitor Bureau (510-839-9000; oaklandcvb.com) 463 11th Street, Oakland.

Livermore Chamber of Commerce (925-447-1606; livermorechamberblog.org) 2157 1st Street, Livermore.

HELPFUL WEB SITES
Trivalleycvb.com
Livermorewine.com
Oaklandtribune.com

GETTING THERE *By air:* **Oakland International Airport** (oaklandairport .com) 1 Airport Drive, Oakland. The airport has some of the best flight deals around and serves not only the East Bay, but also San Francisco.

By bus: **Greyhound** (greyhound.com) 2103 San Pablo Avenue, Oakland. The main hub for the East Bay is located in Oakland, but you can get to Hayward, Emeryville, and Livermore by bus.

By car: To get to the East Bay off I-5, head west on I-580 (expect traffic around Livermore). From US 101, take I-880 north. From San Francisco, you have to cross the Bay Bridge. And from the Sacramento, take I-80 south.

By train: **Amtrak** (Amtrak.com) gets you right to downtown Oakland, with a stop in Jack London Square, or to the Oakland Coliseum. They also stop in Emeryville (right next to Berkeley), Livermore, Fremont, Concord, Antioch, and Hayward.

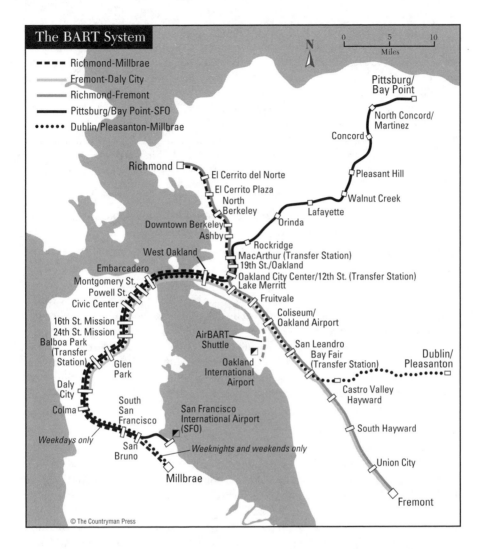

The BART System

- ▬ ▬ ▬ Richmond–Millbrae
- Fremont–Daly City
- Richmond–Fremont
- Pittsburg/Bay Point–SFO
- •••••• Dublin/Pleasanton–Millbrae

0   5   10
Miles

N

Pittsburg/
Bay Point

North Concord/
Martinez

Concord

Richmond

El Cerrito del Norte

El Cerrito Plaza

North
Berkeley

Pleasant Hill

Walnut Creek

Lafayette

Orinda

Downtown Berkeley

Ashby

Rockridge

MacArthur (Transfer Station)

19th St./Oakland

Oakland City Center/12th St. (Transfer Station)

West Oakland

Embarcadero

Montgomery St.

Powell St.

Civic Center

16th St. Mission

24th St. Mission

Balboa Park
(Transfer
Station)

Glen
Park

Daly
City

Colma

Weekdays only

South
San
Francisco

San
Bruno

Millbrae

Lake Merritt

Fruitvale

Coliseum/
Oakland Airport

AirBART
Shuttle

Oakland
International
Airport

San Francisco
International Airport
(SFO)

Weeknights and weekends only

San Leandro

Bay Fair
(Transfer Station)

Dublin/
Pleasanton

Castro Valley

Hayward

South Hayward

Union City

Fremont

© The Countryman Press

GETTING AROUND *By BART:* **BART** (transitinfo.org) serves the East Bay with two lines. You can pretty much get anywhere you want to, by using the train. Note that you have to keep your ticket to exit the train and fees change depending on your destination. If you plan to fly into Oakland and then take BART to your destination, you'll have to catch the BART shuttle ($5—you need exact change).

By bike: Berkeley and Oakland are cities made for biking. Both have Bike Boulevards designated for bikers to have the right-of-way.

By boat: **East Bay Ferry** (510-522-3300; eastbayferry.com) Located in Oakland's Jack London Square, this ferry shuttles people to Angel Island, San Francisco's Ferry Building, and AT&T Park. $6.25 adults; $3.50 youth 5–12; under 5 free.

By bus: **AC Transit** (actransit.org) might not be the best bus service on earth, but it does get you around Oakland, Emeryville, and Berkeley. Buses stop at all BART stations.

By car: I hate driving in the East Bay. Freeways are chaotic, spliced into such quick interchanges that traffic is often at a standstill no matter which direction you are headed. If you must drive in the East Bay tack on an extra bit of time to get to your destination. I-880 runs north and south from San Jose to Oakland, then meets up with I-80, which starts at the Bay Bridge (San Francisco) and takes you northeast through Berkeley, Albany, El Cerrito, Richmond, and all to way to Sacramento. I-580 takes you northwest from I-5 through Livermore, Dublin, and Pleasanton, and into Oakland. From here, you can cut onto CA 24, which passes through Oakland, Orinda, Lafayette, and Walnut Creek. Finally I-680 heads north and south from Dublin, through the East Bay Outback, Walnut Creek, and into the Delta.

MEDICAL EMERGENCIES **Alta Bates Hospital** (510-204-2700; altabates summit.org) 2450 Ashby, Berkeley.

Berkeley Free Clinic (800-6-CLINIC; berkeleyfreeclinic.com) 2339 Durant Avenue, Berkeley.

WEATHER Though people who live in the East Bay like to brag that their weather is better than San Francisco's (and it is by a fraction), to most of you, it will still be chilly. Always have layers with you. Berkeley and Oakland stay pleasant in summer (when the fog cooperates) not getting much warmer than 70 degrees Fahrenheit or so. Inland temperatures reach triple digits in summer. Winter weather is all over the map—you might wear shorts in March or be in a parka dodging pellets of hail in a freak June storm. You just never know.

✳ To See

✐ ☃ **Albany Bulb** At the west end of Buchanan, Albany. What was once the dump for the remnants of the Bay Bridge that fell during the 1989 earthquake now is home to a collection of public art that you sure won't find in the deYoung. In the early 1990s a number of homeless artists moved in and used the refuse in innovative ways. Walk the 0.25-mile path to the end and you won't just get those supreme bay views that you see on postcards, but you also get to see some unique public art. Many of the paintings are made by a dude with a boob fetish; some of the sculptures are withering under the strain of the salty air and fog, but you won't find anything else like this in the bay. While you are there, you might want to explore more than the main trail. If you do, head to the southernmost point to see the castle, then, on a bluff overlooking the bay, there is a bicycle graveyard used in a lot of student films. Just be sure not to tramp through people's houses. Free.

Berkeley City Club See *Lodging*.

✐ ♿ **Chabot Space and Science Center** (510-336-7395; chabotspace.org) 10000 Skyline Boulevard, Oakland. Open Wednesday through Saturday 10 AM–5 PM (until 10 on Friday and Saturday), Sunday noon–5. On a clear night, head up here to use the largest public telescope in the United States and check out the entire bay. There is also a planetarium, the large-screen Tien MegaDome theater, and loads of hands-on science exhibits. The exhibits are mostly geared towards kids, but the new "Beyond Blastoff" exhibit appeals to all ages, showing the workings of everything space station-related, including toilets. $8–15 adult; $7–10 youth.

⚓ ⟁ **Children's Fairyland** (510-452-2259; fairyland.org) 699 Bellevue, Oakland. Open at least 10 AM–4 PM daily in summer; on weekends in winter. If you have to find something to do with the little guys, kids love to see these fairy tales come to life. It may not be worth the steep admission price, but there is an animal farm, puppet show, train rides, and play structures, and it will surely tire the babes out. $6 all ages.

Grand Lake Theater See *Entertainment.*

Heinold's First and Last Chance Saloon See *Entertainment.*

⚓ ⟁ **Lawrence Hall of Science** (510-642-5132; lawrencehallofscience.org) 1 Centennial Drive, UC Berkeley, Berkeley. Open daily from 10 AM–5 PM. Besides the view of the bay, this science center is one of the best around. Hands-on exploration of everything from how the bay was formed, to views of the stars, it is worth a trip up here, if nothing else than for the view. Parents of preschoolers will find plenty to entertain the little guys. $9.50; youth $5.50–7.50.

Museum of Children's Art (MOCHA) (510-465-8770; mocha.org) 538 9th Street, Oakland. Open Tuesday through Sunday 10 AM–5 PM. You've got to love a place that brings art to young people and then allows you to view it for free! Sure, you wouldn't want to pay to see little Tabitha's painting of her dog, but you might find a piece here that strikes your artistic inner child. Free.

Niles Essanay Silent Film Museum (510-494-1411; nilesfilmmuseum.org) 37417 Niles Boulevard, Fremont. Open Saturday 12–4 PM and Sunday 11 AM–3 PM; films on Saturday night. Fans of silent films might want to head out to Fremont on a Saturday afternoon to tour the museum, then grab some Indian food in the neighborhood and come back for a silent film that night. Small fee.

⚓ ⟁ **Oakland Museum of California** (510-238-2200; museumca.org) 1000 Oak Street, Oakland. Open Wednesday through Saturday 10 AM–5 PM and Sunday 12 AM–5 PM. This great museum combines classic and contemporary art with history and natural sciences. As you might expect, the plethora of exhibits makes this museum a great stop for the whole family. Make sure to check out the sculpture garden. $8 adults; $5 youth; children under 6 free.

⚓ ⟁ **Oakland Zoo** (510-632-9525; oaklandzoo.org) 977 Golf Links Road, Oakland. Open daily from at least 10 AM–4 PM. Up in the hills above the bay, the Oakland Zoo teaches kids about mammals, birds, and reptiles. Here you can meet an elephant or a Gila monster, a baby giraffe or a flamingo. $9.50 adults; $6 children 2–14; under 2 free.

⚓ ⟁ **Phoebe A. Heart Museum of Anthropology** (510-643-7648; hearstmuseum.berkeley.edu) UC Berkeley, 103 Kroeber Hall, Berkeley. Open Wednesday through Saturday 10 AM–4:30 PM and Sunday 12–4 PM. It's not every day that you can experience the impact of anthropology. Here you can learn about native cultures throughout the world in changing exhibitions. Free.

Preservation Park (510-874-7580; preservationpark.com) 1233 Preservation Park Way, Oakland. In the late 19th century, Oakland was the second biggest port city in the country and had its fair share of wealthy inhabitants. This park offers a glimpse of what life used to be like, with 16 renovated Victorian houses and many thriving businesses. Head to the office, get a map for a self-guided tour, and wander through these lovely buildings. Free.

Takara Sake USA and Museum (510-540-8250; takarasake.com) 708 Addison Street, Berkeley. Open daily 12–6. Okay, so we're not in Japan, but Berkeley has its own sake factory. You can learn about sake making as well as taste the only local sake made in the Bay Area. Free.

Tao House (925-838-0249; nps.gov) Danville. Tours Wednesday through Sunday 10 and 12:30. The National Park Service is super secretive about the location of Eugene O'Neill's house in the Danville hills: You make a reservation and they pick you up in Danville and shuttle you to the location. Could be because it's where he wrote his final plays like *The Iceman Cometh* and *Long Day's Journey Into Night*. Or maybe they just don't want everyone and their mama coming up here at the same time. Plan two to three hours to tour the property. Reservations are required. Free.

UC Berkeley Art Museum and Pacific Film Archive (510-642-0808; bampfa.berkeley.edu) 2626 Bancroft Way, Berkeley. Open Wednesday through Sunday 11 AM–5 PM (Thursday until 7 PM). The museum attracts the off-the-wall contemporary art you'd expect with a number of must-see events each year. Last time I was there, Yoko Ono had an exhibition that included her calling the museum every so often to talk to visitors. The films you'll catch here, you won't find elsewhere, that's for sure. Museum: $12 adults; $7 youth; under 12 free. Films: $9.50 adults; $6.50 youth (17 and under).

UC Berkeley Campus Tours (510-642-5215; Berkeley.edu/visitors) 101 University Hall, 2200 University Avenue, Berkeley. The 90-minute student-led tours go out daily at 10 AM Monday through Saturday and 11 AM on Sunday. Walk this historic campus and learn about the classic architecture, the radical history, and the brainiacs who currently run the show. Sites not to be missed are the Beaux Arts **Sather Tower (The Campanile)**, **Sather Gate**, **Doe Library**, **Wheeler and California Halls,** and the **Hearst Memorial Mining Building.** Free.

♂ ♿ **UC Botanical Garden** (510-643-2755; botanicalgarden.berkeley.edu) 200 Centennial Drive, Berkeley. Open 9–5 daily. This might be one of the most spectacular botanical gardens around. With much of the international collection of 12,000 plants going to research, you can bet there is some not-to-be-missed greenery to find. Last time I was here, the stinky Odora the Titan was in bloom. $7 adults; seniors and youth: $5; children: $2; under 2 free.

USS *Hornet Museum* (510-521-8448; uss-hornet.org) 707 W. Hornet Avenue, Pier 3, Alameda. Open daily from 10 AM–5 PM. If you ever wondered what it was like to explore a real live aircraft carrier, head over to the island of Alameda. This ship participated in World War II and the Apollo 11 moon mission. $14 adults; $6 youth; under 4 free.

USS *Potomac* (510-627-1215; usspotomac.org) 540 Water Street, at Clay, Oakland. Open for dockside tours Wednesday and Friday 10:30–2 and Sunday 12–3:30. You can either come tour FDR's "floating White House" as it has been deemed, or head out on a two-hour historic sightseeing cruise on a number of Saturdays and Thursdays throughout the summer; call for details. Dockside tours: $5–7; children 12 and under free.

✳ To Do

ATHLETIC EVENTS **Cal Athletics** (800-GO-BEARS; calbears.com) Memorial Stadium, UC Berkeley. With 27 different sport teams, including a very popular football team, the Bears will keep you cheering, even if you are a Stanford fan.

Golden State Warriors (888-479-4667; nba.com/warriors) Oracle Arena, Oakland. So the Warriors might not be the Lakers, but going to a game sure is entertaining—even without a movie star in the front row. It's loud; goofy (entertainment includes a superhero who hands out pizza and overweight dancing men); and the team keeps getting better each year.

Oakland Athletics (877-493-2255; oaklandathletics.com) McAfee Coliseum, Oakland. Going to an As game will not only let you experience a fun baseball team, but you'll also catch a whiff of the diversity of the East Bay in everything from the food to the drummers.

Oakland Raiders (800-RAIDERS; raiders.com) McAfee Stadium, Oakland. Be afraid. Be very afraid. Going to a game at Raider Nation requires you to accept what might be the toughest crowd of football fans in the country.

THE BERKELEY BOTANICAL GARDEN'S ODORA THE TITAN IN FULL BLOOM.

FARMERS' MARKETS **Berkeley Farmers' Market** (ecologycenter.org) Center Street at M. L. King Jr. Way. Saturdays from 10 AM–3 PM. I love riding my bike here in the morning and sampling the array of fresh fruits and veggies. Plus the hippies strumming guitars makes me feel like I took a trip to the 1960s.

Berkeley Farmers' Market (ecologycenter.org) Shattuck Avenue at Rose Street Thursday from 3–7. This all-organic market brings out families, musicians, and people that might make you shake your head at and say "Only in Berkeley."

Grand Lake Farmers' Market Grand and Lake Park Avenues. Saturday 9–2. Sure it may be under a freeway, but don't let that stop you from seeing what makes Oakland so special. The Grand Lake community is one of the most diverse in the bay and the produce proves it.

Jack London Square Farmers' Market Embarcadero and Broadway, Oakland. Sunday 10 AM–2 PM. Come to Jack London's old stomping grounds to shop and munch on fresh produce.

GOLF **Lake Chabot Golf Center** (510-351-5812; lakechabotgolf.com) 11450 Links Road, Oakland. View of the bay makes this a popular spot for golfers. This 27-hole park has been around since 1923. $17–39.

Tilden Park Golf Course (510-848-7373; tildenparkgc.americangolf.com) 10 Golf Course Drive, Berkeley. This lovely golf course, located up in Tilden Park, is the spot to tee off and then space out on the trees. $18–72.

TRAIN RIDES *✈* **Niles Canyon Railway** (925-862-9063; ncry.org) Sunol Depot, 6 Kikare Road, Niles Station, 37001 Mission Boulevard, Fremont. This historic railroad connects Sunol with Fremont, taking folks on rides on Sunday mornings. You can also view artifacts from the old railroad days at the stations. Donations requested.

Steam Train Rides *See* Tilden Park.

WATER SPORTS **California Canoe and Kayak** (510-893-7833; calkayak.com) 409 Water Street, Oakland. Tour Oakland's estuary by kayak on either a day trip or a moonlight tour. Rentals: $15–25.

Gondola Servizio (866-SERVIZIO; gondolaservizio.com) 568 Bellevue Avenue, Oakland. Make a reservation to have a gondolier take you and your sweetheart for a ride on Lake Merritt. Cruises lasting 30 minutes cost $45 for two and $10 per additional person; cruises of 55 minutes will run you $75. Reservations required.

Lake Merritt Boating Center (510-238-2196; oaklandnet.com) 568 Bellevue Avenue, Oakland. You'll see people trying to hold up those sails as they learn the art of being captain of their own sailboat on this mellow lake. For those of you less daring, you can rent kayaks, canoes, and paddleboats.

WINE TASTING Over 40 winemakers are churning out pretty good wines in the Livermore Valley, and most of them don't charge a penny to let you taste their varietals like Petite Sirah. For more detailed winery information visit livermorewine.com and lvwine
.org, or head to the Livermore Visitor Center for a map. I have also included one winery in Emeryville that is worth a stop.

Bent Creek (925-455-6320) 5455 Greenville Rd, Livermore. Open Friday through Sunday 12–4:30. Known for its Petite Sirah and Port, come picnic with vineyards and oak trees all around.

LAKE MERRITT IN OAKLAND.

Concannon (925-456-2505) 4590 Tesla Road, Livermore. Since 1883 Concannon has prided itself on making big reds. Picnic tables are available, and make sure to check out the Victorian on the property. There is talk of starting a Shakespeare festival here.

Garre (925-371-8200) 7986 Tesla Road, Livermore. Open Monday through Friday 11 AM–2:30 PM and weekends from 11:30–3:30. Bordeaux blends are the major draw to this small winery. There is also a café on the property and two bocce ball courts.

La Rochelle (925-243-6442) 5443 Tesla Road, Livermore. Open daily 12–4:30. Pinot Noir is what they do best. You can go on a wine flight with paired food. They also make Portuguese dessert wines.

Periscope Cellars (510-655-7827; periscopecellars.com) 1410 62nd Street, Emeryville. Open Friday through Sunday 12–5 and the second Wednesday of every month from 5–7. This urban winery churns out award-winning wines in an old submarine repair facility. What makes the spot great is the fun Wednesday Happy Hour, where wines are $5 a glass. Free.

Wente Vineyards (925-456-2305) 5565 Tesla Road, Livermore. Livermore's big gun produces a lovely Merlot, offers summer concerts, an 18-hole public golf course, and an outdoor restaurant.

✳ Green Spaces

Albany Bulb See *To See*.

Anthony Chabot Regional Park (888-EBPARKS; ebparks.org) 9999 Redwood Road, Castro Valley. The hills that separate the bay side of the East Bay from the Livermore Valley are rich with hiking trails, lakes, eucalyptus, and oak trees. Access the 31-mile East Bay Skyline National Trail, camp or relax at Lake Chabot (there are 75 tent and RV sites at a first-come first-served basis), mountain bike, or golf at Willow Park.

Crown Memorial State Beach (888-EBPARKS; ebparks.org) 8th Street and Otis Drive, Alameda. Since they refurbished the beach, the trek to Alameda might be worth the effort again. The sand dunes border the bay and the bike trail, making this a popular place to walk your dog. The warm waters attract swimmers, kite-boarders, and windsurfers (rentals are available on spring weekends and during the summer), and kayakers. Parking: $5.

Del Valle Regional Park (925-373-0332; ebparks.org) 7000 Del Valle Road, Livermore. Almost 4000 acres of rolling hills, a wonderful swimming lake, plenty of space to hike, horseback ride, fish for trout, and camp all make this one of the East Bay gems. The marina rents kayaks, canoes, and motorboats. From here you can access the Ohlone Wilderness Trail—a 28-mile stretch of scenic backcountry that

LOOKING TOWARD RICHMOND FROM THE BERKELEY HILLS.

John Hickok

winds through hills and oaks. Book one of the 150 campsites well in advance (888-EBPARKS)—the Family Camp is just steps from the lake.

Eastshore State Park (888-EBPARKS; ebparks.org) From Oakland to Richmond, 8.5 miles of shoreline along the western edge of the East Bay. This is the perfect spot to fish, watch the sunset, or the fog blanket the city, swim, windsurf, walk, and fly kites. Work is still being done to refurbish the area, but today the birds living in the marshes sure look happy, as do the bikers pedaling the entire trail. My favorite spots in this park include the **Berkeley Marina** (at the end of University Avenue), **Emeryville Marina** (off Powell Street), and the **Albany Bulb** (see *To See*).

Huckleberry Botanic Regional Preserve (888-EBPARKS; ebparks.org) On Skyline Boulevard between Broadway Terrace and Snake Road, Oakland. If you are interested in native plants, the 1.7-mile loop weaves through the flowering gems.

Indian Rock Park Indian Rock Avenue at Shattuck Avenue, Berkeley. On a sunny day, even non-rock climbers head up here to watch the sunset, picnic, and soak up the views of the San Francisco Bay. The climb can be a touch difficult, so I probably would leave your out-of-shape relatives at home.

Lake Chabot (888-EBPARKS; ebparks.org) 17600 Lake Chabot Road, Castro Valley. This 315-acre lake attracts water sports enthusiasts eager to fish, hike, kayak, and boat. The Chabot Queen boat takes people on tours of the lake as well. If you prefer hiking or mountain biking, the Live Oak Trail (12 miles of hilly fun) will set you right up. Parking: $5.

Lake Merritt Bellevue Avenue, Oakland. This saltwater lake might not be the cleanest around, but it is the perfect centerpiece to Oakland's downtown. I love strolling around the lake, heading to the farmers' market, or just plopping down on a bench for a picnic. Free.

Mount Diablo State Park (925-837-2525; parks.ca.gov). You can access the park by Mount Diablo Scenic Boulevard, Danville, or North Gate Road, Walnut Creek. On a clear day, you can spot Mount Diablo from almost anywhere in the bay. Rumor has it, with binoculars, you can spot Yosemite's Half Dome from up here! It is our tallest peak (3,849 feet) and stands like a mama bear guarding her offspring. All year you'll find plenty to explore here, but my favorite is in spring when the wildflowers are in full bloom and Donner Falls is going off. Highlights include the wheelchair accessible **Mary Bowerman Trail, Rock City, Sentinel Rock, Deer Flat**, and **Summit Museum** (open 10 AM–4 PM daily). There are a number of campsites (reserveamerica.com).

Ohlone Regional Wilderness (888-EBPARKS; ebparks.org). Access the wilderness through Del Valle, Sunol Regional Park, or Mission Peak Regional Park, by horse or by foot on the Ohlone Wilderness Trail. If you can make it to the top of Rose Peak (3817 feet), you'll be rewarded with views galore and possibly a glimpse of an eagle or tule elk. In springtime the wildflowers are amazing, as is the pumping Murietta Falls. You can camp here but you need to make prior arrangements by calling the above-listed number. $2.

Oakland Estuary See *Water Sports*.

Sunol Regional Wilderness (888-EBPARKS; ebparks.org) 1895 Geary Road, Sunol. These pastoral lands attract hikers and campers, and are the gateway to the

Ohlone Wilderness. View Indian artifacts at the visitor center; check out wildflowers along the creek; or camp (by reservation only). Popular hiking trails include the gentle Indian Joe Creek trail, Canyon View Trail, and the Eagles' View trail.

Tilden Regional Park (888-EBPARKS; ebparks.org) Wildcat Canyon and Grizzly Peak Boulevard, Berkeley. Berkeley locals hold their heads high when talking about this vast park with the fun-to-swim Lake Anza, a carousel, a golf course, a steam train (redwoodvalleyrailway.com), pony rides, miles of hiking trails, and a botanic garden (nativeplants.org; open at least 8:30–5 daily; free). Hikers love Nimitz Way, Inspiration Point, or the East Bay Skyline trails. Free.

✳ Lodging

Bancroft Hotel (510-549-1000 or 800-549-1002; bancrofthotel.com) 2680 Bancroft Way, Berkeley. Popular with people visiting the University, since it is across the street, this 1928 Arts and Crafts building offers 22 simple, quiet rooms. A National Historic Landmark, don't expect elevators, or much more than a small room and a decent continental breakfast. $$.

Berkeley City Club (510-848-7800; berkeleycityclub.com) 2315 Durant Avenue, Berkeley. Julia Morgan designed this California landmark and you can stay in it. This B&B takes you back to a time when couches weren't just for sitting, but were a part of the personality of the room. The 30 rooms have views of the bay and you'll want to spend some time in the indoor pool, fitness center, and enjoying the continental breakfast. $$.

✎ ᴅ ⑂ **Brick Path Bed and Breakfast** (510-524-4277; thebrickpath.com) 1805 Marin Avenue, Berkeley. If I could live in Berkeley, I would select this precious neighborhood, complete with the best food, produce, coffee, parks, and gardens in the East Bay. Instead of living here, you can stay in a room, a cottage, or a suite with gourmet breakfast and comfy beds. I like the East Meets West Cottage, decorated in a spare Japanese fashion. $$.

✎ ᴅ ⑂ **Claremont Resort and Spa** (510-843-3000 or 800-551-7266; Claremontresort.com) 41 Tunnel Road, Oakland. The white palace atop the Oakland Hills, like a dollop of whipped cream, attracts those wanting high-end accommodations without the hustle of the city. However, from most rooms you can still see San Francisco Bay (though lower rooms also allow you to see who drives that Lexus). Like most snazzy hotels, expect the finest in linens, big old tubs, and spacious rooms. Amenities: 279 rooms and suites, 3 restaurants, the fun Paragon Lounge and Café, pool, fitness center, spa, room service, concierge, fitness classes, kids' club, tennis courts, parking (fee). $$$$.

East Brother Light Station (510-233-2385; ebls.org) 117 Park Place, Point Richmond. You'll have to board a boat to get to this B&B. When you arrive, you are greeted with champagne, appetizers, a four-course dinner with wine pairing, a period antique-decorated room, and finally when you wake, you can enjoy a gourmet breakfast. Sure, it's pricey, but this is an experience—staying on a light station on your very own island. $$$–$$$$; if you only stay for one night, there are no showers available to you.

✎ ᴅ ⑂ ❦ **Hotel Durant** (510-845-8981 or 800-238-7268; hoteldurant.com) 2600 Durant Avenue, Berkeley. Newly renovated and taken over by the impressive Joie De Vivre company, this classic building and hotel is the only full-service hotel near campus. Here you'll get 300-thread count sheets, eco-friendly amenities, and Spanish Mediterranean style at a reasonable price. Amenities: 143 rooms and suites, Henry's Gastro-pub, room service, concierge, parking. $$–$$$. At press time, the hotel was still being renovated, prices could go up.

✎ ♿ **Purple Orchid Inn Resort and Spa** (925-606-8855; purple orchid.com) 4549 Cross Road, Livermore. Stay out here in the Livermore Valley wine country and pamper yourself. Part log cabin, part country chic, expect the finest in bath amenities and views of vineyard-covered rolling hills. Amenities: 10 rooms and suites, pool, full breakfast, wine and cheese, spa, fireplace, and Jacuzzi tub. $$–$$$$.

✎ ♿ **Rose Garden Inn** (510-549-2145; rosegardeninn.com) 2740 Telegraph Avenue, Berkeley. The gardens are just what you'd expect from a Berkeley spot—flowering, diverse, fragrant, and sustainable. The five historic mansions seem to hide beneath the flora. Rooms evoke the historic Victorian side of Berkeley rather than the tie-dye you see elsewhere. All 40 rooms include full buffet breakfast. $$–$$$$.

Shattuck Hotel (510-845-7300; hotel shattuckplaza.com) 2086 Allston Way, Berkeley. At press time, this historic downtown hotel was getting a major facelift and closing its doors for months. Unfortunately I couldn't sneak in to give you an update.

✎ ♿ **Waterfront Hotel** (510-836-3800 or 800-729-3638; jdvhotels.com) 10 Washington Street, Oakland. In September of 2008, this hotel in Jack London Square finished a major renovation to turn it into the fine hotel it was meant to be. Besides lovely bay views, a great location, and plenty of hip snazziness that goes with the JDV name, you'll spend your days in Jack London's favorite spot by the bay.

Amenities: 144 rooms, pool, Miss Pearl's Jam House restaurant, shuttle service to BART and downtown Oakland, and room service. $$–$$$.

CAMPING See *Green Spaces*.

✽ Where to Eat

DINING OUT ♿ ♀ **A Cote** (510-655-6469; acoterestaurant.com) 5478 College Avenue, Oakland. Open nightly at 5:30 for dinner. Rustic dining in a bistro setting with low lights and plenty of wine make this Rockridge restaurant a favorite with in-the-know Oakland foodies. Seasonal Mediterranean small plates like gazpacho with shrimp and avocado, mussels with Pernod from the wood oven, fig and pancetta flatbread, and wood-fired salmon keep me returning. Reservations recommended. Small Plates: $–$$.

♿ ♀ **Bay Wolf** (510-655-6004; baywolf .com) 3853 Piedmont Avenue, Oakland. Open Monday through Friday from 11:30–1:45 PM, and for dinner nightly. For over 20 years, Bay Wolf has made cooking an art to behold. Seasonally changing menus highlight Mediterranean regions. Dishes might include a duck charcuterie, a tapas plate, crispy petrale sole with shrimp remoulade, or a cumin-crusted pork loin and belly. Reservations recommended. Lunch: $$; dinner: $$–$$$.

Cesar See *The Gourmet Ghetto*.

Chez Panisse See *The Gourmet Ghetto*.

♿ **Dona Tomas** (510-450-0522; dona tomas.com) 5004 Telegraph Avenue, Oakland. Open Tuesday through Saturday at least 5:30–9:30. This is one of those special Bay Area restaurants that no one tells people about. And not because it's not some of the best Mexican food around. It's already popular—too popular—and no one wants to wait longer to sip margaritas on the candlelit patio, and eat *huitlacoche* and other organic seasonal takes on enchiladas and moles. Reservations recommended. $$–$$$.

✂ ♿ ⚲ **Flora** (510-286-0100) 1900 Telegraph, Oakland. Open Tuesday through Saturday for lunch and dinner (Saturday they serve brunch). After creating the insanely good Dona Tomas, the owners broke into the retro-California dining scene with a hip eatery in a once-shady part of Oakland. Start with absinthe, served in the traditional way—with cold water dripped on a sugar cube into the alcohol. Entrees favor Southern comfort food with pork chops, stuffing, a hard not-to-finish macaroni and cheese, and yummy desserts. Reservations recommended. $$–$$$.

♿ ⚲ **Oliveto Café and Restaurant** (510-547-5356; oliveto.com) 5655 College Avenue, Oakland. Open for lunch and dinner daily; café is open for breakfast. For over 20 years, this Italian restaurant has been a stalwart in the Oakland dining scene. A twofold space with an informal neighborhood café downstairs, where you can get excellent food for a reasonable price; upstairs, Chef Paul Canales completes the menu at 5 PM, depending on what is fresh from the farm, and serves up dishes like local black cod with caramelized fennel, escarole, and brown butter mint sauce. Last time I was here was for a tomato festival, where every course featured the fruit—even dessert! Reservations required for upstairs and not accepted for downstairs. Café: $–$$; Upstairs: $$$.

✂ ♿ ⚲ **Sea Salt** (510-883-1720) 2512 San Pablo Avenue, Berkeley. Open Monday through Friday 11:30–10, Saturday and Sunday from 10 AM–9:30 PM. You never know what a neighborhood lacks until the perfect place appears to fill the gap. That's the case with Sea Salt, a sustainable seafood restaurant in the heart of Berkeley's funkier 'hoods. Casual dining on a tree-shaded patio or inside beneath a tribute to the sea, you can fill up on the freshest oysters, salads, pasta, and seafood around. The menu changes nightly, but you can always come for the happy hour when Chef's Choice oysters are a buck a pop. Reservations recommended. $$–$$$.

Yoshi's See *Entertainment*.

EATING OUT Arizmendi See *Cheeseboard*.

✂ ♿ **Bakesale Betty** (510-985-1213; bakesalebetty.com) 5098 Telegraph Avenue, Oakland. Open Monday through Saturday 7 AM–6 PM, Sunday 7 AM–3 PM. Hipsters stand in line for fried chicken sandwiches, pastries, and coffee. $.

✂ ♿ **Bangkok Thai** (510-848-6483; bangkokthaicuisine.com) 1459 University Avenue, Berkeley. Open Monday through Saturday for lunch from 11:30 AM–3 PM, for dinner from 5–10 PM, and open Sunday from 5–10 PM. Everyone in the East Bay favors a different Thai food spot. Well, this is mine. What it lacks in ambiance, Bangkok makes up for with consistently good food. The *pra-ram*, pumpkin curry, *pad ke mao*, and papaya salads are always just right. $–$$.

Berkeley Bowl (510-843-6929; berkeleybowl.com) 2020 Oregon Street, Berkeley. Open Monday through Saturday 9 AM–8 PM, and Sunday 10 AM–6 PM. You have to see it to believe it. An old bowling alley with the biggest produce section you'll ever see in your life—it's like a supermarket in Mexico, gone Berkeley. Stroll the aisles and you are sure to see some goods you ain't never seen before.

Bittersweet (510-654-7159; bitter sweetchocolatecafe.com) 5427 College Avenue, Oakland. See *San Francisco*.

&. **Breads of India** (510-848-7684; breadsofindia.com) 2448 Sacramento Street, Berkeley or 1358 North Main Street, Walnut Creek. Berkeley location open daily from 11:30–2:30 and 5:30–9:30. Walnut Creek location open Tuesday through Sunday from 11:30–2:30 and 5:30–9:30. Reading the daily changing menu at Breads of India is a lesson in itself. Farms are given recognition for supplying the produce and meats; explanations are given for where each dish comes from; and the list of ingredients will always make me salivate. To call each dish alive with flavor, unique, and super fresh wouldn't do it justice. Make sure to get some bread too, as stuffed as you'll be afterwards, it's a treat. $$.

✔ &. Ⴤ **Chow** (925-962-2469; chow foodbar.com) 53 Lafayette Circle, Lafayette. See *San Francisco*.

✔ &. **Fenton's Creamery** (510-658-7000; fentonscreamery.com) 4226 Piedmont Avenue, Oakland. Open 11 AM–11 PM daily (until midnight on Friday and Saturday). Dating back to 1897 for making ice cream, and 48 years running in this spot, Fenton's is the place to cure that insatiable sweet tooth on a hot September afternoon. They also serve lunch and dinner, but it is only an excuse for ice cream. $–$$.

✔ &. Ⴤ **Firehouse Bistro and Books** (925-449-3473; bistrobooks.com) 2369 1st Street, Livermore. Open daily for lunch and for dinner Tuesday through Sunday. A novel combo: books and a modern bistro located in an old firehouse. The bistro still uses those double doors as a way to bring air and light into the joint. Burgers tend to be better than pastas and the book selection is sparse, but it's still fun to browse while you wait for your date. Call for

information about nightly readings and events. $$–$$$.

✔ &. Ⴤ **First Street Ale House** (925-371-6588) 2086 1st Street, Livermore. Open for lunch and dinner daily. Microbrews and pub food in a casual atmosphere that attracts families and sports lovers makes this one of my favorites in the valley. Don't expect gourmet food, but the beer selection is top notch. $.

Fruitvale Taco Trucks International Boulevard, Oakland. There are so many good places to eat on International Boulevard, but these trucks, parked less than 100 feet apart, duel for your attention. **Mi Grullense** is the most popular (usually parked around 30th Street), but you can't go wrong with the cheap small tacos from most anywhere. Just bring cash and try them all. $.

&. Ⴤ **Jupiter** (510-843-8177; jupiter beer.com) 2181 Shattuck Avenue, Berkeley. Open daily from at least 11:30–1 Monday through Friday, Saturday 12 PM–1:30 AM, and Sunday 1 PM–midnight. When I want good beer, a greasy pizza, a lively outdoor patio, and lots of grad students surrounding me, I head to Jupiter. It's what you would expect from a college bar, but it is still in Berkeley. It's designed after the oldest bar in Berlin. $–$$.

&. Ⴤ **Kirala** (510-549-3486; kirala berkeley.com) 2100 Ward Street, Berkeley. Open Tuesday through Friday 11:30 AM–2 PM, and nightly for dinner. When I first moved to the Bay Area, everyone said that Kirala was the best sushi they had ever eaten. People line up out the door most nights. It is pretty darn spectacular—everything is fresh enough to imagine someone just caught the salmon out back. $$–$$$.

Koryo Wooden Charcoal BBQ (510-548-2525) 2556 Telegraph Avenue #8, Berkeley. Open late, call for hours.

This Korean BBQ joint makes L.A. friends drive up for a monthly fix. Hidden in the back of a mini-mall, this nondescript spot plants heaps of raw meat on your table to grill up yourself. The side dishes are delicately spiced and filling. $–$$.

Lanesplitter (510-845-1652; lanesplitterpizza) 2033 San Pablo Avenue, Berkeley. Open for lunch and dinner daily. Microbrews, calzones the size of a backpack, a sawdust-covered patio with picnic tables, and loud punk music make this one of the better spots to hang out on a Friday night with family or friends. They have another location on Telegraph Avenue in Oakland. $$.

Pasta Shop (510-528-1786) 1786 Fourth Street, Berkeley. When I want to cook a good meal, I head here for fresh pasta, cheese, pre-made salads, and a good baguette. Their lemon ricotta ravioli makes me drool every time. They also have a great selection of food for a picnic and imported Italian sauces and meats.

Pizzaiolo (510-652-4888; pizza iolooakland.com) 5008 Telegraph Avenue, Oakland. Open for dinner from 8–12 Monday through Saturday for espresso, toast, and jam. Charlie Hallowell learned from the best as the pizza dude at Chez Panisse. In 2005, he opened his own spot, which brings city folk out to Oakland to wait an hour for thin-crusted pizza, fresh salads, and possibly a nightly main dish (though the pizza usually does the trick). Go big and be bold—truffles on pizza can be a surprisingly perfect touch. Reservations recommended. $$.

Pyramid Ale House (510-528-9880; pyramidbrew.com) 901 Gilman Street, Berkeley. Open Sunday through Thursday 11:30 AM–10 PM, Friday and Saturday until 11 PM. In summer, when they show movies in the parking lot, grab a pint of apricot ale, some nachos, and chill on a blanket. Inside is as sleek and fun as most microbrew houses, complete with a beer store, loud, drinking students, and sports on TV. $–$$.

Rick and Ann's (510-649-8538; rickandanns.com) 2922 Domingo Avenue, Berkeley. Open for breakfast and lunch daily from 8 AM–2:30 PM, and dinner Tuesday through Sunday 5:30 PM–9:30 PM. You can't go wrong with breakfast at this locally favored country kitchen. Everything feels like it was made with love—from the pancakes to the scrambles, the homemade granola and oatmeal, and even the slices of banana. Come hungry. On Tuesday they serve dinner family style. $–$$.

Tacubaya (510-525-5160; dona tomas.com) 1788 Hearst, Berkeley. Open for breakfast and lunch daily. Why oh why is everything here *so good?* Tamales, horchata, guacamole, tacos, *chilaquiles*, you name it; it rocks. The bummer is that everything is also expensive and served in way-too-small portions. This isn't the spot to bring the kids or a first date, but if you are solo for lunch, head over here and order as much as you can afford. $–$$.

Tamarindo Antojeria (510-444-1944; tamarindoantijeria.com) 468 8th Street, Oakland. Open Monday through Saturday for lunch and dinner (Saturday for brunch). Sometimes you want some ambiance with your tacos. Well look no further. This small-plates kitchen serves up some of the most interesting Cal-Mex food in the Bay—including sopes and shrimp tacos. Exposed brick and candlelight allow you to dine in style without the big prices. Small plates: $–$$.

THE GOURMET GHETTO

It all started with Francophile Alice Waters, who wanted to use fresh California ingredients in quality food. Tired of a Big Mac nation, she started a food trend that would change the way Americans viewed food—both how and what they ate. Her dream transformed the Bay Area into the food mecca it is today. And her restaurant, Chez Panisse, is now surrounded by like-minded eateries in a little North Berkeley neighborhood along Shattuck Avenue, called the Gourmet Ghetto. Below is a list of my favorite places to eat in the area. For a more comprehensive Gourmet Ghetto experience, you might want to contact **In The Kitchen With Lisa** (See *San Francisco Tours*)—she does a great Gourmet Ghetto food tour.

    & ♈ **Cesar** (510-883-0222 or 510-985-1200; barcesar.com) 1515 Shattuck, Berkeley, or 4039 Piedmont Avenue, Oakland. Open daily from 12–12. Expect intense flavors to burst from your tapas while you sip sangria and watch passers-by from an airy patio. Favorites include cucumber gazpacho, *pollo asado* with a lime rub, and rabbit paté. It gets crowded at night, especially right when the work crowd opts for martinis after slaving away on their iMacs. Reservations recommended. $$–$$$.

    ✿ & **Cha Ya** (510-981-1213) 1686 Shattuck Avenue, Berkeley. Open daily 12–2 for lunch, and 5 PM–10 PM for dinner. With about six tables and a small sushi bar, you'd think this sparely decorated vegetarian restaurant wasn't all that. Think again. Berkeley non-vegetarians wait for an hour to eat some of the most delicately created Japanese food I have had in the States. Specials always delight, but my staples here are the Chaya Roll, curry noodle soup, and the seaweed salad. Oh, and the vegan chocolate cake is heavenly. There is a larger San Francisco location on Valencia Street. Cash only. $$.

    ✿ & **Cheeseboard** (510-549-3055; cheeseboardcollective.com) 1512 Shattuck Avenue, Berkeley. Pizza hours are Tuesday through Saturday 11:30 AM–3 PM and 4:30–8 PM. Café hours are Monday 7 AM–1 PM, Tuesday through Friday 7 AM–6 PM, Saturday 8:30 AM–5 PM. In the morning, freshly baked bread, dotted with cheese and fresh vegetables, keeps the bakery packed. But at night, when live jazz and blues pumps out of the small adjoining pizza joint and local Berkeley folks line up around the block for slices of pie, you understand why this co-op has been successful all these years. If you like

✿ & **Vik's Chaat Corner** (510-644-4412) 726 Allston Way, Berkeley. Open Tuesday through Sunday 11 AM–6 PM. Berkeley folks rave about this Indian restaurant that serves street food. I want to love it, but every time I come here, I order the wrong thing. Maybe it is the crowds of people lining up in the warehouse to sit on plastic chairs; or the servers yelling out orders; or the paper plates. Whatever the case, this is a true Berkeley experience. $.

the pastries and pizza, check out Oakland's **Arizmendi Bakery** (3265 Lakeshore Avenue). $–$$.

Chez Panisse (510-548-5525; chezpanisse.com) 1517 Shattuck Avenue, Berkeley. Open Monday through Saturday for two seatings at 6–6:30 and 8:30–9:15. There is also a café, with lunch hours Monday through Thursday 11:30 AM–3 PM, Friday and Saturday 11:30 AM–3:30 PM, and dinner hours Monday through Thursday 5–10:30, Friday and Saturday 5–11:30. What can I say about Alice Waters's restaurant that hasn't already been penned? She changed the way Americans eat with her views on bringing the farm to the kitchen, and after creating the best restaurant in the Bay Area, she started implementing her philosophy into local schools (by creating the best school lunch program around) and by default into most restaurants, where her descendants end up being head chefs. You can eat downstairs for a changing prix fixe dinner with the birthday/anniversary crowd, or do what locals do and head upstairs to the café—which is anything but a café as we know it. Bright, with mounds of vegetables piled around the open kitchen, the smell of the wood-burning stove churning out the best gourmet pizzas around, and an ever-changing menu that will make you pay 6 bucks for a pear, and then come back for more. Reservations required. $$–$$$$.

Epicurious Garden Open Monday through Saturday 11 AM–9 PM, Sunday 11 AM–7 PM (hours may vary by restaurant). Though it isn't the Ferry Building or even Napa's Oxbow, this small collection of restaurants has become one of my *must* stops when I am in North Berkeley. Here you can get killer soup, sushi from Kirala (get the fresh sushi not the packaged one), gourmet chocolate, gelato, and good Chinese food in the back garden.

Gregoire (510-883-1893; gregoirerestaurant.com) Open 11–9 daily. This hole in the wall serves gourmet food to go. You either can sit on the picnic bench out front or take your food home. The menu changes daily depending on what's fresh, but if you are lucky enough to try their mac and cheese paired with any of the chicken or fish dishes, you'll be satisfied. $$–$$$.

Peet's Coffee (peets.com) Walnut and Vine Street, Berkeley. This is the original Peet's Coffee, opened by Alfred Peet in 1966. The philosophy was to use small batches of beans and roast them darker. He inspired the founders of Starbucks and the zillions of coffee makers in every city.

✍ �& ♀ **Zachary's** (510-655-6385; zacharys.com) 5801 College Avenue, Oakland. Open at least 11 AM–10 PM daily. Here's how it goes: You wait an hour in a hot, sweaty space the size of my first apartment (or rather, a closet), then you order big, because you are *starving,* and when you finally sit beneath paintings of pizza, your big, deep-dish pie arrives and you eat two slices and feel like your belly will explode, but you keep going because it is that good. $$.

✳ Entertainment

Ⴤ **924 Gilman** (510-525-9926; 924 gilman.org) 924 Gilman Street, Berkeley. Local musicians Green Day were said to have started their career in this underage punk club.

Ⴤ **1515 Restaurant and Lounge** (925-939-1515; 1515wc.com) 1515 North Main Street, Walnut Creek. This new hip lounge gives the Walnut Creek folks a reason to stay on their side of the bay.

Ⴤ **Albatross** (510-843-2473) 1822 San Pablo Avenue, Berkeley. If you dare battle the brainy grad students, come out for trivia night on Sundays at 8:30.

Aurora Theater Company (510-843-4822; auroratheatre.org) 2081 Addison Street, Berkeley. Smart and relevant theater comes out of this tiny theater.

Berkeley Rep (510-647-2949; Berkeleyrep.com) 2025 Addison Street, Berkeley. This excellent theater company and performance space always puts up innovative and easy-to-watch shows.

Cal Performances (510-642-9988; Calperfs.berkeley.edu) UC Berkeley, Zellerbach Hall. This performance series gets such great world performers it is hard to choose when to see a show.

Ⴤ **First Street Ale House** See *Eating Out.*

Grand Lake Theater (510-452-3556; renaissancerialto.com) 3200 Grand Avenue, Oakland. This historic theater is where I head to see a political film, a blockbuster, or just to see what the owners are thinking—since they post it on the marquee.

Ⴤ **Heinold's First and Last Chance Bar** (510-839-6761; heinoldsfirstand lastchance.com) 48 Webster Street, Oakland. For 125 years, this crooked little bar has stood on Jack London Square. It used to stand on stilts over the coastal mudflats. Today there are still six barstools, the floor tilts, memorabilia hangs off everything, and it is no bigger than 18 by 22 feet. It's the spot for a drink, that's for sure.

Jupiter See *Eating Out.*

Paramount Theater (510-465-6400; paramounttheatre.com) 2025 Broadway Street, Oakland. There is nothing like seeing a diva perform in this historic theater.

Parkway Speakeasy (510-814-2400; parkway-speakeasy.com) 1834 Park Boulevard, Oakland. Closed Mondays. Beer, pizza, couches, and a movie is the perfect recipe for a Sunday night.

Ⴤ **Pyramid Ale House** See *Eating Out.*

Ⴤ **Skates the Bay** (510-549-1900; skatesonthebay.com) 100 Seawall Drive, Berkeley. Though this is also a lovely restaurant, I prefer to come to the bar for a martini and great appetizers, and to watch the sunset over Golden Gate Bridge.

Ⴤ **Stork Club** (510-444-6174; stork cluboakland.com) 2330 Telegraph Avenue, Oakland. One of those Oakland finds, complete with wild outfits, live music, and a great bar.

Ⴤ **The Trappist** (510-238-8900) 460 8th Street, Oakland. With 15 beers on tap and over 100 microbrews by the bottle, this fun new Oakland watering hole satisfies the need for a brew.

& Ⴤ **Yoshi's** (510-238-9200; yoshis .com) 510 Embarcadero West, Oakland. Primo jazz club in the Bay Area not only attracts the top names in music, but also serves up ridiculously good Japanese fusion food.

✳ Selective Shopping

In Berkeley, you can shop for everything from a $0.25 copy of *Kama Sutra* to a $250 pair of jeans. Your first stop has to include Telegraph Avenue, the street that leads to campus—even though it is nothing like it used to be, with a Gap and Urban Outfitters instead of the lines of bookstores. Though I still mourn the loss of Cody's Books, a walk down the street might make you buy a used book or get a tattoo. I like **Shakespeare and Co.** for my used books. Afterwards, head west to 4th Street, where Berkeley's high-end boutiques are located, including **NapaStyle, The Stained Glass Garden, Rabat Shoes**, and **Gardener's**. If you still have energy, head over to Solano Avenue, where you can browse kids' stores and boutiques and feel like the cool yuppies that live here.

In Oakland the best area for shopping is in Rockridge, which spreads across College Avenue. Here are some great galleries, furniture stores, kids' shops, and clothing boutiques. No matter what you do, head to **Diesel Books** to explore the stacks.

If antiques are your thing, don't miss the popular **Alameda Point Antiques and Collectibles Faire** (Antiques-bythebay.net) the first Sunday of month at Alameda Point. Enter through the Webster tube and follow the signs. It costs $15 at 6 AM, $10 at 7:30 AM, and $5 after 9 AM. For a different flea market experience, packed with patchouli and djembe drums, head to the **Berkeley Flea Market** at 1937 Ashby Avenue from 7–7 on weekends.

Walnut Creek's yuppies need somewhere to buy those Manolo Blahniks, and along Main Street is where you'll find upscale shops. In downtown Livermore, you'll find a number of shops, including the great women's boutique **Orghipchick** (925-294-4150; orghipchick.com) on First Street.

✳ Special Events

May–October: **California Shakespeare Theater** (510-548-9666; calshakes.org) 100 Gateway Boulevard, Orinda. During the summer, the hills of Orinda are the spot to catch some great Shakespeare in an outdoor amphitheater. Dress warmly (though they provide blankets) and either bring a picnic or get one there.

June: **Livermore Rodeo** (livermorerodeo.org). If watching wild cow milking is your thing, you won't want to miss the king of local rodeos.

Concerts in Wente Vineyards (925-456-2400; wentevineyards.com) 5050 Arroyo Road, Livermore. Throughout the summer big-name performers step out under the stars and sing their hearts out to people and the wine they happen to be guzzling.

July: **Berkeley Kite Festival** (510-235-5483) Cesar Chavez Park at the Berkeley Marina. Here's why I love Berkeley: Their one waterfront area is so windy it is tough to have a conversation. What do they do? Fly kites and celebrate it. It's beautiful.

August: **Art and Soul Festival** (artandsouloakland.com) This three-day Labor Day festival signals the official end of summer, and the start of good weather in the Bay Area. There is no better way to welcome the heat with local musicians (some of them with an international following), and lots of food.

September: **How Berkeley Can You Be?** (510-644-2204) Downtown Berkeley. I don't want to tell you anything, but do come see this festival at least once in your life. But just in case you doubt me, you'll see art cars, naked folks, music, and Berzerkely in all its glory.

Harvest Wine Celebration (elivermore.com) Livermore. This huge festival celebrates the grape harvest with music, wine tasting, and food.

THE PENINSULA AND SOUTH BAY

Best known for its high-tech gold rush in the last decade, travelers tend to skip over the South Bay when they visit Northern California. And what a shame that is. Though it is considered suburban by most, the hills surrounding Silicon Valley, as well as the coast, offer some of the best exploring in the whole Bay Area. Besides the natural abundance and the insane cumulative IQs of the inhabitants, what make this region so lovely are the compact historic downtowns that would inspire both June Cleaver and Julia Butterfly Hill. From redwood hikes to waterfalls to miles of beach strolls; four-star tasting menus to huge bowls of *pho* for under 10 bucks; from goat farms to the best Tech Museum in the state, the South Bay deserves more than a drive through.

Once you pass **Colma** (the city of cemeteries, where the dead outnumber the living), and the bedroom communities of **Burlingame** and **San Mateo** (a historic suburb with a walkable downtown), you'll find **Redwood City**, an ethnically diverse neighborhood. Though it was once called Deadwood City, the city recently renovated the downtown area in an effort to revitalize itself, and while it is a far cry from San Francisco (or Palo Alto for that matter), it has come a long way. A few miles south is the university town of **Palo Alto** (surrounded by the affluent suburbs of Atherton, Belmont, Woodside, and Los Altos Hills). Known mostly for its brainiacs, Palo Alto also boasts a wonderful art museum, great shopping, and some of the better eateries in the entire Bay. And just a few miles south you'll find **Mountain View**, home to Google headquarters, Indian food galore, and a great downtown area that gets lots of foot traffic in the evening.

The main artery of the region is **San Jose**, a suburban city of mini-malls, 1960s retro buildings, and shops. Usually San Jose gets a bad rap, but if you look hard enough you'll find a rich history of affluence that has helped create some of the Bay's best museums, restaurants, parks, and hiking trails. San Jose's suburbs of **Los Gatos** and **Saratoga** might tie in the South Bay awards for cutest downtowns. Well, unless you count the beach towns.

It is no wonder that the first settlers in San Mateo County picked **Half Moon Bay** as their home. The entire coast, often hidden beneath a thick layer of fog, offers rugged cliffs, with trails to white sand beaches, abundant sea life, and thick redwood forests. As you travel down CA 1, you'll pass the small historic towns of **Pacifica, Montara, Moss Beach,** and **El Granada** to get to Half Moon Bay, the self-proclaimed pumpkin capital of the United States, and a Bay Area hidden gem.

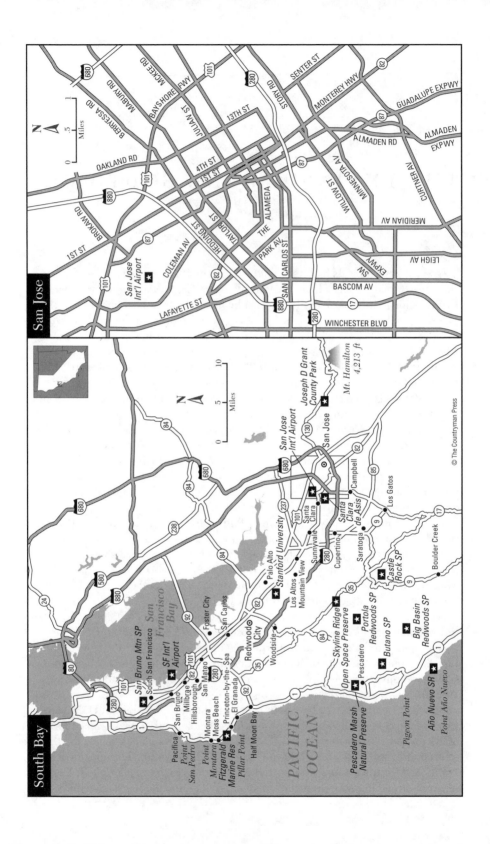

Farther south is the country town of **Pescadero**, fit with farms, roadhouses, and great beach trails.

GUIDANCE **Half Moon Bay Visitor Center** (650-726-8380) 520 Kelly Avenue, 1st floor, Half Moon Bay.

San Jose CVB (800-SAN-JOSE; sanjose.org) 408 Almaden Boulevard, San Jose.

HELPFUL WEB SITES
Sjdowntown.com
Paloaltoonline.com
Metroactive.com
Mercurynews.com
sanmateococvb.com

GETTING THERE *By air:* Visitors fly into either **San Francisco International Airport** (for the north part of the Peninsula) or **Mineta San Jose International Airport.** Both offer connections to most U.S. and international destinations as well as most rental car agencies.

By bus: **Greyhound** (greyhound.com) offers service to most cities along the Peninsula and South Bay. The main Greyhound station for San Jose is at 70 S. Almaden Boulevard, which is 3 miles from the airport, and there is no direct bus service between the two.

By car: Negotiating the Peninsula can often be a task. Traffic, merging highways, and construction tend to be your biggest obstacles. From San Francisco, take I-280 or US 101 south to San Jose; you can access all of the Peninsula and the South Bay from these freeways. I prefer I-280 because it is a nicer drive with less traffic, but there are always speed traps, and if you are going to Palo Alto or Mountain View, you have to add an extra 15 minutes to cross the Peninsula. In San Jose, three major highways cut into the city—the aforementioned I-280 and US 101, plus I-880, which comes from the East Bay. Getting to the San Mateo Coast, take CA 92 west from San Mateo.

By train: **Caltrain** (caltrain.com) runs between San Francisco and San Jose (and all the way to Gilroy during the week. **Amtrak** (Amtrak.com) handles arrivals from outside the Bay Area.

GETTING AROUND *By bus:* **Sam Trans** (samtrans.com) provides bus service throughout San Mateo County and into San Francisco. Or **Santa Clara Valley Transit Authority** (vta.org) runs buses and streetcars throughout San Jose and the vicinity. You can get to Los Gatos, the airport, most attractions, and Palo Alto.

By car: See *Getting There.*

MEDICAL EMERGENCIES Call 911.

Santa Clara Valley Medical Center (408-885-5000) 751 S. Bascom Avenue, San Jose.

WEATHER San Francisco families come to the South Bay valley for a real summer. Other times of the year the climate is the same as the rest of the Bay Area, with moderate temperatures year-round.

✳ To See

Sites listed below from north to south.

✐ Burlingame Museum of Pez Memorabilia (650-347-2301; burlingamepez museum.com) 214 California Drive, Burlingame. Open Tuesday through Saturday 10 AM–6 PM. Over 550 different Pez dispensers have been produced since 1950, and the Burlingame Museum of Pez Memorabilia is the only place in the world to see them all. $3.

✐ Coyote Point Museum for Environmental Education See *Green Spaces*.

San Mateo County History Museum (650-299-0104; historysmc.org) 2200 Broadway Street, Redwood City. Open Tuesday through Sunday 10 AM–4 PM. Museum features exhibits depicting the history of the Peninsula through the times of the Ohlone Indians, the Spanish explorers, the ranchos, pioneer logging, agriculture, dairy farms, whaling, and the Victorian era. You'll also marvel at the largest stained glass dome in a public building on the West Coast. $4 adults; $2 students and seniors.

Filoli Estate (650-364-8300, ext. 507 or 508; filoli.org) 86 Canada Road, Redwood City. Open Tuesday through Saturday 10 AM–3:30 PM, Sunday 11 AM–3:30 PM. Known for its lush gardens and beautiful architectural design from the first part of the 20th century, the estate offers a variety of tours of the rare example of an early 1900s country estate. I enjoy the beautifully preserved Georgian Revival house and the gardens, which was the home of the 1980s television show *Dynasty*. $12 adults; $5 children; free under 5.

Pulgas Water Temple Just off Canada Road by the Crystal Springs Reservoir, Redwood City. Built in 1938, the temple commemorates the completion of the Hetch Hetchy Aqueduct (which brings water to the Crystal Springs Reservoir from the Sierra 150 miles away!) This is one of three temples in the U.S., modeled after those erected near canals and waterways by the ancient Greeks. Free.

Cantor Center Museum (650-723-4177; museum.stanford.edu) Stanford University, 328 Lomita Drive, Palo Alto. Open Wednesday through Sunday at least 11 AM–5 PM. The museum at Stanford University is worth your time—if nothing else, for an excuse to wander through the campus. Besides the Rodin collection, you can meander through the contemporary exhibit, the sculpture garden, and the folk art from around the world. Free.

COOLING OFF IN CESAR CHAVEZ SQUARE, SAN JOSE.

✐ Palo Alto Junior Museum and Zoo (650-326-6338; pajmzfriends.org) 1451 Middlefield Road, Palo Alto. Open Tuesday through Saturday 10 AM–5 PM, Sunday 1–4 PM. This interactive museum and petting zoo is where the peninsula Moms go to entertain the little ones. $3.

✳ To Do

Crystal Springs Golf Course (650-342-0603; playcrystalsprings.com) 6650 Golf Course Drive, Burlingame. Open 6 AM–7 PM daily. This public course is set in a wildlife sanctuary. The course has been recently renovated with new tee boxes, bunkers, and has 18 holes. $26–44.

Watercourse Way (650-462-2000) 165 Channing Avenue, Palo Alto. Open 8:30–11:30 Sunday through Thursday and until 12:30 AM Friday and Saturday. A Japanese-style retreat in the middle of the suburbs. Private soaking rooms, some with steam rooms and saunas, all surrounded by bamboo trees, make this a pleasant escape. $18–27.

✳ Green Spaces:

PARKS For detailed information about San Mateo County parks, contact the County at 650-363-4021 or go to co.sanmateo.ca.us. Or contact the **Midpenisula Regional Open Space District** (650-691-1200; openspace.org). They also provide free maps to hiking trails.

Shoreline Parks (co.sanmateo.ca.us) In San Mateo, along the bay are Ryder Park and Aquatic Playground, and Seal Point Park, which are great places to spend a warm afternoon gazing at the bay and playing in the water. Here you'll find cycling paths, a dog park, and hiking paths with nice views. Bring the little guys to frolic in the water-play area.

San Mateo Central Park, E. 5th Avenue and El Camino Real, San Mateo. This large park in the center of San Mateo has a lovely **Japanese Tea Garden,** which features a teahouse, waterfalls, a pagoda, pathways, trees, and rocks. There is also an electric train for kids and the usual play structures, ball fields, and tennis courts.

Coyote Point Recreation Area (650-342-7755; coyoteptmuseum.com) 1651 Coyote Point Drive, San Mateo. Besides watching airplanes land, letting your little one run around, and trying to find shade, you can also visit the **Museum for Environmental Education**, which exhibits aquariums, computers, games, films, and a wildlife habitat native to the Bay Area. Free (though there is a parking fee).

Palo Alto Baylands (650-329-2506) 2775 Embarcadero Road (east end of Embarcadero Road), Palo Alto. This unique 1,700-acre nature preserve, which is mostly salt marsh, welcomes more than 150 bird species. I like to wander the number of trails, including a boardwalk built over the marsh. Visit the **Nature Interpretive Center** to learn more about this landscape.

Long Ridge Open Space Preserve Skyline Boulevard, about 3.6 miles north of CA 9, and approximately 3.3 miles south of its intersection with Page Mill Road. This popular hiking area is home to the Bay Area Ridge Trail, which offers 13 miles of plant diversity, and the Long Ridge Loop.

Upper Stevens Creek County Park From I-280, exit Page Mill Road (exit 20). Drive west on Page Mill to the junction with Skyline Boulevard (CA 35). Drive south 5 miles. The trail entrance is easy to miss; it's a small, unsigned path on the east side of Skyline. This shaded 5.5-mile loop trail is a great spot to hike in spring and fall.

SAWYER CAMP TRAIL

From Hillcrest Boulevard on the north to Crystal Springs Road on the south. For thousands of years this area was home to the Shalshone Indians, a warlike society who used this trail as a primary means of transportation. Many explorers passed through, but the most notable came on November 4, 1769: Gaspar de Portola and his men camped north of here after descending from Sweeney Ridge, where they were reputed to be the first white men to view San Francisco Bay. After much use this trail became the main highway between San Francisco and Half Moon Bay. Wagons pulled by teams of horses hauled wood over the road; but by 1888, much of the old road was flooded by the Crystal Springs Reservoir—the main water source for the entire Bay Area. The city of San Francisco took over the watershed lands, and in 1978, the San Mateo County Board of Supervisors designated the road a non-vehicular recreation trail, and paved it for bicycles. Today hikers and bikers use the trail, often passing the famed Jepson Laurel, which is over 600 years old and the largest laurel in California.

Portola Redwoods State Park (650-948-9098; parks.ca.gov) Located 6 miles off CA 35, La Honda. Many people go soul-searching in this divine grove of redwoods. While exploring Pescadero Creek, be on the lookout for the tallest redwood in Santa Cruz County—it is over 300 feet! Day use: $6. Campsite: $25; no camping in winter; reservations required.

Windy Hill Portola Road, Portola Valley. Grasslands, Douglas fir, and as you might guess, wind, enchant peninsula hikers—especially when those elusive views of the city occur. The 12 miles of trails include the Anniversary Trail for hikers and the Spring Ridge Trail for mountain bikers.

✱ Lodging

Coxhead (650-685-1600; coxhead.com) 37 E. Santa Inez Avenue, San Mateo. Combining English Country style with Arts and Crafts architecture, Ernest Coxhead built his family home in 1891. Turned into a B&B in 1991, the inn retains the original sensibility while adding unique modern touches like a mural, cozy rooms, and breakfast. $$–$$$.

Dinah's Garden Hotel (650-493-2844; dinahotel.com) 4261 El Camino Real, Palo Alto. Elegant rooms along a koi-filled lagoon make this a charmer. Made for the business traveler (and parents visiting their smarty-pants kids), you can expect the traditional fixings like a pool, a business center, continental breakfast, comfy beds, and an upgrade to suites if you want more space. $$$.

Hotel Avante (650-940-1000 or 800-538-1600; jdvhotels.com/hotels/avante) 860 E. El Camino Real, Mountain View. Called the geekiest hotel in the Bay Area, this Google headquarters favorite offers a boutique hotel experience with in-room Etch-a-Sketches, Rubik's cubes, and Slinkys, plus a groovy Austin Powers lounge. Strangely, all furniture in the rooms is on wheels, so you can move the room around to suit your fancy. Amenities: 91 rooms and suites, pool, business center, Jacuzzi, lounge, fitness room, iPod docking stations, free wine and ale reception, and free chair massages on Tuesday and Wednesday. $$–$$$.

✳ Where to Eat

DINING OUT & **Central Park Bistro** (650-558-8401; centralpark bistro.com) 181 E. 4th Avenue, San Mateo. Open for lunch and dinner daily. This San Mateo mainstay serves up fresh local ingredients in a spare bistro setting. Highlights include the lamb sirloin and the potato-crusted salmon for reasonable prices. You can also get a number of pastas and pizza dishes, great salads, and yummy desserts. Their carefully picked wine list complements the food. $$–$$$.

& ❦ **Evvia** (650-326-0983; evvia.net) 420 Emerson, Palo Alto. Open for lunch Monday through Friday and dinner nightly. This Greek restaurant delights discerning diners—especially those who appreciate the ambiance of eating in a cavernous setting. You can get primo moussaka, ahi pita, and delicately spiced specialties like Kakavia and Kotopoulo. Reservations recommended. Entrees: $$$$.

& **Flea Street Café** (650-854-1225; cooleatz.com) 3607 Alameda de las Pulgas, Menlo Park. Sustainable, organic dining in a casual dining room allows you to really fall in love with Jessie Cool's food. This white-table-cloth restaurant serves lovely starters like raw beet ravioli and squash fritters. For dinner, you can get grass-fed beefsteak or portobello mushroom Wellington. If this high-end experience is out of your budget, they also have an organic café in the Cantor Arts Center at Stanford and a casual café in Menlo Park called **jZ Cool**. Reservations recommended. $$–$$$.

❦ & ❦ **Junnoon** (650-329-9644; junnoon.com) 150 University Avenue, Palo Alto. Open for lunch Monday through Friday, and dinner nightly. You will not find traditional takes on *saag panneer* in this upscale contemporary lounge and restaurant. Instead, you'll be transported into Chef Kirti Pant's creative take on California staples like sea bass and sustainable beef, with freshly ground Indian ingredients. Though the menu focuses on seasonal dishes, some favorites are the coriander and fennel chicken tikka, tangy semolina shells, rice-flaked sea bass, black-pepper steak, and the spiced molten-chocolate cake with ginger ice cream. Reservation recommended. $$–$$$.

❦ & ❦ **Pampas** (650-327-1323; pampaspaloalto.com) 529 Alma Street, Palo Alto. Open for lunch and dinner Monday through Friday and dinner on Saturday and Sunday. Usually these all-you-can eat affairs make me feel like I need someone to roll me home. Chef John Karbowski, who specialized in tasting menus before heading the kitchen at this new loft space, offers a less gluttonous *churrascaria* experience. Most people go for the *rodizio*, all you can gorge on prime cuts of meat and a side bar with innovative accoutrements: coconut couscous, peach caprese, cucumber soup. For those of you not wanting to fill up so intensely, selections from the entrée menu are just as tasty (like the halibut in passion fruit), or just visiting the side bar is a great way to experience Chef John's creative treats for your palate. Reservations recommended. Children's Menu. Rodizio $44; Lunch $–$$$. Dinner: $$–$$$$.

& ❦ **Red Lantern** (650-369-5483; redlanternrwc.com) 808 Winslow Street, Redwood City. Open for lunch Monday through Friday, and dinner nightly. This south-Asian fusion hot spot has infused what some used to call "Dead-wood" City with a little life. Daniel Sudar created a winner with big red lanterns, mod-Asian décor, and an ambitious menu. Check out the communal table in the bar, made from petrified wood. Handmade sauces use local ingredients as much as possible; meat eaters will love the small plates. Reservations recommended. $$–$$$.

&️ ⅄ **The Village Pub** (650-851-9888; villagepub.net) 2967 Woodside Road, Woodside. Open for lunch Monday through Friday and dinner nightly. Don't go expecting a pub serving bangers and mash. This classic restaurant serves some of the most innovative cuisine in the Bay Area. Look for house-made pasta with seasonal vegetables, olive oil-roasted halibut, and an excellent wine list. Also check out the 70-year old mahogany bar. Eat in the pub area for cheaper fare. Reservations recommended. $$$–$$$$.

EATING OUT ✐ **Alice's Restaurant** (650-851-0303; alicesrestaurant.com) 17288 Skyline Boulevard, La Honda. Open 8:30 AM–9 PM daily. This biker bar serves up burgers and garlic fries by the dozens to be enjoyed in outdoor picnic tables on warm days. I like to come here for breakfast before a hike, when it is still mellow. Occasionally there is live music on weekends. $.

✐ &️ **Amber India** (650-968-7511; amber-india.com) 2290 El Camino Real, Mountain View. Open daily for lunch and dinner. I have two words for you: Butter Chicken. After you experience it, you'll know why this mellow Indian restaurant in a strip mall ends up on the *San Francisco Chronicle* Top 100 Restaurants every year. For lunch, the all-you-can-eat buffet is a steal. They recently opened locations in downtown San Francisco, Santana Row, and a cheaper café in Mountain View, but this original location is my favorite. $$.

⅄ **Caffé Del Doge** (650-323-3600; caffedeldoge.com) 419 University Avenue. Open 7 AM–11 PM daily. If a trip to Venice is not in your budget right now, head to this café for the finer side of espresso. Here you won't get paper cups with witty slogans; instead you'll taste a variety of espresso varieties served in a martini glass. Small plates, sandwiches, and desserts can extend your time here. $.

✐ &️ **Chef Chu's** (650-948-2696; chef chu.com) 1067 N. San Antonio Road, Los Altos. Open daily from 11:30–9:30, weekends from 12 PM–10 PM. This Los Altos institution serves up the best Chinese food in the South Bay. This lively two-floor restaurant attracts local families as well as the business crowd. Everything I have had is good. Really. $–$$.

✐ &️ **Sancho's Taqueria** (650-364-8226) 3207 Oak Knoll Drive, Redwood City. Open for lunch and dinner daily. Chef-owner Adam Torres, trained at Boulevard and Village Pub, has mixed his gourmet dining background with his Latino roots. Fish tacos on a warm day are divine. Cash only. $.

&️ **Sirayvah Organic Thai** (650-637-1500) 366 El Camino Real, San Carlos. Open Monday through Friday from 11:30–2:30 and dinner nightly from 5–9:30. You have to love them for creating an all-organic Thai eatery. As you might assume, prices are higher and plates are smaller than most Thai restaurants, but the food is super fresh and the Zen-themed décor gives the illusion that you are on your way to nirvana. Reservations recommended.

✳ **Entertainment**

⅄ **Alberto's Salsa Studio and Nightclub** (650-968-3007; albertos.com) 736 Dana Street, Mountain View. A great place to get your groove on—the South Bay folks pack this salsa club almost every night. Sunday through Thursday are the main dancing nights, with Argentine tango and salsa. On Friday you might enjoy the Bollywood night.

Broadway by the Bay (broadway bythebay.org) 851 Burlwel Road, Burlingame. This theater company presents top-notch musicals and Broadway shows at non-Broadway prices.

Y **Empire Grill and Tap Room** (650-321-3030) 651 Emerson Street, Palo Alto. If you are searching for that constantly packed bar to have a great Bloody Mary, this is the spot. You can get good pub food here too.

Fox Theater (foxdream.com) 2215 Broadway, Redwood City. Since this 1928 theater was renovated in 2001, it has welcomed big-name performers. Check local listings for information.

Palo Alto Children's Theater (650-463-4930; city.palo-alto.ca.us) 1305 Middlefield Road, Palo Alto. Bring the kids for musicals and theater that will not bore them to tears. Check the Web site for scheduled events, times, and prices.

▼ Y **The Savoy** (408-244-6909; club savoy.com) 3546 Flora Vista Avenue, Santa Clara. For 30 years, this lesbian dance club has attracted ladies from around the bay.

Stanford Theater (650-324-3701) 221 University Avenue, Palo Alto. This classic theater shows both first-run films and classic black-and-whites.

✳ Selective Shopping

Aside from hiking, one of the favorite pastimes on the Peninsula is shopping. Most downtown areas have a main street with stores and restaurants. Some of my favorites include Burlingame Avenue in Burlingame, where you'll find the great shoe store **Rabat;** Palo Alto's University Avenue houses shops selling more rugs than you'll find in a Moroccan street market; and Mountain View's Castro Street is home to the spacious **Books Inc**.

✳ Selective Seasonal Events

Stanford Lively Arts (Stanford.edu) World-class musicians, authors, and celebrities come to Stanford to show their stuff throughout the year.

SAN JOSE AND VICINITY

Cathedral Basilica of Saint Joseph (408-283-8100; stjosephcathdral.org) 80 S. Market Street Open 8–5 daily. St. Joseph's was the first church in the Pueblo de San Jose, built in 1803. After a couple renovations, and a massive fire in 1875, the present building became one of the remaining examples of 19th-century architecture. The cathedral is filled with hand-painted murals, stained glass windows, and a custom-built organ.

✐ ⅖ **Children's Discovery Museum** (408-298-5437; cdm.org) 180 Woz Way. Open Tuesday through Saturday 10 AM–5 PM. When the heat becomes too much to handle in summer or rain drenches the playgrounds in winter, families head to this excellent children's museum. There is something for everyone—from crawlers to older children—including a bubble exhibit, a fun water-play area, and lots of interactive odds and ends to play with. $8; children under 1 free.

Rosicrucian Egyptian Museum (408-947-3635; egyptianmuseum.org) 1342 Naglee Avenue. Open 10 AM–5 PM weekdays and 11 AM–6 PM weekends. Built to mimic the Temple of Amon in Karnak, this is the largest collection of Egyptian artifacts in the western U.S. Over 4000 artifacts, including real mummies, always intrigue the little ones. $9 adults; $5–7 children.

San Jose Museum of Art (408-271-6840; sjmusart.org) 110 S. Market Street. Open 11 AM–5 PM Tuesday through Sunday. This wonderful museum hosts internationally known artists. Mainly focusing on 20th- and 21st-century artists, new media, paintings, and sculpture, you may see an exhibit on robots, by Nara, or Joan Miro. $8 adults; $5 children and seniors; under 5 free.

♿ **Santana Row** (408-551-4611; santanarow.com) 355 Santana Row, at Winchester. This mixed-use shopping, restaurant, and entertainment area used to be orchards owned by the famed San Jose Winchester family. Now people from all over the South Bay gather here. I especially like it on warm evenings when bars serve al fresco cocktails, live music wafts through the streets, and families gather on the grassy area near the play structure.

✎ ♿ **The Tech Museum of Innovation and IMAX Theater** (408-294-8324; thetech.org) 201 S. Market Street. Open 9–5 Monday through Wednesday and 9–9 Thursday through Sunday. Though I am not much of a techie, I love visiting this museum. Exhibiting everything from how the Internet works to how to make your house green, from IMAX movies to lessons on how to make musical instruments out of everyday objects, this educational museum will keep you (and the family) entertained for hours. IMAX admission included in the ticket price. $8.

✎ **Winchester Mystery House** (408-247-2101; winchestermysteryhouse.com) 525 Winchester Boulevard. Open daily at 9 AM. Often called one of the weirdest museums around, this huge Victorian mansion appeals to architecture and American History buffs, and those enchanted by a dash of spookiness (though don't expect to see any ghosts in the séance room). Believed to have been erected for the spirits of those killed by the Winchester rifle, Sarah Winchester built this house 24 hours a day for 38 years. Basic tours last an hour. Teens might enjoy the allure of a door that opens into a two-story fall, or the stairway that leads to the ceiling, but for the most part you will probably rather have a margarita and pedicure at Santana Row across the street. $31 adults for mansion tour; $28 children; no children under 10 allowed on tours.

❇ To Do

ATHLETIC EVENTS ✎ **San Jose Earthquakes** (web.misnet.com) Soccer fans crowd this major league soccer stadium, even when the Earthquakes aren't playing well.

✎ **San Jose Sharks** (sharks.nhl.com) My English students skip class to watch these hockey players play at HP Pavilion each year—especially when they get into the playoffs. Games are quite the lively scene.

FARMERS' MARKETS **Downtown Friday Market** (408-279-1775 x 40; sjdowntown.com) San Pedro Square. May through December from 10 AM–2 PM. In summer the best of local farms show off in Downtown.

Los Gatos Farmers' Market (los-gatos.ca.us) W. Main Street and S. Santa Cruz, Sunday 8–1:30. Make sure to check out the array of authentic Mexican food at this affluent community market.

Santana Row Market Santana Row, Sunday from 10 AM–3 PM. This is the San Jose market to purchase carrots and clothes.

GOLF **Cinnabar Hills Golf Course** (408-323-5200; cinnabarhills.com) 23600 McKean Road, San Jose. This beautiful public green is made up of three courses: The Canyon, The Lake, and The Mountain. Monday through Thursday $37–80; Friday through Sunday $47–100.

Coyote Creek Golf Club (408-463-1400; coyotecreekgolf.com) 1 Coyote Creek Golf Drive, San Jose. This 36-hole public course features a Jack Nicklaus design. $70–99.

San Jose Municipal Golf Course (408-441-4653; sjmuni.com) 1560 Oakland Road, San Jose. This 18-hole public course has the best deal in town. Greens fees: $32–46.

HORSEBACK RIDING **Garrod Farms** (408-867-9527; garrodfarms.com) 22647 Garrod Road. You can go on horseback riding trips that last an hour. Even more fun is to combine a ride with a wine tasting. $40–75.

SPAS **Being Spa** (408-227-2227; beingspausa.com) Dolce Hayes Mansion, 200 Edenvale Avenue. I love that traditional massages here last 90 minutes. Last time, my masseuse used hot stones to work out the kinks in my back. Asian-themed, with a pool, Jacuzzi, wet room, and sauna, Being Spa makes a perfect place to laze the day away.

WATER SPORTS **Outback Adventures** (408-551-0588; outbackadventures.org) 1158 Saratoga Avenue. These guys offer everything from kayak classes to full-moon kayaking trips to backpacking, surf lessons, and rock climbing. Most kayak trips will run you about $85.

✳ Green Spaces

For more information, visit the **Santa Clara County Parks and Recreation** (408-355-2200; parkhere.org).

PARKS **Big Basin Redwoods State Park** (831-338-8860 (recorded info) or 831-338-8861 (ranger) Take CA 9 and drive up the hill to Skyline Ridge and then continue over the other side for 7 more miles to CA 236. Bear right and drive about 10 miles to Boulder Creek. Berry Creek Canyon is one of the best Bay Area parks. You will see the 70-foot Berry Creek Falls, and less than a mile up is the 50-foot Silver Falls. Whatever the season, you will surely appreciate this 12-mile loop in the region's oldest redwood park. You can also camp here. Day use: $6.

Hakone Gardens (408-741-4994; Hakone.com) 21000 Big Basin Way, Saratoga. Open at least 11 AM–5 PM daily. This is the oldest Japanese estate and retreat in the West. Wander through 18 acres of Japanese-inspired gardens, meditating on the most peaceful place to escape the mini-malls of the South Bay. $5

⚲ & **Kelley Park** Keyes and Senter Road. A huge park that spreads between at least three big city blocks is a great spot to spend the day. With everything from a **History Park** (a reenactment of how San Jose once looked) to a Japanese garden and even a zoo (which is being renovated but is slated to reopen in September 2009), I love hanging out here when the concrete gets to me. My favorite stop is the **Japanese Friendship Garden** (408-277-2757; scu.edu), which is open Tuesday through Sunday 10 AM–4 PM.

Uvas Canyon County Park (parkhere.org) Morgan Hill. Drive to the end of Almaden Expressway, turn right onto Harry, left onto McKean. McKean turns into Uvas Road. Turn right onto Croy. Getting here is a trek, but this 3.2-mile Waterfall Loop takes you through a series of waterfalls, including the 30-foot Black Rock Falls, and is worth it. Other falls on this hike include Swanson Falls, Triple Falls, Basin Falls, Granuja Falls, and Upper Falls. Parking: $5.

✳ Lodging

"ᵀ" ⚲ & ◯◯ **Dolce Hayes Mansion** (408-226-3200; dolce-hayes-mansion .com) 200 Edenvale Avenue. The original mansion, built in 1904, offers a glimpse of San Jose's rich history. Now you can feel like one of the classy folks who used to live here. Small rooms, with 1000-thread count duvets, flat screen TVs, and fluffy spa robes, surround the pool. Amenities: 214 rooms and suites, two restaurants, including the excellent Orlo's and one of the biggest Sunday brunches in San Jose, pool, indoor and outdoor hot tub, fitness room, sauna, steam room, Being Spa (see *Spas* above), adjacent park for tennis, golf, free tennis racquets and balls, lounge, parking (free), conference rooms. $$–$$$$.

THE HISTORIC DOLCE HAYES MANSION.

⚲ & ◯◯ "ᵀ" **Hotel De Anza** (800-843-3700; hoteldeanza.com) 233 W. Santa Clara Street. This Art Deco classic hotel in downtown San Jose is a San Jose gem. Built in 1931 and renovated in 1990, you might still imagine what it felt like to stay here when hotel visits were reserved for the rich. Rooms are simple yet include comforts like down comforters, plush towels, and room service. My favorite part of the hotel is their late-night Raid the Pantry, where you can literally raid the cabinets for cereal, coffee, and midnight snacks. Other amenities include breakfast (fee), La Pastaia restaurant (see *Dining Out*), VCR, business center, concierge, lounge with live jazz on weekends, and parking (fee). $$–$$$$.

"ᵀ" & ♀ **Hotel Montgomery** (408-282-8800 or 888-823-0530; hotelmont gomerysj.com) 211 S. First Street, San Jose. This neoclassical 1911 hotel, renovated in 2004 to Renaissance Revival hip standards, is located in downtown San Jose. Mixing the old with the new: Think red-circled wallpaper, furry chairs, creaky elevators, plenty of geometry, faux-wood bamboo sinks and accents, all in a part-salvaged, part-hip kind of way. Amenities: 86 rooms and suites, Paragon restaurant, iPod docking stations, bocce courts, CD library, room service, concierge, parking (fee). $$–$$$$.

⚲ ⚹ ⚐ ⚑ **Hotel Valencia** (408-551-0010 or 866-842-0100; hotelvalencia .com) 355 Santana Row, San Jose. This contemporary hotel caters to business travelers and those who want their hotels to offer a dash of modern Zen mixed with classic European touches. Outdoor lounge areas and uniquely lit rooms inspire the savvy business traveler to return. I enjoyed the heavy wood panels and desk, leather chair, big comfy beds, room service, nice bath products, and how they incorporated the four elements into rooms. Though the décor hints at mod, it also feels timeless. You can order any type of pillow you want including buckwheat or restorative. Amenities: 213 rooms, extended continental breakfast, Citrus Restaurant, pool, AYOMA Spa, concierge, business center, parking (free). $$$–$$$$; on weekends you'll get better deals.

⚑ ⚹ **Inn at Saratoga** (877-413-8848; Saratoga-california.com) 20645 4th Street, Saratoga. This luxurious full-service inn in the heart of the picturesque town of Saratoga makes a nice escape from the humdrum. Rooms are spare, yet lovely, with hints of white—imagine marshmallowy duvets, jetted tubs, and a yummy breakfast in the morning. $$$–$$$$.

✳ Where to Eat

DINING OUT ⚲ ⚹ ⚐ **Arcadia (a Michael Mina steakhouse)** (408-278-4555; michaelmina.net/arcadia) Marriott, 301 S. Market Street, San Jose. Open for lunch and dinner daily. Even if the word steakhouse makes you think of cowboys and horseshoes, you have to try out this clean, classic San Jose dining experience. Michael Mina has turned the traditional Ameri-

can steakhouse into a contemporary lair for fine dining. Imagine *ahi* tuna tartare or sinfully good lobster corn dogs—and those are just the appetizers! Steaks, seafood, pasta dishes, sandwiches with duck-fat fries, and amazing desserts round out the menu. Reservations recommended. $$–$$$$.

⚹ ⚐ **E&O Trading Co.** (408-938-4100; eotrading.com) 96 S. 1st Street. Open 11:30–10 weekdays, 5–10:30 Saturday and 5–9 Sunday. Asian fusion dining in this lofty and modern restaurant makes me feel like I am in another country. Most dishes are better shared, so bring a lot of friends. Creative cocktails and fried appetizers are highlights. Black cod with green-tea rice works as an entrée. Reservations recommended. $$–$$$.

⚲ ⚹ **La Pastaia** (408-286-8686; la pastaia.com) 233 W. Santa Clara Street. Open for lunch and dinner daily—the café serves breakfast as well. Even with big windows, this spacious dining room feels intimate and rustic. I like sitting by the open kitchen and watching the chef throw pizzas into the hearth. The food can't be beat—the pasta is super fresh and you can order half-orders to try more types. Many of the dishes are seasonal, but you can always bet on the tiramisu. Reservations recommended. $$–$$$.

⚹ **Manresa** (408-354-4330; manresa restaurant.com) 320 Village Lane, Los Gatos. Open for dinner Wednesday through Sunday. Chef-owner David Kinch combines ingredients in unheard-of ways, using vegetables harvested daily from his biodynamic garden. You can only get a four-course menu or the tasting menu, so save up and relish the joy of eating at this fine, fine dining establishment. The interior appears way more casual than the food—but I suppose that's the draw—

Kinch lets the food do the talking. Reservations required. Tasting menu and four-course menu: $$$$.

⎷ ♈ **The Plumed Horse** (408-867-4711; plumedhorse.com) 14555 Big Basin Way, Saratoga. Open for dinner nightly. Recently re-imagined, this Saratoga institution for over a half century is in a fresh pair of loving hands now. A look around reminds you of a glass exhibition—hanging lights, a barrel ceiling, and a glass wine-wall. The vegetable tasting menu will make you appreciate greens in a new way. Reservations required. $$$$.

✐ ♈ ⎷ **Trevese** (408-354-5551; trevese .com) 115 N. Santa Cruz Avenue, Los Gatos. Open daily from 4:30–9 PM, Sunday brunch 10:30–2:30. This eco-friendly restaurant arrives at hominess despite being housed in a big old Victorian mansion, though the clean lines, glass-covered open kitchen, and mod décor remind you that you aren't in Grandma's kitchen. On warm days the outdoor patio makes a perfect place for Sunday brunch; and on chilly nights the wine bar pumps heat into your veins. And the food? Modern takes on classic dishes, including a lovely vegetarian tasting menu, a seasonal seared-scallops with soba, and huge dinner portions of dishes like salmon with lemon tarragon and chamomile-scented lentils, a tater tot with Brie center, and giant cuts of meat. Reservations recommended. $$$–$$$$.

EATING OUT ✐ ⎷ ♈ **19 Market** (408-280-6111; 19market.com) 19 N. Market. Open for lunch and dinner daily. The owners of the hopping downtown lunch spot put everything into making Vietnamese food accessible to the work crowd. A sleek interior with lots of plants, you can't go wrong with spring rolls and lemongrass chicken. Make sure to have dessert—the tapioca is out of this world. $–$$.

Barefoot Coffee Roasters (408-248-4500; barefootcoffeeroasters.com) 5237 Stevens Creek Boulevard. Open 7 AM–10 PM. Focusing on the art of espresso drinks from the bean to the cup, here you won't only experience café culture at its finest, but also one of the best lattes in the South Bay. They also serve pretty good pastries.

✐ ⎷ **Bill's Café** (408-294-1125; bills cafe.com) 1115 Willow Street. Open daily from 7 AM–3 PM. Partly a place where Granny goes to have her biscuits and gravy and partly where the college kids cure their hangovers with greasy eggs and fluffy pancakes. The Willow Glen location is cuter, if that matters to you. $.

⎷ ♈ **Consuelo** (408-260-7082) 377 Santana Row, San Jose. Open at least 11:30 AM–9 PM, brunch starts at 10 AM on weekends. With almost 400 types of tequila, how can one not like this cantina? The owners have tried to accomplish sophisticated Mexican food that specializes in central Mexican small plates. Regulars order a bunch of appetizers like the quesadillas, salmon tacos, ceviche, freshly baked tortillas, and table-side guacamole, and sit at the bar. $$.

Dasaprakash (408-246-8292) 2636 Homestead Road, Santa Clara. Super cheap South Indian food is the winner here at this hole-in-the-wall in Santa Clara. Go for the thalis, or dosas, and be prepared to be won over. $.

✐ ⎷ **Fleur de Cocoa** (408-354-3574; fleurdecocoa.com) 39 N. Santa Cruz Avenue, Los Gatos. Open Tuesday through Sunday from at least 8 AM–4 (some nights as well). You can't come to Los Gatos without stopping for the best pastries and hot cocoa in the area. Their cheese croissant is perfect. Chocolate ganaches, chocolate anything, really will make your eyes roll back in your head.

STORY ROAD VIETNAMESE DISTRICT:
BETWEEN US 101 AND LUCRETIA AVENUE.

There has been some controversy over the name of the Vietnamese community in San Jose, but one thing can't be debated, this is the spot for good *pho* or Vietnamese sandwiches. Below are some great spots to stop and check out the cheap eats in this collection of strip malls and asphalt.

Grand Century Mall 1111 Story Road, San Jose. The food court in the back of the mall is chock-full of Vietnamese restaurants. Some of the most interesting are as follows: **Hanoi's Corners** serves a killer Cha ca (catfish). **Café Paloma** doesn't discriminate about regions and merely serves food from everywhere in Vietnam, but the *bun rien* is a highlight. I love *bahn xeo* (rice flour pancakes) and this is the spot to find them. **Thuan Phat** serves up excellent pork buns. And **Hien Khanh Dakao** offers desserts including the smelly durian.

Bun Bo Hue An Nam (408-993-1211) 740 Story Road. Most people have heard of *pho,* but Vietnamese people line up for the *bun bo hue,* another noodle soup that is even more popular.

Pho Ga An Nam (408-993-1211) 740 Story Road. *Pho* at its best is a deep bowl of chicken noodle soup. Here you'll get 47 kinds of chicken dishes, included the famed soup.

✐ ⛭ **La Victoria** (408-993-8230; la vicsj.com) 131 W. Santa Clara Street. Open daily. San Jose State students frequent this busy taqueria for cheap burritos and tacos, nachos, and other traditional Mexican fare. They aren't the best tacos around, but you can't beat these cheap eats—at least in downtown. Once you ask around, you'll learn that people can't get over their orange sauce. $.

✐ ⛭ **Peggy Sue's** (408-294-0258) 183 Park Avenue, San Jose. Open for breakfast, lunch, and dinner daily. A classic 1950s diner with friendly servers, checkered floor, and tons of posters on the wall, you order at the counter and dine on burgers and fries, or standard breakfast fare for next to nothing. They've been around since 1958 and are most popular for the 17 types of burgers. They also serve tuna melts and veggie burgers. The San Pedro Square location is another breakfast option. Children's menu. $.

✐ ⛭ **Pizza Antica**, (557-8373) Santana Row, San Jose. Open daily for lunch and dinner. This popular pizza place specializes in thin-crust gourmet pizzas, using seasonal ingredients. A family-friendly spot, serving good salads and pastas, but everyone gets hearth-baked pizza. New locations are springing up around the Bay Area, but this is my favorite. Reservations recommended. Outdoor seating. $$.

✴ Entertainment

▼ ♈ **Mac's Club** (408-288-8221) 39 Post Street, San Jose. This gay bar gets crowded and has a great happy hour.

Montalvo Arts Center (408-961-5800; montalvoarts.org) 15400 Montalvo Road, Saratoga. Big names perform in this 175-acre redwood forest. Wouldn't you? Either hear music in the 1912 plantation mansion, the garden theater, or the carriage house.

♈ **Motif** (408-279-1888) 389 S. 1st Street, San Jose. A new two-story venue with music, food, and pricey cocktails has a suspended black obsidian glass installation hanging from the ceiling. Part lounge, part dance club, this spot is still trying to define itself.

Mountain Winery (408-741-2822; mountainwinery.com) Pierce Road, Saratoga. Sitting outdoors with a glass of white wine on a summer evening, listening to pop stars sing their hearts out, attracts people from all over the bay.

San Jose Repertory Theater (408-367-7266; sjrep.com) 101 Paseo de San Antonio. This major theater company puts up great shows year-round.

♈ ♪ ♿ **Santana Row.** Off Winchester Boulevard and Stevens Creek Boulevard. Since this live/work space opened, San Jose's nightlife scene has seen a renaissance. Here you'll find beautiful people scantily dressed, families hanging out on the grass listening to music, and plenty of people trying to get into the hopping bars. There is a movie theater, a gigantic chess set, a wine bar, shade from oak trees when the weather heats up, and some not-to-be-missed bars. **El Jardin Tequila Bar** is open seasonally and makes a great stop to drink margaritas under the sun. **Sino** offers dim sum and cocktails for the Benetton crowd. **Blowfish Sushi to Die For** (408-345-3848) has loads of fusion appetizers and sushi. **Straits Café**, a Singapore

restaurant, attracts the well-dressed young San Jose crowd. **Village California Bistro and Wine Bar** serves California cuisine and loads of local wines. Finally, if your sweet tooth is kicking, head to **Joseph Schmidt Confections** for delightful truffles or **Cocola,** a hopping bakery café.

♈ ♿ **Seven Restaurant and Lounge** (408-280-1644) 754 The Alameda, San Jose. Packed with foodies, this restaurant's jazzy lounge area is the spot to grab dinner and a couple martinis.

♈ **Three Degrees Restaurant and Bar** (408-395-7070) 140 S. Santa Cruz Avenue, Los Gatos. Elegant, sophisticated, and way more expensive than Black Watch dive bar up the street, this is where the BMW drivers sip chardonnay and dine on California cuisine.

♈ **Voodoo Lounge** (408-286-8636) 14 S. 2nd Street, San Jose. Offering music for almost everyone, here you might hear live reggae, rocking rock bands, or even some hip-hop.

✴ Selective Shopping

The Flea Market (408-453-1110; sjfm.com) 1590 Berryessa Road, San Jose. Open dawn to dusk Wednesday through Sunday. Since 1960, this flea market has been going strong. Plenty of food and up to 2000 vendors, playgrounds, music, and more attract loads of folks looking for a bargain.

At **Santana Row** (santanarow.com) you'll find expensive kids' shops, boutiques, and chain stores. **San Carlos Street** is the spot for antiques and vintage clothing: Check out the **Antiques Colony** (sancarlosstreet.com). My choices for shopping are the towns of **Los Gatos** (along N. Santa Cruz Avenue and W. Main) and **Saratoga** (along Saratoga Avenue). If it is bargains you are hunting for, head to Gilroy for the **Gilroy Premium Outlets** (408-842-3732) 681 Leavesley Road.

✳ Special Events

Note: **South First Fridays** (southfirst fridays.com) The SoFA district in Downtown San Jose comes to party on the first Friday of every month. Galleries open their doors for art, food, and music.

June: **San Jose Gay Pride** (sjgay pride.com) Discovery Meadow. This two-day festival celebrates LGBT folks with music, comedy, food, and performance art.

Zero One Festival (01sj.org) Innovative artists share their newest work at this biannual festival.

June through August: **Music in the Park** (sjdowntown.org) Plaza de Cesar Chavez. Thursday nights during the summer, San Jose heats up with live music from big-name musicians like local Pete Escondito.

Music in the Other Park: (sjdown town.org) St. James Park. In June, you can catch live jazz, reggae, alternative, and rock at this downtown park.

Cinema San Pedro/Cinema St. James (cinequest.org) San Pedro Square and St. James Park. Bring a picnic and a blanket and watch movies under the stars. Classic first-run films like *American Graffiti* and *Best in Show,* bring out the masses.

August: **San Jose Jazz Festival** (sanjosejazz.org) Downtown San Jose. Loads of South Bay people come to see over 100 performers on 10 stages throughout downtown.

September: **San Jose International Mariachi Festival** (mhcviva.org). This two-day outdoor festival celebrates mariachi, with plenty of food and music.

October: **Spirit of Japantown Festival** (spiritofjapantownfestival.com). Music and the smell of food fill the air as San Jose comes to honor its Japanese community.

Rock and Roll Half Marathon. If you need some music to help you run, this half marathon might be the ticket. Major musicians play the finish line.

THE COAST

✳ To See

⚓ **Montara Lighthouse** (650-728-7177) 16th Street and Cabrillo Highway (CA 1), Montara. Established in 1875, the preserved historic lighthouse and turn-of-the-century buildings now welcome overnight guests as a hostel. See *Lodging.*

Pigeon Point Lighthouse (650- 879-0633) CA 1 and Pigeon Point Road, Pescadero. Built in 1872, this lighthouse in Pescadero is one of the tallest lighthouses in the U.S. The views from here always make me catch my breath. Docent-led tours to the top of the tower take place on Saturday and Sunday in summer and on most Sundays throughout the rest of the year. See *Lodging.*

Half Moon Bay Jail 505 Johnson Street, Half Moon Bay. This 1911 structure is now home to the Spanishtown Historical Society Museum, but once held hardened criminals.

✳ To Do

⚓ ♿ **Coastal Trail** This 6-mile paved trail spans from Princeton to Half Moon Bay. It is a great walk or bike ride. My husband goes on runs here whenever we are in town and loves that he can hit up a bunch of beaches along the way to cool off.

THE PEACEFUL SAN MATEO COAST.

CYCLING **Bike Works** (650-726-6708) 20-G Stone Pine Center, downtown Half Moon Bay. This outfitter rents bikes and beach cruisers.

FARM VISITS AND FARMERS' MARKETS ✐ **Harley Farms** (650-879-0480; harleyfarms.com) Pescadero Creek Road, Pescadero. Open from 11 AM–5 PM. I love visiting this goat farm, touring the property, and learning about farming. Plus you can purchase super-fresh chèvre!

Coastside Farmers' Market (650-726-4895; coastsidefarmersmarket.org) Kelly Avenue and CA 1. Every Saturday from May through November. When May arrives, we all get excited in Northern California. The markets open, and the fare is so super fresh it makes it impossible to live anywhere else. To test me on this, hit up the Half Moon Bay market in mid-August and take a bite of a peach.

✐ **Phipps Ranch** (650-879-07872; phippscountry.com) 2700 Pescadero Road. Open from at least 10 AM–5 PM. You can visit the farm and store to buy up some lentils, berries, or whatever happens to be in season. Afterwards, you'll want to tour the farm, pick some berries yourself, and relax in the tranquil environment. $3 for ages 5–59; U-pick berries: $3 per pound.

Yerba Buena Nursery (650-851-1668; yerbabuenanursery.com) 19500 Skyline Boulevard, Woodside. Open from Tuesday through Saturday 9–5. This nursery specializes in native California plants and ferns, and often offers tea service.

FISHING **Riptide Sport Fishing** (888-RIPTIDE; riptide.net) Pillar Point Harbor. Charter a boat with this outfit to try your skill at catching local halibut.

GOLF **Half Moon Bay Golf Links** (650-726-4438; halfmoonbaygolf.com) 1 Miramontes Road. The greens roll along the ocean offering dramatic coastline views. With two courses to choose from, the old course or the ocean course, both lure folks from around the country. Reservations accepted 14 days in advance. $150–195. Twilight specials $50–95.

HELICOPTER TOURS **Bay Aerial Helicopters** (650-281-8282; bayaerial .com) 364 Fletcher Drive, Atherton. This helicopter tour operation specializes in scenic coastal tours. You might see whales, dolphins, lighthouses, sea caves, and if the waves are kicking, the famed Mavericks surf spot. They will also arrange extended tours of the redwoods or San Francisco. $550 per hour, up to three people included.

HORSEBACK RIDING 🐎 **Sea Horse Ranch** (650-726-2362; horserentals.com) Half Moon Bay. When you are walking on a white sand beach and see all the horse poop, you will probably curse the horses that meander down the coast. But then you'll see how much fun the riders are having, and you might want to arrange a tour. $55–75.

SPAS **Ritz Carlton Spa** (650-712-7000; ritzcarlton.com) Open 8–8 daily. A treatment at this seriously decadent spa is worth your last paycheck. The massage therapists are heavenly. And the robes make you feel like Madonna. They specialize in a pumpkin wrap year-round, and offer a full menu of spa services, sauna, steam room, Jacuzzi, and gift shop.

WATER SPORTS

Kayaking
California Canoe & Kayak (800-366-9804; calkayak.com) 214 Princeton Avenue, Princeton. Open from 9 AM–6 PM. Rent a kayak or canoe for $15–25 per hour to tour the calm waters and estuaries.

Half Moon Bay Kayaking (650-773-6101; hmbkayak.com) 2 Johnson Pier, Half Moon Bay. Open Friday through Monday, 9–5. You can arrange trips or rentals through this tried-and-true outfit. Tours are the way to go for beginners—especially if you want to spot sea life in the mellow bay. Kayak rentals: $15–40 per hour.

Whale Watching
Riptide Sport Fishing (888-RIPTIDE; riptide.net) Pillar Point Harbor. Whale-watching trips go out from the harbor from January through April. You'll likely see California gray whales frolicking in the waves. $75.

WINE TASTING For a great map of the wineries in the area, visit the **Santa Cruz Mountain Wine Growers Association** (Scmwa.com).

La Nebbia Winery (650-726-9463; lanebbiawinery.com) 12341 CA 92, Half Moon Bay. The only winery located in Half Moon Bay, you can try hand-blended wines, and picnic in the gardens. They also have a bocce ball court.

Ritz Carlton Wine Room (650-712-7000; ritzcarlton.com) 1 Miramontes Point Road. Open every evening. Wine flights, chocolate flights, cheese or charcuterie flights are the game here at this lovely little tasting room. With views of the ocean, you can't beat this spot. Plus, they have local growers come and give wine-tasting events. It's pricey, but what do you expect?

Thomas Fogarty Winery (650-851-6777; fogartywinery.com) 19501 Skyline Boulevard, Woodside. The best winery in the region; enjoy sweeping views and taste some excellent varietals.

THE HALF MOON BAY GOLF LINKS AND THE SWANKY RITZ CARLTON

Woodside Vineyards (650-851-3144; woodsidevineyards.com) 340 Kings Mountain Road, Woodside. This is the oldest winery in San Mateo County. These guys produce Chardonnay, Pinot Noir, Zinfandel, and Cabernet Sauvignon. You can tour the winery by appointment.

✳ Green Spaces

PARKS ✆ **Año Nuevo State Reserve** (650-879-0227 or 800-444-4445) New Year's Creek Road, Pescadero (off CA 1, 27 miles south of Half Moon Bay). Open year-round, you have to make a trip here in winter, when the gigantic elephant seals battle for the affections of the blubbery females, who also give birth during this time. It can get loud and ugly. The rest of the year, you can still see the seals, but they are not as entertaining. Daily access to the reserve during winter is available only via guided walks. Advance reservations are recommended. From April through November, you can wander around the reserve without a guide, although docents are there to answer questions. $12.

Butano State Park (650-879-2040) Located 5 miles south of Pescadero on Cloverdale Road and off US 1, from Gazos Creek Road. Acres of trails meandering though a redwood grove. There is a 5.5 mile-hike through the trees to the Butano Rim and Trail Camp. This is a little known campground and chances are you won't find many other people here. $6.

✆ **Fitzgerald Marine Reserve** (fitzgeraldreserve.org) Located between Moss Beach and Pillar Point. Take CA 1 to Moss Beach, head west on California Street, drive to the end. Harbor seals, octopuses, starfish, anemones . . . so much sea life, you won't be able to remember it all: A wander through these tidal pools is a San Mateo Coast *must!* The walk is a bit treacherous, so wear sturdy shoes you don't mind getting wet. Go at low tide; at high tide you'll wonder what all the fuss is about. Free.

McNee Ranch State Park (aka Montara Mountain) (650-726-8819; bahiker .com/southbayhikes/mcneeranch). On the mountain side of CA 1, between Pacifica and Half Moon Bay. If you want a challenging hike or bike ride, try the 8-mile climb to the top of Montara Mountain. You'll be rewarded for your sweat with devine ocean views.

Pescadero Marsh South of Half Moon Bay and CA 84, turn west into the Pescadero Beach parking lot; from the south, it's the second parking lot, just after the bridge. If you get to Pescadero Road, you've gone too far. The walk is 1.4 miles out and back through Pescadero Marsh. This marsh is on the Pacific Flyway and nearly 200 species of birds hang out in the area. Winter viewing is best.

Pillar Point Marsh (650-728-3584) Between Pillar Point and Mavericks, in Princeton. You can find 20 percent of all North American bird species at this marsh. This is a lovely spot to kayak or walk along the path.

Purissima Creek Trails and Creekside Trails (650-691-1200; openspace .org) Higgins Purissima Road. This is a great place to hike through the redwoods. Just a short 0.25-mile hike gets you deep in the redwoods and along a creek. The Whitmore Gulch Trail is not the kind of hike for Great-Grandma, since you head up 1600 feet into the sky. The redwood trail is good for strollers and wheelchairs.

BEACHES Most of the beaches in the area are remote, quiet, and foggy. Chances are you will have most of the sandy area to yourself. Call the **San Mateo County Parks and Recreation** (650-363-4021) for details about specific beaches and services.

The surrounding area has many beaches that make for an enjoyable day of surfing. **Montara Beach, Miramar Beach, Pacifica Beach,** and of course the world famous **Mavericks** (see Sidebar), just to name a few. For information on surfing, check out beachcalifornia.com or coastsidelive.com.

CHECK OUT THE LAZY SEALS AT
FITZGERALD MARINE RESERVE.

Beaches listed from north to south.

Pacifica State Beach The beach is located off CA 1 in downtown Pacifica. When the sun comes out, I head to this surf and sand beach to play in the water. Loads of families and dog lovers come here too. There are bathrooms and showers, plus a Taco Bell with stellar views.

Gray Whale Cove State Beach North of Montara on CA 1. The only available automobile parking is on the east side of CA 1. Crossing to the ocean side of the highway can be both difficult and dangerous, but this lovely beach is worth it.

Montara State Beach Approximately 20 miles south of San Francisco. The big beach is located 8 miles north of Half Moon Bay on CA 1 and is a local favorite. With great surf and lots of sand, it is a fun place to hang for the day.

James V. Fitzgerald Marine Reserve See Parks above.

Mavericks See Sidebar below.

BIG WAVE SURFERS: ADVENTURERS OR LUNATICS?
Mavericks (maverickssurf.com) Off Pillar Point Marsh and Shoreline, 0.5-mile offshore, in Princeton. After strong winter storms in the Northern Pacific Ocean, waves can routinely crest at over 25 feet (8m) and top out at over 75 feet (23m)—though they have been recorded at 100 feet. The annual surf contest, Mavericks, occurs anytime during the winter months, with competitors from around the globe ready to fly here with only 24 hours advance notice. If you are lucky to be in town when the big wave gurus arrive, you're in for a treat. Thousands of people line the beach (that for the rest of the year is relatively mellow—ideal for walking) and cheer these brave guys as they are towed out on Jet Skis and ride the monster waves. Afterwards there is a huge party at Half Moon Bay Brewing Co.

THE ELEPHANT SEALS AT AÑO NUEVO
OFFER A DRAMATIC WINTERTIME SHOW.

Pillar Point Harbor Beach Just south of the harbor, by the pier, you'll see a bunch of surfers and a little patch of sand. Novice surfers look no further.

Half Moon Bay State Beach Just west of downtown Half Moon Bay. You can either park at the paid lot, or enter the beach from one of the paths to the north or south. Families walk on the beach, barbeque on warm days, and play Frisbee next to the rough surf. You'll find bathrooms here as well.

Año Nuevo State Park See Parks above.

✳ Lodging

HOTELS AND RESORTS ✧ ♿ "ⓣ"

Costanoa Coastal Lodge and Camp (650-879-1100; costanoa.com) 2001 Rossi Road, Pescadero. Designer camping in warmed beds in a heated canvas tent is the closest I'll get my parents to the wilderness, but Costanoa delivers on luxe-rustic allure. Group comfort areas, hot tub, fire pits, and dining hall make this feel like summer camp. Staying here is a treat. You have the perks of an eco-friendly environment without roughing it. At night the wind blows through the tent, and you have to walk outside to the bathrooms, but you don't have to squat and pee on your PJs. Amenities: 72 rooms, cabins and tents, campsites and RV areas, no TV, sauna, heated bathroom floors, spa, restaurant, store, beach access, BBQ. $–$$$$.

ⓒⓓ **Oceano Hotel and Spa** (650-726-5400 or 888-OCEAN01; oceanohalfmoonbay.com) Half Moon Bay Harbor, 280 Capistrano Road, Half Moon Bay. The newest luxury property to grace Half Moon Bay has been long in the works. For years I have passed this place, wondering if it could combine the casual funkiness of Princeton By the Sea with the luxury it boasted to offer. And it does. At 30 years in the making, this lovely resort is coming into its own. Most of the 95 rooms offer views of the harbor, two TVs, fireplaces, and super-plush towels and sheets. Additional amenities: Crab Landing restaurant, bar, spa, pool, hot tub, mall, conference rooms. $$$–$$$$.

✧ ⓒⓓ **The Ritz Carlton Half Moon Bay** (650-712-7000; ritzcarlton.com) 1 Miramontes Point Road, Half Moon Bay. You have to love a resort that specializes in fire and wine by the sea. Even if it is one of the major hotel chains, I had to include this emblematic Half Moon Bay resort, because a stop here should factor high on your itinerary. Even if you can't afford the decadently expensive rooms, with super luxe bathtubs and bath products, fire pits on some of the balconies, and marshmallow-like beds, you'll probably head here to gaze longingly at the sea while you sip wine. Or at least you should. Amenities: 261 rooms and suites, pool, Navio restaurant, the Conservatory lounge, a wine-, cheese-, and chocolate-tasting room, hot tub, access to two golf courses, tennis (plus free rackets and balls), bicycles, beach access, kids' club, the excellent spa, salon, concierge, fitness center, and wellness classes. $$$$, plus resort fee.

INNS AND B&BS Seal Cove Inn
(650-728-4114; sealcoveinn.com) 221
Cypress Avenue, Moss Beach. Four
Sisters' Inns rely on your desire for
quiet elegance in the most sought-after
locations. And this one does not disappoint. Lovely gardens, a walk to
Fitzgerald Marine Reserve, and ele-
gantly appointed rooms invite you to
relax. The 10 rooms include king beds,
fireplaces, teddy bears on your bed,
and full breakfast. $$$–$$$$.

✍ ⅙ "▯" **Beach House Inn** (650-712-
0220; beach-house.com) 4100 N.
Cabrillo Highway, Half Moon Bay. Sit-
ting in front of the fire on a foggy
evening, playing cards, and glancing
across the bay to Mavericks while the
lighthouse chimes in the distance is
not a bad way to experience the coast.
Luxurious New England-style rooms
with blue and yellow accents, marble
tiles, and million-dollar views from the
patio make this one of my top picks,
especially on summer weekends. I love
the rubber duck by the tub. Amenities:
54 rooms and suites, kitchenette, con-
tinental breakfast, fireplace, balcony/
patio, ocean views, pool, Jacuzzi, in-
room massage treatments, concierge,
business center, fitness center.
$$–$$$$.

Cypress Inn (650-726-6002; cypress
inn.com) 407 Mirada Road, Half Moon
Bay. This luxurious B&B offers beach
style at big prices. In a quiet location,
just steps to a great beach, gallery, and
restaurant, these modern-decorated
rooms offer a perfect getaway. Amenities: 18 rooms, full breakfast, afternoon
social, beach access, some rooms with
jet tubs, fireplace, kitchenette, and
heated bathroom floors. $$–$$$$.

"▯" ❦ **Half Moon Bay Inn** (650-726-
1177; halfmoonbayinn.com) 401 Main
Street, Half Moon Bay. Reminiscent of
a small inn in southern Europe or on
the Mexican coast, the designers of

this boutique inn show off their good
taste at every turn. The old building,
with its exposed pipes and high ceil-
ings, acts as a backdrop to the pillow
top beds, wool throw blankets, antique
Latin art, heavy dark wood furniture,
marble tiled baths, and refined com-
fort. This is a good option if you want
to feel like you have your own apart-
ment. There are no real services here.
Try for king-bed rooms 9 or 10, where
you won't hear the restaurant as much.
$$–$$$$.

∞ "▯" **Mill Rose Inn** (650-726-8750;
millroseinn.com) 615 Mill Street, Half
Moon Bay. Old English inn with gardens galore is located steps from
downtown Half Moon Bay. Rooms
address a need for elegance with hand-
painted fireplaces and claw-foot tubs,
Japanese dressing robes and high-end
antique furnishings, but also allow for
the technological comforts of modernity. The gourmet breakfast is a treat.
$$$–$$$$.

✍ **San Benito House** (650-726-3425;
sanbenitohouse.com) 356 Main Street,
Half Moon Bay. Built in 1905, this old
house has been renovated by the new
owners and now offers European style
charm in an old California atmosphere.
Gardens, small rooms, great breakfast,
and a down-home local bar, are just
some of the perks of staying at this
little inn. $–$$.

HOSTELS ✍ ⅙ "▯" **Point Montara
Lighthouse** (650-728-7177; norcal
hostels.org) In Montara off CA 1. An
1881 lighthouse in Mayo Beach, Mas-
sachusetts, disappeared and recently
experts realized this lighthouse was
brought to San Mateo County. Now it
is a hostel perched over the sea. Single, dorm, or family rooms available,
plus kitchens, linens, games, and an
espresso bar. $.

⊘ ⴲ "↑" **Pigeon Point Lighthouse**
(650-879-0633; norcalhostels.org) CA 1
and Pigeon Point Road., Pescadero.
One of the tallest lighthouses in the
U.S., built in 1872 following a string of
shipwrecks, now serves as a youth hostel. You get some fantastic views from
the point of sea life, the ocean, and the
fog rolling in. Bunk rooms and private
rooms available, plus a hot tub and
three kitchens. $.

❋ Where to Eat

DINING OUT ⴲ ⅄ **Mezzaluna** (650-
728-8108; mezzalunabythesea.com)
459 Prospect Way, Princeton. Open
weekdays from 11:30–3 and 5–10; on
weekends from 11:30–10. Contemporary Southern Italian food in a little
house by the sea, sounds divine, does-
n't it? Vegetarian friendly, and consis-
tently great service and cuisine, dining
in this modern Mediterranean-style
restaurant gets rave reviews from
locals. They serve lovely pizza, pasta,
fish, and meat at reasonable prices.
$–$$$$.

ⴲ ⅄ **Moss Beach Distillery** (650-728-
5595; mossbeachdistillery.com) 140
Beach Way, Moss Beach. Open for
lunch and dinner daily, Sunday brunch
11 AM–3 PM. Who doesn't want to dine
with ocean views? This seafood and
steak restaurant is one of my favorite
places for cocktails and appetizers—
super-fresh oysters or crab cakes—
especially when the fog isn't lingering,
so I can sit on the patio. They use local
organic ingredients and have vegetari-
an options. Ask about their "Blue
Lady" ghost. $$$–$$$$.

⊘ ⴲ ⅄ **Cetrella** (650-726-4090;
cetrella.com) 845 Main Street, Half
Moon Bay. Open for dinner Tuesday
through Sunday This is the best restau-
rant in Half Moon Bay. Newly renovat-
ed, this huge exposed-beam ceiling
restaurant offers views of the open
kitchen, fireplace dining, live music on
weekends, excellent service, and fine
Mediterranean-influenced cuisine. A
daily changing menu highlights locally
caught seafood. Last time I was here I
had a whole sea bream and am still
singing its praises. Reservations recom-
mended. $$$–$$$$.

⊘ ⴲ ⅄ **Pasta Moon** (650-726-5126;
pastamoon.com) 315 Main Street, Half
Moon Bay. Open for lunch Monday
through Saturday and dinner nightly.
For the last 17 years, this neighbor-
hood Italian restaurant has served up
fresh hand-cut pasta, delicious comfort
food, and tasty wood-fired pizzas. The
all-Italian wine list complements
everything from mushroom tagliatelle
to eggplant parmesan. And the
desserts are sinful. Reservations rec-
ommended. $$–$$$.

⊘ ⴲ ⅄ **Sam's Chowder House**. (650-
712-0245; samschowderhouse.com)
4210 N. Cabrillo Highway, Half Moon
Bay. Open for lunch and dinner daily.
Adirondack chairs, fire pits, indoor and
outdoor seating, this casual restaurant
offers fresh seafood at gigantic prices.
Sometimes I think it is worth the price.
I prefer to come here for a drink and
oysters, calamari, and clam chowder.
They brag about their famous "lobsta"
roll, but I can never get myself to pay
so much for a sandwich. $$–$$$$.

EATING OUT **Archangeli Grocery
Company and Norm's Market** (650-
879-0147; normsmarket.com) 287
Stage Road, Pescadero. Since 1929,
they have been serving up their country-style breads, sandwiches, and gourmet treats. The artichoke bread is so
good you should buy two, so when you
finish the first one in the car you won't
have to drive back. $.

Café Classique (650-726-9775; cafe
classique.com) 107 Sevilla Avenue, El
Granada. Open daily from 4 AM–3 PM.

I have been coming to the area for years and just found this little shack. Serving good Kona coffee, granola, fruit, and huge house-made pastries, egg dishes, and sandwiches, you can't go wrong here. On summer evenings, they occasionally have live music. $.

Cameron's Pub and B&B (650-726-5705; cameronsinn.com) 1410 S. Cabrillo Highway, Half Moon Bay. Open daily. This British-style pub, complete with double-decker buses, 20 draft beers and 65 bottled ones, isn't the best place to eat on the coast, but it is a worthy stop. After a couple pints, you won't care what you eat, but you'll be happy to know they serve everything from pasties to mozzarella sticks. If you are too drunk to drive, they have a B&B—no breakfast though, just beverage. $–$$.

Chez Shea (650-560-9234; chez-shea .com) 408 Main Street. Open from 11:30–3 Monday through Friday, and 5–8:30 Tuesday through Saturday, weekend brunch from 11 AM–3 PM. Organic international cuisine from the creators of Café Gibraltar has brought many a smile to the faces of locals lately. This little café serves up everything from enchiladas to moussaka, *bobotie* to curry. At dinner they add a nice tapas menu. In-the-know locals head here for breakfast on weekends, where the Mexican-themed egg and griddle fare shine. The hidden back patio attracts families. $$.

♂ Ⴤ **Duarte's Tavern** (650-879-0464; duartestavern.com) 202 Stage Road, Pescadero. Open 7 AM–9 PM daily. Duarte's doesn't look like much. An old diner, a little tired, past its prime. But disregard that first impression, sit at the bar, and order the famous artichoke mixed with green chile soup and a slice of olallieberry pie. Or, if you are really hungry, go for the crab cioppino. $$–$$$$.

Flying Fish Grill (650-712-1125; flyingfishgrill.net). On the southwest corner of Main Street and CA 92. Open 11:30–8 Tuesday through Sunday. Since 1922, this fish market and café has been serving fried seafood, cod tacos, and the famed artichoke bisque to hungry fishermen. This little shack has plastic tablecloths and not much ambiance, but the draw is the food. They only serve artichoke bisque on weekdays, so hopefully you get to try it. $–$$.

♂ Ⴤ 🐾 Ⴤ **Half Moon Bay Brewing Co.** (650-728-2739; hmbbrewingco .com) 390 Capistrano Road, Princeton. Open daily from at least 11 AM–10:30 PM, food service stops between 9:30 and 10). The Brewing Company is responsible for my initial adoration of the Half Moon Bay area: patio dining by fire pits with dogs and kids playing, brews flowing and good bar food, with views of the harbor. The new chef has introduced recipes that rely heavily on locally caught fresh seafood; make sure to check the specials. My staples are the scallops, a hefty plate of nachos, fish and chips, and the beer sampler or a Bloody Mary. On weekends they have live music. $–$$$.

Raman's Coffee and Chai (650-712-1257; ramanschai.com) 101 Main Street. Open daily. After a turbulent battle to have his little chai stand survive the arrival of Peet's coffee, Raman recently opened his own café. Don't expect yummy food—in fact about all you'll find are packaged chips and convenience store sweets. People come here for probably the best homemade chai tea outside of India. $

San Gregorio General Store (650-726-0565; sangregoriostore.com) CA 84 and Stage Road. Open 9–6 daily. The first time I came upon this store, hopping with locals, live music, and an indescribable energy, I was astounded that I had never heard of its existence. A walk through the store, a cup of coffee or beer, and a sandwich always sets me up just fine. On weekends, hear live music in the early afternoon. $.

✎ **Taqueria Tres Amigos** (650-726-6080) 200 N. Cabrillo Highway. Open for lunch and dinner daily. They've upped the prices and the décor, but this big taqueria is still a decent spot for cheap Mexican food. Go for the tacos or tostadas. The last time I was here the quesadilla was embarrassingly messy. $.

PUMPKINS AT THE HALF MOON BAY PUMPKIN FESTIVAL.

✳ Entertainment

Coastal Repertory Theatre (650-569-3266; coastalrep.com) 1167 Main Street, Half Moon Bay. You can get tickets for as cheap as $15 per head to see some live local theater.

The Bach Dancing & Dynamite Society (650-726-4143; bachddsoc .org) Douglas Beach House, 311 Mirada Road. Sunday from 4:30–7:30. For almost 50 years, the BDDS has been showcasing world-renown jazz on Miramar Beach. This is not a restaurant; instead it is more a salon for music, where they offer light snacks, beer, and wine. Feel free to bring your own bottle. Call for reservations as it often fills up. $30.

✳ Selective Shopping

Along **Main Street** in Half Moon Bay you will find a number of stores, boutiques, and garden shops.

✳ Special Events

The Annual Half Moon Bay Art & Pumpkin Festival Main Street, Half Moon Bay. On the Saturday and Sunday following Columbus Day. Started in 1971, this huge ode to the pumpkin has put Half Moon Bay on the map. Traffic on CA 92 is insane, so try to come really early or stay over. And make sure to check out the world's largest pumpkins. The ones photographed here were over a thousand pounds.

THE NORTH BAY

While the rest of the Bay Area works its bootie off, Marin sits casually, enjoying her slice of nature, her almost suburban serenity. Yes, most inhabitants of Marin are no longer the hippie renegades who escaped to this region to mountain bike, grow pot, and fight the man. Now most of the people who live in these rolling hills are the man. But don't hold that against them, chances are you'll spend some time in the area, and start trying to figure out how you can afford to live with views of San Francisco, the bay, and the expanse of nature.

Starting from the south, many visitors ride their bikes to the European-like hamlet of **Sausalito**. Characterized by hills dotted with super-luxe houses, touristy shops, and overpriced restaurants strewn along the bay, Sausalito marks that perfect place to spend a sunny afternoon and then leave for edgier pastures. However, stay a while and the true charm of this town emerges. Salty seagoing folks sip coffee at Café Trieste, women wearing tie-dye and walking their dogs greet you, and the rugged Headlands remind you why this area is prime real estate.

Farther up the coast is the hidden enclave of **Tiburon**, known mostly to tourists because of the ferries to Angel Island (see *San Francisco*). In addition to its waterfront location, this small town boasts great restaurants (many with bayside decks), and a tight-knit community that comes out to play on summer Friday nights.

Head inland a bit and you reach the affluent communities of **Mill Valley, Larkspur, San Anselmo,** and **Ross**. Known for housing the rich and famous, houses perch in the shadow of the North Bay's tallest mountain,

LONELY BEACHES CHARACTERIZE MARIN'S COAST.

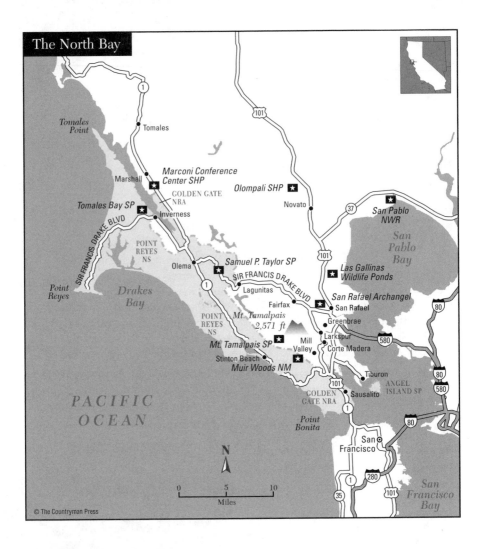

Mount Tamalpais, restaurants offer world-class cuisine, while shoppers for boutique goods, eco-friendly furniture, and antiques rejoice in the abundance. This area used to be prime real estate for hippies in the 1960s and 1970s. Now the hippies have grown up and brought their eco-friendly sensibilities with them. Expect to be wowed by idyllic front gardens, and the insane amount of organic produce available. Accessible from Mill Valley is **Muir Woods**, a redwood grove that rates as a must stop on most tourist radars, Mt Tam State Park, and the coast.

The largest town in Marin, **San Rafael**, was made famous by local resident George Lucas, and since being featured in *American Graffiti*, downtown hasn't changed much. Here you'll still find local kids hanging in public squares eating ice cream, families lining up at local restaurants, and young professionals sipping brews.

Heading towards the coast, you begin to see why Marin lures folks of all types.

With over 40 percent of the land being parkland, the farther west you go, the less suburban and crunchier the locals get. Especially in the hippie town of **Fairfax**. One of my favorite Marin spots, this town represents much of what the Bay Area stands for—organic food, fair-trade gifts, and parks that stretch for miles.

Just past Fairfax, your cell phone stops working and you get far enough from San Francisco to feel like you've landed on another planet; **Point Reyes National Seashore** offers that dreamy escape to the coastal farmlands of Marin. Known internationally as the hub of organic farming, when Prince Charles and the Duchess of Cornwall visited the U.S., they spent a day exploring the Farmers' Market and

JUST ACROSS THE BRIDGE FROM SAN FRANCISCO EXISTS ANOTHER WORLD.

local farms around the town of **Point Reyes Station**. Even more dazzling, the hiking, coast, lighthouse, and wildlife viewing from the plentiful parkland makes Bay Area folks glad this foggy, windswept coast has stayed a secret. Around the pastoral area are the blink-and-you'll-miss-them towns of **Bolinas, Inverness, Olema,** and **Tomales Bay**, which don't offer much for day-trippers, but are great places to stay over and explore the park.

TULE ELK GUARD THE BLUFFS AT POINT REYES NATIONAL SEASHORE.

GUIDANCE **Marin County Visitor Bureau** (866-925-2060; visitmarin.org) 1 Mitchell Boulevard, San Rafael.

Sausalito Visitor Center (415-332-0505; Sausalito.org) 780 Bridgeway, Sausalito.

HELPFUL WEB SITES
Bohemian.com
Fairfaxcoc.com
Millvalley.org
Sananselmochamber.org
Sanrafaelchamber.com
Stinson-beach.org
Tiburonchamber.org

GETTING THERE *By air:* Most people fly into **San Francisco International Airport** (See *San Francisco*) or **Santa Rosa Airport** (see *Sonoma*). Visitors choosing to fly into SFO can take the **Marin Airporter** (415-461-4222; marinairporter .com) to destinations throughout the North Bay.

By boat: **Golden Gate Ferry** (goldengateferry.org) operates frequent ferry service between San Francisco and Larkspur or Sausalito daily. **Angel Island Ferry** (415-435-2131; angelislandferry.com) shuttles passengers between Tiburon and Angel Island daily.

By bus: **Golden Gate Transit** (goldengatetransit.org) motors over the Golden Gate Bridge to Marin and Sonoma Counties, offering a respite from the traffic clogging the bridge.

By car: Few sites match driving across the Golden Gate Bridge into Marin County. To do so, you'll follow the US 101 signs in San Francisco, weaving through the city, onto the bridge. US 101 cuts right through the center of Marin. To get here from the East Bay, travel west on I-580 to San Rafael. To get to Point Reyes off US 101, take Sir Francis Drake Road west until it ends.

GETTING AROUND *By bus:* In addition to **Golden Gate Transit** (see *Getting There*), if you are traveling around West Marin, you can opt to use **West Marin Stage Coach** (marintransit.org), which stops at Mt. Tam, Point Reyes, and Stinson Beach.

By car: Aside from traffic around San Rafael, it is fairly easy to negotiate traveling around Marin County. If traffic annoys you like it does me (especially on vacation), you'll want to check out 511.org to get to know traffic patterns. It is good to know that in summer, the roads to Muir Woods and Stinson Beach get backed up to US 101, so either go early or take the bus.

MEDICAL EMERGENCIES **Marin General Hospital** (415-925-7000) 250 Bon Air Road, Greenbrae.

WEATHER In many ways Marin often feels like a schizophrenic outpatient. In later portions of this chapter, you'll come to see why, but here we are talking about the weather. Along the coast most of the year expect wind, fog, and chilly air like the majority of the Northern California coast. Inland, you often get sunny skies and warmer temperatures—though many days the inland areas reach the same brrr quotient as the coastal regions. Rule of thumb in Northern California, learn it now: always bring layers, a sweater, a hat, a scarf, shoes, and socks.

✳ To See

✂ ⅙ **Bay Area Discovery Museum** (415-339-3900; baykidsmuseum.org) 557 McReynolds Road, Sausalito. Open Tuesday through Friday 9–4 and weekends 10 AM–5 PM. Note that the museum closes for two weeks at the end of September each year. A wonderful world of knowledge and exploration for the little tykes in your group, this museum beats out all other children's museums. Toddlers will love the huge play area, complete with dress up, touch tanks, and safe crawling areas. Older kids (up to about eight) screech as they run towards the model ship and bridge with views of the Golden Gate Bridge. On rainy days there are plenty of indoor activities as well, including a re-creation of a port and the bay. In case you forgot lunch, there is a café here as well. $10 adults; $8 kids 1–17.

✂ **Bay Model** (415-332-3871; spn.usace.army.mil/bmvc) 2100 Bridgeway, Sausalito. Open 9–4 Tuesday through Saturday. A 1.5-acre re-creation of the entire San Francisco Bay and Sacramento Delta, this wonderful exhibit puts the area in perspective. Focusing on tides and currents, geography, topography, ecology, and the history of the area, this educational center is worth a stop. Free.

Frank Lloyd Wright Civic Center
(415-499-7009; co-marin.ca.us) 3501 Civic Center Drive, San Rafael. Tours are held on Wednesday at 10:30 ($5). Dubbed Frank Lloyd Wright's most important piece, this local landmark features dramatic lines throughout the halls, arches, and terrazzo stairs. His atriums were some of the first to be implemented in buildings. Make sure to visit the Hall of Justice (and pop into the yummy café), the gardens, and the library. Free.

Historic Downtown Larkspur
(ci.larkspur.ca.us) Magnolia Avenue, Larkspur. This lovely downtown hidden in a redwood grove has retained its past grandeur with false storefronts, a 1937 Art Deco theater, a Mission-style church, Queen Anne Victorians, and a 1920s Revival bank.

Marin History Museum
(415-454-8538; marinhistory.org) 1125 B Street, San Rafael. Open 11 AM–4 PM Tuesday through Friday and the first Saturday of the month. Tour the Gothic Victorian museum, complete with gardens and rotating exhibits detailing Marin's history, to see historic artifacts. Free.

THE BAY AREA DISCOVERY MUSEUM ATTRACTS KIDS OF ALL AGES.

Marin Museum of the American Indian (415-897-4064; marinindian.com) 2200 Novato Boulevard, Novato. Open Tuesday through Friday 10 AM–3 PM and weekends 12–4 PM. Located in Miwok Park, this museum holds many valuable artifacts from local Indians.

🐾 ♿ **Marine Mammal Center** (415-289-7330; tmmc.org) Fort Cronkhite, Marin Headlands, west of Sausalito. Open daily from 10 AM–4 PM. At press time this great facility was undergoing a major renovation to bring more activities and exhibits to educate us all about marine mammals. Free.

Mission San Rafael Arcangel (415-464-5100; saintrafael.com) 1104 5th Avenue, San Rafael. Open daily from 11 AM–4 PM. You can miss this striking mission in the heart of San Rafael. Rebuilt in 1949 to replicate the original 1817 structure, this was the second-to-last mission in the state. Tour the museum and chapel or attend a service. Free.

Miwok Village (415-464-1164; nps.gov) A 0.5-mile walk from Bear Valley Visitor Center in Point Reyes National Seashore. If Indian history intrigues you, take a hike out to this re-created village to see a sweat lodge, ceremonial house, and homes. Free.

Olompali State Historic Park (415-892-3383; parks.ca.gov) At 2.5 miles north of Novato off US 101. Since 500 A.D. people have inhabited these 700 acres. Today you can tour the land that features historic buildings, including an adobe house once belonging to the last headman of the Miwok Indians. There are plenty of hiking trails with views of the bay. Day use: $6.

Point Bonita Lighthouse (415-331-1540; nps.gov) Golden Gate National Recreation Area. Access only by reserved guided tours. Explore this 1877 lighthouse from 12:30–3:30 Saturday through Monday and on full moon tours. Still active, this lighthouse offers stellar views and the chance to brag that you've stepped on the southern tip of Marin.

Point Reyes Lighthouse (415-669-1543; nps.gov) Drive to the western edge of Point Reyes National Seashore, then walk 308 stairs to the lighthouse. Open 10 AM–4 PM Thursday through Monday. Come here to see whales in winter—there is no better spot from shore to see the coast's largest inhabitants. On your first trip to Point Reyes, a visit to this lighthouse is a must. Sometimes the lighthouse is closed due to high winds. Call for tour reservations on the day of your visit. Free.

San Quentin Museum (415-454-1460). The East Gate of San Quentin State Prison. Appointment only. We often joke that Bay Area prisons get the best real estate. The case is pretty true with this prison, which is home to some of California's worst offenders. If you are interested in prison life (or in a bleak mood and need to be reminded that your life isn't so bad), you can tour the museum and learn about the gas chamber and dungeon.

✴ To Do

CYCLING Marin County gave birth to mountain biking as a sport. In the early 1970s Joe Breeze, Gary Fisher, Otis Guy, and Charlie Kelly refurbished old balloon-tire bicycles from the 1930s and 1940s to use for riding off-road. Today the network of bike paths weaving through the almost 150,000 acres of parkland allow for the best opportunity to explore the mountains. Every park, most streets, and even coastlines offer places to cycle. For the most comprehensive guide to biking

Marin, contact **Marin County Bicycle Coalition** (marinbike.org) or visit cycle pointreyes.com.

For family-friendly trails you can cross the Golden Gate Bridge and take the ferry back, explore **Samuel Taylor Park**, or in **Tomales Bay State Park** take the trail to Marshall Beach.

Serious mountain bikers will want to explore **Point Reyes National Seashore, China Camp State Park** (Shoreline trails), **Samuel P. Taylor Park** (Ridge trail to Mt. Barnabe), **Mt. Tamalpais** (Eldridge Grade to East Peak), and the **San Geronimo Ridge** (Pine Mountain Loop). For trail maps and more specific information check out marintrails.com and marincyclists.com.

Guided Trips

Mountain Biking Marin (415-717-2263; mountainbikingmarin.com) 801 Spring Drive, Mill Valley. These adventurers offer two- to three-hour tours for $150 per person or full-day tours starting at $200 per person. Rates do not include gear.

Rentals

Bikerx Depot (415-407-8960; bikerx.com) 247 Shoreline Highway, Mill Valley.

Cycle Pt. Reyes (415-663-9164; cyclepointreyes.com) CA 1, Point Reyes Station.

Summit Bicycles (415-456-4700; summitbicycles.com) 1820 4th Street, San Rafael.

FARM TOURS **Cowgirl Creamery** (415-663-9335; cowgirlcreamery.com) 80 Fourth Street in Point Reyes Station. Open on Wednesday through Sunday from 10 AM–6 PM. Using organic milk from the Straus Dairy, Cowgirl churns out 3,000 pounds of handmade cheese each week. It's a treat to watch the cheese makers work, then buy a hunk of triple-cream Brie for a hike or to pair with a fine wine.

Hog Island Oysters (415-663-9218 x 208; hogislandoysters.com) CA 1, Marshall. Open Tuesday through Saturday 9–5 by appointment only. Arguably the best oysters in the West are farmed right here. Operated by marine biologists, this company grows and sells more than 3 million crisp, juicy, sea-sweet oysters. These guys also have a restaurant in both San Francisco's Ferry Building and Napa's Oxbow Market. Fee: $10.

✐ **Slide Ranch** (415-381-6155; slideranch.org) 2025 Shoreline Highway, Muir Beach. This nonprofit offers its visitors a chance to learn about organic food, gardening, animals, tide pools, and hiking trails. Call for appointment.

Tomales Bay Oyster Company (415-663-1242; tomalesbayoysters.com) 15479 CA 1, Marshall. Open 8–6 daily. Come prepared and you will dig this bay front picnic area. Bring beer, oyster sauce of your choice, charcoal, and a hungry belly to eat fresh-farmed oysters right from the sea. Since 1909 locals have rushed up here at the first sign of coastal sun to gorge on these delicacies.

FARMERS' MARKETS **Fairfax Farmers' Market** (800-897-FARM; marin countyfarmersmarkets.org) Parking lot of the Fairfax Theatre in downtown Fairfax. Wednesdays from 4–8 from June through September. This market has a great local following, because it's a wonderful place to find organic produce.

The **Larkspur Certified Farmers' Market** is held in the Larkspur Landing Shopping Center, 8:00 AM–1:00 PM every Saturday from May through October.

The Marin Civic Center Certified Farmers' Market (800-897-FARM; marin
countyfarmersmarkets.org) Veteran's Memorial auditorium parking lot, Avenue of
the Flags, San Rafael. Open 8–1 on Thursday, and on Sunday it is at the Civic
Center parking lot, Civic Center Drive, San Rafael during the same time. This is
the largest, oldest, and (arguably) best farmers' market in the county—and maybe
even the country.

Point Reyes Farmers' Market (415-663-1535; marinorganic.org) Toby's Feed
Barn on CA 1 in Point Reyes Station. When Prince Charles and the Duchess of
Cornwall visited this market, it finally got the support it deserves for offering fine
locally grown organic produce, baked goods, artisan cheese, olive oils, homemade
preserves, grass-fed beef, oysters, bee products, and flowers.

San Rafael Farmers' Market (415-457-2266) Fourth Street every Thursday
night from 6–9 from April through September. You'll find 150 vendors along the
five-block long festival, free entertainment, arts and crafts, barbeque and international dinners, clowns, balloons, and activities for children.

FISHING Anglers head to Marin to explore the plentiful fishing opportunities
along both the coast and the bay. Popular fishing spots include **McNear's Beach
Pier** in San Rafael, **China Camp State Park, Paradise Beach Park**, and **Miller
Park Boat Launch** in Tomales Bay. Marin also has seven fishable lakes (marin
water.org).

Fishing charters are available out of **Loch Lomond Marina** in San Rafael. Or you
can contact **Butchie B Sportfishing** (415-302-1650; sfsalmon.com) who take people out to find salmon for about $100 per head—not including equipment.

GOLF **McInnis Park Golf Center** (415-492-1800; mcinnisparkgolfcenter.com)
350 Smith Ranch Road, San Rafael. Views of the San Francisco bay make this one
of the loveliest 9-hole courses in the country. $17–20.

HORSEBACK RIDING **Baywood Canyon Equestrian Center** (415-460-1480)
59 Baywood Canyon Road, Fairfax. This outfit takes people out on trail rides in the
hills surrounding Fairfax.

Five Brooks Stables (415-663-1570) 8001 CA 1, Olema. Not much can surpass a
horseback ride around Point Reyes. These guys rent horses and gear, plus they
lead educational tours for one to six hours. Rates range from $40–180.

KAYAKING **Blue Waters Kayaking** (415-669-2600; bwkayk.com) CA 1, Marshall, about 0.13-mile north of the post office. Perhaps the supreme kayak tour in
the Bay Area, you'll get to explore the bountiful Tomales Bay, seeing Tule elk,
birds, and Drake's Estero. You can even take a moonlit tour, a combination oyster-
tasting and kayak tour, or a naturalist-led hike/kayak trip. Tours vary in length
between three to six hours and range in price from $68–98.

Outback Adventures (415-461-2222; outbackadvenures.com). 12 E. Sir Francis
Drake Boulevard, Larkspur. This outfit rents kayaks for $15 per hour and takes
people out for tours of Angel Island.

SPAS **Tea Garden Springs** (415-389-7123; teagardensprings.com) 38 Miller
Avenue, Mill Valley. The lovely tea garden is just the beginning of your journey

into relaxation at this wonderful spa. Get a massage, a facial, or a combination of both, then let the world melt away while you sip tea to the sound of water dripping on stone.

SURFING AND WINDSURFING I hate to be a buzzkill, but these icy waters are known for great white shark attacks (it's called the Red Triangle). It doesn't happen every year, but enough to warrant me to warn you of them. If that doesn't frighten you off from riding the waves, let me also inform you that you'll find some decent surf spots in Marin, though not as appealing as those in Santa Cruz. Surf spots include **Fort Cronkhite/Rodeo Beach, Stinson Beach, Bolinas Jetty,** and **Point Reyes**.

Lessons and Rentals
2 Mile Surf Shop (415-868-0264; 2milesurf.com) 22 Brighton Avenue, Bolinas. These guys rent boards and wetsuits from $10–$35. Lessons range from $50–100.

Live Waters (415-968-0333; livewatersurfshop.com) 3450 Shoreline Highway, Stinson Beach. These are the go-to people in the Stinson Beach area.

WINERIES **Pacheco Ranch Winery** (415-883-5583; pachecoranchwinery.com) 235 Alameda Del Prado, Novato. Open Tuesday through Saturday from 9–4 and Sunday from 10 AM–3 PM. Call for an appointment to visit. A two-story Italianate home, built by Gumesindo Pacheco in 1876, now houses this winery run by his family. Try out Cabernet Sauvignon and Chardonnay.

Point Reyes Vineyard (415-663-1011; ptreyesvineyardinn.com) 12700 CA 1, Point Reyes Station. Open from 9–5 on weekends, or by appointment. Farmed and operated by the Doughty family for three generations, this tasting room features Merlot, Chardonnay, Zinfandel, and Pinot Noir.

Ross Valley Winery (415-457-5157; rossvalleywinery.com) 343 San Anselmo Avenue, San Anselmo. Open 1–7 Tuesday through Saturday. Taste Merlot, Sauvignon Blanc, and Zinfandel at this downtown Ross Valley tasting room. Then explore the antique shops and the family-centered town of San Anselmo.

✳ Green Spaces
PARKS **Angel Island State Park**
See *San Francisco*.

China Camp State Park (415-456-0766; parks.ca.gov) N. San Pedro Road, 4 miles east of San Rafael. Popular with hikers, mountain bikers, fishermen, and campers—especially in summer when the migrating birds are hiding beneath the blanket of wildflowers—locals love to explore the marsh, the Chinese shrimp-fishing village, and the 15 miles of trails. The most popular trails include the Shoreline and Bay View Trails, which offer 4.5 miles of views. You can camp here (first-come, first-served) as well. Day use: $6.

YOU'LL LIKELY SEE THIS GUY OR HIS MATES IN THE POINT REYES WATER.

VIEWS LIKE THIS ONE GREET YOU THROUGHOUT THE MARIN HEADLANDS.

Marin Headlands (415-561-4700; nps.gov) From US 101 heading north, exit Alexander Avenue and turn left on Bunker Road, drive through the tunnel. Home to miles of hiking trails, beaches (including nude beaches), views of San Francisco, Fort Cronkhite, Kirby Cove, the Marine Mammal Center, the Point Bonita Lighthouse (see *To See*), a hostel (visit norcalhostels.org), an artists' colony, and the wildly-popular Tennessee Valley hiking trail, Marin Headlands is a local gem not to be missed. You can hike down to the Kirby Cove campsite (800-365-CAMP; $25), which affords views of the Golden Gate Bridge and San Francisco. My favorite trail in the area is Tennessee Valley (though I share that love with probably every other family in the bay)—a 3-mile (round trip) stroller friendly trail to the beach. To get here from the south, take the first Mill Valley exit off US 101 and head west until you see the farm stand on the left, turn left and drive until the road ends. The 2-mile trek takes you on an easy stroll through marsh and chaparral to the beach, or up and over the hills to Muir Beach. Free.

Mt. Tamalpais State Park (415-388-2070; parks.ca.gov or reserveamerica.com) 801 Panoramic Highway, Mill Valley. Take the West Marin Stage Coach to reach the visitor center. The spectacle of this park is the 2,571-foot peak, dotted with redwoods and oaks. Views from the top are unbeatable, often offering glimpses of

THE DIPSEA TRAIL

The Dipsea Trail has enchanted hikers and runners for years. A distance of 6 miles each way, runners have participated in a race from Mill Valley to Stinson Beach and back since 1905. Some crazy folks (or inspiring, depending on your view of athletic ability) have run the race every year since the 1930s and even crazier, they don't just do the 6- or 12-mile route, but the 18-mile one—there and back and there again. For the rest of us who want a challenging hike, expect steep grades, mossy trees, and views like you've never imagined. I like to hike to Stinson Beach for lunch, then hike back to Mill Valley. Access the trail from Muir Woods or Stinson Beach.

the elusive Farallon Islands. After the gold rush, some wise guy had the idea to build a railroad on these slopes, and it was soon dubbed the Crookedest Railroad in the World. In 1930 the railroad was abandoned after a fire damaged the tracks. Today, more than 50 miles of hiking and biking trails lure adventurers up this peak. Popular hiking trails include the Railroad Grade (which reaches the West Point Inn, see *Lodging*), Verna Dunshee wheelchair-accessible trail, and the Fern Creek Trail (6 miles). In summer, rangers host Astronomy Nights and local thespians put up Broadway shows at the Mountain Theatre (mountainplay.org). You can also camp in tent cabins at the **Steep Ravine Environmental Campground** overlooking Stinson Beach (seven campsites and nine cabins; reservations required) and the wheelchair accessible **Pantoll Campground.** The Watershed area is home to a variety of lakes and waterfalls, including Kent Lake, Alpine Lake, Bon Tempe Lake (great trout fishing), Phoenix Lake, Carson Falls, and Cataract Falls. To access the trails, park along Bolinas Ridge Road or San Geronimo Ridge Road, near Fairfax (Marin Watershed publishes a great map: marinwater.org). Day use: $6.

Muir Woods National Monument (415-561-4700; nps.gov). From US 101, follow the signs from Mill Valley. Most people who pass through San Francisco visit the 100-year old Muir Woods redwood grove. The interpretive trail offers loads of information about these giant trees and allows you to get up close and personal, and then hike above them (I made it all the way to the coast once by taking the Dipsea Trail). In summer, the best way to get here is to take the free shuttle (415-921-5858; goldengate.org) off US 101 (Muir Woods exit). $5.

Point Reyes National Seashore (415-464-5100 or 415-663-8054; nps.gov) 1 Bear Valley Road, Point Reyes Station. To get here from US 101, take Sir Francis Drake Boulevard west until it ends (about an hour drive); drive north to Bear Valley Road and follow the signs. Visit the Bear Valley Recreation Center to get park information for this wildlife sanctuary, coastal wonderland, and wealth of hiking trails. This 71,000-acre park offers scenic diversity, spring wildflowers, and plenty of great beaches to see wildlife. On hikes here I have passed snakes, deer, elk, sea otters, sea lions, dogs, and birds. Trails that wow visitors include the Coast Trail (16 miles one way), the Sky Trail, Estero Trail (7.8 miles round-trip), Alamere Falls (which also grants access to Bass Lake, 8.4 miles round-trip), Chimney Rock (2.8 miles round-trip), Tomales Point Trail (6 miles), and Limantour. Head out to Pierce Ranch for elk, Point Reyes Lighthouse for whales in winter, birds and wildflowers at Limantour, and deer in the Meadow Trail. Campers like the boat-in Tomales Bay site, the Wildcat camp, or Coast Camp on the Coast Trail, or the Sky Camp along the Sky Trail—though you need permits to camp ($15). Beach stars include Limantour, Drakes Beach, McClure's Beach, Kehoe Beach, Sunset Beach, Kelham Beach, Marshall Beach, and South Beach. There is also a hostel in the park, visit norcalhostels.org for details.

Samuel P. Taylor State Park (415-488-9897; parks.ca.gov or reserveamerica .com) Go 15 miles west of San Rafael on Sir Francis Drake Boulevard. Locals come here to get lost in the redwoods, madrones, oaks, and Douglas fir trees. Salmon spawn in Papermill Creek, so you are not permitted to fish here. Hikers love to ascend Barnabe Peak, the Bay Area Ridge Trail to Bolinas Ridge, or Bill's Trail to get to Stairstep Falls (though the sign is wrong and you actually have to hike 3 miles more to get to the falls). Campers head to Creekside or Orchard Hill (both handicapped accessible) to stay the night ($15–$20).

THE TENNESSEE VALLEY TRAIL TO
TENNESSEE BEACH.

Tomales Bay State Park (415-669-1140; parks.ca.gov) 1208 Pierce Point Road, Inverness. Surf-free beaches blocked from wind by Inverness Ridge, Bishop pine groves, wildflowers, wildlife, and excellent kayaking opportunities await you at this wonderful park that often shrinks in the shadow of her neighbor, Point Reyes. Hike the Johnstone Trail from Heart's Desire Beach to Jepson Memorial Grove (3 miles round-trip) and to Shell Beach add another 8 miles. $6.

BEACHES For more beaches, including those in Point Reyes National Seashore and Golden Gate National Recreation Area, see *Parks*.

Kirby Cove (415-331-1540; nps.gov) From Vista Point on the west side of the Golden Gate Bridge, hike 40 minutes down to the sea. This amazing beach offers unsurpassed views and camping. See *Golden Gate National Recreation Area*.

Rodeo Beach Marin Headlands, at Fort Cronkhite. A lovely black sand beach to spend the day hiking to, and then top off your day with a dip in the icy water and a picnic on the shore.

Tennessee Beach To access the beach, you must hike about 2 miles from Tennessee Valley Road. Once you arrive, you are in for a treat. This beach offers the perfect spot for picnicking, watching the waves crash, and reading a book on warm days.

Muir Beach Off CA 1. Not my favorite beach, but this spot offers coastal access without much of a hike—though adventurers can hike here from Rodeo Beach.

Stinson Beach Off CA 1, in the town of Stinson Beach. The first year I lived in the Bay Area, every time the sun came out, I drove the twisty road to get here. It is the ideal beach for sunbathing, dipping your toes in, and having that beach town experience without the masses. In summer there is also a wonderful Shakespeare production with views of the sea.

Bolinas Beach Off CA 1, past Stinson Beach. The only catch with trying to find this expansive stretch of sand is that the locals in Bolinas want their town to stay hidden so they take off the sign indicating where to turn. If you get here, most of the beach will be yours, along with the sharks and sea lions that congregate here.

McClure's Beach Point Reyes National Seashore. See *Parks*.

Heart's Desire Tomales Bay State Park, 4 miles past Inverness off Pierce Point Road. This lovely beach often scores with less wind than anywhere else in the area, thanks to Inverness Ridge. And this being a bay, you won't get the waves like the beaches at Point Reyes. $6.

❋ Lodging

In addition to the listings below, you will find some economical cabins, hostels, and campgrounds listed in the *Green Spaces* section.

Inner Marin County

⚓ ♿ 🍷 ⊙⊙ **Casa Madrona Hotel and Spa** (415-332-0502; casamadrona.com) 801 Bridgeway, Sausalito. Since 1885 this inn has brought luxury to Sausalito visitors, with views of the bay and plush interiors. Choose between a classic kingly room complete with vintage touches like poster beds, loveseats, and big candlelit tubs, or a contemporary room with clean lines and private balconies. All 31 rooms offer pillow-top beds and dream machines. This is the only full service hotel in Sausalito, complete with a restaurant and spa. $$$–$$$$.

⚓ ♿ 🍷 ⊙⊙ "ᵻ" **Cavallo Point** (415-339-4700; cavallopoint.com) 601 Murray Circle, Sausalito. In the works for years, this lodge at the Golden Gate has transformed the historic Fort Baker parkland into one of the finest accommodations in the Bay Area. Combining history with community events, the 152-room lodge not only offers historic and contemporary lodging with high wooden ceilings, big windows, locally constructed furnishings, and fireplaces, but also art and culinary classes, eco-friendly building and conservation methods, a Healing Arts Center complete with yoga, Pilates, and herbologists; plus a popular restaurant and bar. Choose between historic or contemporary rooms, though all offer organic bedding, flat panel TVs, radiant heated floors, iPod plug-ins, and interesting art. $$$–$$$$.

♿ **Gables Inn Sausalito** (415-289-1100; gablesinnsausalito.com) 62 Princess Street, Sausalito. This quiet and simple inn offers a touch of class without the pretentiousness of most Sausalito hotels. Rooms are small, but still manage to offer fireplaces and comfy beds. If you can afford a suite, you'll feel like you have your own apartment right across the Golden Gate. Amenities: 13 rooms and suites, continental breakfast, afternoon wine and cheese social, concierge, and free parking. $$–$$$$.

⚓ ♿ 🐾 "ᵻ" **Gerstle Park Inn** (415-721-7611 or 800-726-7611; gerstleparkinn.com) 34 Grove Street, San Rafael. Spread across 2.5 acres, this mansion offers Asian and European antiques with modern touches. The lawn and gardens, gourmet breakfast, wine hour, croquet, and Jacuzzi tubs do it for me. You'll feel like you are in the country, yet close to a number of great attractions and restaurants. $$–$$$.

⚓ ♿ **Inn Above Tides** (415-332-9535 or 800-893-8433; innabovetide.com) 30

THE SUNSET OVER ANGEL ISLAND FROM YOUR DECK AT INN ABOVE TIDES.

El Portal, Sausalito. When you enter your room at this waterfront inn, a pamphlet sits on your bed indicating all the sites you see from your floor-to-ceiling windows and private balcony perched over the bay. As my neighbor walked out to look at Angel Island, San Francisco, Tiburon, Berkeley, Alcatraz, and Oakland, I heard her remark that the view was stunning. An understatement, especially as a kayaker, then a sea lion passed. Interiors deserve hype in their own right. Asian touches like soaking tubs, tree stump tables, and deeply sensuous beds add to the allure. Amenities: 30 rooms and suites, expanded continental organic breakfast, wine and cheese hour, concierge, parking (fee), binoculars in room, DVD players. $$$$.

✍ ♿ ❝❞ **Mill Valley Inn** (415-389-6608 or 800-595-2100; jdvhotels.com) 165 Throckmorton Avenue, Mill Valley. Even my staunchest city friends love this hamlet, tucked beneath redwoods and madrones. The 25 rooms recall a European sensibility, with French doors and iron beds, expanded continental breakfast, AC, some fireplaces and soaking tubs, and balconies. $$–$$$$.

✍ ♿ ❝❞ **Waters Edge** (415-789-5999; jdvhotels.com) 25 Main Street, Tiburon. Nautical, lofty, and modern don't always fall in the same category, but the Waters Edge hotel achieves this unlikely mix. The wooden cathedral ceilings with exposed beams and pipes, the 23 rooms that appear to hang over the bay, the plush linens and robes, the marble desks and leather chairs, all contribute to the calming vibe. The best rooms are 221 and 220, which have large patios with million-dollar views. The afternoon wine reception, best enjoyed on the deck that overlooks Angel Island, is a great way to avoid the crowds at nearby Sam's. Amenities: continental breakfast delivered to your room, wine and cheese reception, balconies, soaking tubs, parking (free). $$$$.

West Point Inn (415-646-0702; westpointinn.com) Mt. Tam State Park, park at the Pantoll parking area, 2 miles from the Matt Davis Trail to the Nora Trail. Possibly the best cheap bed in the Bay Area, this rustic hike-in vintage inn offers nothing by way of amenities, unless you consider privacy and a kitchen to cook in, and the views of the fog rolling onto the bay amenities (I sure do!). Bring warm clothes and linens (it gets chilly at night) plus food and water. $35 per person.

West Marin

Blackthorne Inn (415-663-8621; blackthorneinn.com) 266 Vallejo Avenue, Inverness. Built from redwood, cedar, and Douglas fir trees, this four-room inn relies on reputation to draw Bay Area folks looking for a little rustic relaxation. Imagine sloped ceilings, bridges to take you to your own private nest of a room, circular stairwells, and cathedral ceilings, then throw in country bedding, hot tub, and a big old breakfast. Even if you don't stay in it, check out the Eagles Nest, which will make woodworkers drool. $$–$$$$.

✍ **Black Heron Inn** (415-663-8621; blackheroninn.com) 51 Cypress Road, Point Reyes Station. If loquacious B&B owners make your skin crawl, this no-host inn might be the perfect choice for you. Spacious rooms offer bay views, breakfast in the fridge when you arrive, and decks perfect for morning tea. The three country-style rooms wouldn't appeal to Martha Stewart, but they're just right for a weekend in the country. $$–$$$.

♿ ◎ **Manka's Inverness Lodge** (415-669-1034; mankas.com) 30 Callender Way, Inverness. A few years ago, Manka's restaurant burned to the ground, leaving a scar on the face of the local dining scene. However, 10 rooms, cabins, and a boathouse offer Hansel and Gretel's forest abode meets 1910 hunting lodge accommodations. Rooms offer bay views, deep soaking tubs, leather chairs, and plush beds. Most options include an ocean-stone fireplace, wood walls, and outside areas. Another perk to staying here is while they rebuild the restaurant, lodge guests can enjoy fine farmers' market fresh cuisine prepared each night and delivered to your room ($$$$). This is a top choice for a romantic getaway. Rooms: $$$–$$$$.

✎ ⅃ ♚ "↑" ∞ **Nick's Cove** (415-663-1033 or 866-63-NICKS; nickscove .com) 23240 CA 1, Marshall. And along came the luxury to the Point Reyes Seashore, inviting the contemporary urbanites to the country. Its 12 cottages look out onto the bay, offering heated floors, leather chairs, wooden walls, stone fireplaces, soaking tubs, and plenty of space (400–500 square feet). Beds beg for you to sink into them, with plentiful pillows and cushy linens. Staying here combines the nautical with the rustic, the decadent with the simple, and the urban desires of city folk with the country charm of salty air. Don't miss the restaurant. $$$$.

✎ ⅃ ♚ ∞ "↑" **Old Point Reyes Schoolhouse** (415-663-1166; old pointreyesschoolhouse.com) Point Reyes Station. For 25 years Karen Gray has welcomed guests to this lovingly restored 1879 schoolhouse. Don't expect her to chat you up; guests rarely see her. Gardens offer serenity and splashes of color (as they should with Karen's degree in landscape architecture), creating the ideal place to read, or drink wine. Entering the cottages, you get the impression that you are staying at someone's house, with touches like walls of books that you actually

want to thumb through, interesting décor (Gray's Retreat has a massive butterfly piece of art), a full kitchen, fireplace, and even bocce ball. A real treat for families is to stay at the Barn Loft and let the kids sleep in the Sheep Wagon. If you are with a large group, consider renting the schoolhouse for a step back in time. $$–$$$$.

✎ **One Mesa** (415-663-8866; onemesa .com) 1 Mesa Road, Point Reyes Station. Last time I was here, I stayed in the Sunset Cottage, a perfect retreat for sleepy parents, with a full kitchen (though I never cooked because we opted for breakfast delivered to our cottage), wood burning stove, and a big cushiony bed. Our patio afforded us views of the colorful gardens and Eddie and I each took turns enjoying the hot tub with views of the pastoral lands below. This is the ideal spot for couples looking for romance, or weary new parents. $$–$$$.

⅃ **Pelican Inn** (415-383-6000; pelican inn.com) 10 Pacific Way, Muir Beach. Handsomely decorated rooms akin to an English hunting cottage present an air of regality. After a dinner and pint in the pub, head back to your room to relax in wood-beamed poster beds, with portraits of stodgy British fellows above, Persian rugs below, and curtains draped around beds. Tudor architecture enhances the stay, while fresh copper vases of flowers and hearty breakfasts appear at your door. $$–$$$.

✎ "↑" **Redwood Haus** (415-868-1034; stinson-beach.com) Belvedere and CA 1, Stinson Beach. The four colorful rooms evoke nautical themes, and the occasional mismatched chair allows you to feel as if you are staying in someone's home. The Crow's Nest room is the largest, with sloping ceilings and tributes to sea blues, while the redwood room, awash in its namesake, feels like a country cabin. $$.

✴ Where to Eat

DINING OUT

Inland Marin

⌀ ♿ ♈ **Buckeye Roadhouse** (415-331-2600; buckeyeroadhouse.com) 15 Shoreline Highway, Mill Valley. Open for lunch and dinner daily, and Sunday brunch. This yuppie favorite, where SUVs and BMWs populate the parking lot, seems like more of an LA scene than a steak house along the highway. Indulge in a gourmet iceberg wedge, ribs that melt off the bone, and S'mores pie. Reservations recommended. $$–$$$$.

⌀ ♿ ♈ **Insalatas** (415-457-7700; insalatas.com) 120 Sir Francis Drake Boulevard, San Anselmo. Open at least 11:30–2 and 5:30–9 (until 10 on weekends). Locals won't talk about this cavernous restaurant unless prodded. Seems the secret is out, but no one will admit that this Mediterranean favorite has been "found" by more than Marinites. Come here for the Middle Eastern-inspired vegetarian platter or a roasted honey-glazed duck breast. Reservations recommended for dinner. $$–$$$.

⌀ ♿ ♈ **Murray Circle** (415-339-4750; murraycircle.com) Cavallo Point, 602 Murray Circle, Sausalito. Open 7 AM–10 AM, 11:30–2 and 5:30–10 daily. A new addition to the Sausalito dining scene, this mostly organic and constantly changing menu offers views, a touch of class, and excellent food at big prices. The restaurant attracts the people who can afford a $13 cup of soup—which makes me head to the bar for an appetizer and organic margarita. If you can spring for it, go big with a log of a rib eye, or the 10-course tasting menu (oh la la). Reservation recommended. $$–$$$$.

⌀ ♿ **Picco** (415-924-0300; restaurant picco.com) 320 Magnolia Avenue, Larkspur. Open for dinner nightly. Bruce Hill found a niche in the dining scene in this historic neighborhood. California Italian cuisine served in a sleek environment using the best local ingredients—think fresh risotto made on the half hour, tuna tartare, and for dessert you can't pass up the soft-serve ice cream with sea salt and olive oil. Reservations recommended. $$–$$$.

⌀ ♿ ♈ **Poggio** (415-332-7771; poggio trattoria.com) 777 Bridgeway, Sausalito. Open for breakfast, lunch, and dinner daily. For five years this has been the winner in the Sausalito tourist dining scene, beating out other waterfront locations like Scoma's and Horizons with better Italian-style cuisine, house-made salumi, and limoncello. Terracotta and mahogany arches, an outdoor patio, and specialties like house-made burrata make me pine for Italy and then be smugly satisfied with Sausalito instead. Reservations recommended for dinner. $$–$$$.

⌀ ♿ ♈ **Sushi Ran** (415-332-3620; sushiran.com) 107 Caledonia, Sausalito. Open for dinner nightly. A mainstay in the Bay Area dining scene, this sushi spot attracts local Marinites and city dwellers into its small, spare dining room for pricey, but tastes-like-it-was-just-caught delicacies. Reserve a table in the main dining room to enjoy the full sushi menu, or sit in the more casual outdoor café and bar next door. Highlights include the salmon firecracker roll and the crunch roll. Their wine and sake menu draws vinophiles. Reservations highly recommended. $$–$$$.

West Marin

Drake's Beach Café See *Eating Out*.

Manka's See *Lodging*.

⌀ ♿ ♈ **Nick's Cove** (415-663-1033 or 866-63-NICKS; nickscove.com) 23240

CA 1, Marshall. Open for breakfast, lunch, and dinner daily. I have a sweet spot for Nick's Cove Restaurant. When my son was three months old, we came here for my birthday dinner. Colicky, he screamed his head off throughout the entire meal, and instead of the diners in this nautical-themed restaurant complaining or leaving, it seemed everyone pitched in—the waitress, other diners, the bartender—to hold him. You hopefully won't share that experience, but what you will share is an affinity for their oysters and freshly prepared fish, served in this spacious bay view dining room. Reservations recommended. $$–$$$$.

& ⍦ **Olema Inn and Restaurant** (415-663-9559; theolemainn.com) 10000 Sir Francis Drake Boulevard, Olema. Open for lunch and dinner daily. Inside the white-tablecloth, wood-floored restaurant, you get a dash of class served with your wine and oysters. I always sit outside on the deck, drink margaritas, and gorge myself silly on oysters and salads. Everything is organic; everything is wonderful. Reservations recommended. $$$–$$$$.

EATING OUT

Inland Marin

✦ & ⍦ **Broken Drum Brewery and Wood Grill** (415-456-4677; broken drum.com) 1132 4th Street, San Rafael. Burgers, brews, and locals, bottom line. When the traffic on US 101 gets too intense, pull off to enjoy sweet potato fries, salads, and pub grub in a festive environment. $–$$.

✦ & **Café Trieste** (415-332-7660; cafetrieste.com) 1000 Bridgeway, Sausalito. Open 6:30–10 (until midnight on Friday and Saturday). Salty old gentlemen, Italian tourists, families, and local coffee aficionados hang out here all day, soaking up the bohemian vibe and great strong coffee, paninis, and salads. $.

& **Cottage Eatery** (415-789-5636; thecottageeatery.com) 114 Main Street, Tiburon. Open for lunch and dinner Tuesday through Saturday; dinner only on Sunday. Not much to look at, but you'll sure get quality food. Most come to Tiburon for views, but on a cold, foggy night, who cares? These guys specialize in soup. Menus fluctuate with the seasons, so last time I visited I had fennel gratin that blew me away. Reservations recommended. $$–$$$.

✦ & **The Depot Bookstore and Cafe** (415-383-2665; depotbookstore .com) 87 Throckmorton Avenue. Open 7–7 daily. A friend and I used to sit in the outdoor patio, after browsing the wonderful collection of books and eating fresh sandwiches, and watch the moms negotiate their kids, strollers, and dogs. This family-friendly spot might be the best in the North Bay for inspiring you to move to Marin or to swear off having children. $–$$.

✦ & **Dipsea Café** (415-381-0298; dipseacafe.com) 200 Shoreline Hwy, Mill Valley. Open 7–3 Monday through Thursday and 7–9 Friday through Sunday. Named for the famed Dipsea Race (see *The Dipsea Trail*), this popular café serves up big portions of American fare for families, bikers, and hikers along the creek just outside of downtown Mill Valley. Inside sit by the fire and enjoy blueberry pancakes, or outside eat a big ole burger with a root beer float. $–$$.

✦ & **Fish** (415-331-3474; 331fish.com) 350 Harbor Drive, Sausalito. Open 11:30–4:30 and 5:30–8:30 daily. Even if you don't care where your fish comes from (though you should, you really should), a visit to Fish is a must. Using only sustainable seafood (no farmed, no dyed), this is the spot that city dwellers bring out of town visitors to for an authentic Sausalito experience. Order at the fish market counter, sit on picnic tables with views of the bay, and eat the freshest oysters, fish tacos, fish burgers, and even a wonderful grilled cheese. Cash only. $$–$$$.

✆ ♿ **Joe's Taco Lounge** (415-383-8164) 382 Miller Avenue, Mill Valley. Open for lunch and dinner daily. If only I had the guts (or the palate) to try one of the zillion hot sauces along the walls here. Instead I stick to traditional Mexican favorites—burritos, nachos, fish tacos—and am always satisfied after my meal. $–$$.

✆ ♿ **Lotus Cuisine of India** (415-456-5808; lotusrestaurant.com) 704 4th Street, San Rafael. Open Monday through Saturday 11:30–2:30 and daily from at least 5:30–9. Though I haven't had the chance to eat here, friends who know good food swear it is the best Indian food in the Bay Area (I might have to put up my fists to argue that one). Vegans and vegetarians will find plenty of options, even during the lunch buffet. Favorites include the Goa fish curry and chicken *tikka masala*. $–$$.

✆ ♿ **Northpoint Coffee** (415-331-0777; northpointcofee.com) 1250 Bridgeway, Sausalito. Open 6:30–6:30 daily. A trip to the North Bay would not be complete without a stop at this homegrown coffeehouse, complete with a bayside deck, grilled oysters, live music, smoothies, and good coffee. This is the spot to bring the *New York Times* and spend the entire Sunday reading it. $.

✆ ♿ **Pizzeria Picco** (415-924-0300; pizzeriapicco.com) 320 Magnolia Avenue, Larkspur. Open at least 5–9 Monday through Friday and 12–9 weekends. Unofficially, my husband and I have been indulging in a pizza taste test to find the best pie in Northern California. No matter where I go, none of them tastes as good as Pizzeria Picco's. Sure, I am smitten with sitting on the patio, sipping fine white wine near redwood trees and historic buildings; sure, I adore that any pizza can be *piadine* (with a salad on top); of course, I love the roasted olives, soft-serve ice cream with sea salt and olive oil; but the real reason I go out of my way to come here is the pizza. The margarita is my favorite, but I'll tell you a secret, their pepperoni makes me cheat on my diet every time. Crust is thin and flaky, cheeses are melted just right, and the sauce is both perfectly sweet and tangy. All pies, named after Italian road bicycles, inspire. $–$$.

✆ ♿ 🍸 **Sam's Anchor Café** (415-435-4527; samscafe.com) 27 Main Street, Tiburon. Food served 11 AM–10 PM on weekdays and 9:30 AM–10 PM on weekends (bar stays open until 1:30). Though the food is not the draw of this bayside salty bar and grill, people end up eating here. The Bloody Marys,

PIZZERIA PICCO ON A WARM AFTERNOON.

margaritas, beers, and big deck almost force you to stay. $$–$$$.

✇ ♿ **Sol Food** (415-451-4765; sol foodrestaurant.com) 901 Lincoln Avenue, San Rafael or 732 Fourth Street for takeout. Open daily 11 AM–10 PM, until 2 AM on Friday and Saturday). Puerto Rican cuisine never was so popular in the bay. Order at the counter, then sit at communal tables with big buckets of utensils, a mason jar of limeade, and fill up on gigantic plates of rice and beans, plantains, and your choice of meat. This friendly, loud, fast, colorful spot forces you to talk to your neighbors, tap your foot to the music, and eat until your gut needs to bust. $

✇ ♿ **Three Twins Ice Cream** (415-492-8946) 641 Del Ganado Road, San Rafael. Making a splash in the ice cream scene, this organic creamery serves up delicious and fresh scoops of your favorites and even offers the most expensive ice cream cone on the planet. $

West Marin

✇ ♿ **Bolinas Coast Café** (415-868-2298; bolinascafe.com) 46 Wharf Road, Bolinas. Open 11:30–2 Tuesday through Friday, 7:30–2 weekends and for dinner nightly (except Monday). If you can find this coastal restaurant, you are in for a treat. Serving up locally harvested seafood, organic produce, and Niman Ranch burgers, everyone in the family will enjoy the wealth of food options in a casual setting. $$–$$$.

✇ ♿ ☿ **Café Amsterdam** (415-256-8020; cafeamsterdamlive.com) 23 Broadway, Fairfax. Open Monday through Wednesday 4 PM–11 PM, Thursday 11 AM–11 PM and Friday through Saturday 8 AM–midnight. The woodsy oak interior is overshadowed by the sunlight streaming through the big windows, and the happy diners sipping one of 13 beers on tap and eating

big plates of chicken parmesan or poached salmon. Family-friendly and a good pub, this place often has live music on weekends. $–$$.

Cowgirl Creamery See *Farm Tours.*

✇ ♿ **Drake's Beach Café** (415-669-1297) 1 Drakes Beach Road, Point Reyes. Open for lunch and dinner Thursday through Monday. This white-tablecloth restaurant is the only place to eat in Point Reyes National Seashore parkland. The trek takes a while, but the experience is worth it. As with most places around here, all food is organic and seasonal. Lunches tend to be beach fare like sandwiches and salads. However you'll talk about the dinners long after you've left. Prix fixe four-course meals are served on Friday and Saturday. Imagine a carrot soup with tarragon, lamb cooked with lentils, or halibut with corn and tomatoes. Desserts wow diners, using the best of local fruits. Kids are very welcome for the evening meals and even get their own choices—albeit grilled cheese or nitrate-free hot dogs. Reservations required for dinner. Lunch: $–$$. Dinner: $$$$.

✇ ♿ **Fat Angel Bakery** (415-455-9127; fatangelbakery.com) 71 Broadway Boulevard, Fairfax. Open 6 AM–3 PM Thursday through Tuesday. I stop here on my way to Point Reyes religiously for the farmers' market scone, the almond pillow, and the muffin of the moment. Don't know what they put in their sweets, but it's addictive. $.

✇ ♿ **Pine Cone Diner** (415-663-1536; thepineconediner.com) 60 4th Street, Point Reyes Station. Open 7 AM–3 PM daily. Only in West Marin will you find a true country diner serving organic milkshakes, burgers and hot dogs, and plenty of egg and griddle fare for breakfast. The biscuits and gravy will take you back to Grandma's house in 1984. And the trout and eggs is a delight. $–$$.

♪ ♿ **Station House Café** (415-663-1515; stationhousecafe.com) 11180 CA 1, Point Reyes Station. Open for breakfast, lunch, and dinner daily. Since 1974, this garden restaurant and its stellar chefs have been serving innovative organic seasonal cuisine to hungry patrons. The ideal place for ladies lunching, family gatherings, and just a good meal post-hike, you'll not want to miss the oyster po'boy, local sole with orange basil beurre blanc, or the oyster stew. On warm days, sit in the garden—though they do have a bee problem. Reservations recommended for dinner. $–$$$.

✳ Entertainment

Inland Marin

Christopher B. Smith Rafael Film Center (415-454-1222; calfilm.org) 1118 4th Street, San Rafael. This revived Art Deco film house is where famous filmmakers often come to talk to audiences and share their new releases before films hit the masses.

Ⴤ **Farley's Bar** 415-339-4750; murray circle.com) Cavallo Point, 602 Murray Circle, Sausalito. Views and wine. Need I say more? Well, I should add that you'll need to bring cash or a credit card, because the Golden Gate Bridge, San Francisco, and bay views inspire costly libations.

Ⴤ **German Tourist Club** (415-388-9987; touristclubsf.org) 30 Ridge Avenue, Mill Valley. Open the first, second, and fourth weekends of the month from 1–6, though they do close randomly; call before hiking up here. You have to hike to this beer garden, just up the hill from Muir Woods, to get some of the oldest German beer on tap, and sausages. You can also get

here via the Dipsea Trail, call for directions. You can bring kids as well.

Marin Theater Co. (415-388-5208; marintheatre.org) 397 Miller Avenue, Mill Valley. Check local listings to see which plays this wonderful theater company currently has on the roster.

Mountain Theater See *Mount Tamalpais State Park.*

Ⴤ **No Name Bar** (415-332-1392) 757 Bridgeway, Sausalito. Crusty and seemingly a hole-in-the-wall, this old bar has great drinks, live jazz, and a hopping back patio.

Ⴤ **Sam's Anchor Café** See *Eating Out.*

♪ **Starbase Video Arcade** (415-459-7655; starbasearcade.com) 1545 4th Street, San Rafael. For almost three decades this has been the best video arcade in the North Bay.

Ⴤ **Sushi Ran** See *Dining Out.*

Ⴤ **Sweetwater Saloon** (sweetwater saloon.com) This favorite live music venue recently closed. Owners are working on revamping a new space to bring you more music and booze. See Web site for details.

West Marin

Ⴤ **19 Broadway** (415-459-1091; 19broadway.com) 17 Broadway, Fairfax. Come here to hear live music and drink plenty of booze.

Café Amsterdam See *Eating Out.*

Ⴤ **Nick's Cove** See *Dining Out.*

Ⴤ **Smiley's Schooner Saloon** (415-868-1311; coastalpost.com) 41 Wharf Road, Bolinas. Live music and drinks bring out locals and tourists who can find this saloon.

❉ Selective Shopping

If you are dying for that perfect souvenir, Sausalito is probably the place to go. Strewn along Bridgeway you'll find everything from **Art That Makes You Laugh** to **Real Napa**.

But the real draw for shopping in Marin (besides fresh produce) is antiques. Movie set makers, Martha Stewart, and in-the-know interior designers hoof it out to the main streets of San Anselmo and San Rafael to explore the bounty of shops here. In San Anselmo look for **Antiques Legacy** and **Modern I 1950s**, two of the 110 antique dealers in town.

Along 4th Street in San Rafael you'll find boutique shops like **Viva Diva** and **Clogs Unlimited**.

❉ Seasonal Events

June: **Summer Fridays in Tiburon** (tiburonchamber.org) Sleepy Tiburon wakes up on Friday evenings in summer, when restaurants put tables on the streets and live music attracts dancers, street performers, and families. Through August.

Shakespeare at Stinson (nbshakes .org) In summer, pack up and bring a picnic to see live Shakespeare on the beach. Through August.

September: **Sausalito Art Festival** (sausalitoartfestival.com) Sausalito. Since 1952 this festival has brought out artists from around the globe.

October: **Mill Valley Film Festival** (415-383-5256; mvff.com) Mill Valley. Big-name actors and filmmakers show up in the small hamlet of Mill Valley to showcase their films.

The Central Coast and Southern San Joaquin Valley

SANTA CRUZ AND VICINITY

MONTEREY, PACIFIC GROVE,
CARMEL, AND VICINITY

BIG SUR

SALINAS AND VICINITY

INTRODUCTION

I magine the Central Coast as a family of sisters. **Santa Cruz**, the hippie environmentalist, welcomes anyone, from that tattooed renegade to the bookish college student hoping to change the world of science. Home to some of Northern California's best surf beaches, redwood groves, and vegetarian-friendly restaurants, even the most conservative visitors can't help but be taken with this radical town. Santa Cruz's neighboring communities of **Davenport, Felton, Capitola, Soquel, Aptos,** and **Moss Landing** might not be as well known, but they surely are as beautiful (and nearly as radical).

Monterey then would be the perky cheerleader that everyone knows, but is a woman with a secret side (think Laura Palmer from *Twin Peaks*). She lures visitors to the area with clear blue seas perfect for diving, the best aquarium in the country, and a bustling Cannery Row tourist district. Often people are so entranced with her outgoing side they miss out on the understated allure of this diva: that of gourmet restaurants, quiet walking paths, and historic buildings. Surrounding her to the north, the stepsister towns of **Marina, Seaside,** and **Sand City** get overlooked so much, they might as well be characters in an unread novel. Since the military base closed (and California State University Monterey Bay took over), this is where locals eat, live, and play on the giant sand dunes.

POINT LOBOS'S EMERALD COVE.

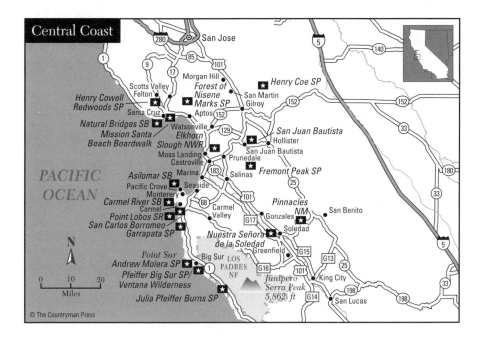

To the south, **Pacific Grove**, the prim and proper sister, paints little butterflies on her binder and dreams of a better world. Pacific Grove (AKA Butterfly City U.S.A.) tempts human travelers with stellar beach strolls, wonderful restaurants, intact Victorian architecture from the late 1880s, and the idyllic Asilomar State Beach.

The prom queen, **Carmel**, probably didn't submit her name for the most-popular contest. She would rather be in the back of the class with her artsy cousin Big Sur; alas, this one-time renegade now dresses in designer clothes, only dating guys with fancy cars and million-dollar houses. Yes, Carmel has come a long way from her missionary or even her art colony roots. Now the Arts and Crafts-style houses, boutiques, high-end restaurants, and inns burst at the seams with tourists almost every weekend. But what really pushes her to prom queen status is her natural beauty: Situated between 17-Mile Drive, Point Lobos, **Carmel Valley** (whose wine country is threatening to be the next big thing), and the pounding sea, this little village might be the most picturesque on the California coast.

Big Sur takes elements from all her sisters—as the rugged adventurer who hikes, paints, gets massages, then sleeps in a bed with zillion thread-count sheets. Plagued by a torturous fire season in 2008 that did a number on the tourism industry, Big Sur, like a phoenix, rises again to welcome visitors. Here you can explore the rugged coastline, the steep cliffs and redwood groves, see passing whales, relax in the mountains, and allow the artist in you to shine.

And then there is the hardworking, no-nonsense farm girl—**Salinas**. Salinas Valley is Steinbeck Country, but she's even more aptly nicknamed "America's Salad Bowl." With her sprawling fields of diverse agriculture ranging from lettuce and tomatoes to mushrooms and artichokes, this area provides the majority of the United States with its veggies. Salinas has had her hard times, especially during the Great Depression, and appears in many of Steinbeck's novels, including *Of Mice* *and Men, East of Eden,* and *The Grapes of Wrath.* Along with its expansive farm-steads, this region also houses some dynamic missions and state parks. Though not as much of a destination, people pass through Salinas to peek into John Steinbeck's life (the National Steinbeck Center is located here), explore agriculture, and hike.

GUIDANCE **Monterey County Convention and Visitor Bureau** (831-657-6400; montereyinfo.org) 150 Olivier Street. This is the main source of information about the whole county, with an extremely helpful staff.

Carmel Chamber of Commerce and Visitor Center (831-624-2522 or 800-550-4333; carmelcalifornia.org) San Carlos between 5th and 6th. Open daily 10 AM–5 PM. The visitor bureau helps arrange same day reservations and has a ridiculous amount of literature and information for tourists.

Carmel Valley Visitor Center (831-659-4000; carmelvalleychamber.com) 13 West Carmel Valley Road.

Santa Cruz CVC (831-425-1234; santacruz.org) 1211 Ocean Avenue, Santa Cruz.

HELPFUL WEB SITES
Pacificgrove.org
Carmelvalleychamber.com
Monterey.org
co.monterey.ca.us/parks

MUSTS FOR FIRST-TIME VISITORS
1. Visit Monterey Bay Aquarium.
2. Hike Point Lobos.
3. Take a surf lesson in Santa Cruz.
4. Go on a whale-watching tour in Moss Landing.
5. Dine at Pacific Grove's Passionfish.
6. Hike Julia Pfeiffer Burns State Park.
7. Gallery hop in Carmel.
8. Bike the 17-Mile Drive.
9. Light a campfire at Asilomar Beach.
10. Ride Santa Cruz's Giant Dipper.

MUSTS FOR REPEAT VISITORS
1. Take a ride on the Roaring Camp Railroads.
2. Hike the redwoods at Big Basin or Henry Cowell.
3. Eat at Café Brazil.
4. Get a spa treatment at Bernardus Lodge or Ventana Inn.
5. Taste wine in Carmel Valley.
6. Explore the Marina Dunes State Park.
7. Take the kids to the Dennis the Menace Park.
8. Visit the Henry Miller Memorial Library.
9. Tour Monterey's Historic Buildings.
10. Dive in Monterey Bay.

GETTING THERE *By bus:* **Greyhound** (greyhound.com) travels from San Francisco to Santa Cruz, Monterey, and Salinas daily.

By car: Driving to Santa Cruz from the Bay Area on weekends gets hectic. Hordes of people from the valley motor over CA 17 to cool off at the beaches; so if you head here on the weekends, go early. In winter, rain (and even sometimes snow) makes the trip over CA 17 even harder. An easier (but longer commute) is to take CA 1 south from San Francisco. To get to the Monterey, Carmel, and Big Sur area from US 101, take CA 156 or CA 68 west to CA 1 south. Follow the signs. The most beautiful drive in all of Northern California is the CA 1 trip from Morro Bay to San Francisco, which takes about eight hours, even though it is less than 300 miles.

By plane: **Monterey Peninsula Airport** (831-648-7000; montereyinfo.org) 200 Fred Crane Drive. **American Eagle** (aa.com), **Delta** (delta.com), **United** (united .com), and **US Airways** (americawest.com) offer flights from San Francisco, Los Angeles, Phoenix, Denver, Long Beach, LA/Ontario, and San Diego. **Allegiant Air** (allegiantair.com) recently jumped into the game with a direct flight from Las Vegas. You can find a number of car rental agencies at the airport.

By train: **Amtrak** (Amtrak.com) stops in San Jose and Salinas on the Seattle-Los Angeles route. To get to the coast from Salinas, take Monterey Salinas Transit (see below) and from San Jose, you can hop on SCMTD (see below).

GETTING AROUND *By bike:* Many people rent (or bring) a bike to explore the region. All towns are bike-friendly, though you still need to look out for vehicles. Another notable detail is that Santa Cruz police will ticket bikers for not following the rules of the road.

By bus: **Monterey Salinas Transit** (831-899-2555; mst.org) offers bus service throughout the county. In summer, the free trolley shuttles visitors between downtown Monterey and Cannery Row.

Santa Cruz Metro Transit District (831-425-8600; scmtd.com) offers service throughout Santa Cruz County and into San Jose.

By car: As with most parts of the Northern California region, having a car is the best way to explore. CA 1 is the major artery connecting the Central Coast. It is slow going on summer weekends, so be patient.

MEDICAL EMERGENCIES **Dominican Hospital** (831-462-7700; dominican hospital.org) 1555 Soquel Drive, Santa Cruz. **Community Hospital of Monterey Peninsula** (831-724-4741; chomp.com) 23625 W.R. Holman Highway, Monterey.

WEATHER For most, this coastal region makes you hug your fleece tight and spit a frustrated *brrr*. Never—even when inland temperatures reach triple digits—come to the coast without a warm sweater. If you are looking for sun, generally you will get a peek in September and October. The rest of the year brings fog and wind, perfect conditions for redwoods and reading.

SANTA CRUZ AND VICINITY

✳ To See

Aptos History Museum (831-688-9514) 7605 B Old Dominion Court, Aptos. Open daily from 10 AM–4 PM. Aptos, the small town just south of Santa Cruz, has a rich history of Indians, pioneers, redwoods, and fog-covered beaches.

✿ **Bigfoot Discovery Museum** (831-335-4478; bigfootdiscoverproject.com) 5497 CA 9, Felton. Open at least Wednesday through Friday 1–6 and weekends 11 AM–6 PM. The goal of this new museum is to flesh out the hairy guy's dossier. In other words, this museum exhibits sightings, hoaxes, and all things related to the big old dude supposedly living in many forests. Free.

Capitola History Museum (831-464-0322; capitolamuseum.org) 410 Capitola Avenue, Capitola. Open Wednesday, Friday through Sunday from 12–4. Most people come to Capitola to mosey down the pier, shop in beachy boutiques, and dine on fresh seafood. But you might want to pop into this museum to learn about how Capitola is the oldest Pacific resort town on the West Coast.

Mission Santa Cruz (831-426-5686) 130 Emmet Street, Santa Cruz. Open Tuesday through Saturday 10 AM–4 PM and Sunday 10 AM–2 PM. In 1791 this mission became California's 12th to be established. After a rich beginning (until gamblers lured the Indians away from God), this mission collapsed from earthquake damage. Now home to a Catholic church and a small replica of the original, you can explore the site and view original art. You'll also want to visit **Santa Cruz Mission State Park** (144 School St) to view the museum. Free.

Museum of Art and History at McPherson Center (831-429-6289; santacruzmah.org) 705 Front Street, Santa Cruz. Open Tuesday through Sunday 11 AM–5 PM. Besides being the only art museum between San Francisco and Monterey, this small house showcases the history of the area, including exhibits on logging, the boardwalk, the Ohlone people, and contemporary art. $5; under 17 free.

✿ **Santa Cruz Municipal Wharf** (831-420-6025; santacruzwharf.com) Beach Street, Santa Cruz. Of all the wharves I have walked on in my time, this one makes the top of the list. Not because of the wealth of restaurants, fish markets, views of the Boardwalk, and beach or boat rides that you find on most California piers, but because of the sea lions. Hundreds of these barking mammals hang around the wharf, entertaining children and adults for hours. This is about as close as you can get to these big guys, without getting in the water. Free.

✍ ⑤ **Santa Cruz Museum of Natural History** (831-420-6115; santacruz museums.org) 1305 E. Cliff Drive, Santa Cruz. Open Tuesday through Sunday 10 AM–5 PM. The bones of a life-sized whale, a touch tidal pool, and plenty of information on native people and wildlife make this a fun and educational stop when the beaches are too cold to play on. $2.50; under 18 free.

✍ ⑤ **Santa Cruz Surfing Museum** (831-420-6289; santacruzsurfingmuseum.org) Mark Abbott Memorial Lighthouse, W. Cliff Drive, Santa Cruz. Open in winter Thursday through Monday from 12–4 and in summer on Wednesday through Monday from 10 AM–5 PM. Surfing lures the crowds here, so why not check out the world's only surf museum. See vintage boards, the first wetsuit, and learn how surfing came to be the big business it is. The museum is located in the spot where Hawaiian princes first brought the sport to North America. Free.

✍ ⑤ **Seymour Marine Discovery Center at Long Marine Lab** (831-459-3800) 100 Shaffer Road, Santa Cruz. Open Tuesday through Sunday 10 AM–5 PM, Sunday 12–5 PM. Docents lead you through this public aquarium, where you can touch hermit crabs and anemones, and see a blue whale skeleton. $6 adults; $4 children and seniors.

Wilder Ranch State Park (831-426-0505; santacruzstateparks.org) 1401 Old Coast Road, Santa Cruz. Open 8 AM–dusk daily. Walking this old dairy farm, complete with Victorian compounds, wetlands, marshes, a plover sanctuary, and mountain trails, will hint at what the area used to be before SUVs or biodynamic foods. Hikers and bikers can explore the myriad of trails leading up the mountain of this 5000-acre park. $6.

✳ To Do

BOAT TOURS ✍ **Elkhorn Slough Safari** (831-633-5555; Elkhornslough.com). Moss Landing Harbor. Head out on a pontoon boat tour to see otters, pelicans, seals, and the wealth of bird life throughout the slough. Reservations required. Tours run two hours and cost $28 (adults) and $20 (children).

Original Stagnaro's Fishing and Boat Cruises (831-427-2334) 32 Municipal Wharf, Santa Cruz. This Santa Cruz family has been taking folks out to fish and tour the bay since before I can remember. You can take either a sunset or a bay cruise. They also offer whale-watching trips and fishing charters. Cruises fee: $13–25 adults. Fishing fee: $49–70.

✍ **Sanctuary Cruises** (831-917-1042 or 800-979-3370; sanctuarycruises .com) Dock A, Moss Landing Harbor. Conservation-conscious whale-watching cruises search for whales year-round. Trips last three to four hours and knowledgeable guides go out of their way to find whales (including orcas and gray whales) and explain whale patterns, habits, and lifestyles. Trips can get cold and bumpy—so bring warm clothes and something to help with seasickness (they sell bands on the boat). When I was out, we got

ABUNDANT SEA LIFE GREETS YOU ON A WHALE-WATCHING CRUISE.

so close to the humpbacks that we smelled their breath—yuck! $40–46 adults; $30–36 kids.

Santa Cruz Sportfishing See *Fishing.*

CYCLING Miles of trails, bike paths, and coastline beckon cyclists. Popular places to ride include the mellow seaside **Recreation Trail** along East and West Cliff Drive in Santa Cruz, **Natural Bridges State Park, Wilder Ranch State Park, Big Basin, Castle Rock, Fall Creek,** and **Nisene Marks**. Inquire at the bike rental places listed below for trail maps.

Rentals

Bicycle Trip (831-427-2580; bicycletrip.com) 1127 Soquel Avenue, Santa Cruz. Open at least 10 AM–5 PM daily.

Family Cycling Center (831-475-3883; familycycling.com) 914 41st Avenue, Santa Cruz.

DIVE BOATS **Aqua Safaris Scuba School** (831-479-4386; aquasafari.com) 6896 A Soquel Avenue, Santa Cruz. Though its sister Monterey gets all the fame for its diving, you can head out into the cold waters of this side of the bay as well.

FAMILY FUN ✪ **Mystery Spot** (831-423-8897; mysteryspot.com) Mystery Spot Road, Santa Cruz. Open daily 9–7. Observant readers will notice the slew of bumper stickers advertising this strange destination before ever seeing it. You'll be tempted to see for yourself whether this nutty local area, where balls roll uphill and trees grow in ways they shouldn't, is worth the hype. $5, plus $5 parking.

✪ **Roaring Camp Railroad** (831-335-4484; roaringcamp.com) CA 17 and Mt. Hermon Road, Felton. Trains run at 11, 12:30, and 2 daily. A ride through the redwoods down to the beach boardwalk and back is a great way to experience the history and natural beauty of the area. Trips last 90 minutes. If you want to spend more time, pack a lunch and hop off the train at the Bear Mountain Picnic Area (you have about an hour before the next train arrives). Adults: $19.50; Children 3–12: $13.50; Kids under 3: free.

MILES OF BIKE TRAILS GRACE SANTA CRUZ.

✪ **Santa Cruz Beach Boardwalk** (831-423-5590; beachboardwalk.com) 400 Beach Street, Santa Cruz. Open daily Memorial Day to Labor Day, on weekends and holidays the rest of the year. The last remaining oceanfront amusement park on the West Coast attracts thousands of visitors each day. With over 30 rides, including the octogenarian Giant Dipper roller coaster, and the 1911 Looff Carousel with 70 hand-carved horses and music from the original 342-pipe organ. Plenty of carnival games, and three video arcades,

THE BEACH BOARDWALK IN SANTA CRUZ.

including the fun Neptune's Kingdom (open year-round), plus a mile of shoreline and family-friendly beach, the kids will never want to leave. I nearly forgot to mention the laser tag, bowling alley, mini-golf course, picnic areas, and Casino Arcade (open year-round) too. Note that on summer weekends and holidays, parking lines are backed up for ages; try parking in downtown and taking the bus here. It's cheaper and quicker. For rides, you need to purchase tickets. On average, rides cost between $2.25 and $5. Around Christmas bring the kids for the holiday train ride, complete with lights, caroling elves, and a Santa visit.

FARM VISITS ✑ **Swanton U-Pick Berry Farm** (831-469-469-8804; swanton berryfarm.com) 25 Swanton Road, Davenport. Open in summer from 8–8; call for winter hours. If you ever wanted to pick your own berries, this is the spot to try.

✑ **UCSC Farm and Garden** (831-459-3240; casfs.ucsc.edu) UCSC, 1156 High Street, Santa Cruz. Open daily 8–6. As if you need another excuse to tour this beautiful campus, where deer, streams, and redwoods outnumber buildings, this organic farm and garden beckons. Learn about sustainable farming and even buy some fruit. There is an arboretum here as well (see *Green Spaces*).

FARMERS' MARKETS **Felton Farmers' Market** (831-425-3331) St. John's Catholic Church, CA 9, Felton. May through November, Tuesday 2:30–6:30.

Santa Cruz Community Farmers' Market (831-454-0566; santacruzfarmers market.org) Cedar and Lincoln Streets, Santa Cruz. Wednesday 2:30–6:30 year-round.

FISHING There are a number of superb fishing spots that you can access from land or by boat. Popular locations include **Capitola Fishing Wharf, Cement Ship** (State Park Drive, Aptos), **Greyhound Rock** (Davenport), **Twin Lakes State Park,** and **Santa Cruz Municipal Wharf.**

Santa Cruz Sportfishing (831-426-4690; santacruzsportfishing.com) Santa Cruz. This crew takes anglers out to hunt for salmon, rock cod, and albacore. They also lead whale-watching trips.

Stagnaro's Fishing Trips See *Boat Tours.*

GOLF De Laveaga Golf Course (831-423-7212; delaveagagolf.com) 401 Upper Park Road, Santa Cruz. From the top of a hill you can see the entire Monterey Bay and try your skill at the 18 holes. $19–68.

Pasatiempo Golf Club (831-459-9155; pasatiempo.com) 18 Clubhouse Road, Santa Cruz. Views abound at this Alister Mackenzie-designed course. $200.

KAYAKING Kayak Connection (831-724-5962 or 831-479-1121; kayakcon nection.com) Elkhorn Slough, Moss Landing, or Santa Cruz Yacht Harbor, Santa Cruz. The most interesting way to come face-to-face—almost literally—with the abundant sea life is by kayak. Otters might swim onto your kayak, seals approach to check you out, and I even saw brave paddlers get so close to a whale I was sure they communicated (though it is illegal to paddle so close to sea life that you change their behavior). $33–45 for a half day.

SPAS Tea House Spa (831-426-9700; teahousespa.com) 112 Elm Street, Santa Cruz. Open daily from 11 AM–midnight. A stop at this Zen-inspired hot tub, sauna, and spa retreat is a must. Aside from the aforementioned body-numbing attributes, the doors in private hot tub rooms open to offer views of a Japanese garden.

Well Within (831-458-9355; wellwithinspa.com) 417 Cedar Street, Santa Cruz. Open daily from 10 AM–midnight. This lovely spa is another favorite in Santa Cruz. Offering private hot tub rooms with gardens, massage, and ski therapy treatments, the Well Within always makes for the perfect post-surf treat.

SURFING When I write that surfing is the most popular pastime in Santa Cruz, you will not hear any argument. In fact, if you live here and don't surf, chances are folks are going to wonder what's wrong with you. These waters are also populated by visitors—Valley folks who drive in from San Jose; tourists who want to try their skills at Surf City USA; and newbies hoping to learn in these cold, kelp-guarded waters—who all fight for space in the waves.

A few things to note about the surf here—first and foremost, it is cold—water temperatures rarely get above 60 degrees Fahrenheit and that's in the peak of summer. You need a wetsuit, a good one, with a hood and booties. Second, locals are extremely territorial. When the surf is up, expect to have to prove yourself for a spot. The best way to navigate territorial locals is to abide by common decency surf guidelines (if you don't know them, don't bother going out here) or go out at less-crowded hours. Also, do not try to surf in areas you are not qualified for. As with most of California, winter brings the best waves, sometimes reaching well over 20 feet overhead.

Surf spots to know about include **Capitola Jetty** and **Cowell's Beach** for beginners, **26th Avenue, The Hook** (end of 41st Avenue), **Pleasure Point** (which also includes Privates), **Natural Bridges**, and **Steamer Lane** for intermediate to advanced surfers.

Cowell's Surf Shop (831-427-2355; cowellssurfshop.com) 30 Front Street, Santa Cruz. Open at least 8–5 daily. Rentals, lessons, gear, all across from the beginner-friendly Cowell's Beach.

Paradise Surf Shop (831-462-3880; paradisesurfshop.com) 3961 Portola Drive. These ladies run the only all-women surf shop that sells and rents boards and gear.

WINE TASTING Big business in the Santa Cruz Mountains, you can find a number of fine wines and unpretentious tasting rooms. For maps of local wineries, contact the **Santa Cruz Mountain Winegrowers' Association** (831-685-VINE; scmwa.com).

Bargetto Winery (831-475-2258; bargetto.com) 3535 N Main Street, Soquel. Open 12–5 daily. Though you don't really need another excuse to explore this quiet beach town, tasting handcrafted wines that the growers have been perfecting since 1933 is a treat. Free.

Bonny Doon Tasting Room (831-425-7777; bonnydoonvineyard.com) 328 Ingalls, Santa Cruz. Open 11 AM–5 PM daily. Their dessert wines rule. You can sip Muscat in their new tasting room in downtown Santa Cruz.

Hallcrest Vineyards/The Organic Wine Works (831-335-4441; hallcrestvine yards.com) 379 Felton Empire Road, Felton. Open 12–5 daily. Since 1941 these guys have been creating wonderful Chardonnay. And sipping it here, surrounded by redwoods in one of the Central Coast's funkiest towns, is a treat.

✱ Green Spaces

✐ ⅙ **UCSC Arboretum** (831-427-2998; arboretum.ucsc.edu) UCSC, 1156 High Street, Santa Cruz. Open 9–5 daily. This large public garden shows off its collection of plants and trees from around the world. The California native plant garden is a highlight and the views are worth the drive up the mountain. $5 adults; $2 kids.

Big Basin Redwoods State Park (831-338-8860; bigbasin.org, or parks.ca.gov) Go 25 miles northwest of Santa Cruz, off CA 9 and 236. Park is open from 6 AM–10 PM daily. The oldest of the California State Parks, Big Basin is well worth your time. The park stretches across the Santa Cruz Mountains and towards Los Gatos on the eastern ridge. With so many hikes it is hard to choose. Skyline to Sea trail, Boulder Creek, Berry Creek Canyon (this trail is tough, but rewards you with waterfalls), the hike to Sempervirens Falls, and the Redwood Trail are good places to start. Get a trail map from the visitor center. Mountain bikers use fire roads and the paved North Escape Road. There are 146 campsites in the park, located in 4 campgrounds (you'll need to reserve ahead for these at 800-444-7275 or reserve america.com). You can also rent tent cabins ($65; minimum night stay on weekends). Campsites range in fees from $23–25. Day use fee: $6.

Castle Rock State Park (408-867-2952; parks.ca.gov) 15000 Skyline Boulevard, Los Gatos. Open 6 AM–sunset. This park connects to Big Basin and is located along the crest of the Santa Cruz Mountains. With 32 miles of trails that pass through riparian forests, chaparral, and redwood trees, Castle Rock offers people tired of the beach a way to get in the shade. The most rewarding hike on the Santa Cruz side of the park is to Castle Rock Falls. Contact the visitor center for a trail map.

PELICANS IN LOVE.

There are primitive campsites for backpackers ($10).

Elkhorn Slough National Estuarine Research Reserve (831-728-2822; elk hornslough.org) 1700 Elkhorn Road. This might just be the best spot for wildlife spotting in Northern California. These tidal marshlands make Elkhorn Slough (pronounce *slew*) an important stopover for birds migrating on the Pacific Flyway, plus this area is a shelter spot for seals and otters. What makes this estuary unique is that it only has freshwater part of the year. The best time to see wildlife spans from November through March, but I was here in June and saw loads of whales, otters, and sea lions. You can kayak or take a pontoon boat tour (see above), or view birds from the public boat launch in Moss Landing and Kirby Park. In addition to the sea celebrities listed above, you might view bat rays, leopard sharks, sardines, slugs, and over 250 species of birds, including herons, clapper rails, eagles, falcons, and black-necked stilts. $2.50 (adults 16 and over).

Forest of Nisene Marks State Park (831-763-7063; santacruzstateparks.com) Aptos Creek Road and Soquel Drive, Aptos. The wildest state park in the area, here you can explore 10,000 acres of second-growth forest, with trails leading to the lovely Maple Falls. A number of primitive campsites are located in the forest, which you need to reserve in advance. Day use: $6. Camping fee: $5.

Henry Cowell Redwoods State Park (831-335-4598 or 831-438-2396; santa cruzstateparks.org or reserveamerica.com) 101 N. Big Trees Park Road, Felton. Open sunrise to sunset; campground closes in winter. Visitor center is open 10 AM–4 PM daily. Zayante Indians once called this redwood forest home, and today it looks much the same as it once did. Massive redwoods, Douglas firs, madrones, and pines show off the best of Northern California coastal forests. Trees are approximately 1400–1800 years old and can reach 285 feet tall. Any hiking or biking trail you take here will delight, but the Fall Creek area offers the most rugged terrain. Campsite Fee: $25. Day use fee: $6.

Portola Redwoods State Park See *South Bay—Green Spaces.*

Wilder Ranch State Park See *To See.*

BEACHES **Capitola City Beach** Esplanade and Monterey Streets, Capitola. In summer, do not drive here. Take the shuttle from inland Capitola/Soquel area and you'll have way more time wandering the restaurants and shops lining this lovely beach. Free.

Davenport Landing Beach (831-454-7956; scparks.com) Davenport Landing, Davenport. This protected cove used to be the site of a whaling town located on these shores.

East Cliff (831-454-7956; scparks.com) 12th Avenue to 41st Avenue, Santa Cruz. Surfers and locals won't tell you about this stretch of surf that causes guys to get territorial even with women. You won't find many places to laze on the sand, but when the tide is out, this is a great area for tide pooling. You need to hike down steep steps to access the water. Surf is the area's best.

Main Beach/Cowell's Beach (831-454-7956; scparks.com) Beach Street, Santa Cruz. As the name implies, this is the main beach in Santa Cruz. Basically this is where you find more visitors than locals, but for a good reason—it's a great beach for families, sunbathing, and swimming.

Manresa State Beach (831-724-3750; santacruzstateparks.org) 400 San Andreas Road, La Selva Beach. Take CA 1 south of Aptos to San Andreas Road. What a lovely place to spend the day. You can laze on the sand, surf, fish, explore tide pools, and then hike to the Uplands, where you can pitch a tent for $25 a night with ocean views. Day use: $6.

Moss Landing State Beach (831-649-2836; Parks.ca.gov) Jetty Road, off CA 1. Bird-watchers, picnickers, and surfers like this mellow stretch of sand, away from the Santa Cruz crowd and populated by wildlife.

Natural Bridges State Beach (831-423-4609; santacruzstateparks.org) 2531 W. Cliff Drive, Santa Cruz. Open 8 AM–sunset. Besides being home to the annual monarch butterfly migration, this lovely beach also beckons people to explore her natural rock bridge, tide pools, wildflowers, wetlands, shorebirds, and even passing whales. Day use: $6.

New Brighton State Beach (831-464-6330 or 800-444-7275; santacruzstateparks .org) 1500 Park Avenue, Capitola. The Chinese immigrants who once had their fishing village on top of the bluffs overlooking these 93 acres of shoreline knew what was up. Today, you can camp on the bluffs, hike the area, or frolic in the water. Camping Fee: $25–35 for premium ocean-view sites and RV hookups (in winter no need to reserve, just come). Day use fee: $6.

SANTA CRUZ'S NATURAL BRIDGES STATE PARK.

Palm State Beach (831-763-7063; santacruzstateparks.com) End of West Beach Street, Watsonville. Seemingly endless shores make this a popular spot for dogs and their owners, fishing, and swimming. Day use: $6.

Seabright State Beach (831-685-6500; santacruzstateparks.com) E. Cliff Drive at Seabright Avenue, Santa Cruz. Between the boardwalk and the harbor, this long sandy beach is popular for bonfires and picnics. Free.

Seacliff State Beach (831-685-6442; santacruzstateparks.com) 201 State Park Drive, Aptos. Popular for swimming, RV camping, fishing, and exploring the USS *Palo Alto* (a WWI cement ship), this is a great place to bring the kids. This park is adjacent to Rio Del Mar, a wide strip of sand perfect for taking the doggie for a walk. Day use: $6. RV camping: $39–44; reservations required (800-444-7275).

Sunset State Beach (831-763-7063; santacruzstateparks.com) 201 Sunset Beach Road, Watsonville. Though there are many reasons to explore this park, here are the main highlights: Bottle-nosed dolphins hang out here in summer and fall, 3 miles of shoreline make for great strolls, a wooded campground surrounded by farmland allows families to relax by the beach, and 200-foot dunes scream to be climbed. Campsite fee: $25. Day use fee: $6.

Twin Lakes State Beach (831-429-2850; santacruzstateparks.com) E. Cliff at 7th Avenue, Santa Cruz. Miles of sandy shoreline attracts swimmers and picnickers, while bird-watchers head to the adjacent Schwann Lake. It is the area's warmest beach. Free.

Waddell Creek Beach CA 1, 1 mile south of San Mateo/Santa Cruz county line. Surfers have paved the way for locals to get to this secret, though adored gem of a beach. Pat yourself on the back if you hike Big Basin and end up here at this remote stretch of sand. Windsurfers populate the waters. Free.

✳ Lodging

If none of these options appeals to you, contact **Bed and Breakfast Inns of Santa Cruz County** (santacruz bnb.com). Motels line the streets surrounding the boardwalk, and usually vacancies abound. Also check out santacruzmotels.com.

✐ "🍴" **The Adobe on Green Street** (831-469-9866; adobeongreen.com) 103 Green Street, Santa Cruz. One of the only B&Bs a couple minutes walk to downtown, this four-room inn makes you feel like you are visiting an old friend. Décor leans more towards *Sunset* magazine than Granny, with heaps of pillows, gardens, claw-foot tubs, and even in-room toothpaste. Breakfasts favor organics rather than Costco muffins. $$–$$$.

Babbling Brook B&B (831-427-2437 or 800-866-1131; babblingbrookinn .com) 1025 Laurel Street, Santa Cruz. A traditional B&B in an untraditional location, this 13-room Victorian offers glimpses of the Boardwalk and the sea, and easy access to the action down the hill. Antique-decorated rooms have whirlpool tubs and fireplaces, making this an ideal off-season locale (especially because the prices drop dramatically). Expanded continental breakfast is just fine to start the day. $$–$$$$.

♿ **Captain's Inn at Moss Landing** (831-633-5550; captainsinn.com) Moss Landing Road. A nautical-themed 10-room B&B, mere steps to the harbor and outfitted with binoculars (for coastal sea life watching), an in-room wildlife and bird guide, and even a toy boat in your bathtub. Newer boathouse rooms are the way to go: close to the river, beds that feel like plush lifeboats, an actual boat in your room, views, and some even come with fireplaces and Jacuzzi tubs; all include full breakfast. $$–$$$; two-night stay on weekends.

✷ & "♪" ⚭ **Casa Blanca Inn and Motel** (831-423-1570; Casablanca -santacruz.com) 101 Main Street, Santa Cruz. The 33 varieties of rooms offer plenty to choose from—motel rooms with ocean views, apartments with kitchenettes, basically there is something for the whole extended family. Popular with weddings, rooms lean towards the regal rather than the beach bum, with deep red linens and four-poster beds. Amenities include continental breakfast, excellent Casablanca Restaurant (great for Sunday brunch), and room service. $–$$$$.

✷ & "♪" ⚭ **Chaminade Resort Spa** (831-475-5600 or 800-283-6569; chaminade.com) 1 Chaminade Lane, Santa Cruz. *The* boutique hotel in Santa Cruz, this 156-room resort charms even the toughest sell of a vacationer. Recently renewed rooms offer a touch of Spanish décor, with woven headboards, primary colors in geometric patterns, granite bathrooms, and delightfully soft bedding. Guests love the spa, the private patios, pool, Jacuzzi, fitness center, breakfast, tennis courts, the personal attention, and the landscaped gardens. $$$$.

✷ & **Davenport Roadhouse at the Cash Store** (831-426-4122) 1 Davenport Road, Davenport. This new boutique inn sits on a cliff overlooking the ocean. The eight eco-friendly rooms use natural woods, and reflect the calm environment with blanket ladders, can-

dles, spare beds, and wraparound porches with rocking chairs. Everyone gets continental breakfast. For the ultimate in romance, upgrade to breakfast in bed and champagne packages when you arrive, and make a reservation at the restaurant. $–$$$; fee for third person over 13.

✷ & **Dream Inn** (831-426-4330; dreaminnsantacruz.com) 175 W. Cliff Drive, Santa Cruz. Location, location, location you'll cry, as you throw open the green shutters to take in the ocean below. This is the only beachfront hotel in Santa Cruz. Need I say more? Okay, I will. The 165 rooms, decorated in blues, oranges, and yellow might initially take you back to the 1970s, but modern amenities like flat-screen TVs, iPod docking stations, plush linens, pool, and restaurant room service help you work through that. $$$–$$$$.

"♪" **Inn at Depot Hill** (800-572-2632; innatdepothill.com) 250 Monterey Avenue, Capitola. This 12-room inn used to be home to the train depot and now offers one of the finest accommodations in the region. Sporting fireplaces, canopy beds, jet tubs, and a fab locale in the heart of Capitola, you won't want to leave. Cream-colored rooms, the gourmet breakfast, and hot tub invoke relaxation. $$$–$$$$.

"♪" **Pleasure Point Inn** (831-475-4657; pleasurepointinn.com) 2-3665 E. Cliff Drive, Santa Cruz. More akin to Southern California than the beachy neighborhood it resides in, this four-bedroom modern retreat in the funky Pleasure Point part of town serves up spare design rather than doilies and teddy bears. You can't help but love the hand-painted tiles, heated bathroom floors, fireplaces, the ocean view hot tub, the breakfast, and those big tubs. $$$.

CAMPING See *Green Spaces*.

✳ Where to Eat

DINING OUT ♪ ♿ ☿ **Davenport Roadhouse** (831-426-4122) 1 Davenport Road, Davenport. Restaurant open Tuesday through Friday from 10 AM–3 PM and 5 AM–9 PM; on weekends from 8 AM–9 (until 8 on Sunday). Café open Monday 8 AM–12 AM, Tuesday through Sunday 8 AM–5 PM. Looking for seasonal, organic California cuisine with an ocean view? Specialties include seafood pasta or leek and artichoke lasagna. Enjoy live music on weekends and discounts on Tuesday through Thursday. Reservations recommended for dinner. Breakfast and lunch: $–$$; dinner: $$–$$$. Café: $–$$.

♪ ♿ ☿ **Nuevo Southwest Grill** (831-475-2233) 21490 E. Cliff, Santa Cruz. Open for dinner nightly and brunch on weekends. Every time I sit in this colorful dining room, I am reminded why Santa Cruz rocks. First of all, the food here is stellar—fresh guacamole, mole dishes, breakfast treats like huevos rancheros. The margaritas do the trick and the art hanging on the walls creates a contemporary, almost urban, space. This is a great place for mom and dad to enjoy quality food with the kids. $$–$$$.

♪ ♿ **O'Mei Restaurant** (831-425-8458) 2316 Mission Street, Santa Cruz. Open for dinner nightly. Wildly popular with those-in-the-know, this Chinese restaurant dubs itself upscale and serves inventive contemporary Asian fare at bigger than usual prices. Start with a glass of artisan wine and a small plate, then try the rock cod, *mushu,* or dumplings. Note that service is inconsistent and if you order take-away, you will be charged an extra 10 percent on your bill. $$–$$$.

Oswald (831-423-7427; premierline .com) Front and Soquel, Santa Cruz.

Open Monday through Saturday 5:30–10. Santa Cruz's finest dining establishment, at press time was relocating to the new location listed above, call for details. $$–$$$.

♪ ♿ ☿ **Ristorante Avanti** (831-427-0135; ristoranteavanti.com) 1711 Mission Street, Santa Cruz. Open for lunch Monday through Friday and dinner nightly. Though it's a casual, rustic environment that feels more like a tavern in Florence than a beach town eatery, this Italian restaurant is a must experience. Avanti highlights the meaning of eating locally, using mostly organic produce grown within a 50-mile radius. Traditional Italian fare showcases eggplant parmesan, house-made sausage, Niman Ranch skirt steak, and striped bass. Reservations recommended. $$–$$$.

♪ ♿ ☿ **Shadowbrook** (831-475-1511; shadowbrook-capitola.com) 1750 Wharf Road, Capitola. Open for dinner nightly and Sunday brunch. You hear that places are "institutions" in a particular area, but none quite represent the best a town has to offer like Capitola's almost 70-year old fine dining superstar. Situated on a creek, this red barn brings foodies out for seasonal entrees such as prime rib or grilled local mushrooms while sitting under a wood-beamed ceiling that recalls another time. Reservations highly recommended. $$–$$$$.

☿ **Soif Wine Bar** See *Entertainment*.

Theo's (831-462-3657; theosrestaurant .com) 3101 N. Main Street, Soquel. Open for dinner Tuesday through Saturday. Chef Nicci Tripp's Maine lobster mac and cheese haunts my dreams, though the vanilla-seared halibut comes a close second. Menu items change, but you can always count on a French-Cal medley of sweet and savory in one of the Central Coast's best-kept secrets. If you want to go really big, try the tasting menu. Reservations recommended. $$$–$$$$.

EATING OUT ✍ ♿ **Café Brazil** (831-429-1855; cafebrazil.us) 1410 Mission Street, Santa Cruz. Open daily from 8–3. The secret is out. I can write about my absolute favorite restaurant south of San Francisco without regret. Seems every student at UCSC waits in line for *moquecas, gallo pinto,* banana pancakes, *acai* bowls, and freshly squeezed juices (try *abacaxi*). You'll wait over an hour on weekends to sit inside the colorful little house, but it is worth it. $–$$.

Caffe Pergolesi (831-426-1775; theperg.com) 418 Cedar Street, Santa Cruz. Open 7 AM–11 PM daily. In an old Victorian building in downtown, you'll find this classically Santa Cruz café, serving up coffee, pastries, bagels, and beer. Sit on the patio and hear all the wacky locals debate politics, or inside where there is probably live music happening.

Coffeetopia (831-425-6583 or 831-477-1940; coffeetopia.com) 1723 Mission Street and 3701 Portola Drive, Santa Cruz. My favorite coffee shop in town is the kind of spot where the baristas take their time with your lattes, they brew each cup just for you, dogs outnumber people, and you want to stay a while.

✍ ♿ ♉ **Crow's Nest** (831-476-4560; crowsnest-santacruz.com) 2218 E. Cliff Drive, Santa Cruz. Open for lunch and dinner daily. Popular more for its harbor-front location than the food, you can be sure you'll get a decent meal with the best views around. I prefer to have oysters on the deck in the late afternoon. $$–$$$$.

Davenport Roadhouse Café See *Dining Out.*

✍ ♿ **Dharmas Restaurant** (831-462-1717; dharmaland.com) 4250 Capitola Road, Capitola. Open 8–9 daily. Vegetarians breathe a sigh of relief when they enter this cafeteria-like organic haven, made just for them. Asian, Mexican, and American fare, made with the freshest natural ingredients around, attracts surfers and families to this casual spot. $.

The Farm Bakery and Café (831-684-0266) 6790 Soquel Avenue, Aptos. Open for breakfast and lunch daily. Though you can get a variety of sandwiches, salads, cookies, cakes, and coffee drinks, the draw here is the fruit tarts—flaky, creamy, and too good to pass up.

✍ ♿ **Fiesta Tepa Sahuayo** (831-724-3492) 15 1st Street, Watsonville. Open from 9–9 daily. People search high and wide for that perfect Oaxaquenan

"LAFFING" SAL IS AN INSTITUTION IN DOWNTOWN SANTA CRUZ.

restaurant, and who would have thought to look in a tiny strip mall in Watsonville for the ideal one? Floor-to-ceiling arts and crafts fade by comparison to the *huitlacoche* enchiladas, mole, and chili rellenos. Don't come here for burritos or nachos, this is for the folks looking for authentic southern Mexican food, and if you are lucky, grasshoppers might be on the menu. $–$$.

Ice Cream by Marianne's (831-458-1447) 1020 Ocean Street, Santa Cruz. For 50 years this has been the beach shack where you get classic flavors of ice cream.

♂ ᵬ **La Bruschetta** (831-335-3337) 5447 CA 9, Felton. Open for breakfast on weekends, lunch during the week, and dinner nightly. An Italian friend of mine is hard to please and she swears by this little Sicilian joint in the redwoods, complete with a hippie vibe and motherly love. Pastas are the way to go. Don't forget dessert. Reservations recommended for dinner. $–$$.

♂ ᵬ ❦ **Manuel's** (831-688-4848; manuelsrestaurant.com) 261 Center Street, Aptos. Open 11 AM–midnight daily (until 11 on Sunday). Owner Manuel Santana's art abounds in this popular Mexican restaurant, but the draws are the beach views and the food. Don't come here looking for funky Cal-cuisine. Instead try the traditional dishes like enchiladas and guacamole. Reservations recommended on weekends. $–$$.

Marini's Ice Cream Parlor (831-423-3299; mariniscandies.com) 1308 Pacific Avenue, Santa Cruz. Come here for old-fashioned stools, black-and-white photos, sundaes in glass dishes, and big scoops of traditional favorites.

New Leaf Community Market (831-425-1793; newleaf.com) 1134 Pacific, Santa Cruz. Find this great natural foods market in Felton, Half Moon

SEA LIONS HANG BY THE PIER AS YOU DINE AT OLITAS.

Bay, and scattered throughout Santa Cruz.

♂ ᵬ ❦ **Olitas Cantina and Grille** (831-458-9393; olitassantacruz.com) Municipal Wharf, Santa Cruz. Open for lunch and dinner daily. Usually restaurants on tourist piers charge ridiculous prices for small amounts of food. Not Olitas. Watch sea lions frolic in the sea while you sip strong margaritas and eat appetizers (the guacamole is addictive, be warned), enchiladas, and fish tacos. $–$$.

♂ ᵬ **Phil's Fish Market and Eatery** (831-633-2152; philsfishmarket.com) 7600 Sandholdt Road, Moss Landing. Open for lunch and dinner daily. After a blustery whale-watching excursion, opt for a hot bowl of cioppino, a grilled artichoke, and a bottle of wine. On some weekday evenings you might be lucky enough to hear some live bluegrass bouncing off the corrugated tin walls. $$–$$$.

♂ ᵬ **Saturn Café** (831-429-8505; saturncafe.com) 145 Laurel Street, Santa Cruz. Open 10 AM–3 AM daily. Since 1975, Saturn Café has been serving up diner fare for those kindhearted hippies that refuse to eat anything that once lived. Milkshakes, burgers and fries, salads, Mexican fare, and plenty of vegan options are what you get in this retro café. $.

✄ ♿ **Silver Spur Restaurant** (831-475-2725; scsilverspur.com) 2650 Soquel Drive, Santa Cruz. Open from 6 AM–3 PM daily. This funky breakfast and lunch spot specializes in vegetarian cuisine (though they don't ignore the carnivores) for a hung over hipster crowd. Go big with eggs and burgers. $.

✄ ♿ **Taqueria Vallarta** (831-464-7022) 893 41st Avenue, Santa Cruz. Open at least 10 AM–midnight daily. A top choice for burritos, tacos, nachos, and your other Mexican food favorites. $.

Tina Louise (831-229-7373) Dock A, Moss Landing Harbor on Sandholdt Road. Open most weekends, call ahead. If you have a kitchen, you might pop by Tina's boat for some freshly caught fish to cook up. Cash only.

✄ ♈ ♿ **The Whole Enchilada** (831-633-3038) CA 1 and Moss Landing Road. Open for lunch and dinner daily. This colorful Mexican restaurant specializes in seafood. Dine on the outdoor patio, enjoy views of the harbor, a margarita, and lobster and crab enchiladas. This local family also owns the **Haute Enchilada Art Café** (831-633-5843; 7902-A Sandholdt Road), which is a more casual affair with plenty of folk art and decent coffee. $$.

✳ Entertainment

Like most college towns, Santa Cruz offers more than enough watering holes, music venues, and theaters. For the most up-to-date entertainment information, including which performers are in town when you visit, pick up a free copy of *Metro Santa Cruz.*

▼ ♈ **Blue Lagoon** (831-423-7117) 923 Pacific Avenue, Santa Cruz. Santa Cruz's oldest gay bar attracts folks of all sexual persuasions to dance to techno and disco and get hammered on Flaming Dr. Peppers.

♈ **Bocci's Cellar** (831-427-1795) 140 Encinal Street, Santa Cruz. Big band, jazz, swing, and rock musicians come to this small space to play for an adoring crowd.

♈ **The Catalyst** (831-423-1336; catalystclub.com) 1011 Pacific Avenue, Santa Cruz. This is the place to hear live music in Santa Cruz. Everyone from Ani DiFranco to Pearl Jam has showed off on this stage. They serve food as well.

♈ **Clouds** (831-429-2000; clouds downtown.com) 1100 Church Street, Santa Cruz. Popular for food and drink, I prefer their cocktails to the Asian fusion fare.

♈ **Club Dakota** (831-454-9030) 1209 Pacific Avenue, Santa Cruz. All types come to get down at this DJ club.

Del Mar Theater (831-469-3220) 1124 Pacific Avenue, Santa Cruz. The latest art house flicks flicker on the restored screen in this 1930s Art Deco theater.

♈ **El Palomar** (831-425-7575; elpalo marrestaurant.com) 1336 Pacific Avenue, Santa Cruz. Locals love the cocktails at this popular downtown restaurant, making this one of those see-and-be-seen types of joints.

Kuumbwa Jazz Center (831-427-2227; kuumbajazz.org) 320-2 Cedar Street, Santa Cruz. Jazz greats inhabit this wonderful nonprofit club. Check local listings for details.

♈ **Moe's Alley** (831-479-1854; moes alley.com) 1535 Commercial Way, Santa Cruz. Locals head here for live down-home music, including great blues.

Nickelodeon (831-426-7500) 210 Lincoln Street, Santa Cruz. As if you need more to do in Santa Cruz. At night this four-plex shows indie and art films.

℞ **Red Room** (831-426-2994) Santa Cruz Hotel, 1003 Cedar Street, Santa Cruz. You'll make new friends at this enthusiastic downtown bar, or if nothing else, you'll leave more enthusiastic than you arrived.

Rio Theatre (831-423-8209; rio theatre.com) 1205 Soquel Avenue, Santa Cruz. Vintage art house shows art films, but also welcomes live music performances and spoken word.

℞ **Seabright Brewery** (831-426-2739; seabrightbrewery.com) 519 Seabright Avenue, Santa Cruz. Microbrews on a patio make this a locally favorite spot. Tuesday nights you get discount pitchers and Friday offers live music.

Shakespeare Santa Cruz (831-459-2121; shakespearesantacruz.org) UCSC, 1156 High Street, Santa Cruz. Shuffling between the Performing Arts Theater and the outdoor redwood pavilion, this wonderful company puts up innovative productions of old greats.

℞ **Soif Wine Bar** (831-423-2020; soifwine.com) 105 Walnut Avenue, Santa Cruz. Open for dinner and drinks nightly. Wine lovers come here to taste over 50 vintage wines by the glass, eat small plates, and feel urban. They serve full gourmet dinners as well.

UCSC Presents (831-459-2826) UCSC, Santa Cruz. World-class universities bring world-class performers to their campuses and UCSC is no different. Singers, musicians, acrobats, dancers, and more grace the stage throughout the school year.

✺ Selective Shopping

In downtown Santa Cruz you can score on a unique thrift-store sweater for a few bucks or get those hundred-dollar Seychelles. Some shops worth a peek along Pacific Avenue include **Bunny's Shoes**, **Bookshop Santa Cruz**, **Sock Shop and Shoe Company,** and **Perfumer's Apprentice**. Elsewhere, check out **Westside Stories** (847 Almar Avenue) for used books, the **Patagonia Outlet** (415 River Street), the original **O'Neill's Surf Shop** (1115 41st Avenue), and the women's-only **Paradise Surf Shop** (3961 Portola Avenue). Antique hunters head to the **Antique Street Faire**, the second Saturday of the month on Lincoln Street.

Capitola reigns as the quaint capital in the area, offering many galleries and boutiques to browse. Most of the shops are located along Capitola and Stockton Avenues, other highlights include the **Capitola Book Café** (1475 41st Avenue) and **Pacific Trading Company** (504 Bay Avenue). And head to Davenport for a few great galleries on Old Coast Road and Davenport Avenue.

✺ Seasonal Events

January: **Fungus Fair** (831-420-6115; santacruzmuseums.org) Loudon Nelson Center. For two days, Santa Cruz honors the fungus that grows in its rich forests with food tasting and displays.

February: **Migration Festival** (831-423-4609) Learn about migrating creatures at all the parks in the area. The best spot is to head to Natural Bridges to see the monarch butterflies, but you can also check out birds and whales at Seacliff, New Brighton, and Henry Cowell State Parks.

Santa Cruz Clam Chowder Cook Off (831-423-5590) Santa Cruz Boardwalk. You've got to experience this wacked-out clam chowder festival at least once.

March: **Santa Cruz Jazz Festival** (831-662-3368; scjf.org) UCSC. Two days of jazz in the redwoods is the perfect way to experience the best of Santa Cruz.

May: **Santa Cruz Bluegrass Faire** (831-459-0908; scbs.org) San Lorenzo Park, 137 Dakota Avenue, Santa Cruz. For over 20 years this festival has been offering free bluegrass to Santa Cruz.

Watsonville Fly-In and Air Show (831-763-5600; watsonvilleflyin.org) Watsonville Airport, 100 Aviation Way, Watsonville. Three days of military splendor, air shows, fireworks, and more.

Santa Cruz Longboard Club Invitational (831-917-4371) Steamer Lane at Lighthouse Point. You've got to experience a surf contest at least once. Seeing one here, at the spot where Hawaiians brought the sport to the Mainland, always amazes me.

Santa Cruz Blues Festival (831-479-9814; santacruzbluesfestival.com) Aptos Village Park, Aptos. For almost 20 years people have celebrated blues music here at this popular festival.

June: **Surf City Classic: Woodies on the Wharf** (831-420-5273; santacruz wharf.com) Municipal Wharf, Santa Cruz. Views and classic cars on the wharf make for a fun family outing.

Capitola Summer Twilight Series (831-475-7300; ci.capitola.ca.us) Esplanade Park, Capitola. Through

August, come out on Wednesday evenings from 6–8 to hear live music.

Friday Night Bands on the Beach (831-423-5590; beachboardwalk.com) Beach Boardwalk, Santa Cruz. Musicians from the 1960s, 1970s, and 1980s, a la Eddie Money, grace the boardwalk stage for free concerts at 6:30 and 8:30. Through August.

July: **Cabrillo Festival of Contemporary Music** (831-420-5260; cabrillo music.org) Santa Cruz Civic Auditorium, 307 Church Street, Santa Cruz. The see-and-be-seen venue for contemporary symphonic music in the U.S., this festival draws the best of the best. Through August.

Capitola Begonia Festival (831-476-4484; begoniafestival.com) Main Beach and Soquel Creek, Capitola Village. Parades, sculptures, movies, and great food make this more than a tribute to a flower.

September: **Greek Culture and Food Festival** (831-429-6500) 223 Church Street, Santa Cruz. For almost 30 years this homage to food has been lauded as the best festival in Santa Cruz. Come taste for yourself.

Capitola Art and Wine Festival (831-475-6522) Capitola Village, Capitola. The name says it all: Drink and view new work by local artists. Plus you can taste gourmet food and hear live music.

Santa Cruz County Fair (831-724-5672) County Fairgrounds, Watsonville. For six days the fair comes to town, complete with rides, games, and food.

MONTEREY, PACIFIC GROVE, CARMEL, AND VICINITY

✳ To See

Towns listed from north to south.

Marina

♿ **Sculpture Habitat at Marina** (831-384-2100; sculptureparkatmarina.org) 711 Neeson Road. These bronze sculptures are created by some locally famous sculptors: Santa Cruz artist Jack Zajac, Fred Parhad, Carmel sculptor Loet Vanderveen, and Carmel Valley artist Richard Mayer. A walk through this outdoor sculpture garden is quite the sight. Free.

Monterey

Cannery Row (831-372-8512; canneryrow.com) Between Prescott Avenue and David Avenue. Is it because John Steinbeck immortalized this strip of land in his novel *Cannery Row* that thousands of tourists flock here each year? Most wander up and down the street imagining what this area used to be like when it was the sardine capital of the world. Some eat seafood above the turquoise sea, shop for souvenirs or antiques, or head to the Aquarium (see below). Live music, an IMAX theater, plenty of wine-tasting rooms, and bars give tourists plenty to do at night. Just at the end of Cannery Row, you'll find **Fisherman's Wharf** (831-649-6544; montereywharf.com) at the end of Calle Principal. What Cannery Row misses in authenticity, Fisherman's Wharf delivers, sort of. Though it may seem authentic (fish smell and all), this isn't a working wharf anymore. You'll only need to come here if you want good clam chowder (see *Eating Out* below) or to venture out on whale-watching cruises (see below).

✐ ♿ **Monterey Maritime and History Museum** (831-372-2608; monterey history.org) Stanton Center, 5 Custom House Plaza. Over 75 years of celebrating Monterey's nautical history, this museum chronicles the history of the Ohlone Indians, Spanish explorers, and local sardine fishermen, plus it showcases the original Fresnel lens from the Point Sur Light Station, which contains 580 glass prisms.

Monterey State Historic Park (831-649-7118; parks.ca.gov) 20 Custom House Plaza. Open daily from 10 AM–4 PM. The fine people at this park preserve the architectural history of Monterey's adobe houses and gardens, then allow you to step back in time and tour them. This is a great way to view the Mexican/Victorian combination that makes these adobes unique. Guides lead tours of all the buildings on Monday, Wednesday, and Friday at 10:30 (call to reserve). If you would rather explore the buildings on your own, grab a "Path of History" map at the **Stanton Center** (831-372-2608; montereyhistory.org; 5 Custom House Plaza) and follow the markers on the sidewalk. Entrance to most buildings is $5 (for the ones that allow you to enter, that is). Here are some not to be missed stops:

Casa Soberanes (336 Pacific Street) Inside you'll find the history of Monterey from when Mexicans ruled to the present. Outside, enjoy the gardens, complete with a whalebone and abalone path, and a rose-covered trellis.

Colton Hall (351 Pacific Street) Open daily from 10 AM–4 PM. Built of Carmel stone, this building was the site of two important California firsts: the first newspaper printing, the first constitution. Now you can linger in the expansive gardens, visit the old jail, or tour the museum.

Cooper-Molera Adobe (Polk and Munras). Open daily from at least 12–4. Guided tours available. Wander through three historic properties, visit with farm animals, and relax in the lovely garden.

Custom House (10 Custom House Plaza). The oldest government building in California—though it was used for the Mexican government. The museum isn't as interesting as the building's history, unless you are taken with 19th-century cargo.

Larkin House (Jefferson and Pacific) Open for tours Wednesday, Friday, and weekends. In 1835 this two-story pink adobe became one of the most architecturally striking structures in the area. And it still is. Inside is a collection of period antiques from Mr. Larkin's home state of New Hampshire.

& **Pacific House Museum** 10 Custom House Plaza. Open Friday through Monday and Wednesday from 10 AM–4 PM. Built in 1847 to house U.S. military supplies. Now you can learn about the history of everyone from Indians to gold rush-era folks, and explore the Sensory Garden.

Presidio of Monterey Museum (831-646-3456) Corporal Ewing Road, in the Presidio Historic Park. Open Monday 10 AM–1 PM, Thursday through Saturday 10 AM–4 PM, Sunday 1 PM–4 PM. The museum and outdoor park area highlight the military presence in the Monterey area. Views from here can't be beat.

Royal Presidio Chapel (831-373-2628; sancarloscathedral) 500 Church Street. Open daily from at least 9 AM–4 PM. This was the original mission, founded by Junípero Serra before he switched to the Carmel location.

Stevenson House (831-649-7118; 530 Houston Street) Only open for tours; call ahead for specific times. Robert Louis Stevenson slept here, and now this old hotel houses a collection of his first editions, his wife's art, and some interesting artifacts and antiques from his life.

✒ & **Monterey Bay Aquarium** (831-648-4888; montereybayaquarium.org) 885 Cannery Row. Open at least 10 AM–6 PM daily. Nothing brings visitors to the Monterey Coast as much as the sea, and this recently renovated tribute to all things oceanic does its part to lure visitors westward. And for a good reason: This is quite possibly the best aquarium in the country. At the forefront of conservation, research, and sustainability (check out their Seafood Watch card), you'll most likely be astounded by the experience. Highlights include the sea otter tank, the giant tuna, penguin feedings, the cosmic jellyfish exhibit, the sharks, the anchovies, the petting area, the outdoor tide pools, and for kids, the upstairs play area. For the best deal, go at the end of the day and get your ticket stamped to return the next morning. Adults: $24.95, Children: $15.95.

&. **Monterey Museum of Art** (831-372-3689; montereyart.org) 720 Via Mirada and 559 Pacific Street. Open Wednesday through Saturday 11 AM–4 PM, Sunday 1 PM–4 PM. The Via Mirada location showcases Asian and Californian works of art in a 19th-century adobe building, plus there is a nice garden area. Docents lead tours of this museum at 2 on weekends. The Pacific campus shows some interesting photography and folk art. Call for information about the Friday evening Art Lounge parties, where the bar scene meets the art world for a night of music, cocktails, and of course art. Adults: $5, for both museums; under 12 free.

✔ **MY Museum** (831-649-6444; mymuseum.org) 425 Washington Street. Open Monday through Saturday from 10 AM–5 PM (Closed Wednesday), Sunday from 12–5 PM. At press time, this children's museum was relocating to a bigger (and bolder) location. Plans are in the works for exhibits geared towards children of all ages, with highlights including a giant kaleidoscope, replicas of California architecture, a treehouse, and an interesting agriculture exhibit that teaches kids how their food gets to the table. $7; children under 2 free.

Pacific Grove

Asilomar Conference Grounds (see sidebar below)

✔ **Monarch Grove Sanctuary** (831-648-5716) Ridge Road at Lighthouse Avenue. Open daily. Each winter thousands of Monarch butterflies arrive in Pacific Grove. They cannot survive the freezing winters elsewhere, and if you look up in the trees, you'll notice they cluster together (almost to the point of being invisible). Amazingly, these individual insects have never been to this location before, and yet, year after year they arrive, giving Pacific Grove the moniker: Butterfly City U.S.A. This magical sight (at its peak between October through February) is not to be missed. Free.

✔ &. **Pacific Grove Museum of Natural History** (831-648-5716, pgmuseum .org) 165 Forest Avenue. Open from 10 AM–5 PM Tuesday through Saturday. On a cold, foggy afternoon, you might pop in here to learn about native plants, animals, and peoples of Monterey County. If you can make it to the spring wildflower show, you are in for a treat. Free.

✔ **Point Pinos Lighthouse** (831-648-5716; ci.pg.ca.us) Asilomar Avenue between Lighthouse Avenue and Del Monte Boulevard. Open Thursday through Sunday from 1–4. Built in 1855, this is the oldest continually operating lighthouse on the West Coast. You can take a one-hour self-guided tour of the lighthouse and museum of 19th-century California maritime history. $1–2 donation.

CARMEL **San Carlos de Borromeo de Carmelo Mission** (831-624-1271, carmelmission.org) 3080 Rio Road. Open Monday through Saturday 9:30 AM–5 PM, Sunday 10:30 AM–5 PM. In 1771 Junípero Serra planted a cross at this site in Carmel, and construction was completed in 1797. Though the building has changed dramatically since its conception, the furnishings, statues, and paintings are originals. The chapels still inspire brides and grooms, as well as classical musicians who fill the parish with music during the annual Bach Festival. The Harrie Downie, Munras, and Convento museums showcase original artifacts and altarpieces. I like to wander the grounds, especially after a chaotic day of shopping in Carmel. Call for docent tour times. Adults: $5; children: $1.

THE CARMEL MISSION.

Robinson Jeffers Tor House (831-624-1813; torhouse.org) 26304 Ocean View Avenue. Newly married Robinson and Una Jeffers built one of the original Carmel cottages by the sea and now visitors can tour this lovely house, climb Hawk Tower, and wander through the gardens. Who knows: This spot might make you want to write your own poetry. Tours on Friday and Saturday from 10 AM–3 PM (children over 12 welcome). $7 adults; $2–4 students.

✳ To Do

CYCLING See also Scenic Walks, Drives, and Bike Trails.

Adventures By the Sea (831-372-1807; adventurebythesea.com) 299 Cannery Row. Open 9 AM–sunset. For $7 an hour, this outfit will set you up with a bike, helmet, and lock to explore the Coastal Trail.

FAMILY FUN ✍ **Earthbound Organic Farm** (831-625-6219; ebfarm.com) 7250 Carmel Valley Road (just 3.5 miles east of CA 1). Open daily from 8–6:30 (9–6 Sunday). Whether you are interested in bugs, organic produce, or just like to eat, the good folks at Earthbound Farms welcome you with plenty of kindness and information. I love the harvest walks, where you can wander through the fields and pick as much produce as you can carry. Most events take place April through October and cost $15–20. A visit to the farm is free.

FISHING CHARTERS **Monterey Sport Fishing** (831-372-2203; montereywhalewatching.com) 96 Fisherman's Wharf, Monterey. Half- and full-day trips are available to test your luck on local catches. $39.95–50.

GARDENS **Monterey Museum of Art at La Mirada** (831-372-3689; montereyart.org) 720 Via Mirada. See *Museums* in *To See* above.

Seaside

Bayonet and Black Horse Golf Course (831-899-2351; bayonetblackhorse.com) 1 McClure Way. This public course offers 36 holes. $30–84.

Pacific Grove

Pacific Grove Golf Links (831-648-5775; ci.pg.ca.us) 77 Asilomar Boulevard. If you want to golf, but can't be bothered to fork over the big bucks for the famed Links along 17-Mile Drive, this municipal golf course will set you up. $35–40.

Links at Spanish Bay (831-624-6611 or 800-654-9300; pebblebeach.com) North end of 17-Mile Drive. Sand dunes and coastal marshes make this a challenging course, but the views can inspire. Reserve a tee time up to two months in advance. $250, cart included for Pebble Beach hotel guests.

Pebble Beach Golf Links (831-624-3811 or 800-654-9300; pebblebeach.com) 17-Mile Drive, at the Lodge at Pebble Beach. Golfers dream about teeing off here, save up, and sojourn to the king of golf courses. Views on this super-challenging course might make you okay with forking over the big bucks to play here. Non-resort guests can reserve a time one day in advance. $495.

Peter Hay (831-625-8518) 17-Mile Drive. If you can't get a reservation (or can't afford) the famed Pebble Beach greens and just have to play, this 9-hole course may suffice. $20.

Poppy Hills (831-625-8518) 3200 Lopez Road, at 17-Mile Drive. This Robert Trent Jones Jr.-designed 18-hole course is less popular than its siblings. Reservations one month in advance. $195.

Spyglass Hill ((831-624-3811 or 800-654-9300; pebblebeach.com) Stevenson Drive and Spyglass Hill Road. The hardest and most beautiful of the Pebble Beach courses, Spyglass Hill lures pros and amateurs. Reservations up to one month in advance. $330; cart included for Pebble Beach hotel guests.

ALONG THE CENTRAL COAST BIKE PATHS, YOU'LL ENCOUNTER MANY PICTURESQUE NOOKS.

Carmel Valley

Quail Lodge (888-828-8787; quail lodge.com) 8205 Valley Greens Drive. People come from all over the country to lounge at this golf resort. Views of the mountains and sunny weather characterize the allure. $80–200.

SCENIC WALKS, DRIVES, AND BIKE TRAILS 17-Mile Drive (pebblebeach.com) For the best views, enter off CA 68 in Pacific Grove. If you are a fan of mansions, coastal bluffs, wildlife, and golf, a drive on the famed 17-Mile Drive is not to be missed. Highlights include the views from Shepard's Knoll, Huckleberry Hill, the Restless Sea, Bird Rock, a picnic at

Seal Rock, and the lone Cypress tree. Golfers will be in heaven to know that the route weaves through the famed Pebble Beach links. The best way to truly enjoy this experience is to bike it. Car fee: $9.

Monterey Bay Coastal Trail (mtycounty.com) This path spans from Marina to Lover's Point in Pacific Grove and delights bikers and walkers with stunning coastal views, wildflowers, towering sand dunes, and rolling hills. For bike rentals, see below.

Carmel
Carmel Walks (831-642-2700; carmelwalks.com) Meet in the courtyard of the Pine Inn on Ocean Avenue and Lincoln Street. Every time I come to Carmel, I fantasize about living in one of the cottages. If you do too, you might appreciate getting to know the town a bit better with this wonderful walking tour, filled with trivia, glimpses at where the famous people lived, and movie locations. Tours Tuesday through Saturday 10 AM (on Saturday they offer a second tour at 2). Reservations required. $25.

SPAS The Spa at Bernardus Lodge (831-658-3560; bernardus.com) 415 Carmel Valley Road, Carmel Valley. Open daily, but call in advance for specific hours as they vary with the season. In-the-know travelers head to this spa for decadent treatments and pure relaxation. With a private outdoor tub, steam and sauna rooms, warming room, heated pool, and meditation garden, spa-goers get more than just a treatment. If I had the money, I would go for the Bernardus Melange, two 25-minute treatments of your choice (like the Oligomer bath in the private outdoor tub, or the Wild Lime Blossom hot stone treatment), and a 60-minute massage. Other highlights are the Chardonnay facial, or a vinotherapy treatment called Grape Impressions.

WATER SPORTS Monterey Bay National Marine Sanctuary Extending over 2 miles deep into the ocean, Monterey Canyon is twice as deep as the Grand Canyon. For most of us, that fact won't actually hit home. We won't see the wealth of sea life thriving in this unique environment: the jellyfish, sharks, whales, lantern fish, kelp forests, rocky shores, reefs, eelgrass beds, whales, and other elusive fish. Even divers can only see a smidgen of what the canyon offers. In order to fully appreciate this ecologically special place, begin with a visit to the **Monterey Bay Aquarium** (see *To See*). Afterwards, you will surely be tempted to get in the water. Below are a few ways to begin to appreciate this natural wonder.

Diving
With 5,300 square miles of water and 300 miles of coastline, there is no shortage of areas to snorkel or dive in the **Monterey Bay National Marine Sanctuary.** The best spots to head out include the **Breakwater** in Monterey, **Lovers Point** in Pacific Grove, the **Pinnacles** at Carmel Bay, and **Whaler's Cove in Point Lobos State Park.** Water temperatures average in the mid-50s year-round with temperatures dropping into the 40s at deeper sites. The following companies take novices and advanced divers out to explore the canyon.

Aquarius Dive Shop (831-375-1933; aquariusdivers.com) 2040 Del Monte Avenue. These guys are the best crew to teach you how to dive. But if you already know how, they will take you on a private guided tour for $65–85.

Monterey Bay Dive Company (831-656-0454; mdbcscuba.com) 225 Cannery Row. These guys take you out on charter boats, rent equipment, and teach dive "virgins" how it's done. A basic guided tour runs about $60.

Kayaking

Adventures By the Sea (831-372-180; adventuresbythesea.com) 299 Cannery Row, Monterey. Open 9 AM–sunset. For $30, these guys will let you meet sea life face to face. They'll gear you up, and teach you how to kayak, then set you off to the sea. You can either explore the crowded bay near Cannery Row, or near Lover's Point in Pacific Grove. Plus you can explore sea caves, kelp forests, and even see whales.

Surfing, Lessons, and Rentals

The best surf spot in the area is **Asilomar State Beach**.

On the Beach (831-646-WAVE; onthebeachsurfshop.com) 693 Lighthouse Avenue. Open at least 10 AM–6 PM daily. These dudes rent surfboards ($20 for a half day and $30 for a full day), wetsuits ($10–15), and surf racks for your car.

South Bay Surfriders (915-0362, southbaysurfriders.org). For $85 you can battle the waves in a two-hour beginner surf lesson. Class comes with a surfboard and wetsuit.

Whale Watching

See *Santa Cruz—To Do* for more Whale-Watching opportunities.

✔ **Monterey Bay Whale Watch** (831-375-4658; montereybaywhalewatch.com) 84 Fisherman's Wharf, Monterey. Getting up close and personal with local whales is a treat, especially since the whales hang out around here all year long. The best time for spotting migrating gray whales is in winter when it is COLD, so dress really warm. In summer, humpbacks and blues hang around the coast, feeding on anchovies. These cruises tend to get crowded and can be bumpy. Trips last three to five hours, depending on the season, and cost $36–45 (adults) and $25–35 (children under 12); children under 3 free.

Sanctuary Cruises See *Santa Cruz—To Do.*

WINE TASTING

Monterey

A Taste of Monterey (831-646-5446; tastemonterey.com) 700 Cannery Row. Open daily from 11 AM–6 PM. Wine tasting with views of the bay and no driving through the winding roads of Carmel Valley. For a foggy coastal afternoon, this might be the perfect way to learn about local varietals.

Carmel Valley

If you don't want to drive, take the **Carmel Valley Grapevine Express** (888-MST-BUS1; mst.org) departs from Crossroads Shopping Center at 30 minutes past the hour. 9:30 AM–6:30 PM; $4.50 all day fare.

Bernardus Winery (831-659-1900; bernardus.com) 415 Carmel Valley Road. Open daily from 11 AM–5 PM. Located in Carmel Valley, this tasting room has a fun atmosphere and great wines. Tasting: $5–10.

Chateau Julien Wine Estate (831-624-2600; chateaujulien.com) 8940 Carmel Valley Road. Open Monday through Friday. 8 AM–5 PM, Saturday and Sunday

11 AM–5 PM. One of the classic tasting rooms in the area, this winery boasts delicious wines, gardens, picnic areas, and tours by reservation.

Heller Estate Organic Vineyards (831-659-6220; hellerestate.com) 69 W. Carmel Valley Road. Open daily 11 AM–5:30 PM. This tasting room also has a lovely outdoor sculpture garden and picnic tables. Make sure to try some Merlot-filled chocolate.

✳ Green Spaces

Marina
Fort Ord State Park (831-649-2836) To get here, drive to the University and walk into the dunes from there. These sand dunes are millions of years old, from the Pleistocene era. Here you can see plants and birds not found elsewhere: the snowy plover, Monterey paintbrush, and the Menzie's wallflower.

Monterey
El Estero Park Complex (831-646-3866) Between Del Monte Avenue and Camino Aguajito, Fremont Avenue, and Camino El Estero. This 45-acre recreation area offers paddle boating on a lake, group BBQ areas, and plenty of green shady spots, but it is mostly known for the amazing **Dennis the Menace Park** (777 Pearl Street). The playground is open daily from 10 AM–dusk (closed Tuesday from May through September). If you are traveling with a child, look no further; this mega-complex will tire out the little tykes, with a ton of play structures, a mini-hedge labyrinth, a train to explore, and much more. Free.

Carmel
Point Lobos State Reserve (831-624-4909; pt-lobos.parks.state.ca.us/) CA 1, Carmel. Open 8 AM–sunset daily. By far the best place to hike in the Carmel-Monterey area, the sweeping coastal views, hidden cypress groves, and bounties of birds make this a delightful place to spend the day. You can tag along tours led by the park docents, or you can go on your own. My favorite hikes are the **Cypress Grove Trail** and **Bird Island Trail** (on this one take your binoculars and check out the cormorants' mating ritual, that shock of blue is like nothing you've seen in nature). You can also tour the **Whaler's Cabin Museum**, where you can observe relics from Portuguese whaling times, including harpoons, photographs, and whale vertebrae. It's not much, but the hike down here is great. Day use fee: $6.

Garland Ranch Regional Park (831-372-3196) 700 W. Carmel Valley Road. Views of Los Padres Mountain, waterfalls, ponds, wildlife, and great picnic areas make this a popular local hiking spot. Visit the visitor center in the parking lot for trail information. Also, you might want to inquire about their star parties, where they set up 12 telescopes in the park for you to star gaze.

BEACHES

Monterey
Monterey State Beach Sand Dunes Drive. This beach stretches from the Monterey Wharf to Seaside, and offers lots of sand, sun, and views of dunes.

MacAbee Beach Cannery Row between McClellen and Prescott. People launch kayaks from here because the sandy beach is so mellow. Kids also play in the gentle surf.

San Carlos Beach Cannery Row. A grassy area with a little sand at the edge of Cannery Row marks the spots where divers head out on trips. You'll also find **Breakwater Cove**, a harbor with a decent, but pricey, snack bar, and toilets.

Pacific Grove

Asilomar State Beach At Asilomar Boulevard and Sunset Drive. This sandy stretch of beach welcomes surfers, swimmers, and beach goers. A wood-planked path allows wheelchair access all the way to Inn at Spanish Bay and makes for a wonderful beach stroll. Locals also have bonfires down here.

Fanshell Beach Signal Hill Road and 17-Mile Drive. Feel like rubbing elbows with the rich and famous? This small beach offers just that. Plus sea otters often congregate around here.

Carmel

Carmel Beach At the end of Ocean Avenue. A white sand beach with a paved path above, overlooking the turquoise sea and the plentiful dogs and kids running on the sand, is an ideal beach to soak up the occasional non-windy day. Campfires are okay. But don't try to swim; it's pretty dangerous.

Carmel River State Beach Scenic Road at Carmelo Street. This beach offers supreme views of Point Lobos and Pebble Beach. With water on both sides of the sand, a marsh, and the excellent **Mission Ranch** restaurant close by, this is a good choice for families, dogs, and bird-watchers.

✴ Lodging

In Monterey you can find everything from budget motels along North Fremont to big-name resorts along Cannery Row. In case you love the chain hotels, you might be interested to know that at press time, the **Fairmont Seaside Resort** (Fairmont.com) was hard at work on a new luxury property in Monterey, while **Intercontinental The Clement** (ichotelsgroup.com) opened the newest luxury property to Cannery Row in June 2008. Other chain hotels in Monterey are the **Marriott** (discovermontereymarriott.com) and the **Hyatt Monterey** (monterey.hyatt.com).

For the whole Monterey Coast area, finding unique accommodations can be costly—unless you want to take out a second (or third) mortgage on your house. Bear in mind that many of the buildings do not have elevators or good handicap access. Also note that almost every accommodation requires at least a two-night minimum stay on peak sea-

son weekends (from April through October) and some even require a third night. Finally, during peak season weekends most places double their prices. I recommend booking far in advance.

If you are traveling with your pet, make sure to inquire about pet fees. Most places (especially in Carmel) accept pets, but charge for it.

HOTELS AND RESORTS

Monterey

♂ Ꮣ ⁗Ꭵ⁗ **Casa Munras** (800-222-2446; hotelcasamunras.com) 700 Munras Avenue. With 171 newly renovated rooms, a lobby, and the Esteban restaurant, this yellow and brown hacienda, built in 1824, now caters to a modern crowd. Rooms, spread over 4.5 acres, feel private, with bougainvillea and sage draping down and around the buildings. Go for a second floor room off the street, which are quieter. $$–$$$$.

⁰†⁰ Monterey Hotel (800-727-0690; montereyhotel.com) 406 Alvarado Street. Built in 1904, this hotel was recently renovated to celebrate the heritage of the original structure, but not feel crotchety. The hotel is located in the center of downtown and is awash in floral touches, pink walls, carved wood fireplaces, and antique furniture. Continental breakfast comes with all 45 rooms. $$–$$$.

⁰†⁰ Monterey Plaza Hotel and Spa (831-372-2628; woodsidehotels.com/ Monterey) 400 Cannery Row. For the crowd who wants some bling in their beach, this oceanfront hotel caters to those who like marble floors, valets who wash your car windows, and bell-hops who offer help if you look the slightest bit lost. If you are going to spring for a night here, go big and get that ocean view room, otherwise you

♿ ⁰†⁰ ⊙ ASILOMAR STATE BEACH AND CONFERENCE GROUNDS AT ASILOMAR STATE PARK

(831-372-8016; visitasilomar.com) 800 Asilomar Avenue. Part of me doesn't want anyone to know about this refuge by the sea, while in my heart, I know that everyone deserves this unique experience. These 28 newly renovated lodges spread across 103 acres of forest, dunes, and coastline. This used to be a YWCA conference grounds and summer camp, designed by the Bay Area phenom Julia Morgan from 1913 to 1928. These Arts and Crafts-style lodgings use the open space, lots of light, and wood as accents. A great way to learn about the architectural history of Asilomar is to take the two-hour self-guided audio tour.

Rooms are simple and plain, with no TVs or phones. Try to get one in the North Woods, facing the sea and set away from the commotion of the conference centers. Julia Morgan historic rooms—Tide Inn, Hill Top, Scripps, and the Lodge—are good budget options as long as you don't mind hearing your neighbor's conversation.

You might be taken aback when you arrive on Friday and face long lines of conference attendees checking in; consider putting off your arrival until after dinner if crowds bother you.

At the end of the day, the draw here is the location. On a state park, with access to one of the best beaches on this stretch of coast, you can wander on a mile of coastal trail, which begins near the buildings and leads you past native grasses, deer, dunes, and forest until you reach the shore. My favorite way to spend the evening is a walk south to Inn at Spanish Bay—take the coastal trail all the way—for a cocktail, dessert, and live jazz.

Amenities include 314 rooms and cottages, full breakfast, bike rentals, beach access, business center, pool, games, store, billiard tables, ping pong, volleyball courts, bonfire areas, and free shuttle service around the grounds; some rooms have a fireplace or balcony. $$–$$$.

are looking at Cannery Row. The 290 rooms were recently renovated. Amenities include fitness center, spa, two restaurants, business center, AC, and parking. $$$$; plus resort fee; children under 17 free in parents' room.

♂ ⚐ "♟" **Portola Hotel and Spa** (831-649-4511; portolahotel.com) Two Portola Plaza. Recently renovated, this 379-room hotel offers sophisticated lodging in a casual atmosphere. Besides being in the heart of downtown, I like the seal toy in the bathtub, triple-sheeted comfy beds, and their concierge, who is the best in Monterey Bay. Amenities include pool, business center, two restaurants, lounge, fitness center, concierge, renovated spa, and parking (fee). $$$–$$$$.

Pacific Grove

⚐ "♟" **Casa Palmero** (831-647-7500 or 800-654-9300; pebblebeach.com) 1518 Cypress Drive, Pebble Beach. Of the Pebble Beach resorts, this understated 24-room Mediterranean-style hideaway appeals to people who don't want to be seen. Though not on the beach, Casa Palmero, hidden beneath trellised walkways, sits on the fairways of the Pebble Beach Golf Links. Guests are pampered beyond belief, from oversized spa tubs to continental breakfast baskets, balconies or private patios, a seriously helpful staff, radiant heated bathroom floors, and use of the Pebble Beach facilities—you can even "borrow" a Lexus for a couple hours. And you'll pay for the attention too; in fact you'll pay more per night here than I paid for my first studio apartment. But you'll also rub elbows with the rich and famous. Amenities include breakfast basket, fireplace, three golf courses, tennis courts, spa, beach access, pool, shuttle service to airport (free), and afternoon cocktail social. $$$$.

♂ ⚐ "♟" **Inn at Spanish Bay** (831-647-7500 or 800-654-9300; pebble

beach.com) 2700 17-Mile Drive. Like its own little village, Inn at Spanish Bay offers a high-end resort vacation experience in an isolated oceanfront setting. Most of the 269 rooms have a fireplace and patio or balcony, marble tiled bathrooms, plush linens, and views of the ocean, golf course, or forest. I like the lobby lounge in the evening, complete with families, couples toasting champagne, a fireplace inside, fire pits (with carefully placed blankets) outside, bagpipers, jazz musicians, and great wine and desserts. Though you'll spend big bucks here, it still feels homey and friendly. And you get to take advantage of the two wonderful Roy's restaurants, café, bar/lounge, four golf courses, newly built tennis club, bike rental, pool, Jacuzzi, room service, spa, access to all Pebble Beach resort facilities, concierge, and beach access. $$$$.

"♟" ⚐ ❀ **Lodge at Pebble Beach** (831-647-7500 or 800-654-9300; pebblebeach.com) 1700 17-Mile Drive. From the Rolex clocks poised outside the shopping area, to the hordes of tourists that pass through wanting a glimpse of the celebrity golf circuit, this is the granddaddy of California golf resorts. If you are not a golf fan, you'll probably not appreciate the draw of this pricey locale. Since partial ocean view rooms can be iffy, just suck it up and go for the full ocean view room. Packed with amenities, the 161 rooms and suites allow access to the three restaurants, including the famed Club XIX, tennis, golf courses, spa, access to other Pebble Beach Resort facilities, gym, pool, Jacuzzi, access to beach, shopping, concierge, and most rooms have a balcony and fireplace. $$$$.

Carmel

♨ ♂ ⚐ ∞ "♟" **La Playa Hotel** (831-624-6476 or 800-582-8900; laplaya hotel.com) Camino Real at 8th Avenue. The only part of the original 1904 mansion still in existence is the stone and stained glass bell tower, but this Mediterranean villa still inspires guests to feel like royalty. Sweep past the marble fireplace, ascend the tiled staircase to your third- or fourth-floor room (which have the best views), and delight in the mermaid motif headboards, hand-loomed rugs, and royal treatment. If you have the money (or a few friends you really like to travel with), the newly renovated modern cottages are the way to go—especially the two-bedroom Tradewinds Cottage. All 82 accommodations allow you to experience the Terrace Grill restaurant (which is a great place for Sunday brunch), room service, heated pool, and spa. Rooms: $$–$$$; cottages $$$$.

Carmel Valley

♂ ⅙ ∞ ⁰ᵀ⁰ **Bernardus** (831-658-3400 or 888-648-9463; bernardus.com) 415 Carmel Valley Road, Carmel Valley. Built in 2000, this 57-room resort actually makes people choose to visit Carmel Valley over picturesque Carmel—and pay big bucks. It feels like Napa, but close to the ocean and completely unpretentious. Here you'll get all the treats: limestone fireplace, featherbed, Italian linens, French doors, private deck, wine and snack pantries, two-person tubs, wine and cheese at arrival, and pure country decadence with European style. Here you'll also get two restaurants (see Dining Out and Eating Out below), award-winning spa (see To Do above), tennis courts, croquet, bocce ball, golf, pool, and hot tub. $$$$.

INNS AND B&BS ⁰ᵀ⁰ **Jabberwock B&B** (831-372-4777 or 888-428-7253; jabberwockinn.com) 598 Laine Street. Perched at the top of Laine Hill overlooking Cannery Row, but far enough away to actually feel like you are staying in Monterey instead of tourist central. This lovely seven-room B&B evokes the Lewis Carroll poem of its namesake: It's the kind of place you don't want to touch anything for fear you'll break it, yet the whimsical gardens and waterfall might make you feel like you've tripped down a rabbit hole. Amenities include full breakfast, concierge, wine and cheese social; some rooms have fireplace, Jacuzzi, and bay views. $$–$$$.

♂ ⅙ ⁰ᵀ⁰ **Monterey Bay Inn** (831-373-6242 or 800-424-6242; montereybay inn.com) 242 Cannery Row. This is the spot for water sports enthusiasts. Steps to San Carlos Beach and Breakwater Cove, this nautical-themed 47-room inn will make you want to open the doors to your balcony, pop open a bottle of local wine, or indulge in the continental breakfast delivered to your room. then take in that salty air while watching sea life frolic in the bay. $$$–$$$$.

⁰ᵀ⁰ **Old Monterey Inn** (831-375-8284 or 800-350-2344, oldmontereyinn.com) 500 Martin Street. This 1929 half-timbered English Tudor inn is the perfect place to cuddle up with your honey. Nestled in eucalyptus, nine rooms, suites, and the cottage feature pine interiors, featherbeds, floral bedspreads, fireplaces, spa tubs, and good lighting; most people never want to leave. Delicious breakfasts can be delivered to your room, making it easy not to get out of bed until noon. $$$–$$$$.

⁰ᵀ⁰ **Spindrift Inn** (831-646-8900 or 800-841-1879; spindriftinn.com) 652 Cannery Row. You can probably spit from your room into the sea, though most people consider this a romantic spot and probably won't be hocking loogies out the window. If antique

brass beds, marble baths, wood-burning fireplaces, and ocean view sunsets inspire romance, this is your stop. Guests in the 42 rooms receive continental breakfast delivered to your room, and parking (fee). $$–$$$$.

Pacific Grove

▼ "⼀" **Anton Inn** (888-242-6866; antoninn.com) 1095 Lighthouse Avenue. These simple, yet classy 10 rooms with masculine appeal are located just a block from the ocean. You won't find Grandma's doilies here. Continental breakfast, soaking tubs (in some rooms), electric fireplaces, contemporary art (check out those window shades!), and the minimalist aesthetic all appeal to the urban crowd. $–$$$$.

✇ ♿ ☻ "⼀" **Lighthouse Lodge and Resort** (800-858-1249; lhrs.com) 1150 and 1249 Lighthouse Avenue. Kids running around, the smell of BBQ, timbered cabins close to water, dogs lounging by the pool, and trees—plenty of cypress trees and pines. The budget-conscious folks will appreciate the Lodge. If you can, spring for the Resort Suites, which are across the street from the ocean, modern and luxurious. All 64 units include breakfast, afternoon barbeque (lodge) or wine and cheese (suites), pool, spa, and kitchenettes. Rooms: $–$$; Suites: $$$; House: $$$$.

✇ ♿ "⼀" **Martine Inn** (831-373-3388; martineinn.com) 255 Ocean View Boulevard. Septuagenarian Don Martine runs his 25-year old Mediterranean-style inn as he does his MG race cars. Offering guests the finest antique furniture (Mott fixtures, 1895 China bathtubs, tiled kitchens, the intricate lace drapery) in all 25 rooms, ocean views, a full three-course gourmet breakfast served on the same china as the White House, hot wine and appetizer hour, homemade cookies and milk at bedtime, Jacuzzi, and con-

stant upgrading to meet his high standards. And if you don't believe me, you can view his race cars and see how well he cares for them, then you'll know you're in good hands. Be sure to ask Don about his racing tales. $$–$$$$.

"⼀" **Seven Gables Inn** (831-372-4341; pginns.com) 555 Ocean View Boulevard. When I first passed this yellow Victorian, the sun glittered off the many chandeliers in the house. Everyone in the car murmured, "Wow." Entering this inn did not disappoint. Spring for an ocean view room in the front of the main building (since all 25 rooms and the cottage are touted to have ocean views). You get a full buffet breakfast, wine and cheese hour, milk and cookies at bedtime, fireplace, and canopy beds. $$$–$$$$; guests 12 and older welcome.

Carmel

"⼀" ☻ **Cypress Inn** (831-624-3871 or 800-443-7443; cypress-inn.com) 7th Avenue and Lincoln. Owned by Doris Day, this aging 44-room Mediterranean hotel is popular with people traveling with pets. Mission revival architecture, sand-colored rooms, extended continental breakfast, cocktail bar with tapas, pool, nightly jazz, room service, and a helpful staff give this property a classic ambiance. However, the rooms are not as luxurious as the price. Children over 12 are welcome. $$–$$$$.

✇ ♿ ☻ "⼀" **Hofsas House** (831-624-2745 or 800-221-2548; hofsashouse .com) 4th and San Carlos. I searched for an affordable hotel in Carmel, and this is the best I found. In winter, you can stay here for under a hundred dollars, but come summer, the 38 rooms in this pink-and-black Swiss-alpine hotel double in price. Most rooms come with kitchenettes, balcony, and continental breakfast. Guests also get partial ocean views and use of the pool.

Rooms: $–$$$; two-bedroom suite: $$$$.

⁰Ṭ⁰ L'Auberge Carmel ((831-624-8578; laubergecarmel.com) Monte Verde at 7th. Built in 1929, this gabled-roof, frame and stucco inn is made for romance. You might not even miss hearing the ocean. Upon arrival, heat up the bathroom floors, and slip into one of the baths (you either get a Japanese soaking tub or whirlpool free-standing bath—with a bowl of bath salts). Nothing has been overlooked in the 20 rooms, from the brocaded curtains and down bedding to the chiseled door handles and warm tones. Amenities include an insanely good restaurant (see *Dining Out* below), partial ocean views, free breakfast, room service, and spa services. $$$–$$$$; no children under 16.

∅ ☙ Lamplighter Inn (831-624-7372; carmellamplighter.com) Ocean Avenue and Camino Real. On a small lot a couple blocks from the ocean, these 10 Hobbit–like, yet lofty A-frame cottages and rooms offer modern touches, antique furniture, some ocean peeks, and just the right dash of luxury. The friendly staff delivers breakfast to your room, where you might hide out, soaking up the marble bath, fireplace, cascade showers, flat screen-TVs, and super-soft down comforters. $$–$$$$.

∅ ⅙ ⓒⓓ Mission Ranch Resort (831-624-6436 or 800-538-8221; missionranchcarmel.com) 26270 Dolores Street. White buildings dotted across emerald grass, overlooking turquoise waters, rocking chairs on private patios, sleeping in a farmhouse on the ocean's edge; the cypress and eucalyptus trees, and the sheep grazing by the water just steps from your room give this 31-room inn a special allure. For the best views, spring for the cottages or meadow view rooms. Amenities include continental breakfast, tennis

SMARTLY DECORATED ROOMS AT L'AUBERGE CARMEL.

courts, gym, restaurant (see *Dining Out* below), and some rooms have a whirlpool tub and fireplace. $$–$$$; fee for extra person.

∅ ⁰Ṭ⁰ Tickle Pink Inn (831-624-1244 or 800-635-4774; ticklepinkinn.com) 155 Highland Drive. Get over the name and bring your sweetheart to the most romantic spot in Carmel. This 35-room inn, originally the site of Senator and Mrs. Tickle's home, now offers one of the only lodging options in the Carmel area deserving of the price. Secluded above the Pacific, most rooms offer cushiony king-sized beds, wood-burning fireplaces, Jacuzzi tubs, robes, and balconies with binoculars for whale watching, plus continental breakfast, outdoor hot tub access, and free movies. Guests receive freshly baked cookies, champagne, and truffles upon arrival, plus one of the best wine and cheese socials in the region. Oh, and guys, you won't find much pink around here. $$$–$$$$; fee for additional person.

⁰Ṭ⁰ Tradewinds Carmel (831-624-2776; tradewindscarmel.com) Mission Street and 3rd Avenue. Though I didn't get a chance to visit this hotel, I have all the confidence in the world recommending it to you. After a big remodel, this 28-room inn combines Asian, modern, and tropical décor with the natural beauty of Carmel. Expanded continental breakfasts are included. $$$–$$$$.

🐾 🐾 "🦮" **Vagabond's House Inn** (831-624-7738 or 800-262-1262, vaga bondshouseinn.com) 4th and Dolores. This might be the best deal for your money. Spacious rooms surround the tranquil gardens. The lobby is a tribute to toys and collectibles from yester-year, and wood-paneled rooms make you want to sip the complimentary in-room sherry by the fireplace, while reciting Romantic poetry. Expect continental breakfast delivered to your room, wine and cheese reception, fire-places, and kitchens. No children under 10 allowed in the 14 rooms and 2 cottages. $$–$$$; cottages $$$$.

Carmel Valley

♿ 🐾 🐾 **Carmel Valley Lodge** (831-659-2261 or 800-641-4646; valleylodge .com) Carmel Valley Road at Ford Road. Once you get your dog in the funky room and find your S'mores package by the wood-burning fire-place, you'll probably understand why this 31-room Mom and Pop lodge has been around for over 30 years. They plan to remodel this year, which is good because the rooms are a little tired. Rates include breakfast, books, movies, games, and use of the pool. $$–$$$$.

🐾 ♿ ◯ "🦮" 🐾 **Los Laureles Lodge** (831-659-2233 or 800-533-4404; loslaureles.com) 313 W. Carmel Valley Road. The knotty-pine paneled walls of the Vanderbilt's former hunting lodge transports you to the 1800s. Once a horse stable, the 33 small Courtyard rooms are the best deal around. Just

know that this is a rustic experience; don't expect room service and some-one to clean your windows, though you can expect continental breakfast, a restaurant and pub, and a pool. $–$$$$.

VACATION RENTALS

Monterey Bay

Monterey Bay Property Management (831-655-7840; Montereyrentals .com) 601 Wave Street. For that oceanfront villa, the cozy beach cottage and everything in between, this rental agency has been serving up vacation rentals for over two decades. Most rentals range from $$$–$$$$.

Pacific Grove

🐾 "🦮" ◯ **Andril Fireplace Cottages** (831-375-0994; andrilcottages.com) 569 Asilomar Road. Families love these—seven rustic studios, and up to five-bedroom cottages with full kitchens, fireplaces, and Jacuzzis. Owned by the Smith family since 1960, you can indulge in renting your own cottage by the sea, without paying the big prices. $–$$$$.

✳ Where to Eat

DINING OUT

Monterey

🍸 ♿ **Esteban** (831-375-0176; esteban restaurant.com) Casa Munras, 700 Munras Avenue. Open daily 11:30–10. Monterey residents are smitten with this new tapas restaurant. Reminiscent of all things Spanish, this sandstone and marble décor hot spot offers 20 types of small plates, like pan-fried barramundi. Reservations recommend-ed. Lunch: $$. Dinner: $$$.

♿ 🐾 🍸 **Montrio Bistro** (831-648-8880; montrio.com) 414 Calle Principal. Open daily from 4:30–10 (11 on Friday and Saturday). While you gaze at the fabric swaying from the ceiling, the exposed brick walls, and the packed tables, enjoying chef Tony Baker's delicious appetizers, know that you have made it to Monterey's *it* destination. Crab stars on the menu, as do seasonal vegetables and lamb. Yet, you can also get a decent burger. I lean towards the small plates, so I can try a variety of tastes. Children's menu. Reservation recommended. $–$$$.

⚓ ♿ ⅋ **Old Fisherman's Grotto** (831-375-4604; oldfishermansgrotto.com) 39 Old Fisherman's Wharf #1. Open from 11 AM–10 PM daily. Their steaks and sustainable seafood dishes have lured diners to the wharf for over 50 years, though I like to come here for clam chowder with a view. You can also order chowder from the street stand and eat outside for cheaper. Reservations recommend. $$–$$$.

♿ ⚓ ⅋ **Sardine Factory** (831-373-3775; sardinefactory.com) 701 Wave Street. Open for dinner nightly. Serving up sustainable seafood a block from the bay, this is the place to dine as if you are on vacation. Order abalone, prime rib, or crab ravioli in the windowed conservatory, or head to the lounge where there is also live entertainment. Reservations recommended. $$–$$$$.

Pacific Grove

⚓ ♿ ⅋ **Fandango** (831-372-3456; fandangorestaurant.com) 223 17th Street. Open from 11:30–2:30 and 5–9 daily. A giant-timbered old barn with distressed walls, exposed stone, and white tablecloths adds to the character of this popular Italian eatery. At Sunday brunch you can dine on everything from blintzes to rack of lamb. Reservations recommended. $–$$$.

♿ **Passionfish** (831-655-3311; passionfish.net) 701 Lighthouse Avenue. Open daily for dinner at 5 PM. I can't recommend this spare, yet modern, restaurant enough. Ted and Cindy Walters have devoted their lives to ecologically sound dining by educating and serving guests their delicious, sustainable seafood. Though the menu changes daily, you could enjoy oysters with cucumber relish, or sturgeon in coconut curry and zucchini fritters. There are always vegetarian and meat items on the menu as well. Reservations highly recommended. $$–$$$.

Pebble Beach

Peppoli (831-647-7433; pebblebeach.com) Inn at Spanish Bay, 2700 17-Mile Drive. Open for dinner nightly 6 PM–10 PM. Super ritzy and catering to the indulgent golf crowd, head here if you crave Tuscan cooking with ocean views for big prices. Though the menu changes, dishes like wild boar, osso buco, and decadent desserts enchant. Reservations recommended; resort attire required. $$$$.

MONTEREY'S CANNERY RESTAURANTS BECKON DINERS TO ENTER.

Carmel

THE CENTRAL COAST AND SOUTHERN SAN JOAQUIN VALLEY

 ♿ **Bouchee Restaurant** (831-626-7880; boucheecarmel.com). Mission Street between Ocean and 7th Avenue. Open for dinner Tuesday through Sunday. If you can't afford L'Auberge and want to celebrate a special occasion, this recently remodeled candlelit bistro is worth your time. Chef David Fink serves up seasonal items that might include the organic braised short ribs, foie gras, or olive oil–poached wild salmon. Reservations recommended. $$$–$$$$.

♿ ♻ **California Market** (831-620-1234; highlandsinn.hyatt.com) Highlands Inn, CA 1. Open 7 AM–10 PM daily. I always search for a place to have sunset cocktails, overlooking the sea. I don't even really care how good the food is. However, California Market's casual setting, with stellar views, an outside patio with binoculars on your table, and mussels served in a bowl of garlic sauce, paired with some local white wine, while the whales frolic in the sea works for me. $$–$$$.

♿ ♻ **Cantinetta Luca** (831-625-6500; cantinettaluca.com) Dolores between Ocean and 7th Avenue. Open daily from 12–2:30 and 5–9:30. The youngest child of the L'Auberge family, this neighborhood Italian restaurant and bar with an all-Italian wine list evokes a casual old Italian ambiance, with modern flair. Think red and green walls, brick ceilings, candles, wood-fired pizza, and house-cured salumi. Reservations recommended. Lunch: $–$$. Dinner: $$–$$$.

♿ ❄ **Grasing's** (831-624-6562; Grasings.com) 6th Street and Mission. Open daily from 11 AM–3 PM and 5 PM–9 PM. Kurt Grasing gets a lot of press for serving up delicate coastal cuisine with local ingredients. His paella is legendary enough to bring your sweetheart, order a bottle of wine, and dine on the pet-friendly patio. To save a bit of cash, you might consider having lunch here. Or if it is a special occasion, the prix fixe menu won't break the bank. Reservations recommended. Lunch: $$–$$$$. Dinner: $$$$.

♿ **L'Auberge Carmel** (831-624-8578; laubergecarmel.com) Monte Verde at 7th. Open 6–9:30 Wednesday through Sunday. In the Central Coast, the dining room at L'Auberge is unsurpassed in class, style, and taste. I head to this 10-table restaurant for special occasions for a market fresh four-course prix fixe and wine-pairing menu worth every penny. Highlights might include foie gras–stuffed squab, Dungeness crab bisque served in a coffee press, and an ongoing supply of freshly baked olive rolls with three types of sea salt. After dinner, diners receive a signed menu from Chef Christophe Grosjean. Reservations required. No children under 18. $$$$.

♻ ♿ ♻ ☯ **Mission Ranch** (831-625-9040; missionranchcarmel.com) 26270 Dolores Street. Bar opens nightly at 4 PM; dinner served from 5 PM–9 PM; Sunday champagne brunch from 10 AM–1:30 PM. Here you'll get the kind of food you would expect from an old California dairy ranch owned by Clint Eastwood: three-mushroom pasta, prime rib sandwich, or a roasted half-chicken. The best way to enjoy this spot is to come for the live piano jazz and check out the lovely view of Carmel River and Point Lobos. Children's menu. No reservations except on special weekends. $$$.

♻ ♿ ♻ **Terrace Grill** (831-624-6476 or 800-582-8900; laplayahotel.com) Camino Real at 8th Avenue. Open from 7 AM–10 PM. There aren't many spots in Carmel to dine overlooking the sea. Enjoy Sunday brunch on the patio, or dinner of seafood *posole* or the super-rich eight-cheese macaroni and cheese delight. The bar stays open until 11:30 PM. Reservations recommended. Lunch: $–$$. Dinner: $$–$$$.

Carmel Valley

& **Marinus** (831-658-3550; bernardus .com) Bernardus Lodge, 415 Carmel Valley Road. Open from 6–10 nightly. Cal Stamenov is culinary royalty in these parts. Often referred to as a lesser-known Thomas Keller, his restaurant consistently wins awards for its wine list, delicate tastes, and local flavors. Like most great-tasting menus, chef Stamenov only serves what is fresh in local farmers' markets, so a true sampling of the menu is impossible. Since I didn't get a chance to eat here, I can only tell you that I have heard rumors about Scottish partridge and black truffle banana splits sending folks to heavenly places. Reservations required. $$$$.

& ⛾ **The Covey** (831-620-8860; quail lodge.com) Quail Lodge, 8205 Valley Greens Drive. Open from 6–9 Tuesday through Sunday. California Mediterranean food from local organic farms makes this a popular choice for tourists in Carmel Valley. The small plates shine at this gourmet destination offering Monterey Bay snapper or Sonoma duck. I like to come to the bar for happy hour and get a couple appetizers to fill up, feel fancy, but not spend my whole paycheck. Reservations recommended. $$$$.

EATING OUT

Sand City

✎ & ⛌ **Ol Factory Café** (831-394-7336; olfactorycafe.com) 1725 Contra Costa Street. Open daily at 7 AM. In an old warehouse in a quiet stretch of Sand City, find Monterey County's best coffee shop. Not only do they serve

perfect lattes, but they also have great breakfast items (huevos rancheros, oatmeal, omelets), lunch and dinner, weekly spelling bees, performance art, visual art, and the earliest happy hour on the peninsula (noon). Plus, they strive to be one of the greenest businesses in town. $.

Seaside

✎ & **Fishwife** (831-394-2027; fishwife .com) 789 Trinity Avenue. Open daily from 11 AM–9 PM, until 10 PM on weekends. People rave about this Caribbean seafood joint, calling their Baja fisherman's bowl, tilapia Cancun, and ceviche the best around. I'd rather drive to Phil's in Moss Landing. Reservations highly recommended. $$.

Monterey

✎ & **Ambrosia Indian Bistro** (831-641-0610; ambrosiaib.com) 565 Abrego Street. Open for lunch and dinner daily. Those of you familiar with Amber India in Mountain View will be happy to know that their former chef has brought the butter chicken recipe to Monterey. Chef Singh combines California concepts, a colorful outside patio, and traditional Indian cuisine. $$–$$$.

& **East Village Coffee Lounge** (831-373-5601; eastvillagecoffeelounge.com) 498 Washington Street. Open daily from at least 7 AM until late. I am always surprised to find an urban coffee shop in a beach town, complete with exposed-stone walls, art, Buddha statues, and loads of laptop-toting students. This is the best place to get organic coffee in Monterey. Plus you can sip beer, wine, or munch on organic sandwiches, bagels, and fruit during one of their poetry slams. $.

✎ ⛾ **Monterey's Fish House** (831-373-4647) 2114 Del Monte Avenue. Open for lunch and dinner. This hole-in-the-wall is a local favorite for big portions of fresh seafood, so make a reservation, or be okay with sitting at the bar, ordering oak-grilled oysters and wine, and seeing why locals hesitate to tell anyone about this casual hideaway. $$$–$$$$.

🍴 ♿ **Rosine's** (831-375-1400; rosines monterey.com) 434 Alvarado. Open for breakfast, lunch, and dinner daily. Family-friendly dining in this casual eatery is a local secret. Yes, the home-made lasagna is legendary, but the highlight is dessert: Cakes and pies on steroids, big enough for four people to share and still not finish. $–$$.

🍴 ♿ **Turtle Bay Taqueria** (831-333-1500; fishwife.com) 431 Tyler Street and (831-899-1010) 1301 Fremont Street, Seaside. Open daily at 11 AM. A colorful and cheaper alternative to their other venture, Fishwife, this taqueria serves tacos and seafood high-lighting the flavors of Mexico and Belize. Get the wild-caught salmon tacos or burritos. $.

🍴 ♿ 🍸 **Willy's Smokehouse and All American Grill** (831-372-8880; willy smoke.com) 95 Prescott Avenue. Open 11:30–10 (until 11 on weekends). This casual American BBQ spot, with cowhides framed on the wall, has a young staff slinging Texas-style por-tions of oak-smoked beef and ribs. Sit on the patio or head to the bar for a fun night of cocktails. $–$$.

Pacific Grove

"**T**" ♿ 🍴 **Central Avenue Bakery** (831-373-200; centralavenuebakery .com) 173 Central Avenue. Open daily at least 7 AM–7 PM in winter and until 10 (most nights) in summer. Catering to the vegetarian and vegan crowd, this organic bakery and café might not have the tastiest pastries, but give them some love for trying. Breakfast and lunch are decent options, with cheap (and good) egg dishes and sandwiches. Plus the cute coffeehouse vibe might be a welcome break from the touristy Cannery Row. $.

🍴 ♿ **First Awakenings** (831-372-1125; firstawakenings.net) 125 Ocean-view Boulevard. Open daily from 7 AM–2 (until 2:30 on weekends). The pancakes at this local gem are to die for. The chocolate chip sundae is also a selling point. It's located across from the Aquarium and gets very crowded on weekends. $–$$.

🍴 ♿ 🍸 **Fishwife** (831-373-7107; fish wife.com) 1996 ½ Sunset Drive. See Seaside.

🍴 ♿ **Red House Café** (831-643-1060; redhousecafe.com) 662 Lighthouse Avenue. Open Tuesday through Sun-day for lunch and dinner; breakfast on weekends. Literally a red house, this country-style kitchen serves up dependable California cuisine with European accents. Lunch relies heavily on sandwiches and salads, while dinner might get you penne pasta with seafood or a rack of lamb. $–$$

🍴 ♿ **Thai Bistro II** (831-372-8700) 159 Central Avenue. Open for lunch and dinner daily. In a little Victorian at the north end of Pacific Grove, this Thai restaurant offers what you'd expect from a southeast Asian/ Monterey beach spot: Pad Thai, panang curry, Tom Kha Kai. It's not the best Thai food you'll ever have, but it is worth a visit if you are tired of California cuisine and looking for some spice. Lunch: $. Dinner: $$.

Carmel

5th Avenue Deli (831-625-2688; 5thavenuedeli.com) 5th and San Carlos Avenue. Open Monday through Satur-day from 11 AM–4 PM and Sunday 12–3 PM. From breakfast pastries to a taco and sandwich bar with gourmet fixings, head here for cheap food in Carmel. $.

Carmel Valley Coffee Roasting Company (831-626-2913; carmel -coffee.com) Ocean Avenue. Open daily at least 7 AM–6 PM. This is my favorite place for coffee in Carmel.

Though expensive, you can guarantee that your beans are freshly roasted and their options are plentiful. They also hawk pastries.

☕ 🐾 🍸 ♿ **Forge in the Forest** (831-624-2233; forgeintheforest.com) 5th and Junipero. Open 11:30–9 (later on Friday and Saturday). Since 1944 loads of people have hit the patio with their dogs, drinking beer by the fire pit. Inside is another world: brass walls, wine-bottle cork curtains, oak bar, relics of a machine shop, and cluttered walls. Though the food won't rock your world, you can get decent items for less than most places in town—grilled steak, chocolate chip cookie dream, Reuben egg rolls, Castroville artichoke, pork loin—plus they have a low-carb menu and a *doggie* menu. Reservations recommended. $$–$$$$.

🐾 ♿ **Katy's Place** (831-624-0199; katysplacecarmel.com) Mission between 5th and 6th. Open daily from 7–2. Truck driver portions of breakfast favorites bring locals and tourists to wait in long lines on weekends. Kids stroll up to the counter to get toys, adults chat over coffee, and the waiters sprint past carrying hefty plates of omelets, Benedicts, and pancakes. Expect country-style needlepoint wall hangings, baskets of jams, and lots of early morning chaos. Cash only. $–$$.

Carmel Valley

🐾 ♿ 🍸 **Bahama Billy's Island Steakhouse** (831-626-0430; bahamabillys .com) 3690 The Barnyard. Open daily from 11:30–9 or 10. Though Billy Quan does not have a hand in running the place anymore, this island-style steak and seafood spot is still a local favorite. I could spend hours gorging on fried *pupus*, crab mango bisque, the free cheese bread, sweet potato fries with coconut and cashew, plus sweet cocktails. On nice days the fire pit on the patio is a great place to hang with

your pooch and pals, listen to reggae, and pretend you are surrounded by palm trees, instead of in a fancy strip mall. Lunch: $$, Dinner: $$–$$$.

🍸 **Café Rustica** (831-659-4444; cafe rusticacarmel.com) 10 Delfino Place. Open for lunch and dinner Tuesday through Sunday This casual restaurant and bar is so popular with locals, they won't even tell you about it when you ask for a good place to eat. You can get everything from escargot to big salads, wood-fired pizzas to beef goulash. $$–$$$.

🐾 ♿ **Earthbound Farms Organic Kitchen** (831-625-6219; ebfarms.com) 7250 Carmel Valley Road. Open daily from at least 9–6. I head over here for cheap and good organic sandwiches, pizzas, and salads. Not much of a selection for the prepared food, you can also pick up pre-made salads, hummus, fruits, and veggies for a picnic in the garden. $.

🐾 ♿ 🌸 **From Scratch** (831-625-2448) 3626 The Barnyard. Open from 8 AM–3 PM daily. Outdoor dining in this strip mall attracts people who want good country breakfasts. Authentic biscuits and gravy, *huevos rancheros*, crab cake Benedict, or for lunch you can get a decent chicken and avocado melt. $.

🐾 **Taqueria De La Valle** (831-659-1373) 19 W. Carmel Valley Road. Open Tuesday through Saturday from 11:30–2:45 and 5–8. Cheap Mexican food, endless chips and salsa, and a decent salmon quesadilla are what you get at this hole-in-the-wall with yellow chairs and brightly colored tablecloths. $.

🐾 🍸 ♿ **Wickets** (831-658-3550; bernardus.com) Bernardus Lodge, 415 Carmel Valley Road. Open from 7 AM–11 PM daily. The best place to come when the fog lingers over the sea and you are craving some sun and excellent food. Using organic, local vegetables and meats, they specialize in wood-fired pizza, Waygu beef burgers with pomme frites, and amazing focaccia. Children's menu. $$–$$$.

♂ & ⅄ **Will's Fargo Dining House and Saloon** (831-659-2774; willsfargo .com) 16 E. Carmel Valley Drive. Open daily for dinner 4:30. Chef Cal Stamenov serves up prime and choice cuts of naturally raised meats, organic vegetables, and fish in a western-style dining room. Antiques and timber-lined walls accent vegetable lasagna and steak tartare. Reservations recommended. $$–$$$.

✳ Entertainment

The best place to find out about local music and entertainment events is in the *Monterey Weekly*. You can find free copies of them everywhere. Most bars stay open until 2 AM.

Monterey

Crown and Anchor (831-649-6496; crownandanchor.net) 150 W. Franklin Street. With a great selection of beer on tap, British pub food, and a decent outdoor patio, locals and tourists get lured into this dark pub and don't often emerge until closing.

Hippodrome (831-646-9244; hipp club.com) Club Octane, 321-D Alvarado Street. Four dance floors playing everything from salsa to house brings out the young crowd.

Monterey Live (831-375-LIVE; montereylive.org) 414 Alvarado Street. Come to hear rock bands perform live.

Sly McFly's (831-649-8050) 700 Cannery Row. If you would rather have a mellow evening, this is a great place to hear live jazz and blues.

Carmel

Brophys (831-624-2476) 4th and San Carlos. Open 11:30 AM–11 PM. Locals go here for microbrews, cheap tacos,

and prime rib specials on Fridays. Here you'll find drinks, sports, and an unpretentious vibe.

Bubbly Fish (831-626-8226) Paseo San Carlos Courtyard, San Carlos between Ocean and 7th Avenue. Looking for something a little fancier? This champagne lounge offers 30 champagnes and wines by the glass, a small plate menu, and live music.

Cypress Inn (831-624-3871 or 800-443-7443; cypress-inn.com) 7th Avenue and Lincoln. In the hotel bar lobby, you can hear live jazz in the evenings. Bring your dog, they like them more than kids.

Forge in the Forest See *Eating Out*.

⅄ **Hog's Breath Inn** (831-625-1044; hogsbreathinn.com) San Carlos and 5th. Open daily 11:30 AM–3 PM and 4 PM–10 PM. This bar and grill used to be owned by Clint Eastwood and is still a popular spot. Grab a beer, plop down outside by the cobblestone fireplace, and eat a Dirty Harry cheeseburger.

Mission Ranch Restaurant See *Dining Out*.

Pacific Rep Theater Company (831-622-0100; pacrep.org). Plays in four venues, including outdoor events in the forest, shows geared toward young and old, Carmel's popular theater company is a valuable part of the community. Call for details.

Carmel Valley

Bahama Billy's See *Eating Out*.

Wickets See *Eating Out*.

✳ Selective Shopping Areas

People find plenty of shopping in Monterey. On Cannery Row, you'll likely be inundated with touristy T-shirts of the MY GRANDMA WENT TO MONTEREY AND ALL I GOT WAS THIS STINKIN T-SHIRT variety. A notable stop is the **Cannery Row Antique Mall** (831-655-0264; canneryrow antiquemall.com) 471 Wave Street. Open daily. This two-story old Carmel Cannery Building, cluttered with relics of the olden days, might be just the place to find that old record, toy, or bracelet. Downtown Monterey shopping (along Alvarado Street and Washington Street) will mostly get you clothing, music, and a few kids' boutiques, and **Book Haven** (831-333-0383; abebooks.com; 559 Tyler Street).

In Pacific Grove along Lighthouse Avenue, you'll find garden shops, clothing, kids' shops, and galleries. I like **The Works** (831-372-2242; the workspg.com; 667 Lighthouse Avenue) for books by local authors.

Stretching down Ocean Avenue and then extending out along from Junipero to Monte Verde in Carmel are loads of shops to keep you entertained. This is the best shopping area in Monterey County and will likely have you wanting way more than you can afford.

Carmel Valley's **The Barnyard** (831-624-8886; TheBarnyard.com; 3618 The Barnyard) offers 43 shops and restaurants weaving through a landscaped outdoor shopping center, including **Tee to Green**, Carmel's only golf store with a women's selection, and **Bountiful Basket** with wines, olive oils, and vinegars.

✳ Seasonal Events

February: **AT&T Pebble Beach Pro-Am Golf Tournament** (831-649-1533, attpbgolf.com) 1 Lower Ragsdale Drive Bldg. 3, Carmel.

April: **Big Sur Marathon** (831-625-6226) Hard-core runners travel from Carmel to Big Sur during one of the most beautiful treks in the United States.

May: **Festival of Winds** (marina festival.com) Kites of all sizes soar over the sand for this fun tribute to air.

June: **Monterey Bay Blues Festival** (831-394-2652; montereyblues.com) Monterey Fairgrounds.

July: **Carmel Bach Festival** (831-624-1521) During July and August you won't want to miss the celestial Bach Festival, which attracts musicians and music lovers from around the globe.

September: **Monterey Jazz Festival** (831-373-3366) This is the big guy of jazz festivals, attracting big names in many varieties of music as well as the stars of jazz and blues.

Annual Sand Castle Contest West end of Ocean Avenue, Carmel. For almost 50 years this festival has attracted the best sand artists around.

BIG SUR

✳ To See

Bixby Creek Bridge CA 1, south of Garrapata State Park. You've seen it in photographs, and will likely take some of your own of this 1932 bridge. Just make sure to pull over before snapping photos; the road can be a nail-biter.

Henry Miller Library (831-667-2574; henrymiller.org) CA 1, Big Sur. Open Tuesday through Sunday 11 AM–5 PM. If I had the money, I would have gotten married here, in the redwood and pine gardens, steps from the tribute to Henry Miller, who fell in love with Big Sur and resided here for quite some time. A visit to the library offers a tranquil destination, plus a glimpse at rare books about the region. Free.

New Camaldoli Hermitage (831-667-2456; contemplation.com) There is a small sign and wooden cross on the mountain side of CA 1, just past Lucia Lodge. You can visit this monastery for Camaldose Benedictine monks and eat some of the best brandy cakes around. This is a great place to find some solitude and if you are really inspired you can stay here—call for details.

Point Sur Light Station State Historic Park (831-625-4419; parks.ca.gov or pointsur.org) CA 1, 0.25-mile north of Point Sur Naval Facility. At the edge of a hazardous bluff, this light station was constructed in 1887 to warn incoming vessels of this often fog-covered piece of volcanic rock. You can tour the station (which is one of the only ones open to the public) or take a guided tour. Tours are by reservation (or if you are lucky and come a half hour before the tours are scheduled), and occur on weekends year-round (weather permitting), and by moonlight April through October. They take two or three hours and require a steep 1-mile hike (round-trip). $8 adults; $4 children 6–17; free for kids under 6.

✳ To Do

BIRD-WATCHING Big Sur is known for its animal visitors and birds are certainly a part of that equation. The best park to spot winged critters is **Andrew Molera State Park**, which has a bird sanctuary in the lagoon of the Big Sur River.

BOAT TOURS See Monterey—To Do.

CYCLING With 90 miles of coastline and wilderness surrounding the region, pedalers will not be at a loss for ways to explore the region by bike. To get from

Carmel to Big Sur, take the **Old Coast Road**, an 11-mile stretch with heart-stopping views, rather than the bumper to bumper CA 1. Mountain bikers will find trails within **Garrapata State Park** and **Andrew Molera State Park**. Note that mountain biking is not permitted in Wilderness Areas, otherwise, you are good to go in most parks. For detailed maps of bike trails visit fs.fed.us.

FISHING After you secure your fishing license, you are free to cast your line into the waters at **Garrapata State Park, Andrew Molera State Park, Pfeiffer Big Sur State Park, Limekiln State Park**, and the **Los Padres National Forest** areas of Nacimiento-Fergusson Road, Mill Creek, and Jade Cove Beach.

HORSEBACK RIDING Molera Horseback Tours (831-625-5486; molerahorsebacktours.com) Andrew Molera State Park. Take a tour on horseback to the beach and explore Andrew Molera State Park. Tours range from hour-long morning rides to sunset rides to three-hour redwood exploration tours. $40–70.

John Hickok
BIG SUR'S TASSAJARA CREEK.

SCENIC DRIVES To call the stretch of CA 1 between Monterey and San Simeon scenic is like calling the queen royal—*duh*. This is quite possibly the most beautiful drive in the United States. A two-lane highway weaves along dramatic bluffs, over bridges, and past the raging Pacific Ocean below. Everyone drives slowly, so be patient. It is too stunning to drive any faster. And note that there are plenty of turnoffs where you can take pictures. Please don't put yourself or other drivers in danger by slowing too much to photograph whales, the Bixby Bridge, or the waves below.

SPAS AND HOT SPRINGS Allegria Spa (831-667-4222; ventanainn.com) Ventana Inn, CA 1, Big Sur. Signature treatments include a Fusion Massage, an organic seaweed muslin wrap, and a wine wrap. For the ultimate in relaxation, try the Zen garden massage.

Esalen (831-667-3002; esalen.org) 55000 CA 1, Big Sur. Guests staying at this retreat center get the honor of lazing all day in the natural hot spring baths perched above the Pacific Ocean. If you aren't staying here, you can either book a massage (with aforementioned views), which gets you an hour in the hot springs, or head here between 1 AM–3 AM (yes, you read it correctly), to take a dip. If you choose the latter option, you must make a reservation and fork over $20. Go either at the full moon to view the ocean or at the new moon to have a stellar view of stars. Also note that nudity is common at the pools and on the living-roof massage deck. The shy readers might choose to swim elsewhere. Inquire about retreats and classes so you can stay the night ($$); especially when famous musicians like Joan Baez are performing.

Post Ranch Spa (831-667-2200; postranchinn.com) CA 1, Big Sur. This spa offers the finest in organic products for massages and facials, yoga classes, and the royal treatment. The organic garden facial and duet massage (four hands, whoopee!) send you to higher ground. Expect to pay the big bucks, but surely you'll find it worth the splurge.

Tassajara Hot Springs (415-865-1895; sfzc.org/tassajara) From CA 1 turn left at Carmel Valley Road and follow it until you reach Tassajara Road on the right. Turn onto Tassajara Road and continue until you reach Jamesburg, where you can park your car and board the stage ($45, reservations required) or continue driving into Tassajara on a very rough dirt road. From May through September you can visit the Zen Center and take a dip in the hot springs. Cash only. $25 adults; $12 children. Make a reservation for their gourmet vegetarian lunch as well.

WATER SPORTS **Big Sur Kayak Adventures** (888-5-BIGSUR) These knowledgeable guides take brave kayakers out into the rough seas of Big Sur to explore the southern reaches of the Monterey Canyon. Head out on the Andrew Molder-Point Sur Adventure to paddle one of the calmer stretches of sea—though you'll still need a helmet and a thick wetsuit—which they supply. $75.

✳ Green Spaces

STATE PARKS AND NATIONAL FORESTS **Andrew Molera State Park** (831-667-2315; parks.ca.gov) CA 1, north of Old Coast Road. Andrew Molera State Park is a must for hikers, bird-watchers, and beach lovers. Take the mile-long trail from the parking area to the bird sanctuary to search for sea otters, ducks, and grebes, then stroll the 2-mile stretch of sandy beach. There is a campground here with 24 sites available at a first-come, first-served basis. Or take a horseback riding tour through the park—see *Horseback Riding*. For the intrepid, the park has a nude beach. Day use: $6.

Garrapata State Park (831-624-4909; parks.ca.gov) CA 1, 2 miles south of Malpaso Creek. This is what Big Sur is about—granite peaks drop dramatically into the sea, whales pass below, and hiking trails through the 2,879-acre park. The **Sobersanes Canyon Trail** (6.7 miles south of Rio Road) is like a Best Of Big Sur trail. You can also hike to the waters below and play in the tide pools at low tide, or wander through the redwoods and mossy oaks.

Julia Pfeiffer Burns State Park (831-667-2315; parks.ca.gov) CA 1. To find the beach access, look for the only paved, ungated road west of CA 1 (Sycamore Canyon Road), between the post office and the State Park, drive for 2 miles. This is Big Sur's diva of a beach park: arch shaped rock formations and rugged cliffs, redwood trees, sycamores, oaks, and views. Other highlights include the **Paddington Cove** (on the east side of the highway), **Saddle Rock,** and **Waterfall Cove**. This is also where locals come to whale watch from land in winter. Camp at one of the 214 sites (800-444-7275; reserveamerica.com)—but reserve way in advance for summer ($16–25). Day use: $6.

Los Padres National Forest (831-385-5484; fs.fed.us) Ranger Office, 406 S. Mildred Avenue, King City. A guided hike at **Brazil Ranch** every Saturday by reservation, takes you deep into the forest for either the Ocean Ridge or Sierra Ridge trails (both are about 2 miles, with the latter being more strenuous). Anglers, hikers, and picnickers head to **Willow Creek** and **Mill Creek.** Campers will appreciate the handicap-accessible Carmel Valley **Arroyo Seco Campground** (49 sites; $20). The **Kirk Creek Campground** (33 sites; $22; campone.com) is located on a bluff overlooking the ocean (reservations are required in summer at recreation .gov); or if you are lucky to score one of the 8 sites at first-come, first-served **Pfeiffer Beach** or **Mill Creek Campgrounds** (free), you'll be rewarded with ocean views galore. If you really want to get away from it all, explore the **Ventana Wilderness** and **Silver Peak Wilderness** areas. For parking in the forest, you'll need to obtain an Adventure Pass from the ranger station. $5.

Palo Colorado Redwoods Palo Colorado Road, south of Garrapata State Park. This redwood canyon is best admired on a foggy day, when you can stop cursing the chilly air and appreciate why these giant trees can grow only here. Farther inland, you can find the **Bottchers Gap Campground** (campone.com; $12), which also leads you to the Ventana Wilderness. $5.

Pfeiffer Big Sur State Park (831-667-2315; parks.ca.gov) CA 1. Surrounded by redwood trees, creeks, and the stunning **Pfeiffer Falls**, this wonderful state park has been attracting visitors for over 75 years. Take the Valley View trail from Big Sur Lodge to the falls, or camp by the river (reservations required: reserveamerica .com). At press time the park was undergoing some major construction and it is slated to close through 2009. $6.

Point Sur Light Station State Park See *To See.*

BEACHES Andrew Molera State Park See *Green Spaces.*

Garrapata State Park See *Green Spaces.*

Jade Cove Off CA 1, 10 miles south of Lucia. You need to hike down a steep path to the cove, where you'll find wonderful views (especially in spring when the wildflowers are in bloom) and if you are lucky, bits of jade. Divers frequent this cove.

Kirk Creek Beach CA 1, 4 miles south of Lucia. Kirk Creek joins the ocean here, where beachcombers and campers gather to enjoy the sandy beach. For camping information see *Green Spaces.*

Pfeiffer Beach See *Julia Pfeiffer Burns State Park.*

Sand Dollar Beach CA 1, 11 miles south of Lucia. Picnickers, hang gliders, and beach strollers love this picturesque stretch of sand.

Willow Creek Beach CA 1, 14 miles south of Lucia. Anglers and picnickers frequent this rocky beach.

✳ Lodging

✐ ⚹ **Big Sur Lodge** (800-424-4787; bigsurlodge.com) Pfeiffer-Big Sur State Park, 47225 CA 1, Big Sur. Stay in a simple rustic lodge surrounded by state park land, including redwoods, oaks, and the striking craggy coast below. Staying here also affords you free access to numerous state parks in the Big Sur area. It is not the most luxurious of Big Sur accommodations, but surely one of the most family-friendly. If you bring the whole crew, consider reserving the kitchen suite to save on dining out. Amenities: 60 rooms and suites, some with kitchen and fireplace, all have decks, no TV or phones, restaurant, espresso café. $$–$$$$.

Ⓨ **Deetjen's Big Sur Inn** (831-667-2377; deetjens.com) 48865 CA 1. In the early 1930s, before Big Sur reached its stride, Helmuth Deetjen (a Norwegian native) camped in this very spot, deciding to devote his life to the beauty of Big Sur. Today, 20 cabins still retain the original ambiance of country-meets-the-sea with redwood walls, French toile, velvet-covered beds, some rooms with shared baths, some with fireplace, no TVs or phones or cell phone reception, and furniture made by Grandpa Deetjen. Most rooms view the redwood forest and creek. This is the ideal place for budget-conscious travelers. And the restaurant offers superb dinners. $–$$$; children over 12 welcome.

Esalen (831-667-3002; esalen.org) 55000 CA 1. In order to stay here, you must either register for a workshop retreat or plan your own "Personal Retreat." For the latter, call the week you intend on visiting to see if there is space in the bunkhouse or cabins, then plan whether you will engage in a massage weekend, a yoga or meditation getaway, or merely soak in the hot springs until your toes swell up. In general, weekends and holidays are full, so your best chance of scoring a spot at this heavenly destination is by coming on a Tuesday. For more information see *Spas and Hot Springs.*

✎ ⓣ **Glen Oaks** (831-667-2105; glenoaksbigsur.com) CA 1. After reading a list of nos—no pets, no TVs, no phones—you might wonder what's so special about this renovated motor inn. In the center of Big Sur (with a restau-

rant), 15 rooms offer modern design coupled with bamboo furniture and fireplace for a dash of luxury. Since you'll probably spend most of your time outdoors, you don't have to spring for a cottage room, the King rooms are fairly spacious. $$–$$$; no credit cards accepted.

♿ ⓣ **Post Ranch Inn** (831-667-2200 or 800-527-2200; postranchinn.com) CA 1. For a romantic vacation that will rate high on your Best Of list, the Post Ranch Inn is up to the task. Recently renovated, one the most luxurious inns of Northern California ascended to new heights, with 10 new rooms and an infinity pool that seems to drop off the edge of the cliff. Eco-friendly bungalows perched on literally an edge of the earth, with living roofs that make you feel like you are lodging in nature, at the Post Ranch Inn you'll be tempted to hijack the keys to the room, so you can stay just a few minutes more. They offer every amenity you might imagine—sunken whirlpool tubs, fireplaces, cloudlike beds, free yoga classes, wine tasting—plus a fine restaurant, continental breakfast, hot tub, spa, and hiking trails. Book early, the 40 rooms are sold out year-round. $$$$; no children allowed.

✎ **Ripplewood Resort** (831-667-2242; ripplewoodresort.com) CA 1. Sold out six months in advance, these very rustic 17 cabins overlooking the river and the redwoods take you back to Big Sur's simpler roots. Don't come expecting anything more than knotty-pine walls, carpet, couches that hurt your butt if you sit on them too long, plastic chairs on your private deck, a restaurant, some fireplaces or kitchens, and you won't be disappointed. $$.

✎ ♿ **Tassajara Zen Center** (415-865-1895; sfzc.org/tassajara) From CA 1 turn left at Carmel Valley Road and follow it until you reach Tassajara Road on the right. Turn onto Tassajara Road to Jamesburg, where you can park your car and board the stage ($45—reservations required) or continue driving into Tassajara on a very rough dirt road. If staying in the middle of the forest, surrounded by gardens and tranquil hot springs, in oil lamp-lit cabins with no water or showers—while butterflies flutter past and Zen students prepare organic vegetarian cuisine for your stay—sounds like a small piece of heaven, get your car tuned up. From May through September stay in a redwood cabin, dorm, room, or yurt with light-filled simplicity, wood floors, a bed, access to hot springs, and three vegetarian meals. You can meditate with the Zen students or on nature as you explore the surrounding wilderness and allow yourself to slowly ease into nirvana. $$–$$$.

✄ ♿ 🐾 ⊕ **Treebones** (877-4-BIG-SUR; treebonesresort.com) 71895 CA 1, Gorda Springs. You won't believe what plush accommodations this eco-friendly resort creates out of 16 yurts. Once a fad of hippies and renegades, here you'll find that sleeping under the canvas in a comfy bed, overlooking the sea, with a symphony of nature lulling you to dreamland is the perfect recipe for relaxation. As long as you are okay not having a toilet in your room, you'll be just fine. If you are going to spring for a night here, go for the ocean view yurts with fireplaces. They also have a guest house (with a restroom), pet-friendly campsites, casual home-cooked dinners (fee), waffle breakfasts, and board games. $ (campsites); $$–$$$; children over 6 welcome.

♿ ♈ ⁙ ⊕ **Ventana Inn and Spa** (831-667-0573; ventanainn.com) CA 1. This 243-acre inn and spa inspires romance without asking you to check your desire for simplicity at the door. Unlike most resorts of this caliber, the

60 Ventana Inn rooms are inspired by nature, with wood-walled accents, a fireplace (in most rooms), high cathedral ceilings, and earth-toned décor. Don't expect the uber-mod look here—rather, soft touches like throw blankets and rocking chairs with ocean views, continental breakfast, spa, Cielo restaurant, yoga classes, guided hikes, and private spa on the deck, or fireplace (some rooms). The inn also has a renovated campground ($). No children allowed. $$$$.

CAMPING In addition to the campgrounds listed under *Green Spaces,* see also **Ventana Inn and Spa** and **Treebones Resort.**

✳ Where To Eat
DINING OUT ♈ **Cielo** (831-667-2331; ventanainn.com/dining) CA 1. After a structural fire in the summer of 2008, Cielo closed. As of this writing, hopes were for the restaurant to reopen to non-hotel guests in April of 2009. When it does you'll be in for a treat—the most divine views (both indoor and *alfresco*), coupled with organic seasonal cuisine that will surely delight.

✄ ♿ ♈ **Nepenthe Restaurant** (831-667-2345; nepenthebigsur.com) CA 1. Open 11:30 AM–10 PM daily. Many of you will pine for the ideal place for a glass of wine and good food. Though Nepenthe delivers on both regards, offering the best location in the Central Coast and decent food, expect to fork over your paycheck for the honor. Here you'll find burgers, steaks, and salads. I prefer to head indoors to the cheaper Café Kevah (which has the same view) for breakfast and lunch. Reservations recommended. $$–$$$$.

♿ ♈ **Sierra Mar** (831-667-2200 or 800-527-2200; postranchinn.com) CA 1, Big Sur. Open for lunch and dinner daily. For your anniversary or birthday dinner kick it up a notch and visit Sierra Mar, which offers fine California cuisine, perched over the sea. Go big and get the prix fixe menu, where chef Craig von Foerster shines with specialties like an ahi tuna tasting, roast rabbit, or apple beignets with apple sorbet. Reservations requested for lunch and dinner; or come for appetizers and drinks on the patio at sunset. $$$$.

EATING OUT ✎ & **Big Sur Bakery and Restaurant** (831-667-0520; bigsurbakery.com) 47540 CA 1. Open daily at 8 AM for breakfast and lunch; for dinner on Tuesday through Saturday. Using a wood-fired oven, this bakery/restaurant heats up some wonderful food—including hearth-baked breads and pastries, pizza, braised rabbit, or California yellowtail. Reserve a table for dinner in this stone-columned one-of-a-kind local favorite. $–$$$.

✎ & **Big Sur Roadhouse** (831-667-2264; bigsurroadhouse.com) CA 1.

Open for dinner 5:30–9 Wednesday through Monday. Somehow Marcus and Heather Foster have created a down-to-earth eatery that also delivers fine Cal-Latin cuisine that will delight food snobs. I am a fan of the enchiladas, or the sweet bell pepper risotto cake. There is a children's menu and outdoor dining as well. Make sure to check out the copper bar. Reservations recommended on weekends. $$.

Café Kevah See *Nepenthe Restaurant—Dining Out.*

Deetjens Restaurant See *Lodging.*

Tassajara Zen Center See *Lodging.*

✳ Entertainment

Though nightlife is scarce in Big Sur, it's not hard to find the occasional live music program. Check with local businesses and at Esalen Institute for information about happenings and events.

✳ Seasonal Events

See Big Sur Marathon—Carmel.

SALINAS AND VICINITY

✳ To See and Do

Aquablue Skin and Body Spa (831-422-2500; aquabluespa.com) 229 Main Street, Salinas. People travel from all over the Central Coast to come to this new spa for facials and massage treatments.

✏ & **Gilroy Garden Family Theme Park** (408-840-7100; gilroygardens.org) 3050 CA 152, Gilroy. Open May through November, call for hours. Situated between Salinas and San Jose, once deemed Bonfante Gardens, this nonprofit now has a new name, a new manager (Paramount Theme Parks), plus new rides and water park attractions. Bring the kids to explore the gardens, complete with butterflies, a train, and an antique car. $32.00–42.99; online specials cut the entrance fee almost in half.

Guglielmo Winery (408-779-2145; guglielmowinery.com) 1480 E. Main Street, Morgan Hill. Come taste wine at this 82-year old winery and tasting room, then gather some gourmet foods and have a picnic outside. Free.

Mission San Antonio de Padua (831-385-4478; missionsanantonio.net) Jolon Road, through the entrance to Fort Hunter Liggett (you need a current driver's license, vehicle registration, and insurance card to enter the gate). On July 14,

MISSION SAN ANTONIO.

John Hickok

1771, Father Junípero Serra founded the third mission of his career. From then until the 1880s construction continued, making this adobe structure into a great representation of early Spanish-style architecture. Donation of $5 recommended for a tour.

Mission San Juan Bautista (831-623-4528; oldmissionsjb.org) 406 2nd Street, San Juan Bautista. Founded in 1797, this was the 15th of the 21 missions on Father Serra's mission. Of all the missions around Northern California, this, completed in 1817, is one of the finest. The museum, garden, and main altar are lovely spaces to tour, while attending a live performance (see *Entertainment*) borders on celestial. Donations accepted.

National Steinbeck Center Museum (831-775-4721; steinbeck.org) 1 Main Street, Salinas. Open 10 AM–5 PM daily. The main attraction in the agricultural town of Salinas deserves a visit. Located in historic downtown Salinas (grab a self-guided walking tour map while you are here), you can learn about John Steinbeck's life, see his truck, or lunch in the **Steinbeck House**. A rotating collection of art both depicting themes in Steinbeck's work and that of local interest are equally interesting. Come on Saturdays and make sure to visit the **Oldtown Farmers' Market** outside. $10.95 adults; $5.95–7.95 children.

Pessagno Winery (831-675-WINE; pessagnowines.com) 1645 River Road, Salinas. Taste Pinot Noir and snag a bottle at a super low price. Free tastings.

✿ **Vision Quest Safari** (831-455-19011 visonquestsafari.com) 400 River Road, Salinas. Tours at 1 PM daily. Come visit wild animals used in film and TV: Everything from elephants to tigers, and you even get to meet some of them up close. They also have a couple B&B rooms, where the elephants deliver your breakfast to your door ($$–$$$).$10 adults; $8 kids.

✳ Green Spaces

Anderson Lake County Park (408-774-3634; sccgov.org) 19245 Malaguerra Avenue, Morgan Hill. The 3,144-acre Anderson Park allows access to the Coyote Creek Parkway trails, the **Jackson Ranch** historic park site, the Moses L. Rosendin Park, the reservoir, and the Burnett Park area. This is a magnet for powerboat enthusiasts, bicyclists, equestrians, picnickers, and nature lovers. Minimal fee.

Fremont Peak State Park (831-623-4255; parks.ca.gov) Off CA 156, 11 miles south of San Juan Bautista on San Juan Canyon Road. Aside from offering lovely (and relatively mellow hiking through the mountains and forests east of Big Sur) here you can visit the observatory and view the planets after dark. The 1-mile Fremont Peak trail offers a hint at the uniqueness of this park, with views of the valley on one side and Monterey Bay on the other. There are a number of campsites ($11–15; reserveamerica.com). Day Use: $6.

Henry Coe State Park (408-779-2728; coepark.org or parks.ca.gov) 9000 East Dunne Avenue, Morgan Hill. The largest Northern California State Park was once the home to the Ohlone Indians. Today you'll find 87,000 acres of rugged terrain to explore. Start at the visitor center to get trail maps ideal for bikers or hikers, then head out to fish in the streams and creeks, or wander the 250 miles of trails. Recommended trails include the Monument, Middle Range, and Fish Trails, which offer views of the hills and in spring, a wealth of wildflowers. Day use: $5; camping: $3 (backcountry) to $12.

John Hickok

PINNACLES NATIONAL MONUMENT.

Pinnacles National Monument (831-389-4485; nps.gov/pinn) 5000 CA 146, Pinnacles. Discover 26,000 acres packed with 30 miles of trails that pass stone spires and crags, the collapse of an ancient volcano, and extensive displays of wildflowers in spring. You can rock climb, explore the Talus caves (Bear Gulch Cave and Balconies Cave both require flashlights and closed-toed shoes), and search for condors. In summer it gets too hot to do much of anything but fan yourself and pray for rain (which never arrives). Before coming, do some research about the current artist in residence—often they show their work that has been inspired by the monument. Popular hikes start from the Pinnacles Campground, Bear Gulch, Old Pinnacles Trailhead, or the western Chaparral entrance. **The Pinnacles Campground** offers 99 tent sites ($23) and 36 RV sites ($36), a general store, and a pool (831-389-4462; pinncamp.com or recreation.gov). Day use: $3–5.

Toro County Park (888-588-CAMP) CA 68 between Salinas and Monterey. Hiking trails and picnic areas draw locals out on warm weekends. Wander the open spaces, past oaks and up on hillsides in this 4700-acre space, to be greeted by views of the rolling hills. Free.

✳ Lodging

 ♧ ⊘ **The Inn at the Pinnacles** (831-678-2400; innatthepinnacles.com) 32025 Stonewall Canyon Road, Soledad. More like staying at an aunt's country home than a B&B, this six-suite inn might be overpriced, but it is the best you'll find along US 101. Large suites boast amenities like clawfoot tubs, antique furniture, breakfast,

wine tasting, and the kind of space you only find away from the city. $$$.

Vision Quest Safari See *To See and Do.*

✳ Where to Eat

♪ ♧ **First Awakenings** (831-784-1125; firstawakenings.net) 171 Main

Street, Salinas. Open for breakfast and lunch daily. Blue germ pancakes, wheat germ pancakes, huevos rancheros, crepes . . . whatever you get here is worth the wait. Note that these are some big portions, so splitting a plate is the way to go. $–$$.

♂ ও **Gino's Fine Italian Food** (831-422-1814) 1410 Main Street, Salinas. Open Monday through Friday 11 AM–3 PM and 5 PM–9 PM (until 10 on Friday) and Saturday from 4 PM–10 PM. For 30 years the Bozzo family has prided itself in serving up the finest traditional Italian food in Monterey County. Colorful murals, a friendly staff, and the freshest local produce (with Gilroy garlic being the star), this is the spot to taste Salinas agriculture, Monterey County wine, good cannelloni, and fettuccine. Reservations recommended. $$–$$$.

♂ ও ♈ **Hullaballoo** (831-757-3663; hullaballoorestaurant.com) 228 Main Street, Salinas. Open 11:30 AM–9 PM Monday through Thursday; 11:30 AM–10 PM Friday; 4 PM–10 PM Saturday and 4 PM–9 PM Sunday. One of the better places to eat in Salinas, this colorful restaurant claims to serve "bold American cooking" the likes of artichoke and garlic fondue. Spinach salad, burgers, a 12-hour brisket, fried chicken, and meatloaf are popular choices. The three-course dinner for $16 is a worthy option, as are the $10 lunch specials. $$–$$$.

✳ Entertainment

El Teatro Campesino (831-623-2444; elteatrocampesino.com) 705 4th

Street, San Juan Bautista. Come see live theater performed in the historic Mission in both Spanish and English.

♈ **Penny Farthing Tavern** (831-424-5652) 9 E. San Luis Street, Salinas. If you give your drivers license to the bartender you can enter the drinking contest. This is where locals come to shoot darts, sip good beer, and stumble home.

✳ Selective Shopping

The small towns along US 101 offer antique shopping, including the downtown **Morgan Hill**. For more mainstream shopping, head to the **Gilroy Outlets** (681 Leavesley Road, Gilroy) for cheap deals on last year's styles.

✳ Seasonal Events

Ongoing: **First Friday Artwalk** (831-758-9126; artistasunidos.org) 100-300 block of S. Main Street, Salinas. See art and hear music in historic old town Salinas.

July: **Gilroy Garlic Festival** (408-846-6886; gilroygarlicfestival.com) 7050 Miller Avenue, Gilroy. The biggest thing to hit Gilroy, well, since garlic. This self-proclaimed garlic capital of the world celebrates that potent veggie with the biggest festival in the area. Music, food, games, and garlic ice cream attract so many people, traffic is at a standstill. Go early.

September: **California International Airshow** (salinasairshow.com) Salinas Municipal Airport. If watching daredevils defy gravity is your thing, you don't want to miss this annual air show.

Wine Country

SONOMA VALLEY, RUSSIAN RIVER
VALLEY, SONOMA COAST

NAPA COUNTY

INLAND MENDOCINO AND
LAKE COUNTIES

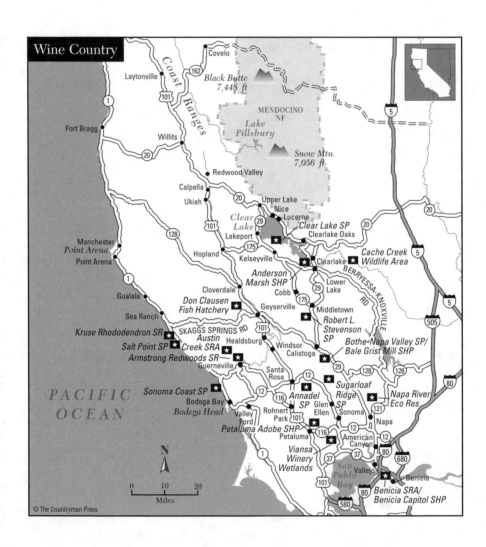

Wine Country

Covelo
Laytonville
162
Black Butte
7,448 ft
MENDOCINO
NF
Lake
Pillsbury
Snow Mtn.
7,056 ft

Coast Ranges

Fort Bragg
1
101
Willits
20
Redwood Valley
Calpella
Ukiah
20
Upper Lake
Nice
Lucerne
Clear Lake
29
Clear Lake SP
Lakeport
Clearlake Oaks
20
175
Kelseyville
Clearlake
Cache Creek
Wildlife Area
5
Manchester
Point Arena
Point Arena
128
Hopland
Anderson
Marsh SHP
Cloverdale
Cobb
Lower
Lake
BERRYESSA-KNOXVILLE RD
Gualala
Don Clausen
Fish Hatchery
Geyserville
175
29
Middletown
505
Sea Ranch
SKAGGS SPRINGS RD
101
Robert L.
Stevenson
SP
5
Kruse Rhododendron SR
Austin
Creek SRA
Healdsburg
Windsor
Calistoga
Bothe-Napa Valley SP/
Bale Grist Mill SHP
Salt Point SP
Armstrong Redwoods SR
Guerneville
Santa
Rosa
12
29
128
128
80
PACIFIC
OCEAN
Sonoma Coast SP
Bodega Bay
Bodega Head
12
116
Annadel
SP
Glen
Ellen
Sugarloaf
Ridge
SP
Sonoma
Napa River
Eco Res
121
Napa
Valley
Ford
Rohnert
Park
101
Petaluma Adobe SHP
Petaluma
116
American
Canyon
12
80
680
N
Viansa
Winery
Wetlands
37
37
San
Pablo
Bay
Vallejo
Benicia
0   10   20
Miles
101
580
80
Benicia SRA/
Benicia Capitol SHP

© The Countryman Press

5

SONOMA VALLEY, RUSSIAN RIVER VALLEY, SONOMA COAST

SONOMA VALLEY

Often treated like Napa's undesirable hippie cousin placed at the kids' table for Thanksgiving, Sonoma Valley often gets shunned by Wine Country visitors. Like a fine aged wine, this area has grown on folks since its inception. Over time this plentiful land has been ruled by the English, Miwok Indians, Russians, Spanish, Mexicans, gold rush pioneers, Bear Flag land thieves, and now the mighty grape and dollar. Today, with everything from rugged beaches to world-class wineries, rafting adventures to Northern California's top restaurants, Sonoma County is definitely worth getting to know.

The 17-mile Sonoma Valley usually begins with a visit to **Sonoma** town. Built around a central plaza, this Spanish-style hamlet welcomes a rush of tourists year-round, who delight in the excellent restaurants next to the mission, tasting rooms where you can take your wine outside to drink in the park, galleries, and inns. Heading up CA 12 you arrive in **Glen Ellen** and **Kenwood**, both rich with wineries, restaurants, romantic inns, and some of the best hiking in Wine Country. To the west on US 101, are the over a century-old farming towns of **Petaluma** and

DOWNTOWN SONOMA'S HISTORIC SQUARE.

Sebastopol: Both boast picturesque downtowns, with parks, tasting rooms, and plenty of families gathering outside in the evenings.

In the heart of Sonoma County is **Santa Rosa**, a sprawling community that feels closer to a suburb than wine country's biggest city. Though there are plenty of historic buildings, museums, great restaurants, a tribute to one-time local resident Charles M Schultz, and even some terrific hiking spots, Santa Rosa hasn't yet arrived at the level of sophistication of her sister cities, but there is hope.

Healdsburg used to be the town that kids wanted to escape the second they turned 18. About 10 years ago, developers moved in and started building high-end restaurants and tasting rooms, hotels, and galleries around the main square. Now that hordes of tourists congregate in town, battling for space with the retirees who live here, real estate has gone way up. Straddling the Russian River, Healdsburg makes a perfect destination for people (including families) who want to explore the **Alexander, Russian River,** and **Dry Creek** valleys, **Geyserville, Cloverdale,** and the newly developed **Windsor Green** town square in **Windsor**.

Heading west along the Russian River, summers make the resort communities of **Forestville, Occidental, Guerneville, Monte Rio,** and **Duncan's Mills**, which are primarily gay- and family-friendly, the place to be. Home to plenty of bearded ladies, couples who want to hide out in the redwoods, and a very elite Republican men's club, this region brings surprises at every turn.

When the unbearable summer heat gets the best of the Sonoma Valley, locals head to the coast to cool off and explore the rolling hills, redwood groves, sharp cliffs, giant rocks, brush, estuaries, and foggy coastline. **Bodega Bay** is the main "town" around here, though it is not much more than a few inns, overpriced restaurants, shops, and an amazing coastline. Up the coast, **Jenner** and the affluent community of **Sea Ranch** are even smaller, but both allow visitors the allure of privacy not found in many places along the Northern California coastline.

GUIDANCE **Sonoma County Chamber of Commerce** (707-996-1033; sonoma chamber.com) 651-A Broadway, Sonoma.

Russian River Chamber of Commerce (707-869-9000; russianriver.com) 16209 1st Street (at the Historical Bridge), Guerneville.

HELPFUL WEB SITES
bodegabay.com
visitsantarosa.com
visitpetaluma.com
sebastopol.org
pressdemocrat.com
wineroad.com
sonomawinegrape.org
sonomawine.com

GETTING THERE *By air:* **Charles M. Schultz Sonoma Co. Airport** (sonomacountyairport.com) Located 6 miles northwest of Santa Rosa off US 101. This airport welcomes incoming

RELAX ON THE RUSSIAN RIVER.

flights from Los Angeles, Las Vegas, Portland, and Seattle.

By car: US 101 runs through Sonoma County. From US 101, to get to the town of Sonoma, take CA 12 east and follow the signs. If you are headed to the coast, you can take CA 12 west to the coast. For the Russian River Valley and Jenner by the Sea, take CA 116.

By bus: **Greyhound** (greyhound.com) 435 Santa Rosa Avenue, Santa Rosa. From the bus station use the **Sonoma County Transit** (sctransit.com) bus to get to neighboring towns.

Getting Around

By bus: Visit **Sonoma County Transit** (sctransit.com) for schedules.

By bike: A popular sport in Sonoma County is to cycle to wineries—that way you can drink a little more and get to soak up the lines of vineyards along the way. See *To Do* for bike rental information.

By car: Please do not ever drink and drive. Cops are out in full force in Wine Country. For the most part, getting around Sonoma County is easy, signs are plentiful, and most roads are two-lane highways with minimal stoplights. It is wise to know that distances between towns are deceiving. Even though Santa Rosa and Sonoma are only about 20 miles apart, when you get within spitting distance of Santa Rosa, you'll hit traffic. To drive the 40 miles between Sonoma and Bodega Bay, expect to be in the car for over an hour.

MUSTS FOR FIRST-TIME VISITORS
1. Raft the Russian River.
2. Walk along a Bodega Bay Beach.
3. Ride a bike through the Alexander Valley.
4. Taste wines in the Healdsburg Square.
5. Dine at Cyrus.
6. Visit Cornerstone.
7. Take a safari at Safari West.
8. Hike Sugarloaf.
9. Taste cheese at Cowgirl Creamery.
10. Shop in downtown Sonoma.

MUSTS FOR REPEAT VISITORS
1. Take a balloon ride over the valley.
2. Taste wine at Locals.
3. Soak in Osmosis Enzyme Baths.
4. Water-ski Lake Sonoma.
5. Swim in the Russian River.
6. Attend a movie night at a winery.
7. Visit a Healdsburg Farmers' Market.
8. Attend a Harvest festival.
9. Lunch at girl and the fig.
10. Ride horses through the redwoods.

MEDICAL EMERGENCIES **Palm Drive Hospital** (707-823-8511) 501 Petaluma Avenue, Sebastopol. **Santa Rosa Memorial Hospital** (707-546-3210 or 707-525-5300) 1165 Montgomery Drive, Santa Rosa.

SONOMA VALLEY

✳ To See

Petaluma

Petaluma Adobe State Historic Park (707-762-4871; petalumaadobe.com) 3325 Adobe Road, Petaluma. Open daily from 10 AM–5 PM. This redwood and adobe brick house served as the center of General Mariano Guadalupe Vallejo's 66,000-

UNWIND ON THE SONOMA COAST.

acre (100 square miles) working ranch between 1836 and 1846. $3; good for admission into the Sonoma State Historic Park as well.

Petaluma Historical Library and Museum (707-778-4398; petalumamuseum .com) 20 4th Street, Petaluma. Open Thursday through Saturday 1–4 and Sunday 12–3. The former library now houses Petaluma poultry, dairy, and Miwok Indian history exhibits from the 1850s. Built in 1904, the library itself is a work of art. They also lead historic tours through Petaluma. Free.

THE SMALL TOWN OF PETALUMA FEELS LIKE A CROSS BETWEEN *MAYBERRY* AND *HAIR*.

Sonoma

🛈 ⊕ **Cornerstone** (707-933.3010; cornerstonegardens.com) 23570 CA 121, Sonoma. Open daily from 10 AM–5 PM. Art lovers, families, gallery shoppers, and wine drinkers head to these creative gardens to view an unexpected local treasure. The students of various landscape architecture schools have created exceptional gardens. Lunch in the café on the property, shop, or sip wine at the one of four tasting rooms. Free.

🛈 **Depot Park Historical Museum**: (707-938-1762; vom.com/depot) 270 First Street. Open 1–4:30 Wednesday through Sunday. On June 14, 1846, a group of Americans rode into Sonoma, captured General Mariano Vallejo, raised the Bear Flag, and proclaimed California a free republic. The Bear Flag Revolt was achieved peacefully, but the republic lasted only 25 days, until a U.S. Navy officer, a grandson of Paul Revere, rode into town and replaced them with American rule. See exhibits marking the history of the revolt, the Miwok Indians, as well as a railroad caboose. Free.

🖉 Sonoma Train Town Railroad (707-938-3912; traintown.com) 20264 Broadway, Sonoma. Open 10 AM–5 PM daily in summer and Friday through Monday the rest of the year. Parents, take the kids for a train ride, then explore the collection of locomotives. The little ones can be entertained for hours. Train rides: $4.25.

Sonoma Valley Museum of Art (707-939-7862; svma.org) 551 Broadway, Sonoma. Open Wednesday through Sunday 11 AM–5 PM. When you get tired of wine, this museum makes an interesting pit stop. This sophisticated museum showcases art from Sonoma County as well as around the world. $5; $8 families; Sunday free.

SONOMA'S CORNERSTONE GARDENS.

Santa Rosa and Vicinity

🖉 Charles Schultz Museum (707-579-4452; schulzmuseum.org) 2301 Hardies Lane, Santa Rosa. If you ever liked Snoopy and Charlie Brown, you must stop at this wonderful museum to pay tribute. You'll see Shultz's studio, a re-creation of Snoopy's house, plus rotating cartoon exhibits. Adults $8, Youth and Seniors $5

Luther Burbank Home and Gardens (707-524-5445; lutherburbank.org) Santa Rosa Avenue at Sonoma Avenue, Santa Rosa. Open Tuesday through Sunday 10 AM–4 PM. Luther Burbank is honored all over the county, but nowhere as well as this lovely garden complex. Docents lead tours every half hour, teaching about the man who brought even more flora to the area. Free.

Sonoma County Museum (707-579-1500; sonomacountymuseum.org) 425 7th Street, Santa Rosa. Open Tuesday through Sunday 11 AM–5 PM. With over 25,000 artifacts, including a great collection of contemporary art, this museum sets out to bring *haute couture* to the wine country. $5.

✳ To Do

CYCLING Winery hopping by bike is a favorite activity in Sonoma County. Every town has bike shops with rentals, but by far the most popular place to start off from is Healdsburg. Popular routes include **Dry Creek Valley**, **Alexander Valley**, **Russian River Valley**, and **Valley of the Moon**. Get a map from the bike shops listed below.

SONOMA STATE HISTORIC PARK

(707-939-9420; parks.sonoma.net) Downtown Sonoma. A number of Mexican-era buildings line old town Sonoma. Visit them and imagine what the town was like when generals, Indians, and revolutionaries fought for this fruitful land. I have included only the highlights of this park. $2 adults and $1 kids allow you to view all the buildings as well as the Petaluma State Historic Park (see above).

Mission San Francisco Solano 363 3rd Street West. In 1840 to 1841 the present chapel was constructed and furnished by General Vallejo in order to provide Sonoma with a parish church. After 1881 the chapel and its adjoining residence building were sold and used as a hay barn, winery, and blacksmith shop. The buildings became a state monument in 1903.

THE SONOMA MISSION.

Sonoma Barracks 363 3rd Street W. The two-story adobe barracks facing Sonoma's central plaza was built to house Mexican army troops under the command of General Vallejo. In the years after 1835, more than 100 military expeditions set out from Sonoma with the objective of subduing the Wappos, Cainameros, or Satisyomis Indians (who more than once rose up and attempted to throw off Mexican domination of their homeland). The barracks later housed a number of Bear Flag followers until July 9, 1846, when the Stars and Stripes were first raised at Sonoma. Thereafter the barracks were used by various U.S. military forces. In 1860 Vallejo remodeled the building to serve as a winery. In later years under other owners it was used as a store, law office, and private residence.

Lachryma Montis (800-777-0369 or 916-653-6995; parks.ca.gov) W. Spain and 3rd Street, Sonoma. Open daily from 10–5. View General Vallejo's 20-acre estate. The Latin name means "Tears of the Mountain" after the abundant springs near the house. You can tour the museum and the grounds.

Spoke Folk Cyclery (707-433-7171; spokefolk.com) 201 Center Street, Healdsburg. They rent advanced touring bikes (including helmet, lock, and an area map) for $10–15 per hour ($30–50 per day), tandems, or kid trailers.

Wine Country Bikes Touring Center (866-922-4537; winecountrybikes.com) 61 Front Street, Healdsburg. Tour the Russian River and Dry Creek valleys with these guys and they give you coupons for taxi service to get to your bike. Rentals $33–95 per day; or tour with local guide $129.

BALLOONING *✄* **Up and Away Ballooning** (800-711-2998; up-away.com) There's a lot of competition for balloon rides up here, so in addition to the traditional champagne brunch trip most outfits offer, these guys throw in chocolate-dipped strawberries. Adults: $245; Teens: $215; Children 6–12: $205.

FARM TOURS Nothing says Sonoma County more than farms. Here you can pick your own produce, play with goats, and of course taste some of the world's best wines. Below is a list of some special farms you can visit. For a comprehensive list of all farms in the area, pick up the informative (and free) "Farm Trails" (farm trails.org) brochure from the Sonoma Valley Visitor Center. You can find wineries listed under *Wine Tasting*.

✄ **Bear Foot Honey Farms** (707-570-2899; bearfoothoney.com) 2971 Guerneville Road, Santa Rosa. Open Monday through Saturday 10 AM–6 PM. Tour this honey farm, learn about beekeeping, and hopefully rid yourself of any aversion you have to honeybees.

✄ **Barlas Boer Goats** (707-762-4476; barlasboergoats.com) 555 Bailey Avenue, Petaluma. Call for appointment. Kids will love meeting and learning about goats here at this sustainable farm.

✄ **Cowgirl Creamery Tasting Room** (866-433-7834; cowgirlcreamery.com) 419 1st Street, Petaluma. I know someone who has his triple-cream Brie shipped to him in Palm Desert. It's that addictive. The new tasting facility offers tours for $30. Reservations required.

✄ **Field of Greens** (707-939-3648; myfieldofgreens.com) 1777 W. Watmaugh Road, Sonoma. Open Tuesday through Friday 2–5, Saturday and Sunday 12–4. These guys have it all: hayrides, pumpkin patch, carriage rides, pick your own produce, sustainable farming practices, and animal viewing.

Full House Farm (707-829-1561; fullhousefarm.com) 1000 Sexton Street, Sebastopol. Call for appoint-

BIKE PAST FIELDS OF GRAPES.

SAFARI WEST

(707-579-2551 or 800-616-2695; safariwest.com) 3115 Porter Creek Road, Santa Rosa. Advanced reservations required. If you have ever flirted with taking a safari in Africa, but can't afford it, Nancy and Peter Lang have created the ideal "staycation" in an unexpected location. Day-trippers can head out in a safari vehicle to view the dozen giraffes, zebras, rhinos, and hundreds more. You can also book a private safari or take the Behind the Scenes tour—you get to feed the giraffes! But the best way to experience this wonderful African camp is to stay overnight. Tent cabins are more luxurious than most B&Bs in the state, with heat, plush beds, and views of the giraffes in the morning. Plus you get to hear the animals all night (which isn't as annoying as it sounds), eat a fine camp style breakfast and dinner, then sit around a campfire telling ghost stories, singing songs, and roasting S'mores. Lodging: $$$. Safari: $65 adults; kids are half price.

ment. Here you can learn about farm life, stay in Christine Cole's vacation rental (see *Lodging*), or participate in her interesting Harmony With Horses workshop.

Hallberg Butterfly Gardens (707-823-3420; hallbergbutterflygardens.org) 8687 Oak Grove Road, Sebastopol. Open by appointment April through October from 10 AM–4 PM on Wednesday through Sunday, This butterfly and wildlife sanctuary give the word *peaceful* another meaning.

✿ **Love Farms** (707-433-1230; lovefarms.com) 15069 Grove Street, Healdsburg. Open March through November daily from 10 AM–6 PM. Certified organic flowers, herbs and produce is one reason to visit. Excellent U-pick strawberries is the other. Tour free with purchase.

Luther Burbank's Gold Ridge Farm (707-829-6711; wschs-grf.pon.net) 7781 Bodega Avenue, Sebastopol. Open year-round, call for appointments. Docents lead tours around Luther Burbank's original Sonoma garden.

McEvoy Ranch (707-778-2307; mcevoyranch.com) 5935 Red Hill Road, Petaluma. Tours by appointment only. This ranch grows olives that they press into some of the best olive oil in Northern California. $25.

Nana Mae's Organics (707-829-7359; nanamae.com) 708 Gravenstein Highway North, Sebastopol. Call for appointment from July through December. Warning: Their applesauce is addictive—I warn you now—it's the only kind my son will eat.

Olive Press (707-939-8900; theolivepress.com) Jacuzzi Winery, 24724 CA 121, Sonoma. Open daily from 10 AM–5:30 PM. Though it is not exactly a farm, if you are interested in learning about olive oil, pay these guys a visit. Many of the local wineries also grow olives and this mill presses these olives into some of the best oil in the country. You'd never know olive oil could taste so good. And it's all organic! Free.

FARMERS' MARKETS Healdsburg Markets On the plaza, Healdsburg. There are two markets in summer. The first is Saturday 9–12 and the second is Tuesday 4–6:30.

Santa Rosa Farmers' Markets Veteran's Building (east parking lot) Wednesday and Saturday 8:30–noon, year-round. In summer, there is another market at B Street and Santa Rosa Plaza downtown, from 5–8:30 on Wednesday.

Sebastopol Downtown Plaza. April through November, Sunday 10 AM–1:30 PM.

Sonoma Plaza On Friday from 9–12 and from April through October on Tuesday from 5:30–8:30.

GOLF **Oakmont Golf Club** (707-539-0415; oakmontgc.com) 7025 Oakmont Drive, Santa Rosa. With the east course and west course, you can play 36 holes of golf in the Valley of the Moon. $30–65.

Tayman Park Municipal Golf Course (707-433-4275; taymanparkgolfcourse .com) 927 S. Fitch Mountain Road, Healdsburg. This 18-hole course is a popular place for local weddings, and good wine. $15–25.

HORSEBACK RIDING **Triple Creek Horse Outfit** (707-887-8700; triplecreek horseoutfit.com) Sonoma and Napa County. If you like horses and want to explore Bothe-Napa Valley Park, Jack London Park, or Sugarloaf Park by horse instead of foot, give these guys a call. All riders must be over eight years old and weigh less than 220 pounds. Wear closed-toed shoes and long pants. $60–80.

SPAS **Health Spa Healdsburg** (707-433-9990; healthspahealdsburg,com) 530 Healdsburg Avenue, Healdsburg. Open 9–9 daily. This new spa and garden is a welcome addition to the Healdsburg area. I had an amazing water-flow massage here, but my husband says their stone massages are just as nice.

Kenwood Spa (707-833-1293; kenwoodinn.com) 10400 Sonoma Highway, Kenwood. Life doesn't often get as good as this: Lazing in a wine barrel bath at the top of a tower, overlooking vineyards that seem to spread for miles below. Kenwood Spa specializes in Arcona vinotherapy, so suck it up and at least have the wine barrel bath. Many people just come here for the day to relax by the pool, drink wine, and eat fantastic healthy food. $35 day use fee.

Osmosis Enzyme Bath See *Russian River Valley*.

WATER SPORTS **Rivers Edge Kayak and Canoe** (707-433- 7247; riversedgekayakandcanoe.com) 13840 Healdsburg Avenue, Healdsburg. All trips offer beautiful and scenic spots to swim, fish, or picnic. Most trips also offer an abundance of opportunities for wildlife viewing. Trips are family-friendly, but no children under 5 are allowed, and basic swimming skills are required. Reservations recommended. Hourly kayak and canoe rentals start at $15, and packages such as the afternoon float on the river start at $65.

KENWOOD SPA HAS POLISHED THE ART OF LUXURY.

PADDLING DOWN THE RUSSIAN RIVER AFFORDS YOU VIEWS YOU WOULDN'T GET OTHERWISE.

SOAR Inflatables (707-433-5599; soar1.com) 20 Healdsburg Avenue, Healds-burg. When Russian River Adventures owner Larry said I could bring my nine-month old on a trip (or my dog, if I had one), I wasn't so sure about the whole gig. But Larry and his staff offer one of the safest adventures around. Paddle 8 miles down the Russian River in an inflatable kayak, stopping at as many beaches and rope swings as you can find. Trips last from four to eight hours, depending on your speed. $45 adults; children $22; dogs: $10.

WINE TASTING

Valley of the Moon

Bartholomew Park Winery (707- 935-9511; bartpark.com) 1000 Vineyard Lane Sonoma. Open daily 11:30–4. Known for their Merlot, Cab and Sauvignon Blanc, this winery is located in an unusual spot—a former women's prison. $5.

Benzinger Family Winery (707-935-3000; benzinger.com) 1883 London Ranch Road, Glen Ellen. Open 10 AM–5 PM daily. Noted for their Merlot, Chardonnay, and Pinot Blanc, you might want to go on a tram tour through the vineyards to learn how this family has become so famous in the wine world. $5–10.

Buena Vista (800-678-8504; buenavistacarneros.com) 27000 Ramal Road, Sono-ma. Open 10 AM–5 PM daily. This historic stop is my choice for a picnic. You can do a traditional tasting, an estate tasting, or a food and wine pairing. Go for the big reds. $5–20.

Gloria Ferrer Caves and Vineyards (707-996-7256; gloriaferrer.com) 23555 CA 121, Sonoma. Open 10 AM–5 PM daily. You might feel more like you are in Spain than Wine Country in this hacienda, but once you travel into the caves, or sit on the deck overlooking the vineyards and taste some brut, you'll remember exactly where you are. $10.

Gundlach Bundschu (707-938-5277; gunbun.com) 2000 Denmark Street, Sono-ma. Open 10 AM–5 PM daily, call for tour appointment. The oldest winery in the area, for 150 years these guys have been churning out competitive wines. You can tour caves, vineyards, and the estate, plus attend concerts. $20.

⚓ **Landmark Vineyards** (707-833-0053; landmarkvineyards.com) 101 Adobe Canyon Road, Kenwood. Open 10:30–4 daily. Bocce ball, croquet, horse drawn carriage rides, geese in the pond, and tributes to the famed John Deere (the owner is a descendant), all make this winery a pleasant place to bring the kids, too. Try out their Chardonnay—it's the specialty. They also have a couple vacation rentals on the property (see *Lodging*). $5–10.

Merry Edwards (888-388-9050; merryedwards.com) 2959 Gravenstein Highway N., Sebastopol. You'll have to call for an appointment to taste these lively Pinot Noirs crafted by one of the first female Sonoma County winemakers.

Moon Mountain (707-996-5870; moonmountainvineyard.com) 1700 Moon Mountain Drive, Sonoma. Open Tuesday through Saturday 10 AM–4 PM, by appointment only. Located high in the mountains, this beautiful wooden winery is a lovely place to spend some time. $5.

Muscardini Cellars and Ty Caton Vineyards (707-833-0526; muscardinicellars .com) 8910 Sonoma Highway, Kenwood. Open 11 AM–6 PM daily. This new (and unlikely pair) of Sonoma wine stars have teamed up and opened a new tasting room. It is all about reds.

Santa Rosa

Siduri (707-578-3882; siduri.com) 980 Airway Court, Suite C, Santa Rosa. Located in a warehouse, this winery creates single-vineyard Pinot Noirs that get Eddie Vedder singing their praises. Call for an appointment. Free.

Dry Creek, Alexander Valley, and Russian River Valley

In downtown Healdsburg, there are a number of tasting rooms around the square. If you don't feel like driving (or riding a bike) out to the vineyards, this is the way to get a taste of some local producers, artisan winemakers, and classic Sonoma wines. Notable stops are **Rosenblum Cellars** (try out those Zins), **Thumbprint Cellars** (for local micro-wines), **Mayo** (an institution around these parts, you can also do a food and wine pairing), **Kendall Jackson** (the name says it all), and the famed **Gallo**. Grab a *Healdsburg Winery Walk* flyer when you get to town.

Bella Vineyards (866-572-3552; http://www.bellawinery.com) 9711 West Dry Road, Healdsburg. Open 11 AM–4:30 PM daily. Named for the children they carried around while picking grapes, Bella gives a new name to family winery. Tastings take place in the caves. $5.

Dry Creek (707-433-1000; drycreekvineyard.com) 3770 Lambert Bridge Road, Healdsburg. Open daily 10:30–4:30. Or you can book an appointment for a tour. An institution in this part of Sonoma County, you'll want to try out those whites. $5.

Ferrari-Carano (707-433-6700 or 800-831-0381; ferrari-carano.com) 8761 Dry Creek Road, Healdsburg. Open 10:30–4. Call for tour appointments. This palace of a tasting room feels like it belongs in St. Helena rather than the Dry Creek Valley. They have a wine shop and a swanky lounge on the property. Try the Chardonnay. $15.

Ironhorse (707-887-1507; ironhorsevineyards.com) 9786 Ross Station Road, Sebastopol. Open 10 AM–3:30 PM daily. This is one of the best outdoor tasting rooms around—if you like Chardonnay, Viognier, Pinot Noir, rolling hills, and views galore. $10.

J Vineyards (707-431-36461; jwine.com) 11447 Old Redwood Highway, Healdsburg. Open daily 11 AM–5 PM. The hippest winery in Sonoma County. A steel bar, a lounge with cushy chairs, and oh-so-good sparkling wines, you might ride your bike here and end up hanging for longer than you expected. $20 for a four-wine flight.

Lambert Bridge (800-975-0555; lambertbridge.com) 4085 W. Dry Creek Road, Healdsburg. Open daily 10:30–4. Known for their Bordeaux blends and the idyllic location, not to mention the wood-fired pizzas that they serve on weekends. $10.

Locals (707-857-4900; tastelocalwines.com) Geyserville Avenue and CA 128, Geyserville. Open Wednesday through Monday 11 AM–6 PM. Artisan winemakers often can't afford tasting rooms. So Locals became one of the first to unite a number of small wineries and offer a place for you to try out wines you might never know about. Free.

Lynmar (707-829-3374 x 118; lynmarwinery.com) 3909 Frei Road, Sebastopol. Open daily from 10 AM–5 PM. Pinot Noir and Chardonnay grow well here in the Russian River Valley, and Lynmar delivers on both fronts. They add to your tasting experience an organic garden for picnicking, food- and wine-pairing adventures by their chef, pizza Fridays, and tours. $10–25.

Michel-Schlumberger (707-433-7427) 4155 Wine Creek Road, Healdsburg. Tours led at 11 or 2 daily. Hidden away from the rest of the crowd, this green winery offers private tastings, tours of the estate, vertical tastings of library wines, artisan cheese and wine pairings, "Green" tours, hillside tastings, and even classes. Reservations required. $25.

Moshin Vineyards (707-433-5499; moshinvineyards.com) 10295 Westside Road, Healdsburg. Open 11 AM–4:30 PM daily. Though this family-owned vineyard feels closer to Guerneville than Healdsburg, it is worth the trek to try out those famed gravity flow Pinot Noirs. Rick used to be a teacher in the Bay Area and made wine out of his garage, now he is one of the foremost wine producers in the area. Get him to take you on a tour; you'll learn more about wine making than you ever knew possible. In summer they show films in the vineyards. Free.

Passalacqua (707-433-5550 or 877- 825-5547; passalacquawinery.com) 3805 Lambert Bridge Road, Healdsburg. Open daily 11 AM–5 PM. One of my favorite gardens to picnic in, complete with views, fountains, and a redwood shaded deck. Try the Zinfandel. $10.

Preston (707-433-3372; prestonvineyards.com) 9282 West Dry Creek Road, Healdsburg. Open 11 AM–4:30 PM. Organic grapes and olives are grown on this family farm. Check out that marble bar in the tasting room while you sip on their famous red varietals. $5.

Rosso & Bianco (877-767-7624; rossobianco.com) 300 Via Archimedes, Geyserville. Open daily at 11 AM. Francis Ford Coppola's new winery got a facelift in 2009. Try out their Chardonnay, picnic in the organic garden, or enjoy the new restaurant for a lovely brunch. You can also do barrel tastings. $10.

✳ Green Spaces

PARKS **Annadel State Park** (parks.ca.gov) 6201 Channel Drive, Santa Rosa. What a find! Wildflowers bloom around Lake Ilsanjo in spring. And you can find miles of hiking trails, fishing for black bass and bluegill, and birds around Ledson Marsh. A popular hike is the Cobblestone Trail. Mountain bikers love it here; in fact people come from around the state to ride, so watch your back. Day use: $4.

Howarth Park (707-543-3424; ci.santa-rosa.ca.us) 630 Summerfield Road, Santa Rosa. Open at least 6–6 daily. Families flock to this park for tennis, fishing, hiking trails, boating on Lake Ralphine, mountain biking, pony rides, train rides, and the carousel. In summer they offer movie nights in the park as well. This 152-acre community park is one of Santa Rosa's hidden delights. Amusement rides: $2. Kayak, canoe and paddleboat rentals: $8 per hour.

Jack London State Park (707-938-5216; jacklondonpark.com) 2400 London Ranch Road, Glen Ellen. Though not much of an outdoor area, fans of Jack London will appreciate a stop here to see where the writer lived. There is a museum in the House of Happy Walls, plus a dam, a lake, and a bathhouse built by the writer himself. There are a few trails where you can bike or ride horses. Inquire at the visitor center. $6.

Lake Sonoma (707-433-9483; corps.lakes.us/sonoma) Milt Brandt Visitor Center, 3333 Skaggs Springs Road, Geyserville, off Dry Creek Road, Open at least 8:30–5:30. This lake has 50 miles of coastline and is a great place to swim when wine country heats up. Enjoy great fishing for bass, catfish, and perch; Jet Ski, wakeboard, or water ski; hike the 40 miles of trails around the lake, or you can also rent boats (lakesonoma.com) for $10 an hour. **Lake Sonoma's Liberty Glen Campground** (reserveamerica.com) sits on a ridge with views of Warm Springs.

Mayacamas Mountain Sanctuary (707-473-0601) 108 Phillip Drive, Healdsburg. 1400 acres of grassland, chaparral, evergreens, streams, and a vernal pool bring bird-watchers and green enthusiasts all the way out here. Free.

Spring Lake Park (707-539-8092; Sonoma-county.org/parks) 5390 Montgomery Drive, Santa Rosa. This lovely lake offers hiking trails, swimming areas, fishing, and campsites. I like to come here in the morning, when the fog hangs over the lake and locals jog with their dogs. $6.

Ragle Ranch Park (707-823-7262) 500 Ragle Road, Sebastopol. This 225-acre park has tennis courts, trails, a dog park, a peace garden, and excellent bird-watching. Free.

Sugarloaf Ridge State Park (parks .ca.gov) 2605 Adobe Canyon Road, Kenwood. The gem of Sonoma County, hiking at this state park will get you unsurpassed views of wineries stretching for miles, wildlife, and forests. You can bike or hike the 21 miles of trails in the Mayacamas Mountains, climb Bald Mountain (which overlooks Napa

THE MORNING FOG HANGS OVER SPRING LAKE IN SANTA ROSA.

Valley), see redwood trees, maples, madrones, and the springtime 25-foot waterfall along Sonoma Creek. In winter and spring, you can fish in Sonoma Creek. There is also a lovely campground (reserveamerica.com) near Sonoma Creek, with 49 sites, toilets, and BBQs (no showers). Visit the visitor center by the campgrounds for a map of trails.

GARDENS **Bouverie Audubon Reserve** (707-938-4554) CA 12, Glen Ellen. This lovely 500-acre property is known for the spring wildflowers that erupt with color. There are also a number of birds that live here, excellent trails, and plenty of trees to escape the summer heat. Call for docent tour reservations. $15 donation recommended.

Quarryhill Botanical Gardens (707-996-3166; quarryhillbg.org) 12841 Sonoma Highway, Glen Ellen. Open Monday through Saturday 9–4. Docent led tours are at 10 AM on the third Saturday of the month. These gardens offer 20 acres of plants brought from Asia that you won't see anywhere else in North America. There are some steep hikes through plants such as orchids, rhododendrons, and irises, as well. $10 adults, $5 kids and seniors, $15 docent-led tours.

SWIMMING SPOTS ✿ ♿ **Healdsburg Veterans Memorial Beach** (707-433-1625; sonomacounty.org) 13839 Healdsburg Avenue. Part of what makes Healdsburg such a great wine country town is its combination of nature and sophistication. Nothing shows that off more than this river beach. After sipping some great wine, you can swim in the river or have a BBQ. Day use: $6 summer and $5 the rest of the year.

Lake Ralphine Park (707-539-8092) 5390 Montgomery Drive, Santa Rosa. See *Howarth Park.*

Lake Sonoma See *Parks.*

✿ **Morton's Warm Springs** (707-833-5511; mortonswarmsprings.com) 1651 Warm Springs Road, Glen Ellen. Open May and September weekends and holidays, and Tuesday through Sunday in June through August, all from 10 AM–6 PM. Cool off when the summer heat gets to be too much in mineral pools. $8 adults; $7 kids (3–12) and seniors; children under 3 free.

Spring Lake Park See *Parks.*

✳ Lodging

Towns listed from south to north.

HOTELS

Petaluma
✿ ◎ ♿ ⫴ **Metro Hotel and Café** (707-773-4900; metrolodging.com) 508 Petaluma Boulevard S. This 140-year old building was restored in 2004 to bring a bit of Paris to the farmlands of Petaluma. Imagine high ceilings, blond hardwood floors, IKEA furniture mixed with some salvaged finds, and primary-colored accents. Ground floor rooms have a small patio. You can also choose to stay in the Airstream. Amenities: 19 rooms and cottages, full breakfast, hot tub, concierge, and restaurant. $–$$.

Carneros
Carneros Inn See *Napa.*

Sonoma
If you are a fan of chain hotels, you might want to check out Marriott's

The **Lodge at Sonoma** (Marriott .com) and the **Fairmont Sonoma Mission Inn** (Fairmont.com), which is pretty far from Sonoma square.

✦ ♿ "♪" ⊙ **El Dorado Hotel** (707-996-3220; eldoradosonoma.com) 405 1st Street West. If you can't afford Hotel Healdsburg, but are looking for something sleek, you'll enjoy the four poolside bungalows. The 23 rooms in the historic building offer less privacy and can get loud with restaurant and bar noise. But this isn't the place to come to sleep—folks come here to party. $$–$$$.

Kenwood

♿ "♪" **Kenwood Inn and Spa** (707-833-1293 or 800-353-6966; kenwoodinn.com) 10400 Sonoma Highway. In the midst of a major renovation, this 18-year old Mediterranean-style compound is one of the most romantic places to stay in the valley. Circling a courtyard packed with avocado and persimmon trees, you'll find 11 different room types. Unifying the property is the faux finish, travertine floors, ornate painted flooring, Italian linens, fountains, water mills, and pools winding through herb gardens and jasmine. Even if you don't stay here, a visit to the restaurant and wine bar or the spa will allow you to enjoy the rustic royal character. Amenities: 30 rooms and suites, full organic breakfast, saline-heated pool, two hot tubs, no TV, room service. plunge tub, and steam room. $$$$; no one allowed under the age of 18.

Santa Rosa

✦ ♿ "♪" **Hotel La Rose** (707-579-3200 or 800-527-6738; hotellarose .com) 308 Wilson Street. Located in Santa Rosa's Old Railroad Square, this decade-old hotel is an integral part of the city. The 47 rooms spread across two buildings; I like the fourth floor rooms in the original exposed-stone

building, with their slanted ceilings, nice light, and fine antiques. Rooms include European-style breakfast, concierge. and access to Josef's restaurant. $$–$$$.

Healdsburg

✦ ♿ 🐾 "♪" **Hotel Healdsburg** (707-431-2800 or 800-889-7188; hotelhealdsburg.com) 25 Matheson Street. Its 55 rooms and suites offer furniture so hip that the concierge printed a list of where the designers shopped. That way you can purchase your own rustic teak floors, unique lighting fixtures (with holes poked in lamps for effect), Merlot and Chardonnay accent rugs, leather furniture, big cushy beds with goose down comforters, 6-foot gray stone soaking tubs, teal mosaic bathroom tiles. Rooms facing the square and courtyard offer the best views, but can get a little loud when folks party at the brewery downstairs. Amenities: continental breakfast; heated pool and Jacuzzi in jasmine, camellia, and grapevine-landscaped garden; hammocks; cabanas; Dry Creek Kitchen restaurant (see *Dining Out*); café;

THE LOUNGE AT HOTEL HEALDSBURG.

lounge with jazz on weekends; concierge; DVD player and movies; room service; computer terminals throughout the building; fitness room; and private balconies. $$$–$$$$.

INNS AND B&BS Also visit **Sonomabb.com**, which lists all of the B&Bs in the area.

Sonoma
Bungalows 313 (707-996-8091; bungalows313.com) 313 1st Street E. Denise and Tony Salvo are all about European elegance in a remote and quiet setting, yet their one- and two-bedroom bungalows are only a half block from the Sonoma square. Imagine crème and marble walls and floors, kingly beds, private patios, kitchen or kitchenette, breakfast, and wood-burning fireplaces. $$–$$$$.

⁙ ✏ **Hidden Oak Inn** (707-996-9863 or 877-996-9863; hiddenoakinn.com) 214 E. Napa Street. Small and quaint, you'll feel like a guest in Valerie and Don's house when you stay at this three-suite B&B. Floral-printed rooms, bed runners, beige and maroon accents all highlight the 1914 architecture. On weekends you get a candlelit full breakfast and on weekdays a continental breakfast, plus access to the pool. $$–$$$.

✏ ✻ ⁙ **Inn at Sonoma** (888-568-9818; innatsonoma.com) 630 Broadway, Sonoma. Two blocks from downtown, this 19-room inn knows that people like to be able to walk to where it's at, but also leave the party without the music coming home with you. As you might imagine from a Four Sisters Inn, you get mismatched country furniture, fireplace, hot tub, and yummy breakfasts—blueberry pancakes or maybe an Italian egg. $$–$$$$.

✏ ✻ ⁙ ⊙ **Macarthur Place Inn and Spa** (707-938-2929; macarthur place.com). 29 East Macarthur Street. No one mixes country charm with Victorian elegance quite like the designers of Macarthur Place. From the flowering garden with sculptures dotting the lawn, to beds that make you want to melt, these 64 rooms, suites, and cottages will delight those of you who want a classic wine country experience. Amenities: continental breakfast, wine and cheese reception, small pool, hot tub, business center, film library, DVD player, spa, and bike rentals. $$$$.

✏ **Sonoma Chalet** (707-938-3129 or 800-938-3129; sonomachalet.com) 18935 5th Street W., Sonoma. Private and located in a wooded country area of Sonoma, a short drive to the plaza and wineries, this unique property takes you back to the 1940s. You'll find antique stoves, patchwork quilts, clawfoot tubs, Navajo art, and views of the Sonoma Valley. Go with the private cottages, which have a kitchen. Seven cottages, suites, and rooms (with shared bath) include continental breakfast and use of hot tub. $$–$$$; children allowed in cottages only; inn is closed on Tuesday and Wednesday.

✏ ✻ **Sonoma Creek Inn** (707-939-9463; 888-712-1289; sonomacreek inn.com) 239 Boyes Boulevard, Sonoma. This is a decent budget option with simple queen beds and no frills. Road noise can get loud, and it isn't in the most picturesque setting, but you're getting a hotel for under $200 on a weekend, in Sonoma. $–$$.

Glen Ellen
✏ ⁙ **Beltane Ranch** (707-996-6501; beltaneranch.com) 11775 Sonoma Highway (CA 12), Glen Ellen. You won't find many ranch-style inns built in 1892 with vineyard views that offer clean and comfortable accommodations. The wraparound porch offers guests their own access to the outdoors. Complete with floral bed run-

ners and rocking chairs, this is the spot for folks who want to remember that wine grows in the country. Five rooms and a cottage include full country breakfast and use of tennis courts. $$–$$$; no credit cards accepted.

ʿłʾ ▼ ⓪ **Gaige House Inn** (707-935-0237 or 800-935-0237; gaige.com) 13549 Arnold Street, Glen Ellen. Probably one of the most famed B&Bs in Sonoma County, Ken and Greg have worked hard to create a Zen-themed oasis in the middle of Glen Ellen. Enjoy the Japanese gardens, in-room orchids, hammocks, creek trails, and pool, or just relax in the temple-like beds near the fireplace and the oh-so-nice Japanese soaking tubs. Chef Charles Holmes cooks up a mean breakfast: I have heard rumors of an artichoke and pistachio blini that will make you sing. $$–$$$$; no one under 18 years old allowed.

Sebastopol

ℰ ʿłʾ ▼ **Avalon B&B** (707-824-0880 or 877-328-2566; avalonluxuryinn.com) 11910 Graton Road. Down a long red-wood-forest road, you arrive at this whimsical B&B. Before you arrive, Hillary will research meals to accompany your diet—gluten free, vegan, bacon addict—and then prepare breakfasts like banana pancakes with organic sausage, and homemade syrup. The inn has a grass-covered shingled roof, brick walls, a common TV area that smells like popcorn or cookies, and a cockatoo in the small gym. All rooms have their own entrances and are individually decorated. Common themes include pastel colors, murals painted by local artist Paul Nicholson, marble floors, radiant heated bathrooms, granite or glass bowl sinks, fireplace, hot tub, and a basket of goods you might have forgotten, including sunscreen. $$$–$$$$.

Santa Rosa

ℰ ʿłʾ **Melitta Station Inn** (707-538-7712; melittastationinn.com) 5850 Melitta Road. Homey (and solar-paneled) rooms filled with relics of another time, like brass beds, floral curtains, Posturepedic beds, soft towels, plus modern amenities like flat screen TVs, and access to the radiant-heated Jacuzzi—you can't go wrong here. Steps to Annadel Park and Spring Lake, plus a short drive to the Kenwood wineries and Santa Rosa attractions, I like the central location. Breakfast at this English country-style inn is one of the best aroundOn my stay I had artichoke frittata, French toast soufflé with baked peaches. $$–$$$.

Healdsburg

Belle de Jour Inn (707-431-9777; belledejourinn.com) 16276 Healdsburg Avenue. If you want to feel like you are in the French countryside, with a fantastic breakfast, close to wineries and solace, head over to this five-cottage B&B. Private uncluttered cottages and a carriage house on 6 acres make the word *quaint* feel like an understatement. Designed for couples and romance, you'll want to whisk your honey into one of the cottages, smell the fresh flowers, light a fire, slip into the Jacuzzi tub, drink wine, and laze away in sun-dried sheets $$$–$$$$.

ℰ ☗ ʿłʾ **Camellia Inn** (707-433-8182 or 800-727-8182; camelliainn.com) 211 North Street. This might be the best deal in Healdsburg, especially considering you'll be staying in an Italianate Victorian 1869 farmhouse. Canopy beds, antique armoires, English gardens, and fireplaces are just some of the elegant touches that transport you to another era. If you are a chocolate fan, you'll love Chocolate Covered Wednesdays—a decadent tribute to cocoa. Some of the nine rooms come with a whirlpool tub and fireplace; all rooms have access to the pool, full breakfast, and Friday night wine tasting. $$–$$$.

"I" & **Grape Leaf Inn** (707-433-8140; grapeleafinn.com) 539 Johnson Street. Spiking into the air on a quiet street in downtown Healdsburg, you'll see the Cabernet-colored Victorian. Decorated with antique French country beds and armoires, murals, floral wallpaper, and oriental rugs, each room has its own personality. The designers used the natural light, sloped ceilings, and old world charm to bleed luxury into the entire property. Amenities: 12 rooms and 3 cottages, some rooms have Jacuzzi tubs and fireplaces, AC, multi-course gourmet breakfast, fresh flowers, lovely gardens, plush towels and allergy free bedding, boutique wine and cheese reception in their "speakeasy," and spa services. $$$–$$$$.

"I" **Honor Mansion, a Resort Inn** (707-433-4277; honormansion.com) 14891 Grove Street, Healdsburg. Steve and Cathi Fowler have turned an 1883 Victorian into a luxurious B&B resort. Set on 4 acres of landscaped grounds, nestled in a sea of vineyards, staying in this mansion might make you feel like Audrey Hepburn. Dream about velvety pillows, four-poster beds, a mural of cherubs floating on the walls, claw-foot tubs, private sundecks, and one of the best breakfasts around. Amenities: 13 rooms and suites, tennis, bocce ball, croquet, putting green, lap pool, fireplaces, outdoor spa tubs, spa services, room service, afternoon wine and refreshments, cookies, a butler's basket of everything you might have forgotten (including a bathing suit!), and plenty of sherry. $$$–$$$$. Adults only.

& "I" ⊙ **Madrona Manor Inn** (707-433-4231 or 800-258-4003; madrona manor.com) 1001 Westside Road. Just as you are about to head into the Russian River Valley, you get a glimpse of a driveway seeming to dissolve into the forest. Behind the wall of greenery sits the palace of the Madrona Manor.

Rooms feel like they belong in a Jane Austen novel, with original antiques from the 1881 Victorian. You know the deal: cherry armoires, pedestal sinks, bed runners, French country gardens, fireplaces, and the grand treatment. Amenities: 18 rooms and suites, fantastic restaurant (see *Dining Out*), pool, buffet breakfast, no TV, pillow-top mattresses, fireplace, some balconies or jet tubs. $$$–$$$$.

♪ **Piper Street Inn** (707-433-8721; piperstreetinn.com) 402 Piper Street. Located on a quiet street a couple blocks from the Healdsburg plaza, this 1882 Victorian attracts artists, food snobs, and families. The suite and cottage include breakfast at Flying Goat Coffee, and a fun mix of salvaged antiques and modern art pieces. Spring for the two-bedroom private cottage in back with a Jacuzzi tub. $$–$$$.

Forestville

"I" **Case Ranch Inn** (707-887-8711; caseranchinn.com) 7446 Poplar Drive. A Sonoma County historical landmark built in 1894, Case Ranch Inn's powder blue farmhouse and cottage make a lovely place to relax in wine country. Like most B&Bs, you have your share of floral wallpaper and bed runners, but you also get a yummy organic breakfast, and custom-made beds. $$–$$$.

"I" ▼ **Farmhouse Inn and Restaurant** (707-887-3300 or 800-464-6642; farmhouseinn.com) 7871 River Road. The yellow farmhouse dates back to 1872, and the brother and sister owners are fifth-generation Forestville folks with one goal in mind: to make your stay original and delicious on every level. Here are some reasons why I adore the Farmhouse: the restaurant (see *Dining Out*); the spa (including yoga classes); the fresh baked cookies and gourmet breakfast; the salvaged décor, including iron railings, bread tables as doors, and pedestals for sinks; redwood doors; and the oh-so-insanely relaxing radiant-heated tub that fills from the ceiling (you have to see it to believe it). I could go on and on: the pool, the Hemingway quotes on the walls of some rooms, the masculine, warm tones, the fire pit (with S'mores), the free bath salts made by a local organic artist, and yummy snacks. $$$–$$$$; three-night minimum stay.

Geyserville

✐ "❢" **Hope-Bosworth & Hope-Merrill Houses** (707-857-3356 or 800-825-4233; hope-inns.com) 21238/53 Geyserville Avenue. You heard it here first: Geyserville is coming up. Get in now while it is still reasonably affordable, because in the next couple years, this adorable Victorian inn will be able to double its rates. Lovely antiques and a delicious full breakfast, fireplaces, pool, claw-foot tubs, and the kind of gardens that will lure you to finish reading *The Corrections* well into the evening. $$–$$$. Children allowed only in the Bosworth house.

Cloverdale

"❢" **Old Crocker Inn** (707-894-4000; oldcrockerinn.com) 1126 Old Crocker Inn Road. This peaceful B&B on the historic 5-acre Crocker Ranch in the hills above Cloverdale used to be a hunting ranch. Now you'll enjoy wildlife surrounding the property, four-poster beds, and breakfast on the porch overlooking the rolling hills. This is a great location for people who want to be close to wineries, but also enjoy country privacy. Eight rooms and suites include gas fireplace, luxurious linens, access to the pool, and evening wine and hors d'oeuvres. $$–$$$.

VACATION RENTALS So many vacation rentals, so little time. The **Sonoma Valley Visitor Bureau** (sonomavalley.com) has the most comprehensive list of affordable cottages and super luxurious villa rentals.

Kenwood

✐ ⬟ **Landmark Cottages** (707-833-0053; landmarkvineyards.com) 101 Adobe Canyon Road, Kenwood. If you ever dreamed of owning your own vineyard and living off the land, these cottages will let you fantasize in style. The suite has two beds and is perfect for friends traveling together, while the cottage works for families, with a kitchen. Landmark offers free wine to those staying in the cottages, which you can enjoy on your private patio, near the bocce ball courts, or as you walk into Sugarloaf State Park. $$–$$$.

Sebastopol

✐ ⬯ **Full House Farm** (707-829-1561; fullhousefarm.com) 1000 Sexton Road, Sebastopol. Hidden in the trees above Christine Cole's horse ranch is this newly renovated three-bedroom vacation rental. Besides the comfy charm of staying on a ranch, you'll also enjoy sitting on those Adirondack chairs overlooking the valley, sipping on fine wine, and eating fresh-off-the-farm produce (that you pick yourself). $$$, plus cleaning fee.

Healdsburg

Healdsburg-Home Away (866-771-3010; homeaway.com). Whenever I walk the neighborhoods of Healdsburg, I flirt with getting myself a little cottage and enjoying the wine country life. You can do it too, with this vacation rental company that has everything from that tiny cottage to mansions.

CAMPING See *Green Spaces.*

✳ Where to Eat

DINING OUT

Sonoma

♿ **Café la Haye** (707-935-5994; cafelahaye.com) 140 E. Napa Street. Open

Tuesday through Saturday from 5:30. Simplicity is a lost art in restaurants. Café la Haye is attempting to bring it back. With a rotating nightly risotto dish, pan-seared chicken, a pork tenderloin with cherry stuffing, and a Meyer lemon cheesecake, you'll be reminded how good produce can taste in the right hands. Reservations recommended. $$$.

✒ ♿ ♈ **Della Santina's** (707-935-0576; dellasantinas.com) 133 E. Napa Street, Sonoma. Open from 11:30–3 and 5–9:30 daily. Flocks of tourists smell the garlic and head over to this local Italian favorite. Part rotisserie, part wine bar, the chef makes fresh pasta, luscious desserts (panna cotta anyone?), and great picnic goods next door. Reservations recommended. $$–$$$.

✒ ♿ ♈ **El Dorado Kitchen and Kitchenette** (707-996-3030; eldorado sonoma.com) 405 First Street. Open daily from 11 AM–2:30 PM and 5:30 PM–9 PM. Bar stays open until 11, serving off a bar menu. Sleek interiors draw a hip young crowd to sit by the pool or inside at the communal table (which is an old bridge from Vermont). Though my experience with the food hasn't made me sing, the warm pistachios, great mojitos, and edible appetizers make me want to hang out here all night. They also have a cheaper café and coffee bar open during the day. Reservations recommended. $$$–$$$$.

✒ ♿ ♈ **the girl and the fig** (707-938-3634; the girlandthefig.com) 110 West Spain Street. Open 11:30–10 daily (until 11 PM Friday and Saturday); Sunday brunch from 10 AM. One of those special places you find and keep talking about long after you get home, Sondra Bernstein and her executive chef, John Toulze, work wonders with local produce. On summer days there is no place I would rather be than on

the shaded back patio by the fire pit, eating charcuterie, Brie, truffled macaroni and cheese, or fresh fruit cobblers, while sipping on Rhone wines. Inside makes me want to speak French and say *oui* to anything the waiter offers me at that antique bar. $$–$$$.

♿ **Harvest Moon Café** (707-933-8160; harvestmoonsonoma.com) 487 1st Street West. Open daily from 5:30–9 (until 9:30 Friday and Saturday). Wine country is a tough market to break into; the husband and wife duo who created this newer café took a big risk, and it paid off. Mediterranean cuisine changes nightly, but imagine a Spanish tortilla appetizer, Liberty Farms duck confit, and a Scharffenberger pot de crème that will make you dream of living in Candyland. Reservations recommended. $$$.

♿ ♈ **Maya** (707-935-3500; maya restaurant.com) 101 E. Napa Street, Sonoma. Open for lunch and dinner daily. Okay, so you come to wine country for wine, but sometimes you just need a margarita and some gourmet Mexican food. I love the exposed stone, the colorful Latin art, the wood chairs and tables, and the celebratory atmosphere of Maya. It feels closer to Mexico City than anything you'd find in these parts. Plus, there are loads of vegetable items, creamy guacamole, and gourmet tacos, and if all else fails, a spacious bar to laze the afternoon away. Lunch: $–$$; Dinner: $$–$$$.

Glen Ellen
The Fig Café and Wine Bar (707-938-2130; thegirlandthefig.com) 13690 Arnold Drive, Glen Ellen. See Sonoma.

Santa Rosa and Sebastopol
♿ ♈ **K&L Bistro** (707-823-6614) 119 S. Main Street, Sebastopol. Open Monday through Saturday from 11:30–3 and 5–9 (until 10 on weekends). Karen and Lucas Martin opened

up in 2001 to serve farm-fresh French food. An intimate French bistro with white tablecloths and creative cuisine, you'll want to bring someone you love to try out the charcuterie, rabbit liver mousse, Meyer lemon and asparagus risotto, house-made *Boudin blanc* sausages, and the plentiful array of wine. Reservations recommended. $$$–$$$$.

✧ & **Stark Steakhouse** (707-546-5100; starkssteakhouse.com) 521 Adams, Santa Rosa. Open Monday through Friday from 11:30–2:30 and daily from at least 5–9. Many people are jumping into the steakhouse game in Northern California, and now the Sonoma crew from Willi's is trying their hand at it. Here you can find good cuts of American Kobe Barette from Snake River Farms, with eight different sauce options, including truffle aioli, and your choice of steak toppers (foie gras, truffled fried egg, popcorn sweetbreads, roasted bone marrow). Other winners are the macaroni and cheese, and fried chicken. Reservations recommended. $$$–$$$$.

✧ & ⵁ **Zazu Restaurant and Farm** (707-523-4814; zazurestaurant.com) 3535 Guerneville Road, Santa Rosa. Open for dinner Tuesday through Sunday. This modern farmhouse, located way out in the sticks of Santa Rosa— yes, keep driving even when you think you've gone too far—brings the farm (literally, it is outside) to your table. The menu changes depending on what your server picked on the farm that day, and what the chef decides to create. Last time I visited, I ate calamari pasta with fresh fava beans, roasted tomatoes and garlic, and a chocolate fondue with peanut butter cookies and banana that I still talk about. Reservations recommended. $$–$$$.

Healdsburg

& ⵁ **Barndiva** (707-431-0100; barndiva.com) 231 Center Street, Healdsburg. Open for lunch and dinner Wednesday through Sunday and for brunch Saturday and Sunday. Aside from being a happening bar in an old barn with funky wire sculptures hanging from the ceiling (yes, the sculptures are for sale at **Artists and Farmers** next door), the Sunday brunch in the gravel patio offers some of the best fish and chips you'll find in the area. Other highlights include an omelet with truffle oil, an egg panisse, burgers, and pastries galore. The mixologist, Lucca, keeps the 30-foot bar packed most nights. Reservations recommended. Brunch $–$$; dinner: $$–$$$$.

ⵁ **Cyrus** (707-433-3311; cyrus restaurant.com) In Les Mars Hotel, 29 North Street, Healdsburg. Open nightly from 5:30–9:30. Chef Douglas Keene is arguably the best chef in Sonoma County, which is why you have to reserve a table at this prix fixe dining establishment two months to the day in advance. Expect to drop a paycheck, especially if the caviar and champagne cart passes by. The local trick is to head to the bar, where mixologist Scott Beattie uses only local ingredients to make the best cocktails in town—and you can eat without a reservation (go early). Reservations required. $$$$.

ⵁ & **Dry Creek Kitchen** (707-431-0330; hotelhealdsburg.com) In Hotel Healdsburg, 317 Healdsburg Avenue. Open daily from 5–9:30 (Friday and Saturday until 10), and from 11:30–2:30 on Friday through Sunday. Indoor and outdoor fine dining in a country chic atmosphere allows this restaurant a place on the wine country map. Though the tasting menu is pricey, it is the best way to experience what the chef finds at the market. If you are here Monday through Thursday, you can get the Sonoma neighbor three-course tasting for just over $30 ($50 for wine pairing). The menu changes daily but the pork cheeks and beef are usually featured. Last time I was here, my husband and I had tempura-fried oysters, oyster chowder, pork cheeks over wok-fried rice, and Bellwether Farms pecorino ravioli with spring peas. Desserts shine, with rich takes on pot de crème, or a peanut-butter chocolate bar. Trust the staff—when they tell you it's good, it is. Plus, the wine list is all Sonoma wines, with free corkage on Sonoma bottles. Reservations recommended. $$$–$$$$.

& **Madrona Manor** (800-258-4003; madronamanor.com) 1001 Westside Road, Healdsburg. Open Wednesday through Sunday 6–9. I haven't yet dined in this 1890s Victorian mansion known for French California food, accommodating finicky eaters, and the tableside liquid-nitrogen ice cream made on a cart, but I have heard it is spectacular. Reservations required. $$$$.

Forestville

& **Farmhouse Inn Restaurant** (707-887-3300 or 800-464-6642; farmhouseinn.com) 7871 River Road, Forestville. The mural of the owners' family history along the main dining-room wall hints that this is a special experience,

DESSERT AT THE FARMHOUSE INN RESTAURANT.

complete with all local ingredients, a farmhouse vibe, a stellar wine list, and attention to detail. Not often would I recommend spending 40 bucks for a steak, but Farmhouse knows how to have you singing that this is the best meat you've ever had. When I was here, the poppy seed-crusted halibut also blew me away. If you are vegetarian, let the chef know in advance so he can prepare you something special. However, if you are bold, they are known for the "rabbit rabbit rabbit." Reservations required. $$$$.

Geyserville

& Y **Santi** (707 857 1790; tavernasanti.com) 21047 Geyserville Avenue. Open Monday through Saturday from 5:30–9 and Sunday from 5–9; lunch on Wednesday through Saturday from 11:30–2. It is probably not fair to attribute the popularity of this restaurant to the rise of Geyserville as a destination, but Santi sure has done its part to lure a loyal following of wine snobs up north to this one-street town. What makes it so great? Where to begin . . . a trellised patio, surrounded by the herb garden (which the chefs use liberally), house-made charcuterie, fresh pasta, and high quality wine. Reservations recommended. $$–$$$$.

EATING OUT

Petaluma

✄ & **Central Market** (707-778-9900; centralmarketpetaluma.com) 42 Petaluma Boulevard. Open at least 5:30–9 daily. Organic local food served in an exposed-brick bistro attracts fans of Petaluma farmers. The raw bar and cheese selections are top notch. Wood-fired grouper, pizzas, pastas, and plenty of meat selections keep me coming back. $$–$$$.

✄ & Y **Velasco's** (707-773-0882; velascosrestaurant.com) 190 Kentucky

Street. Open for lunch and dinner daily. If you are craving Mexican food, this is the stop for hearty plates of enchiladas, burritos, and nachos. The huge menu offers heaps of options, from a seafood tostada to combination plates that will make you need to walk home. $–$$.

🍴 ♿ **Water Street Bistro** (707-763-9563) 100 Petaluma Boulevard N., Petaluma. Open Monday through Saturday at least 7:30–4, Sunday 8:30–2:30; also Friday and Saturday from 5–8:30. Trained at French Laundry, the new owner/chef of Water Street Bistro has created a niche for herself: waterfront dining in a casual setting, serving up a cheap, good breakfast. The waffles are dreamy. $.

Sonoma

Della Santina's See *Dining Out.*

El Dorado Kitchen See *Dining Out.*

🍴 ♿ **Taste of the Himalayas** (707-996-1161 464 1st Street E., Sonoma. Open daily from 11 AM–2:30 PM and 5 PM–10 PM. If you need some ethnic food for reasonable prices, Taste of the Himalayas delivers. It may not be the best momos or curry you'll find on this side of the Pacific, but the lunch buffet will fill your belly with spice enough to keep you drinking more beer at the pub across the street. $–$$.

Kenwood

🍴 ♿ **Café Citti** (707-833-2690) 9047 Sonoma Highway. Open daily from 11 AM–3:30 PM then 5 PM–8:30 PM (no lunch Sunday). There aren't many cheap eats along the Valley of the Moon, and most people opt for a picnic. Here's one place to stop for sandwiches, pastas, and pizza, written up on a white board. Locals love this café for its simplicity: fresh roasted turkey, lasagna, fresh bread, tons of salads, polenta with your choice of sauce, and a wickedly garlic-filled Caesar salad. $–$$.

Flying Goat Coffee (707-575-1202; flyinggoatcoffee.com) 10 Fourth Street. Open 7–6 daily. Quite possibly the best coffee shop in Sonoma County, you'll want to pop in here for your caffeine fix. There is another location near the Healdsburg Plaza.

🍴 ♿ **Hank's Creekside Restaurant** (707-575-8839) 2800 Fourth Street. Open for breakfast and lunch daily, starting at 6 AM. Food Network hosts rave about this place, but before they created all the hype, locals were lining up for pancakes, eggs, and coffee in this little diner. $.

🍴 ♿ ♎ **Hopmonk Tavern** (707-829-7300; hopmonk.com) 230 Petaluma Avenue, Sebastopol. Open for lunch and dinner. A Gordon Biersch cofounder has created a modern take on a rustic pub, with Douglas fir floors and a celebratory atmosphere. The new local choice for spending a warm summer evening, drinking in the beer garden, listening to live music, and munching on a burger or salad. There are 16 beers on tap, a full bar, and small plates like mashed sweet potatoes or grilled cheese. $–$$

Mom's Apple Pie (707-823-8330; momsapplepieusa.com) 4550 Gravenstein Highway North, Sebastopol. Open daily 10 AM–6 PM. I have to admit, I don't come to this 25-year old diner for the tuna salad sandwich. I have a soft spot for apple pie. And Mom's Gravenstein apple pie does the trick. $.

Patisserie Angelica (707-827-7998; patisserieangelica.com) 6821 Laguna Park Way, Sebastopol. Open Tuesday through Saturday from 10 AM–5 PM. This little house is home to some of the finest pastries in Sonoma County. Every time I pass through Sebastopol, I just have to pop in for a fix. They bake artsy wedding cakes that are photographed for magazines. $

⌀ ⚐ ⚑ **Rosso Pizzeria and Wine Bar** (707-544-3221; rossopizzeria.com) Creekside Center, 53 Montgomery Drive. Open daily from 11:30–10. Since it has been getting a ton of hype around the Bay Area and wine country, you might want to reserve a table. People travel distances for fresh wood-fired pizza topped with salad, salumi, and great wine. This is a far cry from Domino's, folks; expect artisan-puffy pizza, heat from those ovens, and to come back one more time before you leave town. $$.

⌀ ⚐ **Screaming Mimi's** (707-823-5902; screaminmimisicecream.com) 6902 Sebastopol Avenue, Sebastopol. Open 11 AM–10 PM (11 on weekends). You can't pass up this fun and popular ice cream shop. Freshly made ice cream in a colorful atmosphere creates a disco in your mouth! All flavors are sinfully sweet and made with local ingredients.

⚑ **Willi's Wine Bar** (707-526-3096; williswinebar.net) 4404 Old Redwood Highway. Open Sunday and Monday 5–9; Tuesday through Saturday 11:30 AM–9 PM (until 9:30 on weekends). Reminiscent of an old roadhouse, this building was constructed in 1886. Ever since the restaurant opened in 2002, locals have flocked to the cozy seating on the covered patio. Besides wine, you can eat eclectic small plates, like baked mac and cheese with roasted Brussels sprouts, or take a wine flight. $$.

⌀ ⚐ **Willow Wood Market** (707-823-0233; willowwoodgraton.com) 9020 Graton Road, Graton. Open Monday through Saturday 8–9:30 and Sunday 9–3. This is the spot for a delicious breakfast enjoyed in the garden. Their polenta couldn't be creamier; just thinking of the smoked trout salad makes me hungry; the coffee and freshly baked pastries make we wish

for morning. Once you come here, you'll know why locals whisper the name and hope it doesn't show up on the tourist radar. I hear its sister restaurant **Underwood** (across the street) is a good high-end option, but I haven't eaten there. $–$$.

Healdsburg and Vicinity

⌀ ⚐ ⚑ **Bear Republic Brewing Co** (707-433-BEER; bearrepublic.com) 345 Healdsburg Avenue. Open at least 11:30–9 daily. Good beer, decent pub food, and a family-friendly attitude can be a tough find in wine country. Bear Republic pulls it off. $–$$.

⌀ ⚐ **Bovolo** (707-431-2962) 106 Matheson Street. Open daily from at least 9–6 (until 9 on Friday and Saturday). Locals won't tell you about this small counter in the back of Copperfield's Books, owned and operated by Santa Rosa's famed Zazu Farms. They serve fresh pizza, sandwiches (the pork cheek is a favorite), house-made salumi, and super-sweet handcrafted gelato, to be enjoyed on the back patio. $–$$.

⌀ ⚐ **Costeaux French Bakery** (707-433-1913; costeaux.com) 417 Healdsburg Avenue. Open at least 7–3 daily. When I ate the bread at Dry Creek Kitchen, and the waitress informed me that they get it from Costeaux, I knew I had to head over. These cosmic homemade pastries have been in the works since 1923. Sit on the rustic outdoor patio and try out their panini, breakfast sandwich, house-made granola, morning bun and the selection of cheese. $–$$.

⌀ ⚐ ⚑ **Diavola Pizzeria** (707-814-0111; diavolapizzeria.com) 21021 Geyserville Avenue, Geyserville. Open Wednesday through Sunday 11:30–9 and Monday 5:30–9. One of the better gourmet pizzas in Northern California, the good people of Santi have created another winner. Exposed brick, floating candles, an espresso machine that is a work of art, and excellent wine, all add to the appeal of these wood-fired gourmet pizzas and house-made salumis. $$.

𝄞 & **Downtown Bakery and Creamery** (707-431-2719) 308 Center Street, Healdsburg. Open daily from 7–5. The secret in town is they serve breakfast on Friday through Sunday. Other days you'll find one of Alice Waters's ex-chefs whipping up organic pastries for you to drool over on copper tables. $.

Flying Goat Coffee See *Santa Rosa*

Jimtown Store Alexander Valley (707-433-1212; jimtown.com) 6706 CA 128. Open 7–5 daily (opens at 7:30 on weekends). Whenever I ask people about their favorite spots in Sonoma County, Jimtown Store appears on the list. Their Brie and chopped olive sandwich is heavenly. $.

Oakville Grocery (707-433-3200) 124 Matheson Street. If you have ever driven through Napa Valley on a summer weekend, you might have noticed people lining up out the door of a little market. They aren't giving anything away. Neither is their popular second location in Healdsburg. Here you'll pay big for huge gourmet sandwiches, cheese, wine, and picnic goods. $–$$.

𝄞 & ♈ ✿ **Ravenous Café** (707-431-1302) 420 Center Street, Healdsburg. Open 11:30–2:30 and 5–9 Wednesday through Sunday. Chef Joy Pezzolo focuses on local organic ingredients, served in a casual, yet elegant bistro indoors. I prefer to sit in the jasmine-scented garden and eat huge salads, vegetarian chili, and hearty burgers. Locals swear by this place for a reason. The smaller, more upscale bistro of the Ravenous duo just isn't as sweet as this one. $$.

♈ **Ruth McGowan's Brewpub** See *Entertainment*.

𝄞 & ♈ **Willi's Seafood and Raw Bar** (707-433-9191; willisseafood.net) 403 Healdsburg Avenue. Open 11:30–9 (until 10 on Friday and Saturday); closed Tuesday. Popular with locals who swear by the food, the Willi's crew has a recipe that works. On summer days the patio goes off with locals drinking wine and munching on tapas. $$–$$$.

✳ Entertainment

For entertainment listings pick up the free weekly *North Bay Bohemian*.

Petaluma

♈ **Graffiti Restaurant** (707-765-4567) 102 Second Street. Vodka martinis are the specialty. You can get food, but don't even think about it without a stiff drink.

♈ **Mystic Theater and Dance Hall** (707-765-2121; mystictheater.com) 23 Petaluma Boulevard N. Local bands and international musicians pass through this classic theater. Or, if you want grub and drink, head next door to **McNear's Saloon and Dining House** for a sports and music memorabilia-filled cocktail.

Sonoma and Vicinity

♈ **Dry Creek Kitchen** See *Dining Out*.

♈ **Harmony Lounge at the Ledson Hotel** (707-996-9779; ledsonhotel.com) 480 Street East. If you can't afford the decadence of this luxe hotel, at least pretend you can by sitting on a plush chair and sipping estate-grown wines.

♈ & **Murphy's Irish Pub** (707-935-0660; sonomapub.com) 464 1st Street East. Head over here for shepherd's pie, bangers and mash, pasties, sandwiches, and some well-poured Guinness. This place gets packed in the afternoon and evenings, when live music fills the alley and people spill onto the concrete.

Y **The Saloon at Jack London Lodge** (707-996-3100) 13740 Arnold Drive, Glen Ellen. Cheap wine and popcorn. Need I say more?

Santa Rosa and Vicinity

Third Street AleWorks (707-523-3060; thirdstreetaleworks.com) 610 3rd Street. Open from at least 11:30 AM–12 AM daily. An outdoor beer garden for those of you tired of sipping wine. Here you'll find local microbrews, pub grub, and locals.

Ace in the Hole (707-829-1ACE; acecider.com) CA 116 at Graton Road, Graton. Open at least 11:30–9:30 daily. If you are a pear cider fan, head over to this pub to sip this intense libation and hear live music.

Y **Hopmonk Tavern** See *Eating Out.*

Y **Russian River Brewing Co** (707-545-2337; russianriverbrewing.com) 745 Fourth Street. Besides the reasonably priced pub menu, locals venture here for barrel-aged beers and Belgian-style ales.

Santa Rosa Symphony (707-546-7097; santarosasymphony.com) 50 Santa Rosa Avenue. This company presents classical, jazz, and youth performances year-round.

Sonoma County Repertory Theater (707-823-0177; the-rep.com) 104 N. Main Street, Sebastopol. This company performs classic plays, like *Taming of the Shrew,* in an intimate setting.

Y **Upper Fourth** (707-573-0522; upperfourth.com) 96 Old Courthouse Square. Mixologists concoct an array of drinks at this popular nightspot.

Y **Willi's Wine Bar** See *Eating Out.*

Healdsburg and Vicinity

Y **Barndiva** See *Dining Out.*

Y **Lounge at Hotel Healdsburg** (707-431-2800) 25 Matheson Street. Maybe the hippest lounge in town, this is the spot for live jazz, a cocktail, and daydreaming in front of the fireplace.

Raven Performing Arts Theater (707-433-6335; raventheater.org) 115 North Street. Come see movies and live performances.

Y **Ruth McGowan's Brewpub** (707-894-9610; ruthmcgowansbrewpub.com) 1st and Main, Cloverdale. Packed with loud locals populating the bar, this is where the winemakers come for big burgers, beer-battered fries, and a good brew.

✳ Selective Shopping

Antiques, art, and the clothing you might expect earth mamas to wear are what you can expect to find in Sonoma County. Starting in the south, in Petaluma, a walk down Petaluma Boulevard will get you all of the above. I like **Splendid Little Shoppe** (707-763-7467) and **Tall Toad Music** (707-765-6807). Farther out of town on Petaluma Boulevard North are Premium Outlets (premiumoutlets.com).

In Sonoma, around the plaza are a number of high-end boutiques, art galleries, and craft stores. Santa Rosa is where you'll find the malls: **Montgomery Village** (707-545-3844) and **Coddingtown Mall** (707-527-5377). Along Main Street in Sebastopol, you'll find places like **Incredible Records and CDs** (707-824-8099), or tons of antique shops on Gravenstein Highway—check out the **Antique Society** (707-829-1733).

Up in Healdsburg, around the plaza it is pretty much the same deal as Sonoma. Make sure to pop in **Artists and Farmers** (next door to Barndiva), and **Baksheesh** (on the square).

BOOKSTORES **Copperfield's Books** (copperfields.net) is a local wine-country chain. You'll find outposts at 140 Kentucky Street in

Petaluma; in Montgomery Village in Santa Rosa; at 138 N. Main Street in Sebastopol; and at 104 Matheson Street in Healdsburg. You'll also find **Readers' Books** (707-939-1779; read ersbooks.com; 130 E. Napa Street) in downtown Sonoma.

✳ Special Events

February: **Olive Festival** (707-996-1090; olivefestival.com). The Sonoma Valley doesn't forget grape's cousin, olive, with this weekend celebration.

March: **Savor Sonoma Valley** (866-794-WINE; heartofsonomavalley.com). Over 20 wineries offer barrel tastings at this two-decade old festival.

April: **Apple Blossom Festival** (877-828-4748; sebastopolappleblossom .com). Sebastopol is known for its apples, and for over 60 years the town has hosted a parade and festival to honor their famed fruit.

Passport to Dry Creek Valley (707-433-3031; wdcv.com). If you want to learn about wine, taste the best the Dry Creek appellation has to offer, and eat well, this festival is calling your name.

May: **Cloverdale Celebration** (707-894-4470; cloverdale.net). I grew up going to country festivals like these, where everyone and their granny participates in bathtub races.

Luther Burbank Rose Parade and Festival (707-542-7673; roseparade festival.com). Everything seems to be in bloom as this annual festival and parade rolls into Santa Rosa.

Sonoma Jazz (866-468-8355; sonoma jazz.org). This festival offers four days of jazz in Sonoma, and, of course, lots of food and wine.

Healdsburg Jazz Festival (heals burgjazzfestival.org). For 10 days in May and June, big names in jazz pass through Healdsburg.

June: **Harmony Festival** (707-861-2035; harmonyfestival.com). For 30 years this music and healthy-living festival has attracted big names, hippies, and curious folks wanting to learn about aromatherapy and peaceful rock music.

Summer Nights on the Green (707-838-5382; townofwindsor.com) Windsor Green. Live concerts, farmers' market, food, and movies bring the town of Windsor out on Thursday nights in summer. Through August.

Taste of the Valley (888-289-4637; alexandervalley.org). It is Alexander Valley wine appellation's time to shine in this two-day festival celebrating food and wine. You can tour caves, vineyards, and learn about how to make wine.

July: **Sonoma County Fair** (707-545-4200; sonomacountyfair.com) Big names from the 1980s and 1990s music scene entertain the adults, while carnival rides, magic, and food take care of the little tykes.

Hot Air Balloon Classic (707-837-1884; townofwindsor.com) Windsor. For two days, tethered balloons take people into the skies to get a taste of this 200-year old sport.

August: **Gravenstein Apple Fair** (800-207-9464; farmtrails.org) Sebastopol. There aren't many Northern California festivals celebrating fruit. So head out to eat, drink, and shop in honor of this biblical superstar.

Sonoma Wine Country Harvest Weekend (800-939-7666; sonoma wine.com) The whole county celebrates the biggest weekend of the year with auctions, lunches, tastings, and a bang-out party where people come from all over the world to participate in the harvest.

October: **Sonoma County Harvest Fair** (707-545-4200; harvestfair.org)

Santa Rosa. Imagine over 500 wines all under one roof. Then throw in carnivals, tasting booths, music, and a grape stomp, and you have fun for all ages.

November: **A Wine and Food Affair**: (800-723-6336; wineroad.com). This month, 57 wineries open their doors and allow you to taste varietals, sample food, and get recipes to try out at home.

RUSSIAN RIVER VALLEY

❋ To Do

✎ **Armstrong Woods Pack Station** (707-887-2939; redwoodhorses.com). This riding company caters to both beginning and advanced riders. Trail rides are great fun for kids. For the full-day rides, there is a two-person minimum during off-season and a four-person minimum in season. They also offer an overnight ride at $380, which includes a gourmet lunch, dinner, and breakfast the next morning. Most rides range from $65–70 for 90 minutes. They also offer full-day rides from $175–225.

Burke's Canoe Trips (707-887-1222; burkecanoetrips.com) Forestville. Paddle from Forestville to Guerneville, which is a fun 10 miles. The return shuttle is included. Canoe, paddle, and life vest for $58 per canoe.

King's Sports (707-869-2156 guernevillesport.com) 16258 Main Street, Guerneville. Offers guided and self-guided canoe and kayak rentals, and fishing gear rentals, along with expertise on some excellent local fishing locations. Guided canoe and kayak rentals are $80–100. Full day kayak or canoe rentals: $30–55 for canoes.

Korbel Champagne Cellars (707-824-7000; korbel.com) 13250 River Road, Guerneville. Open daily 10 AM–4 PM. Whether you are interested in how to make sparkling wine or wandering through rose gardens, a visit to these champagne caves is a worthy ticket on the itinerary. There is a deli on the property as well. Free.

Osmosis (707-823-8231; osmosis.com) 209 Bohemian Highway, Occidental. Open daily from 9–8. This Japanese-style retreat offers a full range of spa treatments, such as massages, facials, and skincare. However, their signature treatment is the cedar enzyme bath that includes hot tea and a special blanket wrap. This place will stop the aging process—or at least make you feel like it.

✎ **Pee Wee Golf Course** (707-869-9321) 16155 Drake Road, Guerneville. Open 11 AM–10 PM daily. A quirky and slightly surreal peewee golf course features statues such as two cannibals cooking a man, and a T-Rex. $7.

Russian River Outfitters (877-775-2925) 25375 Steelhead Road, Duncan's Mills. Open in summer season. It is a blast to paddle the river. Here you can rent a single-seat kayak from $45–65, and a double-seat kayak from $65–85.

Russian River Wine Road See *Sonoma Valley Wineries.*

❋ Green Spaces

✎ ♿ **Armstrong Redwoods State Reserve** (707-869-2958; parks.ca.gov) River Road, Guerneville. Be dwarfed by redwoods and learn a little, too. This amazing

COOL OFF AT A RUSSIAN RIVER BEACH.

park is slated to be closed because of budget cuts; it seems safe now, but go while you can. A very easy trail weaves through these giant trees.

Austin Creek State Recreation Area (707-869-2015; parks.ca.gov) Just 2 miles north of Guerneville off Armstrong Woods Road, in the Redwoods State Reserve. Here you can fish, hike, horseback ride, and camp in Bullfrog Pond Campground.

Johnson's Beach (707-869-2022; johnsonsbeach.com) 16241 First Street, Guerneville. Open 10 AM–6 PM daily, mid-May through early October. Beach has canoes, kayaks, and paddleboats for rent, along with beach chairs, umbrellas, and inner tubes for water fun. There is a snack bar with reasonable prices, plus a roped-off kiddie pool area for the little ones.

Monte Rio Public Beach and Park (707-865-2487; mrrpd.org/monteriobeach .com) Off River Road in Monte Rio. There is a great covered picnic area as well as volleyball and horseshoe pits. Locals and visitors come to fish, swim, launch boats, and be seen in their best summer gear, and even less.

✳ Lodging

Boon Hotel & Spa (707-869-2721; boonhotels.com) 14711 Armstrong Woods Road, Guerneville. White paint and spare modern furniture are what you'll find at this eco-friendly 14-room lodge. Imagine fair-trade cotton sheets, a solar-heated saline pool, fireplace, organic French press coffee with breakfast, and poolside massages. $$–$$$.

Creekside Inn and Cottages (707-869-3623 or 800-776-6586; creeksideinn.com) 16180 Neeley Road, Guerneville. Tucked in the redwoods just south of the Russian River, the Creekside Inn is a solar-powered gem. Blue jays and meadows surround the 22 A-framed cabins. Buildings have recently been renovated (and lifted to save from river flooding), and most come with full kitchens. The 22 nature cottages, cabins, and houses (some with fireplace), plus 5 B&B rooms and suites (with full breakfast) allow access to the pool, pool table, games, movies, and ping pong. $–$$$.

Dawn Ranch Lodge (707-869-0656; dawnranch.com) 16467

River Road, Guerneville. This 100-year old ranch is nestled amidst redwoods on the banks of the river. With beautifully landscaped gardens, it offers private yellow cottages without telephones or televisions. This is an ideal spot for lovers and families who want to spend quality time together, as the 55 studio and two-bedroom cottages allow river and pool access. The Roadhouse Restaurant on-site is a decent choice. $$–$$$$.

🐾 🏠 ⁱⱮⁱ **Ferngrove Cottages** (707-869-8105 or 888 243-2674; ferngrove .com) 16650 CA 116, Guerneville. Cute cottages built in the 1920s, ranging from studio to one and two bedrooms. While all come equipped with a private bath and a TV, some more upscale amenities include full kitchen, spa tubs, continental breakfast, and working fireplaces. $–$$$.

& ⊙ ⁱⱮⁱ **Inn at Occidental** (707-874-1047 or 800-522-6324; innatocci dental.com) 3657 Church Street, Occidental. Occidental is sort of a local secret. Snuggled away deep in the redwoods, surrounded by antique shops and great food, this inn is the perfect place to escape the world. Rooms are colorful and filled with family heirlooms, without feeling as if you are in a thrift store. The 18 rooms and suites (some rooms have fireplace and jet tubs for two) include breakfast, afternoon wine and cheese, and concierge. $$–$$$$.

🐾 ▼ & ⁱⱮⁱ ⊙ **River Villa Beach Resort** (707-865-1143; riovilla.com) 20292 CA 116, Monte Rio. Imagine summer camp with a dash of beer and jetted tubs, and you have arrived at the River Villa. The rooms are nothing to speak of, but the views, the river access, and the great BBQ area are worth the price of this little inn. Continental breakfast included. $$.

▼ & ⁱⱮⁱ **Village Inn** (707-865-2304; villageinn-ca.com) 20822 River Boulevard, Monte Rio. This gay-owned bed-and-breakfast has excellent views of the redwoods and river. The house is filled with antiques. Plus the Oxygen mattress pads and Odeja wool covers make the beds oh-so-comfy. The 10 rooms and suites come with expanded continental breakfast. $$–$$$.

CAMPGROUNDS 🐾 ⊙ ⁱⱮⁱ 🐾

Casini Ranch Family Campground (800-451-8400; casiniranch.com) 22855 Moscow Road, Duncan's Mills. This RV park/campground is located by the Russian River, just minutes away from the ocean. The 110 acres of campsites line a mile of the river. Facilities include the Moscow General Store, with laundry and a video arcade, and the rustic upstairs dance hall. The campground has restrooms with hot showers, and watercraft rentals. $26 daily; Two- to three-night minimum on summer weekends.

THIS SWING HAS AN ENCHANTING VIEW OF THE RIVER AT RIVER VILLA RESORT.

✍ ❀ **Schoolhouse Canyon Campground** (707-869-2311) 12600 River Road, Guerneville. Open May through September. Set amidst a 200-acre wildlife sanctuary, near Korbel Champagne Winery, beaches, and lots of hiking areas. $.

✳ Where to Eat

DINING OUT ♿ **Applewood Inn** (707-869-9093; applewoodinn.com) 13555 CA 116, Guerneville. Open Tuesday through Saturday at 6 PM. Chef Bruce Frieseke serves up farm-fresh food in a farmhouse with an elegant flair. Get the a la carte or tasting menu for specialties like saffron calamari, or pan-roasted duck with brown-butter celery root. Reservations recommended. $$$-$$$$.

♿ ✍ **Bistro des Copain** (707-874-2436; Bistrodescopain.com) 3782 Bohemian Highway, Occidental. Open Sunday through Thursday 5–9 PM, Friday and Saturday 5–10 PM. Provençal food, with an extensive wine list highlighting both French and local wines, this is a local treasure nestled in the redwoods. Favorites include the *Epaule d'Agneau* (a rosé-braised shoulder of Sonoma lamb) and the *Filet de Loup de Mer* (branzino Mediterranean-style). Vegetarians will go hungry here. Reservations Recommended. $$-$$$.

Farmhouse Inn See Sonoma Valley *Dining Out*.

♿ ☿ **The Restaurant at the Village Inn** (707-865-2304; villageinn-ca.com) 20822 River Boulevard, Monte Rio. Open for dinner at 5:30 Wednesday through Sunday This wildly popular dining establishment offers views of the river from a historic farmhouse. Wine drinkers will love the selection of 75 Sonoma County wines, while diners usually enjoy classic takes on a rack of lamb or vegetable pasta. Reservations recommended. $$-$$$.

EATING OUT ✍ ♿ **Cape Fear Café** ((707-865-9246) 25191 CA 116, Duncan's Mills. Open for breakfast, lunch, and dinner daily. Excellent Southern-style food served with Southern kindness at casual, decent prices. I am a fan of the oyster po'boy, tandoori chicken, salmon-crab cakes with aggressive aioli, shrimp grits, corn-meal-fried oysters, and anything with fries. Food heaps off plates, but chances are you won't want to leave any. Breakfasts, with seven types of Benedicts, will make you want to go back to sleep or go on a 10-mile hike. Breakfast and lunch $-$$; Dinner $$-$$$.

✍ ♿ **Coffee Bazaar** (707-869-9706) 14045 Armstrong Woods, Guerneville. Open 6 AM–8 PM daily. This organic-coffee shop serves pastries, sandwiches, and smoothies to the urban folks who can't live without a latte. Art and big open windows, dogs outside, and lots of noise, you'll find the Bay Area folks surfing the net when they take over the town in summer. $.

✍ ♿ **Gold Coast Coffee and Pizza** Off CA 116 in Duncan's Mills. Open daily from at least 7–5 PM. This little shop makes some of the best espresso, smoothies, pizza, and buttery pastries in the area. The bear claw is decadent. People planning to pass through end up hanging out in the forested patio, sitting on Adirondack chairs for hours—or at least we do. $.

❀ **Guerneville Taco Truck** (707-869-1821) In the Safeway parking lot, at 16632 CA 116, Guerneville. Open from 11:30–9 daily. Ever since this taco truck showed up in a gourmet food magazine, the wait has gotten longer, but the food is still as cheap and good as it has always been. You can sit on one long picnic table with everyone else—while the uninspiring flea market folks hawk trinkets—and eat tacos, quesadillas, burritos, or burgers. $.

♪ ♿ **Howard Station Café** (707-874-2838) 75 Main Street, Occidental. Open from 6:30 AM–2:30 PM daily, until 3 on weekends. For big country breakfasts, it seems Howard's has the monopoly. Everything is good. Plates are huge. And people drive here from the Bay Area to eat eggs—enough said? $–$$.

Wild Flour Bread (707-874-2938; wildflourbread.com) 140 Bohemian Highway, Freestone. Baking Friday through Monday 8:30–6. You can't come to the area without hearing murmurs about this wood-fired baked bread. Choose from items ranging from the classic sticky bun, to the exotic Egyptian—with pear, fig, and candied ginger. There is also a coffee bar. Chances are you'll stop by for a loaf of bread and drive back for another to take home—it's that good. $.

THE FAMED PINK ELEPHANT BAR ALONG THE RUSSIAN RIVER.

☀ Entertainment

♪ ♿ ⚱ **Main Street Station** (707-869-0501; mainststation.com) 16280 Main Street, Guerneville. Open 12 PM–10 PM daily during summer, winter hours slightly vary. This is a fun place to hear live jazz, blues, and comedy. They serve a pretty good pizza, too. Reservations suggested.

Pegasus Theater (707-522-9043; pegasustheater.com) Pegasus Hall, 20347 CA 116, Monte Rio. Socially conscious theater in the mountains? Who knew? Call for details.

⚱ ✿ **Pink Elephant** 9895 Main Street, Monte Rio. When local kids turn 21, they all head here to party in this lively bar. Live music and bar food round out the experience.

♪ ♿ **Rio Theater** (707-865-0913; rio theater.com) Corner of Bohemian Highway and CA 116, Monte Rio. Closed Monday and Tuesday. Eat a hot dog and enjoy a classic film in this old-school theater.

⚱ ♿ **Rocker Oysterfellers** (707-876-1983; rockeroysterfellers.com) Valley Ford Hotel, 14415 CA 1, Valley Ford. Open for dinner Wednesday through Sunday from 5–9 and Sunday brunch 10 AM–2 PM. Though it is a popular dinner spot, I like to come to the bar here for a dash of local flavor.

⚱ **Stumptown Brewery** (707-869-0705; stumptown.com) 15045 River Road, Guerneville. Open from Noon–12 AM on weekends, and Monday, Thursday, and Friday from 2 PM–12 AM. Live music, beer, and pub food on the river; as you might expect, this place fills up.

☀ Selective Shopping

You won't find much except antiques in the Russian River area. The best places to look are along Bohemian Highway in Occidental, along CA 116 in downtown Guerneville, and in Duncan's Mills.

✳ Special Events

June: **Russian River Blues Festival** (707-869-1595; russianriverfestivals .com). Johnson's Beach becomes a big party to welcome this world-class blues festival.

Russian River Rodeo (707-632-5754; russianriverrodeo.org) Duncan's Mills. Cowboy hats and boots arrive in Duncan's Mills to rope in the cattle.

July: **Civil War Days** (707-865-2256; civilwardays.com) Casini Ranch Campgrounds, 22855 Moscow Road, Duncan's Mills. The town of Duncan's Mills celebrates the Civil War—if you want to call a reenactment of the war a celebration.

September: **Russian River Jazz Festival** (707-869-1595; russianriver festivals.com). Johnson's Beach comes alive again to welcome jazz stars.

SONOMA COAST

✳ To See

⚓ **Bodega Marine Lab** (707-875-2211; bml.ucdavis.edu) 2099 Westside Road, Bodega Bay. The UC Davis Marine Lab offers free tours of the aquariums on Friday from 2–4. Here you can learn about Northern California tides, anemones, and marine life. Free.

Children's Bell Tower (707-875-3422; nicholasgreen.org) Community Center of Bodega Bay, 1.5 miles north of Visitor Center on ocean side of CA 1. Seven-year-old Nicholas Green was shot in Italy in 1994. To commemorate this senseless killing, people came from around the globe to build this tribute—130 bells of all types. Free.

THE RUGGED SONOMA COAST.

✳ To Do

Bird Walk (707-565-2041) 355 CA 1. Next to Doran Beach, this trail is still being constructed. This marsh path offers glimpses of dozens of bird species, including shorebirds, herons, egrets, and plovers. Bodega Bay is the best spot for bird-watching in Sonoma County. August through October and March through May, you'll see the dozens of species of migrating shorebirds.

Bodega Bay Kayak (707-875-8899; bodegabaykayak.com) 1580 Eastshore Road, Bodega Bay. Open at least 10 AM–6 PM daily. A great way to explore Drake's Bay Estero. These guys will shuttle you for free. They rent single kayaks for $45 (four hours) and offer three-and-one-half-hour guided tours for $85.

Bodega Bay Pro Dive (707-875-3054) 1275 CA 1. Since 1991, this outfit has been taking locals and tourists scuba and abalone diving. Call for tour information.

Bodega Harbour Golf Links (866-90-LINKS) 21301 Heron Drive, Bodega Bay. Robert Trent Jones Jr. designed this 18-hole course, which boasts amazing bay and ocean views. I hear their Bluewater Bistro is a great place for lunch. $60–90.

Bodega Surf Shack (707-875-3944; bodegabaysurf.com) 1400 CA 1. Open at least 10 AM–6 PM daily. Owner Bob Miller does it all: Board rentals ($15), surf lessons, kayak rentals and trips (see *Bodega Bay Kayak* above), kiteboarding lessons, and sells gear and clothes.

🐎 **Chanslor Guest Ranch** (707-875-2721; chanslorranch.com) 2660 CA 1. Ride horses along white sand beaches of the rugged Sonoma Coast or up into the redwood trails. From the 30-minute wetlands ride for $30 or the 90-minute beach ride for $70, you are in for an adventure. For kids there is a 10-minute pony ride for $15.

Will's Bait and Tackle (707-875-2323; bodegabayfishing.com) Deep-sea fishing boat captains take folks out fishing or on three- to four-hour cruises in search of some of the 15,000 migrating gray whales that pass the Pacific Coast each year.

✳ Green Spaces

STATE PARKS **Pomo Canyon** On the west side of CA 1, turn into the paved parking lot for Shell Beach, cross the street, and head up the mountain. Last time I hiked this steep trail, I had just gotten my first expansive view of the river spilling into the ocean and was about to turn back, when a shoeless hippie said we have to keep going for a magical trip into a redwood grove. I second his advice. The hike is tough and about 5.5 miles round-trip, but totally worth the groovy views.

A LOOK AT THE GLASSY WATER AND YOU'LL WANT TO KAYAK THIS BAY.

North of Jenner
Fort Ross State Historical Park (707-847-3286; parks.ca.gov) Go 12 miles north of Jenner on CA 1. You can either have a history lesson on how the pioneers lived, visit Russian Orthodox

historical churches, or indulge in outdoor activities like scuba diving, fishing, hiking, and camping. The North Headlands trail is a gentle hike to the water. $3.

Kruse Rhododendron State Reserve (707-847-3221; parks.ca.gov) CA 1, north of Jenner at mile marker 43. Miles of hiking through rhododendrons, horseback riding, and second-growth redwoods make this a fantastic visit, especially in spring when the flowers are in bloom. $6.

Salt Point State Park (707-847-3221; parks.ca.gov) On CA 1, 20 miles north of Jenner. The 6000 acres of hiking trails, rugged beaches, biking, scuba diving, fishing, and camping make this a local favorite. Most travelers don't get up this far, so you may even have most of it to yourself. $6.

BEACHES In order of preference.

With 17 beaches in 12 miles, separated by giant rocks, the **Sonoma Coast State Beach** offers a secluded bit of coast on this dramatic shoreline. Characterized by rough surf, cold water, and the occasional shark appearance, novices tend to stay out of the water—and for good cause. If you dare, **Salmon Creek Beach, Dillon Beach**, and **Doran Beach** are the best surf spots in the area.

🐚 **Doran Beach Park** (707-565-2267; Sonoma-country.org) This windy beach attracts walkers, campers, kayakers, and surfers. This is the only beach recommended and gentle enough for kids and novice swimmers. You can hike to Pinnacles Beach (0.5 mile south) from here to see spring wildflowers. RV hook ups. Day use: $6; Camping: $20.

Salmon Creek Just north of Bodega Bay on CA 1. A shark attack happened here, but it hasn't stopped locals from heading out to surf on nice days. A wide expanse of beach at the point where Salmon Creek meets the ocean makes this a great choice for families. Surfers find this one of the best places to catch a wave, kids like the spot for skimboarding, and the youngest in your group can splash in the calm waveless waters of the creek.

Bodega Head Just south of Salmon Creek off Westshore Road. You have to hike to get to this rocky headland. This is the spot to watch for migrating whales and access private coves.

Portuguese Beach Just 3 miles north of Bodega Bay on CA 1. One of the best beaches for walking, you'll find one of Sonoma Coast's most expansive beaches, with lots of sand between the steep interior cliffs and the ocean.

Goat Rock North of Bodega Bay, take River Road to CA 1, go left, and you'll run into it in Jenner. This is the spot for kayakers and those who simply enjoy a great view. Goat Rock juts out from the ocean floor, providing a landmark for those who visit the coast. You will see harbor seals and ospreys.

✷ Lodging

🦮 ♿ ⌾ 🍴 **Bodega Bay Lodge and Spa** (707-875-3525 or 800-368-2468; bodegabaylodge.com) 103 CA 1, Bodega Bay. This shingled resort overlooking the bay and Doran Beach offers water views from every room, and the Jacuzzi with the best vista in Bodega Bay. Peace is the key word here: Birds fly up to your balcony, the sunsets beg for wine, and the rooms are set quietly away from civilization. For my money, I would spring for the nautical-themed

GOAT ROCK BEACH IN JENNER.

king whirlpool room, with an amazing 6-foot Jacuzzi tub, vaulted ceiling, and the salty scent of the bay just steps away. Amenities: 86 rooms, fireplace, excellent restaurant (see *Dining Out*), spa, sauna, gym, and wine hour. $$–$$$.

🐾 🐕 ♿ **Bodega Harbor Inn** (707-875-3594; bodegaharborinn.com) 1345 Bodega Avenue, Bodega Bay. Since the 1930s, this simple inn has offered a quiet place to sleep for weary travelers. Across the street from the bay, this is a great option for families and people on a budget. I especially like hanging out on the Adirondack chairs on the grassy lawn overlooking the water. The 14 rooms and 5 houses include continental breakfast in summer and on winter weekends. $–$$.

🐕 ♿ ◎ "🍴" ▼ 🐾 **Jenner Inn and Cottages** (707-865-2377 or 800-732-2377; jennerinn.com) CA 1, Jenner. For almost 30 years, Richard Murphy has been giving visitors a home away from home. All units are individually decorated, and are everything from a kingly oceanfront suite, to a wicker and trundle bed-decorated cottage. The buildings might be old with no TVs, but once you sit on those decks, you'll relax into the peaceful vibe. Meatless breakfast served in the dining room; in summer there is a full restaurant as well. The 23 rooms, cottages, suites, and houses (some have hot tubs and fireplaces) include full breakfast and free wine tasting. $$–$$$.

River's End (707-865-2484) 11048 CA 1, Jenner. I love these five rustic (and wind-blown) cottages that slope down a hill overlooking the bay and ocean. It's the kind of place where you hide out in bed for a weekend. The five cottages are small, lack TVs, and only offer wood walls and doors, decks, and down comforters. But you come here to chill, not get fancy amenities. Cabin 5 has a glass shower with ocean views and a large deck. And the restaurant above is a great place to begin and end the day. $–$$. No children under 12.

♿ "🍴" 🐕 🐾 **Sea Ranch Lodge** (707-785-2371; searanchlodge.com) 60 Sea Ranch Drive, Sea Ranch. Built by the same folks responsible for the Hotel Hana in Maui, these guys know how to create a resort. This one mirrors the natural landscape of the Sonoma and Mendocino Coast with early 1970s-period architecture, including bluff-top ocean views, in a resort setting unlike anywhere else on the Sonoma Coast. The 20 rooms (some with fireplace and hot tub) include complimentary gourmet breakfast. The restaurant will be your favorite place. $$–$$$$.

VACATION RENTALS **Bodega Bay and Beyond** (707-875-3942; sonoma coast.com) 575 CA 1, Bodega Bay. You can find a number of cottages, houses, and rentals at this agency.

CAMPING **Wrights Beach** (707-875-3483; reserveamerica.com) 3095 CA 1, Bodega Bay. You have to make a reservation ages in advance to camp here, but you'll be stoked you did. This is a great beach with easy water access for all ages. The best sites are 1 through 9, which have ocean views. 30 sites, no showers. $25–35.

✳ Where to Eat

DINING OUT ✍ ♿ ♈ **Duck Club** (707-875-3525; bodegabaylodge.com) Bodega Bay Lodge and Spa, 103 CA 1, Bodega Bay. Open daily 8 AM–10:30 and 6–9. This ocean-view restaurant is the best spot to eat in Bodega Bay. Dinner features California contemporary cuisine, but I prefer breakfast for good pancakes and omelets. Reservations recommended. Dinner: $$$–$$$$; Breakfast: $–$$.

✍ ♿ ♈ **Rivers End Restaurant** (707-865-2484; ilovesunsets.com) 11048 CA 1, Jenner. Open daily from 12–3 and 5–9. Fine dining in a casual family-friendly setting with stellar views. Local favorites in this dark-wooded restaurant are the duck confit sandwich, fish and chips, and the vegetarian Neapolitan. Have a cocktail at the bar and watch the sunset over the ocean. Reservations recommended. $$–$$$.

✍ ♿ ♈ **Sea Ranch Restaurant** (707-785-2371; searanchlodge.com) 60 Sea Ranch Drive, Sea Ranch. Open for dinner from 5:30–8:30. They serve breakfast and lunch as well. Spectacular ocean views and California cuisine make this restaurant a highlight on the Sonoma Coast, however, it is a trek to get here. It is easier if you are headed up to Mendocino County. If you do get here, don't miss the pomegranate duck breast. Reservations recommended. $$$–$$$$.

✍ ♿ **The Tides Wharf** (707-875-3652 inatthetides.com) 835 CA 1, Bodega Bay. Open daily 7 AM–10 PM. Even if you don't want to fork over the big bucks for a meal (and if you do, I recommend breakfast) there is an excellent fish market in the facility selling clam chowder and fresh fish. Diners can take in the great views or see pictures of historic Bodega Bay (including a great fisherman's shot by the door, and ones depicting Hitchcock's *The Birds* set, as filmed here). $$–$$$$.

EATING OUT **Emma's Organic Coffee and Pastries** CA 1, Jenner. Open at least 8–5. Coffee and morning pastries (made by Gold Coast in Duncan's Mills) on a patio, overlooking the bay and redwoods, while you order paninis to go, and enjoy the morning. Cash only. $

✍ ♿ **Sandpiper** (707-875-2278 sandpiperrestaurant.com) 1410 Bay Flat Road, Bodega Bay. Open at least 8 AM–8 PM. Locals love this low-key restaurant with bay views. I am not the biggest fan. If you like big plates of fried food with sea views, you might want to try it out. $–$$$.

✍ ♿ **Spud Point Crab Co** (707-875-9472; spudpointcrab.com) 1860 Westshore Road, Bodega Bay. Open 8:30–5 Thursday through Tuesday. Day-trippers come from Santa Rosa for the crab sandwich and clam chowder. Locals frequent this shack for Taylor Maid coffee and donuts in the morning. Later on, everyone sits on picnic tables by the wharf and grubs on heaping sandwiches. $–$$.

✳ Special Events

April: **Bodega Bay Fisherman's Festival** (707-875-3866) Bodega Bay. Wine and music, bathtub races and parades greet the fishing fleet.

August: **Bodega Seafood, Art and Wine Festival** (winecountryfestivals.com) Bodega Bay. A fun tribute to all that makes this town go.

NAPA COUNTY

Native Americans named this 30-mile valley Napa, which means Land of Plenty. Today we might amend the name to Land of Overabundance. With well over 400 vineyards and tasting rooms, some of the finest restaurants and hotels in the country, healing hot springs, and hordes of tourists flooding the oak-dotted hills each year, the valley seems to be bursting at the seams with more than its share.

But that hasn't always been the case. Since the 1840s, people have been trying their luck at reaping riches from the land, starting with lumber and quicksilver mines, but soon the mines dried up. Resilient pioneers planted vineyards, realizing the moderate climate made for ideal grape-growing conditions. But a grapevine disease, then the Prohibition, halted the Napa Valley wine industry.

It wasn't until the 1976 Judgment of Paris blind-tasting wine competition, when Calistoga's **Chateau Montelena's** Chardonnay beat out the best of French wines that the world started to take Napa Valley seriously. Today it might seem that Napa Valley takes itself *too* seriously, often keeping itself out of reach for most tourists— with wine-tasting fees and appointments to visit wineries; restaurants requiring reservations months in advance (to even score the 5:30 or 9 PM seating); restaurants that sneer at families; and hotels charging fees equal to a monthly paycheck for a closet-sized room. However, if you look hard enough, there are still some wonderful restaurants and lovely inns that won't make you take out a second mortgage, and family-owned tasting rooms that offer homegrown barrel-tasting tours.

Starting from the south, you'll find the actual city of **Napa**, the largest in the area. Until the last few years, this wharf town wasn't much of a destination. Today, the downtown is going through a renaissance. With the arrival of new hotels and inns, media-hyped restaurants, and the fantastic **Oxbow Market,** visitors to Napa don't have to wander through downtown scratching their heads and asking, "Where is it?" To the east of Napa, you'll find the strip mall-studded towns of **American Canyon** and **Vallejo**, which don't offer much for tourists, plus the day-tripper favored **Lake Berryessa**.

Just north on CA 29, **Yountville,** which doesn't look like much at first glance, deserves a peek inside. Hidden in the stone buildings you'll find some of the best restaurants in the United States, including the $240-per-person **French Laundry**. Founded by George Calvert Yount, the first settler in Napa Valley, this region (and the surrounding hamlets of **Rutherford** and **Oakville**) attracts the rich and famous, who hide out beneath the canopy of oaks and the maze of vineyards, enjoying the high life.

On the quaint scale, **St. Helena** rates pretty darn high. The historic Main Street is dotted with original antique streetlights, antique shops, boutiques, and delightful restaurants. Add to that the wealth of wineries, parks, and nearby hiking trails, and you begin to see how Wine Country is more than swirling Viognier and swallowing foie gras.

My favorite, the town of **Calistoga,** makes for the ideal getaway. Hot springs, wineries, small inns, fancy resorts, and miles of hiking trails attract people of all persuasions. Retaining its historic western downtown along Lincoln Avenue, complete with old train cars, antique galleries, and boutiques, Calistoga treats visitors to a small-town experience with big-city amenities.

A CLASSIC NAPA VALLEY VIEW.

GUIDANCE **Calistoga Chamber** (707-942-6333; calistogachamber.com) 1506 Lincoln Avenue, Calistoga. Quite possibly the most helpful stop you'll make in Napa Valley, the fine people at the visitor center are a wealth of information on everything from wineries to kids' activities.

COPIA (707-259-1600; copia.org) 500 1st Street, Napa. Open 10 AM–5 PM daily, closed Tuesday. As of press time in 2009, COPIA had filed for bankruptcy and shuttered its doors. However, press liaisons have hinted that they plan to reopen and continue to showcase Napa Valley's bounty, offering the best resource in food, wine, and art in the valley. Check the Web site for details.

Napa Valley CVB (707-226-5813; legendarynapavalley.com) 1310 Napa Town Center, Napa. The visitor center is open daily from 9–5.

Yountville Chamber of Commerce (707-944-0904; Yountville.com) 6484 Washington Street, Yountville. Open 10 AM–5 PM daily.

HELPFUL WEB SITES
Napavalley.com
Silveradotrail.com
Napavintners.com
Winecountry.com
Napadowntown.com
Napavalleycarfree.com
Napanow.com

GETTING THERE *By air:* Either fly into **Santa Rosa Airport** (see *Sonoma*), **Oakland Airport** (see *East Bay*), or **San Francisco Airport** (see *San Francisco*).

By boat: **Baylink Passenger Ferry** (877-64-FERRY; baylinkferry.com) You can take a ferry from Fisherman's Wharf or the Ferry Building in San Francisco to Vallejo, which is close to Napa. From there you can either take the **VINE** bus route #10 to Napa, or arrange a taxi at the station.

By car: Driving into Napa Valley, the suburban landscape morphs into agricultural land, which suddenly turns into rolling hills studded with vineyards. To get here from San Francisco, take US 101 north to CA 37 east. Drive north on CA 29, which takes you to all Napa Valley towns.

GETTING AROUND *By bike:* One of the best (and safest) ways to experience wine country is by bike. The roads are made for leisurely pedals along the lines of vineyards. For bike rental information see *To Do.*

By bus: Napa Valley's **VINE** bus service (707-253-1160; nctpa.net/vine) serves the region. Though it is not the finest bus service you'll ever experience, it is better than a DUI.

Napa Downtown Trolley (707-251-2800; napavalleyVINE.net). This trolley operates daily from at least 11 AM–6 PM. Free trolleys run every 30 to 45 minutes around the downtown loop to the outlets, Fuller Park, and Oxbow Public Market.

By car: Most people drive from winery to winery, which line CA 29 and the Silverado Trail to the east. Note that if you are one of these brave souls, cops are out in full force. It is best to have a designated driver (bring a pregnant friend, maybe?) or hire a driver—see tours below.

TOURS **Beau Wine Tours and Limousine Service** (707-257-0887; beauwine tours.com) Tours range from private limo tours to organized tours of Napa or Sonoma. They start at $99 and go way up.

Blue Heron See *San Francisco.*

California Wine Tours (707-253-1300) Head out in a limo to explore Wine Country. Tours start at $69 per person and go up.

In the Kitchen with Lisa See *San Francisco.*

Wine Country Concierge (707-252-4472; winetrip.com). If you have the big bucks to spend, Jackie Richmond, a 22-year veteran of Napa Valley, will choreograph a vast itinerary ideal for the first-time visitor. She knows all the major players and can score you a tasting or a seat at a restaurant with a mere phone call. She doesn't drive you around, so you'll want to hire a driver.

MEDICAL EMERGENCIES Of course, with anything major, dial 911.
Queen of the Valley Hospital (707-252-4411) 1000 Trancas Avenue, Napa.

WEATHER In many ways, Napa Valley has the ideal California climate: hot summers and cool winters without snow. That being said, I have been here in summer and needed a sweater (the valley still gets morning fog) and have been here in March and worn a summer dress.

✳ To See

Bale Grist Mill (707-942-4575) 3369 CA 29, St. Helena. Open 10 AM–5 PM daily. This used to be the wheat-growing capital of California. Stroll down the path to see the authentic waterwheel and mill house, where you might get to taste some bread. $6.

MUSTS FOR FIRST-TIME VISITORS

1. Indulge in a wine and food pairing experience.
2. Eat at a Thomas Keller Restaurant.
3. Picnic on the grounds of a winery.
4. Hike in Napa's Bothe-Napa Valley State Park.
5. Relax the muscles in one of Calistoga's many hot springs.
6. Visit Chateau Montelena Winery.
7. Take a cooking class at the Culinary Institute of America.
8. Have a cocktail at Auberge du Soleil.
9. Take a balloon ride over the valley.
10. Get a spa treatment at Carneros Inn or Villagio Spa.

MUSTS FOR REPEAT VISITORS

1. Visit the di Rosa Preserve.
2. Taste wine along the Silverado trail.
3. Lunch at a Cindy Pawlcyn restaurant.
4. Shop in St. Helena.
5. Explore Calistoga's farmers' market.
6. Visit Lake Berryessa.
7. Eat at Oxbow Market.
8. Tour the art gallery at Clos Pegase.
9. Wander around Villa Ca'Toga.
10. Hike the Petrified Forest.

For More Musts—see *Sonoma*.

⚓ **Castello di Amorosa** (707-967-6272; castellodiamorosa.com) 4045 CA 29, between St. Helena and Calistoga. Open 9:30–6 daily (until 5 in December and January). Tour this 12th-century Tuscan-castle winery. There are 107 rooms, 8000 tons of stones, 900 feet of caves, Italian frescoes, a drawbridge, a dungeon and torture chamber (hmmmm, what's that for?), a medieval church, and a lake. At 10 AM there is a young adults' tour (minimum age 10); otherwise adults reserve a spot to tour the castle and do a barrel tasting; tours last 90 minutes. $25 adults; $15 kids.

COPIA: the American Center for Wine, Food, and the Arts (707-259-1600; copia.org) 500 1st Street, Napa. Open 10 AM–5 PM daily, closed Tuesday. At press time, this giant ode to food, art, and wine had filed for bankruptcy and closed its doors. Rumor has it, they will reopen, but for now, check the Web site or call for any updates or events.

Culinary Institute of America at Greystone (707-967-1100; ciachef.edu) 2555 Main Street, St. Helena. This castle of a culinary academy will force you to reevaluate your kitchen accessories. Their café, in-house **Wine Spectator Greystone** restaurant, cooking classes, and gardens will also inspire the chef in your inner child.

✎ **Di Rosa Preserve** (707-226-5991; dirosapreserve.org) 5200 Carneros Highway, Napa. Gallery open Tuesday through Friday 9:30–3; tours of the sculpture meadow, residence, and permanent collection from April through October on Tuesday through Saturday at 10, 11, and 12 (at 1 on weekdays); reservations required for tours. The 217 acres of vineyard and meadows offer 2,200 works of art by 900 artists dotting the outdoor areas, and two galleries, combining art and nature in the funkiest of ways. Spread across a pond and wildlife preserve, this is the ideal spot to bring kids, art and nature lovers, and anyone who wants something to do besides swirl and sip. $3 gallery fee; tours: $10–15.

Napa Valley Museum (707-944-0500; napavalleymuseum.org) 55 Presidents Circle, Yountville. Open Wednesday through Monday 10 AM–5 PM. This lovely collection honors local history, nature, and contemporary art. $4.50 adults; $2.50 youth; children under 7 free.

Sharpsteen Museum (707-942-5911; sharpsteen-museum.org) 1311 Washington Street, Calistoga. Open 11 AM–4 PM daily. Though part of the museum tells you more than you care to know about the Sharpsteen family, this small museum makes a good quick stop to freshen up on your Napa County history. You can view a miniature Calistoga and plenty of artifacts. $3; children under 12 free.

Silverado Museum (707-963-3757; silveradomuseum.org) 1490 Library Lane, St. Helena. Open 12–4 Wednesday through Sunday. Though Robert Louis Stevenson only honeymooned with his wife on Mt. St. Helena, then wrote about the region in *The Silverado Squatters*, St. Helena has devoted a library/museum to his legacy. Free.

VILLA CA'TOGA'S OLD WORLD SCULPTURE GARDEN.

Villa Ca'Toga (707-942-3900; catoga .com) 1206 Cedar Street, Calistoga. Tours on Saturday at 11 AM from May through October. Artist Carlo Marchiori crafted his palace and now allows visitors to explore it, peeking into the psyche of this whimsical (and prolific) artisan. Highlights include trompe l'oeil frescoes, Roman ruins hidden by the stream in the garden, the cow-themed bedroom, the outdoor sculptures, and the astrological ceiling in the study. Afterwards you'll want to visit Marchiori's Galleria D'Arte in downtown Calistoga to shop for something whimsical to bring home. $25; no children under 12.

✳ **To Do**

AIR TOURS ✎ **Bonaventura Balloon Company** (800-FLY-NAPA; bonaventuraballoons.com) Offering a wealth of excursions, including international getaways and three-day adventures, the main attraction is the passenger flights. Soar over upper Napa Valley at sunrise, help pack up the balloon, sip some champagne, and then head to Meadowood for breakfast. No children under 5. $235 adults; $145–175 kids; breakfast $29.

🎈 **Napa Valley Balloons** (800-253-2224; napavalleyballoons.com). You'll launch at sunrise to float over miles of vineyards and soak up the peace of the Napa Valley skies. Enjoy a continental breakfast before and champagne breakfast afterwards. $240 adults; $115 kids 5–9.

Wine Country Helicopters (707-226-8470; winecountryhelicopters .com). This crew offers so many tours of Northern California, you'll be dazzled with all the selection. You can explore the skies above Wine Country, alternate between a helicopter ride and a kayak, land to taste reserve wines, and even head down to Big Sur for a spa treatment. Rates range from $1200–15,000 for 1–4 people!

TAKE A BALLOON RIDE AT SUNRISE.

CYCLING A bike can be your best friend in Wine Country. Not only can you explore the small farm roads, stopping to imbibe at your leisure and take a rest in a vineyard, but you can also head into the hills for some good mountain biking. Near Calistoga, head up Oak Hill Mine Road, into Bothe-Napa State Park, Skyline Park in Napa, or up Mt. St. Helena.

Tours and Rentals

Calistoga Bikeshop (707-942-9687; calistogabikeshop.com) 1318 Lincoln Avenue, Calistoga. Bike rentals start at $7 per hour and you can get everything from Italian road bikes to mountain bikes.

Napa Valley Bike Tours (707-251-8687; napavalleybiketours.com) 6488 Washington Street, Yountville. Riding a bike through the small vineyard-surrounded streets is the best way to

HIKE THROUGH MOSSY OAK FORESTS.

experience Napa County—especially if you want to drink. From this outfit, you can either rent a bike for $30–65 per day or go on a personalized bike tour starting at $115.

FAMILY FUN ✎ **Old Faithful Geyser** (707-942-6463; oldfaithfulgeyser.com) 1299 Tubbs Lane, Calistoga. Open at least 9–5. Unless you are a geologist, this geyser that erupts about every 30 minutes (unless there is an earthquake on the horizon), could be a bit of a letdown. Sure it's fascinating that like clockwork, scalding water will spray 60 to 100 feet into the air, and yeah, there are some farm animals to feed, but is it worth 8 bucks? Children: $3; under 6 free.

✎ **Petrified Forest** (707-942-6667; petrifiedforest.org) 4100 Petrified Forest Road, Calistoga. Open at least 9–5. Naturalist-led tours Sunday at 11. See examples of a Pliocene fossil-forest, and tour the meadow with a naturalist who can explain how volcanic activity literally petrified the forest. Also, hike through coastal redwoods and visit the museum. $6 adults; kids and seniors $5; children 6–11: $3.

Safari West See *Sonoma*.

✎ **Six Flags Discovery Kingdom** (707-644-4000; sixflags.com) 1001 Fairgrounds Drive, Vallejo. Open daily in summer and on weekends and holidays the rest of the year from at least 10:30–7. Roller coasters, entertainment, activities, and food make this a great spot to bring the kids while in Wine Country. They also have a Marine World (with walruses) and African U.S.A. animal park area. $44.99; kids: $29.99; online tickets dramatically lower.

OLD FAITHFUL DOES IT AGAIN.

FARMERS' MARKETS **Calistoga Farmers' Market** Washington Street parking lot in front of Sharpsteen Museum, Calistoga. May through October, Saturday from 8:30–noon. This is the best market in the area, with live music, food, and plenty of produce.

Napa Downtown Market COPIA Parking Lot, Downtown Napa. May through October, Tuesday from 7:30 AM–noon. Not the best market in the region, but there are quite a few produce stands and it is close to Oxbow, so you can get breakfast.

St. Helena Market Crane Park, Grayson Avenue, St. Helena. May through October, Friday from 7:30–11:30 AM. Popular with locals, this market hawks goods from some of the best farms around.

THE POOL AT CARNEROS INN IN WINTER.

Yountville Market V Marketplace Parking Lot, Yountville. May through October, Wednesday from 4 PM–dusk. This is where the chefs shop.

GOLF Chardonnay Golf Club (707-257-8950; chardonnaygolfclub.com) 2555 Jameson Canyon Road, Napa. These three 9-hole courses meander through vineyards. $47–79.

Mt. St. Helena Golf Course (707-942-9966; napacountyfairgrounds.com) Napa County Fairgrounds, Calistoga. Not the most scenic or even the best club in Napa Valley, but definitely the cheapest. $10–24.

Vintners Golf Club (707-944-1992; vintnersgolfclub.com) 7901 Solano Avenue, Yountville. This is the choice for locals, who come to tee off with stellar views and good food waiting afterwards. $20–45.

HORSEBACK RIDING Triple Creek Horse Outfitters See *Sonoma*.

SPAS AND HOT SPRINGS ✔ **Calistoga Spa and Hot Springs** (707-942-6269; 866-822-5772; calistogaspa.com) 1006 Washington Street, Calistoga. Open daily from 8:30 AM–9 PM. Bring the whole family to wade in the four mineral springs pools. People camp out all day, eating picnics and sipping wine. Mom and Dad might want to indulge in a mud bath or have a massage in their sky-lit treatment rooms. If you are here on a summer weekend and want to use the pools, go early. Pools fill up quick and you have come-and-go privileges until closing. Day use for the mineral pools: $10–25.

Carneros Inn (707-229-4850; thecarnerosinn.com) 4048 Sonoma Highway, Carneros. Head here for top-notch spa treatments, use of the eucalyptus steam room, and pools. If you come during the week and spend over $300, you can unwind in a bungalow for the day.

Dr. Wilkinson's Hot Springs (707-942-4102; drwilkinson.com) 1507 Lincoln Avenue, Calistoga. I have a soft spot for Dr. Wilkinson and his retro bathhouse. So far from the Zen-like affair most spas put on, come here and take a mud bath in the industrial-sized room, where you hear other people moaning through massages. And leave feeling your Jell-O-y muscles wiggle.

Golden Haven Spa (707-942-8000; goldenhaven.com) 1717 Lake Street, Calistoga. I'll tell you a secret: This is my favorite place to come in winter, when the Napa Valley crowds thin and the rain starts. They offer great deals on couples' mud baths and massage treatments. And though the massages aren't the best in the valley, this is the best deal in town.

Harbin Hot Springs See *Lake County*.

Indian Springs Spa (707-942-4913; indianspringscalistoga.com) 1712 Lincoln Avenue, Calistoga. Read a book at the Buddha Pond after having a volcanic-ash mud bath or massage. Their Olympic-sized pool is the ideal place to spend the day.

Lavender Hill Spa (707-942-4495; lavenderhillspa.com) 1015 Foothill Road, Calistoga. When I asked a Calistoga friend where she gets her spa treatments, without hesitation she said, "Lavender Hill." Tranquil gardens, great massage treatments, baths, and salt glow treatments are just some of the highlights here.

Spa at Villagio (707-948-5050; villagio.com) 6481 Washington Street, Yountville. Luxurious spa treatments for discriminating spa-goers are on the menu at the newest venture of the V crew. Outdoor soaking-baths, private suites, scrubs, and some of the finest masseurs around are just some of the elements that make this one of the finest spas in Napa County.

WINE TASTING 101

A kind tasting-room manager once explained the proper way to taste wine, which I'll impart to you. But before I do, you should know a few details. When you arrive at a winery, you will often have choices. The most typical way to taste wine is at the tasting bar in a winery. Fees in Napa generally range from $10–40 per tasting experience and you usually taste up to five different wines (often vintners waive your tasting fee when you buy a bottle). The big bucks tasting fees allow you to sip wines that might be out of your price range. For many wineries, you need an appointment, and when it is a sit-down affair, paired with food, or barrel tasting, that is almost always the case. It is best to call at least a day before to reserve your space for a tasting, but I have gotten in the day of my visit.

As for varietals, Cabernet Sauvignon helped place Napa Valley on the map, but you'll find excellent Zinfandel, Chardonnay, Sauvignon Blanc, and Pinot Grigio growing here as well.

So now that you have the lowdown, here's how to taste: When the wine is poured, tip the glass sideways over a white piece of paper to see if there is anything floating in your wine. If all is good, set the glass down on the counter (or table) and give it a good swirl (the wine should move around in the glass for up to a minute, really opening up the nose, or aroma). Stick your nose in the glass and give it a good sniff. Try to decipher (before looking at the cheat sheet) what you smell. Is it tobacco? Earth? Peaches? Citrus? My husband always smells armpit in white wine. Don't be afraid to say what kind of nose you detect—it's part of the fun. Next, take a very small sip to wake up the taste buds, followed by a sip about three times bigger than the first. Hold that second sip (or gulp) on your tongue for one and a half rounds of "Happy Birthday to You." Swallow. And that's it.

TRAIN RIDES **Napa Valley Wine Train** (707-253-2111; winetrain.com) 1275 McKinstry Street, Napa. This three-hour train ride through the wine country in vintage rail cars is basically a tourist trap. But how lovely to dine in Kelly Macdonald's restaurant, sipping wine and waving at the poor fools stuck in their cars. Here are the bummers: Nothing is included in the steep price but your ride, and there are no on-and-off privileges. Come for lunch, dinner, family trips, or murder mystery adventures. $49–127.

WATER SPORTS **Lake Berryessa Boats and Jet Ski Rental** (707-966-4204; lakeberryessaboatsandjetskis.com) Markley Cove Resort, 7521 CA 128, Napa. Their name says it all.

Napa River Cruises (707-224-4768; napariveradventures.com) Strenblow Drive, at Kennedy Park Boat Dock, Napa. Take a two-hour guided cruise down the Napa River. This cruise is a great way to see the region without your car. $40.

WINE TASTING

✐ ✺ **Alpha Omega** (707-963-9999; aowinery.com) 1155 Mee Lane, off CA 29, Rutherford. Open 10 AM–6 PM daily, no appointment necessary. Their Proprietary Red Wine is described as "having the balance of Gandhi, the body of Brad, and the depth of Freud." Even better, this is one of the few family- and dog-friendly wineries in Napa. Their picnic area is a nice place to hang out for a while.

Artesa Vineyards and Winery (707-; artesawinery.com) 1345 Henry Road, Napa. Open 10 AM–5 PM daily. Pass by Artesa and you might not even notice the sloped building covered in native grasses. Step inside and taste multi-appellational wines that the Spanish Codorniu family has been perfecting since 1872—the Cabernet, sparkling wine, and Pinot Noir are my favorites. Check out the modern art by Gordon Huether. On weekends, reserve a wine and cheese pairing or tour. Go early, this place gets packed in the afternoon. $10–15.

Bell (707-944-1673; bellwine.com) 6200 Washington Street, Yountville. Open daily from 10:30–4 by reservation only. Anthony Bell seeks out vineyards in a variety of microclimates to find grapes with unique *terroir*. He takes on the French philosophy that the art of wine starts in the vineyard, and crafts fine Cabernet Sauvignon and Viognier (grown in Santa Cruz). $15–250; grape-to-glass tours on weekends $45.

Beringer (707-963-8989; beringer .com) 2000 Main Street, St. Helena. Open at least 10 AM–5 PM daily. The oldest continuously operating winery in Napa Valley might be best known for being the home of the White Zin served from a box at Christmas dinner, but the winemaker will change your mind. Make a reservation for a private tasting in the wine caves. $5–35.

Bouchaine (800-654-WINE; bouchaine.com) 1075 Buchli Station Road, Napa. Open 10:30–4 daily. Close

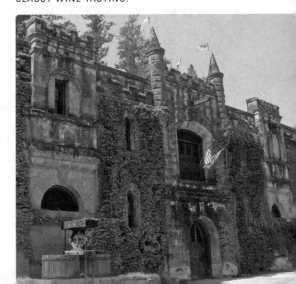

CHATEAU MONTELENA DELIVERS ON CLASSY WINE TASTING.

to San Francisco, Bouchaine is a popular stop for day-trippers wanting to taste Pinot Noir and Chardonnay in a casual setting. If you want to picnic, you'll need to make a reservation. $5.

Cakebread Cellars (800-588-0298; cakebread.com) 8300 St. Helena Highway, Rutherford. Open daily from 10 AM–4 PM by appointment only. Quite the scene with the LA crowd, this family-owned vineyard has been cranking out good Cabernet in a redwood winery since 1973. Try the Chardonnay and Sauvignon Blanc as well. The wine and food pairing experience on weekends uses ingredients from their lovely gardens. $10–40.

Castello di Amorosa See *To See.*

Chateau Montelena (707-942-5105; montelena.com) 1429 Tubbs Lane, Calistoga. Open 9:30 AM–4 PM daily. Come see the winery that made Napa the worthy snob she is. Winner of the Judgment of Paris blind tasting in France in the 1970s, Chateau Montelena became a celebrity, crafting fine Chardonnay and Cabernet Sauvignon on the world stage. Reserve a seat for a library tasting, where you sample $250-per-bottle wines. After you taste, meander down to the lake to feed the birds and have a picnic. $15–25.

Clos Pegase (707-942-4981; clospegase.com) 1060 Dunaweal Lane, Calistoga. Open daily from 10:30 AM–5 PM; tours at 11:30 and 2. No winery shows off the symbiotic relationship of art and wine better than Clos Pegase. From the artisan wine-bottle labels to the sculpture garden and modern paintings, to the Bacchus-inspired caves, this winery reminds you that wine is in fact an art form to be appreciated as much as the paintings on the wall. Free tours are wonderful, as are the wines and the picnic area to enjoy your purchases. They get busy, so come early. $10–20.

Domaine Chandon (707-944-2280; chandon.com) 1 California Drive, Yountville. Open 10 AM–6 PM daily. Sit in the salon and sip bubbly surrounded by vineyards and flowers, eat oysters on the patio in summer, or if you prefer to tour the facility, make an appointment for an informative (and very generous tasting menu) experience. This tasting room gets packed with tour-bus crowds on weekends. Come early, late, or during the week. $16.

Frank Family (707-942-0859; frankfamilyvineyards.com) 1091 Larkmead Lane, Calistoga. Open daily 10 AM–5 PM. Visit this historic winery, established in 1884, for Cabernet Sauvignon and champagne. Free.

Frazier Winery (707-255-3444; frazierwinery.com) 70 Rapp Lane, Napa. Open 10 AM–4 PM by appointment only. The Frazier family produces small lots of Napa Valley Cabernet Sauvignon and Merlot. They've just planted their first round of white grapes, too. Here's a chance to meet a small winemaker before they hit the big time. $30, includes a barrel sampling.

Girard Winery (707-968-9297; girardwinery.com) 6795 Washington Street, Yountville. Open daily from 10 AM–6 PM. This new rustic-meets-modern tasting room in Yountville offers visitors the chance to taste five wines in a traditional tasting. If you can spring for it, the food- and wine-pairing education experience with the director of wine education allows you taste all their wines (including the reserves) and learn about the synergy between food and wine. Reservations required for food pairing, which lasts 90 minutes. $5–40.

Grgich Hills Estate (707-963-2784; grgich.com) 1829 S St. Helena Highway, Rutherford. Open 9:30 AM–4:30 PM daily. Using biodynamic and organic farming

NAPA VINEYARDS SPREAD FOR MILES.

practices, this family-owned estate churns out wonderful whites. During harvest you can come stomp grapes, and on all Fridays come taste from barrels. Friendly service and a casual setting remind you what Napa is all about. $10.

Hall (866-667-HALL; hallwines.com) 401 St. Helena Highway, Rutherford. Open daily from 10 AM–5:30 PM. If you want to experience at least one hoity-toity winery worth the fuss, head to Hall. With a new site created by architect Frank Gehry, and great wines, this winery packs a mean punch. You can either have a private tour and tasting at the Rutherford location or hang with the masses at the St. Helena site. Make an appointment for private tours and barrel tastings, or come for a picnic. $10–20.

Honig Vineyard and Winery (707-963-5618 ext 318; honigwine.com) 850 Rutherford Road, Rutherford. Open 10 AM–5 AM daily. I had to include Honig, my favorite organic Sauvignon Blanc made by Kristin Belair. You need to make an appointment to visit this casual vineyard and learn about their sustainable practices. $10.

Keever Vineyards (707-944-0910; keevervineyards.com) Vineyard View Drive, Yountville. Open by appointment only. Keever's small-lot productions of Cabernet Sauvignon and Sauvignon Blanc shine. Taste with views of the valley, then get a tour of the artisan winery, learning how this family operation hand-sorts their grapes to get the delicate tastes they are known for. This is the antithesis to the big tasting rooms. Tasting and tour: $20.

Kelham Vineyards (707-963-2000; kelhamvineyards.com) 360 Zinfandel Lane, St. Helena. Make an appointment to taste excellent Cabernet and Merlot at this under-the-radar family-owned winery. Here you get to experience a down-home family vibe, complete with lots of dogs tramping around the property, Mom pouring Sauvignon Blanc, and the wine-making sons laughing it up with visitors.

Palmaz Vineyards (707-226-5587; palmazvineyards.com) 4029 Hagen Road, Napa. Open by appointment. Science geeks take note: This is the largest underground gravity-flow winery in the world. The Argentine Palmaz family and their crew create a Bordeaux-style blend that rocks. Two-hour food and wine pairing tours: $60.

Peju Province Winery (707-963-3600; peju.com) 8466 St. Helena Highway, Rutherford. Open 10 AM–6 PM daily. I have a soft spot for Peju's simple red table wine. Ignore the bustling, touristy tasting room, where the staff makes goofy jokes and you are surrounded by tour bus folks, and just try cheap good wine. $10.

Plumpjack Winery (707-945-1220; plumpjack.com) 620 Oakville Crossroads, Oakville. Open daily from 10 AM–4 PM. Sit in the garden, sip Cabernet and Merlot, and feel as worldly as owner Gavin Newsom. Occasionally the tasting room can feel like a frat party, but the wine is so good it doesn't matter. $5.

Quintessa Winery (707-967-1601; quintessa.com) 1601 Silverado Trail, Rutherford. Open by appointment only. This is where New Yorkers and urbanites tired of the country come for a dash of sophistication: all gray stone and dark wood, with little bistro tables for tasting, and a proper staff. Biodynamic perfectionists, Quintessa only makes one wine a year. Guided private tours, including tasting and cheese: $65.

Robert Sinskey Vineyards (707-944-9090; robertsinskey.com) 6320 Silverado Trail, Napa. Open 10 AM–4:30 PM daily; culinary tours by appointment. A winemaker's wine, Robert Sinskey's organic biodynamic wines show up on many Napa Valley restaurant lists. The tasting room is both casual and refined, with a koi pond and picnic tables. $20.

Schramsburg Vineyards (707-942-4558; schramsberg.com) Schramsberg Road, Calistoga. To visit this historic house of bubbly, you must take an educational tour of the 120-year old caves, or take a tour and then indulge in a sparkling wine and food pairing. Tours are at 10, 11:30, 12:30, 1:30, and 2 and last over an hour. $35–60.

HIKE IN BOTHE-NAPA VALLEY STATE PARK.

❋ Green Spaces

Bale Grist Mill State Park See *To See.*

Bothe-Napa Valley State Park (707-942-4575 or 800-444-PARK; parks.ca .gov) 1301 St. Helena Highway North, Calistoga. When you can't sip wine anymore and need a bit of nature, head out for a hike along the second-growth redwoods, or stroll along oak-shaded trails along a creek. Trails include the Ritchey Canyon, Redwood, Coyote Peak, South Fork, and History trails. Also of note is the Native American garden, the handicapped-accessible pool (open from June through Labor Day from 12–6), and 50 campsites that need to be reserved from March through October. Day use: $6. Camping: $20–25.

Lake Berryessa (707-966-2111; usbr.goc) 5520 Knoxville Road, Napa. Visitor Center open weekends from

10 AM–4 PM. This reservoir is one of the largest bodies of freshwater in the state. With 165 miles of shoreline, you'll find plenty of space to hang out, fish, swim, and boat. Recreational day use areas include Oak Shores and Smittle Creek, where you can swim, kayak, picnic, and fish. Coyote and Acorn Beaches are pleasant enough swimming areas, perfect for families. There are also a number of "resorts" that cater to families, fishermen, and campers, though at press time many of the resorts were closing temporarily. If you are interested in staying out here or camping, visit the Web site above to check for current accommodations. For boat rentals, fishing gear, and food, head to **Markley Cove Resort** (800-242-6287).

Napa River Sinewy and underappreciated by everyone but the local farmers, the Napa River makes a lovely place to spend the day fishing, kayaking, or wandering along the riverfront trails. Head to Kennedy Park (CA 221, just south of Napa Valley College) to launch your boat or kayak, or to Trancas Street in Napa to connect to the Napa River trail. Napa River Adventures rents kayaks (see *To Do*).

Robert Louis Stevenson State Park (800-444-PARK; parks.ca.gov or reserve america.com) Just 7 miles north of Calistoga on CA 29. After spending his honeymoon atop Mt. St. Helena, author Robert Louis Stevenson fell in love with the region's rough chaparral slopes and evergreen forests. After his departure, St. Helena has claimed him as an honorary son and named this park for him. Today this 2,700-acre mountain park is yours to enjoy. Hike to the top of the mountain (5 miles) or explore Oak Hill Mine Road trail just outside of Calistoga.

Skyline Wilderness Park (707-252-0481; skylinepark.org) 2201 Imola Avenue, Napa. Open at least 9 AM–dusk. Come to this 850-acre wilderness area to hike and mountain bike to Lake Marie, or explore the Martha Walker Native Plant Garden. Other hiking trails include the Buckeye, Skyline, Chaparral, Toyon, Toyon Creek, and Rim Rock trails. You can also camp here. Day use: $4. Camping: $8–14.

✳ Lodging

HOTELS AND RESORTS

Carneros

✿ ⚲ ⁙ **The Carneros Inn** (707-299-4900 or 888-400-9000; thecarnerosinn .com) 4048 Sonoma Highway, Carneros. If I had to make a hierarchy of places to stay at least once in your life, the Carneros Inn would sit comfortably at the top of the list. Sure, other resorts boast views, spacious cottages without neighbors, and luxury up the wazoo, but the Carneros Inn offers a dash of that je ne sais quoi that breathes relaxation. Could it be the undulating hills dotted with vineyards, surrounding the cottages and house rentals; the steam rising from the pools; the outdoor fireplaces emitting a warmth that draws you to sip wine outside; or the community-like setting with gourmet market, restaurants, and communal area complete with games, movies, and computer? Maybe it is the womblike beds facing the fireplace; the spare design; the radiant-heated floors; deep soaking-tubs; or indoor/outdoor showers? This is the spot that I dream of escaping to when it's rainy and I want to hide out inside watching Hitchcock films. Amenities: 86 cottages and private home rentals, three restaurants, two pools (including an infinity adult one) and hot tub, spa, bocce ball, gourmet market, yoga classes, fitness room, bikes, concierge. $$$$.

Napa

✿ ⚲ ⁙ **Chateau Hotel and Conference Center** (707-253-9300; chateau hotel.com) 4195 Solano Avenue. Don't expect much from this retro hotel that never left the 1980s, and you'll be pleasantly surprised with one of the cheapest accommodations in Napa County. Facilities include 115 rooms and suites with access to the pool and hot tub. $–$$.

Yountville

At press time **Bardessono Inn and Spa, Hotel Luca,** and **The French Laundry Hotel** were breaking ground at new luxury properties in Yountville. The opening dates keep being postponed, so check online for details.

♂ ♿ "⏸" **Napa Valley Lodge** (707-944-2468 or 888-944-3545; woodside hotels.com) 2230 Madison Street. Part motor inn, part Tuscan retreat, this is the ideal hotel for families and people who want full-service amenities, from a pool and spa to a nice continental breakfast buffet spread in the courtyard. Understated rooms evoke a business traveler's ideal—a desk, flat screen TV, private balcony, and views of the pool and vineyards. Amenities: 55 rooms and suites, private terrace, fireplace, champagne continental breakfast, tea and cookies, spa treatments, hot tub, wine hour on Fridays. $$$–$$$$.

Rutherford

♿ "⏸" **Auberge du Soleil** (707-963-1211; aubergedusoleil.com) 180 Rutherford Hill Road. Known for its views of the vineyards spilling down the hills, this luxurious resort is all it promises to be: Private Mediterranean-decorated cottages, with fireplaces and terraces, blend into the hillside's oak and native grass. Fit for the most special of special occasions, once you're sure she or he's the one, come here to indulge in candlelit deep soaking-tubs, a glass of champagne by the adults-only pool, fine gourmet food delivered to your door, and plenty of free midnight snacks in the fridge. Additional amenities: 50 private cottages and rooms, two excellent restaurants and a bar, spa for guests only, two pools, art gallery and sculpture garden, tennis courts, two hot tubs, espresso machines, fresh fruit in room, and oversized king-sized pillow-top beds. $$$$.

St. Helena

♂ ♿ **Meadowood Napa Valley** (707-963-3646 or 800-458-8080; meadowood.com) 900 Meadowood Lane. There is no shortage of luxury in Napa Valley, but Meadowood surpasses most by providing 250 acres of wooded

THE VIEW FROM AUBERGE DU SOLEIL IS UNPARALLELED.

accommodations that fit into the natural environment by incorporating the earth, oaks, and stones into the design. Staff go out of their way to make you comfortable, including traveling by golf cart to your room to deliver wine, and leaving bottles of water stashed up the hiking trails that weave through the property. Cathedral ceilings, sunken tubs, two TVs, pillowy beds, and decks with views of the sun setting over the pines and oaks all add to the appeal. They'll have to kick you out when it's time to check out. Amenities: 85 rooms and suites, three restaurants, including the Restaurant at Meadowood, two pools, a spa, fitness room, 9-hole golf course, croquet, seven tennis courts, bike rental, wine reception, concierge, children's program, and babysitting. $$$$.

Calistoga

✍ ♿ **Calistoga Spa Hot Springs Inn** (707-942-6269 or 866-822-5772; Calis togaspa.com) 1006 Washington Street. This family-friendly motel with the mineral pools in the center is a throwback to the 1970s. Though it can get loud when the pools are going off, this is an ideal (and affordable) hotel for pampering yourself without breaking the bank. The 57 units, with kitchenettes, have access to the four pools all day, spa, fitness room, and aerobics classes. $$.

✍ ♿ "¶" **Wilkinson's Hot Springs Resort** (707-942-4102; drwilkinsons .com) 1507 Lincoln. Quite the mainstay in Calistoga, this hot springs resort offers a mishmash of lodging options, from the Victorian House to the Patio rooms. Here you can expect 42 small rooms for reasonable prices that offer kitchenettes and access to the pools. $$–$$$.

✍ ♿ **Golden Haven Hot Springs** (707-942-8000; goldsenhaven.com) 1713 Lake. My choice for affordable accommodations in Calistoga, especial-

ly when it is cold and I can take advantage of the indoor hot-spring pool, the couples' mud bath specials, and massage treatments. The 28 rooms are nothing special, more like a motel than a resort. $–$$$.

✍ ♿ **Indian Springs Resort** (707-942-4913; indianspringscalistoga.com) 1712 Lincoln Avenue. Ideal for families or romance, this historic hot springs resort is California's oldest continuously running pool and spa facility. The Wapoo Indians used to bathe in the warm waters, and now you can enjoy the geyser-fed Olympic-sized pool and volcanic ash spa treatments, then saunter back to your modernly decorated cottage or lodge room to sip wine. Lodge rooms offer queen beds, Frette linens, and stone floors, while cottage rooms (which are perfect for families), built in 1940, evoke a country charm that will make you want to stay longer. Book early, this property sells out fast. The 42 rooms and cottages have access to pool, spa, and tennis. $$$–$$$$.

✍ ♿ "¶" **Mount View Hotel and Spa** (707-942-6877; mountviewhotel.com) 1457 Lincoln Avenue. Constructed in 1912, this historic hotel has been renovated to offer individually decorated plush rooms that are part Art Deco, part Gothic, and part Clockwork Orange. If you are looking for something out of the norm—you know, nothing frilly or country, yet not something super sleek with no flavor, this hotel is calling your name. Spring for the artist cottage if you can afford it. For a kick, check out an easel and paints and head to the vineyards to create your masterpiece. Amenities: 31 rooms, suites and cottages, two wonderful restaurants (Bar Vino and JoLe—see *Dining Out*), pool, Jacuzzi, spa, concierge, breakfast. $$–$$$$.

✍ ♿ ♈ "¶" **Solage Calistoga** (707-226-0800 or 866-942-7442; solage calistoga.com) 755 Silverado Trail. This new cosmopolitan resort brings the beautiful urbanites out to the Calistoga country to ride sleek black cruisers, laze by the pools, or hide out in one of the cabana studios. The interiors look like they just jumped off the pages of *Dwell* magazine, with lofty rooms, earth tones, stone showers, textured pillows and blankets, and views of the nearby mountains. Solar panels and recycled woods add to the allure—you can just imagine Leonardo DiCaprio touting the virtues of spending your paycheck for a night in this hip eco-friendly resort. Amenities: 89 studios, full service spa, Solbar Restaurant (see *Dining Out*), bikes, fireplace, bocce courts, and organic linens. $$$$.

INNS AND B&BS

Napa

⚓ ♿ **Blackbird Inn** (888-567-9811; blackbirdinnnapa.com) 1755 1st Street. Stay in an early 1900s Craftsman-style house in the heart of downtown Napa. You might imagine you are sleeping in a farmhouse as you lay on the big king beds, staring at the fireplace and hugging the teddy bear left for you. Warm tones and big windows, plus friendly service, breakfast, fireplace, spa tub, and wine hour make this a good choice for people looking for an authentic B&B experience. $$–$$$.

🍴 ♿ **Candlelight Inn** (707-257-3717 or 800-624-0395; candlelightinn.com) 1045 Easum Drive. On the banks of Napa Creek, this 75-year old Tudor mansion, constructed of blackened-oak timber and redwood, offers romance fit for royalty. If 10 rooms with vaulted ceilings, floral wallpaper, drape runners, gourmet breakfast, spa tubs, fireplaces, and plush bedding get your heart pumping, head here. $$–$$$$.

⚓ 🍴 **La Belle Epoque** (707-257-2161 or 800-238-8070; napabelle.com) 1386 Calistoga Avenue. This over-a-century-old Queen Anne Victorian, with stained glass windows in almost every room, offers fine accommodations. Walk through the fragrant gardens to view the heirloom roses, and towards your antique-decorated room. This is an ideal getaway for folks who appreciate fleur de lis wallpaper, high thread-count sheets, spa tubs, fireplaces, formal breakfast, and country French accents. $$$–$$$$.

♿ **Millikin Creek Inn and Spa** (888-593-6175; millikencreekinn.com) 1815 Silverado Trail. This 19th-century stagecoach stop along the Napa River now boasts one of the chicest inns in Northern California. Forget period antiques, here you'll find 12 suites with refurbished bamboo floors, sleek sunlit rooms, warm earth tones, deep tubs, and decadent bedding that scream for romance. Enjoy a picnic breakfast delivered either to your door, in-room, or out in the gardens. Millikin Creek is the finest accommodation in Napa city. $$$$; no children allowed.

🍴 ⊙ ♿ **White House Inn and Spa** (707-254- 9301; napawhitehouseinn .com) 443 Brown Street. For those of you who remember the 1801 First Inn fondly, they have changed their tune and have gone Hollywood, with eco-friendly, hip rooms in a historic downtown Napa mansion. Sleek and modern interiors with contemporary furniture complement the unique sloped ceilings and multi-textured linens and carpets. This inn is sure to appeal more to San Francisco couples than Wal-Mart shoppers. Amenities: 17 rooms, gourmet buffet breakfast, afternoon wine and cheese, spa, some rooms have a fireplace or spa tub. $$$$.

Yountville

⚓ ♿ **Maison Fleurie** (800-788-0369; maisonfleurienapa.com) 6529 Yount Street. Take a step into the French countryside here in Yountville, with an ivy-covered mansion and floral-appointed rooms. For folks on a budget, go for the stone-walled cozy queen, while those looking for luxury will appreciate the king rooms in the Bakery Building. Amenities: 13 rooms, pool, hot tub, breakfast buffet, cookies, afternoon wine and hors d'oeuvres, some rooms have no TV. $$–$$$.

"1" Napa Valley Railway Inn (707-944-2000; napavalleyrailwayinn.com) 6523 Washington Street. This is a great option for people on a budget. You don't get much but a clean room near the railroad tracks, and passes to the fitness center down the street. $$–$$$.

✄ ⅙ "1" Villagio Inn and Spa (707-944-8877 or 800-351-1133; villagio.com) 6481 Washington Street. A stay at this indulgent inn begs you to slow down, sip wine from your complimentary in-room bottle, laze by the heated pool, and then return to your wine-colored room to soak in the big jet-tubs. This is the ideal vacation spot for Mom and Dad, Grandpa, or even picky Aunt Susie. And the champagne breakfast is the best in the valley. Amenities: 112 rooms and suites, afternoon tea, full service spa (see *Spas*), bicycles, tennis courts, concierge, room service, fireplace, wine cellar. $$$$.

"1" ❀ ⊚ ⅙ Vintage Inn (707-944-1112 or 800-351-1133; vintageinn.com) 6541 Washington Street. If you can't go to France, the Vintage Inn is your next best option. Decorated in toile du Jouy fabrics that offer hints of pastoral France in the 1800s, with vaulted beamed ceilings, private balconies, fireplaces, and an oh-so-relaxing two-person tiled soaking tub, this inn, and the surrounding gardens and vineyards, inspires guests to snuggle up with their sweetheart and relax. If you can swing it, spring for the brick villas, reminiscent of the French countryside. Amenities: 92 rooms, suites, and villas, pool, champagne continental breakfast,

spa, tennis courts, bike rentals, concierge, and movie rentals. $$$–$$$$.

St. Helena

"1" Inn at Southbridge (707-967-9400 or 800-520-6800; innatsouthbridge.com) 1020 Main Street. Wine Country simplicity in the heart of St. Helena makes this a great option for travelers looking for refined sophistication. Imagine 20 rooms with white plush bedding, cherry-wood headboards, matted black-and-white photos, private balconies, continental breakfast, and a fireplace. $$$–$$$$.

"1" ⅙ The Wine Country Inn and Gardens (707-963-7077 or 888-465-4608; winecountryinn.com) 1152 Lodi Lane. For over 30 years, the kind people of this St. Helena inn have been offering friendly service in a lovely setting. Country antique-filled rooms with their own personalities allow guests a fine place to relax after a day of exploring. Second floor rooms are a bit older, but have better views. Amenities: 20 rooms, 4 suites, and 5 cottages, spa services, pool, hot tub, spa tubs, fireplaces, gardens, outdoor whirlpool tub, wine tours, breakfast buffet, wine social. $$–$$$$.

Calistoga

✄ "1" Calistoga Inn (707-942-4101; calistogainn.com) 1250 Lincoln Avenue. The 18 simple, classic rooms on the second floor of this locally favored restaurant and brewery are perfect for budget-conscious travelers. You'll share bathrooms and won't get many amenities besides continental breakfast, but aside from camping, this is as cheap as it gets. $–$$.

⅙ "1" Chanric Inn (707-942-4535 or 877-281-3671; the chanric.com) 1805 Foothill Boulevard. This is not your Great Aunt Bessie's B&B. Sleek rooms with designer furniture look like they jumped out of a Restoration Hardware catalog. This fine inn is ideal for an urban couple looking for a bit of romance, a pool, and a decadently delicious breakfast. $$$–$$$$.

🐾 ⁽ᵀ⁾ **Craftsman Inn** (707-341-3035; the craftsmaninn.com) 1213 Foothill Boulevard. One of the newest inns in town, located in a refurbished Craftsman cottage, offers luxury amenities in a casual environment. The highlight of my stay here (besides the Jacuzzi tub and our private terrace) was the food—homemade yogurt, fresh scones and cookies, eggs and Sunday morning champagne. This is a wonderful place for couples looking for a Wine Country escape. Since the inn is on CA 29, request a room in the back. The owners also run the less expensive **Wine Way Inn** down the street, which I didn't get a chance to see. Inquire about winter cooking classes. $$–$$$.

🐾 🐾 **Mountain Home Ranch** (707-942-6616; mountainhomeranch.com) 3400 Mountain Home Ranch Road. If you're looking for something unpretentious that will take you back to the real country roots of this region, you can stay in a rustic cottage or a B&B room (most with shared bathrooms) up in the mountains between Calistoga and Sonoma County. The 23 rooms and cottages have access to a pool. $–$$.

VACATION RENTALS 🐾 🐾 ⁽ᵀ⁾
Washington Street Lodging (707-942-6968; washingtonstreetlodging .com) 1605 Washington Street, Calistoga. Ideal for families, couples traveling with pets, or people who want to stay in Calistoga a little longer, these cottages surround a shared patio area and nestle up to a creek. You can expect country décor and a full kitchen to whip up some pancakes. Room 3 has a private deck along the creek. $–$$.

CAMPING See *Green Spaces*.

BISTRO DON GIOVANNI'S HERB GARDEN.

✳ Where to Eat

DINING OUT

Napa

🐾 ♿ 🍷 **Bistro Don Giovanni** (707-224-3300; bistrodongiovanni.com) 4110 St. Helena Highway. Open at least 11:30–10 daily (until 11 on weekends). It's not a secret that this family-friendly restaurant is one of the best in Northern California. For 15 years, they have served pan-fried chicken, fresh lasagna, and ravioli to an adoring crowd (who wait for hours in the landscaped gardens while their kids run around the fountains and whimsical sculptures) to stuff themselves silly, and then top it all off with the best tiramisu this side of the Atlantic. Parents note that there is a great kids' menu (including a cheese pizza with fries on top and no green stuff). Reservations required. $$–$$$.

🐾 ♿ 🍷 **Ubuntu** (707-251-5656; ubun tunapa.com) 1140 Main Street. Open for lunch and dinner daily. Even carnivores should not pass by this vegetable restaurant/yoga studio. Step into the eco-friendly lofty space, complete with a giant wine rack behind the spacious bar and funky sculptures that will transport you to a world that Nelson Mandela might actually sanction. Friendly and healthy servers help you navigate through Chef Jeremy Fox's creative takes on seasonal produce grown in their biodynamic garden. Yoga classes let out just as your cauliflower claypot arrives. Strangers sip wine at a communal table, while the young eaters enjoy a kids' tasting menu that makes veggies taste like ice cream. Dinner offers a tasting menu that I would not miss. But I like to come here for lunch, when the sun streams through the floor-to-ceiling windows and I can take my time eating pizza, artichoke, burrata, and a finger-licking fennel salad. Reservations highly recommended. $$–$$$.

Yountville

&. ⴗ **Ad Hoc** (707-944-2487; adhoc restaurant.com) 6476 Washington Street, Yountville. Open 5–9 daily and 10:30–2 on Sunday. Originally this was a temporary experiment, but the buzz

NAPA'S "IT" SPOT: THE VEGETARIAN UBUNTU RESTAURANT.

of an accessible (and relatively casual) Thomas Keller restaurant within reach of the masses was too much for diners, who still line up every other Monday and Wednesday for the fried chicken dinner. Rumor on the street is that Keller buys chickens fed with milk powder, so they are juicier (alas, the reason bloggers post the fried chicken schedule). Every night, a prix fixe menu of four courses for $48 is offered (they post the day's menu online at 2 PM or you can get them e-mailed to you each day). Dishes are served family-style. Reservations strongly advised. $$$$.

&. ⴗ **Bistro Jeanty** (707-944-0103; bistrojeanty.com) 6510 Washington Street. Open daily from 11:30–10:30. Take a trip to the French country in this bucolic ode to cuisine. Philippe Jeanty creates his own tour de France with a delectable cream of tomato soup, *daube de boeuf,* and cassoulet. Desserts range from a collection of fine cheeses to a chocolate mousse crème brûlée. Reservations recommended. $$–$$$.

&. ⴗ **Bouchon** (707-944-8037; bouchonbistro.com) 6534 Washington Street, Yountville. Open 11:30–midnight daily. I can't help it, whenever I am in the region, I have to stop into Thomas Keller's foray into France. Sometimes I just walk through the restaurant inhaling the fresh bread, the rich aromas of steak frites, *truite aux amandes,* and tarte au citron—which of course makes me want to heave that cute little old lady waiting for a table aside and scream, "Please let me eat— I'm starving!" More often than not, I reserve a table on the patio (and even settle for inside the lofty bistro). And when all else fails, I head to the bakery/café for a pastry and tartine to go. Reservations required. $$$–$$$$.

&. **French Laundry** (707-944-2380; frenchlaundry.com) 6640 Washington Street. Open for dinner from 5:30 PM–9 PM daily as well as lunch 11 AM–1 PM on Friday through Sunday. What can I say about Thomas Keller's world-famous nine-course chef's tasting menu (or vegetable tasting menu) that hasn't already been said? My friend calls this the Superbowl of food—worth every cent of the hefty $240 per person tab (not including wine). Wear your finest digs and prepare for the royal treatment. Reservations required; they need to be made two months to the day of your visit (or try your luck on opentable.com—I hear they release two tables for each night). The best nine-course tasting menu ever: $$$$$$$$$$$.

&. ♈ **Redd** (707-944-2222; reddnapavalley.com) 6480 Washington Street, Yountville. Lunch (11:30–2:30), and dinner (5:30–10) served nightly in the

THE EASY GUIDE TO WINE AND FOOD PAIRING

If you're visiting the Wine Country, it's a given that your trip is going to include, what else, lots and lots of wine! While winery tours and tastings are a great way to try different varieties and begin to figure out your specific likes and dislikes, at some point you will be sitting down to dinner at one of the many fabulous dining locations, and the inevitable question will arise—what wine should I order to go with my glazed salmon? This guide is intended to be a crash course about some wine-pairing basic tips. Of course, this is supposed to be fun! Never get too hung up on the rules, because pairing your wine and food is absolutely a matter of personal taste and expression. This guide is merely to offer basic guidelines and suggestions, not rules set in stone, so experiment.

An ideal food and wine pairing should accomplish something that neither the food nor the wine can do on its own; in other words, they should complement one another. Wine will have different flavors, or notes, that are only brought out when paired with food. A great way to experience this is to pair wine and cheese together. Generally, white wines are going to complement a broader range of cheeses than reds, primarily because the flavors in red wines are often larger and juicier, sometimes stripping the cheese of its complexity. When having a creamier cheese, such as Brie or goat's milk cheese, a wine with some lively acidity will balance it out nicely. This is because the acidity of the wine will counteract the creamy, mouth-coating texture of the cheese, and act as a palate cleanser that enables you to taste the flavors more completely. For a white wine with great acidity, try a Sauvignon Blanc, or a Pinot Gris. If in doubt, it is hard to go wrong with a light, fizzy wine such as a Prosecco or a Moscato d'asti, both from Italy.

Although it is common knowledge that red wines generally pair better with meat dishes, while whites are complemented by lighter dishes such as salads and fish, this is not always the case. An easier, and more general

dining room, and you can get bar food all day. Green and brown tones, with white walls and big windows, allow you to focus on Richard Reddington's creative and elegant food rather than being caught up in the décor. Here you will experience California cuisine at its finest, from hamachi sashimi, to a Liberty Farms duck breast and Swiss chard crepe on celery root and chocolate sauce. The tasting menu highlights the creativity that makes this restau-

rant shine, while the bar menu offers favorites like gourmet fish tacos, pizza, and potstickers. Reservations recommended. $$–$$$$.

Rutherford
Auberge Du Soleil Restaurant See Eating Out.

St. Helena
& ⅋ **Martini House** (707-963-2233; martinihouse.com) 1245 Spring Street. Open from 11 AM–10 PM daily. Restau-

rule to follow is to pair delicate or lighter wines with lighter food, and to pair heavier or stronger-flavored food with a stronger wine that can stand up to the intensity. For example, in addition to being a wonderful match for creamy cheeses, a Sauvignon Blanc works well with grilled pork, trout, and salmon as well, for the flavors are on the lighter side. On the other hand, a heavier wine, such as a Cabernet or a Syrah, needs a dish such as a steak or game dish. Try a savory dish such as lamb with a spicy red wine like Cabernet Sauvignon. A lighter red wine such as a Merlot or a Pinot Noir might work better with a slightly lighter meat flavor, such as a veal or poultry that has been baked or roasted. However, sometimes, contrary flavors can be fantastic in food and wine pairings, as well. A good example of this is Chardonnay, which can be buttery, oaky, or crisp. If you were to pair a buttery Chardonnay, such as a Selby, with a cream-based sauce, this might be a little too close in flavor.

If you want your dessert to be on the lighter side, such as a fruit base, a white wine with some of corresponding fruit flavors is a great choice. For a fresh fruit dessert, a California Viognier pairs excellently. If your dessert is custard-based, try a sparkling wine such as Champagne or even a dry Spanish Cava, the bubbles will cut through the creaminess nicely. However, if you are like me and your dessert just has to include chocolate, this gives you the most options for a wine pairing. Typically, a red wine will pair the best with a chocolate dessert. If it is a lighter and somewhat sweeter chocolate dish, such as a chocolate mousse, try a really ripe Cabernet or a Merlot (from California of course). If the dessert is a dark or more bittersweet chocolate, try a Port or a big and bold Petite Sirah, such as the Napa Valley Girard. The latent cocoa flavors in the wine will explode when they come into contact with the chocolate. And when it comes down to it, that is the overarching goal of any food and wine pairing, to experience a feeling, flavor, or taste that would not have been possible if you had not tried the two together. So the rest is really just field research.

—Taylor Williams

rant designer Pat Kuleto and executive chef Todd Humphries have devised one of the most creative restaurants in Napa Valley: To evoke the Native American history of the region by using foraged, wild ingredients. Working with sustainable farms (including White Crane—a favorite for foraged salad greens from deep in the redwood forests), Humphries creates house-cured charcuterie, a terrine of foie gras, and a mushroom-tasting menu that will inspire praise from the most finicky eaters. Reservations recommended. $$$$.

Ỵ Restaurant at Meadowood (707-967-1205; meadowood.com) 900 Meadowood Lane. Open for dinner nightly. If you are looking for a collection of small tastes presented like delicate objects in a Miro painting, while being served by folks who believe in the gospel of their fine dining establishment, the Restaurant at Meadowood is made for you. This is not the spot for the kids or people with big appetites—you should head downstairs to the slightly more casual Grill (their breakfast is one of the best around)—but rather where couples celebrate their 50th anniversary. Reservations required. Tasting menu: $$$$.

& Ỵ Terra (707-963-8931; terrarestaurant.com) 1345 Railroad Avenue. Open for dinner Wednesday through Monday. For an anniversary dinner, it would be tough to pass up the stone-walled candlelit dining room at Terra. Chef-owners Hiro Sone and Lissa Doumani meld California cuisine with Asian accoutrements. Highlights include the broiled-sake black cod and shrimp dumplings with a shiso broth, and the grilled quail with bacon-bread pudding. Reservations recommended. $$$$.

Tra Vigne See *Eating Out.*

Calistoga

& Ỵ Bar Vino (707-942-9900; bar-vino.com) 1457 Lincoln. Open nightly for dinner. Most people don't expect to find a hip restaurant in Calistoga. Bar Vino's arrival (with JoLe and Solbar following close at her heels) brings urban sensibilities to the country with textured walls and bar, red on silver on black décor, good wine, and fine food. Chef Dominic Orsini's mostly Italian-themed small plate menu focuses on innovative ingredients such as wild boar gnocchi, pancetta wrapped dates, and wild mushroom pizza. $$–$$$.

♂ & Ỵ Brannan's Grill (707-942-2233; brannansgrill.com) 1374 Lincoln Avenue. Open for lunch and dinner daily. If this steakhouse, with live jazz on weekends and an evolved wine list, were in Columbus, Ohio, it might be one of the best restaurants in town. Being located in such close proximity to Thomas Keller's dynasty both helps and hurts Brannan's. Suddenly people who wouldn't pay 30 bucks for a filet, come here thinking they scored a deal. Big, loud, bright, and fun, this is the spot to have a nice dinner with the whole family. Reservations recommended. $$$–$$$$.

♂ & Ỵ JoLe (707-942-5938; jolerestaurant.com) 1457 Lincoln Avenue. Open at least 5–10 daily (until 11 on weekends). After husband-and-wife Chefs Matt and Sonjia Spector succeeded in creating Matyson, one of the hottest restaurants in Philadelphia, they sold it and headed west to open this modern farm-to-table organic restaurant. Menu items change daily, made for you to explore a variety of small plates. Savory favorites include the mushrooms and polenta, and the rib eye. Save room for Sonjia's desserts, which take you back to Grandma's kitchen with S'mores, cream pies, and chocolate galore.

Reservations recommended. Small plates: $–$$ (you'll need to order two to three plates per person to fill up).

✐ & ⸸ **SolBar at Solage** (707-226-0850; solagecalistoga.com) 755 Silverado Trail, Calistoga. Open from 7:30–3 and 5:30–11 daily. If the ladies from *Sex in the City* came to Napa Valley, they would surely sip Chardonnay by the pool as they enjoyed a summery meal of Dungeness crab salad, sand dabs (well, maybe only decadent Samantha would appreciate the butter-laden dish), and maybe even share a thin-crusted pizza. The see-and-be-seen loungy vibe will surely attract the oversized-sunglasses crowd of Angelenos. Reservations recommended for dinner. $$–$$$$.

EATING OUT

Napa
✐ & ⸸ **BarBersQ** (707-224-660; barbersq.com) 3900 D Bel Aire Plaza. Open 11:30–9 daily. Even though it is in a strip mall, foodies frequent this down-home barbeque restaurant. Concrete floors, a wall of wine, and plenty of black-and-white photos of Napa only add to the allure of the finger-licking food. Imagine if Grandma got together with the organic farmer down the road—you'd get organic BBQ chicken, honey-butter cornbread, melt-in-your-mouth macaroni and cheese, ribs that fall off the bone, and freshly grilled seafood. Reservations recommended. $$–$$$.

✐ & **Boonfly Café** (707-299-4900; theboonflycafe.com) Carneros Inn, 4048 Sonoma Highway. Open 7 AM–9 PM daily. Breakfast and brunch in this barn-meets-loft with exposed silver pipes and big windows takes me back to my farm-girl days. Sit outside on the porch swing to wait for your table, then enjoy a breakfast flatbread, green eggs and ham, a smoked-trout BLT, or

a Kobe burger in a down-to-earth setting perfect for the whole family, or for sitting at the counter and reading the *Chronicle* on a rainy Sunday. $$.

Napa Valley Roasting Company (707-224-2233) 948 Main Street, Napa or 1400 Oak Street, St. Helena. Though not the best coffee in Napa, it is up there. The St. Helena location attracts local winemakers and families, while the Napa location is a tourist destination.

✐ & **Oxbow Public Market** (oxbow publicmarket.com) 610 1st Street. Open at least 9–7 daily (10–5 Sunday). This long-awaited artisan marketplace began a renaissance in downtown Napa. It doesn't get much better than this. Sit on the deck along the Napa River and eat an *arepa* from **Pica Pica Maize Kitchen**, a croissant from **Model Bakery**, an ice cream from **Three Twins Organic Ice Cream**, or a fresh peach from the **Produce Market**. Or maybe you want a latte from San Francisco's **Ritual Coffee Roasters**, a milkshake and burger at **Taylor's Refresher**, or to sit at **Folio Enoteca** for seasonal sandwiches and a glass of Viognier. Other favorite stops include the **Olive Press** (see *Sonoma*), **Hog Island Oysters, Kanaloa Seafood,** and **Fatted Calf**.

Rutherford
& ⸸ **Auberge Du Soleil Bar** (707-967-3111; aubergedusoleil.com) 180 Rutherford Hill Road. Open from 11–11 (the restaurant has abbreviated hours). Most of us can't afford a four-course tasting menu at the fine Auberge restaurant ($98 a person), but almost all of us deserve to feel as entitled as the celebrities who dine there, so why not opt for a seat at this bar/restaurant. Only in Napa can you sit atop a Mediterranean villa that slopes down a mountain, and drink one of 25 wines by the glass while eating

the best burger and fries in the valley. The views are the best in the Wine Country, so even if you don't want food, come for a drink by the fire. You can also order off the restaurant menu if you are so inclined. $$–$$$.

Yountville

Bouchon Bakery See *Dining Out.*

✍ ♿ ♆ **Hurley's** (707-944-2345; hurleysrestaurant.com) 6518 Washington Street, Yountville. Open for lunch and dinner daily, plus late night they serve at the bar. Tired of pretentious dining that leaves you hungry afterwards? Hurley's is where locals go for huge entrees, casual friendly service, and great cocktails. The horseradish-crusted salmon, crab cakes, and daily specials are always right on target. Save room for the ice cream sandwich. Reservations recommended—try to get a seat on the patio, where there are heat lamps and they bring you blankets. $$–$$$.

✍ ♿ ♆ **Mustard's Grill** (707-944-2424; mustardsgrill.com) 7399 St. Helena Highway. Open for lunch and dinner daily. Cindy Pawlcyn's original outpost to her deserved food empire started as a gourmet diner. At night, you need reservations to gorge on hearty California cuisine like the seafood tostada, a calf liver, or chipotle-rubbed quail, while for lunches you'll wait with her adoring fans for seasonal Wine Country staples like gourmet burgers and salads. I'd bring Mom here for her birthday lunch. $$–$$$.

✍ ♿ **NapaStyle Paninoteca Cafe** (707-945-1229; napastyle.com) V Marketplace, 6525 Washington Street. Open from at least 11 AM–4 AM daily. It's tough to find good cheap food in Yountville, but at Michael Chiarello's new location of his NapaStyle store, you can eat and still have cash left to shop. The house-cured salumi, chicken or pulled-pork paninis, and of course

the wine, are winners. Add to that a spacious patio for the kids to run around in (or adults to relax in between tasting visits) and you'll be smitten. $.

Oakville Grocery (707-944-9902) 7856 St. Helena Highway, Oakville. You'll likely drive through the town of Oakville on a weekend and spot hordes of people lined up out the door of a pocket-sized market. It will behoove you to park your car (not in the lot madness, but down the street) and get in line to order humungous gourmet sandwiches at the deli counter. Just prepare to rub elbows with your neighbor for a good chunk of time and take your sandwich elsewhere. $–$$.

Redd See *Dining Out.*

St. Helena

✍ **Azteca Market** (707-963-4963) 789 Main Street. Open at least 8–6 daily. Tacos, pork tamales, and carne asada for under 10 bucks—this is exactly what you need when visiting the valley. After you are done being fancy, come here to get back down to earth, by eating cheap good tacos on picnic tables outside. Vegetarians will go hungry here. $.

✍ ♿ ♆ **Cindy's Backstreet Kitchen** (707-963-1200; cindysbackstreet kitchen.com) 1327 Railroad Avenue. Open 11:30–9 daily. All day eager diners fill Cindy Pawlcyn's country restaurant to sit under the fig tree, sipping wine and enjoying the mostly Latin-inspired California comfort food. Specialties include the grit, chard, and mushroom tamale, slow-roasted pork, and a S'mores dessert that will send you back to third grade summer camp. $$–$$$.

✍ ♿ **Gillwoods Café** (707-963-1788 or 707-253-0409) 1313 Main Street, St. Helena or 1320 Town Center, Napa. Open for breakfast and lunch. If you are tired of the chichi Napa Valley restaurants serving up toenail-sized portions of food then charging you a hundred (or $240) bucks, deposit your bootie in line here at this cozy diner, which serves cheap, massive portions of breakfast favorites. $.

☍ ♿ 🍷 **Go Fish** (707-963-0700; gofish restaurant.com) 641 Main Street. Open for lunch and dinner daily. Chef Cindy Pawlcyn, of Mustards and Cindy's Backstreet Kitchen fame, and Sushi Hana Chef Ken Tominaga have created a sushi haven in St. Helena. Nautical mixed with industrial décor doesn't much complement the exquisite sushi offerings, like Ken and Cindy's combination plates, or even the wide variety of seafood or meat entrees (like the arctic char in a fennel pomegranate jus) prepared to your liking, but you're here to eat, and with these two running the kitchen you can bet it'll be good. Reservations recommended. $$–$$$$.

The Grill at Meadowood See *Dining Out—The Restaurant at Meadowood.*

☍ ♿ 🍷 **Market: An American Restaurant** (707-963-3799; markets thelena.com) 1347 Main Street. Open daily from 11:30–10. When I grilled three different friends in St. Helena about where to take my son for lunch, they each emphatically swore by Market. Farmers' market fresh cuisine served in an 1890 building, by Chef Douglas Keane (of Cyrus fame—see *Dining Out* Healdsburg), delights locals who come here to relax in a casual atmosphere and grub on fried chicken, an adult macaroni and cheese, and porcini mushroom ravioli. Check out the back bar, which dates back to the Grand Ballroom of the Palace Hotel and was reportedly taken out during Prohibition. $$–$$$.

Model Bakery (707-963-8192; the modelbakery.com) 1357 Main Street, St. Helena. Open 6:30–6 Tuesday through Friday, 7–6 Saturday, and 7–4 Sunday. For over 80 years this bakery has been home to the best pastries and bread north of San Francisco. Just thinking about their smoked-salmon croissants makes me hungry.

☍ ♿ **Taylor's Automatic Refresher** (707-963-3486; taylorsrefresher.com) 933 Main Street. Open 10:30–9 daily. A one-of-a-kind family-owned burger and fries joint using the finest ingredients from local farms and meat from humanely treated animals charts high on my list of must-visit restaurants in Northern California. The ideal place for a pumpkin milkshake or a microbrew, a big old burger or a Cobb salad, to bring the kids, or to nurse a hangover. This is the original outpost of this local restaurant, but you'll find others in the Ferry Building in SF and at Napa's Oxbow Market. $–$$.

☍ ♿ 🍷 **Tra Vigne** (707-967-9999; tra vignerestaurant.com) 1050 Charter Oak. Open for lunch and dinner daily. Most people know about the fine dining half of this huge restaurant founded by superstar Chef Michael Chiarello, but the trick to getting in at this wonderful Italian spot is to march straight to the pizzeria for great pasta, *piadine*, pizza, and soft-serve ice cream. $–$$.

Calistoga

☍ **Buster's Original Southern Barbecue** (707-942-5605; busterssouth ernbbq.com) 1207 Foothill Boulevard. Open for lunch and dinner daily. Just as you enter Calistoga the smoky haze sends a whiff of serious barbecue your way, and you begin to imagine pork loin, chicken, chili dogs, and pork ribs, those artery-clogging delights more fitting to Arkansas than a Wine Country parking lot. Don't come here for free-range chicken or seitan kebobs, this is the real deal y'all. $–$$.

☍ ♿ 🍷 **Calistoga Inn and Brewery** (707-942-4101; calistogainn.com) 1250 Lincoln Avenue. Open 11 AM–10 daily and Sunday brunch. Locals swear by this historic hotel's creek-side dining (or in winter, inside the classic dining room), complete with the "best" buffalo wings, a smoked turkey and Brie sandwich, peas and pasta, plus live music in the evenings. You might also choose to plop down in the bar for a beer at the brewery. Here you'll meet good ole locals who can tell you about what Calistoga was like before Solage's black cruisers and Dr. Wilkinson's mud baths. $–$$.

♪ ᨆ **Calistoga Roastery** (707-942-5757; calistogaroastery.com) 1426 Lincoln Avenue. Open daily from 6:30–6 PM. This packed coffeehouse serves up great lattes and pastries. I love coming here and listening to locals chatting—it reminds me that this really is a small town.

♪ ᨆ **Café Sarafornia** (707-942-0555) 1413 Lincoln Avenue. Open for breakfast and lunch. When I want a big country breakfast, I head here to eat heaping omelets and pancakes. Don't be fooled with the gourmet fare. This is the spot to regress to simple breakfasts at the counter, and cheap lunches. $.

NIGHTLIFE ᛉ **Anna's Cantina** (707-963-4921) 1205 Main Street, St. Helena. The bar to hit if you are staying in or near St. Helena; they also serve food.

ᛉ **Brannan's Grill** See *Dining Out*.

ᛉ **Calistoga Inn Restaurant and Brewery** See *Eating Out*.

ᛉ **Downtown Joe's** (707-258-2337; downtownjoes.com) 902 Main Street, Napa. Soon this won't be the only happening bar in Napa, but for now, this is where you head to hear live music by the river.

ᛉ **Hurley's** See *Eating Out*.

ᛉ **Hydro Bar and Grill** (707-942-9777; hydrogrillnapavalley.com) 1403 Lincoln Avenue, Calistoga. More like a

bar you'd find in a college town than Calistoga, this restaurant offers pub grub, jazz, and blues, and the occasional rock band or DJ night.

ᛉ **JoLe** See *Dining Out*.

ᛉ **Martini House** See *Dining Out*.

Napa Valley Opera House (707-226-7372; nvoh.org) 1030 Main Street, Napa. Newly renovated, this centerpiece in downtown Napa was constructed in 1879. Today symphonies populate the schedule.

Napa Valley Symphony (707-226-6872) Hopefully the symphony will be in town when you visit; they perform at the Lincoln Theater or the Napa Valley Opera House.

ᛉ **Silverado Brewing Co.** (707-967-9876; silveradobrewingcompany.com) 3020 St. Helena Highway, St. Helena. Sometimes you just want a pint and some fries on a deck with your buddies.

✳ Selective Shopping

In Downtown Napa you'll find many of the stores you see elsewhere, with a few specialized boutiques thrown in. To shop, head to either the Town Center in downtown, **Oxbow Public Market, the Bounty Hunter Wine Shop**, the Premium Outlets (premiumoutlets .com; 629 Factory Stores Drive) where you'll find a Barneys outlet among other brands; or head to the Bel Aire Plaza to find a large **Copperfield's Books**, a few gourmet markets, and a great children's store.

In Yountville, the **V Marketplace** (vmarketplace.com; 6525 Washington Street), built in 1870, hawks boutique finds at **Napastyle**, **Gallery 1870**, **V Wine Cellar**, and a handful of fashion and jewelry stores.

When I want to shop for gifts or stroll through a historic downtown, I head to St. Helena's Main Street. Stores not to miss include the fair trade **Baksheesh**,

Dean and DeLuca gourmet market, St. Helena **Olive Oil Company**, **Main Street Books**, and make sure to pop into the cooking store at the **Culinary Academy**.

Farther north along Lincoln Avenue in Calistoga, you'll find the deals—thrift stores, boutiques, a wonderful kids' clothing store, **Copperfield's Books**, and the local secret on CA 29, just south of Lincoln, is the **Wine Garage**, which sells wines for under $25—they use real gas pump nozzles on the wall to fill jugs.

✳ Seasonal Events

Ongoing: **Calistoga Town Dances** (calistogavisitors.com) On the first Friday of each month, head out to downtown Calistoga for an old-fashioned town dance.

February: **Mustard Festival** (mustard festival.org) In February and March throughout the valley this wonderful festival honors the bounty growing right here in Napa Valley with music, food, wine, and art.

April: **First and Third Thursday Movie Night** (calistogavisitors.com) Through August, Calistoga's downtown offers free movies on Thursday nights.

June: **Saturday on the Plaza** (napa downtown.com) Dwight Murray Plaza, 1st and Main Streets, Napa. Every Saturday through September, come hear free concerts from 4–7.

Robert Mondavi Summer Festival (robertmondaviwinery.com) Oakville. Through August, come out to the winery to hear live music on the main lawn under the stars. Big-name world musicians as well as domestic jazz greats have been known to drop in. Wine and cheese tasting happens at intermission.

July: **Napa County Fair** (napacounty

fairgrounds.com) 1435 Oak Street, Calistoga. Over Fourth of July weekend, this annual county fair offer rides, food, and a parade.

Wine Country Film Festival (wine countryfilmfestival.com) For four weekends in July and August, Napa Valley rolls out the red carpet for Hollywood. You can see world premieres of major films first.

August: **Harvest** From August through October, depending on the weather, Napa Valley's temperature isn't the only thing that heats up. During Crush (or Harvest), people come from around the world to help harvest that year's crop. See how it's done, attend parties, barrel-tasting events, and even get to stomp some grapes. Call wineries for details.

Music in the Vineyards (napavalley-music.org) Throughout August the Napa Valley Chamber Music Festival performs at wineries around the valley.

November: **Carols in the Caves** (carolsinthecaves.com) On November and December weekends, come hear Christmas carols sung in the wine caves—it's heavenly.

December: **Calistoga Lighted Tractor Parade** My friend calls this annual event a "Kick in the head" complete with carolers, live music, Santa and his crew, and of course colorful tractors done up in lights. Though it sounds like a kids-only deal, adults line the street, sipping beer, chuckling with friends, and taking in the arrival of the holidays.

INLAND MENDOCINO AND LAKE COUNTIES

Wines, marijuana, natural foods, and redwoods flourish in the Mendocino County innards. Way ahead of its time (to some points of view), this county was the first to create organic wine, ban genetically modified crops, and make pot smoking legal for personal use. Called the Emerald Triangle for more than its trees, folks farm heaps of marijuana (including organic strains), local radio broadcasts when the DEA flies over, and ballot initiatives constantly pit growers against their neighbors. Lately however, Mendocino wines have been stealing the show, by attracting national attention.

From the south, entering Mendocino County seems like an extension of Wine Country. While from the north, it is reminiscent of Humboldt. The area is a mishmash of crunchy-granola hippies and high-end wineries (Cristal was created here). Blink and you'll miss the towns strung along US 101: **Hopland** (which deftly combines green ideals with old-town charm), **Ukiah** (Mendocino County's largest city, mixes history with modernity), and **Willits** (which allows visitors easy access to redwood parks and wineries). Idyllic **Anderson Valley** doesn't look like much at first glance: a winding road shaded by redwoods, occasionally opening to offer glimpses of rows of vineyards and old farmhouses. This is Mendocino County at its finest. The three hamlets of **Yorkville, Boonville,** and **Philo** are so remote they even created their own language called Boontling to communicate. Settle in and you'll encounter organic roadhouses with farm-fresh cuisine, miles of hiking trails, and the foggy cold that forces people to slow down.

In Lake County, wine country sophistication meets Coors Light-drinking folks along **Clearlake**. Here you'll find reasonably priced accommodations, small historic cities, RV parks, and California's largest freshwater lake to enjoy during the hot summer months.

GUIDANCE For information about Mendocino County, contact the **Mendocino Visitor Bureau** (Gomendo.com) or the **Mendocino County Visitor Bureau** (mendocino.winecountry.com).

Brutocao School House Plaza (707-744-2000; 13500 South US 101, Hopland) houses the Mendocino Wine and Visitor Center in the Albert Building. Not only do they offer lots of info, but you can also play on one of the six authentic championship Bocce Ball courts.

For assistance planning your Lake County adventure, contact the **Lake County Visitor Center** (707-274-5652 or 800-525-3743; lakecounty.com) 5110 E. CA 20, Lucerne.

HELPFUL WEB SITES
Lakecountywinegrape.org
Andersonvalleychamber.com

GETTING THERE Heading north along US 101, you'll encounter Hopland, Ukiah, and Willits. To get to Anderson Valley from US 101, when you enter Cloverdale drive west on CA 128. To get to Lake County from Napa, take CA 29 north. From US 101, drive east on either CA 175 (Lower Lake) or CA 20 (Upper Lake). From the Sacramento area (I-5), take CA 20 west. If you don't have a car, **Greyhound** (greyhound.com) stops in the major cities of both counties.

GETTING AROUND A bummer, but a fact, is that you truly need a car to explore the region properly. The **Mendocino Transit Authority** (4mta.org) travels around Ukiah and to the coast, but it isn't your best option. Lake County's bus system, **Lake Transit** (laketransit.org), services the entire county.

✳ To See and Do

Hopland
The Solar Living Institute (707-744-2017; solarliving.org) 13771 S. US 101, Hopland. Open 8:30–5 daily. Established in 1998 by the founder of the Real Goods Trading Company, this nonprofit educational organization promotes sustainable living through environmental education. They offer guided tours on weekends for $3 and occasionally throw some mean earth-friendly parties.

Boonville
Anderson Valley Brewing Co. (707-895-BEER; avbc.com) 17700 CA 253, Boonville. Open at least 1–6 (until 7 on Friday). To say this brewpub put Anderson Valley on the map might be hyperbole, but it sure helped. Now microbrew lovers sojourn out to this solar-powered brewery to taste award-winning brews like the famous Boont Amber Ale. Every day at 3 PM you can tour the brewery, but be sure to wear closed-toed shoes. The beer garden is my favorite place for an afternoon pint.

Anderson Valley Farmers' Market Boonville Hotel parking lot, Boonville, Saturday morning from 9:45–noon.

Anderson Valley Museum (707-895-3207; andersonvalleymuseum.org) CA 128, Boonville. Open February through November on Friday through Sunday from 1–4. View Pomo Indian artifacts, a sheep-shearing exhibit, and learn about the intriguing history of the Boonville folks. Free.

Ukiah
City of Ten Thousand Buddhas (cttbusa.org) 2001 Talmage Road, Ukiah. Open 8–6 daily. Café open daily except for Tuesday, 12–3. At Wonderful Enlightenment Mountain, you can visit an international Buddhist community established in 1976. You can tour the property, eat at the vegetarian café, or head to the gift shop to learn more about Buddhism. Free.

WINERIES AND TASTING ROOMS

Considered the spearhead in the green wine movement, Mendocino County wines don't merely make you feel proud to tell Al Gore of your wine-drinking habits, but the region is also home to some exquisite Pinot Noirs, sparkling wines, Gewurtztraminer, and Syrah. Farther inland, you can try out the earth-friendly Cabernet, Merlot, and Zinfandels. Down-to-earth, fruit-forward, organic or biodynamic wines, you'll be hard-pressed not to walk away with a bottle (or three).

Lake County's distinct variations in climate and altitude allow growers to create almost every type of wine you can imagine. Another highlight of the region is instead of driving from winery to winery, you can hit up tasting rooms by boat.

Hopland

Jeriko Estate (707-744-1140; jeriko.us) 12141 Hewitt and Sturtevant Road. Open at least 11–4 daily. This Mediterranean villa grows tasty organic and biodynamic wines. They are known for their Brut, so you might want to grab a bottle for a harvest picnic on the grounds.

SIP! Mendocino (707-744-8375; SIPmendocino.com) 13420 US 101. Open 11–6 daily. This is a great place to become acquainted with Mendocino wines. With at least 18 daily glasses to taste, you probably won't get to experience them all, but you will learn about local growing practices. They also serve appetizers and can help you plan your tasting route.

Redwood Valley

Frey Vineyards (707-485-5177; freywine.com) 14000 Tomki Road. Call for an appointment. The oldest organic and biodynamic winemakers in the United States, Frey wins awards for almost every wine they craft.

Lolonis Winery (925-938-8066; lolonis.com) 1905 Road D. Call for appointment. I didn't like white wine until I tried theirs. Now I am hooked. A picnic by the pond with a bottle of wine is unparalleled.

Philo

Handley Cellars (800-733-3151; handleycellars.com) 3151 CA 128. Tasting room open daily from at least 11–5. Tours by appointment. Picnicking in this country-style garden environment with a bottle of Chardonnay or Pinot Noir is a treat. Also, touring Milla Handley's international folk art collection, or trying out one of the Culinary Adventures (where winemakers and chefs pair wines with local food) is worth your time.

Husch Vineyards (707-895-3216; huschvineyards.com) 4400 CA 128. Open at least 10–5 daily. On a warm day, pack a picnic, grab a bottle of their Chenin Blanc or Chardonnay, and enjoy the rustic setting.

Navarro Vineyards (707-895-3686; navarrowine.com) 5601 CA 128. Open at least 11–5 daily. Every time I dine with a local, they bust out Navarro wine. It's that good. Really. You can also purchase cheese and smoked salmon at the tasting room for a picnic.

Roederer Estate (707-894-2288; roedererestate.com) 4501 CA 128. Open 11–5 daily. For those of you who appreciate bling in your wine, head over to the home of Cristal to taste some stellar Brut, Rosé, and other sparkling delicacies.

Scharffenberger Cellars (707-895-2957; scharffenbergercellars.com) 8501 CA 128. Open daily from 11–5. The new winemaker churns out superior Brut and sparkling wines while staying true to the original owner's philosophy.

Ukiah

Parducci (707-463-5357; parducci.com) 501 Parducci Road, just off US 101, north of Ukiah. Open daily from 10–5. Growing, bottling, and corking sustainable wines, this winery is a great place for a picnic.

Tierra (707-468-7936; artgardenwine.com) 312 N. School Road. Open Wednesday through Sunday 12–6; Thursday until 8 PM. If you are looking for those boutique artisan wines that hardly anyone has heard of, this art, garden, and wine-tasting boutique can help.

Lake County

Ceago Vinegarden (707-274-1462; ceago.com) 5115 E. CA 20, Nice. Open daily 10–5. Tours by appointment. Owned by Jim Fetzer, one of the leaders in the Mendocino County biodynamic movement. Picnic in a field of lavender and taste some really good wine. There is a seasonal café on the property as well.

Cougar's Leap Winery (707-279-0651; cougarsleap.com) 9300 Seigler Springs Road, Kelseyville. Open Friday through Sunday 11–5 (May through October only). Wine plus mountains equals a hotbed for creativity here at this solar-powered winery. While sipping their Syrah and Zinfandel, you can gaze across the Mayacamas Mountains at herds of deer.

Terrill Cellars Winery (707-252-8444; terrillcellars.com) 16175 Main Street, Lower Lake. Open 11–4 daily. Located in the Tuscan Village in Lower Lake, you can sip port and Cabernet and pretend you are in Italy.

Grace Hudson and the Sun House Museum (707-467-2836; gracehudson museum.org) 431 S. Main, Ukiah. Open Wednesday through Saturday 10 AM–4:30 PM and Sunday 12–4 PM. This art, anthropology, and history museum showcases photos, paintings, Pomo Indian artifacts, and more. The Sun House, a 1911 redwood Craftsman, was built by the Hudsons; you can tour it with docents and learn about their bohemian lifestyle. Fee.

Orr Hot Springs Resort (707-462-6277) 13201 Orr Springs Road, Ukiah. Hot springs and river water flow together beneath trees, while hippies prance around naked sharing their kombucha. It is best during the week, since they limit the number of soakers. They also offer massage service, cabins, and camping. Reservations required.

Pomo Basketry Museum (707-467-4200) 1160 Lake Mendocino Drive, Ukiah. Open Wednesday through Sunday 9–5. There is a Pomo Native American Museum and Cultural Center on the north shore of Lake Mendocino, where you may learn about the first people to inhabit these lands. Free.

Ukiah Municipal Golf Course (707-467-2832; ukiahgolf.com) 599 Park Avenue, Ukiah. This lovely public course offers great rates and pretty nice views. $21–39.

Vichy Springs Hot Springs Resort (707-462-9515; vichysprings.com) 2605 Vichy Springs Road, Ukiah. Open 9 AM–dusk. This magical hot springs is open for day use. The champagne mineral pools, the 700 acres of hiking trails, and the Olympic-sized pool will make the day go faster than you want it to. Day use fee: $27 (2 hours) or $45 (all day).

Willits

✢ **Ridgewood Ranch (The home of Seabiscuit)** (707-459-5992; willits.org) 16200 US 101, Willits. In summer, you can tour the ranch and view Seabiscuit memorabilia. Call for times and days. Ridgewood Ranch is one of the few existing sites depicting the life of Seabiscuit. Weekday tours: $15 adults; children under 11 free. Weekend tours: $25.

The Skunk Train See *Fort Bragg*.

Lake County

Crazy Creek Gliders (707-987-9112) 18896 Grange Road, Middletown. Take a glider ride over the spring wildflowers and the lake, while riding the hot air from the geysers. Calling it a thrill is an understatement. Reservations required.

Harbin Hot Springs (707-987-2477; harbin.org) 18424 Harbin Springs Road, Middletown. Bay Area folks head up here to escape city life—and their clothing. This hot springs resort has miles of hiking trails, hot and cold

IN MENDOCINO COUNTY, YOU'LL NEVER FORGET YOU'RE IN NORTHERN CALIFORNIA.

plunge pools, camping facilities, and hotel accommodations. You must be a member to enter (a trial membership costs $10). A day pass ranges from $20–35 (adults) and $15–30 (kids).

Hidden Valley Lake Golf Course (707-987-3035; hvla.com) CA 29, north of Middletown. Tee off near this little lake community on a championship course. $45–55.

Historic Courthouse Museum (707-263-4555) 255 N Main Street, Lakeport. Open Wednesday through Saturday 10 AM–4 PM and Sunday 12–4 PM. Built in 1871, this courthouse exhibits basketry, pioneer rifles, and geological timelines. Free.

Kelseyville Farmers' Market at Steele Wines 4350 Thomas Drive, Kelseyville. From Memorial Day through October, Saturdays come alive from 8–12. For more information on growers and farm visits, pick up the "Lake County Farm Trails" brochure from the visitor center.

FISHING

Not only does Lake County get to brag that it has the cleanest air and the largest natural lake in the state, but it also claims to offer the best bass fishing around. You can fish year-round. You just have to make sure to have your fishing license (see *What's Where*). The best spots to fish include **Clear Lake State Park** (Off Soda Bay Road), **Highland Springs Reservoir/Highland Creek Reservoir**, **Horseshoe Bend** (Soda Bay Road, between Soda Bay and Buckingham Park outside of Kelseyville) and **Rodman Slough** (both above and below the bridge of the Nice-Lucerne Cutoff between CA 20 and 29 on the Northshore).

Fishing Guides

It seems everyone and his brother is in the business of being a fishing guide. Here are a few that have been recommended to me; for more listings check out lakecounty.com.

Big George's Fishing Guide Service (707-279-9269; biggeorgesguide.com) Kelseyville. His 25 years of fishing on the lake makes George a pretty reliable guy. He supplies bait, tackle, and gear and you pay him $45–50 per person.

Konocti Guide Service (707-279-0472; mtkonoctiguide.com) Kelseyville. Dave Majestic claims to be the man for your fishing charter needs. He supplies the gear and charges $30–40 per person.

License, Bait, and Tackle Outlets

Clearlake Bait and Tackle (707-994-4399) 14699 Lakeshore Drive, Clearlake.

Konocti Harbor Marina Store See *Water Sports*.

Konocti Harbor Resort Marina (707-279-6628) 8727 Soda Bay Road, Kelseyville. Find any water-sport gear you need here: fishing boats, Jet skis, paddle boats. You name it.

Narrows Lodge Resorts (707-275-2718) 5690 Blue Lakes Road, Upper Lake. These guys rent fishing gear, rowboats, and kayaks to spend the day on Blue Lakes.

Wilbur Hot Springs See *Shasta Cascade*.

✱ Green Spaces

Admiral William Standley State Recreation Area (707-247-3318; parks.ca.gov) North of Willits, 14 miles west of Laytonville on Branscomb Road. Heading east from Westport you'll find this rich redwood forest, the Eel River, and plentiful hiking. Fishermen savor the wealth of salmon and steelhead.

Clear Lake (707-262-1618; lakecounty.com) Off CA 29 in Lake County. This is the largest natural freshwater lake in California. Folks head out for plentiful bass fishing, boating, swimming, and hiking (check out the Dorn Nature Trail, a 1.5-mile loop off CA 29 in Kelseyville). Favorite spots for kayakers are Rodman Slough (off CA 29 near Nice), plus Anderson Marsh State Historic Park and McVicar Preserve in Lower Lake. Beach lovers head to Clear Lake State Park (Kelseyville), Nice Beach, and Davis Beach. There are a number of camping spots around the lake, which you need to reserve in advance.

Hendy Woods State Park (707-895-3141; parks.ca.gov) Go 8 miles northwest of Boonville, south of CA 128 on Philo-Greenwood Road. This 845-acre park of old-growth redwoods was the home to the Hendy Hermit, believed to be a Ukrainian Jewish survivor of World War II. Several of his hermit huts remain along the Hermit Hut Trail. You can camp here for $25 per night, or get a cabin for $50.

Lake Mendocino (lakemendocino.com) Off US 101, follow the signs on Lake Mendocino Drive. Created by the U.S. Army, this recreation area offers a wealth

ESCAPE INTO MENDOCINO COUNTY'S FOREST.

of outdoor activities, including boating, fishing, swimming, hiking, and camping. You can camp in one of four lakefront campsites (only the Kyen Campground is open year-round). Fees range from $8–20.

Mendocino National Forest (707-983-6118; r5.fs.fed.us) North of Willits, take CA 162 east. Outdoor lovers will rejoice at how empty the area feels, how much wildlife you'll encounter, and how much beauty lives in the region. A couple highlights include the tiny Hammerhorn Lake, Eel River, Little Howard Lake, and Lake Pillsbury (a great spot for fishing). As you might expect, there are a bunch of campsites in the area. If you want to be remote, head out to the primitive sites at Trout Creek, Lower Nye, Eel River, and Wells Cabin. Otherwise, join the masses around Lake Pillsbury at the Navy site, Fuller Grove, and Lake Pillsbury Resort.

Montgomery Woods (parks.ca.gov) Go 13 miles east of Ukiah on Orr Hot Springs Road. For a moment in time, Mendocino claimed to have the tallest tree in the world. And though these things change, visitors flocked into the Montgomery Woods redwood area to view the tree, which suffered damage to its roots after the tourist traffic. Now that the park doesn't have bragging rights, you can stroll beneath these giant trees, probably seeing more wildlife than humans.

✳ Lodging

Boonville

Anderson Creek Inn (800-552-1202; andersoncreekinn.com) 12050 Anderson Valley Way. A little like staying with family members, this 16-acre ranch in Boonville offers something no other accommodations in the area do: a pool. In summer, you'll appreciate that, the friendly service, the ranch pets, the full breakfast, the redwoods and oaks, and the five simple country-antique rooms. $$; Two-night minimum on weekends; fee for extra person; no small children allowed.

✐ ☀ ♿ **Boonville Hotel** (707-895-2210; boonvillehotel.com) 14050 CA 128. A 10-room modern roadhouse for people who don't want Aunt Edna's country inn, amenities might include private decks, rocking chairs, comfy beds, continental breakfast, and bright rooms. Book a studio or bungalow room in the back by the creek, since the hotel is on CA 128. $$–$$$; fee for extra person or pet.

✐ ☀ **The Other Place** (707-895-3979; sheepdung.com) Boonville. If it's privacy you crave, head out to this ranch estate for a few nights in these one- and two-bedroom pastoral cottages. Bright, airy, and freshly built, expect IKEA furniture, marble baths, BBQ areas, and plenty of room for the kids and dogs to frolic. The one-bedroom Oaks cottage has a fireplace, views of the vineyards, and, as the name suggests, is sheltered by oak trees. The owners also rent out Long Valley Ranch houses and a studio near Ukiah. $$–$$$.

Philo

The Philo Apple Farm (707-895-2333; philoapplefarm.com) 18501 Greenwood Road, Philo. Some of you, who want room service and daily housekeeping service, won't enjoy the rustic simplicity of crickets and butterflies, farm-fresh apple juice delivered to your door, or the bright sun streaming through the windows way too early. My favorite cottage of the three is the Red Door, with an outdoor shower and wood-stove fireplace. Rates: $$–$$$; two-night minimum on weekends.

Ukiah

Orr Hot Springs Resort *To See and Do.*

"1" Vichy Springs Resort (707-462-9515; vichysprings.com) 2605 Vichy Springs Road, Ukiah. Flowering trellises lead you from one of the 26 rooms or cottages to the mineral pools, and a bit of peace will follow you home. Go for the cottages, which are more private. $$–$$$$, fee for extra guest.

Willits

❀ &️ "1" ❀ Baechtel Creek Inn and Spa (707-459-9063; baechtelcreekinn.com) 101 Gregory, Willits. Located just off US 101 in Willits, this is a lovely place to stop when passing through town. The 46 rooms are simple, clean, and include breakfast. For a more authentic experience, reserve a custom room, decorated with period antiques. $$–$$$; no children under 16 in custom rooms.

Lake County

&️ "1" The Bungalow (707-998-0399; thebungalow.com) 10195 E. CA 20, Clearlake Oaks. Right on the lake, this 1930s Craftsman cottage allows you to enjoy the lake, without being bothered by those roaring boats. Three antique-decorated rooms, a wonderful breakfast, a hot tub, a rose garden, and a private beach give this solar-powered inn a touch of romance. Rates: $$; two-night minimum on weekends.

❀ &️ Harbin Hot Springs (800-622-2477; harbin.org) 18424 Harbin Springs Road, Middletown. Friends stayed at this hot springs resort (where most people wandered around in the buff) and were kept up all night by a deaf couple having loud sex. Hence, this is *not* a place for the prudish, timid, or shy. If I haven't scared you away yet, you'll love the quiet, mellow, anything-goes (except sex in the pools) attitude. You can camp, sleep in a tent cabin or a dorm room, have your own bathtub or your own cottage. Rooms are decorated in period antiques. The newest addition is the domes, which are sort of like yurts, but more Alice in Wonderland. There are three restaurants and a market on the property as well. $–$$$ (you must buy a $10 membership to stay over); children are not allowed in rooms; two-night minimum stay on weekends.

Inn at Kelsey Creek (866-928-9804; innatkelseycreek.com) 16335 CA 175, Cobb. The five cottages come with their own kitchens and fireplaces, privacy, and a charm distinct to wine country. Cute and filled with country decor, these cabins inspire romance. The Orchid room is more masculine, while the others favor a more traditional B&B style. Amenities include kitchens, whirlpool tubs, barbeques, decks, and fireplaces. $$; two-night minimum on weekends; fee for third person.

❀ "1" &️ Konocti Harbor Resort and Spa (800-660-LAKE; konoctiharbor.com) 8727 Soda Bay Road, Kelseyville. This 250-room resort acts as a sort of hub in these parts. Rooms aren't much to speak of, but the beach access, watersport activities, concerts, spa and restaurants, tennis, volleyball, two pools, mini golf, playground, kids' club, three restaurants, and two bars are quite the draw. $–$$$; $10 for third person.

"1" &️ Tallman Hotel (707-275-2244; tallmanhotel.com) 9550 Main Street, Upper Lake. This historic boutique hotel is like nothing else in the area, offering Japanese soaking-tubs in some of the 17 rooms, period antiques that have been selected with care, and the perfect mix of class and homey comfort. While your boater friends head to Konocti, romance-seekers searching for a small dash of luxury will appreciate this low-key option. There is a restaurant on property (see *Dining Out*). $$–$$$.

CAMPING See *Green Spaces*.

✳ Where to Eat

DINING OUT

Boonville

♀ **Boonville Hotel Restaurant** (707-895-2210; boonvillehotel.com) 14050 CA 128. Open for dinner Thursday through Monday. Bright and airy, the chef changes the menu depending on what's fresh, so you might enjoy cornmeal-crusted halibut one night and a rack of lamb the next. Whatever is cooking, you can guarantee that the American comfort food will warm you up on a foggy winter night. Reservations recommended. $$$.

Ukiah

⌀ **Patrona** (707-462-9181; patrona restaurant.com) 130 W. Standley Street. Open Tuesday through Saturday 5–9. Probably the nicest place to eat in Ukiah, here you'll find exposed brick walls, white couches, and a communal redwood table. While the ambiance is urban, the food highlights local farm ingredients like trout, chard crepes, or burgers for the little guys. $$–$$$.

Lake County

& ♀ **Blue Wing Saloon and Café** (707-275-2233; bluewingsaloon.com) 9520 Main Street, Upper Lake. Open for lunch (11–3) and dinner (5–9) daily and Sunday brunch. This is probably one of the best restaurants in Lake County. Here you'll get American comfort food with a California mentality, which means locally grown produce, Lake Country wines, and microbrews. Plus, the dark wood and saloon setting makes everything taste a little better. Reservations recommended. $$$.

EATING OUT

Hopland

⌀ & **Bluebird Cafe** (707-744-1633) 13340 South US 101, Hopland. Open daily for breakfast, lunch, and dinner.

Abundant breakfasts that will fill most any stomach; end up here for lunch, which features great veggie and exotic meat entrees, like a wild boar burger. $–$$.

Boonville

Boonville General Store (707-895-9477) 14077-A CA 128. Open 9–3 Thursday through Monday. Here's where to go for gourmet picnic fixings, espresso, and good cheese. They also whip up breakfast on weekend mornings. $.

⌀ **Lauren's Cafe** (707-895-3869) 14211 CA 128. Open from 5–9 Tuesday through Saturday. Lauren grabbed up the market for family dining in this little renegade town. Serving up an eclectic menu of burgers, pasta, pizza, and Asian dishes, you'll catch locals shooting pool or playing music, while families share potpies. $–$$.

Philo

Libby's (707-895-2646) 8651 CA 128. Open Tuesday through Saturday from 11:30–2:30 and 5–8:30. I heard about this place from a vintner friend in Sonoma, who says that she and her friends fought over who would deliver wine to Boonville so they could get to stop at this little gem. And though service is super slow, the food is as fresh as can be. Everyone raves about the carnitas, so if you don't mind waiting a bit, that's the way to go. $$.

Ukiah

Cheesecake Momma (707-462-2253; cheesecakemomma.com) 200 W. Henry Street. Open 8–4 Monday through Friday. If cheesecake is your thing, a stop here is a must.

⌀ & **Oco Time** (707-462-2422; oco time.com) Open from 11:30–2 on Tuesday through Friday and dinner Monday through Saturday from at least 5:30–8:30. California Japanese cuisine with a healthy selection of vegetarian options, this small funky spot downtown is a good change from the standard American food that abounds in the region. If you are in a hurry, their **Sushi Express** (open Monday through Friday 11 AM–7:30 AM) next door offers a large selection of sushi, bowls, and vegetarian food. $.

☙ ♿ **Schat's Courthouse Bakery and Café** (707-462-1670; schats.com) 113 W. Perkins. Open from 5:30 AM–6 PM Monday through Saturday. The Dutch bakers have been perfecting their recipes since 1893. The *volkoren* (Dutch whole grain bread) is not to be missed. Sandwiches and salads with names such as the Legal Eagle turkey, the vegetarian Not Guilty, and the Courthouse Chef salad will fill you up. $.

☙ ♿ **Ukiah Brewing Co.** (707-468-5898; ubcr.com) 102 S. State Street. Open daily from 11–11 (until 1 AM on Friday and Saturday). This all-organic brewery and restaurant in a lofty wood-paneled space is the place to be in Ukiah. During the day, this is my favorite place to get a pint of Point Arena Pale Ale and a gigantic burrito (vegetarian or carnitas). And at night the live music gets pumping. Expect to pay big for your earthy-friendly pub grub. Lunch: $–$$. Dinner: $$–$$$.

Willits

☙ **Burrito Exquisito** (707-459-5421) 42 S. Main Street. Open 10 AM–10 PM daily. Serving up all-natural Mexican food for great prices, with plenty of vegetarian options and smoothies, three tables, and a colorful tribute to Jerry Garcia, this is the spot to fill your belly and get back on the road. You have a choice of 1- or 1.5-pound burritos, stuffed with superfresh organic ingredients. $–$$.

☙ ♿ **The Loose Caboose** (707-459-1434) 10 Wood Street, Willits. A friend recommended this local lunch spot and I fell in love with their great soups, sandwiches, and milkshakes. Cash only. $.

♿ **Purple Thistle** (707-459-4750) 50 S. Main Street, Willits. Open Tuesday through Saturday from 5–9. People love this simple, small restaurant that offers a generous selection of organic dinner options. Entrees like seared tofu, and organic chicken or steak, paired with local wine, are winners. $$–$$$.

Lake County

Angelina's Bakery Espresso (707-263-0391) 365 N. Main Street, Lakeport. Open Monday through Friday 7–5 and Saturday from 8–2. Come here for decent baked goods and espresso drinks.

Ceago See *Wine Tasting*.

☙ **Marcie's Brick Grill** (707-279-9866) 4015-B Main Street, Kelseyville. Open 7–2 daily. Don't bother going anywhere else for breakfast. The big omelets, potatoes served however you want them, and casual atmosphere draw crowds on weekends. $.

Mt. St. Helena Brewing Co (707-987-2106: beercollections.com) 21167 Calistoga Street, Middletown. Open for lunch and dinner daily. Even if you aren't a fan of microbrews (and after tasting their honey wheat you may sing another tune), head over here for a fun, casual atmosphere, pizza, and pub grub. $.

✳ **Entertainment**

☿ **Konocti Harbor Amphitheater** See *Lodging*.

☿ **Shanachie Pub** (707-459-9194) Hidden behind the Purple Thistle restaurant in Willits, this pub gets rockin' with live music and a good beer selection. Plus, the outdoor beer garden is a great place to spend a warm summer evening.

☿ **Ukiah Brewing Co**. See *Eating Out*.

✳ Selective Shopping

You won't find much in the Inland Mendo area except Tibetan prayer flags, antiques, and heaps of wine to take home. You'll drive right through the commercial districts of Hopland and Willits on US 101. In Willits, you might want to pause at the **Leaves of Grass** bookstore on Main Street. For Ukiah, head downtown to State Street, where there is the great **The Mendocino Book Company** (102 S. School Street, Ukiah).

For Lake County, it's all about antiques and rocks (as in stones and gems), so head to Main Street in Lakeport to get started. If it is books you're after, head to **Watershed Books** on Main Street.

✳ Special Events

Monthly: **First Fridays Ukiah** On the first Friday of every month from 5–8, downtown Ukiah stays open late to show off the work of the local artists.

June: **Sierra Nevada World Music Festival** (snwmf.com) Mendocino Fairgrounds. In June, this three-day camping and music festival takes over the town of Boonville, and brings big-name musicians, playing earth-conscious music to the mountains.

August: **Solfest** (707-744-2017) Solar Living Institute, Hopland. Thousands of people come out for this two-day festival to celebrate all things green.

The North Coast

MENDOCINO COAST—
GUALALA TO WESTPORT

REDWOOD COAST—
LEGGETT TO CRESCENT CITY

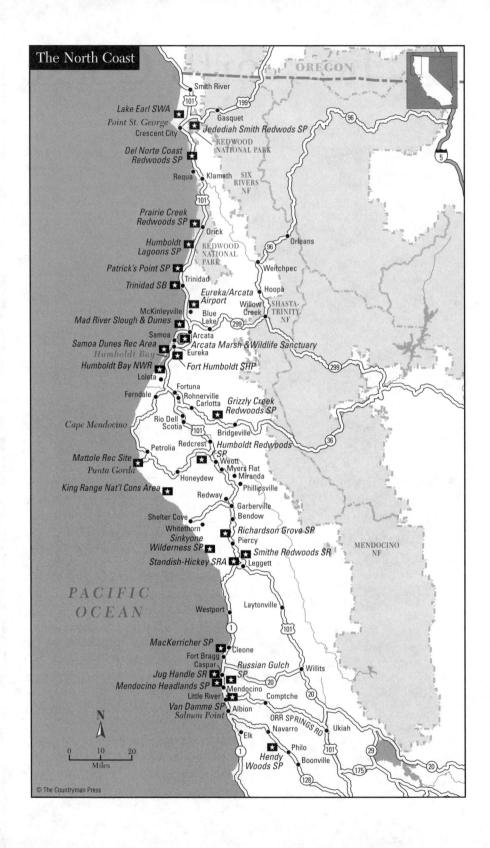

The North Coast

OREGON

Smith River
Lake Earl SWA ★
Point St. George
Crescent City
Gasquet
Jedediah Smith Redwoods SP ★
REDWOOD NATIONAL PARK
Del Norte Coast Redwoods SP ★
Requa
Klamath
SIX RIVERS NF
Prairie Creek Redwoods SP ★
Orick
Orleans
Humboldt Lagoons SP ★
REDWOOD NATIONAL PARK
Weitchpec
Patrick's Point SP ★
Trinidad
Trinidad SB ★
Hoopa
Eureka/Arcata Airport
McKinleyville
Willow Creek
SHASTA-TRINITY NF
Blue Lake
Mad River Slough & Dunes ★
Samoa
Arcata
Samoa Dunes Rec Area ★
Arcata Marsh & Wildlife Sanctuary ★
Humboldt Bay
Eureka
Humboldt Bay NWR ★
Fort Humboldt SHP ★
Loleta
Fortuna
Ferndale
Rohnerville
Carlotta
Grizzly Creek Redwoods SP ★
Cape Mendocino
Rio Dell
Scotia
Bridgeville
Petrolia
Redcrest
Humboldt Redwoods SP ★
Mattole Rec Site ★
Weott
Punta Gorda
Myers Flat
Miranda
Honeydew
Phillipsville
King Range Nat'l Cons Area ★
Redway
Garberville
Benbow
Shelter Cove
Whitethorn
Richardson Grove SP ★
Sinkyone Wilderness SP ★
Piercy
Standish-Hickey SRA ★
Smithe Redwoods SR ★
Leggett
MENDOCINO NF

PACIFIC OCEAN

Westport
Laytonville

MacKerricher SP ★
Cleone
Fort Bragg
Caspar
Russian Gulch SP ★
Willits
Jug Handle SR ★
Mendocino Headlands SP ★
Mendocino
Comptche
Little River
Van Damme SP ★
Albion
Salmon Point
Elk
Navarro
Ukiah
ORR SPRINGS RD
Philo
Hendy Woods SP ★
Boonville

N

0   10   20
Miles

© The Countryman Press

MENDOCINO COAST

One of the first signs that you have arrived on the Mendocino coast will be the disappearance of service on your cell phone. Look out the window: If you can see past the fog, you'll notice empty beaches scattered with driftwood, *wakame*, boulders the size of some buildings, wind-blown redwood and cypress trees, and plentiful wildlife. Once the suppliers of timber to the Bay Area, now these ex-logging towns have become destinations for travelers of the whale, bird, and human variety, not to mention the ideal place to hide out, grow marijuana, and disappear from your life.

Gualala (pronounced wa-lala), the first stop on the coast as you enter Mendocino County, straddles CA 1 and offers a down-to-earth, affordable, and friendly vibe mixed with all the beauty of the Northern California coast: Cypress trees, cliffs, and boulders spill into the rivers and the ocean; kayakers meander up the coast, dogs run on the sand; and people are about as friendly as you can get.

Besides a couple places to stay and a general store, you'll likely pass through Anchor Bay on your way to **Point Arena**, which celebrated its centennial in 2008. This town is becoming a haven for artists and hippies, fishermen, and people wanting the slow life. Victorian houses, a pier where you can fish without a license, a lighthouse, the famed Bowling Ball beach, great abalone diving in the Arena Rock Underwater Preserve, and a couple wonderful restaurants have helped this tiny town attract the tourist industry.

Continue driving north through **Manchester**, the West Coast's closest point to Hawaii. Though tourists love the state park and the lovely beach, the most unusual part of Manchester is what you won't see: the underground telephone service link that connects the mainland to Hawaii and the Far East. Rounding out the southern part of this coast, you arrive at **Elk** (which is also called Greenwood—don't ask, no one really knows). Here you will find luxurious B&Bs, bearded ladies, bikers, divers, and one of the loveliest beach strolls on the coast.

Back on the road, heading north along CA 1 takes you through the renegade hideout towns of **Albion** and **Little River**—known for dramatic cliffs, rivers spilling into the sea, plentiful abalone, family-friendly Van Damme State Park, and super-luxe lodging options—to arrive in the starlet of the coast.

The dollhouse-like town of **Mendocino**, perched on cliffs above a bay, attracts lovers of Victorians, organic food, arts, and romances. It all started in 1852, when the German survivor of a shipwreck, William Kasten, saw the dollar signs of the

THE TOWN OF MENDOCINO.

timber industry and helped create the incentive to build the Victorians you still see today. After the decline of the timber industry, artists flocked to the area, and today you'll find a bustling town bursting with tourists on summer weekends.

Keep driving north until you find timber central: **Fort Bragg**. In the midst of an identity change, this is the cheapest place to stay on the coast. But don't let that fool you. Hidden within the antique shops, industrial buildings, old mills, and renegade hippies are fantastic restaurants, amazing beaches and trails, and the Skunk Train Depot. Once a military town, built to keep the Indians in line (though we're not sure who kept who in line), now Fort Bragg earns its keep through the fishing trade. Keep driving north through the village of **Cleone**, where you will find the handicap-accessible MacKerricher State Park.

Farther north is the town of **Westport**, a country town on the coast (and the gateway to the famed Sinkyone State Wilderness Area), which used to bustle (sort of) until the church fell into the sea—twice—and people moved onward, not trusting the coastal bluffs.

GUIDANCE For a wealth of information about Mendocino County, contact the **Mendocino Visitor Bureau** (Gomendo.com).
Or, if you plan to focus your time primarily on the southern Mendonoma Coast, the **Redwood Coast Visitor Bureau** (800-778-5252; redwoodcoastchamber.com) is located behind the post office in the center of Gualala. Here you will also find the Dolphin Gift Shop and Gallery, which is the showplace and retail outlet for the work of Gualala Arts Center's local artist exhibition.

GETTING THERE Heading north along US 101, when you enter Cloverdale, drive west on CA 128 through Anderson Valley. At CA 1 turn left (south) for Elk and the southern coast and for the northern coast (including Mendocino) head north (right).

If you plan to spend most of your time in Gualala, you might consider taking CA 116 from US 101, which takes you along the Russian River. At CA 1, head north and prepare for a beautiful (though long and winding) drive up the Pacific coastline.

If Fort Bragg or Westport is your destination, from US 101, take the redwood-covered mountain drive along CA 20 west until you meet CA 1 in Fort Bragg.

GETTING AROUND Though you'll see a bus traveling this skinny road every so often, the most reliable way to access this dramatic coastline is by car. CA 1 runs the length of the coast, and almost everything you need is found along this road.

I am assuming that you will explore from south to north, so listings are in that order. Gualala is 15 miles south of Point Arena, which is 19 miles from Elk. Mendocino is 17 miles from Elk. Fort Bragg is 10 miles up the road. Finally, Westport pops up 15 miles north. All in all, if you are driving from Gualala to Westport on these winding coastal roads, expect to be in the car for two hours.

MEDICAL EMERGENCY Mendocino Coast District Hospital (707-961-1234; mcdh.org) 700 River Drive, Fort Bragg.

WEATHER Foggy and windy almost year-round, you might wonder why people would even consider visiting this coastal area. The average temperature lingers around the 60-degree Fahrenheit mark. But on those few sunny days, there is nothing like seeing the sun sparkle over the sea.

MUSTS FOR FIRST-TIME VISITORS
1. Explore the bounty of color at the Mendocino Botanical Gardens.
2. Hike Russian Gulch State Park and see the waterfall.
3. Climb the Jug Handle Ecological Staircase.
4. Wander the bluffs of Mendocino Headlands.
5. Explore the historic Mendocino village.
6. Kayak a river or through a sea cave.
7. Go whale watching.
8. Stroll a lonely beach.

MUSTS FOR REPEAT VISITORS
1. Hike to the Pygmy Forest.
2. Ride a horse on the beach.
3. Take a moonlight flotilla up the Gualala River.
4. Enjoy a sunset cocktail at the Ledford House.
5. Go antique shopping in Fort Bragg.
6. Taste organic wines in Anderson Valley.
7. Hike the redwoods.
8. Dive for abalone.

✳ To See

Gualala Arts Center (707-884-1138; gualalaarts.org) 46501 Gualala Road, Gualala. Open weekdays from 9–4 and most weekends from 12–4. High art nestled into the redwoods? This multi-million dollar arts complex is home to galleries, conference rooms, a hiking trail to the river, a meditation area in old-growth redwoods, a sculpture garden, and a zillion annual events. Free.

Arena Cinema (707-882-3456; arenacinema.com) CA 1, Point Arena. The only movie theater on the coast between Monte Rio (in Sonoma County and Fort Bragg) plays first run and art films, children's movies, live music, and more. The 1928 Art Deco-style theater was restored about a decade ago to its former glory.

Point Arena Lighthouse (707-882-2777; pointarenalighthouse.com) From CA 1, head west on Lighthouse Road (mile marker 17). Open from 10 AM–3:30 PM daily. You can climb to the top of the tallest lighthouse in the Western U.S. and gaze out to sea, spotting whales, birds, and maybe a ship. Rebuilt after being destroyed in the 1906 earthquake, the 1908 building features a 6-foot glass prism lens. Marietta offers daily tours of the lighthouse. If you love it out here, inquire about one of their vacation rentals, which are pet-friendly and rent for $$–$$$ per night. Free.

Point Arena Pier From CA 1, head west on Iverson Avenue, at the southern end of Point Arena; drive to the end. Fishermen love to reel in lingcod from this 330-foot pier. And since you don't need a fishing license, it can get crowded. See Arena Cove for more information. Free.

✳ To Do

🐾 **B. Bryan Preserve** (707-882-2297: bbryanpreserve.com) 130 Riverside Drive, Point Arena. The 90-minute tours of this wildlife preserve will keep the kids entertained. If you go in the late afternoon you can watch them feed endangered species such as zebra, antelope, giraffe, and kudu. Tours cost $20 for adults and $10 for children under 10. Reservations required. They also rent out a two-bedroom vacation rental ($$) on the preserve.

Elk Cove Inn and Spa (707 877-3321 or 800 275-2967; elkcoveinn.com) 6300 S. CA 1. Organic spa treatments at this full service spa will make you melt after a long day of hiking. Hot stone massages, couples' treatments, and sea polishes are some of their specialties.

Gualala Farmers' Market (707-884-3736; mcfarm.org) Gualala Community Center. May through October, Saturdays take on a whole new meaning for local food lovers. Shop for local fruits and vegetables. Open 10 AM–12:30.

Ross Ranch (707-877-1834; rossranch.biz) Private horseback riding trips on Manchester Beach, or through the redwoods near Elk, are offered by a local family, and make for a lovely afternoon. Rides last two hours and will cost you $60 for a beach ride and $50 for a mountain trek.

WATER SPORTS Adventure Rents (888-881-4386; adventurerents.com) Cantamere Center (behind Century 21), Gualala. If paddling through redwoods and along the river sounds fun, this outfit rents single or double kayaks ($40–70 for a full day) and canoes ($70 for a full day) and offers complimentary beginner lessons. In summer, moonlight flotillas, complete with catered sunset dinner and boat rental on the river, run you $50 per adult—reservations required.

Force 10 Ocean Kayak Tours (707-877-3505; force10tours.com) Elk. Two-hour tours on the Pacific Ocean include wetsuit (including booties and gloves), kayak and gear, lessons, and a guide for $115. You'll paddle through kelp, sea caves, and see plenty of marine life. Cash only.

✳ Green Spaces

PARKS **Bower Park** 38040 Old Stage Road, Gualala. Families looking for a shady spot beneath redwoods and oaks will enjoy this mellow park that has tennis, basketball, baseball, trails, a playground, and a duck pond.

Gualala Point Regional Park (707-785-2377; sonoma-county.org/parks) Technically in Sonoma County, head south on CA 1, cross the river and turn right about a mile past Gualala. A visit to Gualala is not complete without a stop at this beautiful park. Wander through meadows, forest, along the river and beach trails, plus find plenty of picnic spots, a BBQ area, and even a campground. Though the sea appears inviting, it is dangerous for swimming.

ABALONE DIVING—ONLY IN MENDOCINO COUNTY

Outlawed in most parts of the California coast, abalone diving brings plenty of folks to the Mendonoma area. Though chilly—you'll want a good wetsuit, year-round—this is one of the only places to hunt for the giant mollusk. However, there are some very strict limits to ensure the sustainability of abalone. Don't tempt the Department of Fish and Game by testing these limits.

You can only catch 3 abalone per day, and no more than 24 during a calendar year.

A Department of Fish and Game tag must be placed on each abalone as soon as it is taken.

You can only take red abalone.

You'll need to have a good measuring device, because abalone need to be at least 7 inches in diameter to take them.

Your abalone iron needs to be in good working condition.

Recreational abalone can be taken between April and November, although during the month of July, you cannot hunt for them.

You cannot hunt for abs in scuba gear.

You must have a fishing license and an abalone fishing report card.

For specific information and licenses visit the **Department of Fish and Game** dfg.ca.gov/mrd/sportfishing and dfg.ca.gov/mrd/abalone.

To rent abalone gear contact **Sub Surface Progression** (707-964-3793) 1860 N. CA 1, Fort Bragg and **Gualala Sport and Tackle** (707-884-4247) 39225 S. CA 1, Gualala. They will also inform you of the current best places to dive.

Stornetta Public Lands (707-468-4000; blm.gov) From CA 1, head west on Lighthouse Road (mile marker 17), Point Arena. These protected lands with limited public access for birding, horseback riding, hiking, and diving make the perfect place to explore the diverse Mendocino coast. With 2 miles of coastline, an estuary, an island, as well as a wealth of endangered species, you won't want to pass up a visit here. To get detailed trail information, speak to Marietta at the Point Arena Lighthouse. She'll tell you the best hikes for you.

Navarro River State Park (707-937-5804; parks.ca.gov) Go 2 miles east of CA 1 on CA 128, Elk. Driving out to the coast on CA 128, you might notice it suddenly got dark: The 11 miles of second-growth redwoods have a way of blocking out the sun in the sweetest way. This park is an excellent place to kayak, canoe, hike, swim, camp, or just hang out and enjoy the splendor of these giant trees, especially since in summer it gets pretty warm here. If you want to pitch a tent, **Navarro Beach Campground** (707-937-5804; parks.ca.gov) is located at the mouth of the Navarro River on the Pacific Ocean. Access road is located on the south side of the Navarro River Bridge, just past where CA 1 and CA 128 merge. Camp where the ocean meets the redwoods in this chilly, but beautiful setting. $20 per vehicle.

BEACHES (*Listed from south to north*) The best surf spot on the southern coast is the Cove at Point Arena Pier.

Fish Rock Beach Just past the hamlet of Anchor Bay on CA 1, turn into the Anchor Bay Campground. Called Fish Rock for the town that disappeared in the 1920s, now this family-friendly beach offers gentle surf, plus less wind and fog most of the year. The south-facing beach changes dramatically, though in summer kids explore tide pools; kayakers, surfers, and divers head out to sea; and couples lounge on the sand. The campground charges a nominal fee for parking.

Bowling Ball Beach and Schooner Gulch State Beach On CA 1 midway between Anchor Bay and Point Arena (mile marker 11.41), there are two 0.5-mile trails leading to the beach. One heads to Bowling Ball beach, where you'll see lines of huge boulders that really look like gigantic bowling balls. Note that boulders are visible at low tide, so adjust your schedule. The other trail leads to Schooner Gulch Beach, which is an excellent spot to spend the day surfing, windsurfing, swimming, or playing in the sand. Just south of Schooner Gulch Beach is the Schooner Gulch Vista Point. This is a great spot for whale watching from December through March.

Arena Cove From CA 1, head west on Iverson Avenue, at the southern end of Point Arena; drive to the end. This little beach cove has some fantastic diving (sunken ships, abalone, harbor seal-viewing locations), a surf spot, a boat launch, and tide pools. Plus there are a couple restaurants (see *Eating Out* below).

Manchester State Beach (707-882-2463; parks.ca.gov) Just north of Manchester off CA 1. This remote beach offers endless stretches of sand, driftwood, grasses, and creeks to explore. People love to fish here as well. There is a campsite here, though make sure to pack your winter jacket.

Greenwood State Beach (707-937-5804; parks.ca.gov) To access the beach from CA 1, park near Queenie's Roadhouse, Elk, and walk down a fairly steep trail. The magical walk down to this azure beach offers views of the fog hanging over the sea caves, seaweed hunters, fly fishermen, and the huge boulders and cliffs protecting this picturesque spot.

✴ Lodging

Additional campgrounds listed under *Green Spaces*.

Gualala

♂ ♿ 🐾 🌿 "¶" **Surf Motel Gualala**
(707-884-3571) 39170 CA 1, Gualala.
The new owners spiffed this 20-room
motel right up. Its bluff-side location
in the heart of Gualala makes this a
simple choice for the budget-conscious. The new beds look like they are
on steroids, with all the comforters and
pillows piled high. At press time, the
owners were adding a new hot tub and
breakfast service. $$.

♂ 🐾 ♿ "¶" **St. Orres** (707-884-3303;
saintorres.com) 95445 CA 1, just north
of Gualala town on the mountainside.
You can't miss this Russian-style lodge,
crafted by hand out of heavy timber,
with minarets and domes. The cheap-
est accommodations are the 6 Euro-
pean-style rooms above the restaurant,
which share a bathroom, while in-the-
know travelers opt for the romantic 13
cottages, nestled in the cypress trees.
Each cottage is different. Some have
an outdoor shower, redwood deck, fire-
place, Jacuzzi tub, ocean view, or king-
sized bed. Full breakfast (cottages get
breakfast delivered to your room in a
basket). Rooms $–$$; Cottages
$$–$$$$.

Anchor Bay

♂ 🐾 **Anchor Bay Campground** (707-
884-4222; abcamp.com) Anchor Bay is
4 miles north of Gualala on the ocean
side. This beachfront campground can
begin to resemble a shantytown on
summer weekends, but the reason
people like it so much is because this
beach often has the best weather on
the coast. $38–42 per night for one
vehicle.

♂ 🐾 **Mar Vista Cottages** (707-884-
3522 or 877-855-3522; marvistamen
docino.com) 35101 S. CA 1. Yellow

A SEAWEED HARVESTER AT GREENWOOD
STATE BEACH.

cottages spread across the mountain-
side of an organic farm (which guests
can harvest for dinner), offer 12 one-
and two-bedroom units. Old-fashioned
kitchens, light and airy rooms with
simple country cottage décor, a fire-
place, down comforters, oak floors, and
no TVs or phones makes this a popular
choice for those who want to curl up
with your sweetheart, a good book, or
play Risk until your eyeballs glaze over.
$$–$$$.

Point Arena

Coast Guard House (707-882-2442;
coastguardhouse.com) 695 Arena
Cove, Point Arena. They used to row
out from this house in tiny boats to
save wrecked sailors, and now owners
Mia and Kevin have decorated the
original structure with Arts and Crafts-
movement decor. The two cottages are
romantic, with views of the sea and
Jacuzzi tubs, while the four rooms in
the main house are understated, with a
classic white-on-white simplicity.

Rooms include breakfast, some Jacuzzi or Japanese soaking tubs, and use of hot tub. $$–$$$.

🗝 ♿ 🐾 **Wharf Master's Inn** (707-882-3171; wharfmasters.com) 785 Iversen Avenue. The original wharf-master's house was built in 1865, and in 1980, the 27-room inn was built around it. Sloping down the hill leading to the wharf, most rooms offer ocean views, queen featherbeds, and two-person Jacuzzi tubs (with candles surrounding them). Little touches make the price worth it: The driftwood sculptures, friendly staff, continental breakfast, restaurant, beach access, and free wine in the restaurant below. $–$$$.

Manchester

Inn at Victorian Gardens (707-882-3606, innatvictoriangardens.com) 14409 South CA 1. Luciano and Pauline Zamboni's labor of love resulted in the most spectacular inn on the

IT IS IMPOSSIBLE NOT TO RELAX IN THE TUBS AT THE INN AT VICTORIAN GARDENS.

southern coast. There are 92 acres of coastal ranch, donkeys, sheep, chickens, gardens, a bocce ball court, and forest surrounding the 1904 Victorian house. My favorite of the four rooms is the light-filled Master Bedroom (one of Pauline's designs), with a bed the color of the Golden Gate Bridge, a Japanese soaking tub, and fir floors. If you want to conceive, check into the small Golden Room—all eight of the children of the original owners were conceived right here. Occasionally Pauline serves a five-course gourmet Italian dinner for parties of six or more; call in advance for details. Full gourmet breakfast included. $$$–$$$$.

Elk

🗝 🐾 ♿ **Greenwood Pier Inn** (707-877-9997 or 800-807-3423; greenwoodpierinn.com) 5928 CA 1, Elk. Fans of the TV show *Twin Peaks* might appreciate the eclectic Greenwood Pier Inn, where you find a colorful staff and unique rooms. In the midst of a renovation, the inn is attempting to redefine itself to highlight those spectacular gardens and ocean views. For now you can expect sponge pink wallpaper, Jacuzzi tubs, fireplaces, cascade showerheads, ailing mismatched furniture, continental breakfast delivered to your room, a restaurant (see *Where to Eat*), no TV or phone, hot tub, and ocean-view decks. $$–$$$$.

🗝 🐾 ♿ "¶" **Griffin House** (707-877-3422; griffininn.com) 5910 S. CA 1. Oceanfront and garden cottages with simple thoughtful touches, like complimentary wine, plush robes, down comforters, and free organic coffee. The eight oceanfront cottages come with full breakfast delivered to your room (most with wood-burning stoves), Bridget Dolan's Pub restaurant, and beach access. This is the best deal in town. $$–$$$.

"1" & Harbor House Inn (707-877-3203; theharborhouseinn.com) 5600 S. CA 1, Elk. The plushest place to stay in Elk, this 1916 Arts and Crafts lodge and cottages offers serious ocean views and access to a private beach. Antique furniture coupled with fine linens and subdued lighting, plus full breakfast and four-course dinner for two at the excellent restaurant (see Dining Out), make this luxury option perfect for rekindling the romance in your life. Six antique house-rooms offer king-sized sleigh beds and flowered wallpaper, while the four cottages have a spare, modern feel. $$$$; no children under 16.

✳ Where To Eat

DINING OUT Pinning down hours for local dining establishments is a challenge. Most places have summer, winter, and something-came-up hours. In general, if I listed that a place serves dinner, you can expect food to be available between 5ish to 9ish. Lunch is the same deal (11:30ish to 2:30ish). Call ahead for specific seasonal hours.

Gualala
Sea Ranch Lodge See *Sonoma Coast*.

& **St. Orres** (707-884-3335; saintorres.com) 95445 S. CA 1. Open nightly from 6–9:30. Lofty, with stained-glass views of the sunset, personalized service, and some of the best food in the area, Chef Rosemary Campiformio offers not just dinner, but an experience. Prix fixe three-course dinners, with a selection of nightly specials that will have you scratching your head—blueberry waffles and venison, apricot soup, garlic flan—but once you taste the food, you'll understand why Rosemary chooses to create her seasonal nightly specials each day. Reservations highly recommended. $$$$.

QUIRKY AND LUSH: THE GREENWOOD PIER INN.

Elk
Harbor House Seaside Dining Room (707-877-3203; theharborhouseinn.com) 5600 S. CA 1. Dinner seating at 6:45. Ocean-view dining in this classic inn offers some of the best food on the north coast. Prix fixe dinners served in an elegant atmosphere appeal to folks wanting sustainable foie gras, or filet mignon served in a puff pastry. Chef David Rosenthal supports local farmers and believes that dining is an experience; and here, it is. Reservation required. Four-course dinner: $$$$.

EATING OUT

Gualala
✐ & **Bones Restaurant** (707-884-1188;) 38920 S. CA 1, Open daily from 11:30–9. This hopping roadhouse serves up heaping plates of BBQ and live music on weekends. Wood-pit smoked barbeque sandwiches, burgers (and veggie burgers too), sausages, smoked oysters, and salads populate

the menu. Texas-style BBQ lovers will appreciate the 4 to 12 hours meats are cooked in the native-oak pits. $–$$.

Laura's Bakery and Taqueria (707-884-3175) Just north of Gualala center on ocean side of CA 1. Open for breakfast and lunch; closed Sunday. This little house is the spot to get a decent breakfast while the masses head to Meza Grille. Though there are no views, you'll get real Mexican food and delicious baked goods like *pan dolces,* empanadas, and *orejas.* $.

❝❞ ♿ **Trinks Café** (707-884-1713) 39140 S. CA 1. This little café, located in a strip mall, butts up to the ocean and offers the best espresso drinks in town. Plus you'll get an array of soups, sandwiches, and desserts. $.

Point Arena

♪ ♈ **Arena Cove Bar and Grill** (707-882-2100) 790 Port Road. Open for lunch and dinner daily. It's hard to find dining with views and prices like these—as long as you are okay with the occasional inexperienced waiter, paint peeling off the walls, and a lot of grease. Locals favor the carved wooden bar, while tourists line the big windows to gawk at the sea. Order fish and chips or chops. $–$$$.

Franny's Cup and Saucer (707-822-2500) 213 Main Street. Open Wednesday-Sunday 8–4. This little bakery/souvenir shop sells luscious baked goods, espresso drinks, and toys. I suspect the toys are to drag Mom and Dad into the store, but it is the sweets that delight. This is the best place in the area to get cappuccino—Taylor Maid Coffee, too. Save the diet for next week. Cash Only. $.

The Record Café and Market (707-822-FOOD) 265 Main Street. Open Monday through Saturday 7 AM–7 PM, Sunday 8–6. This natural food store also has a popular café in the back where you can order healthy fare, sandwiches, and salads for reasonable prices. You might want to stop by here before heading out to Bowling Ball beach. $.

Elk

Elk Market (707-877-3411) 6101 CA 1. Open daily. A great place to gather a picnic lunch, this little deli sells organic produce, fresh deli sandwiches, and plenty of goods to keep you satiated.

♪ ◯◯ ♿ **Greenwood Pier Restaurant** (707-877-9997 or 800-807-3423; greenwoodpierinn.com) 5928 CA 1. Open for breakfast, lunch, and dinner daily. Standard American fare, served by a quirky staff, with live jazz on weekends and a decent Mendocino-favored wine list, attracts locals and tourists. They use organic vegetables from the garden to complement the seafood, meat, and pasta dishes. $$–$$$.

♪ **Queenie's Roadhouse Café** (707-877-3285) 6061 CA 1. Open from 8 AM–3 PM Thursday through Monday. Queenie is no joke: sweating over the grill in the back of her roadhouse diner while her staff keeps the strong coffee flowing. Breakfast is the main attraction, especially on cold mornings when the fireplace is pumping; locals read tarot cards or swap fishing tales, and travelers gorge on big plates of *huevos rancheros* or tofu stir fry-made with organic ingredients. $–$$.

IN CASE YOU WANT TO KNOW WHERE YOU
ARE AFTER EATING AT QUEENIE'S.

✳ Entertainment

Arena Theater See *To See* above.

Beacon Light By the Sea (707-877-3360) 7401 S. CA 1, just past the town of Elk. Open Friday and Saturday from 5 PM–11 PM. In the back of Bob Beacon's house, he serves up spirits and local lore on weekends.

Bridget Dolan's Pub and Dinner House (707-877-3422; griffininn.com) Griffin House Inn, 5910 S. CA 1. Open for dinner nightly. If a pint of Guinness is the ideal way for you to end your day (or start it), you'll want to head over to this Elk local favorite. You can also get pub fare ($$) served with white tablecloths, relaxed atmosphere, lots of locals, and Irish wit.

✳ Selective Shopping

In Gualala along CA 1, you'll find galleries, shops, and **Cypress Village** on the mountain side of CA 1, with high-end cooking supplies, arts and crafts, and **Four Eyed Frog Books** (707-884-1333; foureyedfrogbooks.com), the best bookshop on the southern coast.

✳ Seasonal Events

August: **Art in the Redwoods** (707-884-1138; gualalaarts.org) 46501 Gualala Road. The third weekend of August, the Gualala Art Center hosts this annual music and local art celebration.

NORTHERN MENDOCINO COAST

✳ To See

Mendocino

Ford House Museum (707-937-5397; Mendocino.com) On the ocean side of Main Street. Open daily from 11 AM–4 PM. To understand the history of this natural and architectural wonder of a town, a visit to the visitor center of the Mendocino Headlands Park is a worthy stop. The building, constructed in 1854, is a relic in itself. Free.

Historic Mendocino A wander through the village of Mendocino won't take you long and will likely have you pining for the simple life of white-picket fences, gardening, ocean breezes, and quiet living. As you wander inland, you might recognize the Blair House B&B (on Little Lake Road.), which was the home of Angela Lansbury's character in *Murder She Wrote*. Back on Main Street you can tour the Presbyterian Church (1867) on Saturday from 10 AM–12 PM. Finally, you might want to check out the first houses built in town, on the corner of Lansing and Howard. Free.

Kelley House Museum (707-937-5791; mendocinohistory.org) Across the street from the ocean on Main Street. Open in winter from Friday through Monday 11 AM–3 PM; summer hours are 11 AM–3 PM, closed Wednesday. Built in 1861, this yellow Victorian will enrich your understanding of the historic and economic history of the area. The "Then and Now" photography exhibit showcases the past hundred years in Mendocino history, with modern photos taken by local high school students. Free.

Mendocino Art Center (707-937-5818) Little Lake Street. I love settling into the grass, or wandering through the sculpture gardens and imagining that I am a local artist here in this little town. Other highlights are the rotating exhibit of local artists and a great gift shop. Free.

Point Cabrillo Lighthouse and Reserve (707-937-6122; pointcabrillo.org) From CA 1, turn towards the ocean when you see Russian Gulch State Park. Turn right on Point Cabrillo Drive and follow the signs. Open 11 AM–4 PM daily. You can either park and hike 1.5 miles through the grasslands leading to the ocean, watching deer prance, sighting rare birds, and seeing fog pass overhead; or you can drive to the 1909 lighthouse and hike around the bluffs, tour the lighthouse, or explore the wrecked clipper ship. There are also some lovely rooms and cottages to rent here (see Lodging). Free.

Fort Bragg

Guest House Museum (707-964-4251) 343 N. Main Street. Open 11–2 on weekdays and from 10 AM–5 PM on weekends. Wandering around the three-story redwood mansion is a must if you are curious about the history of this region. Plenty of logging materials, train artifacts, and photos explain the whole deal. Admission is free.

⚓ ⚐ ☗ ⊚ **Mendocino Coast Botanical Gardens** (707-964-4352; gardenbythe sea.org) On the ocean side of CA 1, just south of Fort Bragg. Open at least 9–4 daily. In spring when the rhododendrons bloom, framing the fog-covered sea and cliffs, you'll be transported to another world. In winter, whale watching is excellent, as are the abundant flowering heathers. Adults $10, senior and youth discounts, children under 5 free.

Triangle Tattoo Museum (707-964-8814; triangletattoo.com) 356B N. Main Street. Open daily from 12–6. If art with a pulse is your thing, you can tour the tattoo museum or even get inked yourself. Here you'll learn about the history of tattoos from Maori warriors to the Holocaust, to modern day wonders fit for the circus.

✳ To Do

CYCLING **Catch a Canoe and Bicycles Too** (707-937-0273; stanfordinn.com) CA 1 and Comptche-Ukiah Road. Open daily from at least 9:30–5. These guys rent mountain bikes to explore the Van Damme State Park or Russian Gulch State Park, and offer a comprehensive listing of bike routes to try out.

FARMERS' MARKETS Mendocino Farmers' Market (707-937-3632; mcfarm .org) On Howard and Main Street, May through October, Fridays from 12–2.

Fort Bragg Farmers' Market (707-937-4330; mcfarm.org) 801 N. Main Street, May through October, Wednesdays from 3:30–6.

FISHING All Aboard Adventures (see Water Sports below).

GOLF Little River Inn Golf Course (707-937-5667; littleriverinn.com) 7751 N. CA 1. Two miles south of Mendocino, this 18-hole course beckons deer, raccoons, herons, and golfers who enjoy zoning out on the sea between turns. On weekends an 18-hole round costs $40.

HORSEBACK AND LLAMA RIDING ✍ **Llama Treks** (707-964-7191; lodging andllamas.com) 18301 Old Coast Highway, Fort Bragg. Ever wanted to ride a llama along the coast or through the redwoods, complete with a gourmet wine-paired lunch? The 40-minute tours with lunch will run you $50–60. Children under 10 free.

✍ **Ricochet Ridge Ranch** (888-873-5777; horse-vacation.com) Cleone. The Ten-Mile Beach Trail Ride (though it is only a 7-mile trail that ends at Ten Mile River) heads out at 10, 12, 2, and 4, by appointment only. Children 6 and older are welcome. Tour cost $45 for 90 minutes.

SPAS Creekside Spa (800-731-5535; schoolhousecreek.com) Inn at Schoolhouse Creek, 7051 N CA 1, Little River. Open 9–7:30. Full spa treatments in a yurt next to the creek might be the recipe to turn you into Jell-O.

Indigo Eco Spa (707-937-2810 or 800-421-2810; stevenswood.com) Stevenswood Resort, 8211 N. CA 1, Little River. The only luxury spa on the Mendocino coast offers a variety of treatments using local ingredients like Humboldt salt, ocean lipids, olive oil, and lavender.

Sweetwater Gardens (707-937-4140 or 800-300-4140; sweetwaterspa.com) 955 Ukiah Street, Mendocino. Open daily from at least 1 PM–10 PM. If your accommodations don't include a hot tub, you can use the private hot tubs and sauna for one hour for $15. They also arrange massages. Reservations recommended.

TRAIN RIDES ✍ **Skunk Train** (800-866-1690; skunktrain.com) Fort Bragg Depot is at the end of Laurel Street, The Willits Depot, 299 E. Commercial Street. Depot open from 8–8 Monday through Saturday and 8–5 Sunday. The absolute best way (and what used to be the only way) to see the redwoods between Fort Bragg and Willits is to take a ride on the Skunk Train. Four-

A TYPICAL MENDOCINO GARDEN.

hour Northspur trips, departing at 10:00 AM from Fort Bragg, cost $47 per adult and $22 per child, and wind you through the towering redwoods all the way to Northspur and back. In summer, they add an afternoon trip that includes a BBQ in the redwoods. From Willits, four-hour tours to Northspur depart at 9:45 and cost $35 per adult and $20 per child. This route takes you up the steep summit and back.

WATER SPORTS

Boating

All Aboard Adventures (707-964-1881; allaboardadventures.com) Fort Bragg. Captain Tim Gillespie takes anglers, whale watchers, bay cruisers, and charters out onto the great Pacific. From December through April whale watching along the coast is dynamic. When I went out, I came so close to a whale, we looked each other in the eye. Whale-watching trips last two hours and run $25 per person. Fishing trips head out year-round (either for rock cod or salmon—if you're lucky). Expect to be out for five hours, and rates run between $45–55, not including tackle kits.

Canoeing and Kayaking

The two best places to river kayak in the area are **Big River** and **Pudding Creek Estuary** (enter the river 0.25 mile past Glass Beach in Fort Bragg) where you'll paddle past birds of a zillion varieties, salmon, and endless meadows.

Rentals and Tours

Catch a Canoe and Bicycles Too (707-937-0273; stanfordinn.com) CA 1 and Comptche-Ukiah Road. Open daily from at least 9:30–5. Big River is the ideal place for novice kayakers, and even for some pros. Because it is a protected estuary, paddling through the canyons, past swimming holes and plentiful wildlife is a cinch. This outfit rents a variety of canoes (including outriggers) and both river and ocean-going kayaks from $8–25 per hour.

Kayak Mendocino (707-964-7480; kayakmendocino.com) Van Damme State Park. Tours depart the beach daily at 9, 11:30, 2, and sunset. This outfit guides novice and experienced kayakers out to explore the sea caves. Whether you take the north coast or south coast tour, you are sure to encounter plentiful sea life and some geologically stunning caves. Tours cost $50 and include kayak, wetsuit, booties, helmet, and guide. Sunset tours will run you $100. Reservations required.

Surf, Rentals, and Lessons

The best surf spot on the north coast is Virgin Beach in Fort Bragg. However, this cold-water, rough landscape is known for shark attacks, and surf isn't as stellar as you might desire. If you're still up for it, the following companies rent boards and offer lessons.

Gone Surfing (707-964-3793) 330 N. Franklin. This outfit rents boards and give lessons and will tell you the best places to catch waves on the north coast.

Sub Surface Progression (707-964-3793; subsurfaceprogressions.com) 18600 CA 1. This water-sport rental haven will set you up with gear and information for where to surf during the season.

WHALE WATCHING See Boating

STATE PARKS Van Damme State Park (707-937-5804; parks.ca.gov) Three miles south of Mendocino on CA 1. Outdoor adventurers will adore this 2069-acre state park. Hiking and biking trails lead you up to Fern Canyon; a rocky beach meets the river, where divers, kayakers, cold-water-loving swimmers, and boaters head out to sea; and the famed Pygmy Forest of century-old cypress and pine trees, none taller than 10 feet, might have you scratching your head. And finally, if you love it here so much, 74 campsites (with Wi-Fi) might be just the ticket for a mellow weekend in the forest ($20–25 per night).

Mendocino Headlands State Park (707-937-5804; parks.ca.gov) Surrounding the town of Mendocino, along CA 1. I have spent endless amounts of time browsing these headlands, meandering down to the shore, and exploring the newest addition to this state park: the **Big River Unit**. Named for the size of redwoods growing along the river, this 7440-acre wildlife corridor adjoins Jackson Demonstration Forest with Mendocino Woodlands State Park. Here you'll find wetlands, trails, fishing, birding, an estuary, marsh, a beach, and diverse plant life. For visitor information visit the **Ford House** (see *To See* above).

Mendocino Woodlands State Park (707-937-5804; mendocinowoodlands.org) 39350 Little Lake Road. Enjoy 25 miles of hiking trails up in the sunnier park of Mendocino, with swimming holes, redwoods, plenty of wildlife, retreat campgrounds, environmental center, and that peace you might associate with the woods. If you want to camp, contact one of the groups listed on the "Uncommon Vacations" section of the Web site that are looking to expand their numbers.

Russian Gulch State Park (707-937-5804; parks.ca.gov) Two miles north of Mendocino on CA 1. The 6.5-mile waterfall hike or bike trip is the highlight of many people's Mendocino visit. Here you can hike the endless array of trails, swim, fish, dive, picnic, bike, camp, and gawk at the 60-foot deep blowhole. There are 30 campsites here as well—one of them is wheelchair accessible ($20–25 per night).

Caspar Headlands State Reserve (707-937-5804; parks.ca.gov) North of Russian Gulch, head north on Point Cabrillo Road, turn right on Caspar Drive. Though the residents of Caspar call this small State Reserve home, the geology of the land, filled with wildflowers, coastal bluffs, and unique rock formations, offers vistas worth a peek. You can access the reserve only with an entry permit from the Mendocino Sector Office; visit the Russian Gulch State Park for more information.

Jug Handle State Preserve Ecological Staircase (707-964-4630; parks.ca .gov) Halfway between Fort Bragg and Mendocino on CA 1. And you thought the coastal bluffs were cool? Go check out the 2.5-mile staircase trail from the coast to the Pygmy Forest that displays the ecological succession and landscape evolution. Once sandstone, the terraces (that create a natural staircase) have been weathered for different lengths of time by sea, wind, and tectonic plate movements. **Jug Handle Beach** is an option if you don't want the 5-mile round-trip hike up and down the stairs.

EXPLORE THE MENDOCINO HEADLANDS.

❦ **Jackson Demonstration Forest** (707-964-5674; fire.ca.gov) CA 20 between Fort Bragg and Willits. A sea of redwoods, Douglas firs, hemlocks, tan oaks, madrones, and bay myrtles, perfect for hiking, camping, picnicking, swimming, and inhaling a healthy dose of oxygen. The Waterfall Grove Trail and the Forest History Trail make for excellent treks. Two camping areas (free) have picnic tables, fire rings, and pit toilets, and require permits.

BEACHES **Van Damme State Beach** See *Green Spaces.*

Big River Beach State Park (707-937-5804; parks.ca.gov) Accessible from CA 1, just as you enter Mendocino. This is an excellent beach for spending a sunny afternoon, or for those windswept morning strolls with your leashed dog. From here, you can paddle up the river (see *Water Sports*).

Russian Gulch State Beach (707- 937-5804; parks.ca.gov) Two miles north of Mendocino on CA 1. You can hike to the sandy beach beneath the Frederick W. Panhorst Bridge. Swimming, tide pooling, diving, and fishing are common favorites with locals.

Caspar Headlands State Beach (707-937-5804; parks.ca.gov) From CA 1, drive south on Point Cabrillo Road. The beach is across from the RV Park. If you can't get it together to get a permit to visit the Headlands, you can view a mere section of them from this sandy beach.

Glass Beach Head west on Elm Street. If only the ocean could cure all our problems. This beach was once the site of an old dump; the glass was left on this beach and over time, the sea polished the glass. Today you can walk along the colorful glass. However, you might not want to bring ailing Grandpa on this trail—it can be a bit rough.

& ❝❡❞ **MacKerricher State Park** (707-937-5397; parks.ca.gov) Just 3 miles north of Fort Bragg in Cleone. The 7 miles of sandy beach, wetlands, tide pools, even a lake, a wheelchair-accessible coastal bluff walk, campsites with Wi-Fi, access to the Pudding Creek Estuary (see Kayaking above), fantastic diving, and a great bike trail make this one of Mendocino County's best beaches. The 10 pet-friendly campsites (reserveamerica.com) with full services fill quickly ($20–25 per night).

Sinkyone Wilderness State Park (707-986-7711; parks.ca.gov) To access this area from the south, approximately one hour north of Ft. Bragg on CA 1, look for mile marker 90.88; drive north for 6 miles onto an unpaved, steep, and very narrow road. See *Redwood Coast.*

✳ Lodging

With a zillion inns, B&Bs, and vacation rentals, finding the one for you will be a snap. Note that on busy holiday weekends, you should reserve in advance. In general you can assume that there is a two to three-night minimum stay on weekends and holidays. And when I have noted that pets are allowed at a particular property, without exception it is with a charge. Because they are easy to spot throughout Fort Bragg (there are about a dozen for under a hundred bucks), I have not included motel listings. I have listed campsites under *Green Spaces.*

Little River

✐ ♿ ☕ ◌◌ ⑪ **Little River Inn** (707-937-5942 or 888-466-5683; littleriver inn.com) 7901 N. CA 1. They offer 64 cliff-side cottages (with hot tubs and fireplaces), and rooms you might find at your Auntie's house (complete with family heirlooms and peeks of the bay across the street). Since 1939, this family-owned full-service hotel has been doing something right. Friends like the Mallory House rooms, located in a meadow on the ocean side of CA 1. Resort amenities include restaurant and bar, tennis courts, golf course, and spa. $$–$$$$.

✐ ♿ ⑪ **Stevenswood Spa Resort** (707-937-2810 or 800-421-2810; stevenswood.com) 8211 N. CA 1. This well-oiled 10-room resort caters to a sophisticated eco-friendly crowd—think leather furniture, wood-burning stoves, wine-cork floors, an eco-spa, excellent restaurant, fitness room, two hot tubs, and in-room espresso machines. $$$–$$$$.

Mendocino

✐ ☕ ♿ ◌◌ ♈ **Mendocino Hotel & Garden Suites** (707-937-0511 or 800-548-0513; mendocinohotel.com) 45080 Main Street. Old pictures of Mendocino's first settlers, the dimly lit parlor and its lore about being haunted by spirits, mixed with the fragrant gardens, haunt guests until they return. The only full-service hotel in the village, located across the street from the bluffs, offers 51 rooms, from shared-bath accommodations to suites with tiled marble baths. In general you can assume your room will be decorated in antiques—brass bed, floral-print furniture, silky drapery—and if the ghosts don't rouse you, you'll probably sleep darn good. They also have two restaurants (see Dining Out below), concierge, and spa services. $$–$$$$.

✐ ☕ ♿ **Stanford Inn By the Sea** (707-937-5615 or 800-331-8884; stan fordinn.com) CA 1 and Comptche-Ukiah Road. Joan and Jeff Stanford created this organic oasis atop a meadow overlooking Mendocino Bay. The 43 pine- and redwood-paneled rooms with fireplaces feel cabin-like, yet sophisticated. Enjoy an organic breakfast in the main lodge with your dog, socialize over afternoon hors d'oeuvres, wander through the vegetable gardens, swim in the pool, or chill out in your room with a DVD and a fire. Other amenities: Ravens restaurant, spa, yoga, fitness room, mountain bikes, canoes, and kayaks. $$$–$$$$.

INNS AND B&BS

Albion

♿ ◌◌ **Albion River Inn** (707-937-1919 or 800-479-7944; albionriver inn.com) 3790 N. CA 1. Oceanfront rooms and cottages set atop a cliff, with no neighbors but the campground across the highway, make this a perfect choice for romance. Floral-printed bedspreads, fireplaces, and privacy are some of the perks you can expect from this remote inn. Amenities: 22 rooms and cottages, full breakfast, Albion River Inn restaurant (see Dining Out below), balconies, gardens, CD and video library, no TV. $$–$$$$.

✐ ☕ ♿ ◌◌ **Inn at Schoolhouse Creek** (707-937-5525 or 800-731-5525; school-housecreek.com) 7051 N. CA 1. Built in 1932, this inn offers country-style lodging across the street from the ocean. This is the perfect place for families who don't want to be in the center of Mendocino. The rustic location, individually decorated rooms, giant chess set, games, puzzles, books and movies, ocean views, and fireplaces, make this property feel like a grown-up summer camp. Amenities: 19 rooms and cottages (some cliff side), expanded continental breakfast, wine hour, yurt spa. $$–$$$$.

Fort Bragg

♪ "¶" Grey Whale Inn (707-964-0640 or 800-382-7244; greywhaleinn.com) 615 N. Main Street. Floral wallpaper and wicker furniture, some ocean views and fireplaces, and redwood walls evoke the mishmash of culture you'll find here in Fort Bragg. Cozy and old, this B&B makes a lovely stop if you want to explore the northern Mendocino coast, but still be able to walk to town. The Sunrise and Sunset penthouse suites offer the best ocean views. Amenities: 13 rooms, full breakfast, some kitchenettes, movie library, games, pool table, free local calls. $$.

♪ "¶" Old Coast Hotel (707-961-4488 or 888-468-3550; oldcoasthotel.com) 101 N. Franklin Street. Dating back to 1892, this historic B&B has recently been remodeled to evoke the spirit of the turn of the century without the quality of that time. Brass beds, Granny's furniture, oak hardwood floors, tin ceilings, and the sports bar downstairs add to the old world ambiance. Amenities: 6 rooms, continental breakfast, some rooms with fireplace. $$–$$$.

♪ ∞ Weller House Inn (707-964-4415; wellerhouse.com) 524 Stewart Street. Constructed in 1886, this Victorian is Fort Bragg's oldest building. The 10 individually crafted rooms, which evoke the spirit of Asia, Sweden, England, and France—have redwood walls, marble fireplaces, hand-painted tiles, stained glass, rich dark colors, comfy beds, and come with full breakfast. The newer Water Tower rooms are a treat, since they are in the tallest structure in town. Plus, the hot tub—on the fourth floor of the Water Tower—will take the ache out of those hiking muscles, while offering views of the ocean. $$.

Mendocino

♪ Alegria Inn and Cottages (707-937-5150 or 800-780-7905; oceanfront magic.com) 44781 Main Street. These 11 cottages, suites, and vacation rentals stacked on the bluff are a great choice for romance, or families looking for a kitchen in the center of Mendocino. The Cove cottage is closest to the bay, with bamboo floors and a soaking tub; the A-frame Driftwood cottage was the original owner's studio and now has a kitchen and loft. Down the road, the Village Farm Retreat is an apartment in a decade-old farmhouse, and is a great choice for families. Amenities: full breakfast for ocean side rooms, continental breakfast basket for other properties, games, movies, deck, beach access, and hot tub. $$–$$$.

Blue Heron Inn (707-937-4323; the blueheron.com) 390 Kasten Street. For those of you on a budget who want to be in the center of town, but also want a B&B experience, here you'll get rooms without the frills of many Mendocino area B&Bs. The three rooms have queen beds, shared baths, continental breakfast, access to Moosse Café and gardens, and views of the bay, ocean, or village. $$. No small children.

♿ "¶" ∞ Brewery Gulch Inn (707-937-4752 or 800-578-4454; brewery gulchinn.com) 9401 N. CA 1. Salvaged mineralized-redwood cabinets and doorframes, granite counters, and views of Mendocino's Smuggler's Cove give these individually designed rooms that special allure of romance reserved for rustic, remote lodging. Neither rustic nor particularly remote, guests come here for luxury: leather club chairs in front of the gas-lit fireplaces, down comforters, flat screen TVs and DVD players, iPod docking stations, some rooms have Jacuzzis or soaking tubs. I like the cozy loft rooms—which are less

expensive, but still luxurious. Amenities: 10 rooms, full organic breakfast, afternoon wine and food, some balconies. $$$–$$$$; no children under 12.

⟨Τ⟩ & ⊙ **Lighthouse Inn at Point Cabrillo** (707-937-6124 or 866-937-6124; mendocinolighthouse.point cabrillo.org) 45300 Lighthouse Road. Classy cottages and rooms, just steps from the ocean on this old lighthouse-keeper's property, are unique. Rooms are decorated to enhance the classic feel of the property, with antiques, brick fireplaces, and radiant heating. The six rooms and cottages offer a five-course gourmet breakfast. No children under 15. $$–$$$.

✍ 🐾 ⟨Τ⟩ ⊙ **MacCallum House Inn** (707-937-0289 or 800-609-0492; mac callumhouse.com) 45020 Albion Street. Built in 1882, this iconic yellow Victorian represents Mendocino. Luxury perks such as Jacuzzi tubs, flat screen TVs, hot tub, and plush linens mix with antique four-poster beds, oil lamps, and the occasional river stone fireplace. Broken into four properties, my favorites are the cottages on the Main House property—for both luxury and privacy. Amenities: 44 rooms, cottages, and suites, full breakfast, dinner vouchers, Grey Whale Bar and Café (see *Dining Out*), concierge. $–$$$$.

✍ 🐾 ⟨Τ⟩ **Seagull Inn** (707-937-5204 or 888-937-5204; seagullbb.com) 44960 Albion Street. In the travel business cozy means small, and many of the rooms at this inn are in the blink-and-you'll-miss-them category, but they also evoke the Dutch word *gezellig* (which means having a warm cozy atmosphere). Here you'll find nine antique-decorated rooms, organic breakfast, lush colorful gardens, super-friendly innkeepers, and the best deal in town. $–$$.

⟨Τ⟩ **Packard House** (707-937-2677 or 888-453-2677; packardhouse.com)

45170 Little Lake Street. Looking for a luxury B&B without Grandma's antiques? The Packard House offers four modern rooms with an urban sensibility: fireplaces, fine linens, pillowy beds, flat screen TVs, DVDs, Jacuzzi tubs, choice of a gourmet breakfast in the dining room or a breakfast basket in your room, afternoon wine hour, and calming gardens. Their sister property, the **JD House** (jdhouse .com), offers eight nautical-themed modern rooms for less money. $$–$$$; no children under 12.

✍ 🐾 ▼ ⊙ **Whitegate Inn** (800-531-7282; whitegateinn.com) 499 Howard Street. The classic feel of this 1887 white Victorian, with its colorful gardens and friendly staff, offers a traditional B&B experience. My aunt really likes the French Rose room, with floral carpet, an antique four-poster bed, pink accents, and ocean views. If you are traveling with kids or pets, you might head over to their sister property, **Abigail's Inn**. Amenities: six rooms and cottages, two-course breakfast, afternoon wine and cheese, and concierge. $$–$$$$.

Westport

✍ 🐾 ⟨Τ⟩ **DeHaven Valley Farm** (707-961-1660; dehavenvalleyinn.com) 39247 N. CA 1. The inn is actually a Victorian farmhouse nestled into a meadow, with some ocean-view rooms

THE LIGHTHOUSE INN AT POINT CABRILLO.

and cottages. Rooms feel like Granny decorated them. Families will appreciate the spacious Rose Cottage with a wood-burning stove and a private patio. Amenities: Eight rooms and cottages, some rooms with private bath, gourmet breakfast, hot tub, and dinner served on weekends (fee). $–$$.

☂ ☃ Howard Creek Ranch (707-964-6725; howardcreekranch.com) 40501 N. CA 1. This 60-acre farm, with gardens, animals, redwoods, and country kindness offers Victorian-style accommodations for couples that find oceanfront ranches romantic. Each room owns a unique style—nautical, farm, 1863, and even a rustic wood cottage. Amenities: 13 cabins, cottages, and rooms, some with kitchenettes, full breakfast. $–$$; no children allowed.

VACATION RENTALS Shoreline Vacation Rentals (707-964-1444; 888-942-8482; shorelinevacations.com) 18180 N. CA 1, Fort Bragg. This rental agency handles cottages and houses all along the Mendocino coast. You will find everything from the one-bedroom Le Faux to the four-bedroom Serendipity house. Some facilities accept pets, though there is a charge. On holiday weekends, they have a two- to three-night minimum stay.

✳ Where to Eat

DINING OUT

Albion
☂ Albion River Inn (707-937-1919; albionriverinn.com) 3790 N. CA 1. Open for dinner nightly. Ocean-view dining highlights the local fresh cuisine created by Chef Stephen Smith. Light entrees like the pork stew or burger are good choices for the budget conscious. Or you can go for the big plates of mushroom pasta or seared rock cod and a bottle of wine off Mark Bowery's award-winning wine list. Reservations recommended. $$–$$$.

☂ ☃ ♿ Ledford House (707-937-0282) 3000 N. CA 1, Albion. This is my favorite place to eat in the area. Super-fresh Cal-French cuisine with expansive ocean views, French and Brazilian music (or live jazz on weekends), local artwork, friendly service, and a lovely deck to watch the sunset with a glass of wine, make this perfect for romance or family dining. Specialties include cassoulet, vegetarian gnocchi, and rabbit. The nightly bistro special is a steal: a tummy busting three-course dinner for $25! Reservations recommended. $$–$$$.

Fort Bragg
∞ Mendo Bistro (707-964-4974; mendobistro.com) 301 N. Main Street. Open for dinner nightly. Locals swear by this second-floor restaurant, perched over CA 1. I appreciate the Choice Menu, where you can select from a variety of organic meat, fish, or vegetarian items, pick how you want it cooked (broiled, sautéed, and so on), and which sauce you want (Charmoula, roasted garlic gravy). Loads of pasta selections and great appetizers also will please the whole family. $$–$$$.

Mendocino
955 Ukiah Street (707-937-1955; 955restaurant.com) 955 Ukiah Street. Open for dinner Thursday through Sunday. Walk down a garden path to this hidden, old water-tower mill, where you gaze at the gardens, sip wine, and enjoy classic takes on seasonal California cuisine. Think hard-shell clams, pasta with seasonal vegetables, or chuck steak. Reservations recommended. $$–$$$.

∞ Café Beaujolais (707-937-5614; cafebeaulolais.com) 961 Ukiah Street. Open 11:30–2 and 5:45–9 daily. If I were lauded as the best restaurant in town, I probably wouldn't be so snobby about it. However, if you can get past the blonde cheerleader attitude, the baked breads, seasonal soups, and game are probably the tastiest you'll get in town. Chef David La Monica knows how to combine delicate tastes—nettle and cream, wild mushroom and butternut squash. Reservations required for dinner. Lunch: $–$$. Dinner: $$$–$$$$.

✤ ♈ ⊙ **Grey Whale Bar and Cafe** (707-937-0289 or 800-609-0492; maccallumhouse.com) MacCallum House, 45020 Albion Street, Mendocino. Open for breakfast and dinner daily. Dining by the fireplace in this classic Victorian dining room or along the outdoor patio is a treat. Chef Alan Kantor cooks up local favorites, like the risotto primavera, sautéed sea bass in a coconut curry, or Rosie organic chicken in lemon-thyme sauce. If you are on a budget, head over to the café for tacos, a po' boy, or an organic potpie. Make sure to save room for dessert— the praline cookie taco is divine. Reservations recommended. Breakfast: $–$$. Café: $$. Dinner: $$$–$$$$.

✤ ♿ ♈ **Mendocino Hotel Dining Room and Bistro** (707-937-0511 or 800-548-0513; mendocinohotel.com) 45080 Main Street. Open daily for breakfast, lunch, and dinner. If you are in the mood for classic white-tablecloth service, with tableside Caesar salad preparation, and seven-spiced rack of lamb, the dining room is made for you. Dining under a Tiffany stained-glass dome isn't so bad either. Families and budget-conscious folks who want to glimpse the bay while dining will enjoy the casual bistro and bar. This is one of the few restaurants that stays open all day. Reservations recommended. Bistro: $–$$. Dinner: $$$.

Moosse Café (707-937-4323; theblueheron.com) Blue Heron Inn, 390 Kasten Street. Open for lunch (12–3) and dinner (5:30–9) daily. The wood décor of this bistro-style restaurant lets the food do the talking. Seasonal, local food like the lunchtime cod sandwich, or macaroni and cheese, or the dinner vegetable pavé with lemon-thyme broth keeps me coming back. Reservations recommended. Lunch: $–$$. Dinner: $$$.

✤ ☗ ♿ **Ravens Restaurant** (707-937-5615 or 800-331-8884; ravensrestaurant.com) Stanford Inn, Coast CA 1 and Comptche-Ukiah Road. Open for breakfast and dinner nightly. If organic vegetarian and vegan cuisine with views of the sea and forest (while your pooch sits under the table eating up your scraps) sounds like heaven, head up to the Ravens. Dishes highlight the vegetables grown in the organic gardens (that you can wander through after dinner): Citrus polenta, sea-palm strudel, and tempeh carpaccio are just some of the specialties. Reservations recommended. Breakfast: $$. Dinner: $$$.

EATING OUT

Fort Bragg

✤ ♿ **Café 1** (707-964-0911) 753 N. Main Street. Open daily for breakfast and lunch; dinner on Thursday through Saturday. Hidden on a quiet stretch of CA 1, this organic diner serves up some great breakfast fare in a country setting. The nine-vegetable Hippie Scramble with either organic eggs or tofu, rocks. $–$$.

✤ **D'Aurelio's** (707-964-4227) 438 S. Franklin Street. Open nightly from 5–9. The Coast's most popular casual Italian eatery draws locals to wait in super-long lines for pizza, heaping plates of pasta and sandwiches, and fresh baked breads. Unless you are a teenage football player, go for the half portion. $$.

✤ ♿ **Egghead's Restaurant** (707-964-5005; eggheadsrestaurant.com) 326 N. Main Street. Open 7–2; closed Wednesday. This breakfast institution serves gigantic portions of eggs and griddle fare. The Wizard of Oz-themed murals, friendly staff (even early in the morning), 31 years of service, and the extensive menu keep me returning. $.

  ♿ **Harvest Market** (707-964-7000) 171 Boatyard Drive. Open daily from 5 AM–11 PM. Natural foods, a deli, and a decent selection of affordable local groceries bring locals from around the coast. This is the spot to get a picnic lunch for the Skunk Train or a long hike along the coast.

  ♫ ♿ **Headlands Coffee House** (707-964-1987) 120 E. Laurel Street. Open daily from 7 AM–10 PM (until 11 on weekends). Tie-dye-shirted tarot card readers, gray-bearded folks (men and women!) chanting, loggers, and fishermen drinking beer at 8 AM. The choices for a bagel are from Safeway *or* the famed Café Beaujolais (for the same price), live music, decent coffee and sandwiches, beer, wine, and plenty of Fort Bragg flavor. $.

  ♫ **North Coast Brewing Co.** (707-964-3400; northcoastbrewing.com) 444 N. Main Street. Open from 12 PM–11 PM. This award-winning brewery is not just for drinking—though you'll be hard-pressed not to return for another pint. Resurrecting the old Acme beer label to modern standards, the new brewsters have mastered the Red Seal Ale and the Old Rasputin. One of my favorite stops along the coast, these guys take as much pride in their food as their beers. Pasta, chops, and Kobe beef burgers are the stars of the restaurant, but the way to go is the pub food, where you get great deals. Lunch and Pub: $–$$. Dinner: $$–$$$$.

  ♫ ♿ **Purple Rose** (707-964-6507) 24300 N CA 1. Open Wednesday through Sunday for dinner. You might not think much of it, based on the gravel driveway, but there is a reason this small Mexican joint has locals lining up: Margaritas. The food can be hit or miss; tacos tend to be winners for me. $–$$.

  ♫ ♿ **Sharon's By the Sea** (707-964-0680; sharonsbythesea.com) 32096 N. Harbor Drive. Open daily for lunch and dinner. Casual dining on the harbor in an intimate setting, with an emphasis on Italian specialties, offers wonderful lunchtime views. The fish and chips and fish tacos are worthy options. Reservations recommended. $$–$$$.

Little River

Little River Market (707-937-5133) 7746 N. CA 1. A million-dollar view comes with your deli fare here. Besides groceries, you can put together picnic lunches of salads, sandwiches, and Mexican food.

Mendocino

Bay View Café (707-937-4197) 45040 Main Street. Open daily for breakfast and lunch; dinner on Friday and Saturday. If your inn doesn't offer breakfast, you'll probably head up the water tower to this ocean-view spot. Traditional American fare like breakfast scrambles and omelets, lunchtime burgers, and dinner pastas with a Southwestern tilt. Cash only. $–$$.

Corners of the Mouth (707-937-5345) 45015 Ukiah Street. Open daily from 8–8. Whenever I come to the area, I always pop into this old church that now houses the organic grocery. Though they don't prepare food, you can find enough to fill your belly.

  ♫ **Frankie's Handmade Ice Cream** (707-931-2436) 44951 Ukiah Street. Open 11 AM–9 PM daily. This new addition to the town has people lining up for yummy pizzas and falafels, and organic handmade ice cream. Make sure to try the mushroom ice cream—no joke, it rocks! There is live music here on weekends. If you are in Fort Bragg, head over to **Cowlick's Ice Cream** (where this ice cream is actually made) on Main Street: $–$$.

Mendocino Bakery and Café (707-937-0836) 10483 Lansing. Open 7:30–5:30 daily. This is my favorite place to eat in Mendocino. Not because it is the best food, but the vibe is friendly, the coffee perfect, and the pastries and pizzas are super fresh. $.

Mendocino Café (707-937-2422; mendocinocafe.com) 10451 Lansing Street. Open for lunch and dinner daily. Everyone in town recommends this place. And for a good reason: It is affordable and good. The first time I came here, I was confused at the innovative fusion of flavors like Thai burritos, but everything I try works. On sunny days, the outdoor patio can't be beat. $$–$$$.

✳ Entertainment

Caspar

Caspar Inn (707-964-5565; casparinn .com) 14957 Caspar Road. Open Tuesday through Sunday from at least 6 PM–1 AM. A historic nightclub exists all the way out here. And if you are daring, they even rent rooms. This is the spot for live music, open mic nights, and classic Mendo culture.

Mendocino

Dick's Place (707-937-5643) Main Street. Open daily until 2 AM. This dive bar gets packed on weekends and holidays.

Mendocino Theater Company (707-937-4477; mendocinotheater.org) 45200 Little Lake Road. For over 30 years, this company has put up classic and contemporary plays.

♈ Patterson's Irish Pub (707-937-4782; pattersonspub.com) 10485 Lansing Street. Open daily until 1 AM. This green Victorian on the outskirts of town offers reasonably priced pub grub and great Irish beers to locals and tourists who stumble this far. I've come here many a time to watch a sporting event when my inn didn't have a TV.

✳ Selective Shopping

In Mendocino, along Main Street and Lansing, you'll find the majority of galleries and shops scattered throughout historic buildings. Some places not to miss are **The World of Suzi Long** (707-937-9664; 601 Albion Street), which showcases Suzi Long's art in an old skinny water tower and **Sallie Mac Home and Garden** (707-937-5357; 1040 Lansing Street). **Gallery Bookshop** (707-937-BOOK; gallerybook shop.com) Main Street is open daily from 9:30–6 (until 9 on Friday and Saturday). On a cold afternoon, this is where I go to browse. Their kids' section, local writers' section, and fiction selection are great.

Fort Bragg is an antique shopper's dream. The historic old town has so many antique shops you'll think you stepped back to 1954. Another notable stop includes **Cheshire Books** (707-964-5918; 345 N. Franklin Street).

✳ Seasonal Events

May: **Mendocino Film Festival** (707-937-0171; mendocinofilmfestival.org) Hollywood comes to Mendocino for three days of progressive-minded films and events.

July: **Mendocino Music Festival** (707-937-2044; Mendocinomusic.com) Main Street. In July, Main Street comes alive with two weeks of music, spanning genre, age, and nationality. Tickets range from $21–48. Children under 18: $16.

World's Largest Salmon BBQ Noyo Harbor, Fort Bragg. Coinciding with Independence Day, this giant celebration of the pink fish is worth the $25 admission. Happening since 1970, you know that the recipe has been perfected.

THE REDWOOD COAST

NORTHERN MENDOCINO AND SOUTHERN HUMBOLDT COUNTIES
NORTHERN HUMBOLDT COUNTY AND THE FAR NORTH

This is the most beautiful region in California. Hands down. One time in your life (or many, if you are as smitten with these trees as we Northern Californians), you have to stand in the shadow of a city of redwood trees that dwarf people, cars, even buildings, to understand the magic that these forests evoke. Nowhere else will you see the symbiotic relationship of trees and ocean, moss and mulch, ferns and fog, mountains and sea.

However, as dramatic as the natural beauty of this area is, that is how bleak the towns can feel. Save Eureka and Arcata, you won't find much in terms of culture, industry, or even good food. The lumber industry is about all these folks have up here, and they are struggling to hang on.

Starting in northern Mendocino County, a couple little towns (**Leggett** and **Laytonville**) straddle US 101, which, aside from offering access to beautiful parks, a drive-through tree, wood carvings, and some curiosities like the **Confusion Hill**, tourists will most likely pass right through to get to SoHum (Southern Humboldt County). This region marks the entrance to the sea of redwood trees in the famed **Humboldt Redwood State Park**. Most people camp here and visit the one-shop towns of **Garberville, Redway, Phillipsville, Miranda,** and **Myers Flat** for food and gas. From here you also have access to the mostly unexplored Lost Coast and the town of **Shelter Cove**.

DEEP IN THE REDWOOD FOREST.

THE TOWN OF MIRANDA TAKES YOU BACK TO ANOTHER ERA.

NoHum starts as you head up US 101: The redwood trees begin to part past the ailing lumber towns of **Scotia** and **Fortuna**; while to the west is the touristy Victorian village of **Ferndale,** and way to the east, **Bigfoot Country** (Willow Creek). Most people motor through heading to the twin towns of **Eureka** and **Arcata**; located on opposite sides of **Humboldt Bay Lagoons**, these brothers could not be more different. Eureka is the conservative lumber town, holding on to its roots with an Old Town filled with galleries, cafés and music venues, bearded lumberjacks, gun shops, and mullets. Arcata is the black sheep of the whole North Coast. A funky college town, complete with artists, hippies, and educators, there are more dreadlocks here than mullets, more pot smoke than gun shops, and more organic fare than fast food. Most people stop here for a couple of days to explore the beach village of **Trinidad** and the magical **Redwood State and National Park**.

Once you arrive in Del Norte County, you can feel a shift. Indian reservations and RV parks outnumber hotels and even houses, and everything begins to feel bleaker. However, this area is home to some of the most beautiful—and unexplored!—redwood parks, rivers, and beaches in the whole state. You won't find much in the towns of **Orick, Klamath,** and **Crescent City** except places where over a third of the population is under the poverty line. Much of this poverty can be attributed to the ailing lumber companies and the 1964 tsunami: A 20.78-foot wave destroyed 289 Crescent City buildings and killed 11 people. If you make it all the way up here (and you should) I recommend camping or staying along the **Smith River**.

GUIDANCE **Humboldt County Visitor and Convention Bureau** (800-346-3482; redwoods.info) 1034 2nd Street, Eureka.

Crescent City Visitor Center 707-464-3174 or 800-343-8300; 2chambers.com) 1001 Front Street, Crescent City.

HELPFUL WEB SITES
Arcatachamber.com
exploredelnorte.com

SCENIC DRIVES

Even if you aren't a hiker, you can still access the grandeur of the tall trees on a number of scenic drives. Though US 101 isn't so bad (nor is CA 299 or US 199), on the drives listed below you can get right up in the trees, without leaving your car.

Avenue of the Giants (avenueofthegiants.com) Off US 101 from the south, the drive is north of Garberville, take the Phillipsville exit; or from the north take the Pepperwood exit. In SoHum, nothing beats a drive along these gentle giants. This 31-mile scenic road takes you deep into the forest through 51,222 acres of redwoods and along the Eel River. You will find plenty of places to stop for a hike, a picnic, or to take pictures. Allow at least two hours for the drive.

Newton B. Drury Parkway Just past Orick off US 101. If you are in NoHum, this scenic drive is one of California's best. You will be dwarfed by redwood trees, and maybe even start to understand why Julia Butterfly Hill camped out in one for so long.

Howland Hill Road In Jedediah Smith Redwoods State Park, just south of Crescent City, take Elk Valley Road east to Howland Hill Road. This rough gravel road is about as close as you can get into a massive grove of pristine redwoods. No RVs can make it through here, in fact my Honda Civic barely made it.

DRIVE BENEATH THE TOWERING GIANTS.

Lost Coast Scenic Drive From Ferndale, take Petrolia Road for 6 miles down the coast and keep going on this winding, rough road until you reach Humboldt Redwoods State Park. Allow three or four hours to explore this rugged wilderness—the only coastal wilderness in all of California. For more information see *Lost Coast* Sidebar.

northerncalifornia.net
avenueofthegiants.net
willowcreekchamber.com
humguide.com
northcoastjournal.com
humcity.com

GETTING THERE *By air:* The **Arcata Airport** welcomes flights on Horizon Air (800-547-9308) from Los Angeles, Portland, and Redding. United Airlines (800-241-6522) serves San Francisco, Sacramento, and Portland. Avis, National, and Alamo car rental agencies can be found at the airport.

By bus: **Greyhound** (greyhound.com) and **Amtrak** (Amtrak.com) offer bus service to the area.

By car: US 101 weaves up the coast offering access to all Redwood Coast towns and attractions, plus some of the best views around.

GETTING AROUND Unfortunately, you'll kick yourself if you don't have a car here. Though you can access some of the natural attractions by bus, the best way to get into them is by car—often on seriously winding roads. Everything requires a trek. From Leggett to Garberville it is about 20 miles, but it takes about a half hour to drive it. Eureka is about 70 miles from there and Arcata is another 10 miles to the north. The Redwood State and National Park is about 45 minutes north of town. Crescent City is 77 miles from Arcata. If you hope to stay deep in the forest, you might want to explore Willow Creek area; however make sure you have a full tank and a sense of adventure: this is a trek for some serious solitude.

By bus: **Arcata and Mad River Transit System** (707-822-3775) offer service within Arcata. The **Redwood Transit System** (707-443-0826) serves the NoHum area.

MEDICAL EMERGENCIES **Jerold Phelps Community Hospital** (707-923-3921) 509 Elm Street, Garberville. **St. Joseph Hospital** (707-445-8121) 2700 Dolbeer Street, Eureka. **Humboldt Open Door Clinic** (707-826-7698) 670 9th Street, Arcata.

NORTHERN MENDOCINO AND SOUTHERN HUMBOLDT COUNTIES

✳ To See

✿ **Confusion Hill** (707-925-6456; confusionhill.com) 75001 N. US 101, Piercy. Open at least 10 AM–5 PM daily (longer hours in summer). This is one of those spots you see from the road that your kids will scream to go into. Here you'll find plenty of tchotchkes being hawked, a semi-fascinating gravity house, a train ride through redwoods, a redwood shoehouse, and a few other curiosities. Since there isn't much between Ukiah and Eureka, you'll likely pit stop here. Admission to the gravity house: $5 adults, $4 children, kids under 3 free. Train rides: $7 adults, $5 kids, children under 3 free.

⚲ **One Log House** (707-247-3717; one-loghouse.com) 705 US 101, Garberville. Open daily from at least 8–5 (longer hours in summer). Yes, you can live inside one of those huge redwood trees and here is proof: an entire house inside one log. You can get an espresso here, and connect to the Internet for free. Minimal fee.

✳ To Do

Avenue of the Giants See *Scenic Drives.*

Benbow Resort Golf Course (707-923-2124; benbowinn.com) 445 Lake Benbow Drive, Garberville. Golf surrounded by trees at this lovely course. $24–30.

THE RUGGED NORTHERN CALIFORNIA COAST.

THE LOST COAST

To access this area from the south, approximately one hour north of Fort Bragg on CA 1, look for mile marker 90.88; drive north for 6 miles onto an unpaved, steep, and very narrow road. From the north, 36 miles southwest of Garberville/Redway, take Briceland Road west from Redway; it becomes Mendocino County Road 435. The last 3.5 miles are unpaved, steep, and very narrow.

For over 3,000 years, people have lived here, intentionally distanced from the rest of the world. However, because main highways don't reach this wooded coastal stretch, the moniker "Lost Coast" just stuck. Folks who live here, and plenty of resourceful hikers and campers, know where it is

Drive Thru Tree Park (707-925-6363; drivethrutree.com) Drive Thru Tree Road, Leggett. You'll see the signs, so many signs, and at one of the three drive-through trees in these parts, you'll probably be tempted. This one, the Chandelier Drive-Thru Tree, was carved in the 1930s. There is a small fee to drive through.

Garberville Farmers' Market In the Town Square, Garberville, Friday 11 AM–2 PM.

Shrine Drive Thru Tree Follow the signs off US 101 in Myers Flat. Here's your second chance to drive through a tree. This one is located close to the Humboldt Redwoods Park. As per usual in these trees, expect to wait a while because people stop and take pictures of their cars in the tree. There is a small fee to drive through.

and how to get here. And if you can handle a long, winding, and rough route to get into this real California coastal wilderness, so will you.

The region is broken up into the two main areas of **Sinkyone Wilderness State Park** (Mendocino County) and **King Range National Conservation Area** (Humboldt County), with a few tiny towns scattered down the coast. The main community is in Shelter Cove, a blink-and-you'll-miss-it town with a couple inns and restaurants. Most people come here to escape the fast-paced world—cell phone service doesn't work and since it is so hard to get here, only the brave attempt it. From here, you will have access to both Sinkyone and the King Range.

To camp on the Lost Coast, contact the **Bureau of Land Management Parks and Campgrounds** (707-825-2300). That includes camping in King Range, Black Sands Beach in Shelter Cove, Honeydew Campground, Mal Coombs Park in Shelter Cove, Mattole Campground in Petrolia, and Lost Coast Headlands.

Sinkyone Wilderness State Park (707-986-7711; parks.ca.gov) Once the home to the Sinkyone and Mattole Indians, now the nation's first intertribal state park, it connects to Sinkyone's 7,367 lush acres. Thousands of years ago, the Indians used their proximity to the coast to survive. For a good hike, try the **The Lost Coast Trail**, 2 miles round-trip to Jones Beach, or 4.5 miles round-trip to Whale Gulch. For the serious hiker, you can traverse the entire 6-mile trail (start out at the **Needle Rock Visitor Center**). Look for the herds of Roosevelt elk that roam the park.

Kings Range National Conservation Area (707-561-6640; blm.gov) North of Westport, off CA 1, head up Usal Road. Here, bears thrive and roads don't reach the sea. From Westport, you can access the southern part of this 35-mile park, from Garberville, you can get to the northern part. Mountains spike nearly a mile into the air, then drop towards the sea, offering black sand beaches, tide pools, and some excellent diving with sea mammals. Here you'll also find elk, bald eagles, seals, and much more. There are also plenty of campgrounds ($8). For more information, contact the **Garberville-Redway Chamber of Commerce** (garberville.org)

✴ Green Spaces

STATE AND NATIONAL PARKS Benbow Lake State Recreation Area (707-247-3318; parks.ca.gov) Off US 101 south of Garberville. In summer, the park service dams Eel River to create a lake for swimming and canoeing. There is a campground here (reserveamerica.com) as well as the Benbow Valley RV Resort.

Humboldt Redwoods State Park (707-247-3318; parks.ca.gov) The Visitor Center is off Avenue of the Giants, between Weott and Myers Flat. Spread over 53,000 acres, with 17,000 of those acres populated by untouched redwood groves, this is one of the most pristine places on earth. The Rockefeller Forest boasts the largest remaining old-growth redwood forest in the world, with some of the world's tallest trees. Other favorite trails are the Founders Grove Nature Trail, Bull Creek Flats Loop Trail, the Dyerville Giant (a fallen tree that is 200 feet taller than Niagara Falls), and in the Big Trees area, the Immortal Tree. From within the park, you can access the Eel River and Mattole River, which are great places to fish for salmon and steelhead in winter. For camping information, see *Lodging*.

Kings Range National Conservation Area See *Lost Coast* Sidebar.

Lost Coast See *Lost Coast* Sidebar.

⁑ Richardson Grove State Park (707-247-3318; parks.ca.gov) 1600 US 101, Garberville. Named after the 25th governor of California, this park bisects the south fork of the Eel River and offers plenty of access to redwoods. Here you'll find the ninth tallest redwood tree in the world and a walk-through tree. You can camp here in the Huckleberry or Madrone Campgrounds year-round, and in the Oak Flat campground in summer. Family camping is $20.

Sinkyone Wilderness State Park See *Lost Coast* Sidebar.

BEACHES See *Lost Coast.*

✴ Lodging

𝒮 ♿ ⁑ ▼ **Benbow Inn** (707-923-2124; benbowinn.com) 445 Lake Benbow Drive, Garberville. Humboldt County's only full-service resort in a historic building is an attractive option if you aren't keen on sleeping outdoors. Since 1926, this resort has welcomed everyone from Hollywood stars to RV campers, offering a caliber of service not found in many places. Rooms evoke another time, with rich red velvet, deep wood, and doors painted by Eva Benbow. Amenities: world-class restaurant, golf course, tennis courts, afternoon cocktail reception, bicycles, live entertainment on summer evenings, films, spa services. $$–$$$$.

𝒮 **Miranda Gardens Resort** (707-943-3011; mirandagardens.com) Avenue of the Giants, Miranda. If you don't want to camp, but want to sleep beneath the redwoods, I like the Miranda Gardens. The 16 cottages and rooms nestled in a grove of redwoods, with deer wandering through the playground and around the pool, are both homey and rustic. Families will like the ones with full kitchens and barbeque areas. Others might do just fine in a simple room. $$.

CAMPGROUNDS Humboldt Redwoods State Park (reserveamerica .com) For all these sites, you must book well in advance; they fill up fast.

For all hosted sites, the fee is $20 per family. In addition to those listed below, you can hike to a number of sites. For all of these, register with the Visitor Center, buy a hiking map, and pack out all your trash. Bears are notorious in the area, and there are no bear cans set up. The following are camps with pit toilets and untreated water: **Johnson Camp** (notorious for mosquitoes, especially early in the season), **Grasshopper Camp** (amazing views), **Whiskey Flat** (beneath a grove of old-growth redwoods), **Hansen Ridge** (views of the ocean and King Range mountains), and the quiet **Bull Creek Camp**.

Campsites accessible by car:
Albee Creek Five miles west of the Avenue of the Giants on the Mattole Road. Deep in the Rockefeller Forest, these 40 sites allow you to sleep under second-growth redwoods. Open Memorial Day through mid-October. There are full services here.

Burlington Next to the Visitor Center on the Avenue of the Giants, 1.5 miles south of Weott. Camp in a grove of old- and second-growth redwoods; this campground has 57 sites, and is a short distance from the South Fork of the Eel for fishing and swimming. Open year-round.

Hidden Springs Five miles south of the Visitor Center on the Avenue of the Giants, just south of Myers Flat. Situated on a hillside in a mixed forest, the 154 campsites offer plenty of privacy. Open mid-April through Labor Day.

Hamilton Barn and Baxter Environmental Camps Six miles west of the Avenue of the Giants on Mattole Road. Here you'll find picnic tables, fire rings, pit toilets, and untreated water. With only five sites, you need to book early. Open mid-April through mid-October.

Cuneo Creek Horse Camp Eight miles west of Avenue of the Giants on Mattole Road. This campground is reserved for campers bringing their horses to the park—a beautiful open prairie at the base of a ridge. There are five family campsites, each with two corrals, and two group campsites. There are fire rings, picnic tables, treated water, flush toilets, and coin-operated hot showers. Open mid-April through mid-October.

Other Campsites:
Benbow Lake State Recreation Area See *Green Spaces.*

Richardson Grove State Park See *Green Spaces.*

✷ Where to Eat

DINING OUT ✐ ♿ ♉ **Benbow Hotel Restaurant** (707-923-2124; benbow hotelandresort.com) 445 Lake Benbow Drive, Garberville. Open for breakfast and dinner daily, lunch in summer. Wine lovers, history buffs, and folks who like good food will delight in this classic restaurant. In summer, I like to sit on the garden patio and dine on portobello and Taleggio gratinée, while my husband can't get enough of the sage-roasted sirloin of Sonoma spring lamb. Breakfast is just as delightful. Reservations recommended. There is a dress code of no sandals, shorts, or T-shirts. $$—$$$$.

♿ ♉ **The Cove** (707-986-1197; shelter coverestaurant.com) 10 Seal Court, Shelter Cove. Open Thursday through Sunday 5–9; Sunday 11:30–3. Though the menu is the typical style you'll get from those ocean-view spots up and down the California coast, the view is something else. Specialties include smoked-salmon pasta and steaks. There is nightly music here, as well. $$–$$$$.

&. **The Groves** (707-943-9930; river bencellars.com) 12990 Avenue of the Giants, Myers Flat. Open from 5–9 Thursday through Monday. This famous SoHum dining establishment attracts the foodies from Eureka and Arcata for seasonal and pricey California cuisine. Located in an old barn attached to a tasting room, here you'll get the finest food and wine between Mendocino and Eureka. Chef Bryan Hopper changes his menu daily, but imagine a wood-oven roasted rack of lamb with rosemary couscous, grilled salmon, and wood-fired pizzas that will blow your mind. Reservations recommended. $$–$$$$.

&. **Mateel Café** (707-923-2030; mateelcafe.com) 3344 Redwood Drive, Redway. Open Monday through Friday 11:30–9. Though the wood chairs and picnic tables might place this restaurant as a more casual place to eat, the organic world-fusion cuisine makes this a dining star in the area. Local beer and wine, pizza, sirloin, Thai noodles, pasta, and sandwiches make this a dependable stop for food. $$–$$$.

EATING OUT Chautauqua Natural Foods and Café Minou (707-923-2452) 436 Church Street, Garberville. Open Monday through Saturday 10 AM–6 PM. What a find in this funky little town—an organic natural-food market with a great selection of produce that also has a good deli attached to it. Specialties like rice-crust pizza and salads fill the menu boards, but I am a fan of their plain old turkey sandwich. $.

&. ♈ **El Rio at the Riverwood Inn** (707-943-3333; riverwoodinn.com) Take the Phillipsville exit off US 101, restaurant located on Avenue of Giants, 6 miles north of Garberville. Harley bikers populate the redwood bar, sipping MGD and margaritas, locals return weekly for huge plates of insanely good Mexican food. Burritos are the size of my head, the enchiladas are as good as they get, the homemade salsa and tortillas make me eat well past full. Plus the pool table, the arcade games, the page-long tequila menu, and the *Twin Peaks*-like décor will entertain. $–$$.

WINE TASTING IN THE REDWOODS

Though Humboldt County is not known for their world-class wines, there are a number of good wines to come out of the region. Most of the tasting rooms are open by appointment only. Below is a list and contact information for some of the local tasting rooms.

Briceland Vineyards (707-923-2429) 5959 Briceland Road, Redway. Tasting by appointment.

Elk Prairie Vineyard (707-943-3498; elkprairievineyard.com) 11544 Dyerville Loop Road, Myers Flat. Tasting by appointment.

Riverbend Cellars (707-943-9907; riverbendcellars.com) 122990 Avenue of the Giants, Myers Flat. Open daily from 11–5. Free.

Winnett Vineyards (530-629-3478) 655 Peachtree Lane, Willow Creek. Appointment only. This organic estate-grown vineyard has begun to get a lot of press lately. You might want to go see what all the hype is about.

REGGAE RISING MUSIC FESTIVAL.

Flavors (707-923-7007) 767 Redwood Drive, Garberville. Open from at least 8–5 daily. This is the best place for coffee in SoHum. They also serve sandwiches.

Nacho Mama (707-923-4060) 377 Sprowl Creek Road, Garberville. Open from 11 AM–6 PM Monday through Saturday. In a little shack behind the gas station, you'll find burritos or fish tacos. Most everything is organic. There is nowhere to sit, so call ahead for your order and take it to a redwood park. $.

🍴 ♿ **Woodrose Café** (707-923-3191) 911 Redwood, Garberville. Open 8–2:30 daily. People always recommend this diner with organic and vegetarian specialties, Diestel turkey burgers, and Mexican-style breakfast. Though the food is fine for this area, I wasn't blown away. Cash Only. $–$$.

✳ Entertainment

🍸 **Benbow Inn Restaurant** See *Dining Out.*

🍸 **The Cove** See *Dining Out.*

🍸 **Riverwood Inn Restaurant** See *Eating Out.*

✳ Seasonal Events

Bimonthly: **Arts Alive!** Downtown Garberville. Friday 5–8. Every business boasts an art collection on Fridays, when everyone around SoHum comes to celebrate the local artists.

May: **Avenue of the Giants Marathon** (theave.org) At least you know you can breathe for this eye-popping marathon—there is probably more oxygen here than any other place on earth.

August: **Reggae Rising** (reggaerising .com) Mateel Community Center. Every August the rastas, hippies, potheads, and reggae music lovers saturate SoHum for a weekend of camping and music from around the world. Everyone greets you with, "Happy Reggae," and it sure is a "happy" event. There is more green here than people. And if people watching is your game, this is one of the best festivals to do so.

✳ To See

Scotia, Ferndale, and Vicinity

Ferndale Victorian Village Exit US 101, just north of Fortuna, cross the Fernbridge (a historic bridge) and park along Main Street. Originally built by dairy farmers, the Victorian buildings in this village have been well preserved. The most beautiful buildings are the B&Bs (see *Lodging*). You can also take a carriage ride through downtown—find the horse-drawn carriages along Main Street. Or you might want to check out the **Ferndale Museum** (3rd and Shaw Streets) if you can't get enough of this architecture.

Kinetic Sculpture Race Museum (707-786-4477) Main and Shaw Streets. The Kinetic Sculpture Race is a trip. If you can't be in the area to see this eclectic festival (see *Special Events*) you should definitely stop and check out some of the old floats and people-powered sculptures.

Pacific Lumber Company Museum In the town of Scotia, look for the locomotive; the museum is behind it. Open Monday through Friday from June through August. The company owns the town and offers this museum to learn about the 75 years of lumber industry in the area. There is also an aquarium to learn about local salmon and steelhead. Free.

Eureka

Carson Mansion 2nd and M Streets This Victorian always makes me wonder why we have lost the art of making our houses unique. Built in the late 1880s, it is now an exclusive men's club, closed to the public, but perched high enough to photograph.

Clarke Historical Museum (707-443-1947; clarkemuseum.org) 240 E Street, Eureka. Open Tuesday through Saturday 11 AM–4 PM. Here you can view artifacts from Northern California's Native American population, from baskets to ceremoni-

OLD TOWN EUREKA.

al clothing, plus an array of contemporary arts that will put the wood carvings you see along the road to shame. Free.

✐ **Discovery Museum** (707-443-9694; discovery-museum.org) 517 3rd Street, Eureka. Open Tuesday through Saturday from 10 AM–4 PM; Sunday from 12–4 PM. Kids like exploring this hands-on nonprofit museum where they can learn about art, culture, and science. Especially fun is the Co-op grocery, where kids can shop for their own produce and total it up. $3 for everyone over 3.

Fort Humboldt State Historic Park (707-445-6547) 3431 Fort Avenue, Eureka. Open from 8–5 daily. So when the fighting between the white settlers and the Indians became too intense, the military built this fort to "protect both peoples" (read: Relocate the native people to reservations). You can tour the museum and learn about the internment of up to 300 Indians. The site isn't all that, but the views are pretty good. Free.

Humboldt Bay Maritime Museum (707-444-9440; humboldtbaymaritime museum.com) 77 Cookhouse Lane, Samoa, next to the Samoa Cookhouse. Open Wednesday through Sunday 11 AM–4 PM. Here you can explore the maritime history of the north coast, checking out artifacts from ships, shipwrecks, and lighthouse memorabilia. Free.

Morris Graves Museum of Art (707-442-0278; humboldtarts.org) 636 F Street, Eureka. Open 12–5 Wednesday through Sunday. With plenty of community programs that bring art to Eureka—including films, visual art events, and parties— this newer museum works hard to attract locals and tourists. Free.

✐ **Sequoia Park and Zoo** (707-441-4263; sequoiaparkzoo.net) 3414 W Street, Eureka. Open Tuesday through Sunday from at least 10 AM–5 PM. Not many zoos can boast having a 70-acre old-growth redwood park, too. Kids will like visiting the primates, the birds, and the petting zoo. It's not much, but makes a fun outing on a cool day. Adults: $4; Children: $2; kids under 2 free.

THE LOCAL MONEYMAKER

I recently heard that there is a list of all the people who grow pot in the Mendocino and Humboldt area of Northern California; it is called the Yellow Pages. Yes, the fog is not only good for those giant coastal redwoods, but also for growing some stellar Mary Jane. However, if you have the urge (and if you spend a minute in Arcata or Golden Gate Park for that matter, you'll smell the earthy aroma everywhere), you should know that under federal law having and smoking herb is illegal. Chong (of Cheech and Chong fame) was put in jail for selling bongs; imagine what the Feds do to someone puffing on a carload of hashish? That being said, the Feds rarely patrol the area (except along US 101 between Arcata and Santa Rosa, which locals call "The Gauntlet"). And in California, under state law, it is legal to buy and smoke weed, as long as you have a doctor's note. These days, you'll find a number of dispensaries hawking high-grade pot. Unless you have a note from Dr. Ganja, don't just walk in and order green Lucky Charms. The general rule is, if you got it, don't flaunt it.

CHILLIN' IN THE ARCATA PLAZA ON A
FRIDAY AFTERNOON.

Arcata

⚓ **Natural History Museum** (707-826-4479; Humboldt.edu) 1315 G Street, Arcata. Open Tuesday through Saturday from 10 AM–5 PM. Humboldt State's science museum is a great spot to bring the kids to explore fossils and local natural history. There are plenty of interactive exhibits, live animals, and loads of information about the biodiversity of the area. $3 adults; children: $2.

Phillips House Museum (707-822-4722) 71 E. 7th Street, Arcata. Open Sunday from 2–4 or by appointment. Tour a typical farmhouse from back in the day. This living museum showcases the daily life of an Arcata resident from 1854–1932. The views from here are spectacular. Free.

Trinidad and Vicinity

Sumeg Village (707-677-3570) 4150 Patrick's Point Drive, Patrick's Point State Park, Trinidad. The reconstructed Yurok village includes traditional-style family houses, a sweathouse, changing houses, a redwood canoe, and a dance house. Sumeg is the place name of a former Yurok seasonal fishing camp, not a permanent village. There is an actual village near Trinidad, but it is not accessible to the public, so this is as close as you can get. The trail through the native plant garden leads you to the village. Fee: $6.

THE TRINIDAD LIGHTHOUSE AND BAY.

Edward Broitman

*Telonicher Marine Laboratory** (707-826-3671; Humboldt.edu) 570 Ewing Street, Trinidad. Open 9–4:30 Monday through Friday and 12–4 on weekends during the school year. If you, or your kids, are interested in sea life, head over to HSU's marine lab, where you can get your hands wet and touch some cool invertebrates. Free.

Trinidad Memorial Lighthouse At the end of Main Street. Though it doesn't actually function as a lighthouse anymore, this tower marks one of the best views of the sea on a sunny day. Inside is a 2 ton fog bell.

Willow Creek and Vicinity

*China Flat Bigfoot Museum** (530-629-2653; bigfootcountry.net) CA 299 and CA 96, Willow Creek. Open Wednesday through Sunday, 10 AM–4 PM, mid-April through late October. Though there is plenty of memorabilia of times gone by, the main attraction here is the Bigfoot collection that recently became open to the public. Free.

Hoopa Tribal Museum (530-625-4110) CA 96, north of Willow Creek. Open Monday through Saturday 8 AM–12 then 1 PM–5 PM (from 10 AM–12 then 1 PM– 4 PM on Saturday). You can take guided tours of the Hoopa historical sites as well as visit the museum, which has a nice collection of artifacts from the Hoopa Indians. There is a small fee.

Del Norte County

Battery Point Lighthouse (707-464-3089; cr.nps.gov) Take Front Street towards the ocean, Crescent City. Open Wednesday through Sunday 10 AM–4 PM. The picturesque building you see jutted out of the end of a rock is the Battery Point Lighthouse. The lore is that a ship crashed into the rock here in 1855 and the town decided they needed a lighthouse here—voila!

*Ocean World** (707-464-4900; oceanworldonline.com) US 101, Crescent City. A privately owned aquarium where you can touch sharks—don't get too excited, they aren't the killing type. You can take a 45-minute guided tour to learn about local sea and plant life, including eels, sea lions, and the famed sharks. $9.95 adults; $5.95 children 4–11; under 4 free.

✳ To Do

CYCLING The best places to mountain bike in the area are in the Arcata Community Forest, Lost Man Creek Trail in Trinidad, and the Hammond Coastal Trail in Arcata. For more

CRESCENT CITY'S BATTERY POINT LIGHTHOUSE.

information, inquire at **Adventures Edge** (707-822-4673; adventuresedge .com) 650 10th Street, Arcata. Open Monday through Saturday 9–6 and Sunday 11 AM–5 PM.

FAMILY FUN **Drive Thru Tree** Off US 101, Terwer Valley exit, Klamath. In 1976, a tunnel was made through this 725-year-old redwood so that now you can drive through it. The tree is more than 90 feet tall and the trunk is over 15 feet wide. It takes a while because everyone jumps out of the car and takes pictures. Minimal Fee.

❧ **Humboldt Crabs Baseball** (707-826-2333; humboldtcrabs.com) Arcata Ballpark, 9th and F Streets. On a summer afternoon when you see folks headed past the Arcata Plaza carrying seat cushions, it is time for peanuts and Cracker Jacks. Yes, even Humboldt County has a semi-pro baseball team. The season runs from June through August. $6 adults; $2 children.

❧ **Loleta Cheese Factory** (707-733-5470; loletacheese.com) 252 Loleta Drive, Loleta. Open 9–5 daily. Humboldt County might be known for its redwoods and pot, but the other main industry here is dairy. You can visit a working cheese factory, learn how it works, try cheeses—including 20 varieties of organic, non-GMO-fed kinds—and explore the farm. Free.

❧ **Madaket—the Humboldt Bay Harbor Cruise** (707-445-1910; Humboldtbay maritimemuseum.com) Foot of F Street, Boardwalk Old Town, Eureka. In summer, you can take an 8-mile tour of the Humboldt Bay in an original ferry. In October and May cruises go out on Saturday and Sunday. June through September cruises go on Wednesday through Saturday afternoons. $15 Adults; $7.50 children over 5.

❧ **Trees of Mystery Sky Trail** (707-482-2251 or 800-638-3389; treesofmystery.net) 15500 US 101, Klamath. Open at least 9:30–4:30 daily. Most people come for the seven-minute ride in an enclosed six-person gondola through the redwoods. Others stop at Ted's Ridge for views of the redwoods and the beach, or to photograph the gigantic statue of Paul Bunyan and the blue ox. You can hike back down through redwoods and visit the museum at the end of the trail. Sky Trail: $13.50; kids: $6.50; under 3 free.

FARMERS' MARKETS **Arcata Plaza** It is held from April through November, every Saturday from 9–2.

Eureka Old Town In summer on Tuesday, Old Town wakes up from 10 AM–1 PM.

GOLF **Del Norte Golf Course** (707-458-3214; delnortegolf.com) 130 Club Drive, Crescent City. On the Smith River, this 9-hole course is surrounded by redwoods. $17–20.

Eureka Golf Course (707-443-4808; playeureka.com) 4750 Fairway Drive, Eureka. One of the most sustainable golf courses in the country, green folks will feel good about teeing off here. $20–25; twilight: $12–15.

WATER SPORTS **Bigfoot Rafting Company** (530-629-2263; bigfootrafting .com) Willow Creek. These guys take people on half- or full-day rafting trips down the Trinity River. They also rent inflatable kayaks and take people on fishing adventures. It's a trek to get out here, but it's totally worth it. Trips cost adults $59–85 and kids $55–75.

Hum-Boats (707-443-5157; hum-boats.com) Dock A, Woodley Island Marina, Eureka. These guys do it all—from kayak lessons to rentals, Friday-evening kayak trips with wine and cheese, kayak fishing trips, whale-watching cruises, they might even shine your shoes if you asked. On your selected trip explore the Arcata Marsh, the Mad River slough, Trinidad Bay, lagoon tours, or Humboldt Bay.

Kayak Zak (707-498-1130; kayakzak.com) Orick. When you pass by the expansive Humboldt Lagoons and just have to get out there and explore, call Kayak Zak. He'll set you right up. You can get kayak instruction,

THE LOUDEST SOUND AT THE CRESCENT CITY HARBOR IS THE SEA LIONS.

guided trips, adaptive paddling, kayak rentals, and get the scoop on how to explore the waters of the Humboldt Lagoons State Park, Redwood National and State Parks, Trinidad Cove, Humboldt Bay, Big Lagoon County Park, and other waterways in Humboldt and Del Norte Counties.

The Far North
Klamath River Jet Boat (800-887-JETS; jetboattours.com) 17635 CA 110, Klamath. In summer, these jet boats motor you down the Klamath River. Tours last two hours and leave every three hours, starting at 10 AM. $38 adults; $19 children 4–11; kids under 4 free.

A REDWOOD TREE'S ROOTS.

STATE PARKS Arcata Community Forest (707-822-8184) 14th Street, Arcata. A new 11.5-mile bike path was completed in 2007, making these 790 acres of woodland recreation the spot for mountain bikers and walkers. The **Redwood Park** is adjacent to the Community Forest and offers trail access into the forest. The Park has a playground, picnic areas, and restrooms. Free.

Azalea State Reserve (707-488-2041; parks.ca.gov) Go 5 miles north of Arcata, take the McKinleyville exit off US 101. Drive 2 miles east on North Bank Road and turn left into the reserve. If you arrive here in April or May, you will be wowed by the abundance of rhododendron blossoms scenting the air.

REDWOOD STATE AND NATIONAL PARK

(707-464-6101; parks.ca.gov or nps.gov) US 101, from Orick to Crescent City. Coastal redwoods grow along the Northern California coast from Big Sur to the

Oregon border, but nowhere else will you see trees this tall, this pristine, and groves this populated. Many of these coastal redwoods have lived here for over 2000 years; they grow to over 370 feet tall (higher than a 30-story building!); their bark resists fire and disease; and better yet, the tallest recorded tree in the world—the Hyperion—lives in this massive Redwood Park. But to call the parks merely redwood parks leaves out the joy of smelling the mossy wetness, touching the soft

HE'S 6 FEET TALL AND STILL DWARFED BY COASTAL REDWOODS.

bark of the trees, hearing the birds, the wind, waterfalls, and streams, and walking through canyons of ferns while the sun casts rays of light through the branches so high above.

This portion of the redwood parks in the area is actually broken into sections—Orick, Prairie Creek, Klamath, Del Norte, and Jedediah Smith (the last three being in Del Norte County). Within the park, you'll find more than you can even begin to imagine—black sand beaches, redwood-studded cliffs, lagoons, rivers, bears, elk, and even places where there are no people. To really get a

Freshwater County Park (707-445-7651) Freshwater Road, 7 miles east of Eureka. Open sunrise to sunset. In summer, the county dams up the creek and makes a little swimming area for people to hang out in, have a BBQ, and find some sunshine. Day use $5 per car.

Grizzly Creek Redwoods (707-445-7651; co.humboldt.ca.us) Off CA 36, 17 miles off US 101. This small redwood park is a quiet place to fish, swim in the Van Duzen River, and hike in these magnificent trees. There are 30 campsites here.

Headwaters Forest Reserve (707-825-2300) 1695 Heindon Road, Arcata. The old-growth redwood provides habitat for the threatened marbled murrelet, and the stream systems provide habitat for threatened coho salmon. The Bureau of Land

feel for the area, I recommend camping (see *Campgrounds*), since the only other place to stay is at a hostel (see *Lodging*). Day use fee: $6.

Orick Area The southernmost part of the park system. Start with a stop to the **Kuchel Visitor Center** off US 101. Here you can get a free permit to visit the **Tall Trees Grove**. Only a limited number are offered each day on a first-come, first-served basis, so get here early because this is a treat—to see where the tallest trees in the world grow. Another highlight is the **Lady Bird Johnson Grove**, a 1-mile hike through a dense redwood forest.

Prairie Creek Area Off Newton B. Drury Parkway, visit the visitor center to get trail maps. There are 70 miles of hiking trails in this state park. Not to be missed are **Elk Meadow** (where you can glimpse the Roosevelt elk populating the area—but don't get too close, they can charge), **Big Tree Wayside, Fern Canyon** (a short accessible hike through a dense fern jungle), **Lost Man Creek** (an 11-mile mountain biker favorite, or a beautiful, but rough, drive), **Gold Bluffs Beach**, and the **Coastal Drive**.

Klamath Area The redwood trees spill into the river, lagoons, and the sea. It seems every direction you look is just as dazzling as the last. Check out the **False Klamath Cove** (a protected beach at the mouth of Wilson Creek with excellent tide pools), the **Coastal Trail**, and **Lagoon Creek** (take the Yurok Loop Trail for excellent bird-watching and sublime ocean views).

Del Norte Coast Redwood State Park Headquarters for all of the redwood parks in the area are located in Crescent City at 1111 2nd Street (open year-round). These 8 miles of rugged coastline are hugged by zillions of old-growth mossy redwoods. You can reach the coast on the **Damnation Trail** or the **Footsteps Rock Trail**. Bird-watchers head to Ossagon Creek.

Jedediah Smith State Park Before getting started, head to the **Hiouchi Information Center** (open in summer only), off US 199. This nearly unused state park has some of the tallest trees in the world. To start, you might want to drive the rough Howland Hill Road. It'll take you to **Stout Grove,** the spot with the tallest trees in this northernmost area of the redwood park. The hike is short, but worth it.

Management is out to help this threatened ecological system. You can access from the north along the Elk River County Road, approximately 6 miles southeast of Eureka. The hike from here is 11 miles round-trip and takes you deep into the forest. From the south, you can enter from mid-May through mid-November for a guided hike on weekends. The trail is approximately 4 miles round-trip and runs parallel to the old-growth forest along Salmon Creek.

Humboldt Bay National Wildlife Refuge (fws.gov) Exit 696 off US 101. The Richard J. Guadagno Headquarters and Visitor Center is located at the Salmon Creek Unit. Open daily from 8–5. The Visitor Center has dioramas and telescopes. There are guided walks of the dunes, plenty of wildlife viewing, bay and marsh trails, bird-watching, and spots to view Castle Rock State Park, an island off the coast of the marsh. Friends of the Dunes (friendsofthedunes.org) host free nature walks, contact them directly for the schedule.

Humboldt Lagoon County Park (707-445-7651; co.humboldt.ca.us) Go 7 miles north of Trinidad; take US 101 to Big Lagoon Park Road. Just north of Patrick's Point, you'll find another gem of Humboldt County. This is an adventurer's dream—paddling on smooth waters, finding semi-precious gems like jade and moonstone, hiking the coastal trail, and then camping along the water. There are three lagoons: Big Lagoon, Dry Lagoon, and Stone Lagoon. Camping is first-come, first-served. For kayaking information see *To Do*. Adjacent to this park is the **Harry A. Merlo State Recreation Area**, a popular fishing spot. $2.

Patrick's Point State Park See *Beaches*.

The Far North
Lake Earl Wildlife Area (707-464-2523) Just 5 miles north of Crescent City. A huge space where you'll be awed by nature (as if you don't have enough reason, up here in the redwoods), the wildlife area here stretches for over 5000 acres. Bird-watchers will lose it over the amount of birds around the lake—including Aleutian geese. There is plenty of hiking in the uplands.

Smith River National Recreation Area (707-457-3131) East of Crescent City off US 199. The cleanest river in the world, yet one of the most unexplored areas of Northern California, this is truly the place to escape civilization. For 600 years the Tolowa Indians had this area to themselves, until Jedediah Smith arrived; he claimed to have discovered the redwoods, and sent word back east for folks to come out and see for themselves these marvelous giant trees. Now, this recreation area is a part of the **Six Rivers National Forest**. You can white-water raft, fish for steelhead and salmon, marvel at the blooming rhododendrons, swim, hike for miles (my favorite hikes are Darlingtonia, Stony Creek, and Myrtle Creek. You'll want to pop by the Visitor Center in Gasquet (pronounced "Gas-*key*") for specific trail information. You can camp in the park at Grassy Flat, Big Flat, Panther Flat, and Patrick Creek.

BEACHES **Centerville Beach** (707-445-7651) Just 5 miles west of Ferndale. I like to come here to watch whales pass by in late spring. Others like to come for bird-watching or to marvel at the sandstone cliffs.

Clam Beach County Park (707-445-7651) US 101 North of McKinleyville. At this popular beach park, you can also camp on the sand. There are only 12 tent sites and they are on a first-come first-serve basis.

Gold Bluffs Beach See *Redwood State and National Park*.

Mad River County Park (707-445-7651) Exit west onto the Giuntoli Lane interchange off US 101 north of Arcata; head north onto Heindon Road. Turn left (west) onto Miller Road., right onto Mad River Road. This is one of Humboldt County's best beaches for hanging out on the dunes, or kayaking in the river just across the parking lot. Bird-watchers, be on the lookout for barn owls, American redstarts, and warblers.

Moonstone Beach (707-445-7651) South of Trinidad, take the Westhaven exit and turn onto Moonstone Beach Road. This is the spot for surfing and walking along the headlands.

🏊 ♿ ⌒ **Patrick's Point State Park** (707-677-3570; reserveamerica.com) 4150 Patrick's Point Drive, Trinidad. There is so much to do at this redwood beach park, you'll have to schedule another vacation to do it. Hiking, camping, biking, exploring a re-creation of an Indian village, picnicking, beachcombing, walking through a native plant garden—I said there was a ton to do here. Plus, the dense spruce, fir, and hemlock stand guard over the dramatic coastline and make for a breathtaking view. Also, you might want to check out **Wedding Rock,** where for over a hundred years locals have been getting married. Agate Beach is a popular spot to play in the water. There are 124 RV or tent sites in the Abalone and Agate Beach campsites. Family fee: $20.

Samoa Dunes Recreation Area (707-825-2300) Samoa. Though the beaches are dirty and the water is freezing, this is one of the closest spots to Eureka to get to the waves.

Trinidad State Beach (707-445-7651) Off Main Street, Trinidad. You can walk a beautiful coastal trail to get to this beach. On both sides of the sand, there is water, which makes this beach unique. On one side is the windy swimming area and on the other is a boat launch with a pier. To the north is College Cove, a sheltered spot that makes this a perfect spot to laze in the sun (when it appears out here).

The Far North

For information about surf spots and board rentals, contact Rhyn Noll Surf and Skate Shop at (707-465-4400; 275 L Street).

Crescent City State Beach Go 2 miles south of Crescent City on Enderts Beach Road. A sandy beach with great surf makes this a popular choice in town.

Enderts Beach Off Enderts Beach Road, Crescent City. This long expanse of sand, usually shrouded in fog, is a great place to walk while gazing up at the redwoods.

Tolowa Dunes State Park (707-464-6101; parks.ca.gov) Just 2 miles north of Crescent City off US 101; take Northcrest Drive to Lake Earl Drive. Follow the signs. Wetlands and walking go hand in hand here in this huge park. Stroll through redwoods, wildflowers, and sand dunes, or explore the wealth of bird life at Earl Lake. You can also camp here, but first you have to register at Jedediah Smith Redwood State Park.

ON A SUNNY DAY, NOTHING BEATS THE VIEWS AT TRINIDAD STATE BEACH.
Edward Broitman

Ferndale

℡ Gingerbread Mansion (707-786-4000 or 800-952-4136; gingerbread-mansion.com) 400 Berding Street. This turreted and gabled Victorian in Ferndale village offers 11 rooms with garden views, old fashioned tubs, gourmet breakfast, and fireplaces (with fireside bubble baths). $$–$$$$; no children under 12.

℡ Victorian Inn (707-786-4949 or 888-589-1808; a-victorian-inn.com) 400 Ocean Avenue, Ferndale. These rooms allow you to dip into another era, of Jane Austen novels and romantic poets. Dream away in comfy beds, surrounded by plush linens and floral wallpaper. Amenities: 16 rooms and suites, breakfast, Curley's Restaurant. $$–$$$.

Eureka

If you are looking for cheaper options, there are motels along Broadway Street.

✐ ♿ 🐾 ℡ Carter House Inn (707-444-8062; carterhouse.com) 301 L Street. One of the finest inns in the area, this 1880s mansion is comprised of four restored Victorian buildings. Imagine four-poster beds, wooden antiques, lacy bedding, and modern amenities like flat-screen TVs and DVD players. There are rooms dubbed "Really Nice Rooms," and that is true. Amenities: breakfast, Restaurant 301 (see *Dining Out)*, spa tubs, fireplaces, room service, wine and cheese social. $$–$$$$.

✐ ℡ The Ships Inn (707-443-7583 or 877-443-7583; shipsinn.net) 821 D Street, Eureka. Lovely renovated rooms in an old Victorian stand out from the crowd with their individual flavor and thoughtful details. The Mission Room, a tribute to Frank Lloyd Wright, relies on soft colors to show off the oversized king bed and wooden antique furnishings. Rates: $$. Facilities and amenities: three rooms and a cottage, fireplace.

Arcata

✐ ♿ ℡ Hotel Arcata (800-344-1221; hotelarcata.com) 708 9th Street, Arcata. Located on the town square of historic Arcata. The 32 small rooms offer turn of the century décor, including claw-foot tubs and period antiques. Plus, the best Japanese restaurant in town is located in the building. This isn't the finest accommodation around, but the hotel is well priced and in a good location and offers continental breakfast. $–$$.

✐ ℡ Worthington House Inn (707-668-1889 worthingtonhouseinn. 521 First Avenue, Blue Lake. Head to this Italianate Victorian, built in 1887, and later restored into a five-room garden inn, for a relaxing vacation away from the crowds. The breakfast includes dishes such as French toast and egg soufflés. $$.

Vacation Rentals

Arcata Stay (877-822- 0935; arcata stay.com) Arcata. Offers six different accommodations on the Plaza, or in nearby quiet residential neighborhoods.

Trinidad

✐ ♿ ⊙ Lost Whale Inn (707-677-3425 or 800-677-7859; lostwhaleinn .com) 3452 Patrick's Point Drive. If there were a competition for the perfect mix of mountain, trees, and ocean, Trinidad might win. This four-room inn combines all the aspects that make Trinidad exceptional under one roof— sea colors, earthy accents like plants and wood floors, big windows, throw blankets, plus breakfast, wine social, spa services, and some rooms have wood stoves. $$–$$$$.

℡ Trinidad Bay B&B (707-677-0840; trinidadbaybnb.com) 560 Edwards Street. One of the loveliest properties on the coast, this four-room B&B specializes in ocean views, and handsomely decorated rooms that could have popped out of the pages of *Sunset* magazine. Washed in red, blue, and green accents, you'll get local art, a zillion thread-count sheets, breakfast, and luxury service. $$$.

Willow Creek

♂ ❤ "❦" **Coho Cottages** (530-629-2263 or 800-722-2223; cohocottages .com) On the Trinity River, in the middle of the largest Douglas fir forest in the world, this is the perfect nesting place for nature lovers who want cosmopolitan amenities like down comforters, bathrobes, private outdoor areas with gas BBQs, concierge service, and kitchens (some). Themed rooms like the Tao House (Japanese-themed with bowl sinks and cobblestone flooring) and the Spa Retreat (with a soaking tub) allow you to indulge. The family of owners has been in the area for over 100 years and can give great advice on where to hike, fish, or swim. $$.

Klamath

♂ ❤ **HI Redwood Hostel** (707-482-8265 hihostels.com) 14480 US 101 at Wilson Creek Road, Klamath. The only beds to sleep on in Redwood National Park, this perfectly placed hostel can accommodate up to 30 guests in dorm beds or private rooms. Guests whale watch from the decks, explore the ocean across the street, and hike the redwoods. There is a large kitchen to share. $.

The Far North

In Crescent City along US 101, you'll find a number of motor lodges, some even with beach views. Below I have listed places you might not find on your own. They are a bit of a trek up the hill from Crescent City.

♂ ❤ ▼ **Patrick Creek Lodge** (707-457-3323; patrickcreeklodge.net) 13950 US 199, Gasquet. Located by the Smith River, which is the cleanest river in the U.S., this lodge takes you

back in time to when a log cabin meant big huge logs stacked on top of each other. You could call the rooms rustic, or drab, but you stay here for the history and location, not the thread count of the sheets. Amenities: 17 rooms and cabins, swimming pool, no TV, restaurant, and bar. $$.

♂ **Smith River Retreat** (707-457-3477; smithriverretreat.com) US 199, Gasquet. If you ever dreamt of moving to the country, growing your own garden, and living off the grid, this is the place to try it. Kris and Mike have built an empire, complete with their own swing bridge to cross the river to access their property (people afraid of heights take note), a private beach, two swimming holes, and the cutest cottages around. As long as you bring your own food to cook, you'll be happy here. $–$$.

CAMPGROUNDS To reserve a site contact reserveamerica.com. Make reservations early as most of these sites fill quickly. Below I have listed campgrounds in Redwood State and National Park, for others, see *Green Spaces*.

Redwood State and National Park

❤ **Elk Prairie Campground** Prairie Creek Redwood State Park. Open all year. If you are a fan of elk, this is the spot for you. There are 75 tent and RV sites with full services. $20.

Gold Bluff Beach Prairie Creek Redwood State Park. Open all year. High in demand, you can camp right on the sand. It's a short walk to Fern Canyon, and the campground is surrounded by redwood and fern-covered bluffs. All services. 29 sites. $20.

Mill Creek Campground Del Norte Coast Redwood Park. Open from May 1 through September 30. There are 145 tent and RV sites here under the redwoods. All services. $20.

Jedediah Smith Campground Jedediah Smith Redwood State Park. Open all year. Tucked beneath redwoods, this site has all services and 106 tent and RV sites. $20.

✳ Where to Eat

DINING OUT

Eureka

&. ♉ **Avalon** (707-445-0500; avalon eureka.com) 3rd and G Street, Eureka. Open for dinner Tuesday through Saturday. With an award-winning wine list and some of the best organic steak and seafood around, this classic Eureka spot brings the elite of the area to dine on farm-fresh food. It's fun to order their signature salmon, which arrives to your table on fire. There is also live music and plenty of local art featured here. Reservations recommended. $$–$$$$.

♦ &. ♉ **Hurricane Kate's** (707-444-1405; hurricanekates.com) 511 2nd Street. Open 11:30 AM–2:30 PM, and 5 PM–9:30 PM. Closed Sunday and Monday. It's tough to find a good family-friendly restaurant that doesn't rely on grease to appease the kids. Hurricane Kate's serves a world-fusion menu that does just that, including oysters and wood-fired pizza. $$-$$$

&. **Restaurant 301** (707-444-8062; carterhouse.com/restaurant-301) 301 L Street. Award winning, this garden-to-table restaurant farms their own vegetables and is a strong supporter of the slow food movement. You can get a la carte and prix fixe menus, but the highlight is the nine-course chef's tasting menu. To give you an idea of the food, imagine a bell pepper *piemontese* on grilled *ciabatta*, Humboldt albacore tuna, or a twice-baked cheese soufflé. Make sure to try out their house wine, Envy, made in Calistoga. Reservations highly recommended. A la carte menu $$–$$$. Prix fixe or tasting menu: $$$$.

Arcata

♦ &. ♉ **Abruzzi's** (707-826-2345; abruzziarcata.com) 780 7th Street. Open 5:30 PM–9 PM daily. Walking into this classic Italian dining room, you'll probably be swept back into time. Wood-covered, dark, and almost romantic, you can't go wrong with a visit to Abruzzi's. A popular dish is the spaghetti carbonara, with pancetta and a creamy Alfredo sauce. $$–$$$.

&. **Folie Douce** (707-822-1042; holy folie.com). 1551 G Street. Open Tuesday through Saturday at 5:30. When you walk in, you smell the wood-burning stove doing its magic, and know your meal will be good. Part modern, part rustic, Folie Douce might be the best affordable restaurant in the area. Serving local organic and seasonal foods, the menu changes weekly, but expect lovely pizzas and pastas, meat and seafood. $$–$$$$.

&. ♉ **Jambalaya** (707-822-4766; jam balaya-restaurant.com) 915 H Street. Open Tuesday through Sunday from 5:30–9 PM (until 9:30 on Friday and Saturday). Bistro seating, complete with dark wood and live music, highlights the Arcata take on the fusion of Cajun, Creole, and American cuisine. If a little spice freaks you out, try the Humboldt grass-fed beef burgers. I go for the salmon that changes preparation nightly. $$–$$$.

Trinidad

♦ &. **Larrupin Café** (707-677-0230; larrupincafe.com) 1658 Patrick Point's Drive, Trinidad. Open 5–9 Thursday through Sunday. Famous for their beef brisket and pork ribs, both served with the Larrupin barbeque sauce (bottled and sold on the premises), folks come from around Humboldt Bay for finger-licking cooking. Cash only. $$$–$$$$.

&. ♉ **Moonstone Grill** (707-677-1616; moonstonegrill.com) 100 Moonstone Beach Road, Trinidad. Open Wednesday through Sunday, 5–8:30. Perched above the bay in Trinidad, this local favorite serves a decent rack of lamb. There are a couple vegetarian options, but it isn't their strong suit. The lobster and the locally smoked tuna wontons are popular as well. Reservations recommended. $$–$$$$.

EATING OUT

Ferndale and Fortuna

✍ & ⅄ **Curley's Grill** (707-786-9696) 400 Ocean Avenue, Ferndale. Open Monday through Saturday 11:30 AM–9 PM, and Sunday 9–9. On the ground floor of the historic Victorian Inn, this is a popular choice with locals and tourists. They are best known for their daily specials, often featuring fresh fish. Reservations recommended. $–$$$.

& ⅄ **Eel River Brewing Co** (707-725-2739; eelriverbrewing.com) 1777 Alamar Way, Fortuna. Open daily for lunch and dinner. They claim to be the first organic brewery in the U.S. Plus they have the largest beer garden on the North Coast. Come for fish and chips and India Pale Ale, and you'll be smiling all day. $–$$.

Poppa Joe's (707-786-4180) 409 Main Street, Ferndale. Open daily from 6 AM–2 PM (until 12 PM on weekends). This is where to find hearty breakfasts. Since 1880, this building has been a gathering spot for locals; today you can still get coffee for a buck and traditional American-style breakfasts of eggs, bacon, and toast. Cash only. $.

Eureka

✍ & ⅄ **Café Waterfront** (707-443-9190) 102 F Street, Eureka. Open for breakfast, lunch, and dinner daily. A friend recommended this bay-view restaurant that specializes in seafood, steak, and pasta. Part roadhouse, part tourist trap, if you are looking for a burger and a view, this is the place to go. Sometimes there is live music here. $–$$$.

✍ & "⅄" **Lost Coast Brewery** (707-445-4480; lostcoast.com) 617 Fourth Street, Eureka. Food served 11 AM–midnight, bar open until 1 AM. This is a favorite watering hole/lunch spot and dinner pub. The food is hearty and good, but the highlight is the beer. Their signature Downtown Brown ale has won numerous awards. $–$$.

✍ & **Mazzotti's** (707-445-1912) 305 F Street, Eureka. Open daily from 11:30 AM–9 PM (until 10 on Friday through Sunday). Everyone raves about this fun Italian restaurant. Accessible and kid-friendly, eat ravioli and eggplant parmigiana for reasonable prices. $$–$$$.

North Coast Co-op (707-822-5947 or 707-443-6027; northcoastco-op.com) 811 I Street, Arcata. 1036 5th Street, Eureka. Open from 6 AM–9 PM daily. You can find just about anything you need at this giant co-op. The bakery, deli, espresso bar, vegan and vegetarian food, meat and seafood selection, and bulk items are the best around. If you are headed north to camp, a stop here is recommended.

Obento (707-268-1298) 317 F Street, Eureka. Open 11 AM–5:30 PM daily (until 7 PM Friday and Saturday). Quite the little surprise, to stumble into this Japanese snack and sushi stop. Rolls with local names such as the Trinidad (lox and cream cheese) and the Humboldt County (smoked tofu, cream cheese, and avocado) mix with more traditional *unagi*, rice bowls, and salads. $.

"⅄" & **Old Town Coffee** (707-445-8600; oldtowncoffeeeureka.com) 211 F Street, Eureka. Open daily from at least 7 AM–9 PM. Located in a historic brick building, this coffee shop is where locals gather to catch up on events, read the paper, drink fine coffee, and hear live music on weekends. They also offer tea, fudge, and chocolates.

✐ & ♈ **Ritz** (707-443-7489; cincin-ritz
.com) 240 F Street, Eureka. Open
daily from 11:30–2 (sushi only) and
dinner from 5:30–9. A walk past this
old building will probably have you
thinking this is more a dive bar than a
popular sushi and teppanyaki spot.
Sushi is fresh—sit at the bar for the
best options. But the highlight is their
teppanyaki. The cook prepares fish and
meat at your table. Reservations rec-
ommended for teppan tables. $$–$$$$.

Samoa

✐ & **Samoa Cookhouse** (707-442-
1659; samoacookhouse.net) Across the
Samoa Bridge, off Cookhouse Road,
Samoa. Open 7 AM–10 PM daily. The
last surviving cookhouse in the West
serves an abundance of good food, in
the style of a lumber camp: red-and-
white checkerboard tablecloths, mis-
matched chairs, a big plate of fish or
meat, salad, veggies, potatoes, bread,
and dessert. People line up for insane-
ly huge portions of American fare, with
views of Eureka. You don't get much
choice, but you do get an experience.
$–$$.

Arcata

✐ & ♈ **Café Brio** (707-822-5922) 791
G Street, Arcata. Open for breakfast,
lunch, and dinner daily. If I lived in
Arcata, this would be my hangout—I
would be a big fat pastry-loving, cof-
fee-drinking mess; you'd have to drag
me away from the Blue Bottle Coffee,
the organic pastries, and the farm-
fresh sandwiches and salads. Sit inside,
bathed by the sunshine of the big windows, or outside with views of the
square. The wine bar fills early. $.

✐ & **Crosswinds** (707-826-2133;
arcatacrosswinds.com) 860 10th Street,
Arcata. Open Wednesday through Sunday, 7:30 AM–2 PM. Head to this old
Victorian for their weekend brunch of
buckwheat crepes, vegetarian biscuits
and gravy, and loads of egg dishes,

which are accompanied by complimentary muffins and champagne. $–$$.

✐ & **Los Bagels** (707-822-3150; los
bagels.com) 1061 I Street, Arcata.
Open Monday, Wednesday through
Friday from 6:30 AM–5 PM, Saturday
7–5, Sunday 7–3. This place is
packed—all the time. Locals come for
bagels with Mexican toppings; visitors
tend to stick to traditional lox and
cream cheese. There is another location in Old Town Eureka, but I like
this one better. $.

Mazzotti's See *Eureka Eating Out.*

✐ & **Muddy Waters Coffee Co** (707-
826-2233; ilovemud.com) 1603 G
Street, Arcata. Open daily from 6 AM–
12 AM. Live music, a patio crammed
with Arcata hippies, and good coffee
makes this north town coffeehouse a
fun place to meet the community.

North Coast Co-op See *Eureka Eating Out.*

✐ & **Renata's Creperie** (707-825-
TRUE) 1030 G Street, Arcata. Open
Tuesday through Sunday 8–3, and Friday and Saturday 5–9. I waited for an
hour last time I was here—on a Friday
afternoon. I was prepared to like my
crepe, but not to *love* it. Sweet and
savory crepes, like spinach and
almond, or the super-sweet Righteous
Babe with raspberries, strawberries,
and Nutella, rule the menu. The décor
reminds you why Arcata has its reputation for attracting artists and hippies—
with large portraits of Ani DiFranco
and Michael Franti, a gold and maroon
paint job, and enough dreadlocks to
make hair stylists shiver. $–$$.

& ♈ ✐ **Tomo Japanese** (707-822-
1414) 708 9th Street, Arcata. Open
Monday through Saturday from
11:30–2 and 5–9:30 (on Sunday from
5–9). Sometimes it is hard to find good
Japanese food outside a major city.
Aside from the fact that last time I was

here, my tuna roll was canned tuna, this very popular spot works for the Arcata sushi lovers. Go for traditional rolls because some creations are a bit too ambitious. Reservations recommended. $–$$.

✂ ♿ **Wildflower Café and Bakery** (707-822-0360) 1604 G Street, Arcata. Open daily for breakfast, lunch, and dinner. Everyone loves the vegetarian cuisine at this funky eatery. The vegan mac and cheese, spelt biscuits and almond gravy, and almost any breakfast dish, rock. You can get smoothies, organic espresso drinks, and vegan pastries too. $–$$

Trinidad
Katy's Smokehouse (707-677-0151; katyssmokehouse.com) 740 Edwards Street, Trinidad. Though not an actual restaurant, you should head to this little shack for smoked fish, including excellent smoked salmon.

✂ ♿ **Seascape Restaurant** (707-677-3762) 1 Bay Street, Trinidad. Open Monday through Sunday 7 AM–9:30 PM. This place gets mixed reviews. But there isn't any other place around that you can have these views (when it isn't too foggy) and eat clam chowder, fish and chips, and blackberry pie. I prefer breakfast here. Most dishes: $$–$$$.

Crescent City
✂ ♿ **Good Harvest Café** (707-465-6028) 700 Northcrest Drive, Crescent City. Open daily from 7:30 AM–2 PM. This charming café, decorated in rustic willow, offers decent breakfast options for the health conscious. $.

Harvest Natural Foods (707-464-1926) 265 L Street, Crescent City. Open 10 AM–6 PM daily. If you have your own kitchen (and around here you should), a stop to this small natural food market is about the best you can do. There is no meat here, but you can find pasta, sauce, some fresh produce, and dairy.

✂ ♿ ♉ **Patrick Creek Lodge** (707-457-3323; patrickcreeklodge.net) 13950 US 199, Gasquet. Open daily for breakfast, lunch, and dinner. I really want to love this restaurant. Don't get me wrong, it isn't bad—my server was sweet, the décor (in a solarium overlooking the forest) is ideal. I'll say this, the baked potato is good, the drinks are cheap, and if you like prime rib, they serve hunks of it on Friday and Saturday. Sunday brunch is another option. $$–$$$.

✂ ♿ **Thai House** (707-464-2427) 105 N Street, Crescent City. Open daily from at least 11 AM–9 PM. Though not the best Thai/Vietnamese cooking in California, it will satisfy the craving for something, anything, other than fish and chips. The yellow curry is a safe bet. $

✳ Entertainment
The best spot to find local entertainment information is in the free weekly *Times Standard*.

Ferndale
Ferndale Repertory Theater (707-786-5483; Ferndale-red.org) 477 Main Street, Ferndale. Community theater in a Victorian village, how Hollywood.

Eureka
Arkley Center for the Performing Arts (707-447-1956; arkleycenter.com) 412 G Street, Eureka. When big names come to town, which isn't too often, they tend to show their faces in this lovely theater.

♉ **Art of Wine** (707-268-0626; humboldtartofwine.com) 208 2nd Street, Old Town Eureka. Serving almost all local varietals (or those within a reasonable drive), locals come and are schooled about wine.

North Coast Repertory Theater (707-442-6278; ncrt.net) 300 5th Street, Eureka. If you are interested in seeing local productions of classic plays, contact these guys to see what they currently are performing.

Redwood Curtain (707-443-7688; redwoodcurtain.com) Call for directions. Care for cutting-edge theater? This is the stop for edgy productions.

Arcata

🦪 ⚇ 🍷 **Humboldt Brews** (707-826-2739; humboldtbrews.com) 856 10th Street, Arcata. Open daily at least 11:30 AM–9 PM. This is the spot for live music, good beer, and pub food ($–$$).

🍷 **Jambalaya** See Arcata *Dining Out.*

🍷 **Libation Wine Bar** (707-825-7596; libation.com) 761 8th Street, Arcata. Open Friday and Saturday 3–9. Each weekend you'll find three flights of wine, or you can taste individual wines. They also serve cheese.

The Far North

🍷 **Patrick Creek Lodge** See *Eating Out.*

✳ Selective Shopping

Aside from wood carvings, that you will notice start repeating themselves as you drive along US 101, the only shopping in the area is located in Eureka Old Town and Arcata Plaza. In Eureka expect art galleries, antique shops, and some great bookstores (**Everything for the Traveler, Consider the Alternative,** and the **Booklegger**).

In Arcata, besides **Adventure's Edge,** there are a number of clothing boutiques and galleries around the square, and a number of great booksellers along H Street, (including **Rookery Books** and **Northtown Books**).

✳ Special Events

First Saturday of each month: **Arts Alive!** (707-442-9054) Between 6–9, everyone comes out to celebrate the artistic vision of local musicians, fire dancers, sculptors, and visual artists. Free.

Second Friday of each month: **Arts! Arcata** (707-822-4500) Locals and tourists gather to celebrate the art and artists of Arcata for this free event downtown.

May: **Kinetic Sculpture Race** (kinetic universe.com) Possible the biggest thing to hit Humboldt County since kush arrived from Pakistan, this man-powered sculpture race sends folks between Arcata and Ferndale for a crazy ride. Part art, part insanity, if you are anywhere near the area when it's on, you have to see it to believe it.

Summer: **Eureka Summer Concerts** (707-442-9054) From mid-June through August, on Thursday evenings from 6 to 8 in Old Town Eureka, it seems the whole town rocks with live music. Free.

August: **Blues by the Bay** (707-445-3378) Halvorsen Park, Eureka. This two-day blues festival draws big names and a fun crowd.

Del Norte County Fair The first weekend in August, Crescent City heads to the fairground to ride Tilt-a-Whirls and spinning teacups.

Bigfoot Days Celebration (800-628-5156) Willow Creek. So this is the largest celebration of the big guy and everyone wonders every year if he'll show up, too. Guess you have to go to see for yourself.

September: **North County Fair** (707-822-5320) Arcata Plaza. This two-day annual festival features live music, yummy food, and a parade.

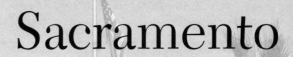

Sacramento

SACRAMENTO AND VICINITY

SAN JOAQUIN VALLEY AND THE
DELTA

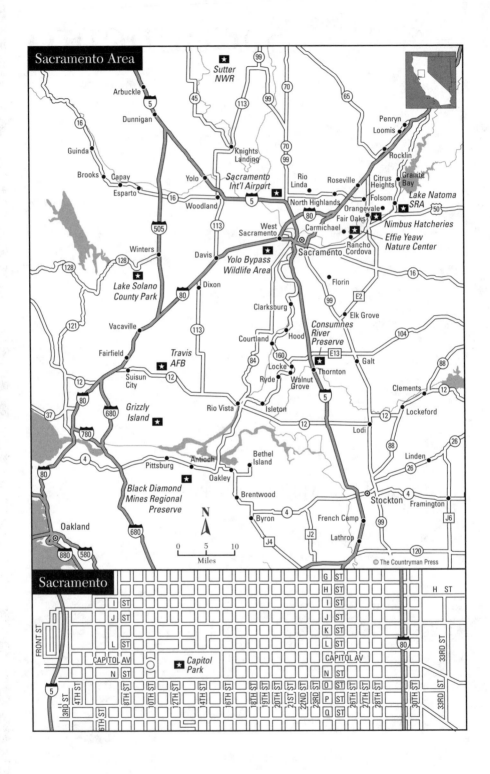

SACRAMENTO AND VICINITY

Sacramento has always been seen (by its sister California cities) as a suburban farmland, complete with cowbells, farmers, big trucks, and miniskirts. Since the beginning of its journey into city-hood (and capitaldom), the majority of folks who flocked here were of a different mind-set than those who arrived in San Francisco and Los Angeles. They farmed, mined, and built railroads—the phrase *salt of the earth* was made for them. Today the state capital is experiencing an identity shift. Sure, there are still Ford F-150s, generic miniskirts, and bovine varietals, but the arrival of hip young folks, looking to cash in on the cheap real estate has created an urban (gasp!) downtown. Past the tourist haven of Old Sacramento, the Midtown neighborhood (or the Grid as locals call it) boasts tree-lined streets, alfresco dining, museums, and great parks. Farther out in East Sacramento you'll find gourmet restaurants, mansions fit for kings in the Fabulous Forties neighborhood, and some great swimming spots in the American River.

However, once you leave the city, agriculture (and Tundras and cows) rules the sprawling suburbs and rural areas. Around the towns of **Folsom, Woodland, Stockton,** and **Modesto,** you'll find a mixture of the kindest small-town country folks and that particular brand of backwardness that accompanies pastoral living. On the other hand, **Davis**, a compact university town, prides itself on being the most bike-friendly town in the country, while **Lodi**, a historic town, has made a name for itself in the wine world.

Connecting Sacramento and Stockton with the Bay Area, you'll find the **Delta**. During the gold rush, this waterway became the main source of steamboat travel. However, automobiles and railroads became cheaper transportation options and so steamboat travel concluded its short life. Today, the Delta is a highly used recreation area for boat lovers, hikers, and bird-watchers.

GUIDANCE **Sacramento Convention and Visitor Bureau** (916-808-7777) 1608 I Street, Sacramento. Open 9–5 Monday through Friday.

Sacramento Visitor Center (916-442-7644; discovergold.org) 1002 2nd Street, Sacramento. Open 10 AM–5 PM daily.

Yolo County Visitor Bureau (530-297-1900; yolocvb.org) 105 E Street, Suite 300, Davis.

Lodi Convention and Visitor Bureau (209-365-1195; visitlodi.com) 115 S. School Street, Lodi.

SACRAMENTO

Downtownsac.org
sacbee.com
sacdine.com
oldsacramento.com
midtowngrid.com
visitstockton.org
californiadelta.org
visitmodesto.com

GETTING THERE *By air:* **Sacramento International Airport** (916-929-5411; sacairports.org) 6900 Airport Boulevard, Sacramento. There are a number of car rental agencies at the airport, including **Avis** (avis.com) and **Enterprise** (enterprise.com).

Stockton Metropolitan Airport welcomes flights on Allegiant Air (allegiantair .com) from Las Vegas and Mesa, Arizona.

By bus: **Greyhound** (greyhound.com) 715 L Street, Sacramento. You can also access Stockton, Modesto, Lodi, and Davis by bus.

By car: I-80 and US 50 cut through Sacramento going east/west. I-5 and CA 99 go north/south. Along I-5 you have access to the valley, including Modesto, Stockton, Lodi, and Woodland. I-80 gets you to Davis and the Delta, as well as Folsom Lake.

By train: **Amtrak** (Amtrak.com) 401 I Street, Sacramento. In Davis, the station is located at 840 2nd Street In Stockton the station is at 735 S. San Joaquin Street.

Altamont Commuter Express (acerail.com) connects the valley with the East and South Bay Areas.

GETTING AROUND *By bus:* **Regional Transit Buses, Light Rail,** and **Trolley** (916-321-BUSS; SacRT.com) Every time I come to Sacramento, I want to use public transportation; unfortunately the buses never deliver me where I want to go. If you choose to travel by public transport, buy a daily pass or a single fare ticket (valid for two hours).

To travel around the Valley by bus, contact **San Joaquin RTD** (sanjoaquinrtd.com).

By car: Sacramento is an easy city to navigate. Most sites of interest to tourists are located on the grid (downtown Sac). Number streets run north/south and letter streets run east/west. Parking in downtown Sacramento can be tricky. Bring a bunch of quarters or find some pay lots in the mall or under the freeway. The suburbs of Sacramento sprawl in all directions for miles. And chances are, besides going to East Sacramento to play in the American River or eat (or if you are going to a basketball game or the airport), you won't need to visit here.

The smaller cities in the area are mainly accessible by car. You find either sprawling strip-mall towns (Manteca and Tracy) or suburbs that have compact downtowns (Lodi and Davis).

By foot: I have walked the entire downtown Sacramento in a day, but if you would like some guidance contact **Hysterical Walks and Rides** (916-441-2527; hystericalwalks.com): They offer guided comedy walks through downtown. Or check out **Sacramento Podcast Tours** (916-808-777; discovergold.org.podcast) to learn about the discovery of gold, the Pony Express, the transcontinental railroad, and how Sacramento became the capital.

For the remainder of the towns in the area, you probably won't be able to explore on foot, with the exceptions being Davis, Stockton, and Lodi's historic downtown areas.

By velocab: **Velocabs** (916-498-9980; ridevelocab.com) These environmentally friendly open-air pedicabs take you around downtown to major sites.

WEATHER The Valley and Delta get *hot* in summer. Winters are the exact opposite. Though you won't get snow, you should expect temperatures to drop into the 30s.

MEDICAL EMERGENCIES **Sutter Medical Center** (916-454-2222) 2801 L Street, Sacramento. **Dameron Hospital** (209-944-5550) 525 W. Arcadia, Street, Stockton.

SACRAMENTO AND VICINITY

✳ To See

✧ ⅙ **Aerospace Museum** (916-643-3192; aerospacemuseumofcalifornia.org) 3200 Freedom Park Drive, McClellan. Open 9–5 daily (from 10 AM–5 PM on Sunday). Airplane enthusiasts will appreciate California's first aerospace museum that showcases a biplane by one of the Wright Brothers, an original Norden bomb sight, an Air Force art collection, restored engines, and a flight simulator. $8 adults; $5–6 children; under 6 free.

✧ ⅙ **California Museum for History, Women, and the Arts** (916-653-7524; californiamuseum.org) 1020 O Street. Open Tuesday through Saturday 10 AM–5 PM, Sunday 12–5 PM. Maria Shriver, during her tenure as California's First Lady, has created this museum tribute to remarkable California women. Strangely, you'll see more famous women's clothing than actual feats by ladies. $5 adults; $3.50 kids 6–13; under 6 free.

✧ **California State Capitol Park and Museum** (916-324-0333; capitolmuseum.ca.gov) 10th and L Streets. Open daily 8–4. Free walking tours or

MUSTS FOR FIRST-TIME VISITORS
1. Tour Old Sacramento.
2. Take a boat cruise down the river.
3. Visit the State Capitol.
4. Swim in the American River.
5. Visit the California State Railroad Museum.
6. Hang out in William Land Park.
7. Dine on the Delta King.
8. Sip wine in Midtown.
9. Pedal through Davis.
10. Hike Cache Creek Canyon.

MUSTS FOR REPEAT VISITORS
1. Wakeboard the Delta.
2. White-water raft the American River.
3. Visit a Yolo County farm.
4. Shop in Midtown.
5. Visit the Crocker Art Museum.
6. Lose your voice at a Kings basketball game.
7. Have breakfast at the Tower Café.
8. Explore the Davis wetlands.
9. Take a Delta Seaplane Tour.
10. Ride the rails on the Sacramento River Train.

SACRAMENTO BLENDS ART AND POLITICS.

self-guided tours of the building and gardens. Inside, a collection of artwork, murals, contemporary pieces chosen by senators, and a number of antique artifacts line the walls. Free.

California State Indian Museum (916-324-0971; parks.ca.gov) 2618 K Street. Open daily 10 AM–5 PM. California's Indian population included 150 tribes that spoke at least 64 languages. Most Indian museums in Northern California display the artifacts of one or two of those tribes, this one exhibits artifacts from a number of them. $2 adults; $1 youth; under 6 free.

California State Railroad Museum (916-445-6645; california staterailroadmuseum.org) 125 I Street. Open daily 10 AM–5 PM. Kids from around Northern California sojourn here to learn about trains. A fascinating collection of old steam engines, dining car china, and toy trains, plus steam train rides and films, make this a worthy stop if you are 6 or 60. $8 adults, $3 kids; under 6 free.

Crocker Art Museum (916-264-5423; crockerartmuseum.org) 216 O Street. Open Tuesday through Sunday 10 AM–5 PM. Tour the 1872 Victorian, the classic art gallery on the second floor, and the small but innovative contemporary art exhibit. In summer, the third Thursday jazz series in the park is worth your time. At press time, they were constructing a new wing. $6 adults; $3 youth; under 6 free.

Discovery Museum History Center (916-575-3941; the discovery.org) 101 I Street. Open daily from 10 AM–5 PM. In winter on Tuesday through Sunday at least 12–5. Kids will find this gold rush history museum interesting. Plenty of artifacts, plus an information display on agriculture, really brings home the importance of this region on California's past and present. $5 adults; $3–4 youth; under 3 free.

Discovery Museum Science and Space Center (916-575-3941; the discovery.org) 3615 Auburn Boulevard. Open daily from 10 AM–5 PM. Winter open Tuesday through Sunday at least 12–5. The Challenger and the Space and Science Center both focus on teaching kids about science's advances in space, geology, and physical sciences. $5 adults; $3–4 youth; under 3 free.

Fairytale Town (916-264-5233; fairytaletown.org) 3901 Land Park Drive. Open March through October, daily 9–4; November through February, Thursday through Sunday 10 AM–4 PM. Besides being located in one of the most kid-friendly parks in the city, this young people's adventure land has a host of events, from films to concerts. In the park, the kids can run through a variety of exhibits depicting fairy tales, plus they can meet the animals. $3.75 (weekdays), $4.50 weekends and holidays; under 2 free.

Leland Stanford Mansion State Historic Park (916-324-0575; parks.ca.gov) 8th and N Streets. Open daily 9:30–5. After a huge renovation, the famed railroad baron's mansion is open for us little folks to see how the other 1 percent lives. Leland Stanford was the governor of California from 1862 to 1863 and when he moved in, he remodeled—twice. Marvel at the 17-foot ceilings, the bronze and crystal light fixtures, the artwork, and the sheer decadence of the mansion. $8 adults, $3 youth; under 6 free.

✄ & **Old Sacramento State Historic Park** (916-445-6645; parks.ca.gov) Front and I Streets. Open daily. Over 50 historic buildings from the gold rush days attract visitors looking to reenact the Wild West. Carriage rides, plays, classic boats, candy shops, souvenir stores, and wine bars make this a tourist trap, but everyone around will tell you this is Sacramento's pride and joy. Free.

Sacramento Historic City Cemetery (916-448-0811; oldcitycemetery.com) Broadway at 10th Street. As dark as it sounds, this is a lovely place to picnic, surrounded by gardens and tombstones dating back to the gold rush days. Free guided tours daily as well as the occasional full-moon tour ($15).

✄ & **Sacramento Zoo** (916-264-5888; saczoo.com) 3930 W. Land Park Drive. Open daily from 9–4. This is a pretty darn good zoo, working to save animals and educate visitors about the impact of their environmental choices. The lemurs and African animals are highlights. $6–9.

Sutter's Fort State Historic Park (916-445-4422; parks.ca.gov) 2701 L Street. Open daily 10 AM–5 PM. In 1839, John Sutter scored a land grant from the Mexican government. He created an agricultural empire and established Sacramento's earliest settlement (or at least the first non-Indian settlement). In 1847, Sutter sent aid to the Donner Party, a group of immigrants trapped in a winter storm in the Sierra Nevada. Word spread and Sutter became known for his hospitality and for providing temporary refuge to travelers. This reputation made his empire a destination for early immigrants to California. Gold seekers soon overran his area and this fort is all that remains. $6.

✄ & **Towe Auto Museum** (916-442-6802; toweautomuseum.org) 2200 Front Street. Open 10 AM–5 PM daily. You car lovers are in for a treat. View cars from the beginning of automotive history through the present. $7 adults; $3 youth.

Davis
✄ & **Explorit Science Center** (530-756-0191; explorit.org) 2801 2nd Street. Open Tuesday through Friday 2–4:30 and weekends 11 AM–4:30 PM. This hands-on science museum might actually make your kid want to be a scientist. $4; under 3 free.

Woodland
Heidrick Ag History Center (530-666-9700; aghistory.org) 1962 Hays Lane. Open at least 10 AM–4 PM daily. I don't know about you, but every time I am in the area, I become fascinated with where my food comes from. This history of agriculture museum scratches that itch, with plenty of information about how agriculture works in these parts and the advances we've made over time. $7 adults; $4 youth; under 5 free.

Folsom

Folsom History Museum (916-985-2707; folsomhistorymuseum.org) 823 Sutter Street. Open Tuesday through Sunday 11 AM–4 PM. As if we need another museum in the area, this one brings it all together, focusing on the Indians who first inhabited the area, gold rush seekers, railroads, mining history, and more. $3 adults; $2 youth; under 12 free.

✳ To Do

ATHLETIC EVENTS ✍ **River Cats** (916-376-4700; rivercats.com) 400 Ball Park Drive, Sacramento. On a warm summer night, head out to watch the triple-A affiliate of the Oakland As.

✍ **Sacramento Kings** (nba.com/kings) Arco Arena, 1 Sports Parkway, Sacramento. A game here is an experience, complete with cowbells and some excellent basketball.

CYCLING This area breeds cyclists. Not only are downtown Sacramento and Davis ideal places to work out the legs, you can also find some great trails. Check out sacbike.org for information and trail maps. The best trails to cycle are the **American River Bike Trail,** the **Jedediah Smith Memorial Trail,** and **Lake Natomas.**

Bike Rentals
B&L Bike Shop (530-756-3540; blbikeshop.com) 610 3rd Street, Davis. Open 8–9 weekdays and at least 10 AM–5 PM weekends.

City Bicycle Works (916-447-2453; citybicycleworks.com) 2419 K Street, Sacramento. Open at least 11 AM–5 PM daily.

BOAT TOURS ✍ ♿ **Sacramento Yacht Charters** (916-552-2933; sacyachts .com) 110 L Street, Sacramento. On the **Spirit of Sacramento,** a paddle wheeler, they offer dinner and dance cruises, lunch, or just sightseeing down the river ($25–50). The **Trolley Boat** is a sightseeing cruise on Wednesday through Sunday ($25 adults; $15 children). Another option is to take a smaller **River Otter Taxi Co.** trip from Old Sacramento to the Riverbank Marina or Sturgeon Marina ($10 adults; $8 youth).

FAMILY FUN ✍ **Sacramento River Train** (800-866-1690; sacramentoriver train.com) 341 Industrial Way, Woodland. The Great Train Robbery is a must for families—as long as your kids don't mind the loud fake gunshots (though the actors do give a speech about gun safety afterwards). Couples might prefer the evening dinners, murder mystery rides, or the Sunday brunch. $45–64; children (on the Great Train Robbery) $25.

FARM TOURS **Buzzards Roost Ranch** (530-795-4084; buzzardsroostranch .com) 8290A Pleasants Valley Road, Winters. Call for appointment. Take a carriage ride through the orchards, buy organic apricots and walnuts, or rent a cabin.

Pacific Star Gardens (530-666-7308) 20872 County Road 99, Woodland. Open daylight hours. In the spring you can pick your own organic strawberries and apricots; in summer it's tomatoes, melons, and watermelon.

FARMERS' MARKETS Cesar Chavez Plaza Market 10th and J Streets, in front of City Hall. Wednesday from 10 AM–2 PM (May through October only).

Davis Farmers' Market (davisfarmersmarket.org) Central Park, 4th and C Streets, Davis. On Saturday from 8–1, year-round. For over 30 years, this huge market has been selling fresh off the farm goods. Check out the Hotdogger for gourmet dogs.

Denio's Farmers' Market (denios.org) 1551 Vineyard Road, Roseville. Friday through Sunday. Since 1947, this produce market and swap meet has attracted shoppers.

THE GREAT TRAIN ROBBERY ABOARD THE SACRAMENTO RIVER TRAIN.

Sacramento Central Market 8th and W Streets, underneath I-80. Sunday from 8–noon. This is the big guy in these parts.

GOLF Ancil Hoffman Golf Club (916-368-PUTT; ancilhoffman.com) 6700 Tarshes Drive, Carmichael. This 18-hole course has greens fees of $28–47.

Haggin Oaks Golf Center (916-489-6799; hagginoaks.com) 3645 Fulton Avenue, Sacramento. This golf complex has two affordable courses and a driving range open 24 hours a day. $20–54.

SPAS Spa La Le (916-379-5980; lerivagehote.com) Le Rivage Hotel, 4350 Riverside Boulevard, Sacramento. Pampering packages are called "bundles," the longest lasting more than four hours.

Skin Sanctuary (916-444-5824; skinsanctuary.com) 3260 J Street, Sacramento. A mix of eastern and western spa treatments allows this sanctuary to live up to its name.

WATER SPORTS American River Raft Rentals (916-635-6400; raftrentals.com) 11257 S. Bridge Street, Rancho Cordova. In summer, you can bob down the American River on a raft or kayak. You'll negotiate some rapids in the area, but not the big ole ones people brag about surviving. No children under 5. Kayak rentals: $30–50. Raft rentals: $48–144.

GLIDE OVER LAKES AND CITIES IN A SEAPLANE

Delta Seaplane Tours (916-837-8952; deltaseaplanes.com) These seaplane pilots offer four types of trips, but each are guaranteed to thrill as you glide over either the Delta, San Francisco Bay, Sacramento, or the valley farms and Folsom Lake. A trip costs between $350–490. If you can afford the Ultimate Pilot's Experience, travel all the way to the San Francisco Bay, then splash down on the Delta and see the waterway in all its windy glory.

Cache Canyon River Trips (800-796-3091; cachecanyon.com) Operating from April through Labor Day. You can go on one- or two-day white-water rafting adventures. One of the only self-guided tours you'll find, you'd better be confident in your abilities. One-day trips go out on Thursday, Saturday, and Sunday. $30–45.

Sacramento State Aquatic Center (916-278-2842; sacstateaquaticcenter.com) 1901 Hazel Avenue, Gold River. Located at Lake Natomas, this outfit rents sailboats, kayaks, and canoes. Rates are as good as you'll get, with kayaks and canoes from $9–14. They also rent bikes.

WINE TASTING All around the area are some fantastic wine growers. For specific wineries within a day's drive, check out the *Sierra Foothills, the Delta, the Sacramento Valley,* and of course the *Napa* and *Sonoma Wine Tasting* sections.

58 Degrees and Holding Co (916-442-5858; 58degrees.com) 1217 8th Street, Sacramento. Open at 11 AM daily. This low-lit bistro and wine bar has a pretty good local wine list.

Discover California (916-443-8275; discovercal.com) 114 J Street, Sacramento. Open daily from 12–7 (until 9 on Friday and Saturday). I am a sucker for these types of wine bars, where the wines come to you, instead of driving from one winery to the next. Taste Northern California wines or take wine classes. Would that be an easy A or what?

Frasinetti Winery (916-383-2444; frasinetti.com) 7395 Frasinetti Road, Sacramento. Open 11 AM–8 PM daily. Sacramento's oldest winery not only offers a taste of their wines, but also dinner and lunch service. Free.

Revolution Wines (revolution-wines.com) 2116 P Street, Sacramento. Open at least 12–6 PM daily. This urban winery prides itself on being the sole pioneer on that frontier. Free.

Rominger West Winery (530-747-2044; romingerwest.com) 4602 2nd Street, Davis. Open Monday through Friday 8 AM–5 PM and Saturday 11 AM–4 PM. Davis's first winery allows you to taste and tour the winemaking facilities—this is especially monumental because the up-and-coming winemakers of Northern Californiastudy here at U.C. Davis, so you can learn more about wine than you thought possible. Free.

✳ Green Spaces

American River Parkway (916-875-6961; co.sacramento.ca.us) This 23-mile river system has a wealth of trails, rafting, picnic areas, and swimming holes. Anglers head to the **Rossmoor Bar, Sacramento Bar, Upper and Lower Sunrise,** and the **Sailor Bar**. Other highlights include **Ancil Hoffman Park** (Tarshes Drive, Carmichael), home to the **Effie Yeaw Nature Center,** a golf course, and almost 400 acres of trails. **Discovery Park** stretches across the north part of downtown Sacramento, and offers a boat launch, a bike and walk trail, and a swimming area (it gets sketchy at night). **Howe Avenue River Access** (Off US 50, take Howe Avenue towards the water) offers a boat launch, beaches for swimming, and access to the 32-mile Jedediah Smith Memorial Bike Trail. $5 per car.

Sacramento Parks

✇ **McKinley Park** (916-277-6060; cityofsacramento.org) Alhambra and McKinley Boulevard. This huge park begs you to chill out in the pool, take the kids to the playground, or read the newspaper.

☙ **William Land Park** (916-277-6060; cityofsacramento.org) Sutterville Road and 17th Avenue. Sacramento's monster-of-all park: with a zoo, a children's play land, pony rides, picnic areas, golf, and plenty of shade.

Parks in the Surrounding Areas
Cache Creek Canyon Regional Park (530-666-8115; yolocounty.org) CA 16, Rumsey. Head out to white-water raft, hike, fish, and horseback ride in this 700-acre park. There are 45 campsites ($17–19). Day use: $6.

& **Cosumnes River Preserve** (916-684-2816; cosumnes.org) 13501 Franklin Boulevard, Galt. Visitor Center open Saturday and Sunday 9–5 (in summer open 8–12). This 80-mile river and wildlife preserve is fragile. You can only access the area surrounding the visitor center. Popular trails include the 1-mile wheelchair-accessible Lost Slough Wetlands Walk, which gets you up close and personal with the birds and marshes; the 3-mile Cosumnes River Walk trail, which winds through riparian forest and oaks; and the 7-mile Rancho Seco Howard Ranch Trail, which gets you to some vernal pools, the Rancho Seco Lake, and seasonal wetlands. The mellow river offers great kayaking, canoeing, and fishing. $5.

Folsom Lake State Recreation Area (800-444-7275 or 916-988-0205 (camping reservations); american.parks.ca.gov) 7806 Folsom-Auburn Road, Folsom. A bit of a beerfest in summer, but hey, you're hot, want to jump in a lake, or camp near water. Boaters are out in full force, as are hikers, picnickers, and bikers. The Oaks Nature Trail is a short handicapped-accessible walk with lovely lake views. You can camp at this 18,000-acre park. Plus, there are horse rentals at Beal's Point Campground. $5.

UC Davis Arboretum (530-752-4880; arboretum.ucdavis.edu) 1 Shields Avenue, Davis. Open 24 hours a day. The 100 acres of gardens make this one of my favorite spots to relax in Davis. I especially like the native plant garden. Free.

Yolo Basin Foundation (530-757-3780; yolobasin.org) Between Davis and Sacramento you'll think you're seeing things, but those really are thousands of birds flying around the wetlands. Public tours of the area take place on the second Saturday of the month from September through June. The park is open from sunrise to sunset year-round. Free.

✳ Lodging

Sacramento
⁙ **Amber House B&B** (916-444-8085; amberhouse.com) 1315 22nd Street. Besides the great location in midtown, this B&B offers elegance in a classic environment that puts it above the standard of most options. Named after European composers and writers, 10 classy rooms offer lovely touches like marble fireplaces, deep tubs, full breakfast, Frette linens, and super-plush beds. $$–$$$$.

☙ & ∞ **Delta King Hotel** (916-444-5464; deltaking.com) 1000 Front Street. At least one time in your life, you have to sleep aboard a ship, and why not this antique paddleboat/hotel, docked in Old Sacramento? You'll feel a little rocking, just enough to lull you to sleep, but not enough to warrant Dramamine. The 44 rooms are small, but what do you expect from a boat? Spring for river views: It's as close as you can get in town. Plus there is continental breakfast, two restaurants, and a bar. $–$$.

SLEEP ON THE WATER AT THE DELTA KING HOTEL.

✏ ♿ ⑂ **Hostelling International— Sacramento Hostel** (916-443-1691; norcalhostels.org) 925 H Street. Most hostels can't offer a night in a gold rush mansion for cheaper than you can get a sushi dinner. Go for the river city suite, which is a private room with a bathroom. Other private rooms share a bath, or you can sleep in a dorm room. All guests can use the kitchen. $.

✏ ♿ ⑂ **Le Rivage Hotel** (800-323-7500; lerivagehotel.com) 4350 Riverside Boulevard. On the banks of the Sacramento River, this luxury hotel is just far enough from downtown (2 miles) to not cater only to business travelers—though you wouldn't know it from the masculine rooms. There are 100 dark wood-colored rooms with marble bathrooms, claw-foot tubs and rain showerheads, Italian linens, balconies, and views of the river or city. Amenities include a spa, Scott's Seafood, town cars to downtown, concierge, room service, pool, fitness center, bike rentals, and parking (fee). $$$–$$$$.

✏ ♿ ⑂ 🐾 ⑩ **Sheraton Grand Sacramento Hotel** (916-447-1700; Sheraton.com) 1230 J Street. Close enough to Midtown (but also mere steps from a slightly dodgy area), this is a great option for families. Besides the Sleep Sleeper beds, the 503 rooms aren't much to speak of. It's about proximity, the lobby designed by Julia Morgan, and having the amenities (pool, restaurant, lounge, concierge, fitness center, paid parking) of a big hotel. $$–$$$.

⑩ **Sterling Hotel** (800-365-7660; sterlinghotel.com) 1300 H Street. This mansion transports you to another time, when these 17 rooms were considered "Sleeping Rooms" and offered two-story high ceilings, deep Jacuzzi tubs, big windows, and fluffy beds. New owners hope to take this classic property to a new level. Make sure not to get the downstairs room next to the stairs on a Thursday night. Continental breakfast and Chanterelle Restaurant round out the experience. $$–$$$.

In the Surrounding Areas
✏ ♿ ⑂ **Aggie Inn** (530-756-0352; aggieinn.com) 245 1st Street, Davis. Folks with cash to spend prefer the cottages to the 33 standard rooms. Located next to UC Davis, it is a bit pricey for what you get, but there are slim pickings in town. Amenities include continental breakfast, pool, fitness room, and spa. $$–$$$.

✏ ♿ ⑂ **Cache Creek Casino Resort and Spa** (888-77-CACHE; cache creek.com) 14455 CA 16, Brooks. In the pastoral Capay Valley, this 200-room resort deems itself luxurious. I suppose for the area, this is about as fancy as you can get: duvet covers, deep soaking-tubs, airy rooms with valley views, a massive glassed-in shower, the choice of Vietnamese noodles or a porterhouse, and access to a pool, spa, and the casino next door. $$–$$$.

⊕ "I" 🐾 ✎ **Capay Valley B&B** (866-227-2922; capayvalleybandb.com) 15875 CA 16, Capay. This 1898 farmhouse supplies guests with country living and an onsite zoo. Themed rooms like the Wild Wild West and the Patriotic Suites, the cottages with kitchenettes (a great choice for families or folks traveling with Fido), bocce ball, and breakfast, attract those seeking a simple respite from the world. $$–$$$.

Rumsey Canyon Inn (530-796-2400; rumseycanyoninn.com) 2996 Rumsey Canyon Road, Rumsey. Sometimes you just want to get away from it all. And I mean it *all*. Located between Sacramento and Clear Lake, this Craftsman inn expects guests to read a book on the wraparound veranda, enjoy a country breakfast, sip wine by the stone fireplace, and meditate on the orchards that surround the property. $$.

✳ Where to Eat

DINING OUT

Sacramento

𝕐 ♿ **Biba** (916-455-2422; biba-restaurant.com) 2801 Capitol Avenue. Open Monday through Friday 11:30–2 and at least 5:30–9:30, and Saturday 5:30–10. Biba Caggiano moved from Bologna to Sacramento and opened this classic Italian eatery that has attracted foodies from around the world. Don't expect Kandinsky drops of food with foamed vegetables. Instead, you get traditional housemade pastas and lasagna (on Thursday and Friday only) and a salad after your main course. Reservations required. $$–$$$.

𝕐 ♿ ⊕ **The Firehouse** (916-442-4772; firehouseoldsac.com) 1112 2nd Street. Open Sunday through Friday 11:30–2:30 and 5:30–10:30 (Sunday they close at 9) and Saturday 5–10:30.

Built in 1853, this famous Sacramento restaurant both takes you to boomtown days and offers contemporary takes on American cuisine. Inside, the dining room feels more like you are on a ship than an old firehouse, while outside, the tree-covered terrace is the perfect place for alfresco romance. Entrees include Wagyu steak Oscar, Scottish king salmon with an olive *fregola,* and *achiote* duck. Reservations recommended for dinner. $$$–$$$$.

The Kitchen (916-568-7171; thekitchenrestaurant.com) 2225 Hurley Way, Suite 101, (north of Fair Oaks, East of Howe). Dinner served Wednesday through Sunday. If you want a culinary adventure, chef and owner Randall Selland will prepare a four-course demonstration dinner in his "kitchen," while you watch the preparations, sip wine, and experience the freshest in seasonal organic produce. Imagine a Maine lobster thermidor, a porcini-mushroom potpie, sashimi, herb-glazed Liberty duck breast, monkfish short ribs, and a warm Delta blueberry cream tart. Sound good? It better, because this experience will run you $125 per person, not including drinks, tax, or gratuity. Reservations required.

♿ **Kru Restaurant** (916-551-1559; krurestaurant.com) 2516 J Street, Sacramento. Open Mon through Friday from at least 11:30–9:30, Saturday 12–11, and Sunday 5–9:30. Contemporary Japanese cuisine is all the rage in Sacramento. But Kru packs the house, offering small plates and sushi served in a bamboo and red-painted room. Reservations recommended. $$–$$$.

𝕐 ♿ **Restaurant 55 Degrees** (916-553-4100; restaurant55.com) 555 Capitol Mall. Open Monday through Friday 11:30–2:30 and nightly for dinner from at least 5–9. A San Francisco foodie mentality has arrived in Sacramento, and Chef Luc Dendlevel's California cuisine fits the bill (and begs for your entire paycheck). Some of you might enjoy the $80 six-course tasting menu, while the rest of us either dig deep to afford mussels and frites or a Niman Ranch pork chop. Come for happy hour (4–6 weekdays) and have appetizers if the price is out of your range. Reservations recommended. $$–$$$$.

♂ & Ÿ **Rio City Café** (916-442-8226; riocitycafe.com) 1110 Front Street. Open at least 11 AM–10 PM daily. With such an ideal Sac-town location—right on the river in Old Sacramento—you had better hope their hyped Sunday brunch is worth it. Well, the bottomless mimosa helps, but I would head to the bar, have a drink and an appetizer, then, once you get your fill of the view, head over to Indo Café. $$–$$$.

Ÿ & **Waterboy** (916-498-9891; water boyrestaurant.com) 2000 Capitol Avenue. Open for lunch and dinner daily. Focusing on local seasonal ingredients, this French-Italian-Californian restaurant has deposited itself on the short list of romantic spots in Midtown. You have to love a spot that serves chicken under a brick, and panko-breaded fish sticks. Reservations recommended. $$$.

Ÿ **Zocalo** (916-441-0303; zocalosac ramento.com) 1801 Capitol Avenue. Open for lunch, dinner, and weekend brunch. Imagine a warehouse, pumping Latin music, bright colors, and a flavorful menu paired with margaritas and mojitos. I'd rather drink here than eat—especially when they serve up those tequila experiences. $$.

EATING OUT & Ÿ **Aioli Bodega Espanola** (916-447-9440) 1800 L Street. Open Monday through Friday 11:30–3 and 5–11, Saturday 5–11 and Sunday 5–10. Live flamenco music, brightly painted murals, a nice-sized outdoor terrace, and good Spanish cuisine bring Midtown hipsters out to play. *Albondigas todo ajo* and paella are sound options. Reservations recommended. $$–$$$.

♂ & **Ambrosia Café** (916-444-8129; ambrosiacafesacramento.com) 1030 K Street. Open 6:30–5 Monday through Friday and 8–3 on weekends. Doing their part for the environment, this green café composts, uses local products, and serves fair-trade coffee. Highlights include the crème brûlée, French toast, and the eggplant panini. $.

♂ & **Café Bernardo** (916-443-1180; paragarys.com) 2801 Capitol Avenue or 1431 R Street. Open at least 7 AM–10 PM daily. The local restaurant monopoly, the Paragary crew, has done it again with this organic café. The menu changes seasonally, but you can expect yummy egg and griddle fare, salads and sandwiches, great polenta, and just the right amount of fried food to round out the menu. I like the R Street location's urban atmosphere, including the bar next door, and the patio with a park view. $–$$.

Ÿ & **Fox and Goose Public House** (916-443-8825; foxandgoose.com) 1001 R Street. Open for breakfast, lunch, and dinner daily. Most pubs laugh when you tell them you are a vegetarian, then serve you a nice big portion of black-and-white pudding. This popular breakfast spot (and music venue) not only offers bangers and mash, but also tempeh sticks. $–$$.

♂ & Ÿ **Fran's Café** (916-920-0744; franscafeac.com) 1616 Del Paso Boulevard. Open Tuesday through Thursday 11 AM–8 PM and Friday and Saturday 10 AM–10 PM. Fran and her crew have created a sleek, silvery café that speaks to yuppies not wanting to miss out on *everything* when they get that big house. Imagine *Sex in the City* meets

Desperate Housewives, with a plentiful cocktail menu (yep, there are cosmos), paninis, small plates like cumin beef tacos, and a Caesar salad served on a pizza. Every second Thursday, they project films on the wall while you eat a three-course meal and drink wine. Movie night is $35, reservations required. $.

☙ ♿ **Indo Café** (916-446-4008) 1100 Front Street, # 150. Open for breakfast, lunch, and dinner Tuesday through Sunday. Other restaurants in Old Sac want you to shell out heaps of cash for mediocre food, but this family-owned Indonesian café is trying a different tactic: Charge reasonable prices for big plates of good food that you eat either on picnic tables, or in the cafeteria-like room, surrounded by Elvis posters. The *lempurs,* or any rice and noodle dish, are great options for a hungry family. $.

☙ ♿ **La Bonne Soup Café** (916-492-9506) 920 Eighth Street. Open Monday through Friday 10:30–2:30. This dude has a good thing going: short hours, lines out the door, minimal staff, and cheap rent, right next to the Bail Bonds Store in downtown Sac. You want veggie cream soup or a prosciutto sandwich, tell the French chef and he'll make it for you on the spot. Voila! Get here early, or you'll be one of the suckers waiting and waiting and waiting. $.

☙ ♿ **Lemon Grass Restaurant** (916-486-4891; lemongrassrestaurant.com) 601 Munroe Street. Sure, this Vietnamese restaurant is out in the suburbs, but when you have to have Bangkok beef with Niman Ranch meat, or the vegetarian monk's curry, you just gotta have it. My favorite is the coffee, which is more like a milkshake. $$.

♿ **Old Soul Co.** (916-443-7685; old soulco.com) 1716 L Street (entrance on alley). Open daily from 6 AM–11 PM. Find fresh-roasted coffee and some of the better pastries in town at this warehouse in Midtown. Don't say I didn't warn you that the staff doesn't particularly want you to hang out long: There are a couple folding chairs and the attitude that comes with knowing you have a sweet deal.

☙ ♿ **Sacramento Natural Foods Co-op** (916-736-6800; sacfoodcoop.com) 1900 Alhambra at S Street. Open 7–10 daily. Besides a healthy selection of organic produce, natural foods, and nontoxic beauty products, this co-op has a lovely deli counter, serving hot food, sandwiches, and ethnic creations. $.

☙ ♿ **Selland's Market Café** (916-736-3333; the kitchen.com/sellands) 5340 H Street. Open Monday through Saturday 10:30–8. Market-fresh mostly organic food and deli fare, plus a decent wine list, place Selland's on the map of where to go for food-lovers. Turkey sandwiches, flavorful salads, pizzas, and teriyaki chicken are featured on the seasonal menu. $–$$.

☙ ♿ "⫯" **Temple Fine Coffee and Tea** (916-443-4960; templecoffee.com) 1014 10th Street. Open daily 6 AM–11 PM. Aptly named, when I first entered this shrine to coffee, my barista informed me "Coffee is my life." And, after tasting her perfectly foamed latte (using San Jose's Barefoot Coffee Roaster's beans), I knew I would come pray at this coffee shop every time I come back. Their pastries, made by Old Soul, are almost as good as the coffee.

☙ ♿ ♈ **Three Sisters** (916-452-7442) 5100 Folsom. Open for breakfast, lunch, and dinner daily. Colorful, folksy, and family-owned, the three sisters of Midtown's Tres Hermanas opened this new outpost but didn't sacrifice quality in the process. The guacamole, tostadas, and cod tacos accompany the margaritas perfectly. $.

🍴 ♿ **Tower Café** (916-441-0222; towercafe.com) 1518 Broadway. Open at least 8 AM–11 PM daily. On weekends, Sac locals line up for over an hour to wait for international-themed omelets (most with a Latin twist). Inside, it reminds me of the living room of a world traveler gone mad with Mom's credit card, with rainbows of masks, tapestries, and art hanging from every possible surface; outside, the garden patio feels like dining in the jungle. The eggs tower, burgers, and salads are top choices. $–$$.

Surrounding Areas
Aioli Bodega Espanola (530-757-2766) 808 Second Street, Davis. See *Eating Out Sacramento*.

THE HISTORIC TOWER THEATER AND CAFÉ.

🍴 ♿ **Black Rooster** (916-357-7115; blkrooster.com) 807 Sutter Street, Folsom. Open daily at 7 AM until at least 4 (but until 9 on most nights). Before a day at the lake, you'll want to pop in here for fair-trade organic espresso drinks, gelato, sandwiches and salads, and delicious desserts. Dishes: $.

🍴 ♿ **Café Bernardo** (530-750-5101) 234 D Street, Davis See *Eating Out Sacramento*.

🍴 ♿ 🍸 **Caffe Italia** (530-759-7200; dancingtomato.com) 1121 Richards Boulevard, Davis. Open 6 AM–10 PM Monday through Thursday (until 11 on Friday and Saturday); 7 AM–10 PM on Sunday. For 10 years, this restaurant has been the first stop you see when entering Davis. Here you'll find a traditional Italian joint with friendly servers, Italian memorabilia on the walls, and the best breakfast in town. Dishes: $–$$.

Davis Food Co-op (530-758-2667; daviscoop.com) 620 G Street, Davis. Open 8 AM–10 PM daily. Head over to this co-op for all your grocery needs, some decent deli items, and plenty of local foods.

🍴 ♿ 🍸 **Kung Fu Fats** (888-77-CACHE; cachecreek.com) 14455 CA 16, Brooks. Open daily from 11 AM–midnight. Pan-Asian cuisine in a casino resort might not be the highest of haute cuisine, but then you consider that the chef combines three regions of Chinese cooking with Korean and Vietnamese cuisine. Try the congee or adobo. $–$$.

Little Prague See *Entertainment*.

🍴 ♿ **Putah Creek Café** (530-795-2682; buckhornsteakhouse.com) 1 Main Street, Winters. Open at least 6 AM–2:30 daily. Sacramento folks drive the half hour for breakfast on the knotty pine counter. Here, when they say country-style, that's what you can expect, with biscuits and gravy, chicken-fried steak, lemon bars, great oat-meal, and mounds of scrambles. Go early, or expect to wait. $–$$.

🍴 ♿ 🍷 **Seasons** (530-750-1801; seasonsdavis.com) 102 F Street, Davis. Open Tuesday through Friday 11:30 AM–2 PM and 5 PM–9 PM; Saturday 12–2 PM and 5 PM–10 PM; Sunday 11 AM–2 PM and 5 PM–9 PM. As you might imagine, this hippie college town has a slow-food restaurant. Mahogany and cherry-wood interiors, sleek lines, and a nice selection of American fare for kids and adults, make this the ideal place for Mom and Dad to enjoy a bottle of wine, while Junior eats a burger and doesn't whine. Reservations recommended for dinner. $$–$$$.

🍴 ♿ 🍷 **Tazzina Bistro** (530-661-1700; tazzinabistro.com) 614 Main Street, Woodland. Open for lunch and dinner daily (brunch at 10 on weekends). Not the kind of spot you'd expect to find in an old western town. Seasonal menu items might include the tofu ragout, Snake River Farms Kobe burger, and quiche with Kurabata ham. In summer, you can sit at the patio or the bar. $–$$.

Village Bakery (530-750-2255) 814 2nd Street, Davis. Open Monday through Saturday 5:30 AM–9 PM and Sunday 11:30 AM–8 PM. If you want good pizza, this is the spot in Davis. It's cheap, it's gourmet, and it has a huge local following. Dishes: $–$$.

✳ Entertainment

For up-to-date entertainment listings, pick up the free weekly *Sacramento News and Review.*

Sacramento
B Street Theater (916-443-5300; bstreettheater.org) Box office: 2711 B Street. Sacramento's most innovative major theater company.

🍷 ▼ **Badlands** (916-448-8790; sacbadlands.com) 2003 K Street. Open night-

ly until 2 AM. Sacramento's biggest gay dance club has great events like a pillow-fight night and a burlesque show.

🍷 **L Wine Lounge and Urban Kitchen** (916-443-6970) 1801 L Street. This expensive and swanky wine bar attracts the hip want-to-be-seen youth. Wines are extensive and you can eat here as well.

🍴 ♿ **Music Circus** (916-557-1999) 1419 H Street. Shows in July and August. So you like the big top, but also want to see Broadway-quality theater? Head out to the Teflon tent in downtown. Temperatures inside can make you get to know your neighbor a bit more than you might prefer.

🍷 **The Park Ultra Lounge** (916-442-7222; theparkdowntown.com) 1116 15th Street. One of the hippest bars around, you can lounge on beds under a canopy and gaze at the stars while sipping wine. They are attached to Mason's Restaurant and Ma Jong Asian Diner, if you get hungry.

SACT (Sactheater.org) This nonprofit theater company puts up musicals like *Urinetown* and *Fiddler on the Roof.*

🍷 **Torch Club** (916-443-2797; torchclub.net) 904 15th Street. This is the spot to hear blues music and shake your thing.

Zocalo See *Dining Out-Sacramento.*

Davis
🍷 **Little Prague** (530-756-1157; littleprague.com) 330 G Street. Not only is this funky spot known for serving interesting Czech food and calling it Bohemian, but they also have great outdoor seating and live music on weekends.

✳ Selective Shopping

In the **Westfield Downtown Plaza** (between 4th and 7th, and J and L Streets), you'll find most major chain stores that typically dot malls across America. If you are looking for something unique, head to the **Grid** (mid towngrid.com). Most stores and galleries are on J, K, and L Streets, between 17th and 26th Streets.

BOOKSHOPS The Avid Reader (916-441-4400 or 530-758-4040; avid readerbooks.com) 1600 Broadway, Sacramento, and 617 2nd Street, Davis. This is the area's largest independent bookseller.

Beers Books (916-442-9475; beers books.com) 915 S Street. This used bookstore is the best you can find in Sacramento.

✳ Seasonal Events

Ongoing: **Second Saturday Art Walk** (2nd-sat.com) In Midtown and along Del Paso Boulevard in the Uptown Arts District, galleries stay open from 6–9 to celebrate the arts. This is the best monthly event in Sacramento, complete with live music in most alleyways.

March: **California Capital Air Show** (916-808-7777; californiacapitalair show.com) Mather Field. If you like fast planes, stunts, and the blaring Blue Angels, come to town for this monster of a show.

April: **Picnic Day** (yolocvb.org) The University hosts a big all-day festival. The different university departments open their doors and allow regular Joes into classrooms to play.

May: **Friday Night Concerts in the Park** Cesar Chavez Plaza (10th and J Streets, Sacramento). Free music from Sacramento's top local musicians every Friday through mid-August. There is even a beer garden.

July: **Fourth of July at the Cal Expo** Big booming fireworks to music, and lots of patriotism.

August: **California State Fair** (877-225-3976; calexpo.com) The Cal Expo comes alive each year to celebrate California. It's been going on for over 150 years, so you'd think they'd know how to party.

Gold Rush Days (916-808-7777; discovergold.org) Old Sacramento. On Labor Day weekend, tons of dirt gets piled into Old Sacramento and horses prance through the streets to celebrate the gold rush.

December: **California International Marathon** (916-983-4622; runcim.org) Folsom to Sacramento. Gear up for the 26.2-mile trek, or at least come out and watch the physically superior creatures cross the finish line.

SAN JOAQUIN VALLEY
AND THE DELTA

✳ To See and Do

Modesto

Perhaps best known for being the home of George Lucas and the film site of *American Graffiti*, Modesto's downtown has its own appeal—as long as you like a touch of Mayberry with your manure smell.

Castle Air Museum (209-723-2178) Santa Fe Drive, west of Buhach Road, Atwater. Open daily at least 10 AM–4 PM. Currently more than 45 aircraft are on display, including some military planes like the B-52 and B-25. Donations accepted.

Great Valley Museum of Natural History (209-575-6196) 1100 Stoddard Avenue. Open at least 12–4:30 Tuesday through Saturday. Learn about the animals and plants native to the region. $1; under 6 free.

McHenry Museum (209-577-5366; mchenrymuseum.org) 1402 I Street, Modesto. Open Tuesday through Sunday 12–4. Originally the city library, now this museum takes you back to the days of the gold rush with a real blacksmith shop, old mining and firefighting equipment, and cattle brands. You might also pop over to the **McHenry Mansion.** Free.

Stockton

Cambodian Buddhist Temple (209-406-7311; cambodianbuddhist.org) 3732 Carpenter Road. Giant hand-carved statues tell the story of the Cambodian Buddhist experience. Check out the 50-foot reclining Buddha. Free.

✐ ♿ **Children's Museum of Stockton** (209-465-4386; Stockton.gov) 402 W. Weber Street. Open Tuesday through Friday from 9–4 and Saturday from 10 AM–5 PM. Kids love museums that offer adult activities at their height. Here the little guys can play with pint-sized tools, play banker with fake money, and explore what it might be like to be a doctor or a fast-food worker—hmm, what are they training their children for? While you're there, head over to the Events Center to let the little ones cool off in the interactive water-play area. $4.50; children under 2 free.

✐ ♿ ☕ **Delta River Cruises** (209-942-4372; deltarivercruises.com) 445 W. Weber Avenue. Launch from downtown Stockton and cruise the Delta on the *Princess of Whales*, a 149-passenger catamaran. You can choose between a 90-minute sightseeing jaunt, a brunch or sunset cruise, or a full-blown dinner cruise. Sightseeing cruises cost $25.

Haggin Museum (209-940-6300; hagginmuseum.org) 1201 N. Pershing Avenue. Open Wednesday through Sunday 1:30–5 (open until 9 on first and third Thursday). Numerous 19th-century paintings, a Native American village, some tractors, and a mummy are what you'll get in this local museum. An interesting exhibit not to be missed is the collection of accomplishments by local residents, including the inventor of the Caterpillar tractor, Benjamin Holt. $5 adults; $2.50 for youth and seniors; under 10 free.

Micke Grove Golf Links See *Green Spaces.*

✔ **Micke Grove Regional Park and Zoo** See *Green Spaces.*

✔ ♿ **Pixie Woods Children's Fairyland** (209-937-8206; Stockton.gov) Louis Park, west of Occidental and Shimizu. Open at least 11 AM–5 PM in summer. Kids will love this small amusement park, located in a garden. They can ride a train or merry-go-round, or explore the world of pirates and Indians. $3.75; $3 children; under 1 free. There is a fee for the rides as well.

Lodi

Great Valley Serpentarium (209-369-7737) 2379 Maggio Circle, Unit C. Open Tuesday through Sunday at least 11 AM–4 PM. I'll admit, this place creeps me out, but Slytherins out there will enjoy viewing (and holding) over 50 types of snakes and reptiles, including bearded dragons, horned frogs, and tarantulas. Free.

Lockeford Springs Golf Course (209-333-6275; lockefordsprings.com) 16360 N. CA 88. A public 18-hole course surrounded by wine country. $10–65.

Lodi Lake Park See *Green Spaces.*

Phillips Farm (209-368-7384) 4580 W. CA 12. Pumpkins, jam, bread, animals, and just plain ole farm living attract Lodi locals here year-round. Free.

San Joaquin County Historical Museum (209-331-2055) 11793 N. Micke Grove Road. Open Wednesday through Sunday 10 AM–3 PM. Located in Micke Grove Park, this museum showcases life as it used to be in the Valley. You can pan for gold, walk through an old schoolhouse, view the antique tools and tractors, and learn about the Indians that once ruled the area. $2 adults; $1 children.

MINOR LEAGUE SPORTS

California Cougars Stockton Arena, 248 W. Fremont Street. Indoor soccer games at the Arena get loud, so bring some earplugs.

Stockton Lightning Stockton Arena, 248 W. Fremont Street. Indoor arena football games are always entertaining.

Stockton Ports (stocktonports.com) Stockton Ballpark, Fremont and Van Buren Streets. Head out for a baseball game and enjoy the warm summer nights.

Stockton Thunder Stockton Arena, 248 W. Fremont Street. If you like watching hockey and can't get a ticket to a game in San Jose, the Thunder are sure to give you all the head banging you're looking for.

Sierra Adventure Outfitters (209-368-3461) 120 N. School Street. Open 10 AM–6 PM Monday through Saturday. These guys rent kayaks and canoes for adventures in local rivers and can also guide you to the best places to paddle, hike, and more.

The Delta

☙ **Delta Ecotours** (916-775-4021; deltaecotours.com) 13737 Grand Island Road, Walnut Grove. You can take a catamaran tour of the Delta and learn about the ecology of this unique waterway. Tours last two hours and go out on selective Saturdays throughout the year. Call for reservations. Trips cost $35 (adults) and $15 (children 6–12). They also run four-hour tours, and have a flower farm for you to tour before or after your trip.

Delta Meadows River Park Canoe Tours ((916-777-6671; parks.ca.gov) Near the town of Locke, drive into Railroad Slough from the River Road, between Walnut Grove and Locke. Explore one of the few remaining natural islands in the Delta on a canoe tour with a State Park guide. You'll look for river otter, beaver, muskrat, birds, and other wildlife. Tours are offered on Saturdays and Sundays at 10 AM and last between three and four hours. Reservations required. $15.

Delta Seaplane Tours See *Sacramento To Do.*

Delta Watercraft Rentals (925-684-2620; deltawatercraft.com) 3025 Gateway Road, Bethel Island. If you are over 18, you can rent Jet Skis, WaveRunners, and other watercraft.

Fish Hookers Sport Fishing (916-777-6498; fishhookers.com) 1759 Circle Drive, Isleton. Fish on your own in a number of fishing holes (**Lost Slough** and **Decker Island** are local favorites) and catch anything from bass to sturgeon, catfish to salmon. If you would rather have yourself a guide, these folks can take you out, starting at $135.

Sugar Barge RV Resort and Marina (800-799-4100; sugarbarge.com) 1440 Sugar Barge Road, Bethel Island. If you are in the market to rent kayaks, head over to this marina. They can set you up with kayaks for as cheap as $13–18 an hour. Though there is a lot of powerboat activity on the Delta, there are still places where you can paddle reasonably smooth waters. The best places to kayak in the area are **Sevenmile Slough, Old River, Middle River, Mokelumne River, Lost Slough,** and **Brannon Island State Park.**

❋ Green Spaces

The Valley

☙ **Lodi Lake Park** (209-333-6742) 1101 W. Turner Road, Lodi. Seems on a hot summer day the whole town heads to this lake beach (the beach is open May through September). You can rent pedal boats and kayaks, walk on the trails through the riparian zones, and even learn a thing or two at the Lake Discovery Museum. There is a minimal fee to enter the park and swim area.

☙ ♿ **Micke Grove Park and Zoo** (209-331-7400; co.san-joaquin.ca.us/parks) 11793 N. Micke Grove Road, Lodi. Park open 8–sunset. Zoo is open 10 AM–5 PM. Japanese Garden is open from 9–2. With 258 acres of oak trees, a zoo, a Japanese garden, the Funderwoods Amusement Park for kids, the San Joaquin Historical Museum, a playground, and areas for sports and picnics, this popular park fits the bill for most of your green space needs. There is a minimal fee to enter the park and museum.

WINE TASTING TAKES THE EDGE OFF THE DUSTY CENTRAL VALLEY

The newest wine appellation to take charge of the Valley can be found here in Lodi. I know what you're thinking—Lodi? The Delta? Today 70 wineries grow fruit-forward, full-bodied Zinfandel as well as Rhone varieties like Viognier and Syrah. In fact, many of the grapes that go into Napa Valley wines are grown right here. So get here while local growers are still trying to attract visitors, instead of waiting for them to get all pretentious and snobby about their *Wine Spectator* scores.

To obtain a map of the wineries, contact the **Lodi Wine Grape Commission** (209-367-4727), or hit up the helpful **Lodi Wine and Visitor Center** (209-365-0621; lodiwine.com) 2545 W. Turner Road. Open 10–5 daily.

Tasting Rooms

Bogle Vineyards (916-744-1139; boglewinery.com) 37783 County Road 144, Clarksburg. Open at least 11–5 daily. Though this winery is technically in the Delta, Sacramento natives like to claim it as their own. Bring some cheese and buy some Chardonnay to enjoy on the grounds of this six generations-old winery. The light-filled tasting room has great views of the ranch.

cellardoor (209-339-4394) 21 N. School Street, Lodi. Open Tuesday through Wednesday 12–6; Thursday through Saturday 12–9 and Sunday 12–5. Three Lodi winemakers teamed up to create this new tasting room: Michael-David, Jessie's Grove, and Van Ruiten. Here you can taste wine at the marble bar.

Crystal Valley Cellars (209-759-3888; cosentinowinery.com) 16750 E. CA 88, Lodi. Open 10–5 daily. The Cosentino crew is actually a Napa wine grower with a single Lodi vineyard. Here you can try world-class wines without the Napa fees.

Oak Grove Nature Center and Regional Park (209-953-8814) 4520 W. 8 Mile Road, Stockton. Plenty of trails meander through the park. Head over to the Nature Center to learn about the habitat and get information on which trails are currently open. Free.

The Delta

An outdoor enthusiast's paradise with so much to do, you'll need to spend a lifetime exploring this vast network (738,000 acres) of five major rivers, islands, and parks (and you better do it soon, since the water levels are rising quickly, making some of the islands inaccessible). Sure, this area is more popular with crawdad-fishers, fly-fishers, and Bud Light-drinking boaters, but the wealth of wildlife and birds, kayaking and native plants also attracts hikers and kayakers. The entire area is green space, but below are some spots you should not miss.

⁙ **Brannon Island State Recreation Area** (916-777-6671; parks.ca.gov) CA 160, a few miles south of Rio Vista. On weekends, head to the visitor center for a

Grands Amis Winery (209-369-6805; grandsamis.com) 115 N. School Road, Lodi. Open Friday through Sunday 1–5. This small tasting room in downtown Lodi showcases their award-winning Syrah.

Harmony Wynelands (209-369-4184; harmonywynelands.com) 9291 E. Harney Lane, Lodi. Open Monday through Saturday 11–5:30 and Sunday 12:30–5. Wine-grower Bob Hartzell plays the organ when he's not making Zin and Chardonnay.

Jessie's Grove Winery (209-368-0880; jgwinery.com) 1973 W. Turner Road, Lodi. Open daily 12–4. The oldest Lodi-area tasting room helped put the region on the map. Come out for a picnic, to hear live music throughout the summer, and to explore the museum and ranch. A visit wouldn't be complete without trying their "Earth, Zin, & Fire."

Michael David Tasting Room (209-368-7384; lodivineyards.com) 4580 W. CA 12, Lodi. Open daily from 10–5. Popular in the Valley for its 7 Deadly Zins and Earth-quake labels, this rustic tasting room/produce stand gets packed on weekends. After you sip, you might be hungry for some food—well, they have you covered for breakfast and lunch. Tasting: $5.

Van Ruiten Family Winery (209-334-5722; vrwinery.com) 340 W. CA 12, Lodi. Open daily from 11–5. With over 800 acres of vineyards, this Dutch family's farming roots go back over a half century. Try out their Zinfandel and Sauvignon Blanc.

Vino Piazza (209-727-9770; vinopiazza.com) 12470 Locke Road, Lockeford. Nine wineries and an Italian restaurant are housed in this building. For those of you who like one-stop shopping, most of these small winemakers open for tasting opportunities on the weekends.

map of the park, so you can figure out an itinerary to explore the countless islands, marshes, and waterways that make up this large recreation area. Known for its fishing, kayaking, boating, windsurfing (at Windy Cove), and swimming (Seven Mile Slough), this area has a number of great day-use areas. Bird-watchers, be on the prowl for the over 76 species known to live in the park. There are also 140 campsites located in the park (reserveamerica.com) and a number of boat launches.

Delta Meadows River Park (916-777-6671; parks.ca.gov) Near the town of Locke, drive into Railroad Slough from the River Road between Walnut Grove and Locke. Look for a small gravel road just east of the cross channel. Meadows with deer, a natural island, a slough, and plenty of birds attract serious nature lovers. Volunteers lead canoe tours on weekends, call for details.

Frank's Tract State Recreation Area (916-777-6671; parks.ca.gov) Frank's Tract is only accessible by water, and is located southeast of Brannan Island between

False River and Bethel Island. Popular with fly-fishers and bird-watchers, you can get maps of this recreation area at Brannan.

Grizzly Island Wildlife Area (707-425-3828) Take CA 12 east toward Rio Vista. Turn onto Grizzly Island Road and drive until you see the Dept. of Fish and Game office. Over 15,300 acres of marsh and wildlife habitat for exploring bring out all types of folks, from fishermen to hunters, hikers to dog trainers. This is one of the only places in Northern California to see tule elk.

Jepson Prairie Preserve (707-432-0150; solanolandtrust.org) South of Dixon. The reserve protects one of the best few remaining vernal pool habitats, as well as native bunchgrass prairie and the threatened Delta green ground beetle. Volunteers lead tours through the area.

✳ Lodging

The Valley

There are a number of motor inns in both Stockton and Modesto, and for those of you looking for something a bit more high-end, a new **Sheraton** (Sheraton.com) opened in Stockton recently.

⁒↑⁒ ⌾ The Inn at Locke House (209-368-5658; innatlockehouse.com) 7889 E. Harney Lane, Lockeford. Stay at a historic physician's farmhouse near the Lodi Wine Trail. Its five rooms take you back to a world of claw-foot tubs, four-poster beds, country breakfasts, and rocking chairs by the fireplace. A far cry from *Little House on the Prairie*, but not hard to imagine yourself as Laura Ingalls Wilder here. $$–$$$; two-night minimum on weekends.

⁒↑⁒ ⌔ ⚐ Wine and Roses Hotel and Restaurant (209-334-6988; winerose .com) 2505 W. Turner Road, Lodi. Haute elegance in Lodi? Despite the kitschy name, rooms actually deliver a taste of wine country swankiness. The 52 rooms and suites offer fluffy beds, wood beams, geometric designs on pillows, expanded continental breakfast, and modern technology. Choose from historic inn rooms (the best deal), garden rooms, spa rooms (my favorite), or signature suites with a kitchen (these have amazing weekly-stay rates that get you a free spa treatment). $$–$$$$; $20 for extra person.

The Delta

There are more RV parks, camping locations, and rental cottages than you can imagine. For more information, visit californiadelta.org.

⁒↑⁒ Delta Daze Inn (916-777-7777; deltadazeinn.com) 20 Main Street, Isleton. These 10 country-style rooms try a little harder than necessary to be cute, but in the area, this is a decent place to lay your head. Themed rooms (such as the Asian or Celebrity) offer private bathrooms, 1980s style décor, and breakfast. $–$$.

CAMPING See *Green Spaces*.

✳ Where to Eat

DINING OUT

The Valley

Ŷ ⚐ Ernie's on the Brickwalk (209-951-3311) 269 Lincoln Center, Stockton. Open for lunch and dinner daily. Since 1990, Chef Warren Ito has combined classic French dining with California ingredients, and while this is no French Laundry (or Taylor's Refresher for that matter), you might try out the lamb chops, grilled tahini prawns, or Manila clam chowder. $$–$$$.

Ⓨ ⊙ **Wine and Roses Hotel and Restaurant** (209-334-6988; winerose .com) 2505 W. Turner Road., Lodi. Open for lunch and dinner daily from 11:30 AM–1:30 PM and 5–9 PM (until 10 PM on weekends); brunch served from 10 AM–1:30 PM on weekends. Live jazz at the bar and spacious gardens add a dash of romance to this high-end restaurant. Seasonal ingredients change the menu often, but some highlights include truffled macaroni and cheese, fennel-spiced ahi, and seared Scottish salmon. Reservations recommended. Lunch and brunch $$–$$$; dinner $$$–$$$$.

The Delta

▼ **Grand Island Mansion and Spa** (916-775-1705; grandislandmansion .com) 13415 Grand Island Road, Walnut Grove. This Italian Renaissance mansion serves up a lavish Sunday brunch from 10:30–2. Champagne kicks off your soiree into decadence and afterwards you can enjoy quiche, Italian toast, and sea bass. At press time, they were vamping up to offer spa services and hotel rooms. Reservations required. $$$.

EATING OUT

The Valley

& Ⓨ **Adler Market** (209-943-1921; adlermarket.com) 151 W. Alder Street, Stockton. Open for lunch Tuesday through Friday and dinner Tuesday through Sunday. Though it gets mixed reviews, this bistro tapas bar has one of the best deals around. If you are in town on a Tuesday, head in for half price on nearly everything. Just note that their concept of tapas strays from the Spanish original version, with options like hummus, pizza, and deep-fried polenta. There is live music here on weekends. $–$$.

✐ & **Cocoro Japanese Bistro and Sushi Bar** (209-941-6053; cocoro bistro.com) 2105 Pacific Avenue,

Stockton. Open for lunch and dinner Monday through Saturday. This popular Japanese restaurant serves healthy portions of teriyaki and sushi, tempura, Korean barbeque, and more. It is very popular with locals, so get here early or prepare to wait. $–$$.

❝↑❞ **Java Aroma** (209-941-0072) 1825 Pacific Avenue, Stockton. Open at least 7 AM–midnight daily (opens at 6 AM on weekdays). Caffeinated college students hang at this restored theater and surf the net.

& ✐ Ⓨ **Rosewood Bar and Grill** (209-369-0470; rosewoodbarandgrill .com) 28 S. School Street, Lodi. Open for dinner nightly. Owned by the Wine and Roses crew, this restaurant serves similar food for less cash. At night there is live music. Reservations recommended. $$–$$$$.

✐ & Ⓨ **Valley Brew** (209-464-2739; valleybrew.com) 157 W. Adams, Stock-

---

MODESTO TACO TRUCKS

If you are looking for authentically Mexican food, at least four taco trucks compete in downtown Modesto to serve you the best taco around. Below is a list of the better ones, and where they usually park. You can pretty much fill up for 5 bucks.

Mariscos Sinaloa Crows Landing Road.

Tacos Jessica #1 on 8th between H and I Streets. (Note: There are two Jessica trucks parked in the area; try for #1, which tends to have the better tacos).

Vallarta on 14th and D.

Viva Taco on 9th.

ton. Open for lunch and dinner daily. Not sure about you, but something about heat, dust, farms, and strip malls makes me want beer and fried food. You know the deal: beer-battered fries, chicken strips, darn good IPA, and a little patio. $–$$.

✐ ৬ **Yen Du Restaurant** (209-951-3748) 702 Porter Avenue, Suite E, Stockton. Open for lunch and dinner. Stockton swarms with Asian eateries and since it's probably best not to call any one "the best," I will just say this Northern Chinese restaurant serves up nicely sized portions of good, traditional Chinese food at great prices. And it's a hole in the wall, which strangely can be a selling point for Chinese restaurants. $.

The Delta

✐ ৬ ᵞ **Isleton's Joe's Restaurant and Saloon** (916-777-6510) 212 2nd Street, Isleton. Open from 8 AM–9 PM daily. If you want to slurp some mudbugs (and by that I mean crawdads), this is the place. A crawdad cocktail is the perfect remedy for a day of playing out in the sun. $.

✐ ৬ ᵞ **Moore's Riverboat Restaurant** (916-777-4884; mooreriverboat .com) 106 W. Brannan Island Road, Isleton. Open for lunch and dinner daily. Pull up on your boat, heck, dock it there for the night, so you can get well-liquored up at the bar; eat juicy burgers and steak, or carbo-load on pasta. You can dine on the dock and hear live music on weekends too. $$–$$$.

✳ Entertainment

The Valley

ᵞ **856 Restaurant and Lounge** (209-957-7855; 856856.com) 856 Benjamin Holt Drive, Stockton. Martinis and fresh fish fill the menu at this trendy bar in downtown.

Ballet San Joaquin (209-477-4141) 7632 Larkspur Lane, Stockton. This local company performs around town year-round.

ᵞ **Envy Ultra Lounge** (209-951-5555) 600 W. Longview Avenue, Stockton. Stockton's only upscale nightclub has dancing, happy hour, and plenty of drink specials.

ᵞ **Rosewood Bar and Grill** See *Eating Out*.

ᵞ **Stockton Joe's** (209-951-2980; stocktonjoes.com) 236 Lincoln Center, Stockton. This restaurant has the best happy hour in town, and good burgers.

ᵞ **Valley Brew** See *Eating Out*.

ᵞ **Wine and Roses Restaurant** See *Dining Out*.

The Delta

ᵞ **Moore's Riverboat Restaurant** See *Eating Out*.

✳ Selective Shopping

Stockton is packed with the typical chain stores and mini-malls you'll find around the country. Check out **Lincoln Center** (lincolncenter.com) at Benjamin Holt and Center Drive for some independently owned shops like **Ocean Avenue Bed and Bath**. Or head out to **Miracle Mile** (stockton miraclemile.com), where you can walk the streets and find some unique galleries, restaurants, and shops. If you are a fan of flea markets, head to the **Stockton Open Air Flea Market** (209-465-1544) at 3550 N. Wilson Way. It is open 6–5 on weekends. In Lodi, walk along School Street in downtown to find some unique non-franchise stores.

✳ Seasonal Events

Ongoing: **First Friday Art Hop** (209-333-5511; lodiarts.org) 125 S. Hutchins Street, Lodi. From 6–8:30 on the first

Friday of the month, galleries stay open late to celebrate the arts. This is a fine time to sample wines, meet artists, and hear music throughout downtown.

Downtown Stockton Art Walk (downtownstockton.org) From March through September on the second Friday of every month from 5–8, visit a number of galleries, hear music and spoken word, and see the creative side of town.

April: **Stockton Asparagus Festival** (visitstockton.org) Thousands of people visit Stockton during this three-day festival to celebrate this vegetable. You have to head to Asparagus Alley to taste deep-fried asparagus, a Stockton tradition.

May: **Zinfest** (zinfest.com) It seems appropriate that the grape that made Lodi into a wine destination should get its own celebration. Wine makers, food vendors, and musicians set up around the lake.

June: **Concerts in the Park** (stockton gov.com) Victory Park, Pershing Avenue at Acacia, Stockton. From June to August on Wednesday nights 6–8, live music fills the park. Free.

Crawdad Festival (916-777-5880; crawdadfestival.com) For three days in mid-June, Isleton crawls with folks wanting to celebrate their famous friend, the crawdad. Here you'll find live music, 24,000 pounds of boiled crawdads, and a carnival area.

November: **Sandhill Crane Festival** (lodichamber.com) Sixty wildlife tours head out in all directions to find the Sandhill cranes that descend on the area in winter. Besides nature tours, there is plenty of music, food, and wine.

Sierra Foothills (aka Gold Country)

NORTHERN SIERRA FOOTHILLS—
SIERRAVILLE TO PLACERVILLE

SOUTHERN SIERRA FOOTHILLS—
PLYMOUTH TO MARIPOSA

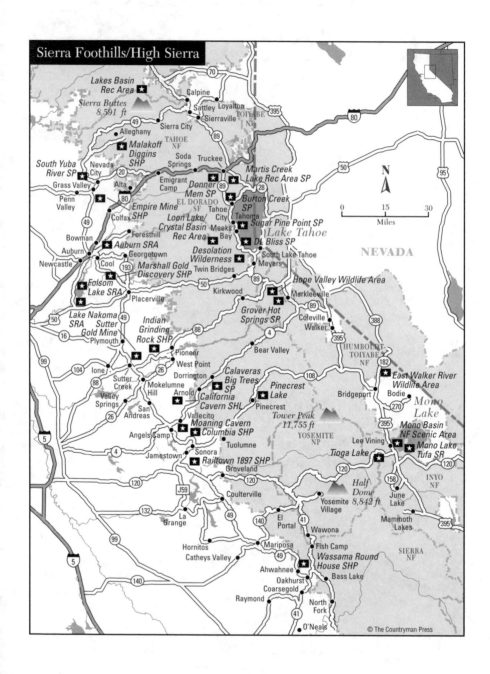

Sierra Foothills/High Sierra

Lakes Basin Rec Area
Sierra Buttes 8,591 ft
Calpine
Sattley Loyalton
Sierraville
Sierra City
Alleghany
TOIYABE NF
Malakoff Diggins SHP
TAHOE NF
South Yuba River SP
Nevada City
Soda Springs
Truckee
Grass Valley
Alta
Penn Valley
Empire Mine SHP
Colfax
Bowman
Foresthill
Auburn SRA
Auburn
Georgetown
Newcastle
Cool
Marshall Gold Discovery SHP
Folsom Lake SRA
Placerville
Lake Nakoma SRA
Sutter Gold Mine
Indian Grinding Rock SHP
Plymouth
Ione
Pioneer
West Point
Dorrington
Sutter Creek
Mokelumne Hill
Arnold
Valley Springs
San Andreas
Vallecito
Angels Camp
Sonora
Jamestown
Railtown 1897 SHP
Groveland
Coulterville
La Grange
Hornitos
Catheys Valley
Mariposa
Emigrant Camp
Donner Mem SP
Martis Creek Lake Rec Area SP
EL DORADO SF
Tahoe City
Burton Creek SP
Loon Lake/ Crystal Basin Rec Area
Tahoma
Meeks Bay
Sugar Pine Point SP
Lake Tahoe
Desolation Wilderness
DL Bliss SP
South Lake Tahoe
Twin Bridges
Meyers
Kirkwood
Grover Hot Springs SP
Markleeville
Coleville
Walker
Hope Valley Wildlife Area
NEVADA
HUMBOLDT-TOIYABE NF
Bear Valley
Calaveras Big Trees SP
California Cavern SHL
Pinecrest Lake
Pinecrest
Moaning Cavern
Columbia SHP
Tuolumne
Tower Peak 11,755 ft
YOSEMITE NP
Bridgeport
Bodie
East Walker River Wildlife Area
Mono Lake
Mono Basin NF Scenic Area
Lee Vining
Tioga Lake
Mono Lake Tufa SR
Half Dome 8,842 ft
Yosemite Village
El Portal
Wawona
June Lake
Mammoth Lakes
INYO NF
SIERRA NF
Fish Camp
Wassama Round House SHP
Ahwahnee
Oakhurst
Coarsegold
Bass Lake
Raymond
North Fork
O'Neals

© The Countryman Press

INTRODUCTION

Saying the Gold Country evokes images of dusty cowboys, eager to strike it rich, Indians fighting against the onslaught of stagecoaches, and forty-niners in gunfights. It all started when, in 1848, James Marshall hollered "Eureka!" along CA 49 in Coloma, sparking the biggest migration westward this country has ever known. Word spread and this region quickly became known as the Motherlode.

Now, the Sierra foothills are home to way more than dusty towns that look like they belong in the movies. Of course you can still pan for gold—and find some!—but a visit here offers more than getting dirty. Besides some of Northern California's best state parks, you can also find excellent swimming holes, lakes, forests, museums, historic towns with galleries, world-class wine, antique shops, and good eateries.

From the north, **Sierra County** is known as the Lost Sierra. It seems the allure of these quiet, historic towns never struck gold in the hearts of modern travelers, leaving some of the most beautiful landscape in Northern California unexplored and relatively mellow. Characterized by alpine lakes, rolling hikes, national forests, and friendly folks, people looking to strike it rich in an off-the-beaten-path locale should head up here.

Nevada County is home to two of the most interesting gold country towns: **Nevada City** and **Grass Valley**. The historic downtown of **Grass Valley** dates back to the 1850s, when the underground mines produced over 900 million dollars worth of gold. Today, visitors shake their heads with wonder when they happen upon this funky tight-knit community and its sister town, **Nevada City**. More bookstores than you can count, organic restaurants that draw urban foodies, swimming holes, great wooded areas, and plenty of Victorian houses make **Nevada City's** historic downtown a unique stop.

Placer County's city of **Auburn** is a gateway to Lake Tahoe (see *High Sierra*). Though its historic downtown is worth a look, most people merely stop for pie at the famed **Ikeda's,** and head farther east. It's a shame because there are a number of forests, state parks, and fishing holes to explore.

It was during a visit to **El Dorado County** that I realized how much this region has to offer travelers. Sure, a sojourn to **Coloma,** where gold was first discovered, is dutiful. But exploring the hills that roll off the High Sierra like wavy hair on a Barbie doll produced some of my favorite Northern California finds. You can't miss the idyllic wine town of **Fair Play**, nor can you pass up a stroll through

Old Hangtown itself, **Placerville**. Plus, this region attracts visitors from around the world to white-water raft on the American River. Being that half of the county is state parks and national forests (okay, it has a running start with South Lake Tahoe in its district—see *High Sierra*), you'll find that you won't want to leave this bountiful region.

Heading south into scenic **Amador County**, you'll come upon plenty of gold rush history, but the draw here is the wine. Piggybacking on the vino-craze erupting along these foothills, you'll find museums, galleries, antique shops, and restaurants in the gold rush towns of **Amador City, Sutter Creek, Jackson,** and **Plymouth**. Yet as a friend recently reminded me, the Wild West isn't completely gone—the bridal shop has an X-rated section in the back, hotels still have tunnels leading to bordellos, towns honor hold-up artists, and saloons qualify as tourist attractions. Of the towns in the area, if I had to pick two to explore it would be Sutter Creek and Jackson, as they offer the most for tourists: walkable historic areas, museums, mine and cave tours, historic buildings, antique shops, and an ice cream store that serves gigantic junior scoops.

Keep driving south and chances are you'll head straight to **Angels Camp**, the only incorporated city in all of **Calaveras County**. In 1864, Mark Twain wrote his first successful short story, "The Celebrated Jumping Frog of Calaveras County," and Angels Camp became linked with frogs apparently for all time. Today the town's main industry is tourism, boasting such attractions as caverns, challenging golf, a beautiful lake, historic buildings, and shopping. But travelers actually want to make a beeline for the village of **Murphys,** which is known for its charming Main Street, wineries, and art galleries.

Tuolumne County, once home to Miwok Indians, reached its heyday in 1848, when gold was plentiful. **Sonora** became quite the cosmopolitan city, attracting lawless renegades, pioneers, and families looking for more than their share. Today, the frontier town is still in its original state, but it has evolved into a home for hippies and country folks. The small gold rush communities of **Columbia** and **Jamestown** attract tourists looking to pan for gold and walk through a slightly Disney-esque collection of restored buildings from the mid-1800s. Heading up into the high country, you'll find the sweet alpine town of **Twain Harte**. On the way to Yosemite, the small settlement of **Groveland** has retained its original gold rush character.

Finally, traveling south on CA 49, you'll reach **Mariposa**, the southern gateway to Yosemite and Gold Country. This land was once part of a land grant from Mexico, and today this region allows drivers a pleasant respite from the long haul between Yosemite and Southern California.

EL DORADO COUNTY FROM ABOVE.

MUSTS FOR FIRST-TIME VISITORS

1. Meander through a North Grove trail at Big Trees State Park.
2. Hike the expansive Stanislaus National Forest.
3. See Clarissa the donkey at the end of Murphys's Main Street.
4. Kayak on an alpine lake.
5. Go to Mercer Caverns.
6. Mountain bike in Downieville.
7. Shop for books in Nevada City.
8. Pan for gold.
9. Raft the American River.
10. Visit Marshall Gold Discovery State Historic Park.

MUSTS FOR REPEAT VISITORS

1. Winery hop in Murphys or Plymouth.
2. Experience the zip lines or cave at Moaning Cavern.
3. Hike Natural Bridges.
4. Float in a hot air balloon over El Dorado County.
5. Dine at Fair Play's Boccanato.
6. Find antique bargains in Amador County.
7. Stroll through a historic gold rush town.
8. Take a dip in Sierra Hot Springs.
9. Tour a gold mine.
10. Swim in a Nevada County swimming hole.

GUIDANCE **Amador County Chamber of Commerce** (209-223-0350; amadorcountychamber.com) 571 S. CA 49, Jackson.

Calaveras County Visitor Center (209-736-0049 or 800-225-3764; gocalaveras .com) 1192 S. Main Street, Angels Camp. Quiet possibly one of the most helpful visitor bureaus in Northern California is located in a little house in Angels Camp.

California Welcome Center (530-887-2111; visitplacer.com) 13411 Lincoln Way, Auburn. Offering a bounty of information about California and Gold Country, if you are passing through Auburn, you'll want to pop in here for maps and assistance.

El Dorado County Visitor Bureau (800-457-6279; visit-eldorado.com) 542 Main Street, Placerville. A visit to this amazingly helpful visitor bureau will present you with so much information,

GOLD STILL ATTRACTS TOURISTS.

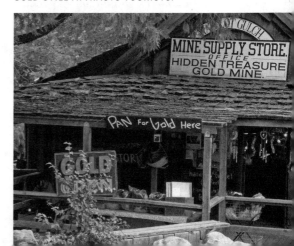

you'll have to extend your trip for weeks on end.

Grass Valley/Nevada City Chamber (530-273-4667 or 800-655-4667; grassvalley chamber.com) 248 Mill Street, Grass Valley.

Tuolomne County Visitor Bureau (209-533-4420 or 800-446-1333; portal.co .tuolumne.ca.us) 542 W. Stockton Road, Sonora.

HELPFUL WEB SITES
Sierracounty.org
Homeofyosemite.com
Historichwy49.com

GETTING THERE *By air:* The closest airport is **Sacramento International Airport** (see *Sacramento*).

By car: You need a car to get the most out of this region. If you imagine that the famed CA 49 is an artery, leading you through most Gold Country towns, you'll easily find your way. However, first you need to get to the two-lane CA 49. To reach the far northern part of the foothills (Sierra and Nevada Counties) from Sacramento area (I-5), take I-80 east. To reach Auburn and El Dorado Counties, drive east on US 50. For Calaveras County, CA 4 connects to CA 49. Heading south along CA 49, you'll pass through Tuolumne and Mariposa Counties.

By train: **Amtrak** (800-USA-RAIL; Amtrak.com) serves the region with stations in Auburn (777 Nevada Street), Grass Valley (125 E. Main Street), Mariposa (5158 CA 140) and Placerville (Mosquito Road and Clay Street).

GETTING AROUND Unless you want to bike the region, the only way to explore the area fully is with a car. Most roads are two-lane highways that slow through towns. Distances can be deceiving. Though Sacramento is 44 miles from Placerville, which is less than 15 miles to Fair Play, the entire journey can take up to two hours on the curvy roads. Plan extra travel time, especially in winter. When there is the possibility of snow, CA 49 stays open, but you will want to call the Highway Patrol (209-754-3541) to check on road closures up the mountains.

MEDICAL EMERGENCIES Dial 911.

Marshall Medical Center (530-622-1444) 1100 Marshall Way, Placerville. **Sierra Nevada Memorial Hospital** (530-274-6000) 155 Glasson Way, Grass Valley. **Sutter Amador Hospital** (209-233-7500) 810 Court Street, Jackson.

WEATHER The foothills offer scorching summers (sometimes reaching triple-digit temperatures) and moderate winters. Though it rarely (if ever) snows in these lower elevations, it can get pretty chilly. Higher elevations like Groveland and Twain Harte get plenty of snow.

NORTHERN SIERRA FOOTHILLS—
Sierraville to Placerville

☀ To See

Counties listed from north to south.

Sierra County

Downieville Museum (530-289-3423) Main Street, Downieville. Open from Memorial Day to early October from at least 11 AM–4 PM. In winter, open on weekends from 11 AM–4 PM. Tours by reservation only. After you stroll down historic Main Street's wooden boardwalks, passing the 1872 Goodyears Bar Schoolhouse and a number of historic buildings, you'll want to pop into this 1852 building. It used to be a Chinese store, and now houses a collection of goodies from Great-Granny's era, including a full-scale model town.

Kentucky Mine Museum (530-862-1310; kentuckymine.org) CA 49, Sierra City. Open in summer Thursday through Monday from 10 AM–5 PM and on weekends in October. Tours at 11 and 2 when museum is open. This historic park offers glimpses of the gold mine (1853) and stamp mill (1863) structures, as well as household goods and photos from that era. In summer, the park offers music at the mine. $1; tours $5.

Loyalton Museum and Historical Park (530-993-6754) 105 Beckwith Road, Loyalton. Open May through September on Thursday through Monday, from 11 AM–3 PM. This research center offers the most comprehensive exhibit on Sierra Valley history, including Native American, logging, mining, and agricultural exhibits.

☙ **Underground Gold Miners Museum** (530-287-3330; undergroundgold.com) 356 Main Street, Alleghany. Open Memorial Day through Labor Day weekends from 1–5. Tour the original 16-1 mine, which has been in business for over a century, by reservation only. This mine has produced over 1 million ounces of gold. Otherwise, you can view artifacts from gold rush days, including mining equipment and historic photos. Tours: $95 adults; $80 youth 13–16; $35 kids 5–12; under 4 free.

Nevada County

Empire Mine State Historic Park (530-273-8522; parks.ca.gov) 10791 E. Empire Street, Grass Valley. Head to this 800-acre state park to learn about hardrock gold mining. This mine operated for over a hundred years and produced almost 6 million ounces of gold. You can tour the area and look deep into the mines to get a feel for how far these single-minded folks would go for a hunk of gold. And check out that fancy pad where the mine owner lived. Day use: $6.

Firehouse Museum #1 (530-265-5468) 214 Main Street, Nevada City. Open in summer, daily from 11–4 and in winter Thursday through Sunday 11–4. History buffs will want to peek into this museum, which houses relics from the ill-fated Donner Party. Other gold rush-era artifacts, Indian displays, and of course, an ode to the firehouse make this Nevada City's most visited museum. Free.

Grass Valley Museum (530-273-5509) 410 S. Church Street, Grass Valley. Open Tuesday through Friday 12:30–3:30. Built in 1865, the building itself is worth a look; it was an orphanage on the grounds of Mt. St. Mary's convent. Today you can explore a gold rush-era classroom or doctor's office, and see period clothing and paintings from the Victorian era. Free.

Malakoff Diggings State Historic Park (530-265-2740) 23579 N. Bloomfield Road, Nevada City. In the center of this 3000-acre park, a historic old town has been reconstructed to show you what life was like in the 1870s. I prefer to wander through the oaks and lakes (where you can swim), and even camp at one of the sites (reserveamerica.com). Day use: $6.

✄ **Narrow Gauge Railroad Museum** (530-470-0902; ncngrrmuseum.org) 5 Kidder Court, Nevada City. Open in summer from 10 AM–4 PM on Thursday through

---

HOW TO PAN FOR GOLD

From 1848 through 1965, the top gold-producing counties of Nevada ($440,000,000), Amador ($200,000,000), Tuolumne ($190,000,000), Calaveras and Sierra ($150,000,000), Placer ($120,000,000), and El Dorado ($110,000,000) have raked in the dough. If those figures get your heart pumping, use these simple tips to try your own luck.

Since you probably don't have immediate access to gas-powered dredges, hydraulic gear (which was outlawed in 1848), or the ability to do some hard-rock mining down a vertical shaft, these techniques might help. If nothing else, they'll entertain little ones for a bit.

Start in a river, hopefully a local will offer advice on the best rivers to try your hand, but if not, head to South Yuba River in Bridgeport, along the American River in Coloma, and the Gold Bug Mine in Placerville. Have a strong 12 to 18-inch gold pan, a small shovel, bucket, spoon, pocketknife, and a little vial for your riches. You can get this equipment from the **Sierra Gold Shop** in downtown Downieville, the **Gold Bug Mine** in Placerville, and **Bekearts Gun Shop** in Coloma.

Dig where heavy gold might settle—around tree roots, upstream in gravel bars, or around old mines. Tilt, then swirl the water, sand, and gravel in your pan, slowly letting materials fall from the pan until you reach black sand, and hopefully, gold. Be patient. And don't settle for that fool's gold, which breaks at the touch.

Monday and on winter weekends from 10 AM–4 PM. Learn about transportation history in the region, from the early railroad era. View an 1875 Baldwin lumber hauler, wooden rail cars, and the restoration shop. For train tours see *Nevada County Traction Company*). Free.

North Star Mining Museum (530-273-4255) Mill Street and Allison Ranch Road, Grass Valley. Open daily from May through October 10 AM–4 PM. People intrigued with Pelton wheels (a water turbine) should visit this mining museum—they have the largest one ever built. Like most museums in the area, view artifacts from mining times. Free.

Placer County
Gold Country Museum (530-889-6500) 101 Maple Street, Auburn. Open Tuesday through Sunday 11–4. Learn about mining history the real way by viewing a miner's cabin, a saloon, a rock mine, and then panning for your own gold ($2). Free.

El Dorado County
El Dorado County Historical Museum (530-621-5865) 104 Placerville Drive, at the Fairgrounds, Placerville. Open Wednesday through Saturday 10 AM–4 PM and Sunday 12–4. Learn about the rich history of the region, from Miwok and Washoe Indian times to the discovery of gold. Here you can learn about the historic buildings in old Placerville, including the **Fountain Tallman Museum,** the oldest building in the area, which you can tour on weekends from 12–4.

✦ **Hangtown Gold Bug Mine and Park** (530-642-5207; goldbugpark.org) 2635 Gold Bug Lane, Placerville. Open daily from 10 AM–4 PM in summer and November through March weekends from 12–4 (weather permitting). Besides being a great park to explore, right in the heart of historic Placerville, you can actually get into the mine and take a self-guided audio tour of the stamp mill, hard rock mines, and Hattie Mine. The museum displays mining equipment and explains various techniques. Tours: $5 adults, $2–3 youth.

✦ **Marshall Gold Discovery State Historic Park** 530-622-3470; parks.ca.gov) CA 48 between Placerville and Auburn. This is the spot that started it all. In 1848, James Marshall shouted "Gold!" or possibly something a little more expletive, and in rode the masses. Quite possibly one of the most important historic sites in California (though folks in L.A. might say the Hollywood sign is more important), today you can visit traces of the Sutter sawmill along the banks of the South Fork of the American River, and tour the restored town of Coloma. See a replica of the original sawmill and over 20 historic buildings, including a working post office (where locals have to come to retrieve mail) and an ice cream shop. There are plenty of interpretive programs throughout the year; the most exciting (I dare say) are the Live History Days. Also, you'll want to tour the Gold Discovery Museum, which tells the story of Sutter, and Marshall's discovery. I've heard visitors talk of being disappointed that this area isn't as vibrant as other historic sites, but the draw here is not to be bombarded with hawkers and souvenir shops; come here to tour California history and go elsewhere to whoop it up. Parking: $5.

✳ To Do

BALLOONING **Sky Drifters** (888-FLY-0484; skydrifters.com) American River Valley, Coloma. Wake up before dawn and head to a pasture near the American

River. Groggily clutching your coffee and pastry from the bakery up the street, watch the balloon inflate, then climb into the basket, hold on tight, and prepare to float over the American River Valley, watching the sun rise, groggy campers wave, trees pass below, and the river pick up speed. Beautiful and just enough of an adventure to get the heart pumping, this balloon experience ends with a champagne brunch along the shores of the river. Bring earplugs. Trips are best for children over five. Plan for about three to four hours for your entire trip, though you are in the air for a little less than an hour. Reservations required. $175–225.

THE SHADOW OF A HOT AIR BALLOON LANDING NEAR THE AMERICAN RIVER.

BOATING Favorite spots to boat near Downieville are at **Jackson Meadow** and **Independence Lake**, and farther north in the **Lakes Basin,** with over 15 lakes to explore (only on small boats with no motors). Nevada County boat launches include **Rollins Lake, Scotts Flat Lake, Englebright Lake, Bullards Bar Reservoir,** and **Lake Spaulding**. In Placer County head to **Sugar Pine Reservoir, French Meadows Reservoir,** and **Kelly Lake**; and in El Dorado County's foothills boaters enjoy **Jenkinson Lake, Union Valley Reservoir,** and **Loon Lake**—though the entire county boasts 160 lakes!

Boat Rentals

Rollins Lake Resort (530-346-6166; rollinslake.net) Off I-80, 2 miles from Colfax. You can rent a variety of watercraft here.

Scotts Flat Lake Marina (530-265-0413) 23333 Scotts Flat Road, Nevada City. The marina at this popular lake rents boats.

CYCLING Mountain bikers: Go to Downieville. Trails include **North Yuba Trail, Halls Ranch, Fiddle Creek Ridge, Downie River Trail**, and the **First, Second, and Third Divide** west of Downieville on CA 49. For committed mountain bikers, the steep **Badenaugh Trail** offers views of eastern California and western Nevada in the Sierra Valley, just east of Loyalton off CA 49.

In Nevada County, mountain bikers can ride the **Osbourne** and **Union Hill Trails**, in Empire Mine State Park; explore the **South Yuba State Park**; and the massive **Tahoe National Forest** network of 600 miles of trails. In Placer County, mountain bikers use the **Burton Creek State Park** and **Foresthill Divide Loop** (off Foresthill Road, 3.5 miles east of Foresthill Bridge).

Cyclists will love to ride the rolling hills of El Dorado County. The **El Dorado Trail** (off US 50, Placerville), the **Placerville/Newtown Loop** (see beautifulvista .com for directions), the **Mosquito Road Loop** (off CA 49 in Placerville), and the historic **Coloma-Georgetown-Cool Loop** (CA 49 at Lotus Post Office—see

beautifulvista.com for specific directions), which I like, just to get to ride through
the town of Cool.

Bike Rentals and Tours
Auburn Bike Works (530-885-3861; auburnbikeworks.com) 350 Grass Valley
Highway, Auburn. Rentals and plenty of information about your biking needs, the
Byrd family opened this store in 1972, and though there are new owners, the shop
is still going strong.

Placerville Bike Shop (530-622-3088) 1307 Broadway, Placerville. The best
resource in the northern Sierra foothills for trail information and bike routes.

Tour of Nevada City Bicycle Shop (530-265-2187; tourofnevadacity.com) 457
Sacramento, Nevada City. They rent mountain bikes for $40 a day. Their Web site
also lists a number of great rides in this area and the West.

Yuba Expeditions (530-289-3010; yubaexpeditions.com) 208 Main Street, Downieville. Closed Tuesday through Wednesday. Besides being a great resource for
trail maps, this group offers bike rentals and shuttles to a number of local trails.

FARM TOURS **Apple Hill** (applehill.com) Over 50 apple ranches, each known
for something different. Head to **Honey Bear Ranch** (2826 Barkley Road,
Camino) for organic apples and a great lunch, **Rainbow Orchards** (2569 Larsen
Drive, Camping) for apple donuts, and to **High Hill** (2901 High Hill Road, Placerville) for fudge, apple wine, and BBQ chicken.

Gold Hill Olive Oil Co (530-621-7073; goldhilloliveoilco.com) 5601 Gold Hill
Road, Placerville. Open Friday through Sunday 10 AM–4 PM. Here you can taste
what olive oil is supposed to taste like.

Lotus Bonsai Nursery and Gardens
(530-633-9681; lotusbonsai.com) 1435
Lower Lake Drive, Placerville. Open
by appointment only. A walk through
the gardens of these bonsai masters
will offer a peace like nowhere else in
the region. Plus, you'll learn about this
ancient art. They also offer classes.
Free.

HOW CAN YOU NOT FALL IN LOVE WITH
THESE ALPACAS?

✐ **Retiredice Alpacas** (530-620-1415;
retiredicealpacas.com) 6899 Mt.
Aukum Road, Fair Play. Open on
weekends from 10 AM–5 PM. Reader
beware, a trip here will make you fall
in love with these Peruvian relatives of
the camel. Free.

FARMERS' MARKETS

Nevada County
Mill Street Farmers' Market (530-
277-5877) Mill Street, downtown
Grass Valley. Thursday evenings from

6–9, come hear live music, shop for produce, baked goods, plants, and arts and crafts.

Nevada City Farmers' Market (530-277-5877) Union Street, downtown Nevada City. Saturday 8–12 from late June to late October.

Nevada County Fairgrounds Farmers' Market (530-277-5877) 11228 McCourtney Road, Grass Valley. Saturday from 8–noon from May to late September.

El Dorado County

Placerville Saturday Farmers' Market Main Street and Cedar Ravine, Ivy House parking lot. On May through October, Saturdays from 8–12.

Placerville Wednesday Farmers' Market Bell Tower, Main Street, Placerville. Wednesdays from 5–dusk, June through October.

FISHING Fly-fishers travel from around the country for trout. Popular places to fish include Sierra County's **Independence Lake**, the **Lakes Basin**, and **Smithneck Creek** in the Sierra Valley (best for German brown trout); Nevada County's **Rollins Lake, Scotts Flat Lake, Grouse Lakes**, and the **South Fork Yuba River**; **Sugar Pine Lake** in Placer County; and in El Dorado County, **Jenkinson Lake, Finnon Reservoir, Webber Reservoir**, and **Cameron Park Lake**.

GOLF **Apple Mountain Golf Resort** (530-647-4700; applemountaingolfresort .com) 3455 Carson Road, Camino. Lovely views of snow-capped mountains make these 18 holes a popular choice for golfers. $49–69.

Dark Horse Golf Club (530-269-7900; darkhorsegolf.com) 113450 Combie Road, Auburn. This is a top-choice course, surrounded by wetlands and oaks. $45–79.

RAFTING AND KAYAKING Whitewater rafting draws thousands to this region. Springtime in Sierra County, when the snowmelt runs into the **Yuba River**, Class IV and V rapids make for an adventure unlike any other. El Dorado County's **South Fork of the American River** (Class III) attracts adventurers of all ages, who can rely on rapids flowing through October. Class III Rating is the highest that First-Time Rafters can go on, and doesn't require previous experience or even the ability to swim. In other words, while getting the heart pumping, it is fairly safe for Little Zach and Grandpa. If that is too much excitement, head to the **Lakes Basin** in Sierra County for mellow paddling. Many outfitters combine a white-water trip with camping and meals.

WHY DOES THE WATER FLOW SO WELL IN THE AMERICAN RIVER? With so many outfitters taking folks out on the American River, you'd wonder if the water ever stops flowing. Well, it used to, until the good folks at the SMUD (Sacramento Municipal Utility District) and PG&E (Pacific Gas & Electric) began a water release program from their main dams holding the water above the river. Now river-rafting guides know when and how much water will flow each day and at what times, making this river the only Class III river that flows year-round.

HEAPS OF PEOPLE RAFT THE AMERICAN RIVER IN SUMMER.

Outfitters and Guides

American Whitewater Expeditions (800-825-3205; americawhitewater.com) To raft the South Fork of the American River, people come to Placerville from around the world. This outfit knows how to take care of everyone from kamikazes wanting to raft Tunnel Chute—the 80-foot ravine blasted by coal miners in the 1850s—to families wanting to take gung-ho Granny down Chili Bar's Class III rapids. $82–149 adults; $72–139 kids.

Ø **Gold Rush Whitewater Adventures** (800-900-7238; goldrushriver.com) 6260 CA 49, Lotus. Want to raft the South Fork of the American River? Tim and his crew are your guys. They offer half- and two-day trips on Class III-IV rapids, run by safe, trained guides. Beginners should opt for the half trip down Chili Bar Run, which is five hours. More advanced riders will love the full river trips (21 miles), which can include meals and camping in their fine facilities along the river. $70–299.

Tributary Whitewater Tours (530-346-6812; whitewatertours.com) See *North High Sierra*.

Wolf Creek Expeditions (530-477-2722; wolfcreekwilderness.com) 595 E. Main Street, Grass Valley. They offer classes, tours, rentals, plus run a great store.

SPAS Sierra Hot Springs (530-994-3773; sierrahotsprings.com) 521 Campbell Hot Springs Road, Sierraville. Hike to a private pool beneath a canopy of oaks; enter a dome pool, built of wood; or meditate in the private Phoenix pools. There are 700 acres of hiking and biking trails nestled within the Tahoe National Forest, and accommodations in a lodge or lovely allergen-free hotel. See *Lodging* for more information. Note that most people are nude: if this creeps you out, try your luck at Calistoga Hot Springs (see *Napa*) instead. To enter, you need to purchase a membership good for a month ($5) and then fork over another $15–20 to soak.

TRAIN RIDES *Ø* **Nevada County Traction Co** (530-265-0896) 420 Railroad Avenue, Nevada City. Take a 3-mile train ride up History Hill and through the Chinese Cemetery, pines, cedars, and gardens. The entire jaunt lasts 90 minutes. $12 adults and $7 for kids 2–12.

Nevada and Sierra County

An unusually high number of wine varieties flourish in the northern Sierra foothills. You'll find everything from Chardonnay, Merlot, and Zinfandel to Cabernet Franc, Barbera, and Tempranillo. For more comprehensive information (including maps) about Nevada County's wine region visit northernsierrawine country.com.

Avanguardia Winery (530-274-9482; avanguardiawines.com) 13028 Jones Bar Road, Nevada City. Open for tasting April through December weekends 12–4, or by appointment. Taste wines made of hybrid grapes from California, Russia, France, and Italy. Free.

Coufos Cellars (530-274-2923) 10065 Rough and Ready Road, Rough and Ready. Open for tasting by appointment. If nothing else, you need to stop by this dairy farm/vineyard to say you've been to the town of Rough and Ready. Organic wines like Syrah make the trip worth it.

Double Oak Vineyards and Winery (530-292-3235; doubleoakwinery.com) 14510 Blind Shady Road, Nevada City. Open Saturday from 11–5 and by appointment. Since 1982, these growers have been perfecting their Zinfandel, Merlot, and Chardonnay. Grab a bottle and picnic high on the foothills with views galore.

Nevada City Winery (530-265-9463; ncwinery.com) 321 Spring Street, Nevada City. Come taste Tempranillo and Chardonnay in a woodsy tasting-room and then shop in their sweet gift store.

Renaissance Vineyard and Winery (800-655-3277; renaissancewinery.com) 12585 Rices Crossing Road, Oregon House. Organic grapes planted between 1975 through 1982 yield a very small crop each year, but the creators of the Bordeaux and Rhone varietals only release the best of them in their fine wines. $10–25.

El Dorado County

Zinfandel put the El Dorado wine country on the national map. Below is just a sampling of the wonderful wineries in the region; for more detailed lists visit fair playwine.com or eldoradowines.org.

THE VIEW FROM GOLD HILL VINEYARD.

Boeger Winery (530-622-8094; boegerwinery.com) 1709 Carson Road, Placerville. Open daily from 10 AM–5 PM. Taste Merlot, Barbera, and Zinfandel in a 19th-century Swiss-Italian stone wine cellar.

Chateau Rodin Winery (530-622-6839) 4771 Green Hills Road, Placerville. Open 11–5 Wednesday through Sunday. Chardonnay, Zinfandel, and Cabs are the way to go. Grab a bottle and enjoy a picnic with views of the foothills.

David Girard Vineyards (530-295-1833; davidgirardvineyards.com) 741 Cold Springs Road, Placerville. Open weekends from 11–5. One of the finest wineries in the region, you can taste Rhone varietals in an elegant setting.

Fitzpatrick Winery and Lodge (530-620-3248; fitzpatrickwinery.com) 7740 Fair Play Road, Fair Play. Open Friday through Monday from 11–5. Irish owners doused the tasting room with splashes of green, but it doesn't mask the friendliness of the Fitzpatricks, nor the quality of the organic wine. The log lodge, lovely gardens, expansive views, and Friday night pizza—baked in the wood oven on the deck—all add to the ambiance. You can also stay here. See *Lodging*.

Gold Hill Vineyard (530-626-6522; goldhillvineyard.com) 5660 Vineyard Lane, Placerville. Open Thursday through Sunday 10 AM–5 PM. Though running a winery and a brewery might sound too ambitious to take seriously, this is a great stop for couples that can't agree on what they want to drink. Grab a beer or Chardonnay and sit on the deck staring at the vineyards below.

Madrona Vineyards (530-644-5948; madronavineyards.com) High Hill Ranch, Apple Hill. Open 11–5 daily. These guys make wonderful wine and are eco-friendly! They're powered by solar energy, wastewater is recycled, cork is recycled, and the grape stems are used to prevent erosion in the vineyard.

WINTER SPORTS Skiers and boarders generally head up to the Tahoe area—which you should—but cross-country skiers and snowshoers will find plenty of space in Sierra County, like **Henness Pass Road, the Yuba Pass Area, Upper Sardine Lake, Little Truckee Summit Winter trails**, and the **Treasure Mountain Loop**.

For snowmobile trails, you first need to acquire a permit at sporting goods shops (916-324-1222). Then you can head to Nevada County to explore the **China Wall Snowmobile Trailhead** (14 miles east of Foresthill).

For a real treat, head out on a custom snowshoe tour with **Cathyworks** (cathy works.com) for $45 per person in the upper Nevada County region.

✳ Green Spaces

A little redundant, since the entire area is basically one big green space, here are some special parks, lakes, and rivers to explore. In El Dorado County the **American River Trail Conservancy** (arconservancy.org; 348 CA 49, Coloma) runs a wonderful nature center, which offers a wealth of information about local flora and fauna, wildlife and trails.

NATIONAL FORESTS **El Dorado National Forest** (530-644-6048; fs.fed.us) 100 Forni Road, Placerville. The El Dorado Forest ranges in elevation from 100 to 10,000 feet above sea level, making it a diverse place for outdoor fanatics. Spread across 780,000 acres, with 346 miles of trails, 611 miles of fishable streams and rivers, 611 lakes and reservoirs, and two major wilderness areas—the Mokelumne and Desolation (See *North High Sierra*)—finding places to explore is not the issue; making time to see it all might be, though. Hikers around Placerville (530-644-2324; Ranger Station: 4260 8 Mile Road, Placerville) explore the **Buck Pasture, Caples Creek, Cedar Park, Cody Lake, Fleming Meadow Lovers Leap, Pyramid Creek,** and **Sayles Canyon** trails through dense forests. Near Georgetown (530-333-4312; Ranger Station: 7600 Wentworth Springs Road, Georgetown) hike the **Bald Mountain Canyon, Bear Flat Oak, Hell Hole, Hunter, Kelliher, Lawyer, Mar Det, Nevada Point**, and **Sugarloaf trails**—contact the ranger station for maps. Campers find that the **Big Meadows, Dru Barner Park, Hell Hole,** and **Stumpy Meadows** in the Georgetown area make for good central spots to set up shop. Near Placerville, camp at **China Flat, Indian Springs,** or **Sand Flat**. Camping: $8–20.

Tahoe National Forest (530-885-5821 or 530-256-4531; fs.fed.us) Ranger Station, 631 Coyote Street, Nevada City. This forest makes up the majority of parkland in the region, stretching from Foresthill to Sierraville, and offering an insane amount of recreational activities. Besides being home to the **Yuba** and **American Rivers,** a Mecca for kayakers and rafters (see *To Do*), **The Lakes Basin, Bullards Bar, Meadow Lake,** and more, hikers, bikers, swimmers, boaters, anglers, and campers will rejoice in the vast amount of space to explore. Most camping areas are open in summer only and require reservations in advance (recreation.gov). In Sierra County, for trail maps and camping reservations, contact the **North Yuba River Ranger Station** (530-288-3231 or 478-6253) Ranger Station, 15924 CA 49, Camptonville. Hikers, bikers, bird-watchers, and campers take advantage of the **Indian Valley area** (recreation.gov) just north of CA 49 near the North Yuba River; from here you can access the six camping areas ($22–24). Mountain bikers will want to pitch a tent at the **Union Flat campground** ($20) to be steps from **Downie River, Empire Creek,** and **Lavezzola** Trails. Nevada County visitors, contact the **Yuba River South District** (530-265-4531) Ranger Station, 631 Coyote Street, Nevada City. Hikers, don't miss the accessible **Independence** trail, the **Grouse Lakes Area** (from CA 20, take Bowman Lake Road to Grouse Ridge Road), the **Pioneer National Recreation** Trail (25 miles each way, from White Cloud campground), and the **Glacier Lake Trail** (from CA 20, take Bowman Lake Road to Grouse Ridge Road). Campers head to **White Cloud** ($20) and **Grouse Ridge** (free) until it snows. Finally, in the south, the **Western States Trail** (a 100-mile route between Squaw Valley and Auburn) is accessible from Sugar Pine and the North Fork of the American River.

STATE PARKS, GARDENS, AND RECREATION AREAS **Auburn State Recreation Area** (530-885-4527 or for Whitewater Recreation call 530-823-4162; parks.ca.gov) Off I-80, from Auburn to Colfax. The main access is from Auburn, on either CA 49 or the Auburn-Foresthill Road. There are 100 miles of trails, including parts of the Western States Trail (see *Tahoe National Forest*) and **Pleasant Avenue** in Auburn. Mountain bikers love the **Confluence** trail. Boaters, anglers, and swimmers head to **Lake Clementine** (Auburn-Foresthill Road, 2 miles from Auburn). Popular in summer, campsites are first-come, first-served, so get here early to pitch a tent at the lovely **Mineral Bar** (off Iowa Hill Road). You can reserve a site (800-444-7275) for the boat-in Lake Clementine. Campsites: $15–25.

Crystal Basin Recreation Area (877-444-6777) Off US 50, take Ice House Road north. The 85,000-acres of fir and pine forests, lakes, reservoirs, granite peaks, and recreational activities draw adventurers year-round. Anglers cast for kokanee salmon, bass, and rainbow trout at the **Union Valley Reservoir** and **Loon Lake**. The **Gerle Creek Summer Harvest Trail** is wheelchair accessible, and offers details of how the Maidu, Washoe, and Miwok Indians gathered food. Cross-country skiers head to Loon Lake in winter. Finally, there are 700 developed campsites, including **the Ice House, Sunset,** and **Wench Creek Campgrounds** near Union Valley Reservoir, the accessible **Gerle Creek,** and the **Loon Lake** Campgrounds ($10–20). For people who just need a bed, the **Van Vleck Bunkhouse**, **Robbs Hut,** or **Loon Lake Chalet** are available by reservation.

Empire Mine State Park See *To See.*

Gold Bug Mine Park See *To See.*

Lakes Basin Recreation Area (530-836-2575 or 877-444-6777; reserveusa.com or fs.fed.us) Off CA 49, east of Sierra City. These 15 lakes offer more than a weekend's share of exploration. Hikers head to the **Gray Eagle Creek** and **Lily Lakes** trails off Gold Lake Highway, **Bear Lakes Loop** from the Lakes Basin campground, and **the Pacific Crest**. Anglers favor **Gold Lake**; though fly-fishers can try their skills in any of the 15 lakes. Campers head to the **Lakes Basin Campground** ($16–32) south of Graeagle off County Road 519. For more information see *Shasta Cascade—Plumas National Forest.*

Malakoff Diggins State Park See *To See.*

Marshall Gold Discovery State Park See *To See.*

Sierra Buttes Recreation Area See *Shasta Cascade.*

Sly Park Recreation Area (530-644-2545 or 530-644-2792; eid.org) 4771 Sly Park Road, Pollock Pines. Surrounded by ponderosa pines, the large **Jenkinson Lake** draws anglers on the prowl for varieties of trout, bass, and bluegill. Boaters, kayakers, and water-skiers congregate here (you can rent gear in summer at the Stonebraker boat launch). People love to hike around the 8.5 miles of shoreline, swim, and camp at one of the 164 hosted sites at **Pinecone, Jenkinson,** or **Chimney Camp**. Day use: $6; camping: $10–20.

&. **South Yuba River State Park** (530-432-2546; parks.ca.gov) 175660 Pleasant Valley Road, Penn Valley. To access the park from CA 49, take Edwards Crossing or Purdon Crossing. This 20-mile stretch of the river extends from Malakoff Diggins State Park to Bridgeport and offers some of the best rafting, kayaking, and fishing around. You'll also find the longest single-span covered bridge in the world and the first wheelchair-accessible trail in the country, the **Independence Trail.** There are loads of swimming holes around the park as well, check with the local ranger station for water levels. Gold panning is a popular activity: Make sure to bring your gear. Day use: $6.

LAKES AND RESERVOIRS **Bullards Bar** See Tahoe National Forest.

Englebright Lake (530-432-6427; englebrightlake.com) Near Smartville, on CA 20, 15 miles west of Grass Valley. This reservoir is popular with house-boaters and water sports lovers. There are 100 developed boat-in campsites (first-come, first-served) at $4–10, boat rentals, picnic areas, and a café. Fish for trout, catfish, bluegill, bass, and kokanee. Day use: $4.

Jenkinson Lake See **Sly Park Recreation Area**.

Lakes Basin National Recreation Area See *State Parks, Gardens, and Recreation Areas.*

Lake Spaulding (530-527-0354) Off CA 20, past Bowman Lake Road. This alpine lake surrounded by pines, sits in a granite bowl. Its 25 campsites, picnic areas, fishing, swimming, boating, and hiking make this a wonderful place to spend a day or a week.

Loon Lake See Crystal Basin Recreation Area.

Packer Lake Packer Lake Road, Sierra City. Fish for trout here at this lovely alpine lake. **Packer Lake Lodge** (530-862-1221) offers six cabins in summer.

Rollins Lake Off CA 174, between Grass Valley and Colfax. The 900 acres of lake and 26 miles of shoreline make this a favorite with campers, anglers, boaters, and water sports enthusiasts. There are four family-owned campgrounds at the lake, including the **Rollins Lake Resort Campground** (530-272-6100), **Orchard Springs Campground** (530-346-2212; osresort.com), **Peninsula Campground** (530-477-9413 penresort.com), and the **Long Ravine Campground** (530-346-6166; longravinecampground.com). Peninsula camp rents boats. To swim, head to Greenhorn Camp/Rollins Lake Resort.

Salmon Lake Take Salmon Lake Road, Sierra City. This lovely alpine lake is stocked with rainbow trout. Swimming is great in summer and boating is ideal. **Salmon Lake Lodge** rents a few tent cabins here as well (salmonlake.net).

Sardine Lake Sardine Lake Road, Sierra City. Though you can't swim here, fishing conditions are perfect in summer. The **Sardine Lake Resort** here has some of the better food in the area (530-862-1196).

Scotts Flat Lake (530-265-5302 or 530-265-0413) East of Nevada City off CA 20. The 7.5 miles of shoreline, dotted with pines, is a popular spot with fishermen, boaters, and families. You can rent watercraft at the marina or camp. Day use: $6.25; Camping: $19–30.

✳ Lodging

Sierra County

⚓ 🐾 **Carriage House Inn** (530-289-3573 or 800-296-2289; downieville carriagehouse.com) 110 Commercial Street, Downieville. Situated on the Downie River, this nine-room inn attracts families and mountain bikers wanting to explore the small town of Downieville. Get a room facing the river rather than CA 49. Rooms include continental breakfast, some have a balcony and bike storage. $–$$.

⚓ **Helms St. Charles Inn** (530-289-0910; goodyearsbar.com) 459 Mountain House Road, Goodyears Bar. Once a stagecoach stop, this four-room B&B offers the same country charm as it had over a century ago. Picnic basket breakfasts delivered to your door so you can eat with a river view; country style, complete with bed runners, floral wallpaper, and motifs throughout. $; reservations required in winter.

High Country Inn (530-862-1530 or 800-862-1530; hicountryinn.com) CA 49 and Gold Lake Road, Sierra City. People looking to spend quiet time in the Lakes Basin will enjoy this four-room riverside B&B with views of the Sierra Buttes. Decorated in antiques that complement the alpine setting, this is the spot to get away from people and spend the day exploring the Yuba River. Breakfast included. $$.

⚓ ♿ **Sierra Hot Springs/Globe Hotel** (530-994-3773; sierrahotsprings .com) 521 Campbell Hot Springs Road, Sierraville. People come for the hot springs pools, the serenity, and the ability to walk in nature in the buff. Historic lodge rooms offer shared baths or dorm beds, with cats roaming the building, while the Sierraville Globe Hotel (a mile away in town) offers more traditional rooms, without the furry friends. This is a crunchy place, with communal kitchens, organic restaurant, massage rooms, and people talking about yoga retreats. You can also camp here. $ (includes your bath access, but not the $5–20 membership fee); children half price.

Sierra Shangri La See *Vacation Rentals.*

Nevada County

¶**Emma Nevada House** (530-265-4415 or 800-916-3662; emmanevada house.com) 528 E. Broad Street, Nevada City. A renovated farmhouse surrounded by gardens, people from around the world sitting down to an elaborate gourmet breakfast, fireplaces, and Jacuzzi tubs make this six-room B&B a prime choice. After a day of activity, retreat to a handsomely decorated room awash in deep earth tones and textured fabrics. $$–$$$; children over 12 welcome.

✎ & ¶ ⊙ **The Holbrook Hotel** (530-273-1353 or 800-933-7077; holbrooke.com) 212 W. Main Street, Grass Valley. Besides hosting Mark Twain, Grover Cleveland, and Benjamin Harrison, this historic mainstay in the Grass Valley community offers 28 of the finest rooms in the foothills. Victorian-era antiques, fireplaces, fluffy brass beds, and claw-foot tubs combine with 21st-century amenities to offer you a classy place to sleep. The restaurant, saloon, and continental breakfast don't hurt either. $–$$$.

✎ & **National Hotel** (530-265-4551; thenationalhotel.com) 211 Broad Street, Nevada City. For over 130 years this historic hotel has offered a bed for weary travelers. Today you won't get the luxury you might find in nearby B&Bs, but antique-decorated

rooms and the central location might be all you need. All 42 rooms and suites have access to the restaurant and pool. $–$$.

Rose Mountain Manor (530-346-1083; rosemountainmanor.com) 233 Plutes Way, Colfax. A little girl's dollhouse all grown up, this B&B's three rooms look like pillowy clouds. Centerpieces for the rooms, the beds invite you to cuddle up, while the pines outside fill the air with fragrance, and the owners prepare a hearty breakfast. $–$$.

✎ ☻ **Swan Levine House** (530-272-1873; swanlevinehouse.com) 328 South Church Street, Grass Valley. If staying in an old hospital doesn't creep you out, you are in for a treat! Owners Howard and Margaret have decorated this hospital like an art-gallery tribute to printmaking and salvaged antiques. After learning about their art, you can head into the studio to create your own. Antiques, poster beds, plush comforters, breakfast, and friendly service make this a great choice for families and couples looking for something different. $–$$.

El Dorado County

✎ ☻ **7 Up Bar Guest Ranch** (530-620-5450 or 800-717-5450; 7upranch .com) 8060 Fair Play Road, Fair Play. Drive a mile down a gravel driveway past vineyards, wild turkeys, and oaks to your country log cabin (there are six). Before slipping off into dreamland in one of the comfy feather beds, sit on the deck, watching the sunset as the zillions of animals sing themselves to sleep. Organic breakfast in the main ranch house is a treat, as are wandering the trails and lazing on the hammock. No TVs or phones. $$.

✎ ⊙ **Barkley Historic Homestead** (530-620-6793; barkleyhomestead .com) 8320 Stoney Creek Road, Fair Play. Located on 67 acres of vineyards, the 1915 main house offers country-style rooms. Think Granny's attic rather than rustic, with the five rooms decorated like a hunting lodge or Fourth of July in a small town. Amenities: hiking trails, fishing pond, vineyards and tasting room, breakfast. $–$$.

Bella Vista B&B (530-622-3456; bellavistainc.net) 581 Cold Springs Road, Placerville. Located atop a hill between Placerville and Coloma, Bella Vista delivers on luxury. More a Mediterranean villa than Gold Country antique, the three suites have ceilings that make Wilt Chamberlain seem short, antique oil paintings, Persian rugs, pedestal sinks, and views galore. Make sure to check out the bed in the Bella Vista Suite. Amenities: gardens with waterfalls, breakfast, afternoon snacks, kitchenette and fireplace in some rooms, private patio. $$–$$$.

♂ ❀ **Coloma Country Inn** (530-622-6919; colomacountryinn.com) 345 High Street, Coloma. Martha Stewart could learn a thing or two from Marjorie Sanborn. Her interior design skills surpass every eastern California B&B. Highlights include the sheet music-wallpapered bathroom, the trellised arches leading to fragrant gardens, the pond, the deer grazing the

COLOMA COUNTY INN.

meadow, the handmade wooden swing, and the salvaged farm antiques—perfectly placed to fit the six rooms and suites in ways you'd never imagine. Breakfast by the pond will make you need to return, even if you aren't into the history of Coloma. $$–$$$.

Fitzpatrick Winery and Lodge (530-620-3248; fitzpatrickwinery.com) 7740 Fair Play Road, Fair Play. Part hunters' cabin, part Irish retreat, this winery and lodge offers guests a chance to explore the wonderful Fair Play appellation, and then come home to a casual environment where you'll pop open a bottle of wine and chill on the deck for hours. The five rooms and suites offer full breakfast, complimentary wine tasting, and a pool. $–$$.

♂ ᵞ **Historic Cary House Hotel** (530-622-4271; caryhouse.com) 300 Main Street, Placerville. Billing itself the "jewel of Placerville" and offering affordable luxury, this historic inn has been a fixture since 1857. Though the original structure was demolished, the new hotel attempts to recreate the original vibe with period antiques. All 38 rooms and suites include continental breakfast. $$.

VACATION RENTALS AND COTTAGES

Sierra County

♂ ❀ **Canyon Ranch Resort** (530-994-1033; canyonranchsierraville.com) 622 Old Truckee Road, Sierraville. Rustic and simple cabins situated on a creek make this an ideal place to escape the crowds. They call themselves the Lost Sierra in these parts, because this area is rich with solitude and beauty. Cabins offer basic kitchens and are close to Sierraville. $.

♂ ❀ **Lure Resort** (530-289-3465; lureresort.com) CA 49, 1 mile east of Downieville. Fly-fishers usually inhabit these camping cottages and house-

THE PIZZA OVEN AND VIEW FROM FITZ-PATRICK WINERY AND LODGE.

keeping cabins, but even if you don't cast your line, you should know about this woodsy retreat. While families prefer the two-bedroom Mallard's Place, couples and smaller groups like the cottages and cabins. The Yuba River flows right outside your door, and you are close enough to town to make a quick beer run, but still far enough to feel isolated. $$–$$$.

✔ **Sierra Shangri La** (530-289-3455; sierrashangrila.com) 12 Jim Crow Canyon, Downieville. This secret Sierra spot sells out so fast that return visitors book their favorites up to a year in advance. Perched above the riverbank, these stone cottages beg you to scramble eggs, bake cookies, and blend margaritas while you chill on the deck and play Risk. Bed-and-breakfast rooms are easier to get and come with a deluxe continental breakfast. Cabins are the way to go, however. $–$$$; a week; minimum night stay in summer.

El Dorado County
American River Resort Campgrounds (530-622-6700; americanriverresort.com) 6019 New River Road, Coloma. Here you'll find 65 tent

sites, 25 RV sites, a pool, a fishing pond, and great views of people careening down the American River. They also have nice riverside cottages, with full kitchens and decks just screaming for a game of poker and some beer. Camping: $20–35; Cabin: $$–$$$ (two-night minimum on weekends).

Campgrounds
There are so many campsites in the Sierra Nevada Mountains and foothills. National Forest Service (877-444-6777; reserveusa.com) sites generally are on a first-come, first-served basis, though there are some you can reserve in advance. These generally have basic services like pit toilets and fire rings. State park campgrounds (800-444-7275; reserveamerica.com) like Empire Mine and South Yuba River must be reserved in advance (do it early, they sell out quickly). For backcountry camping, you'll need a free permit, so contact the Forest Service near the area you wish to camp. I have listed campgrounds under the *Green Spaces* section.

✳ Where to Eat
DINING OUT

Nevada County
& ⌚ **Citronee Bistro and Wine Bar** (530-265-5697; citroneebistro.com) 320 Broad Street, Nevada City. Open for dinner Wednesday through Monday. Expect to pay Bay Area prices for farm-fresh cuisine in this country-French bistro. Chef Robert Perez and his wife, Marianna, offer casual café dining, or fine dining by a fireplace in the exposed brick-walled dining room. Choose between the "grazing" menu, with specialties being hazelnut-crusted goat cheese, Coq au Vin, braised rabbit, or pork bratwurst in a pilsner juice. Reservations recommended. $$–$$$.

🍷 ♿ **New Moon Café** (530-265-6399; thenewmooncafe.com) 203 York Street, Nevada City. Open for lunch Tuesday through Friday and dinner Tuesday through Sunday. Since 1997, this local favorite has been serving fine, organic, seasonal menus in a candlelit-dining room on tables covered first in white cloth, then with tan butcher paper, giving a hint at the vibe here: casual on the outside, yet elegant on the inside. Favorites include the ravioli or fish specials, and the flatiron. Save room for desserts, which change nightly, but if there is something with lemon, order it. Reservations recommended for dinner. $$–$$$.

♿ 🍷 ⌨ **Stonehouse Restaurant** (530-265-5050; stonehouse1857.com) 107 Sacramento Street, Nevada City. Open for lunch and dinner daily, and brunch on weekends. Dine literally in a stone house, though interiors are nothing like what you'd expect from the exteriors. Here you'll find both rustic and modern touches like blond hardwood floors, spacious high ceilings, tiered floors, and artsy wood chairs, plus entrees like the lamb skewer, filet mignon, and a trout with pecan butter. $$–$$$.

Placer and El Dorado Counties

🍷 ♿ 🍷 **Bocconato** (530-620-2493) 7915 Fair Play Road, Fair Play. Open Thursday and Monday 5–9, Friday through Sunday 11–9. Bocconato means big mouthful in Italian, and you will want to take more than your share of big mouthfuls at this surprisingly wonderful restaurant. Interiors evoke a wine-country feel: casual, with large, colorful paintings and a decent-sized patio area. Anything the waiter recommends, eat it. Food is crafted by an artist who picks herbs from the garden—after you order—to use in your meal. The freshly made pasta special changes daily, and appetizers like the

sformati and the *farinata* are winners. Save room for tiramisu. $$–$$$.

♿ **Café Mahjaic** (530-622-9587; cafemahjaic.com) 1006 Lotus Road, Lotus. Open Tuesday through Saturday for dinner. Low lighting gives this brick-walled, white-tablecloth bistro an intimacy not found in restaurants around here. Menus change with the season. You'll get to choose between three to six entrée specials nightly, consisting of naturally raised meats, wild-caught seafood, and organic produce. Examples of menu items include a Himalayan vegetarian dish, chocolate chipotle prawns (this item put them on the dining map), and chicken Grandmere. Reservations recommended. $$–$$$.

♿ 🍷 **Latitudes** (530-885-6500) 130 Maple Street, Auburn. Open for lunch and dinner Wednesday through Sunday, and Sunday brunch. Multicultural cuisine served in a historic building in downtown Auburn satisfies everyone, from tofu lovers to burger eaters. Eat Indian curried tofu, German cider chicken or teriyaki tempeh. $$–$$$.

🍷 ⌨ **Sequoia** (530-622-5222; sequoiaplacerville.com) 643 Bee Street, Placerville. Open 9–9 Sunday, 5–9 Tuesday through Thursday and 11–10 Friday and Saturday; closed Monday. Built in 1853, this was the home to Judge Bennett, who was the reason Placerville got its nickname of Old Hangtown; then it housed Colonel Bee, who was responsible for creating the Pony Express (among other endeavors). Downstairs in the wine cellar, there is rumored to be a tunnel that used to allow "working" gals to get into Placerville without being seen. Plus, there are a number of ghosts in the building. All that should pique your interest enough to head here for a classically decadent meal of grilled fish, steak, or cassoulet. Like most suited-waiter-restaurants, desserts are the highlight. Go big. You're in a mansion. Reservations recommended. $$–$$$.

EATING OUT

Sierra County

☙ ♿ **Bassett's Station** (530-862-1297; bassets-station.com) CA 49 and Gold Lake Road, Sierraville. Open for breakfast, lunch, and dinner daily. This down-home country diner serves hearty breakfasts and big burgers. $–$$.

☙ ♿ **Los Dos Hermanos** (530-994-1058) 100 S. Lincoln Street, Sierraville. Open for dinner. Great *carne asada* and margaritas make this a must if you are anywhere near Sierraville—especially considering the slim pickings in the area. $–$$.

☙ ♿ **Riverview Pizza** (530-289-3540) Main and Nevada, Downieville. Open for breakfast, lunch, and dinner daily. Pretty much the only restaurant in Downieville, they serve up hearty breakfasts and pizzas. $.

Nevada County

☙ ♿ **Briar Patch Co-op and Deli** (530-272-5333; briarpatch.coop) 290 Sierra College Drive, Grass Valley. Open 7 AM–9 PM Monday through Saturday and 8 AM–7 PM Sunday. I come here for groceries, organic coffee drinks, smoothies, sandwiches, and salads. Food offerings range from Rahlene's Beautiful (a sandwich of sunflower seeds, cheese, and avocado) to burgers. $.

☙ ♿ **California Organics Market and Organic Grill** (530-265-9293; californiaorganics.org) 135 Argall Way, Nevada City. Besides coming here for all-organic goods (this is the first certified all-organic market in the state), the grill is pretty great. Weekend brunches range from Benedicts to bison burgers. You can also get milk-

shakes, grilled rib eyes, and tempeh enchiladas. $–$$.

☙ ♿ **Diego's Restaurant** (530-477-1460; diegosrestaurant.com) 217 Colfax Avenue, Grass Valley. Open Monday through Friday 11–9 and Saturday 12–9. Colorful, with mismatched chairs and funky paintings, this is the spot for fish tacos, *rellenos*, and *tres leches*. Specializing in *pescado* with a Mexican/Latin twist, locals crowd the place on Friday, when live music adds even more flavor. Reservations recommended on weekends. $–$$.

☙ ♿ **Ike's Quarter Café** (530-265-6138) 401 Commercial Street, Nevada City. Open 8–8 Wednesday through Monday. Using organic ingredients, this New Orleans-style bistro serves diners either inside the little house or beneath the trees on the patio. The biscuits and gravy, po'boy, gumbo, mac and cheese, and sweet potato pie bring locals back time and time again. Cash only. $–$$.

☙ ♿ **Tofanelli's** (530-272-1468; tofanellis.com) 302 W. Main Street, Grass Valley. Open 7 AM–9 PM daily. If I could sit on the patio, surrounded by fountains and brick, and eat one different omelet a day, it would take me 101 mornings to get through them all. Lunches offer burgers, while dinners head to Europe for Italian specialties. $–$$$.

Placer County

☙ ♿ **Ikeda's** (530-885-4243) 13500 Lincoln Way, Auburn. Open at least 8 AM–9 PM daily. You may already know about it, especially if you have ever trekked up I-80 to Tahoe. It's a produce stand run amok: Known for their burgers, the other side sells homemade pies, produce, nuts, condiments, and munchies of every sort. The Dutch apple pie makes me drool. $.

La Billig French Café (530-888-1491) 11750 Atwood Road, Auburn. Open Tuesday through Saturday for lunch and dinner. French café fare at reasonable prices makes this a great place to stop on your way to Tahoe or the foothills. They have a take-out window for *croque monsieurs* and crepes if you are really in a hurry. $–$$.

El Dorado County

♂ ♿ ♈ **Cozmic Café** (530-642-8481; thecozmiccafé.com) 594 Main Street, Placerville. Open 7 AM–8 PM Monday through Saturday (later for the pub upstairs) and 8–8 on Sunday. Aside from serving some of the best organic vegetarian food (and non-veggie fare too), local wines and microbrews, coffee, and smoothies in the area, this café was once a mine. Today you can walk deep into the mine and even eat a Righteous Rice Bowl or a Thymely Tuna Wrap in the cool environment. At night, come for live music. $.

♂ ♿ ♈ **Gold Vine Grill and Wine Bar** (530-626-4042; goldvinegrill.com) 6028 Grizzly Flat Road, Somerset. Open for dinner Wednesday through Sunday from 5–9. Though I didn't get the chance to eat here, a friend who I trust recommended it. She likes the seafood *vol au vent* or the sesame crusted ahi. $$–$$$.

♈ **Heyday Café** See *Entertainment.*

♂ ♿ **Marco's Café** (530-642-2025) 7221 CA 49, Coloma. Open at least 11–9 daily. Sit outside near the river, beneath the cool misters, and eat Roman-style pizza, curry, salads, and rice bowls. I like the spinach salad, and the brownies are sinful. $–$$.

✳ Entertainment

Sierra and Nevada Counties

♈ **Citronee Wine Bar** See *Dining Out.*

Foothill Theatre (foothilltheatre.org) Nevada Theatre, 401 Broad Street. Come see live theater in this wonderful historic building, and even occasionally, outside in the foothills.

♈ **Golden Gate Saloon at the Holbrooke** (530-273-1353 or 800-933-7077; holbrooke.com) 212 W. Main Street, Grass Valley. Sit at the bar with a whiskey and admire the bar that was brought from Italy in the 1850s.

♈ **Old Nevada Brewery** (530-265-3960) 107 Sacramento Street, Nevada City. Located in a historic building that used to brew beer until the Prohibition. This is a lively spot for a beer and pub food.

Yuba Theatre 212 Main Street, Downieville. Built in 1940, this theater still hosts arts performances. Check local listings.

Placer and El Dorado Counties

♈ **Auburn Alehouse Brewery** (auburnalehouse.com) 289 Washington Street, Auburn. Open daily from 11–11, until 12 on Friday and Saturday. Pub grub takes a backseat to freshly crafted ales.

Auburn Symphony (530-823-6683; auburnsymphony.com) 808 Lincoln Way, Auburn. Known as being one of the better symphony companies in eastern California, check local listings for shows and performances.

♈ **Bootleggers Old Town Tavern and Grill** (530-889-2229; bootleggers auburn.com) 210 Washington Street, Auburn. Belgian brews, a nice wine list, and decent food bring folks out from Sacramento.

♈ **Cozmic Café** See *Eating Out.*

♈ **Heyday Café** (530-626-9700; hey daycafe.com) 325 Main Street, Placerville. Besides great food, this popular café (really popular, you have to wait ages for a table on weekends) is also a hopping wine bar.

THOUGH OAK TREES AREN'T USED FOR HANGING PEOPLE IN THE FOOTHILLS ANYMORE, THE TOWN STILL REMEMBERS.

Old Coloma Theatre (530-626-5282; oldcolomatheatre.com) 380 Monument Road, Coloma. Friday and Saturday nights at 8 PM. Old-fashioned melodrama in this historic setting make for a fun family outing. $10 adults and $5 for kids under 12.

Ⴡ **Sierra Nevada House** (530-626-8096; sierranevadahouse.com) Lotus Road and CA 49, Coloma. Although there is a hotel and restaurant here, locals line up for live music and a hopping bar.

✷ Selective Shopping

Drop me on Broad Street in Nevada City and you won't hear a peep for hours. Known as Booktown USA, there are more books per block than people. Every other store sells new and used titles, making this region a bibliophile's paradise. Favorites include **Mountain**

House Books, Harmony Books, Brigadoon Books, Toad Hall Book Shop, Main Street Antiques and Books, Inner Travel Books, and **Inner Sanctum Books**.

Searching for antiques? Take a jaunt through the historic downtowns of Grass Valley, Sierraville, Nevada City, Auburn, and Placerville for those vintage gems.

✷ Seasonal Events

March and April: **Passport Weekend** (eldoradowines.org) Placerville. This is actually two weekends, but who's complaining? This popular festival sells out every year, when 22 wineries offer wine tasting, pairings, barrel tasting, and entertainment.

May: **Gold Rush Book Fair** (goldrushbookfair.com) Nevada County Fairgrounds, Grass Valley. Enough to make this writer spend her entire paycheck, books on everything you can imagine are up for grabs in Booktown USA.

June: **Coloma Blues Live** (colomablueslive.com) Henningson Lotus Park, Coloma. An all-day blues festival held right on the American River in Coloma.

Music in the Mountains Summerfest (musicinthemountains.org) Through July, music events bring heaps of visitors to Nevada City and Grass Valley.

Gold Rush Days (530-289-1000) Downieville. For two day in June, expect rowdy crowds, rustlers, gun fights, music, a street dance, and lots of period costumes throughout Downieville, as the town recreates the era that put them on the map.

July: **Downieville Classic Bike Race** (530-289-3010) Downieville. Bikers gather in these foothills to race in this three-day event.

Fourth of July Grass Valley and Nevada City take turns hosting the annual parade. Later in the afternoon, everyone heads to the fairgrounds for a party and fireworks.

August: **Nevada County Fair** Nevada County Fairgrounds. Just what you'd expect from a small-town county fair: rides, games, food, and fun.

Sierra Brewfest Nevada County Fairgrounds. Beers from around the West get to show off their hops at this enthusiastic party.

Sierra Shakespeare Festival (foothilltheatre.org) Fred Forsman Amphitheater, Nevada County Fairgrounds. The Foothill Theatre Company presents live Shakespeare in the forest.

September: **Gold Harvest Wine Trail** (866-355-9463) Nevada County. Two days of wine tasting to celebrate the annual harvest.

American River Music Festival (americanrivermusic.org) American River Resort, Coloma. This is a little-known festival, but so much fun. Three days of music, camping, and fun, right on the river.

SOUTHERN SIERRA FOOTHILLS—
Plymouth to Mariposa

✳ To See

Amador County

Amador Whitney Museum Main Street, Amador City. Open weekends 12–4. Though this sneeze-and-you'll-miss-it town doesn't have much by way of hopping tourist spots, this museum is a rare find—it honors the contributions of *women* to the Motherlode region. After you tour the museum's stagecoaches and clothing exhibits, head outside to wander the block called Amador City. Free.

✦ **Black Chasm Cavern** (866-762-2837; caverntours.com) 15701 Volcano Pioneer Road, Volcano. Open at least 10 AM–4 PM daily (longer hours in summer). If you have never toured a helictite cave, surrounded by icy stalactites and stalagmites, you're missing out. Head here for a 50-minute walking tour of the chilly 57-degree Fahrenheit cave. You can also mine for gemstones, explore the visitor center, and see the crystal collection. $14.25 adults; $7.15; kids 3–12.

Chew Kee Store (209-223-4131) Main Street, Fiddletown. Open 12–4 April through October. Fiddletown once housed a prominent Chinese community, who used this herb store for a variety of ills. Today the store is a museum of Chinese artifacts from the 1800s to 1900s. Afterwards, walk through old Fiddletown to see the Chinese Gambling Hall and the Fiddletown General Store, and try to recall the wild mining town Bret Harte wrote about in "An Episode of Fiddletown."

Historic Kennedy Gold Mine Surface Tours See *To Do*.

Indian Grinding Rock State Historic Park (209-296-7488; parks.ca.gov) 14881 Pine Grove-Volcano Road, Pine Grove. Just 8 miles east of Jackson, this little valley once accommodated the Miwok Indians. Here you can see marbleized limestone with 1,185 mortar holes, and a number of petroglyphs. Ancient Miwok women used the holes to grind acorns, and today Indians gather here to celebrate acorns throughout the year, with music, dancing, and food—the biggest bash being the **Native American Big Time Celebration** the last weekend in September (see *Seasonal Events*). Visit the **Chaw'se Regional Indian Museum** to view Indian artifacts. You can also tour the reconstructed Miwok village. And if you are really inspired, you can tent camp or stay in the U'macha'tam'ma—these are bark houses where you'll need to haul all your gear, food, and water 200 yards, to get deep into the ancient Indian ways. Hike the North or South trails to explore the oak environment. To camp here, reserve early. Day use: $6.

Knight and Co. Ltd. Foundry and Machine Shop (209-267-0201; knight foundry.org) 81 Eureka Street, Sutter Creek. Open for guided tours from 10 AM–4 PM on weekends. The only water-powered foundry in the state, this still-working machine shop introduced the Pelton wheel to the area. Today the machine shop creates iron castings. Call for reservations.

Monteverde General Store (209-267-1344; suttercreek.org) 3 Randolph Street, Sutter Creek. Open Thursday through Monday from 10 AM–3 PM. While visiting the well-kept gold mining town of Sutter Creek, pop into this museum to learn about the history of the region, including walking down the aisles of shopping goods along the walls—check out the Chux disposable diapers. You can learn how John Sutter nixed the idea of setting up shop here and instead set up camp along the creek. Sure, Leland Stanford added to his riches by excavating the area, but Sutter Creek was more of a supply town than a gold mine. Free.

Sutter Creek Gold Mining Co. See *To Do.*

Western Hard Rock Mining Museum (209-267-0848; minerspick.com) See *Sutter Creek Gold Mine.*

Calaveras County
Angels Camp Museum (209-736-2963) 753 S. Main Street (CA 49), Angels Camp. Carriage house, barn, wagons, gold mining, logging, farm equipment, carpenter tools, blacksmith shop, rocks, minerals, household items, plus a model stamp mill and train that shows the route of the Angels Camp branch of the Sierra Railway. Free.

Calaveras County Museum Complex (209-754-4658; calaverascohistorical.com) 30 N. Main Street, San Andreas. Open daily 10 AM–4 PM except major holidays. Courthouse, jail yard, and hall of records, with displays dating to the gold rush era, plus an outstanding Miwok Indian exhibit that includes artifacts, photos, and quotes revealing Miwok lifestyle, make this an educational stop.

Ironstone Heritage Museum See *Wine Tasting.*

Tuolumne County
Columbia State Historic Park (2090-536-1672; columbiacalifornia .com or parks.ca.gov) Main Street off CA 49, Columbia. Shops open 10 AM–5 PM daily. Bring the family to this car-free historic town, which is slightly reminiscent of Disneyland, without the crowds, the high prices, and well, the mouse. This Old West town (the capital of the area in its heyday) has been saved from the modern mini-mall Starbucks craze by becoming a state park. Now, you can wander through the Old West imagining the working ladies, the bar brawls, and the dusty prospectors

COLUMBIA STATE HISTORIC PARK.

hoping to make millions. Visit the **William Cavalier Museum** (Main and State Streets) to learn about this town and its part in the gold craze. The **Museum of the Gold Rush Press**, **Columbia Grammar School, Fallon Hotel,** and the **miner's cabin** make for interesting stops; press the buttons outside of buildings to learn their history. There are a couple restaurants and saloons here, but mostly you'll ride the carriage, peek around, slurp some ice cream, and head back to your hotel. Although if you happen to be in town for a murder-mystery weekend, you might want to stick around (call for details), or contact the City Hotel to learn about their creepy Ghost Tours. Free.

✿ ♿ **Railtown 1897 State Historic Park** (209-984-3953; csrmf.org) 5th Avenue and Reservoir Road, Jamestown. Open daily from 9:30–4:30 April through October, and the rest of the year, 10 AM–3 PM. Known as the movie railroad, kids and adults will find more than a museum of past railroad artifacts here. Find out which movie stars rode this train, which films the trains appeared in, and how Hollywood saved the park from turning into a pile of junk. Come in spring, when you can ride a real steam train. Take a self-guided walking tour of the facilities, or a guided Roundhouse tour ($2 adults; $1 kids). Steam Train rides go 6 miles in 40 minutes and will run you $8.

Sonora's Historic Downtown Washington Street, Sonora. Take a walk through this historic downtown area, strolling past antique shops, wine bars, and historic buildings like the lovely **St. Patrick's Church** (1975), which sits at the top of Sonora like a mother bear. Another highlight is the **Tuolumne Courthouse** (1898), which is often the site of local festivals and live music.

Tuolumne County Museum and History Center (209-532-1317; tchistory.org) 1568 W. Bradford, Sonora. Open 10 AM–4 PM daily. People often start with the Old Jail, which shows photos and historical artifacts about each region in Tuolumne County. Also, learn about pioneers, and the get the scoop on Mark Twain's part in Gold Country history. Free.

Mariposa County

Mariposa County Museum and History Center (209-966-2924;mariposa museum.com) 5119 Jessie Street, Mariposa. Open 10 AM–4 PM daily. Sure, most museums in the foothills showcase the same history—Indians, pioneers, gold rush, and a few location-specific artifacts—though this museum's collection is quite extensive and explains the history in a clear and interesting way. $3; children: free.

✳ To Do

AIR TOURS **Springfield Flying Service** (209-532-4103; letsgofly.com) Mike Cano takes folks up on an air tour over Tuolumne County, including Stanislaus Park, Donnell, Emigrant Wilderness, Tuolumne Gorge, and Hetch Hetchy. $220.

Skydrifters Hot Air Balloons See *North Sierra Foothills*.

CAVE AND MINE TOURS

Amador County

✿ **Black Chasm Cavern, National Natural Landmark** (209-736-2708 or 866-762-2837; caverntours.com) 15701 Volcano Pioneer Road, Volcano. Open daily, year-round. Explore beautiful trails and chambers in this enchanting National

Natural Landmark cave on 50-minute guided-walk tours. See sparkling flowstones, stalactites, and huge clusters of rare, crystalline helictite formations. $14.25 adults; $7.15 kids 3–12.

✎ **Historic Kennedy Gold Mine Surface Tours** (209-223-9542; kennedygold mine.com) Kennedy Mine Road, Jackson. Open Saturday, Sunday, and holidays for guided tours. One of the deepest gold mines in the world (almost 6,000 feet), you can tour the area, including taking a peek at one of the biggest stamp mills in the Mother Lode. Though you won't go into the mine, you will learn how gold was processed. $9; $5 ages 6–12; under 6 free.

✎ **Sutter Gold Mine Tours** (209-736-2708; suttergold.com)13660 CA 49, Sutter Creek. Guided tours daily from at least 10 AM–5 PM. Throw on a hardhat and head underground to explore this hard-rock mine, which helped make Leland Stanford so affluent. People like this tour because they can see the Mother Lode from the inside. Board the boss-buggy shuttle, and journey deep underground on a one-hour tour in this modern hard-rock gold mine. See mining gear, techniques, gold, and fool's gold. Tours culminate with a chance to try your luck at finding gemstones. You might also want to explore the **Western Hard Rock Mining Museum** (209-267-0848; minerspick.com) on the property, which houses a comprehensive collection of mining artifacts. $17.50; $11.50 kids 4–12. Not recommended for kids under 4.

TAKE A ZIP LINE TRIP AFTER YOUR MINING EXCURSION.

Calaveras County

✎ **California Cavern State Historic Landmark** (209-736-2708 or 866-762-2837; caverntours.com) 9565 Cave City Road, Mountain Ranch. Open year-round. California's first show cave, delighting visitors since 1850, features an enchanting trail with beautiful crystalline formations in historical and recently discovered pristine areas. $14.25 adults; $7.15 kids 3–12.

Gold Cliff Mine (209-736-2708 or 866-762-2837; caverntours.com) Located at the south end of Calaveras County, Angels Camp. Open year-round by reservation. Step back in time and explore this historic gold mine on a two- to four-hour adventure trip, combining challenging exploration with gold rush history and folklore.

✎ **Mercer Caverns** (209-728-2101; mercercaverns.com) 1665 Sheep Ranch Road, Murphys. View beautiful crystalline formations; stalactites, stalagmites, soda straws, curtains, and Angel's wings. Nature proves herself an artist and welcomes visitors year-round to see her in this magnificent subterranean wonderland. $12.

✍ **Moaning Cavern** (209-736-2708 or 866-762-2837; caverntours.com) 5350 Moaning Cave Road off Parrotts Ferry Road, Vallecito. Open daily, year-round. Descend deep underground on a guided-walk tour, rappel by rope 165 feet, or reserve a challenging Adventure Trip. Above ground, race 0.25 mile on thrilling twin zip-lines. See *California Zip Lines*. $14.25 adults; $7.15 kids 3–12.

CYCLING Popular places to ride include New Melones Lake, Stanislaus National Forest, New Hogan Lake, Lyons Reservoir, Cedar Ridge, Glory Hole Recreation Area, Hammill Canyon, Angels Camp to San Andreas Bike Ride, and the Mokelumne Coast to Crest trail. Or you can take the 14-mile Murphys Winery Bike Tour.

Rentals and Tours
Mountain Pedaler (209-736-0771) 352 S. Main Street, Angels Camp. Full range of bicycles, clothing, and accessories, as well as custom-made bikes, plus local trail maps are available.

FARM TOURS

Amador County
✍ **Daffodil Hill and Amador Flower Farm** (209-245-6660; amadorflower farm.com) From Jackson, turn east on CA 88 for 8 miles to Pine Grove; drive north on Pine Grove-Volcano Road until it turns into Rams Horn Grade, to Daffodil Hill. Open mid-March to mid-April, daily from 10 AM–4 PM. When spring arrives, there is no place I would rather visit than Daffodil Hill. Since 1887, this hill has attracted people awaiting spring's arrival, and today more than 300 varieties of daffodil bloom on the hill. Other seasons, visit the flower farm, which has pumpkin festivities and is a working nursery. Free.

Tuolumne County
Cover's Apple Ranch (928-4689; coversappleranch.com) 19211 Cherokee Road, Tuolumne. Open 6:30–6 Monday through Friday and 8–5 Saturday. Since 1890, this apple, pear, squash, cucumber, and animal farm has been growing sweet produce. Free.

Mariposa County
Country Kitchen Herb Garden (209-742-6363) 5467 Clouds Rest Road, Mariposa. Tour this lovely organic herb garden, pick some herbs to take home, and picnic near a pond while farm animals graze nearby. Free.

FARMERS' MARKETS **Murphys Farmers' Market** (209-728-9112) Thursday evenings from 4–dusk, July through October, by the Vina Moda Winery on Main Street, Murphys. This is one of the best places in town for organic herbs, veggies, and fruits, plus breads and freshly baked treats, handcrafted goods, wine, and music.

Sonora Farmers' Market Downtown Sonora. On Saturdays from 8–noon from May through October, this market showcases the foothill bounty of local produce.

Sutter Creek Market Eureka Street, Sutter Creek. Saturday mornings from 8 AM–11 AM in June through October, downtown Sutter Creek attracts locals, who crowd the market looking for the best in local produce.

FISHING Anglers head to the area to fly-fish and try their skills at catching trout, salmon, bass, and more in **Stanislaus National Forest's** 611 miles of rivers and streams, **Don Pedro Reservoir**, **New Melones,** and **Lake Tulloch.**

Guides and Gear

Mark Cotrell Guide Service (209-536-9364; markcotrellguideservice.com) Sonora. Mark and his crew take folks out on walk- or boat-fishing trips. Full or half day adventures will run you between $250–350.

Springfield Trout Farm (209-532-4623) 21980 Springfield Road, Sonora. Kids will especially like to learn how to fish here.

GOLD PANNING GEAR AND GUIDES Also see *To See* and *To Do*.

California Gold and 49er Mining Supplies (209-588-1635; 49ermining supplies.com). This crew takes people on private mining charters to Woods Creek. Trips last five hours and cost $115 (kids under 12 are free). Wear a wetsuit and prepare to work.

Calaveras County

Books & More (209-736-9020; booksnmore.com) 328 N. Main Street, Angels Camp. With gold prospecting and gold panning equipment, these authorized Keene and Fisher Dealers will set you up.

Roaring Camp Mining Company (209-296-4100; roaringcampgold.com) 12010 Tabeau Road, Pine Grove. Located in the Mokelumne River Canyon, here is a forty-niner gold camp with prospecting cabins and camping, gold panning, gold prospecting, fishing, swimming, adventure tours, and cookout tours. Open May through September.

Tuolumne County

✍ **Gold Prospecting Adventures** (209-984-4653; goldprospecting.com) 18170 Main Street, Jamestown. Choose between using a sluice box for two to five hours (or even up to two days); using a metal detector; various expeditions; the bonanza, where you work through 1000 pans of material an hour; or dig a hole and go for it without a guide. Rates and tours vary, but range between $25–295 for the whole family.

Mariposa County

Jackson's Prospecting Supplies (209-966-4827 or 800-288-7759) 5144 Fair-grounds Drive., Mariposa. Half- or full-day panning excursions, all equipment included.

Paystreak Mining and Recreation (209-742-5777) 5057 CA 140, Mariposa. Gold panning during summer months only. For $5 you get a bag of dirt containing gold; you will be shown how to pan the gold out. For the more serious gold panner, maps of spots are provided, or you can make reservations for a private prospecting lesson. Gold panning equipment sold year-round. Closed Mondays.

GOLF

Amador County

Mace Meadows Golf and Country Club (209-295-7020; macemeadow.com) 26570 Fairway Drive, Pioneer. This 18-hole public course wins awards for being the best course in Amador County. $12–37.

Calaveras County

Greenhorn Creek Resort (209-729-8111; greenhorncreek.com) 711 McCauley Ranch Road, Angels Camp. A 72-par golf course redesigned by Robert Trent Jones II. $35–90 including GPS cart.

Tuolumne County

Mountain Springs Golf Course (209-532-1000; mountainspringsgolf.com) 17566 Lime Kiln Road, Sonora. FYI: this championship 18-hole club expects men to wear collared shirts. $16–40.

JET SKIING AND WATER SKIING **Bev's Boats and Market** (209-785-8500 or 888-760-8600; bevsboatrental.com) 7260 O'Byrnes Ferry Road at Lake Tulloch Resort, Copperopolis. This marina rents boats and water toys, wakeboard, ski, and fishing boats, Jet Skis, and WaveRunners.

New Melones Lake Marina (209-785-3300; newmelones.com) 6503 Glory Hole Road, Angels Camp. This full-service marina, on the third-largest reservoir in California, rents luxury houseboats, fishing, and patio boats.

HORSEBACK RIDING **Horse and Barrel** (209-728-9333; horseand barrel.com) 2000 Nickerson Lane, Murphys. Saddle up with Horse and Barrel for a rural adventure past vineyards and along the foothills. $80–150.

RAFTING AND KAYAKING The **Tuolumne River's** 18-mile section from Meral's Pool to Ward's Ferry is California's best place to raft the big rapids. Highlights include the "T" (Class IV) and Clavey Falls (Class V). Also see *North Sierra Foothills*.

O.A.R.S. Outdoor Adventure River Specialists (209-736-4677; oars.com) 2687 CA 49, Angels Camp. If you're up for an adventure (or some civilized wine tasting and gourmet-food sampling in between your ride down the river) an OARS trip is a must. Trips available for all experience levels.

Sierra Mac River Trips (800-457-2580; sierramac.com) Groveland. For over 35 years, Marty McDonnell has been taking adventurers down the gnarliest part of the Tuolumne River. Either take the 18-mile Tuolumne River trip, or combine that stretch with the Cherry Creek camping voyage. Trips last one to three days, include wetsuits and meals, and run $225–805.

THERE ARE PLENTY OF LAKES AND RIVERS TO EXPLORE IN THE FOOTHILLS.

BLACK BART

Not all Gold Country pioneers got down in the tunnels to earn their riches. One of the most famous—and underhanded—folks to *work* the region was named Black Bart. In the kindest of ways, Black Bart and his double-barreled shotgun jumped in front of a stagecoach and said, "Will you please throw down the express box?" Maybe his mama would be proud of his use of the word please, but locals feared his trademark politeness—in his time, he robbed 28 Wells Fargo stagecoaches. Finally, a lawmaker who had been on his trail for over eight years figured out his true identity, as the quiet Charles Boles of San Francisco, and nabbed him off the streets.

Today, if you are in the area on the third weekend of June, come celebrate **Black Bart Hold Up Days** (suttercreek.org), a weekend of music, reenactment holdups, period attire, and gold panning—just hold onto your wallet.

✒ **Zephyr Whitewater** (209-532-6249; zrafting.com) See *South High Sierra*.

SPAS **Jillian's Day Spa** (209-728- 3939) 488 Main Street, Murphys. Open Saturday through Tuesday, 9–5, Wednesday and Thursday 9–6:30, Friday 9–5:30. Say "yes" to a glass of local wine and relax while having a manicure and pedicure. The Stone Massage will put you into a lovely trance. Jillian's is a full-service salon, offering spa packages.

TRAIN RIDES ✒ **Railtown 1897** See *To See*.

WALKING TOURS **Jackson Walking Tour** (209-223-0350; amadorcounty chamber.com) 125 Peek Street, Suite B, Jackson. Grab a map from the visitor center and explore this gold rush town, once home to a wealth of gamblers, renegades, and working gals. A meander along Main Street takes you past Victorian buildings, stone buildings, and wooden walkways; past the Amador County Museum (See *To See*) and the St. Sava Serbian Orthodox Church. While you're exploring, pop into the antique stores and the Ice Cream Emporium. Free.

Sutter Creek Walking Tours (800-892-2276) American Exchange Hotel, 53 Main Street, Sutter Creek. Reserve a spot for a walking tour (Saturday, 1:30) or bus tour (Saturday, 10:30) of historic Sutter Creek and the region. You'll learn about the historic buildings and church, plus get to know this authentic gold rush-era town. Make sure your guide tells you about the secret bordello tunnel that allowed the gentlemen to pass underground from the hotel without their wives or chatty neighbors getting a look. Call for fees.

WINE TASTING For more information on this up-and-coming wine region, visit amadorwine.com.

Charles Spinetta Winery and Wildlife Art Gallery (209-245-3384; charles spinetawinery.com) 12557 Steiner Road, Plymouth. Open weekends 9–5 and Monday, Thursday, and Friday 8–4. Since 1984, Charles Spinetta has been growing and crafting fine wines in small quantities.

Clockspring Vineyard (209-245-3297) 11811 Steiner Road, Plymouth. Organic Zinfandel populates the land, here at this small operation.

Renwood Winery (209-245-6979; renwood.com) 12225 Steiner Road, Plymouth. Open daily from 10:30–5:30. One of the oldest Zinfandel vineyards, this is the winery to get some big Zin in their pastoral tasting room. Free.

Sobon Estate (209-245-6554; sobonwine.com) 14430 Shenandoah Road, Plymouth. Open daily from 9:30–5. Organically grown grapes, with Zinfandel being the star, have been growing here since 1854. You might also want to stop by their sister vineyard **Shenandoah Vineyards** (209-245-4455; 12300 Steiner Road) to check out the art gallery while sipping big red varietals.

Young's Vineyard (209-245-3005; youngsvineyard.com) 10120 Shenandoah Road, Plymouth. Expansive lawn area and gorgeous landscaping makes Young's one of the best spots to sip Cabernet and share a hunk of Brie with friends.

Calaveras County

Black Sheep Winery (209-728-2157; blacksheepwinery.com) 221 Main Street (near Alchemy), Murphys. Open daily 11–5. Zinfandel is Black Sheep's bedrock. If you like port, sample the newly listed Fortissimo. The Sauvignon Blanc and Lily Pad Rosé were a huge hit at my friend's wedding.

Brice Station (209-728-9893; bricestation.com) 3353 East CA 4, (4 miles east of Murphys). Open Friday through Sunday 12–6, and select Mondays by appointment. At 3,300 feet, grapes drink in the sunshine at the highest-altitude vineyard in the Sierra Nevadas. Taste the wine, then visit the sheep, geese, horses, and llamas. Pottery pieces available from the onsite Quyle Kilns.

Chatom Vineyards (209-736-6500; chatomvineyards.com) 1969 CA 4, Douglas Flat. This vineyard, owned and run by women, is a must-stop. Try the delicious She Wines; partial proceeds go to help women's causes.

Historic Winery Tasting Room
(209-728-0638) 2690 San Domingo Road, off Sheep Ranch Road. Open daily 11–5. Visit the oldest winery in Calaveras County and taste the new Red Rover. Bring the family, grab your bottle, and catch a Theater Under the Stars piece during the summer at the outdoor Murphy's Creek Theater.

WINE BARRELS IN CALAVERAS COUNTY.

Indian Rock Vineyards (209-728-8514; indianrockvineyards.com) 1154 Pennsylvania Gulch Road (just 1 mile down Pennsylvania Gulch off CA 4), Murphys. Open 12–5 Friday through Sunday. Located on a site originally settled by Miwok tribes, the land itself has an historic feel. Sip a Barbera or a Pinot Noir and check out the several year-round springs, which feed two large ponds and hydrate the 14 different varietals. Bring the family and a picnic, or do as the locals do and visit on Saturday afternoons for a free BBQ.

Ironstone Vineyards (209-728-1251; ironstonevineyards.com) 1894 Six Mile Road, Murphys. Open daily 10 AM–5 PM. Ironstone has been described as the 'Vegas' of Murphys wineries, and that I can see. Tour the historic caverns, the museum (with the largest hunk of gold ever found here), and lake; gold pan, shop, or picnic at the gourmet deli. If you're still up for action, attend a silent movie night, concert series, or art show. Make sure to check out the organ downstairs.

Lavender Ridge Vineyard (209-728-2441; lavenderridgevineyard.com) 431 Main Street, Murphys. Stop in for superb specialized Rhône varietals. They grow over 1000 Grosso lavender plants and 50 French olive trees; you can take some of the dreamy scents with you in organic olive oils and lavender bouquets.

ZIP LINES **California Zip Lines** (209-736-2708 or 866-762-2837; caverntours .com) 5350 Moaning Cave Road, Vallecito. Open daily, year-round. Race high above the beautiful Gold Country foothills at up to 40 mph on thrilling twin zips 0.25-mile long. You can also tour the caves here. See *Moaning Cavern*. $39.

✳ Green Spaces

PARKS AND FORESTS **Big Trees State Park** (209-795-2334; parks.ca.gov) Take CA 4 east, 4 miles past Arnold. You can't visit Calaveras County without stopping at Big Trees. This beautiful park dates back to 1931, established to preserve the North Grove of the regal giant sequoias. As a first-timer, you'll want to stroll at least part of the interpretive trail; it introduces you to the Discovery Tree, the first redwood discovered in 1852 among many unique and beautiful others. Day use: $6.

El Dorado National Forest (209-295-5996; fe.fed.us) Amador Ranger District, 26820 Silver Drive, Pioneer. Visit the ranger station to get a detailed map of hiking trails, campsites, and fishing spots along the CA 88 corridor. For more detailed information on the forest see *North Sierra Foothills* and *High Sierra*.

Indian Grinding Rock State Historic Park See *To See*.

Natural Bridges Hike Take CA 4 to Parrots Ferry Road. Go about 4 miles and park at the marked trailhead. This beautiful 2-mile round-trip hike will lead you to spectacular limestone caverns that have been carved out by Coyote Creek.

Stanislaus National Forest (209-532-3671; fs.fed.us) Main Ranger Station, 19777 Greenley Road, Sonora or 24545 CA 120, Groveland. This endless forest encompasses three wilderness areas (see *High Sierra*), nine lakes and reservoirs, and seven rivers. The best way to get to know the forest is to visit a ranger station for maps and information. Anglers head to the **Tuolumne River,** and **Cherry Lake**. Mountain bikers like the 15-mile **Gooseberry-Crabtree Trail**. Hikers explore the kid-friendly **Little Golden Forest Trail** (near Groveland Ranger Station), the area around Cherry Lake (which is great for day-use trips, boating, and swimming, as well), and the 6-mile **Tuolumne River Canyon Trail** (Take Lumsden Road off Ferretti Road, drive 4.5 miles to trailhead). Rafters wanting to take on the Wild and Scenic Tuolumne River on your own, need a permit ($15) from

PEOPLE POSING FOR A PHOTO ON THE CALAVERAS BIG TREES FAMED STUMP.

the ranger station. Camping options abound, but favorites include the **Lumsden Campground** in Groveland (free), **Cherry Valley** ($17) and **Dimond O** ($19).

Table Mountain Up Rawhide Road, just north of Jamestown. Explore Tuolumne County's best-kept secret—this 40-mile mountain, which is home to some of the most beautiful wildflowers, Peppermint Falls, rock formations, and even old mines.

LAKES AND RIVERS **Amador Lake** Off CA 88, west of Jackson. Basically this lake is for fishermen looking to snag bass, catfish, and bluegill. You can camp at the **Amador Lake Resort** (amadorlake.com). There is neither swimming nor motorized boating allowed on this little lake.

Lake Camanche (209-763-5121; camancherecreation.com) 11700 Wade Lane, Burson. Overnight accommodations feature lakeside camping and newly renovated RV sites, plus furnished cottage and motel units. Excellent bass and trout fishing provide year-round fishing access. $8.50 per vehicle.

Lake Don Pedro (800-255-5561; foreverresorts.com) Off CA 120, southeast of Chinese Camp. One of the better deals around is for you and nine friends to rent a houseboat for just under $2000 for four days; for services, head to the Moccasin Point Marina, just off CA 120.

Lake Tulloch (800-894-2267; laketullochcampground.com) Tulloch Road, Jamestown. Boaters, anglers, water-skiers, swimmers, and sunbathers head to Lake Tulloch when temperatures reach triple digits in the foothills. Camp at the **Lake Tulloch Campground**.

Mokelumne River (ebmud.com) Known as the *Rio de la Pasion* to the early Spanish settlers, soon the gold rush pioneers moved in and used so much of the water for energy, the river nearly dried up. Today, the California Dept. of Fish and Game has assisted in helping reroute the water to and from the somewhat bleak Camanche Reservoir to allow the salmon to return. White-water rafters now enjoy the 37-mile section of the river from CA 49 up CA 88, and are trying to make it a wild and scenic river, to preserve its water flow.

New Melones Lake (gloryholesports.com) Sits between Angels Camp, Murphys, and Jamestown on CA 49. This is a large reservoir; if you're looking for fish to fry, New Melones has produced some big beauties. When the water level is low, watch for occasional underwater trees in your path. The dam flooded the river valley, covering the old mining town of Melones—some of the tree tops still reach out of the water.

✳ Lodging

Amador County

⚓ ❝🍴❞ **Foxes Inn of Sutter Creek** (209-267-5882 or 800-987-3344; foxes inn.com) 77 Main Street, Sutter Creek. If you'd like a little luxury, post-gold panning, head to the Foxes Inn. Like a small slice of the east coast, this 1857 house offers rich fabrics, deep wooden furniture, the occasional fireplace, and plush beds. Delicious breakfasts are delivered to your room, so you don't have to make conversation with other guests pre-coffee. $$–$$$$.

Gatehouse Inn (209-223-3500 or 800-841-1072; gatehouseinn.com) 1330 Jackson Gate Road, Jackson. Geared more towards romance than a trip with the fishing buddies, enjoy themed rooms with everything from exposed-brick walls to lace bed-runners, iron beds to floral-print wallpaper. Amenities: four rooms and suites, plus a cottage, full breakfast, solar-heated pool, wood stove, and Jacuzzi tubs in some rooms, AC, wine reception. $$–$$$.

⚓ **Imperial Hotel** (209-267-9172; imperialamador.com) 14202 CA 49, Amador City. Imagine riding up in a stagecoach, weary and excited to arrive in Gold Country, to find this brick hotel with a nice bed awaiting you. Situated along historic CA 49, this 1879 hotel offers small rooms with local art. I'd forgo the main hotel rooms and head to the cottage suites, up the hill. An affordable treat, families and couples will enjoy a night or two here. Amenities: 9 rooms and suites, full breakfast, the wonderful restaurant (see *Dining Out*), the Oasis Bar, no phone or TV, some rooms have fireplaces and Jacuzzi tubs. $$.

⚓ 🌸 ∞ **St George Hotel** (209-296-4458; stgeorgehotel.com) 16104 Main Street, Volcano. This 150-year old hotel makes you want to sit on the porch and watch the shadows pass. Shared bathrooms, small rooms that evoke visions of the 1800s, complete with floral wallpaper, brass beds, and old pictures, characterize the historic hotel rooms. For more space, consider the bungalow annex rooms, or the garden cottage. Note that if you have limited mobility, stairways are steep in the hotel, so inquire about annex rooms. Amenities: 20 rooms, suites and a cottage, continental breakfast, the great restaurant (see *Dining Out*), the Whiskey Flat Saloon. Closed Mondays. $–$$$.

Calaveras County

Also see *Southern High Sierra*.

❝🍴❞ **Dunbar House 1880** (209-728-2897; 800-692-6006; dunbarhouse .com) 271 Jones Street, Murphys. If you like B&Bs, this Italianate home and 1880s country inn offers refined coziness, without the place looking like someone vomited flowers—though rooms are still pretty feminine. Amenities: 4 rooms, afternoon appetizers, local wine, breakfast with edible flowers, fireplace, gardens, Jacuzzi or clawfoot tubs, and yummy cookies. $$–$$$; children over 12 welcome.

⚓ ∞ **Hotel Leger Historic Inn and Restaurant** (209-286-1401; hotel leger.com) 8304 Main Street, Mokelumne Hill. Visit an amazing piece of history, with antique-filled rooms free from the fast-paced world. Go for a room off the street, as walls are thin. Amenities: 14 rooms, pool, restaurant, bar, no TV or phones, pool. $–$$.

Murphys Historic Hotel (209-728-3444; murphyshotel.com) 457 Main Street, Murphys. A registered Historic Landmark Hotel (1856) with a modern lodge and 29 historic rooms. Read the historic guest registry for a kick. This is a fun place to stay if you don't mind some noise from the restaurant and bar, or shared bathrooms. $–$$.

Tuolumne County

⚘ ⓓ 1859 Historic National Hotel (209-984-3446 or 800-894-3446; national-hotel.com) 18183 Main Street, Jamestown. Since 1859 this hotel has offered nine elegant accommodations in the heart of Jamestown. All guests have access to the soaking room, buffet breakfast, and restaurant. And hopefully you'll get to meet the resident ghost, Flo, who occasionally plays silly pranks. $$.

⚘ Bradford Place Inn and Gardens (209-536-6075 or 800-209-2315; bradfordplaceinn.com) 56 W. Bradford Street, Sonora. I imagine Mark Twain probably sat in a room like this—walnut furniture, floral bedspreads and wallpaper, and a big tub to soak those aching muscles—trying to make sense of this wild western town. Today it seems nothing has changed in this luxurious inn, besides TVs with loads of channels and a breakfast delivered to your room. If you can afford it, spring for the Bradford Suite. $$–$$$.

⚘ ⓓ Columbia City and Fallon Hotel (800-532-1479; cityhotel.com) 22768 Main Street, Columbia. These sister hotels, in Columbia State Historic Park, have been restored to their original 19th-century opulence with Victorian-era antiques and sitting parlours. Enjoy one of 66 rooms (with a shared or private bath) that include a balcony, breakfast, and access to the wonderful restaurant and lounge. $$.

⚘ ⚘ ⓓ Groveland Hotel (209-962-4000 or 800-273-3314, groveland.com) 18767 Main Street, Groveland. Built in 1849, then left to disrepair until Peggy and Grover Mosley quit high-paying jobs to embark on a new career in hospitality. The hotel offers feather beds, fine linens, frilly curtains, claw-foot tubs, bath toys, and a wraparound porch perfect for sipping wine and eating some dessert from the restaurant. I recommend booking your stay by phone, as I had a little snafu with my online reservation and didn't have a room for my second night—luckily my brother was camping nearby and had space for us on a Friday night in summer. Rates: $$–$$$. Facilities and amenities: 14 rooms and three suites, saloon, excellent restaurant (see *Dining Out*), room service, full breakfast.

Harlan House B&B (209-533-4862; Harlan-house.com) 22890 School House Road, Columbia. For a steal, you can stay in an antique-decorated

KIDS LIVING THE SIMPLE LIFE AT MURPHYS.

B&B in the heart of Columbia (though the town really has no pulse). Rooms have wood-burning stoves, brass beds, and you get a full breakfast. For my money, I'd spring the extra 40 bucks for the cottage, which has a huge patio area with a private spa, and way more space. $–$$.

♪ "♪" 🐾 **McCaffrey House** (209-586-0757 or 888-586-0757; mccaffreyhouse .com) 23251 CA 108, Twain Harte. Stephanie and Michael (and their spunky dog) created a home away from home between the High Sierra and the foothills. Quilts, big windows, pine-tree views, games, hundreds of movies, and the friendliest dog around, all make this a prime choice in this neck of the woods. Plus, the excellent breakfast— on the wraparound patio beneath the pines—isn't too bad, either. Amenities: 8 rooms, some rooms have a balcony or wood-burning stove, afternoon wine social. $$.

Mariposa County
♪ **Little Valley Inn** (209-742-6204 or 800-889-5444; littlevalley.com) 3483 Brooks Road, Mariposa. Take a trip to the country at this rustic, yet modern B&B. Close to trails and Yosemite, but still billing itself in the foothills, this inn makes a good choice for families. The six rooms are colorful, with warm beds to snuggle up in and read a book, continental breakfasts, and private decks. $–$$.

Yosemite Bug Hostel (see *South High Sierra*).

✳ Where to Eat
DINING OUT

Amador County
♿ **Caffe Via D'Oro** (209-267-9992; cafeviadoro.com) 36 Main Street, Sutter Creek. Open for dinner Wednesday through Sunday. Like most restaurants in the region, expect white tablecloths

with red napkins, in an effort to combine elegant with the past. What makes this spot different is the wall-sized mural and the great Thursday Night Dinners with free wine tasting. Menu highlights include a stuffed portobello mushroom, and the Via D'oro chicken. Reservations recommended. $$–$$$.

🍷 **Imperial Hotel** (209-267-9172; imperialamador.com) 14202 CA 49, Amador City. Open for dinner Wednesday through Sunday. I am often surprised by how evolved the restaurants in the Sierra Foothills are. Dine in this historic dining room on seasonal, organic cuisine, like a bistro steak with garlic rosemary mashed potatoes. Reservations recommended. $$–$$$.

♪ 🍷 **St. George Hotel** (209-296-4458; stgeorgehotel.com) 16104 Main Street, Volcano. Open for dinner Thursday through Sunday, and Sunday brunch. Step back into the 1800s to dine in an elegant (in a Wild West kind of way) room on some of the most interesting food in the region. Come Sundays for the prime rib dinner, or try the smoked salmon linguine. Reservations recommended. $$–$$$.

♿ 🍷 **Taste Restaurant** (209-245-3463; restauranttaste.com) 9402 Main Street, Plymouth. Open Thursday through Monday for dinner. I like Thirteen Dollar Thursdays at the wine bar, or the $30 prix fixe three-course dinner. However, other nights are just as fine. Dine in the burnt-orange dining room, on seasonal, healthy California cuisine like a seared Sonoma foie gras, or oven-roasted guinea hen. Reservations recommended. $$–$$$$.

Calaveras County
♪ ♿ 🍷 **Alchemy Market & Wine Bar/Café** (209-728-0700; alchemy market.com) 191 Main Street, Murphys. The wine and beer selection and the outside seating are the reasons to come here and order a classic lunch or

winemaker's dinner. Though a different place than it once was, you can now enjoy fried calamari, a variety of salads, and excellent burgers, in addition to the deli sandwiches and specialty market fare. $$

✔ ♿ ♈ **CAMPS Restaurant at Greenhorn Creek** (209-729-8181; greenhorncreek.com) 711 McCauley Ranch Road, Angels Camp. Open Wednesday through Sunday, lunch: 11:30–5, dinner: 5–9. Removed from the bustle of town, the quiet atmosphere lends itself to a leisurely lunch or dinner. It's a perfect place to have a romantic dinner and watch the sunset. I love the cozy lounge area, to munch and sip by the fireplace. $$

✔ ♿ ♈ **Firewood** (209-728-3248) 420 Main Street, Murphys. Open daily from 11–9. If you don't mind the line on busy days, this is a good family locale for a casual lunch or dinner. Their wood-fired pizzas from the centerpiece Italian oven, nachos, burgers, and fries delight kids and adults. The south of the border tacos lay beneath a tasty sauce. And the staff is super friendly. $.

♿ ♈ **Mineral** (209-728-9743; mineral restarant.com) 419 Main Street, Murphys. Open Wednesday through Friday 3–9, and Saturday for dinner. This is the place to go without little ones for upscale vegetarian cuisine. Try the Chef's Five-Course Discovery, which includes wontons with miso butter and carrot jelly, the bouillon of red miso and coconut, chili hemp fondue with herb salad, spring green asparagus drizzled with salted plum vinaigrette, and hibiscus black sesame jelly. You'll be more than satisfied, but don't leave without experiencing the decadent Indian Spiced Fried Chocolate. Mineral offers a full sake bar. $$

✔ ♿ ♈ **V Restaurant and Bar** (209-728-0107; victoriainn-murphys.com) 402-H Main Street, Murphys. Serving Wednesday through Sunday beginning at 5. Chef Bob whips up hearty, savory dishes. Eat inside and enjoy the cozy, elegant dining room and bar, or sit on the seasonal patio. I savor the mussels in white wine with its buttery broth, and the petite lamb chops. Don't leave without trying at least one dessert. Co-owner, Mary, makes a scrumptious cheesecake or flourless chocolate cake. $$.

Tuolumne County

✔ ♿ ♈ **Azzo's** (209-984-1173; azzos restaurant.com) 18228 Main Street, Jamestown. Open for dinner. Though it is slim pickings in Jamestown, this restaurant offers a casual, fun atmosphere and pretty good food. Come for pizza, burgers, pasta, salads, veal Madeira, or (on Wednesday and Thursday) gnocchi. $$.

✔ ♿ **Banny's Café and Wine Bar** (209-533-4709; bannyscafe.com) 83 S. Stewart Street, Sonora. Open Monday through Saturday 11–3 and 4:30–9. Simple, eclectic California cuisine, just off Washington Street, offers a dash of sophistication in this small town. Entrees that stand out are the duckling, or the prawns, mussels and vegetable risotto. Reservations recommended. $$.

✔ ♿ ♈ **City Hotel Restaurant** (209-532-1479; cityhotel.com) 22768 Main Street, Columbia. Open Tuesday through Sunday 5–9, and Sunday brunch. This gourmet dining room is staffed by students from Columbia Community College's Hospitality Management Program, and under the expert guidance of Chef Alec Abt, the students turn out top-flight, multi-course dinners. Reservations recommended. $$–$$$.

SIERRA FOOTHILLS (AKA GOLD COUNTRY)

 ☼ ♿ ⅉ ⚭ **Groveland Hotel Restaurant** (209-962-4000 or 800-273-3314, groveland.com) 18767 Main Street, Groveland. Open for dinner; call for seasonal hours. Dine in the Victorian dining room or the outside patio garden on wonderful California seasonal cuisine. Highlights include the Alaskan crab summer roll, super-thin pizzas with house-made sausage, and the pasta of the day. The wine list is superb and service is super-friendly. Reservations recommended. $$–$$$.

♿ ⅉ **Seven Sisters** (209-928-9363 or 877-747-8777; blackoakcasino.com) Black Oak Casino, 19400 Tuolumne Road N., Tuolumne City. Open for dinner Wednesday through Sunday. Though I didn't get the chance to dine here, I've heard it is one of the better restaurants in the region. Elegant meals of organic free-range chicken, prawns, and dayboat scallops attract locals and visitors. Reservations recommended. $$$–$$$$.

☼ ♿ ⅉ **Villa Doro** (209-586-2182) 23023 Joaquin Gulley Road, Twain Harte. Open for dinner; call for seasonal hours. With outside dining under the pines, this Italian eatery creates the perfect alpine ambiance without sacrificing their authenticity. Mint spaghetti is a standout, as is the panko-crusted calamari. This place gets packed on summer weekends. Reservations recommended. $$–$$$.

Mariposa County

Charles Street Dinner House (209-966-2366; charlesstreetdinnerhouse.com) CA 140 and 7th Street, Mariposa. Open for dinner nightly. Heading towards Yosemite, you'll be treated to a number of dining options, but down on this end of the foothills, this is the spot for fine food. Meaty, decorated in wood from floor to ceiling, and a mainstay in the community, if you stay in Mariposa, chances are you'll eat here. $$–$$$$.

Amador County

Amador Vintage Market (209-245-3968) 9393 Main Street, Plymouth. Open Thursday through Sunday 10 AM–5 PM. Gourmet sandwiches and picnic fare in the Amador Wine Country—the perfect ingredients for spending the day exploring. $-$$.

☼ ♿ **Mel and Fayes Diner** (209-223-0853) CA 88 and CA 49, Jackson. Open for breakfast, lunch, and dinner daily. If you are hankering for a burger and fries (or if your lodging doesn't include breakfast and you want a hunk of eggs), this local institution will fill you up. $.

Sutter Creek Ice Cream Emporium (209-267-0543) 51 Main Street, Sutter Creek. Known for dishing up the biggest junior scoop of ice cream in the Gold Country (and maybe Northern California), visitors can't help but stop by for a few licks.

Calaveras County

Angels Food Market & Deli (209-736-4243) 396 N. Main Street, Angels Camp. Family-owned and operated since 1935. Peruse the complete wine and liquor department, produce section, pre-made sandwiches, and don't miss the deli for lunch. $.

☼ ♿ **Aria** (coffee) (209-728-9250) 458 Main Street, Murphys. Open 7–4. Closed Tuesdays. This is my favorite place in town for well-brewed coffee and espresso drinks. Sandwiches, salads, soups, and quiches are served for lunch. Special-order sweets for a picnic or party and pretend you made them. $

☼ ♿ ⅉ **Ironstone Vineyards Delicatessen** See *Wine Tasting*.

☼ ♿ ⅉ **Lube Room Saloon & Grill** (209-795-2118; dorringtonhotel.com) 3431 CA 4, Dorrington. Open daily from 11:30–9. The Lube Room offers cocktails, cold drafts, and family fare including soups, burgers, fries, and old-fashioned comfort food. Located at the historic Dorrington Hotel, the Lube Room Saloon & Grill has been a favorite with the locals for decades. Shoot some pool, play horseshoes in the backyard, and bring some quarters for the jukebox. $–$$$.

✍ ♿ **Mike's Pizza of Angels** (209-736-9246; angelscamp.com) 294 S. Main Street, Angels Camp. Open for lunch and dinner daily. One of the better family-friendly restaurants in the region; though the pizza isn't quite gourmet as adversied, it is quite good. Parents watch sports on the big screen, and good luck pulling your kids away from the video arcade. $.

✍ ♿ **Pickle Patch Deli & Garden** (209-754-1978) 577 W. St. Charles Street, CA 49, San Andreas. Pickle Patch is a must-stop. Locals know they have the best sandwiches and salads in town. Inside, 1950s décor takes you back to a slower time, but service is speedy. Sit in the shade on the patio or under an umbrella, or soak up the sun in the expansive garden. $.

Tuolumne County

See also *Southern High Sierra*.

✍ ♿ **Bon Appetit** (209-532-2355; frenchbakerybistro.com) 51 S. Washington, Sonora. Open from 10 AM–3 PM Tuesday through Saturday and dinner Wednesday through Saturday. I have to admit, whenever I see Brie and apple appetizer on the menu, I drool, so Bon Appetit sort of had me at hello. Then I saw their tartines and knew we were meant to be. Hopefully, this bistro will make your heart sing as much as mine. $.

✍ ♿ 🐾 ♟ **Diamondback Grill** (209-532-6661; thediamondbackgrill.com) 93 S. Washington, Sonora. Open 11–9 Monday through Saturday and until 8 on Sunday. Don't let the weathered-stone walls fool you, this California-

style grill serves up sophisticated fare in a casual atmosphere. Using local ingredients, and some organic products as well, the wildly popular Diamondback Grill keeps the locals waiting at all times of day. I like the Wild Alaskan salmon burger, even though they have 11 burgers to choose from. $.

Mountain Sage (209-962-4686; mtnsage.com) 18653 Main Street, Groveland. Open daily. A surprisingly special place a coffee or smoothie pre- or post-hike. On Friday night and Saturday morning in summer there is a small farmers' market in the garden. The store is worth a peek as well (see *Selective Shopping*).

✍ ♿ ♟ **Iron Door Grill and Saloon** (209-962-6244; iron-door-saloon.com) 18761 Main Street, Groveland. Open 11 AM–2 AM daily. The tradition at this saloon/restaurant is to take a dollar bill (or more if you're so inclined) and dart it up onto the ceiling. I'd bet at least a few hundred bucks can be collected up there. Besides pool, live music, and a hopping bar that seems to date back to the gold rush era, you can get burgers and fries and good beer. $.

✍ ♿ **The Rock Pub and Restaurant** (209-586-2080; therockofth.com) 23068 Fuller Road, Twain Harte. Open for breakfast, lunch, and dinner daily. Pub grub after a day of adventure always seems to be the perfect recipe. The Rock serves pounds of fried food (from mozzarella sticks to fish and chips), burgers, fish, and steaks, plus decent beer. You can sit outside on warm days. $–$$.

What Cheer Saloon (209-532-1479; cityhotel.com) 22768 Main Street, Columbia. Open for lunch and dinner. In the City Hotel, this old-time saloon is a decent place to get burgers and sandwiches, and pretend you are a gunslinger from the old days. $.

✍ ♿ **Woods Creek Cafe** (209-984-

4001) 18256 CA 108, Jamestown. Open for breakfast and lunch. Come here for breakfast in a bread bowl, egg dishes, and a dining room that is a tribute to cows. Expect lines on weekends. Cash only. $.

ENTERTAINMENT ☿ **Black Oak Casino** (877-747-8777; blackoakcasino .com) 19400 Tuolumne Road North, Tuolumne City. Slots and game tables, live music, decent food, bowling, and an arcade will entertain the entire family.

☿ **Iron Door Saloon** See *Eating Out.*

☿ **Jackson Rancheria Casino** (800-822-9466; jacksoncasino.com) 12222 New Ranch Road, Jackson. Try your luck at this casino and bar.

Mariposa Symphony Orchestra (209-966-3155) Mariposa. This musical ensemble performs throughout the year in Mariposa. Call for details.

☿ **Oasis Bar** See *Imperial Hotel— Dining Out.*

☿ **The Rock Pub** See *Eating Out.*

Sierra Repertory Theater (209-532-3120; sierrarep.org) See live theater at Columbia's historic Fallon Theater or at the East Sonora Theater.

Stage 3 Theater (209-536-1778; stage3.org) 208 S. Green Street, Sonora. This theater company presents contemporary works by up and coming playwrights.

Volcano Theater Company (volcano theatre.org) This theater company has been putting up shows since the early 1970s. See a performance in the outdoor amphitheater or at the Cobblestone Theater.

☿ **What Cheer Saloon** See *Eating Out.*

☿ **Whiskey Flat Saloon** (stgeorge hotel.com) St. George Hotel, 16104 Main Street, Volcano. Built in the 1930s, this is the type of bar where you order a burger and a glass of whiskey, then make friends with the random people at the bar.

✳ Selective Shopping

When on the hunt for antique bargains and finds, friends leave the city and head to the foothills. Take a walk through the historic downtowns of Sutter Creek, Amador City, and Jackson in Amador County to find both sadly discarded china and goods from Granny's era, and scores like hand-carved headboards. In Jackson, head for **Real Deal Antiques** (104 Main Street, Jackson) and **Water Street Antiques** (11101 CA 88, Jackson). Another favorite is the **Hein and Company Bookstore and Coffeehouse** (204 N. Main Street, Jackson), which sells used and rare books.

Calaveras County has its share of antiques, but Murphys is the stop for people wanting to visit art galleries. You might also want to visit **Kristine's** and **Mad About Shoes** (209-728-2506), **Murphys Motorcycle Company** (209-728-2350; murphysmotor cyclecompany.com), and **Murphys Village Toy Store** (209-728-8517; murphysvillagetoystore.com).

In Sonora, my favorite stop is the **Legends Books and Antiques, Old Fashion Soda Fountain Shoppe** (131 S. Washington Street) to sift through a wealth of antiques and then slurp real root beer from the historic bar. Others to peek into include **Antiques Etc.** and **Baer's 1851 Antiques** on Washington Street.

In Groveland, the **Hammock Garden at Mountain Sage** (18653 Main Street) sells everything from fair-trade gifts to books to great kids' gear. And in Mariposa, along 5th Street, you'll want to explore the galleries, especially **Mariposa County Arts Council**.

THE CALAVERAS COUNTY FAIR AND JUMPING FROG JUBILEE

(209-736-2561; frogtown.org) Calaveras County Fair Grounds, Angels Camp. Known by locals as The Frog Jump, this annual mid-May event dates back to the gold rush. Writer Mark Twain became famous for his first published work, *The Celebrated Jumping Frog of Calaveras County*. No doubt he could have imagined that it would prove to be inspiration for a genuine event. The competition is open to everyone, and the rules are simple. All frogs must be at least four inches in length from nose to tail. Each frog is dropped onto an eight-inch launch pad, and once a frog makes the first jump from that pad it is illegal for the jockey to touch the frog again. They must find other ways to convince the frog to take the largest possible three hops forward. Frog jumping is indeed a serious sport here.

✳ Seasonal Events

March: **Murphys Irish Day** (murphys irishdays.org) Irish musicians and dancers, food, beer and wine, and Irish fare take over Main Street. A parade marks 11 AM and bagpipes, wee folk, vintage cars, and everything green parades through town in the spirit of the Irish. Free.

The Sonora Celtic Faire (800-350-1814; sonoracelticfaire.com) 220 Southgate Drive, Motherlode Fairgrounds, Sonora. California's oldest and largest Celtic Faire celebrates Celtic culture with a music festival, with something for the entire family. Irish step and Highland dancers, jousting on horseback, Celtic living history, and plenty of crafts, ethnic food, and drink. The knight in full armor that I watched dialing at the phone booth is the image that never ceases to bring a smile to my face.

June: **Columbia Diggings Living History Weekend** Columbia. Come view a tent town reenactment, complete with period clothing, actors discussing current events from that time, and gold panning.

July: **Mother Lode Fair** Mother Lode Fairgrounds, Sonora. Celebrate the region with a big ole county fair.

August: **Ragtime Festival** (sutter creekragtime.com) For three days, come to downtown Sutter Creek to hear ragtime played in the streets, beneath the balconies of the historic buildings.

Sonora Blues Festival Mother Lode Fairgrounds, Sonora. Blues music, microbrews, food, and more make this a fun place to spend the day.

September: **Blues and Brews Festival** (suttercreek.org) For over a decade, Sutter Creek has hosted a lively blues festival that also boasts two beer gardens. Make sure you have a designated driver.

October: **Calaveras Grape Stomp and Street Faire** (209-728-9467; calaveraswines.org) The annual Grape Stomp celebrates the wine community in Murphys Park. Truly a family event, sign up ahead of time for the competitive grape stomping, wear a wild stomping costume, and bring a partner. If you aren't ready to jump into the barrel, the Street Faire is a great place to shop, snack, and people watch.

December: **City Hotel Victorian Feast** Columbia State Historic Park. Come enjoy an authentic 1850s dinner, complete with drama and entertainment. This one sells out, so book early.

The High Sierra

NORTHERN HIGH SIERRA

SOUTHERN HIGH SIERRA

Oliver Reyes

NORTHERN HIGH SIERRA—
Truckee to Markleeville

If you picture a land covered in diamond peaks and sapphire lakes, granite walls and emerald forests, you could maybe begin to visualize the astounding grandeur of the north High Sierra. Some of the most traveled and the most remote Northern California landscape, the northern High Sierra attracts visitors from around the world and keeps them dazzled even on return visits.

Most travelers head straight to the famed Lake Tahoe, the largest alpine lake in North America. It attracts summer adventurers looking to cool off in the waters, and winter snowbunnies braving the world-class slopes. Over a mile up in the mountains and split between the states of California and Nevada, this lake is part hippie and part whore. Her packed shores, resorts, and mountains, cluttered with casinos, live music, and tons of people often eclipse the mellow ambiance these mountains evoke. However, if you head here in spring and fall, you are sure to find the perfect recipe for relaxation.

Since it is 72 miles around the entire lake, you'll find a variety of towns to

LAKE TAHOE IN SUMMER.

explore, the biggest being **South Lake Tahoe**, a stretch of strip malls, resorts, restaurants, and ski lodges. Heading north on the California side, you pass a number of state parks and small resorts before you get to the largest town on the north shore, **Tahoe City**. This is the only area with a truly walkable downtown. Farther north and west is the famed **Olympic Valley**, home to ski slopes and high-end restaurants and hotels. Finally you reach **Truckee**, the mountain town that originally earned its fame by being where the ill-fated Donner Party got stuck in a snowstorm and were forced to eat members of the group. Today, you won't find human leg-eaters around here; rather there are a number of boutique hotels, a historic downtown, great food options, and some wonderful family-friendly ski resorts. Headed south from Tahoe, small towns like Markleeville appear out of nowhere between the richest forests you can imagine.

GUIDANCE **Lake Tahoe South Shore Chamber of Commerce** (530-544-5050 x 229; tahoechamber.org) 3066 Lake Tahoe Boulevard, So. Lake Tahoe.

Tahoe City Visitor Information Center (530-581-6900) 380 North Lake Boulevard., Tahoe City.

Truckee Donner Chamber of Commerce (530-587-2757; truckee.com) 10065 Donner Pass Road, Truckee.

HELPFUL WEB SITES
Tahoechamber.org
Northlaketahoe.com
Tahoeinfo.com
Laketahoechamber.com
Gotahoenorth.com
Bluelaketahoe.com
Gotahoe.com
Tahoesbest.com
Alpinecounty.com

MEDICAL EMERGENCIES **Tahoe Forest Hospital** (530-587-6011; tfhd.com) 10121 Pine Avenue, Truckee.

WEATHER As you might imagine, being located over a mile in the sky brings a variety of weather. In summer, while the weather is a perfect 70 to 80 degrees Fahrenheit, you'll still see snow atop the tallest peaks, reminding you that winters can be blustery. Winter temperatures range from 15–41 degrees Fahrenheit, with plenty of snow, as well as many a bright, sunny day. Whatever the time of year, nights and early mornings are chilly.

GETTING THERE *By air:* If you are going to Lake Tahoe, you might fly into **Reno/Tahoe International Airport** (renoairport.com). Most local carriers fly here. Another possibility is you can fly into **Sacramento Airport** (see *Sacramento—Getting There*) and drive the 90 minutes up the mountain. From both airports, you can find most major rental car companies.

Lakeshore Limousine (877-347-4789), One of the only shuttles to serve the entire Lake Tahoe area, is a good option if you choose not to rent a car.

MUSTS FOR FIRST-TIME VISITORS

1. Ski Heavenly.
2. Kayak Lake Tahoe.
3. Sip a margarita at a lakeside bar.
4. Hike to Vikingsholm and Eagle Lake.
5. Soak in the view of Emerald Bay.
6. Explore Squaw Valley.
7. Pamper yourself with a spa treatment.
8. Hike parts of the Rubicon Trail.
9. Swim in the lake.
10. Wander around Truckee's historic downtown.

MUSTS FOR REPEAT VISITORS

1. Ski Squaw Valley or Kirkwood.
2. Go cross-country skiing.
3. Take a boat cruise on the lake.
4. Hike the Tahoe Rim trail.
5. Explore Desolation Wilderness.
6. Take a dip in Grover Hot Springs.
7. Water-ski or wakeboard on the lake.
8. Dine at Plumpjack Café.
9. Visit the Gatekeeper's Museum.
10. Take a helicopter or balloon ride over the lake.

By bus: The major **Greyhound Station** (800-231-2222; greyhound.com) is located in downtown Truckee across from Commercial Row. From there you can take **TART** (see *Getting Around*).

By car: From Sacramento to get to South Lake Tahoe, take US 50 east. If you are headed to North Lake Tahoe or Truckee, you'll want to take I-80. Note that on most weekends, there is traffic on these two-lane mountain highways, so plan extra drive time. Also be aware that in winter, you need snow chains to drive up into the mountains, but both highways are open year-round.

By train: **Amtrak** (Amtrak.com; 800-USA-RAIL) also stops at the Depot in historic Truckee, across from Commercial Row.

GETTING AROUND *By bus:* **TART** (530-551-1212). Tahoe's regional bus serves the entire lake—though only the North and West Shores year-round. You need exact change, so call for current prices. The buses connect to both the Amtrak and Greyhound stations.

There are also a couple seasonal trolleys serving the lake area (**Nifty 50** in South Lake Tahoe and **Tahoe Trolley** on the North Shore). **Truckee Trolley** (530-587-7451) provides free ski area transportation year-round. Call for specific fare information and schedules.

Trail. Year-round, expect traffic on the two-lane highways—sometimes because of
snow, sometimes someone hit a bear, sometimes people just can't seem to take
their eyes off Lake Tahoe (especially around Emerald Bay).

In Lake Tahoe, you can drive around the entire lake. US 50 takes you around the
South Shore, meeting up with CA 28, which gets you to Tahoe City, and also connects you to CA 89, the connection between South Lake Tahoe and Truckee. It is
72 miles around the lake, and the trip will probably take you a good, long day.

LAKE TAHOE AND VICINITY

✳ To See

Emigrant Trail Museum (530-582-7892; parks.ca.gov) 12593 Donner Pass Road,
Truckee. Open at least 10 AM–4 PM daily. See *Donner Memorial State Park*.

Gatekeeper's Cabin Museum (530-583-1762; northtahoemuseums.org) 120 W.
Lake Boulevard, Tahoe City. Open in summer from 11–5 and in the winter 11–3
(weather permitting). The original cabin housed the gatekeepers who regulated
Lake Tahoe's water level after the Truckee River was dammed. Today, this hand-
carved cabin is home to a collection of artifacts that will take you to another era.
$3 adults; $1 kids; children under 6 are free.

✐ ♿ **KidZone Children's Museum** (530-587-5437; kidzonemuseum.org) 11711
Donner Pass Road, Truckee. Open in summer from 9–1 Tuesday through Sunday;
in winter, call for hours. Sometimes the kids just don't want to hike anymore, so
why not bring them to explore this hands-on museum that celebrates play, science,
history, and the arts. $5–7.

Tallac Historic Site (530-541-5227) CA 89, south of Emerald Bay, South Lake
Tahoe, CA. Open June through September, at least 11–4. These summer estates
for three elite San Francisco families used to make up a grand resort right on the
shores of the lake. Today the area, the homes, and a museum are open to the public. The Baldwin Estate looks like a log cabin and houses the Tallac Museum
(make sure to check out the native plant garden). The 1923 Valhalla Estate
(Valhallatahoe.com) is mostly used for weddings and special events, but there are a
couple galleries in the estate (and a great music festival). The Pope Estate (1894)
is the largest of the three. In summer you can tour the Pope house on Wednesday,
Friday, Saturday, and Sunday at 1 and 2:30. $3

Truckee Donner Historical Society and Old Jail (530-582-0893; truckee
history.org) Jiboom and Spring Streets, Truckee. Open 11–4 on summer weekends.
Try and get out of this 1875 jail and you'll see why it is still standing—steel ceilings, 32-inch thick walls, no windows. A visit today allows you to experience the jail
from the inside and view some memorabilia from Truckee's past. Free.

Vikingsholm Mansion and Visitor Center (vikingsholm.org) Emerald Bay State
Park, 999 Emerald Bay Road, Tahoma. Open 8–4 daily. You'll have to hike a steep
1.7-miles down (and back up) the mountain, or find the 1928 Norse castle by boat.
Magical in location and architecture, if you can get out here and tour the castle,
you won't be disappointed. $5 adults; $3 youths 6–17; children under 6 are free.

Western Ski Sport Museum (530-426-3313) Boreal Ski Area, Soda Springs. Open

Wednesday through Sunday 10 AM–4 PM, winter only. This museum will school you on the history of skiing from the 1850s to the present. Check out the 8-foot long cross-country skis by "Snowshoe Thompson," the mail carrier in the late 1800s. Free.

✳ To Do

AIR TOURS Helitahoe (530-544-2211; helitahoe.com) 1901 Airport Road, Suite 106, South Lake Tahoe. By far the best way to see all the beauty this area has to offer, this tour company offers a variety of flights. The most popular is the Emerald Bay Helicopter Tour (10 minutes; $49 per person). Other options include the Casino tour (10 minutes; $49), Sunset tour (one hour; $279 per person), the South Shore tour (20 minutes; $119) and the Lake Tahoe tour (45 minutes; $229 per person).

Lake Tahoe Balloons (530-544-1221 or 800-872-9294; laketahoeballoons.com) South Lake Tahoe. In summer, I can't think of a more peaceful way to enjoy Lake Tahoe than to take a balloon ride above it. Allow four hours for your flight and expect to get up before the crack of dawn (between 5 AM–7 AM). But the views of the entire lake, the Sierra Mountains, and the foothills are worth it. After your flight, you can sip champagne to help you get back to sleep. $250 per person.

Soar Minden (800-345-7627; soarminden.com) 1138 Minden Road, Minden, NV. This outfit provides one-hour tours with two-to three-passenger flights available over Emerald Bay and Fallen Leaf Lake. If you are feeling adventurous, you might want to go on an acrobatic flight with one of the pilots.

BOAT TOURS ♂ ∞ **M.S. Dixie II** (800-23-TAHOE; laketahoecruises.com) Zephyr Cove Marina, NV. Sure, it is in Nevada, but this 570-passenger paddle wheeler doesn't stay in Nevada. In summer, choose between trips like the Champagne Brunch, the two-hour Family Fun, Emerald Bay Sightseeing or Dinner Cruise, Sunset Dinner Dance, or the Show Boat Dinner Cruise. All trips educate travelers about sustainability and the environment, plus when food is served, they use sustainable products and include child-friendly options. $41–71 adults; $20–41 children.

Tahoe Boat Cruises (775-588-1881 or 888-867-6394; tahoeboatcruises.com) Tahoe Keys Marina, South Lake Tahoe, CA. Head out on a yacht to explore the lake and coast. The West Shore Cruise on the Safari Rose goes out Saturday through Thursday in summer, at 11 AM, and tours the west shore. They also offer a variety of sunset cruises, including martini and margarita Mondays, Wednesday Wine Tasting, Sunday Live Music, and Happy Hour cruises on other days. $59–95 adults; $55 for children under 12.

♂ ∞ **Tahoe Queen** (800-23-TAHOE; laketahoecruises.com) 900 Ski Run Boulevard, South Lake Tahoe. For over 25 years this paddle wheeler has transported visitors back to the turn of the 19th century for cruise options like Mark Twain's Tales of Tahoe, Afternoon Tea with Mrs. Lora J Knight, Captain's Dinner Dance, Ports of Call Dining Experience, and the Voyage Through the Big Water. Trips last between two to three-and-a-half hours and most include a sustainable child-friendly menu. $46–109 adult; $22–69 child.

Woodwind (530-542-2212; tahoecruises.com) Tahoe Keys Marina. Sailing cruises to Emerald Bay go out in summer every day at 11:30, 1:30, and 3:30. You can also take a Happy Hour or Sunset Cruise. Bring a sweater, as it can get chilly on the lake. $26–36 adults; $12 children.

CYCLING Biking in the Lake Tahoe area is a treat. In summer, it seems everyone dons helmets to pedal the bike paths surrounding the lake. There are a number of paved bike paths, serviced by TART, including from **Tahoe City-Dollar Point** (2.5 miles), **Tahoe City-Sugar Pine Point State Park** (9 miles), **Tahoe City-Squaw Valley** (4 miles, with access to Western States Trailhead), **Pope Baldwin Bike Path** (3.9 miles), and the **South Lake Tahoe Bike Path** (this is the most expansive path, connecting to many others). For bike-path trail maps, visit the South Lake Tahoe Visitor Center.

Mountain biking is also massively popular. The season generally runs from July through November. The best places to go include **Kirkwood Mountain Bike Park** (209-258-7357), **Northstar at Tahoe Mountain Bike Park** (530-562-1010), **Sugar Pine Point State Park, Alpine Meadows Western States Trail,** and **The Tahoe Rim Trail**. For other mountain biking areas nearby see *North Sierra Foothills.*

Bike Rentals
Camp Richardson Outdoor Sports Center (530-542-6584; camprichardson .com) 1900 Jameson Beach Road, South Lake Tahoe. Seems everyone lines up at this historic camp to get gear. But with over 1000 bikes in stock, these outfitters have the means to suit you up just fine. They also have trail maps.

Tahoe Bike and Ski (530-546-7437; tahoebikeski.com) 8499 North Lake Boulevard, Kings Beach. These guys will set you up with everything you need for a mountain bike adventure, including helmets, maps, and a bike.

FARMERS' MARKETS **Homewood Mountain Resort** (530-823-6183; foothill farmersmarket.com) June through August, Saturday 8–1.

South Lake Tahoe Market (530-622-1900; edc-cfma.org) American Legion Hall, June through October on Tuesday from 8–1.

Tahoe City (530-583-9000;visittahoecity.com) Commons Beach, May through October, Thursday 8–1.

Truckee River Regional Park (530-622-6183; foothillfarmersmarket.com) June through September, Tuesday 8–1.

FISHING The questions isn't where, but how to find the best spots to cast your line. Besides **Lake Tahoe** itself, anglers will enjoy trying their luck in the **Truckee River**, as well as in the various lakes to the north (see *North Sierra Foothills*) and south around Markleeville (see *Green Spaces*).

Charters and Guides
Tahoe Sport Fishing (530-541-5448; tahoesportfishing.com) Ski Run Marina, South Lake Tahoe. If you want to find a good charter to take you out to the best fishing holes, supply you with gear, then clean and bag your catch, these are your guides. Afternoon charters are slightly less than morning.

GOLF There's a reason why Tiger Woods lives part of the year in Lake Tahoe. The wealth of golf courses with championship greens and stellar views makes this one of the most sought-after golf destinations in northern California. Most courses open in April and close in November, call for specifics.

Lake Tahoe Golf Course (530-577-0788; laketahoegc.com) US 50 between Lake Tahoe Airport and Meyers, South Lake Tahoe. This 18-hole par 71 course is a decent place to tee off in summer. $23–55.

Old Greenwood (530-550-7010; oldgreenwood.com) 12915 Fairway Drive, Truckee. This Jack Nicklaus signature course is set up around trout streams, so if your opponents are too slow, you can fish while you golf—brings a new meaning to go-fish. $100–180.

The Resort at Squaw Creek Golf Course (530-583-6300; squawcrek.com) 400 Squaw Creek Road, Olympic Valley. This 18-hole championship course, designed by Robert Trent Jones Jr., is the spot for serious golfers. $55–110.

Tahoe City Golf Course (530-583-1516) 252 N. Lake Boulevard, Tahoe City. Since 1917, golfers have flocked to this lakeside course. $35–65.

GONDOLA RIDES *ℰ* **Heavenly Village Gondola** (775-586-7000; skiheavenly .com) Heavenly Mountain Resort, South Lake Tahoe. Open 10 AM–5 PM daily in summer. Soar into the air on a gondola, 2.4 miles up Heavenly Mountain, to be rewarded with panoramic views of the lake and the surrounding forest, arriving at the Deck, 9100 feet in the air. $26–30 adults; $20–26 youth; children under 4 free.

ℰ **Northstar at Tahoe** (800-GO-NORTH; northstarattahoe.com) 100 Northstar Drive, Truckee. Open at least 10 AM–4 PM daily in summer. Northstar operates free gondola lift rides in summer for folks to sightsee and hike around the mountain. Season Pass offices offer vouchers. Free.

ℰ **Squaw Valley Cable Car** (530-583-6985; squaw.com) Squaw Valley. Open in summer, call for specific times. The cable car/tram climbs 2000 feet to high camp, where you can eat, hike, and soak up the magnificent views. There are a number of packages including cable-car/skate, one way, cable-car/swim. $10–32 adults; $5–20 kids.

HIKING For most hiking information, see *Green Spaces*. Below are two trails that don't fit in one particular park.

The Pacific Crest Trail See *Sidebar.*

The Tahoe Rim Trail (tahoerimtrail.org) This 165-mile natural wonder circles the ridge around Lake Tahoe. Bikers, hikers, and equestrians love to explore this exciting trail that goes all the way up to 10,333 feet. The 12 different trailheads around the lake make this a fairly easy place to head into the wilderness, even with your baby.

HORSEBACK RIDING *ℰ* **Camp Richardson Corral** (530-541-3113; camp richardson.com) Emerald Bar Road at Fallen Leaf Road, South Lake Tahoe. Since 1934, Roberta and Quint Ross have been taking riders on trails to experience a side of the Tahoe area you can't find elsewhere. In summer, choose between regular Trail Rides ($32; 50 minutes), Extended Trail Rides ($60; two hours) Breakfast Rides ($45; 90 minutes) or a Steak Ride ($65; two-and-a-half hours). In winter they can arrange sleigh rides, as well. No children under 6 years allowed, and you must weigh less than 225 pounds. Reservations required.

THE PACIFIC CREST TRAIL—A TRUE ACCOUNT

"Turn south on this trail, you go to Mexico. Go north, it'll take you all the way to Canada." My first introduction to the Pacific Crest Trail left my spine tingling. It was 1987, we were in Tuolumne Meadows, and I was a 15-year-old on my first backpacking trip. Right there, in the middle of nowhere, was a trail you could hike clear across the country. At 2,658 miles, the idea was beyond daunting.

Fast forward 15 years, it was day 73 and I was over 1,200 miles into the trip. While the trail wound through summer in Northern California, the deserts of Southern California and the snow covered passes of the High Sierra were fading into memory. Another hiker and I emerged from the trees to find a stranger standing in the middle of a remote dirt road. He asked, "Hiking the PCT?" followed by "Ready to eat?" I may be dumb enough to hike 2,600 miles, but at least I'd learned enough on the trip to immediately say yes when food is offered. Our host led us back to his car, where his wife was firing up a car-camping double-burner Coleman stove. At sunrise, I had granola and powdered milk for breakfast, yet again, then suddenly, I am sitting down to heaping platefuls of scrambled eggs, mugs of steaming coffee, watermelon, and brownies for dessert, the whole time enjoying great conversation with brand-new age-old friends.

A few nights later, I was hiking out of Sierra City. It was a warm, moonlit night and I was slogging up a long, never-ending section of trail. Somewhere ahead, a thrashing noise was moving through the woods. After a few minutes, it sank in that the noise was a very large animal moving very fast down the side of the mountain. Before long, I realized that not only was this large animal moving down the side of the mountain, but it was headed directly at me. I ducked behind a stout-looking tree and waited. Seconds later, a big ol' bear flew out of the night, back legs overtaking front legs. In its rush to get somewhere very far away from right there, it never saw me. I caught my breath, than continued up to the ridgeline. It wasn't till I was snug in my bag, tired eyes closing against the star-filled sky, that I wondered what could possibly give a bear such a scare. Sleep was a long time coming.

And that is the nature of the Pacific Crest Trail. From the barren, granite world of the High Sierra, past the deep blue of Lake Tahoe, into the skinny-dipping pools on the middle fork of the Feather River, around Mt. Shasta's snow-covered majesty, in and out of little towns like Burney Falls, Old Station, and Etna, the trail leads you on an unparalleled exploration. The beauty and adventure comes from the mountains, the rivers, and the bears charging past in the middle of the night, but the true magic comes from the amazing people met along the way.

—Dan McGuire

For more information about the Pacific Crest Trail, visit pcta.org.

ICE SKATING **Heavenly Village Outdoor Ice Rink** (530-543-1423) Heavenly Village, South Lake Tahoe. Open 10 AM–10 PM in winter, weather permitting. As if they couldn't find enough for you to do on this mountain, they had to add one more fun, family activity—ice skating. In winter, you can spin like Brian Boitano and fall like yours truly.

Olympic Ice Pavilion (530-583-6985; squaw.com) High Camp, Squaw Valley. Open most of the year except the height of summer. Paired with an exhilarating ride on the cable car, you can twirl and spin on ice. $25 (includes skates, skating, and cable car ride).

OTHER OUTDOOR ADVENTURES **Heavenly Flyer** (skiheavenly.com) Heavenly Mountain, South Lake Tahoe. Open daily in summer from 11–4:30. The longest zip line in the continental United States propels riders at speeds up to 50 mph, as they cruise over the treetops and look out over Lake Tahoe. The total ride lasts about 80 seconds and drops 525 vertical feet. It's a thrill. You must be between 75 and 275 pounds to ride. Reservations recommended. $30–40.

✍ **High Camp Bath and Tennis Club** (530-581-7255; squaw.com) High Camp, Squaw Valley. Open at least 11–4 in summer. Sometimes you want that chlorine smell instead of the lake; I get it. Well you can't beat a swim or hot tub, 8000 feet in the sky. Trips up here include a ride on the cable car, and you can also ice skate for a few more bucks. $16–28.

✍ **Lake Tahoe Adventures** (530-577-2940; laketahoeadventures.com) South Lake Tahoe. If you want to ride an ATV or buggy on the Rubicon Trail, the most challenging 4X4 trail in the U.S., these are the dudes to get you out there. They also lead snowmobile tours 9000 feet up to Hope Valley, which I still remember from when I visited as a kid.

✍ **Squaw Valley Adventure Center** (530-583-7673; squawadventure.com) Next to the Olympic Village Lodge, Olympic Valley. Open daily. If skiing, hiking, boating, biking, snowmobiling, and snowshoeing aren't enough, head over to this adventure center for a ropes course, giant swing, bungee-trampoline, and other heart-dropping activities.

SCENIC DRIVES **Carson Pass** CA 88 from Sacramento to Carson City, NV. This 58-mile scenic drive is one of the most striking you can get. Heading up through alpine forests, you pass a number of insanely beautiful lakes that come in a variety of colors—Red Lake, Blue Lakes, and Silver Lake, plus Caples Lake and Kirkwood Lake. Make sure to stop at Kirkwood Mountain Resort for a lunch break and some majestic mountain views.

Lake Tahoe At Stateline, you'll find the bright lights, music performers, and big spenders hanging out at the major resort casinos lining the lake. Heading west to South Lake Tahoe, you can begin to access the lake at numerous points, including El Dorado, Regan, Pope, and Camp Richardson beaches. The road winds in hairpin turns, up and down the mountain, opening up at the mouth-dropping Eagle Falls and Emerald Bay. Next up is the stunning D. L. Bliss State Park, located a few miles from the turnout for Emerald Bay, which is a great picnic and beach area, or you can continue to Meeks Bay, where you will find another fun beach. About 3 miles north is Sugar Pine Point State Park. From here it is about 7 miles to Tahoe City, one of the more developed spots on the north shore. Continuing the trip around the lake, you next reach Carnelian Bay, another fairly developed community with plenty of restaurants and businesses; Tahoe Vista; and King's Beach, a fun swimming area. Crystal Bay is the northern border between California and Nevada, on the lake. The resort area of Incline Village is 3 miles farther, and just south from here is Nevada's Lake Tahoe State Park, and the lovely beach at Sand Harbor.

SPAS **Massage Therapy Cottage** (530-541-4269; massagetahoe.net) 1169 Ski Run Boulevard, South Lake Tahoe. Seems everyone on the South Shore recommends this spa, so I will too. What a perfect recipe for healing those skied-out muscles—a sugar polish and a massage—ahhhh.

Resort at Squaw Creek Spa (530-583-6300; squawcreek.com) 400 Squaw Creek Road, Olympic Valley. Open at least 9–7 daily. Why not splurge for a massage—you deserve it. And if you can't afford the swanky accommodations at this resort, you might as well spring for a spa treatment instead.

WATER SPORTS ✂ **Camp Richardson Marina** (530-542-6570; camprich.com) 1900 Jameson Beach Road, South Lake Tahoe. They rent everything from boats to water-skis, Jet Skis, WaveRunners, kayaks, canoes, you name it, they have it. They will also take you out on a parasailing trip. They don't take reservations for kayaks, so get here early. Afterwards you can chill on the beach.

Tahoe City Kayak (530-581-4336; tahoecitykayak.net) 521 N. Lake Boulevard, Tahoe City. Here you can rent kayaks and canoes, but the best deals are the guided tours of Emerald Bay. They last five hours and are tough, but once you arrive in this pristine bay, you'll be so proud of yourself, you won't stop bragging. It's hard, so don't bring along your wimpy friends. $95 per person.

✂ **Tahoe Paddle and Oar** (530-581-3029; tahoepaddle.com) 8299 N. Lake Boulevard, Kings Beach. Open daily from 9–5 May through September. This outfit rents kayaks ($20–30 per hour) and canoes. Plus, they take you out on guided kayak tours of Crystal Bay for $90 per person—reservations required.

Tributary Whitewater Tours (800-672-3846; whitewatertours.com) Granite Chief, Truckee. This major outfit has been taking folks on guided white-water

WATER-SKI LAKE TAHOE.

KAYAKING LAKE TAHOE IS MORE CHALLENGING THAN IT LOOKS.

tours in northern California for over 30 years. This trip heads off to ride the rapids on the Truckee River. This is not one of those leisurely self-guided trips, rather an intense, bumpy ride where *you will get wet.* They recommend only bringing children over 7 and Grandma—if she is one tough cookie. Otherwise, send them on the East Carson trip. Allow three to four hours and bring water shoes. $69–79 adults; 10 percent off for children.

Truckee River Raft Company (530-583-0123; truckeeriverraft.com) River Road and CA 89, Tahoe City. Open June through September, 8:30–3:30. These guys give you your own raft and paddles and send you off downriver to float 5 miles to River Ranch. Bring a picnic; 5 miles can work up the appetite. $35 adults; $30 kids 6–12; under 6 free.

WINE TASTING **Picchetti Winery** (530-541-1500) US 50 near the South Lake Tahoe Recreation Center. Open daily from 11–5. Picchetti has three estate vineyards, including 110-year-old Zinfandel vines, estate Chardonnay, and Cabernet Sauvignon. Head over to try out their varietals.

WINTER SPORTS, SKIING, AND SNOWBOARDING

Lake Tahoe is a ski and snowboard haven, attracting pros and novices. Since lift tickets vary by year, and you can often find great deals online, I have included a range for prices, though they too will probably change by the time you read this book. Search for deals—they're out there.

If you don't want to fork over the big bucks at the mountain resorts to rent

FULL MOON SNOW SHOE TOUR (530-525-9920; westshoresports .com) Sugar Pine Point State Park, 10 miles south of Tahoe City. Look for a small yellow "special event" sign on left. Rangers lead people out on the nights of the full moon in winter to explore the park on a 1.5-mile trail. It sells out fast, so make reservations. $10; $5 if there is no snow.

gear, in the South Shore, contact **Tahoe Sports Ltd** (530-542-4000; tahoesport-sltd.com) 4000 Lake Tahoe Boulevard, South Lake Tahoe. For cross-country gear, they have a separate office where US 50 and CA 89 meet. On the North Shore, you'll find a great selection of board and ski gear at **Tahoe Dave's Ski and Boards** (530-583-0400) 590 N. Lake Boulevard, Tahoe City. Cross-country skiers who need gear head to **Hope Valley Cross Country** (530-694-2266; hopevalley-outdoors.com) CA 88 and CA 89, Hope Valley. These guys offer lessons and rentals, plus guide you to their 50 miles of trails.

Lift ticket price range:

$0–30	$
$31–49	$$
$50–70	$$$
over $71	$$$$

South Shore

Heavenly Mountain Resort (775-586-7000; skiheavenly.com) Ski Run Boulevard, South Lake Tahoe. There's so much to say about this iconic Lake Tahoe-area mountain. First of all, it's big: 10,067 feet; nine peaks; two valleys; 91 trails; 4800 acres. And there is something for everyone—beginner slopes (up the gondola or at the California Lodge), kid slopes (the Enchanted Forest), lessons, child care for kids over six weeks. The Sky Express quad chair takes intermediate and advanced folks to the summit; experts head to Mott and Killebrew canyons; and for snowboarders, there are five parks and a super pipe. There is a great ski school, rentals, lifts, and even great food on an expansive deck, for the guy who overdid it yesterday. $$$$.

Kirkwood Ski Resort (209-258-6000; Kirkwood.com) CA 88, west of CA 89, South Lake Tahoe. If you are a serious boarder or skier, you probably already know about this intense mountain park 36 miles south of the lake. This is where the most snow falls in the area (up to 500 feet annually). There is so much to do here: Ski the steep chutes, learn on mellow trails, snowboard at the Stomping Grounds, snowshoe, ice skate, dog sled, mountain bike (in summer), snow skate, cat-ski, and cross-country tracks (50 miles worth). They offer backcountry safety courses as well as lessons for kids 4–12. Mom and Dad will be happy to know there is day care for children aged 2–6. $$$.

Sierra at Tahoe (530-659-7453; sierraattahoe.com) Off US 50 near Echo Summit, 12 miles from Lake Tahoe. The peak of this park reaches 8,852 ft and attracts a slew of snowboarders and their fans. Backcountry skiers will find easy access to uncharted territory. The snow-tubing hill is fun for the kids who haven't quite mastered this mostly intermediate mountain. $$$.

North Shore

Alpine Meadows Ski Area (530-583-4232; skialpine.com) 2600 Alpine Meadows Road, north of Tahoe City. This ski area doesn't get much attention, being in the shadow of these other world-class slopes. But don't let that sway you from trying it out. You'll get a mellow vibe of mostly local intermediate skiers and snowboarders, taking advantage of the dependable snowpack. Novice folks should come here to learn how to navigate the runs; they have a great school. $$$.

Homewood Mountain Resort (530-525-2992; skihomewood.com) CA 89, south of Tahoe City. This is the spot. Not for its reputation—go to Heavenly or Kirkwood for that—rather because this mountain seems to be one with the lake, rising from the shores, offering some of the better conditions for skiing, no matter what the weather. It's not as windy as other ski areas, which makes this a prime spot throughout the season. And kids under 10 run the slopes for free! $$$.

Squaw Valley USA (530-583-6985; squaw.com) 1960 Squaw Valley Road, Olympic Valley. In 1960 Squaw Valley was the site of the 1960 Olympics, catapulting this lovely area into one of the biggest, most famous ski resorts in California. With 100 trails on 4000 acres, all levels of skiers, boarders, and hot-cocoa sippers will enjoy getting to know the six peaks. Tricksters like the three terrain parks, while experts head straight for the famed KT-22. High Camp has enough options to keep beginning and intermediate folks busy. The best part about the mountain (besides the pool and Jacuzzi at High Camp) is the night skiing until 9 PM. Cross-country skiers, head to the **Resort at Squaw Creek** (squawcreek.com) for trail maps and gear. $$$$.

Truckee and Vicinity
There are a number of small parks in the area, which are perfect for families and people not wanting to fork over the big bucks to get out on the slopes. These parks have super-cheap lift tickets ($$) and make great places to learn: **Donner Ski Ranch** (530-426-3635; donnerskiranch.com), **Soda Springs** (530-426-3901; ski sodasprings.com), and **Tahoe Donner** (530-587-9444; tahoedonner.com).

Boreal (530-426-3666; borealski.com) Boreal/Castle Peak exit off I-80. This green, mountain park boasts the only all-mountain terrain area for kamikazes. Though small at 380 acres, they pack a lot of trails onto the mountain, pleasing beginning and intermediate riders. There is a kids' club, lessons, and night skiing. $$.

Northstar at Tahoe (530-562-1010; skinorthstar.com) CA 267, 6 miles southeast of Truckee. Packed in winter, you'll want to get here early to beat the crowds. Intermediate skiers and snowboarders (as well as families and new snow bunnies) love this massive mountain park. The terrain park is one of the best around and Lookout Mountain will keep the experts entertained for hours. There is also a 28-mile cross-country center here. Child lessons and a day care keep the little guys busy. $$$$.

Royal Gorge (530-426-3871; royalgorge.com) Soda Springs/Norden exit off I-80, Soda Springs. Cross-country skiers, head here to enjoy the largest ski resort especially for you. Its 90 trails on 9,172 acres, ski schools, cafés, views, *and* a hot tub make this a wonderful spot to try out those skills. Moms, head over during the week for the special Mom-n-Me days for discounted tickets and a sled to pull sleeping Junior. They also have accommodations, if you are too exhausted to leave the area. $.

Sugar Bowl (530-426-1111; sugarbowl.com) Donner Pass Road, 3 miles east of Soda Springs/Norden exit off I-80. Friends come here from San Francisco for the day to take advantage of the killer snowfall and the variety of slopes. Everyone will find something to do at this oldest ski resort in Tahoe (it was opened by Walt Disney in the 1930s—though don't expect to see singing mice). Although it gets crowded, the park still feels mellow and welcoming to all levels. $$$.

EMERALD BAY.

✳ Green Spaces

STATE PARKS AND RECREATION AREAS

Lake Tahoe
Parks listed south to north.

Heavenly Mountain See To Do.

Washoe Meadows State Park (530-525-7232; parks.ca.gov) Sawmill Road at Lake Tahoe Boulevard, South Lake Tahoe. This is a great, mellow spot to walk, run, and cross-country ski without the masses of people who populate the lake in summer. The meadow doesn't have any marked trails, but you can go for 4 miles.

Pope Baldwin Recreation Area See Tallac Historic Site.

Emerald Bay State Park (530-525-7255; parks.ca.gov) Go 4 miles west of Pope Baldwin Recreation Area on CA 89. The most-photographed spot in California and possibly the United States, this aqua and turquoise 3-mile bay surrounds Fannette, Tahoe's only island. As you wind around the lake in sometimes-scary hairpin turns, you'll be rewarded with jaw-dropping views of the bay on one side and Fallen Leaf Lake on the other. Traffic surrounding the area gets nutty, so to avoid the crowds, go early, park at the **Eagle Falls** picnic area, then hike up to **Eagle Falls** for a spectacular view of the entire bay with less people getting in your photos. I like to take a dip in **Eagle Lake** on the way back from **Upper and Middle Velma Lakes**. The hike is long (6 miles each way) and strenuous, but so worth it. You can also hike down to **Vikingsholm** (see *To See*). You can also camp here in summer at either the family camp or the boat-in sites (reserveamerica.com).

Fallen Leaf Lake (877-444-6777; sf.fed.us) Off CA 89 onto Fallen Leaf Road, South Lake Tahoe. This pristine lake, just on the other side of the road from Emerald Bay, offers a wealth of fishing, hiking, biking, and camping. There are 205 campsites, 17 of them are on a first-come, first-served basis. Otherwise, reserve early. $25.

D. L. Bliss State Park (530-525-7277; parks.ca.gov) Just 3 miles north of Emerald Bay State Park on CA 89. This park, named for a lumber baron who used to own a ridiculous amount of land along the shore, now joins with Emerald Bay State Park to create one of the most beautiful stretches of parkland in the Lake Tahoe area. The best hike is the **Rubicon Trail** (9 miles round-trip), which takes you through fields of trees; in autumn the colors are mind-blowing, and in spring the wildflowers make me want to sing like Julie Andrews. You can get all the way to Emerald Bay and a great beach with warmish water. Another hike is the **Balancing Rock Nature Trail,** a 0.5-mile trek that shows off granite rocks balancing on a small stone base. You can camp here in summer; reservations are required (reserveamerica.com).

Sugar Pine Point State Park (530-725-7982; parks.ca.gov) CA 89, 8 miles north of D. L. Bliss State Park. There are 10 miles of trails at this state park, but it is not filled with sugar pines, as the name implies. You'll find **Ehrman Mansion** (530-525-7982), which you can tour in summer months. There are 2 miles of great beach to explore, but the highlights are the miles of hiking trails around General Creek, the 10-mile bike path to Tahoe City, and the excellent cross-country trails. You can camp at General Creek Campground (800-444-7275; reserveamerica .com), which is one of the only campgrounds in the area to stay open year-round—though the showers only work in summer.

Burton Creek State Park (530-525-7232; parks.ca.gov) On the northeast side of Tahoe City, off Bunker Drive. Quite the secret in these parts, this is a wonderful park to explore when you want to escape the crowds. Trails aren't marked well, but know that Burton Creek separates two nature preserves (Antone Meadows and Burton Creek). This park is mostly used for cross-country skiers. Visit the Tahoe SRA for detailed information.

High Camp at Squaw Valley See *To Do.*

Truckee and Vicinity

Donner Memorial State Park and Emigrant Trail Museum (530-582-7892; parks.ca.gov) Donner Pass Road, off I-80, west of Truckee. Museum is open at least 9–4 daily. It might seem strange to commemorate the cannibalistic Donner Party, a group of pioneers stuck in 22 feet of snow in the Sierra in the mid-1800s, in a park where you can hike, snowshoe, and cross-country ski. I would recommend doing your activity before visiting the museum, which shows a slide show about the group and how they never ate one of their family members but did munch on someone else's leg meat. Day use: $6.

OTHER BEACHES *Beaches listed south to north.*

Regan Beach South Lake Tahoe. This lakeside park is popular for weddings and picnics, as the grassy area has plenty of shade.

Pope Beach CA 89, 2 miles south of Camp Richardson, South Lake Tahoe. This popular family beach offers a mile of beach for swimming and picnicking. Parking $5.

Camp Richardson CA 89, South Lake Tahoe. In summer this popular marina and strip of sand gets packed with families renting water sports equipment, swimming, picnicking, and playing in the water.

Kiva Beach CA 89, turn right at Fallen Leaf Road and look for the Visitor Center. Its somewhat hidden location makes this a less-popular beach with tourists, though the rocky bottom might not make this the best swim spot for little ones. This is a good dog-walking beach, strolling on the sand spot, and place to cool off.

Baldwin Beach Off CA 89, 1 mile north of Fallen Leaf Road. Though there is no shade here, this is where you'll want to hang out for the day. The waters are fairly calm (though watch out for boaters), and the creek meets the lake, which might entertain the kids. Parking: $5.

Emerald Bay See *State Parks and Recreation Areas.*

D. L. Bliss See *State Parks and Recreation Areas.*

Meeks Bay Off CA 89, north of Emerald Bay in Meeks Bay. Families love this great beach, with campsites and inns along the coast. The water is warmer than most places and the area is sheltered from wind.

Sugar Pine Point See *State Parks and Recreation Areas.*

Tahoe City Commons Tahoe City downtown. In the heart of downtown Tahoe City is this wonderful beach park, with grassy area, climbing rocks, playgrounds, BBQs, and live music on summer Sunday afternoons.

Tahoe State Recreation Area (parks.ca.gov) In Tahoe City on the lakeside. This waterfront campsite and recreation area offers 57 acres of beach access and 39 campsites (reservations required).

Kings Beach Recreation Area Along CA 28, downtown Kings Beach. Basically, three beach parks make up this fun recreation area. I love coming here with inflatable rafts and spending a day floating in the sun. You can rent water toys here, and walk to a number of restaurants. There is a playground, BBQs, and summer arts and crafts fairs. Parking fee depends on length of your stay.

WILDERNESS AROUND LAKE TAHOE Surrounded by wild land, those of you wanting to escape the hoopla around the lake won't have any trouble locating an unexplored spot; though you will want a good hiking guide. My favorites are the *Sierra North* and *Tahoe Sierra* both published by Wilderness Press.

To explore these rugged areas, be sure to pack out everything you take in and practice not leaving any trace of your presence in the parks. Also note that bears are plentiful in the area. I assume if you are heading to these parks, you know the bear protocol, but just in case, note that bears like to eat—probably not you, but your almonds and rice cakes tend to attract them. Don't leave any traces of food in your car, avoid wearing scented sprays and lotions, and if you see a furry guy, make lots of noise and do not turn your back.

Parks listed from south to north.

Humboldt-Toiyabe National Forest See *South High Sierra.*

Mokelumne Wilderness (209-532-3671; fs.fed.us) Located along CA 4 and CA 68, near Markleeville. Over 100,000 acres of alpine forest straddles the summit of the three giant national forests in the area. This rugged area has been home to explorers and Indians, and now is protected land with a wealth of recreational activities for daring explorers. Though you need a permit to camp, you do not need one to hike the over 100 miles of trails. Major trailheads on the Stanislaus portion are located at **Lake Alpine, Woodchuck Basin,** and **Sandy Meadow** along

CA 4, on the Eldorado National Forest at **Tanglefoot, Plasse Trading Post, Caples Lake, Woods Lake,** and **Carson Pass** off CA 88, and on the Toiyabe National Forest at **Ebbetts Pass (Pacific Crest Trail), Pleasant Valley,** and **Wet Meadows.**

Grover Hot Springs State Park (530-694-2248 or 530-694-2249; parks.ca.gov) Go 4 miles west of Markleeville at the end of Hot Springs Road. Open year-round except select holidays and two weeks in September. Whether blizzards or scorching day, these two hot springs pools in an alpine meadow and pine forest attract folks who want to go on intense hikes 10,000 feet up and then relax their muscles. The best hike is the 10-mile round-trip **Burnside Trail**, which takes you past a waterfall, granite peaks, and up to Burnside Lake. You can also drive to the lake up Burnside Road. The campsite here welcomes tent and RV sites, by reservation only.

Desolation Wilderness (530-644-6048; fs.fed.us) From CA 89, access the wilderness from Eagle Falls picnic area or Meeks Bay. This popular wilderness area requires you to have a permit even to enter it. Its 100 square miles of rugged trails attract so many people in summer, you need to get your permit three months in advance. Day permits are available at the trailheads, but you need to arrange

---

FIRE AND ICE

Both fire and avalanches are a part of nature. In the past couple years the High Sierra (and all of Northern California, really) has been a hotbed for fires—in 2008 over 1000 fires burned after a freak lightning storm and heat wave hung over the area. In 2007, Lake Tahoe came closer than any of us ever want to come to a forest fire, with the Angora fire burning over 3,000 acres, 242 houses, and almost 70 commercial structures. Bottom line is, you don't want to be the dude sitting in court facing a family that lost all their belongings, including their baby pictures. So you need to be very cautious when out in the wild. Of course you should never smoke. And it is imperative that you make sure only to light a campfire when the visitor center says that fire danger is minimal—that means only a light breeze and non-scorching temperatures. If the temptation for S'mores is too great, you'll need to make sure to put the fire out completely before moving on.

As for avalanches, the first rule of thumb is to never go out alone— especially in backcountry. If you plan to head into backcountry, carry some sort of avalanche safety kit, including a probe and shovel. Most avalanches occur before or after a major storm—but not all—so look out for mountainsides where the slope is greater than 30 degrees and avoid open sloping areas, especially if you see snow rolling down it. The general rule is that if you do get stuck in an avalanche, go with the flow, try to grab a tree, and if that doesn't work, when the slide stops, dig a large air pocket for your head.

WATER WATER EVERYWHERE

The High Sierra has more lakes than Britney Spears has hits on the Internet. It is impossible to categorize them all for you. What you want to know is that when summer comes and the snow melts, swimming, fishing, boating, and hiking in the area can't be topped. Aside from superstar Lake Tahoe and the aforementioned lakes above, here is a list of some other notable stops listed from north to south.

Echo Lake Echo Lakes Road, just south of Lake Tahoe on US 50. This wonderful little natural lake has some great cabins to rent in summer (echochalet.com).

Blue Lakes (916-923-7142) Off CA 88, take Blue Lakes Road south. These four lakes make for excellent trout fishing, swimming, and quiet camping (42 sites on a first-come, first-served basis).

Woods Lake (916-923-7142) On CA 88, west of Carson Pass. This small lake offers swimming, picnic areas, a couple campsites (with pit toilets), and decent fishing.

Caples Lake (530-644-6048; eid.org) Off CA 88, west of Carson Pass. From this large alpine lake, you can access a number of smaller lakes, including **Kirkwood Lake, Round Lake, Emigrant Lake,** and **Meiss Lake.** The lake itself offers plenty of activities, resorts, and campgrounds ($20).

Silver Lake (530-644-6048; eid.org) Off CA 88, 6 miles west of Caples Lake. This granite and blue-water recreation area is where Kit Carson rested for a bit. Today families pack the lake in summer, staying at resorts and camping along the shores. Camp fees: $20.

camping permits through the Forest Service (530-644-6048) There are over 100 lakes in the area and fishing is plentiful. Popular trails include the **Meeks Bay, Echo Lakes, Mount Tallac, Bayview,** and **Eagle Falls**. Permits: $5.

Granite Chief Wilderness (530-265-4531; fs.fed.us) Access the wilderness from Soda Springs, off Soda Springs Road. From Tahoe City, take CA 89 south to Squaw Valley Road, look for the fire station and the trailhead. Officially a part of Tahoe National Forest, this nearly 20,000 acres of wilderness is not as heavily used as Desolation Wilderness and allows access to the headwaters of the American River. Though you don't need a camping or day-use permit, you will need a campfire permit. Hikers find lots of deer, amazing rock formations, and many lakes. Popular trails include the **Pacific Crest Trail** (21 miles) and **the Five Lakes Trail** (which has great summer swimming).

✳ Lodging

High season for lodging generally occurs in summer and on winter holiday weekends (and when fresh snow presents ideal conditions). During high season, many of the hotels have a minimum-night stay. Rates below do not include tax or extra fees for pets or a third person.

HOTELS AND RESORTS If you prefer to stay in chain hotels, you'll be happy to know that **Hyatt Regency** (hyatt.com) is just across the Nevada border and **Marriott** (marriott.com) sits at the base of Heavenly. On the Nevada side, some of the massive casino resorts include **Harvey's** (harveys.com), **Harrah's** (harrahs.com), **Tahoe Biltmore** (tahoebiltmore.com), and **Horizon** (horizoncasino.com).

Lake Tahoe

✿ ♿ ❝Ⴌ❞ ✾ **Deerfield Lodge** (tahoe deerfieldlodge.com) 1200 Ski Run Boulevard, South Lake Tahoe. Eric and Robin Eichenfield have turned the Old Dream Inn into a 12-room boutique hotel complete with luxurious amenities. Though when you pull up it might feel like a motor inn, step inside and see the special touches, like flat-screen TVs, self-cleaning Jacuzzi tubs, continental breakfasts, leather couches, and rain showerheads. For those of you who share a bed with a cover thief, you'll enjoy the individual bedding of fine linens. Breakfast is the only non-luxury item on their menu, but with so many great spots to eat, you probably won't care. Light sleepers might note that the walls are rather thin. From here you can roll out of bed and be at Heavenly in minutes. You can also bring your dog. $$–$$$$.

✿ ✿ ♿ **Historic Camp Richardson Resort** (800-544-1801; camprichardson.com) Off CA 89, a couple miles west of South Lake Tahoe. The word "historic" in the name hints that this is not your ordinary Tahoe accommodation. Built in the 1920s, with the land owned by the Feds, this 40-unit lodge, campsite, and recreation area pulls off the summer camp vibe without draining your wallet. Perfect for large groups, who can either get hotel-style lodging, private cabins with basic kitchens, or camp, all with views of the lake for a steal, compared to other parts of Tahoe. As long as you don't expect the Ritz, you are going to love this spot. Amenities: Beacon Bar and Grill restaurant (see *Eating Out*), marina, water sports rentals, beach, cross-country ski facilities, ice cream shop, general store, horse riding stables, kitchens in cabins, fireplace, no TV or phone. $–$$$.

✿ ♿ ❝ ❝Ⴌ❞ ⦿ **Resort at Squaw Creek** (530-583-6300 or 800-327-3353; squawcreek.com) 400 Squaw Creek Road, Olympic Valley. If you want a resort that you never have to leave, this is your first choice. Here you won't find that cozy cabin feeling, rather you get a 6500-acre complex offering every amenity imaginable—a winter chairlift, a fly-fishing center, waterslide, and ski-in, ski-out lodging. The 405 rooms evoke a corporate feel, with rich warm tones, some kitchens and fireplaces, LCD TVs, pools, tennis, four restaurants, concierge, kids' programs, spa, gym, golf course, and bar. After a recent 65 million dollar renovation, you can bet you'll get what you pay for. $$$$.

✿ ♿ **Sunnyside Steakhouse and Lodge** (530-583-7200 or 800-822-2754; sunnysidetahoe.com) 1850 W. Lake Boulevard, Tahoe City. Rustic and chic, this 23-room lodge represents all that makes Tahoe great. Sloping ceilings, plush bedding, stone fireplaces, and balconies over the lake (for most rooms), you'll definitely feel like you are on vacation here. The great Sunnyside Steakhouse gets loud in summer. Amenities: continental breakfast, Tahoe Grill, room service, and beach access. $$–$$$$.

Truckee

🐾 ♿ 🐾 "🍴" 🍷 **Cedar House Sport Hotel** (866-582-5655; cedarsporthotel.com) 10918 Brockway Road, Truckee. Featuring the finest in hip design, with sleek lines and mod touches like bowl sinks and German down comforters, yet honoring the mountain setting with earthy colors and heated granite floors, this 42-room hotel is calling out to travelers who want the ultimate in luxury. An eco-friendly design, hot tub, and bar add to the allure. $$$–$$$$.

🐾 ♿ "🍴" **Northstar at Tahoe Resort** (530-562-1010 or 800-466-6784; northstarattahoe.com) CA 267, 6 miles southeast of Truckee. This 270-unit megaplex of a resort offers everything from hotel rooms to condos, vacation rentals to houses you can only ski to, plus the arrival of a new Ritz Carlton Resort in 2009 will up the ante. This super family-friendly environment has so many activities to offer (including free lift tickets, pool, bikes, tennis, fitness center, kids' club, golf course, six restaurants, hot tub, and teen center) that you won't need to leave the resort. $–$$$$.

Truckee Hotel (530-587-4444 or 800-659-6921; truckeehotel.com) 10007 Bridge Street, Truckee. Both my husband and I saw a ghost last time we stayed at this 37-room historic hotel in the heart of Truckee. You'll feel the history immediately as you walk into this 1868 lumber-worker hotel, decorated in dark wood and period antiques. Most rooms share a bathroom, and include continental breakfast, but this is one of the best deals in the area. Moody's Bistro and Lounge (see Dining Out) is on the property. $–$$.

Lake Tahoe

🐾 ♿ 🐾 "🍴" **Alder Inn** (530-544-4485 or 800-544-0056; alderinntahoe.com) 1072 Ski Run Boulevard, South Lake Tahoe. If you bring Rufus the Chihuahua and don't want to cart him to the slopes, this inn can hook you up with a pet sitter (who happens to be the same person who will also baby-sit little Max). The 24 rooms are simple, motel-like, and clean, with breakfast, ski shuttles, pool, and hot tub. $–$$.

♿ "🍴" **Black Bear Inn B&B** (530-544-4451; tahoeblackbear.com) 1202 Ski Run Boulevard, South Lake Tahoe. Ski Run Boulevard is becoming Tahoe's Rodeo Drive. This Craftsman-style B&B adds to the allure of the neighborhood with some classic-Tahoe historic stone-and-log architecture. The luxury lodge features farm antiques and the best gourmet breakfast around, for guests in the five rooms and three cabins. Make sure to check out that 34-foot river rock fireplace in the main lodge, and the hot tub. $$$–$$$$; no children allowed.

"🍴" **Cottage Inn** (530-581-4073; the cottageinn.com) 1690 W. Lake Boulevard, Tahoe City. This knotty pine cottage-B&B screams Tahoe style. Wood-paneled walls, stone accents, and themed rooms (like the Hunter's Hideout and Skier's Chalet) show guests how much thought and attention have gone into making this a perfectly romantic getaway year-round. The 23 cottages and suites include full breakfast and beach access. $$–$$$$; no children under 12.

🐾 ♿ 🐾 ⊚ **Fireside Lodge Bed & Breakfast** (530-544-5515; tahoefiresidelodge.com) 515 Emerald Bay Road, South Lake Tahoe. With the forest in the backyard and minutes to Emerald Bay, Fallen Leaf Lake, and beaches, this lovely log cabin lodge offers the perfect recipe for outdoor lovers. Sit around the fire pit sipping wine, after a day of kayaking, then return to your mountain-themed fireplace room and cook up some hearty pasta in your kitchenette. Find nine rooms and suites, plus a vacation home with complimentary bicycles and kayaks, and expanded continental breakfast. $$–$$$.

🌊 ♿ 🐾 **Inn at Heavenly Bed & Breakfast** (530-544-4244; innatheavenly.com) 1261 Ski Run Boulevard, South Lake Tahoe. This inn does it all, offering fireplace rooms, equipped kitchenettes, cabins, homes, and an event center. Its 30 rooms combine rustic comforts with class, allowing you to relax in the pine-shrouded inn. The Inn offers massage, expanded continental breakfast, wine and cheese, bicycles, and kayaks. $-$$$$.

🌊 ♿ ¶ ⊚ **Plumpjack Squaw Valley Inn** (530-583-1576 or 800-323-ROOM; plumpjacksquawvalleyinn.com) 1920 Squaw Valley Road, Olympic Valley. Plumpjack is the ideal location for urbanites. In winter, you ski in and out of this well-designed 61-room inn that offers clean lines, whimsical artsy touches, modern technology, and marshmallow-like beds. What this crew does so well is combine casual elegance with nature, allowing you to be pampered without feeling that someone is hanging over your shoulder ready to spit shine your shoes at a nod—though someone probably would if you paid enough. Amenities: 61 rooms and suites, some with kitchen, gourmet breakfast, patio, pool, hot tubs, ski rentals, fitness room, concierge, two restaurants, and a bar. $$–$$$$.

🌊 ⊚ **River Ranch Lodge** (530-583-4264 or 800-535-9900; riverranchlodge.com) CA 89 at Alpine Meadows Road, Tahoe City. For over 35 years this lodge, tucked into the banks of the Truckee River, has attracted snow bunnies and rafting aficionados. The 19 rooms feature period antiques, and tend to fill quickly, so reserve early. Rooms include continental breakfast, the River Ranch Restaurant. and bar. $–$$$.

⊚ **Rockwood Lodge** (530-525-5273 or 800-538-2463; inreach.com/rockwood) 5295 W. Lake Boulevard, Homewood. Established in 1939, this is Tahoe's first B&B property. Offering Dutch-style comforts like brass and porcelain showerheads, antique décor in all five rooms, hand-painted tiles, wood-paneled walls, pedestal sinks, and plush Laura Ashley linens, not to mention the simple breakfast, if you are looking for comfort look no further. $$–$$$.

🌊 ♞ 🐾 **Rustic Cottages** (888-7-RUSTIC; rusticcottages.com) 7449 N. Lake Boulevard, Tahoe Vista. The name of this little resort says it all. This is the perfect place for families or folks not wanting to fork over big bucks. Beds are comfy and the 22 cottages, situated beneath 2 acres of pines, are across the street from the lake and might be just the recipe. If these guys don't have the cottage you are looking for, their sister property, **Tahoe Vista,** 1 mile down the street, might. Amenities: continental breakfast, kitchenette, fireplace, bikes, sleds, croquet, and snowshoes. $–$$$$.

¶ **Shore House at Lake Tahoe** (530-546-7270 or 800-207-5160; shorehouselaketahoe.com) 7170 N. Lake Boulevard., Tahoe Vista. These nine lakefront cabins offer high-end amenities that still feel like you are in the mountains. Knotty pine walls and wood-burning stoves just scream hot cocoa and a game of Scrabble, while down comforters, the hot tub, and featherbeds will make you want to snuggle up close to your honey. $$–$$$$. .

🕭 🎄 **Tahoma Meadows B&B Cottages** (530-525-1553; tahomameadows .com) CA 89, 8 miles south of Tahoe City in Homewood. These 16 sweet cottages, located in a quiet stretch of Lake Tahoe's west shore, offer simple touches like claw-foot tubs and themed rooms (I like the Sun Room), with fresh flowers and plenty of shady outside areas to frolic. Some cottages get breakfast in the morning, while guests staying in the cottages with kitchens get to make their own pancakes. $–$$$$.

Truckee

🕭 ⁵⁷⁵ **River Street Inn** (530-550-9290; riverstreetinntruckee.com) 10009 E. River Street, Truckee. My favorite part about alpine B&Bs is that they often go for the rustic romance vibe rather than the Granny décor. This old brothel doesn't disappoint, with 11 rooms offering velvety linens, claw-foot tubs, sloped ceilings, and breakfast. $$.

Surrounding Areas

🕭 ⅄ ⁵⁷⁵ ⑳ **Sorenson's Resort** (530-694-2203 or 800-423-9949; sorensons resort.com) 14255 Hwy 88, Hope Valley. Part vacation rental and part B&B, these 33 rustic cabins deliver on alpine ambiance. Hammocks and rocking chairs dot the property, which tends to attract large groups of families and wedding parties. Most cabins come with kitchens and fireplaces, though there are a few bed-and-breakfast rooms, as well. Try to secure cabins off the main highway. The resort is open year-round, and amenities include kids' club, restaurant, no TV, bike rentals. $–$$$$.

VACATION RENTALS Camp Richardson See *Hotels and Resorts.*

🕭 ⅄ **Meeks Bay Resort** (530-525-6946 or 877-326-3357; meeksbayresort .com) 7941 Emerald Bay Road, Meeks Bay. Operated by the Washoe Tribe, this summer-only resort has one of the better locations on the lake. You can camp, rent a cabin (studio to two-bedrooms), or rent out the entire Kehlet Mansion. This is the perfect spot for large groups who want to spend a ton of time frolicking in the warm waters of the lake. Accommodations are rustic, but you will get a kitchen with most of them. Go for the beachfront rooms, which you won't find in many other spots on the lake. The 27 rooms and cabins, 12 tent sites, and 22 RV hookups offer fire pits, beach access, marina, and general store. $–$$$$.

Rustic Cottages See *Inns and Bed and Breakfast.*

Sorenson's Resort See *Inns and Bed & Breakfasts.*

🕭 ⅄ ⑳ ⁵⁷⁵ **Squaw Valley Lodge** (530-583-5500 or 800-922-9970; squawvalleylodge.com) 201 Squaw Peak Road, Olympic Valley. These 142 individually owned studio to three-bedroom condos, right in the heart of Olympic Valley, allow you the many amenities of a resort as well as the perks of having your own home. All condos come with daily maid service, kitchens, and big ole tubs. If you are picky about décor, ask for pictures of your particular rental unit. The loft suites are the airiest of the litter. Amenities: fitness room, spa, six hot tubs, video rentals, games, pool, concierge. $$–$$$$.

🕭 ⅄ **Tahoe Keys Resort** (800-698-2463) Tahoe Keys Marina, South Lake Tahoe. Its 200 vacation homes and condos make this a great choice for families and people who want to stick around for a while. Close to the lake, with first-class amenities (kitchen, fireplace, laundry, views galore) and plenty of activities to keep everyone busy (hot tub, basketball court, lake access, bikes, tennis, pools, and fitness room). Each rental is individually owned, so you never know what to expect, but in most cases, guests receive comfortable studio to six-bedroom units with nearly everything you need to make a home for a week. $$–$$$$.

✎ ♿ **The Village at Squaw Valley** (530-584-6205 or 888-805-5022; the villageatsquaw.com) 1985 Squaw Valley Road, Olympic Valley. The ultimate in condo-tel accommodations, this new complex offers 209 condos with heated bathroom floors, fireplace and kitchens, daily maid service, and multiple rooms—it's like home, but better. You can get a studio or three-bedroom condo and walk to the happening Squaw Valley Village area. $$–$$$$.

Truckee
Northstar at Tahoe See *Resorts and Hotels.*

Markleeville and Vicinity
✎ **Caples Lake Resort** (209-258-8888; capleslakeresort.com) CA 88, Kirkwood. You can either secure a cabin or a bed-and-breakfast room at this lakefront resort, just minutes from Kirkwood Mountain. Try for cabins 9 or 5, because they are closer to the lake. All 15 rooms have been remodeled within the last decade and though they aren't fancy, you will appreciate the simplicity of the complex. Breakfast comes with some rooms, while cabins often have kitchens. $–$$$.

✎ **Kit Carson Lodge** (209-258-8500; kitcarsonlodge.com) CA 88, Kit Carson. On the banks of the beautiful Silver Lake, these housekeeping cottages are a wonderful choice for families and groups who want to escape the crowds. With 22 cottages and hotel rooms, all decorated in knotty pine with down-home mountain furniture, fireplaces, and BBQs, this summer-only resort (except one ski-in unit) is a fun spot way off the beaten track. The restaurant on site is a sound option. $$–$$$$.

CAMPGROUNDS There are so many campsites in the Sierra Nevada Mountains! National Forest Service (877-444-6777; reserveusa.com) sites generally are on a first-come, first-served basis, though there are some you can reserve in advance. These usually have basic services like pit toilets and fire rings. State park campgrounds

JUST A FEW STEPS FROM THE CROWDED CAMP RICHARDSON, GETS YOU ENDLESS SPACE.

(800-444-7275; reserveamerica.com) like Sugar Pine Point and Emerald Bay must be reserved in advance (do it early, they sell out quickly). For back-country camping, you'll need a free permit, so contact the Forest Service of the area you wish to camp in. I have listed campgrounds under the *Green Spaces* section, though there are some options for camping at **Camp Richardson, Meeks Bay,** and **Grover Hot Springs** as well. Note that most sites close for winter.

✳ Where to Eat

DINING OUT

South Lake Tahoe

&. **Café Fiore** (530-541-2908; cafe fiore.com) 1169 Ski Run Boulevard #5, South Lake Tahoe. Open daily for dinner at 5:30. This intimate Italian restaurant attracts locals wanting a fine dining experience without the crowds. Seven tables in the whole restaurant guarantee that you will be taken care of. And the food is exceptional—eggplant crepes, *cappellini bocconcini, pollo* ala Sonoma. Reservations highly recommended. $$–$$$.

&. ♈ **Evan's** (530-542-1990; evanstahoe .com) 536 Emerald Bay Road., South Lake Tahoe. Open for dinner daily. High-end California cuisine at its finest. Located in a little house across from the lake, this expensive spot delivers with creative takes on international dishes, using the finest and freshest ingredients you can find. Entrees include grilled filet with foie gras butter, or breast and confit leg of duck with Grand Marnier duck glaze. Reservations required. $$$–$$$$.

&. **Nepheles** (530-544-8130; nepheles .com) 1169 Ski Run Boulevard, South Lake Tahoe. Open for dinner nightly. California cuisine in a relaxed atmosphere (with a couple hot tubs in back, in case you need extra help unwind-

ing). Favorite entrees include Thai coconut shrimp, and rack of New Zealand lamb. The nightly special could be anything from elk to ahi tuna, depending on what's fresh. Reservations recommended. $$$–$$$$.

♋ &. ♈ **Riva Grill** (530-542-2600; riva grill.com) 900 Ski Run Boulevard, South Lake Tahoe. Open for lunch and dinner daily. Surprisingly, there isn't much chance to dine with a lake view in the South Shore, which is probably why this overpriced restaurant gets packed in summer. The food relies heavily on grease, but the views are worth it. I prefer to come here at sunset for a cocktail and crab cakes, then go somewhere else for dinner. But after a few cocktails, you might not be moving anywhere. $$–$$$$.

Samurai Restaurant (530-542-0300; sushitahoe.com) 2588 Lake Tahoe Boulevard, South Lake Tahoe. Open 5–10 daily. Since 1984 this has been the place to get fine sushi and Japanese fare. Their new addition of healthy grub from around the Asian continent offers a wonderful mint tofu salad. Otherwise, go for the sushi. $$–$$$.

West and North Lake Tahoe

♈ **Graham's of Squaw Valley** (530-581-0454 or 530-581-2199) 1650 Squaw Valley Road, Olympic Valley. Open for dinner daily in winter and from Wednesday through Sunday in summer. Exposed stone and a fireplace make this homey high-end restaurant feel like you are being catered to in a private lodge. Meals are what you would expect, concentrating on game, steaks, and pastas. Reservations recommended. $$$–$$$$.

♈ **Mamasake** (530-584-0110; mama sake.com) Village at Squaw Valley, 1850 Village South Road, Olympic Valley. Open for lunch and dinner daily. Head to this wildly popular sushi and tapas spot for great happy hour specials, with views of the ski run. Though it may sound strange to combine Japanese with Italian and Latin flavors, you'll be surprised at the party that happens in your mouth. Try their Mamas Balls. Reservations recommended. $$–$$$.

✂ ᕦ ♈ **Plumpjack Café** (530-583-1578; plumpjack.com) 1920 Squaw Valley Road, Olympic Valley. Open from 11:30–10. Foodies know that there is nowhere better than this urban-style restaurant that uses the word café in name only. The chef's use of seasonal, organic ingredients is only part of what makes this urban-esque restaurant hip: Here you'll find a stellar wine list and some of the best food around. Reservations recommended. $$–$$$$.

Sunnyside Steakhouse See *Lodging*.

♈ **The West Shore Café** (530-525-5200; westshorecafe.com) 5160 West Lake Boulevard., Homewood. Open in winter for dinner, on Friday through Monday. Open for lunch and dinner from Memorial Day through Labor Day. Elegant dining is the name of the game at this lakefront restaurant. I come here on Monday for the select three-course menu served for only $40. Otherwise, choose between gourmet mushrooms, wild salmon, and lamb rack with crepes. Reservations required. $$$$.

Wolfdale's (530-583-5700) 640 N. Lake Boulevard, Tahoe City. Open for dinner Wednesday through Monday. Lake views with excellent food are few and far between, yet for 30 years, Wolfdale's has delivered. Though they specialize in the F word (fusion, for non-foodies), you'll find interesting takes on seafood with Japanese influences. Reservations a must! $$$–$$$$.

Truckee and Vicinity

♈ **Cottonwood Restaurant and Bar** (530-587-5711; cottonwoodrestaurant .com) Off Brockway Road, Truckee. Open daily from 5:30–9:30. Winner of numerous local-favorite awards, this fine-dining restaurant overlooking downtown Truckee delivers on great wines and cocktails, and creative menu items you won't find elsewhere in town—think butternut squash enchiladas, hormone-free grass-fed burgers, and Caesar salad that begs you to eat with your fingers. Reservations recommended. $$–$$$.

♈ **Dragonfly** (530-587-0557; dragon flycuisine.com) 10118 Donner Pass, Truckee. Open daily from 11:30–2:30 for lunch, 4–5:30 for happy hour sushi and at 5:30–9:30 for dinner. Stop by for the happy hour special weekdays from 4–6. Otherwise, head here for great sushi, and California-fusion cuisine like flatbreads, Asian-inspired seafood, and Kobe steak. Reservations recommended. Lunch: $–$$. Dinner: $$$–$$$$.

♈ **Moody's** (530-587-8688; moodys bistro.com) 1007 Bridge Street, Truckee. Open for lunch and dinner daily, and brunch on weekends. Organic, seasonal, farm-fresh cuisine that changes depending on the whim of the chef. I like to eat outside in summer, before heading inside to hear live music on weekends. If you like pork, try their Big Ass Pork Platter. Reservations recommended. $$–$$$.

Nevada Side

♈ **Elevation 6310** (775-588-6310) 181 US 50, Stateline, NV. Open 11 AM–4 AM daily. This popular late-night dining spot is quite good and worth the trek into the chaos in Stateline. They serve creative organic dishes like a calamari salad, baked Brie and mushroom phyllo wrap, and Zinfandel-marinated tri-tip, accompanied by organic alcohol and infused drinks. $$–$$$$.

South and West Shore Lake Tahoe

Alpina (530-541-7449; alpinacafe.com) 822 Emerald Bay Road, near the "Y." Open 6–6. This is a delightful stop for coffee. Not only because it is pretty good, but also because of the alpine décor, the free Internet access, and the yummy pastries.

✦ ♿ ☼ **Beacon Bar and Grill** (800-544-1801; camprich.com) Camp Richardson, South Lake Tahoe. Open daily for lunch and dinner. There really aren't enough places to dine on a patio and stare at the lake. This is one of them. Though the food is not the best and you have to wait hours to eat, it seems everyone still shows up. Go really early to score an outside table on summer days. $$–$$$$.

✦ ♿ **Blue Angel Café** (530-544-6544; blueangelcafe.com) 1132 Ski Run Boulevard, South Lake Tahoe. Open 8–8 daily. Locals love this healthy breakfast spot. What works for my crew is that I can get granola, my husband can get a frittata, and our crazy friends can order a British Bob's hangover cure. $.

♿ ☼ **Blue Water Bistro** (530-541-0113; bluewaterbistrotahoe.com) Boardwalk Pier, Timber Cove Marina, South Lake Tahoe. Open for lunch and dinner daily. This new lakefront spot specializes in organic seasonal cuisine with a view. Sweet potato Dungeness crab cakes and the lentil nut loaf are both a treat. Reservations recommended. $$–$$$.

✦ ♿ ☼ **The Cantina** (530-544-1233; cantinatahoe.com) 765 Emerald Bay Drive, South Lake Tahoe. Open 11:30–10:30 daily. If you can sacrifice not dining on the lake, this is a great choice for quality Mexican food and butt-kicking margaritas. Hearty burritos, quesadillas, and nachos populate the menu, while the happy hour specials enjoyed at the festive bar or on the patio make for a fun post-adventure snack. $$.

✦ ♿ **Ernie's** (530-541-2161) 1146 Emerald Bay Road, South Lake Tahoe. Open 6 AM–2 PM daily. You have to love a spot where the staff has been there for over 25 years. This popular lumberjack-style breakfast spot brings out all flavors of devoted locals. $–$$.

✦ ♿ **Freshies** (530-542-3630) 3330 Lake Tahoe Boulevard, South Lake Tahoe. Open for dinner daily. Known around town for having the best fish tacos north of San Diego, this spot serves up healthy dishes that actually taste great. Vegetarians will love the selection of meatless offerings. The island décor, the menu (including Hawaiian pork ribs), and the service make this one of the better options in town. $–$$$.

✦ ♿ **Sprouts Natural Foods Café** (530-541-6969) 3123 Harrison Avenue, South Lake Tahoe. Open from 8–8 Monday through Friday, 7–8 Saturday and 8–6 Sunday. If you want healthy fare with a Latin twist, wraps, rice bowls, and smoothies, Sprouts is calling your name. I like to grab a picnic from here to take to the beach in summer, but don't expect to get out of this wood-paneled eatery quickly. On weekends this place is jam-packed. Cash only. $.

North Lake Tahoe

✦ ♿ ☼ **Caliente** (530-546-1000; calientetahoe.com) 8791 North Lake Boulevard, Kings Beach. Open from 11:30–9:30 (bar stays open until 11:30). At happy hour you can enjoy drink specials and half-off appetizers at this Southwestern-themed restaurant. Heavy wooden chairs, colorful décor, and great drinks round out the dining experience. $$–$$$.

◊ & **Fire Sign Café** (530-583-0871) 1785 W. Lake Boulevard., Tahoe City. Open from 7 AM–3 PM daily. Breakfasts rule at this too-popular restaurant. Benedict fans will appreciate that Fire Sign allows you to get two types on one plate. Get here early on Sundays; it can be packed, and you'll want to dine on the patio if it is warm. $–$$.

◊ & ⅋ **Gar Woods Grill and Pier** (530-546-3366; garwoods.com) 5000 North Lake Boulevard, Carnelian Bay. Open for lunch and dinner daily, and brunch on weekends. Broken into two restaurants, the cheaper being the bar café, you'll find an array of weekday specials including half-price appetizers and drink specials, as well as a mish-mash of food like crab sandwiches, fish tacos, and Thai chicken lettuce wraps. $$–$$$.

◊ & **Log Cabin Café** (530-546-7109) 8692 N. Lake Boulevard, Kings Beach. Open 7 AM–2 PM daily and in summer the ice cream shop is open from noon–10 PM. Breakfast doesn't get better than this. Eat massive portions of creative breakfasts in a log cabin. Specialties include a trout scramble, Arizona French toast, and Benedicts. They don't take reservations, but you might try calling ahead to put your name on the list. $$.

◊ & ⅋ **Sol y Lago** (530-583-0358; solylago.com) Inside the Boatworks Mall, Tahoe City. Open for dinner from 5:30 daily, and happy hour starts at 4 PM with discounted drinks and appetizers. The dark interior allows for you to space out on the lake views all around. Food ranges from small plates like *queso fundido* and *lomo saltado,* to tacos, moles, and even burgers. $$–$$$.

Truckee and Vicinity

◊ & **Squeeze Inn** (530-587-4694) 10096 Donner Pass Road, Truckee. Open for breakfast and lunch daily.

The Squeeze Inn breakfast spot is not joking about the name—it's 11-by-60 feet! They also claim to have the 62 Best Omelettes on the Planet. Not sure about that, but they are pretty darn good. As long as you aren't claustrophobic, you'll enjoy breakfast or lunch here. $.

✳ Entertainment

The majority of nightlife occurs in Stateline, Nevada. Here you'll find casinos, late-night bars and dining, and live music. For the rest of the Tahoe area, expect a sleepier nightlife vibe, with a few classy watering holes thrown in for good measure.

South and West Shores

⅋ **Beacon Bar and Grill** See *Eating Out.*

⅋ **The Cantina** See *Eating Out.*

⅋ **FiRE + iCE** Heavenly Village. Head here to sip on martinis around a fire pit.

⅋ **McP's Irish Pub and Grill** (530-542-4435) 4093 Lake Tahoe Boulevard, South Lake Tahoe. This popular Irish pub has led to many a hangover. It even lures folks from the Stateline area to the California side.

⅋ **Riva Grill** See *Dining Out.*

North Lake Tahoe

⅋ **Bridgetender** (530-583-3342) 65 W. Lake Boulevard, Tahoe City. The outdoor bar along the Truckee River keeps locals coming back year after year. Their burgers and waffle fries help too.

⅋ **Caliente** See *Eating Out.*

⅋ **Fiamma** (530-581-1416) 521 N. Lake Boulevard, Tahoe City. This newish wine bar has become the happening spot for local wine lovers and wood-fired pizza lovers.

⅋ **Jason's Beachside Grille** 8338 N. Lake, Boulevard, Kings Beach. This lakefront bar and grill serves burgers and beers on an outdoor deck.

℣ **Mamasake** See *Dining Out.*

℣ **Zenbu** (530-583-9900) Inside the Olympic House at Squaw Valley. Live music and DJs, plus drink specials, make this a hopping spot on all days of the week.

Truckee and Vicinity

℣ **Fifty Fifty Brewing Company** (530-587-BEER; fiftyfiftybrewing.com) 11197 Brockway Road, Truckee. Head here for great beer and pub grub.

℣ **Moodys** See *Dining Out.*

Stateline, Nevada

Besides all-night gambling, there is plenty of nightlife to keep you busy just across the border.

℣ **blu** (775-588-3515; montbleuresort .com) MontBleu Resort and Casino, 55 US 50. This nightclub caters to the younger crowd. For people interested in more of a lounge scene, check out **Opal Ultra Lounge**. Big-name performers also headline at the resort.

Harvey's Outdoor Arena (harveys .com) Harvey's Casino, 12 US 50. Famous musicians play under the stars all summer long.

℣ **VEX nightclub** (800-HARRAHS; harrahs.com) 15 US 50. Come here to dance and be seen on weekends.

✳ Selective Shopping

On the South Shore, shoppers will find plenty to keep them busy at **Heavenly Village** (theshopsatheavenlyvillage .com), including galleries, clothing boutiques (check out **Rainurbana**), and jewelry stores. Rumor has it that the South Shore is also attempting to make Ski Run Boulevard into Tahoe's version of Rodeo Drive, with a number of luxury boutiques. For more high-end shopping, head to **Squaw Valley USA**, where you can find 31 shops and

boutiques, or the newer **Village at Northstar.**

✳ Seasonal Events

May: **Vallhalla Arts and Music** (vallhallatahoe.com) Tallac Historic Site. Through September, this popular festival offers world music, arts and crafts, and cultural events.

June: **Truckee Outdoor Amphitheater Concerts** (530-582-7720; tdrpd .com) Truckee River Regional Park. On Wednesday evenings from 6:30–8:30 through August, hear free live performances by local bands.

Commons Beach Concert Series (visittahoecity.com). On Sundays through August you can listen to live music on the beach from 4–7.

Movies and Music (800-GO-NORTH) Northstar-at-Tahoe. Until the end of August, come out on Thursday through Sunday afternoons to hear live music at this resort. And on weekends at dusk, come see outdoor movies.

July: **Fourth of July** This is a *big* night around the Lake, with parades and fireworks, festivals and BBQs. You can see fireworks at Donner Lake in Truckee, the Boathouse Theater in South Lake Tahoe, and at the beach in Tahoe City.

Lake Tahoe Shakespeare Festival (800-74-SHOWS; laketahoeshakespeare .com) Sand Harbor, NV. This wonderful festival is up there with some of the better Shakespeare festivals around. From July through August, come see outdoor theater with lake views.

Lake Tahoe Music Festival (530-583-3101; tahoemusic.org) Homewood Resort. Through August on select nights, this three-week festival has bloomed so much, they are building a new amphitheater to hold attendees.

Big-name musicians appear alongside local orchestras and students.

Squaw Summer Movie Series (530-584-6266; thevillageatsquaw.com). In July and August, the Village at Squaw projects films at dusk.

Summer Music on the Beach (ntba mainstreet.org) Kings Beach. Thursdays in August, local bands rock the biggest beach in Tahoe.

August: **Concours d'Elegance** (530-581-4700; laketahoeconcours.com) Carnelian Bay. The big guns come out to play for this festival, or rather, the guys with the best boats, come to show off their wooden flotillas. BBQs, rallies, and a boat parade celebrate the week-long event.

September: **Lake Tahoe Marathon** (laketahoemarathon.com). All week leading up to the marathon, those endurance junkies are participating in every type of sport to gear up. If you ever wanted to go for the 26.2 miles, this isn't the worst place to try out your legs.

SOUTHERN HIGH SIERRA—
Ebbetts Pass to Mono Lake

EBBETTS PASS TO SONORA PASS
YOSEMITE NATIONAL PARK
YOSEMITE SIERRA—
FISH CAMP TO OAKHURST
THE EASTERN SIERRA

Climb the mountains and get their good tidings. Nature's peace will flow into you as sunshine into trees.–John Muir.

To fully experience the landscape that captured the heart of John Muir, inspired the photographs of Ansel Adams, and evokes the same sort of grand contemplation and revelation in its visitors, you need to stay a while. In fact, you can't know Yosemite, Bass, and Mono Lakes, or even the heights of Tuolumne and Calaveras Counties without returning throughout the seasons. How can you fully appreciate the pinkish hue over the valley, the tons of water rushing over the granite peaks, the sudden thunder storms, the deer silently sipping water by a lake, the bear cub playing with a piece of bark, the hush of snow, the fields of poppies and lupine, the sudden chill after the sun sets, the echo that bounces off the spires, the burnt orange, red, and yellow of the fall foliage, the swimming holes, the unbelievable heights of sequoias, unless you sit in a field and inhale it all in.

Unfortunately, our busy lives don't allow us to give up our day jobs and head to the mountains like John Muir, Yosemite's theoretical father. So if you do nothing else, plan to return in another season. Though summer offers ideal weather conditions, there is nothing like the Yosemite Valley in spring, nor can you beat a drive to Mono Lake in fall, just when the leaves offer a flashy show, nor a weekend in the opalescent powder, with crystalline waterfalls trickling down the granite peaks.

Though finding (and ultimately helping to protect) this region is often credited to flower child, John Muir, Indians were the first to inhabit the 450-mile slab of granite we call the Sierra Nevada Mountains. Yosemite Valley gets credit for being the most dramatic, with vertical granite walls carved by glaciers, erosion, and earthquakes. However, with more time to explore, you'll find awe-inspiring sequoia groves, alpine lakes, and blankets of lupine throughout the area.

North of Yosemite, two of California's most scenic drives (which are only open when there is no snow or threat of snow), **Ebbetts** and **Sonora Passes,** weave from the Sierra Foothills all the way over the mountains and to the often overlooked eastern edge of the Sierra Nevada Mountains. The small recreation areas and towns of **Arnold, Bear Valley, Pinecrest,** and **Dardanelle** offer uncrowded opportunities to explore nature.

Yosemite National Park needs no introduction. Originally a battleground of fire and ice, with glaciers and volcanoes carving cliffs so stark, meadows so expansive, and waterfalls so lush they flow year-round, this region also has a bloody history. In the mid-1800s, vigilantes hired by the California government stormed the valley, killing off and destroying the village of the local Miwok Indians. Like all travelers, these guys went home and told everyone they met about the abundance of beauty we call Yosemite. And alas, tourism came to the valley. Then John Muir arrived, on a sojourn to connect with God. Enamored with the valley, he wrote *My First Summer in the Sierra,* built a cabin, and, high on nature, lobbied the U.S. government to create a National Park to protect his adopted home. He even convinced Teddy Roosevelt to ditch his secret service detail for three days of camping in the wild—this did the trick, and the valley was protected. Today, especially in summer, loads of cars stream through the park, often bumper-to-bumper, to snap photos of **Half Dome, El Capitan, Yosemite Falls,** and **Bridalveil Falls**— probably not what Muir had in mind.

South of Yosemite, you'll find a number of tourist enclaves created just to house the hordes of people headed west during the gold rush. Though gold was discovered in Coarsegold, this region became more famous for its granite production and lumber business. These days, the lovely towns of **Ahwahnee, Bass Lake, Fish Camp,** and **Wawona** offer a wealth of lodging options for the masses of visitors to Yosemite. The largest town in the region, **Oakhurst,** feels like an authentic mountain town, where you can find antiques, lumberjack-sized breakfasts, and plenty of recreational opportunities within a few miles of driving.

You might call the Eastern Sierra California's outback. The winding roads force you to slow down, and maybe even get out of the car to take in the Jeffrey pines, the singing birds, the mule's ears and lupines enveloping the countryside. Here you'll find a glimpse of the Wild West, where explorers passed through searching for riches, farmers and ranchers still offer supplies for those in need, and now ghost towns filled with piles of dusty tin cans lie dormant. However, outdoor enthusiasts will find so many opportunities to flex their muscles, it might be impossible to leave.

GUIDANCE **Yosemite National Park Visitor Center** There are four visitor centers throughout Yosemite. The only one open year-round is located in Yosemite Village from 9–7 daily. This is always my first stop—the volunteer staff is just as fascinated with the park as you are, and often can tell you where deer or a bear and her cub frequent. Other centers are located in Tuolumne Meadows, open June through September from 9–6; Wawona, next to Wawona Hotel in Hill's Studio, from spring to fall, 8:30–5; and Big Oak Flat, open spring to fall from 9–7.

Yosemite Sierra Visitor Bureau (559-683-4636; yosemitethisyear.com) 41969 Southern CA 41, Oakhurst. Before heading into the park, visit the 24-hour infor-

MUSTS FOR FIRST-TIME VISITORS

1. Tour Yosemite's valley floor.
2. Eat at Erna's Elderberry House.
3. Swim in Pinecrest Lake.
4. Drive the Sonora Pass to Bridgeport.
5. Ski Bear Valley.
6. Visit a sequoia grove.
7. Attend a performance at the Golden Chain Theater.
8. Explore Tuolumne Meadows.
9. Spend an afternoon playing in Bass Lake.
10. Visit Bodie.

MUSTS FOR REPEAT VISITORS

1. Hike Half Dome.
2. View the Yosemite Valley from Glacier Point.
3. Eat brunch at the Ahwahnee.
4. Take a horseback trip into the wilderness.
5. Wander the back roads of the eastern mountains.
6. Explore Hetch Hetchy's waterfalls.
7. Hike to Vernal Falls.
8. Drive a scenic byway.
9. Kayak Lake Alpine.
10. View the Dardanelles.

mation board, chat with the staff, and grab some maps to make your exploring easier.

HELPFUL WEB SITES
Yosemite.com
Thegreatunfenced.com
Homeofyosemite.com
Yosemite-gateway.org
tcvb.com
monocounty.org
gocalaveras.com
Monoco.org

GETTING THERE *By air:* There is no airport serving the region. The closest major one is **Sacramento Airport** (see *Sacramento*).

By bus: **Greyhound** (greyhound.com) doesn't actually make it to Yosemite, but it will get you pretty close (to Merced). From there, you can take **Yosemite Via** (via-adventures.com) to Midpines or Mariposa. **Yosemite Area Regional Transportation System (YARTS)** (209-388-9589; yarts.com) shuttles folks along CA 140 from Merced to the park, as well as CA 120 over the Tioga Pass in summer.

By car: It is possible, but tough, to fully explore the region without a car. Brave souls hike the Pacific Crest trail or take a number of day-long bus journeys from place to place, but the easiest way to explore (sorry, Al Gore) is with your own set of wheels. In summer Ebbetts Pass (CA 4) and Sonora Pass (CA 108) allows people access from CA 49–US 395. CA 120 (also known as Tioga Pass) is open to Yosemite year-round, but closes as a route to Mono Lake in winter. From the south, take CA 140 to the southern entrance of Yosemite. Note that there are no gas stations in the Yosemite Valley, so fill up before heading in. For road conditions, contact **Caltrans** (916-445-7623).

By train: **Amtrak** (Amtrak.com) gets you as far as Merced.

GETTING AROUND *By bus:* **YARTS** (yarts.com) shuttles passengers throughout the region, but not throughout Yosemite National Park. The absolute best way to see the park (without the stress of traffic) is to take the **Valley Shuttle Bus** (yosemitepark.com). This free shuttle transports travelers around the loop, stopping at every major accommodation, restaurant, and valley floor site. Shuttles come every few minutes and erase the stresses that come with negotiating traffic, knowing where to turn, and wanting to photograph the deer in the meadow. In summer, I've never waited longer than five minutes for a shuttle, and I have to say that those were the best five minutes of my last Yosemite visit—I saw a bear cub!

By car: Other than in Yosemite National Park (see *Getting Around by bus*), your car will come in handy. Two-lane mountain roads often get congested in summer, so be patient, bring some good music, and remember that everything you are seeing is nature.

MEDICAL EMERGENCIES If it is a major problem, dial 911.

Community Medical Center (559-683-2992) 48677 Victoria Lane, Oakhurst. **Yosemite Medical Clinic** (209-372-4637) Ahwahnee Drive, Yosemite National Park.

WEATHER Typical alpine climate characterizes this region. Summers offer warm days and cool nights, while winter brings snow. Always have a sweater handy. Up near Half Dome in Yosemite, thundershowers often occur without warning. See also *Northern High Sierra—Fire and Ice.*

EBBETTS PASS TO SONORA PASS

✳ To See and Do

Ebbetts Pass
Bear Valley Adventure Company See below.

Bear Valley Cross Country Ski/Bear Valley Adventure Co. (209-753-2834; bearvalleyxc.com) 1 Bear Valley Road, Bear Valley. Cross-country skiers and snowshoers will love the 40 miles (65 km) of trails and track. Plus there is a great sledding hill for the little guys. They also have ski-in lodging options at the Bear Valley Lodge (bearvalleylodge.com), with rates starting at $109. These are also the go-to guys for mountain biking information (they publish a wonderful trail guide), bike and kayak rentals, and gear.

Bear Valley Ski Area (209-753-2301; bearvalley.com) CA 4 at CA 207, Bear Valley. In-the-know skiers head here to hit the slopes, since Tahoe gets so packed. You'll find 1,280 acres, covered with up to 30 inches of snow annually, 67 runs, lifts, and plenty of terrain for boarders and kamikazes to show off. In summer, mountain bikers take over the area, exploring the trails—for a detailed list of places to pedal visit the Bear Valley Adventure Company (See above). Lift tickets range from $42 for a half day to $59 for peak season. Kids' rates range from $16–49, and children under 5 are free.

Bear Valley Snowmobile (209-753-2323; bvsnowmobile.com) 132 Bear Valley Road, Bear Valley. If you have never explored the innards of a forest by snowmobile, here is your chance. These guys rent by the hour or for a full day, and direct you to groomed trails throughout the Stanislaus National Forest. Rentals start at $49 for a half-hour tour of the village and go way up to $239 for a six-hour tour of Lake Alpine.

Sierra Nevada Adventure Co. (209-795-9310; snacattack.com) 2293 CA 4, across from Meadowmont Center in Arnold. Rent snowshoes, ski equipment, snowboards, and buy outdoorsy clothing. Rates start at $14 per day.

Sonora Pass

Dodge Ridge Ski Area (209-536-5300; dodgeridge.com) 1 Dodge Ridge Road, Pinecrest. Since 1951, this mountain park has been giving winter sports enthusiasts a safe place to play. With a summit of 8,200 feet and 815 acres of land, everyone from beginners to tricksters will be entertained . $42–52 adults; $10–33 youth; under 5 free.

Kennedy Meadows Resort and Pack Station (209-965-3900; kennedymeadows .com) CA 108, Kennedy Meadows. The gateway to the Emigrant Wilderness, here you can ride a horse past tree-lined lakes, reservoirs, and into the forest. Their 90-minute trip is great for beginners, while more advanced riders will appreciate the day-long (or overnight) jaunts into Carson-Iceberg Wilderness. They also arrange pack trips into the forest for one-day trips or overnights. This is also a great starting-off point for hikes, fishing, and uncrowded High Sierra exploring. Fees start at $22.50.

✿ **Leland High Sierra Snow Play** (209-965-4719; snowplay.com) Off CA 108, turn on Leland Meadows Road, Strawberry. The largest snowplay-only facility in the Sierra; bring the kids to tube, sled, and play in the arcade, while Mom and Dad relax by the fire. $18–30.

Pinecrest Lake Resort Marina (209-965-3333; pinecrestlakeresort.com) Pinecrest Lake Road, Pinecrest. The picturesque Pinecrest Lake makes for a wonderful place to kayak, sail, or rent a paddleboat. You can find them all at this resort marina. Kayak rentals start at $15.

✳ Green Spaces

Ebbetts Pass

Calaveras Big Trees See *Sierra Foothills.*

Stanislaus National Forest (209-795-1381; fs.fed.us/ r5/Stanislaus) Calaveras Ranger District, 5519 CA 1, Hathaway Pines. The Calaveras Ranger portion of the forest is one of the most pristine, containing the wonderful Lake Alpine;

PINECREST LAKE.

Highland Lakes (fishing for trout here is supreme); **Mosquito Lakes**; **Spicer**, **Utica**, and **Union Reservoirs**; and all with a plethora of fishing, swimming, boating, and beachcombing opportunities. Mountain bikers are in heaven with Elephant Rock Loop, Lake Alpine Loop, Bear Trap Basin Loop, Jelmini Basin Loop, and Slick Rock Ride. If you only have a day, head out to **Lake Alpine**, or in winter trek to the California SNOPARK at the edge of CA 4's winter closure gate. Hikers will want to explore the Bear Valley to Alpine Lake, Bull Run Lake, Duck Lake, or the mellow Lake Alpine trails. Escapists will want to retreat to the quiet **Mokelumne** and **Carson-Iceberg Wilderness** areas (note that you need to acquire a permit from the ranger station for an overnight stay). With 20 campgrounds to choose from (and a number of backcountry hideouts as well) you won't be at a loss for finding a campground—though in summer, you want to reserve your spot (recreation.gov) at the more popular sites like **Big Meadow** ($17), **Highland Lakes** ($8), **Lake Alpine** ($20), and **Spicer Reservoir** ($20). For all activities, contact the ranger station to get a map, as territorial locals often steal the directional signs.

Sonora Pass

Stanislaus National Forest (209-965-3434; fs.fed.us/r5/Stanislaus) Summit Ranger District, 1 Pinecrest Lake Road, Pinecrest. Along CA 108, you'll be rewarded with hikes unlike anywhere else in the forest. Head to the ranger station to get a map, as local vandals often remove the signs for trailheads, then head off to explore the Trail of the Gargoyles (just past Strawberry), which offers craggy, ancient volcanic formations reminiscent of gargoyles. Or, you might enjoy the Trail of the Ancient Dwarfs, near Niagara Creek Campground off Eagle Meadow Road—the road is very rough, so you might want to park earlier and trek up the road. This trail is a gateway to the Bennett Juniper (See *Sidebar*). Another highlight is the Columns of the Giants Trail (Pigeon Flat Campground), where you will find the largest concentration of basaltic columns in the Sierra. You might really want to get into the wilderness, so you'll need to contact the ranger station for a permit to head into the **Emigrant** and **Carson-Iceberg Wilderness Areas** (see above). Mountain bikers frequent the Sugar Pine Railroad Grade and the Goose-

THE BENNETT JUNIPER

You hear all the hype about redwood trees, and if you are of the same camp of Ronald Reagan, thinking—what's all the hype?—you might not want to read further. For the rest of us tree huggers, a worthy side trip when exploring the innards of the Stanislaus National Forest along CA 108 is to see the Bennett Juniper. This tree is the largest western juniper, at 80 feet tall and 40 feet around, and it is believed to be over 3500 years old. The lucky old gal even has its own caretaker.

To visit the juniper, prepare for a longish journey; though distances are short, it takes 45 minutes to drive 12 miles. Take CA 108 to Eagle Meadow Road and follow the signs. It is best to grab a map at the ranger station.

berry-Crabtree trails—note that it is illegal to ride a bike in a wilderness area. Popular day-use areas include the Beardsley Reservoir (great for fishing), Pinecrest Lake (which is fun to swim and kayak), Donnell Vista picnic area, Kennedy Meadows, and Dardanelle. And, as you might expect there are zillions of campgrounds, which you can reserve at recreation.gov. Favorites include **Dardanelle** ($18–22), **Niagara Creek** ($6), **Meadowview** ($14), and **Clark Fork** ($14).

✳ Lodging

Along the two passes are a number of resorts, nestled near lakes and reservoirs, plus strings of campgrounds throughout the region. If none of these accommodations listed appeal to you, contact the **Calaveras County Visitor Bureau** and the **Tuolumne County Visitor Bureau**. You might also check in *Sierra Foothills* lodging section for additional inns.

Ebbetts Pass

⛲ ⌾ **Arnold Black Bear Inn B&B** (209-795-8999; arnoldblackbearinn .com) 1343 Oak Circle, Arnold. Staying in this log B&B, surrounded by pines, and steps to lakes, ski lifts, and great wine tasting, you enjoy solitude and country charm. Expect cathedral ceilings, wood-burning stoves, Jacuzzi tubs, fireplaces, wine socials, and hearty breakfasts. $$–$$$; no children under 10 allowed during ski season.

Bear Valley

⛲ ⅋ ⌾ **Bear Valley Lodge** (209-753-2327; bearvalleylodge.com) 3 Bear Valley Road, Bear Valley. Steps from the ski lift and surrounded by daisies and pines, this 53-room lodge has a restaurant, a lounge, and makes a good hub for skiers. Winter season offers affordable lift and lodging packages starting at $55. $–$$ (rates double in winter).

⛲ ⅋ ❀ **Lake Alpine Resort** (209-753-6350; lakealpineresort.com) 4000 CA 4, Bear Valley. Stay in a tent cabin or the lodge, right on lovely Lake Alpine. Some cabins offer kitchens as well. Bring the kids for a week so you can let them run around while you relax by the shores of the lake with a microbrew and a book. There is also a restaurant here. $–$$$.

VACATION RENTALS Central Sierra Vacation Rentals (formerly Sierra Vacation Rentals) (800-523-5499; sierrapropertyrentals.com) 908 Moran Road, Arnold. Over 50 Cabins in Big Trees and Arnold areas. Located in Blue Lake Springs, just minutes from Bear Valley Mountain Resort and directly in Arnold's resort community.

✳ Where to Eat

You might also check the *Sierra Foothills* chapter, paying close attention to Twain Harte (for Sonora Pass) and Murphys (along CA 108), which are both close enough for dining, if you are staying up in the mountains.

Ebbetts Pass

✒ ઙ ☗ **Creekside Dining at Bear** (209-753-2325; bearvalleylodge.com) 3 Bear Valley Road, Bear Valley. Serving breakfast Tuesday through Thursday, lunch Tuesday through Sunday, and dinner nightly. Excellent fresh, seasonal dishes by Chef Mikael Blancho, who whips up homemade sauces and delicious desserts at both the Creekside and the Grizzly Lounge (which also serves food nightly). Sit outside in the flower-lined landscape in the summer. $$.

✒ ઙ ☗ **Headwaters Coffee House** (209-753-2708; headwaterscoffeehouse .com) In the Bear Valley Lodge, 3 Bear Valley Road, Bear Valley. Open for breakfast, lunch, and dinner daily. Freshly baked goods, smoothies, ice cream, milkshakes, gourmet pizza, coffee, tea, espresso, wine, and a decent microbrew selection are available here. $.

✒ ઙ **Sarafina's Italian Kitchen** (209-795-9858) 794 CA 4, Arnold. Open Wednesday through Sunday for dinner. Old-world Italy meets contemporary California in this wooded stretch of CA 4. Traditional favorites or uniquely created dishes, like Sarah's favorite, ensure a palate pleaser. If you like garlic, they use it well. Reservations suggested. $$.

✒ ઙ ☗ **Snowshoe Brewing Company** (209-795-2272; snowshoebrewing .com) 2050 CA 4, Arnold. Open for lunch Tuesday through Sunday, dinner nightly. Arnold's own microbrewery handcrafts award-winning ales, then serves them in a family atmosphere. Outdoor dining on the golf course is available in the summer. $.

Sonora Pass

✒ ઙ **Alicia's Sugar Shack** (209-586-5400; aliciassugarshack.com) 24191 CA 108, Sugar Pine. Open 6 AM–2 PM. One of the better surprises of my last trip up CA 108 was to find this idyllic country bakery in aptly named Sugar Pine. Espresso drinks are as frothy as can be and the pastries are divine. $.

✒ ઙ **Café 108** (209-965-4390) 29824 CA 108, Long Barn. Open Monday from 11–2, Wednesday through Friday from 8 AM–7:30 PM, and Saturday and Sunday from at least 9 AM–7:30 PM. A local favorite, especially since owners Fred and Liz moved from Cold Springs to Sugar Pine to enhance their offerings. Breakfast will set you up like a champ in the simple dining room. Or, if you are craving a burger or rib eye, they'll hook you up. Don't expect gourmet—this is the country y'all. Reservations recommended for dinner. $–$$.

✒ ઙ ☗ **Kennedy Meadows Pack Station** (209-965-3900; kennedymeadows .com) CA 108, Kennedy Meadows. Open 6 AM–10 PM daily from the end of April through Columbus Day. Known for the Sunday prime rib dinner and the Wild West-style dining room, Sierra folks head up here for a slab of meat, soup, salad, potato, veggie, and dessert. Sure, you can get other dishes—poultry, burgers—but why would you? $$.

✳ Entertainment

Most people hit the bed early after a long day of being outdoors. The only nightlife to be found is chasing mosquitoes. However, if you want a drink along the Sonora Pass, head to the **Strawberry Inn** (209-965-3662). Or in Arnold, you might want to visit the **Snowshoe Brewing Co** (See *Where to Eat*).

✳ Selective Shopping

People don't come to the Sierra to shop. That being said, if you need any outdoor gear, head to **Sierra Nevada Adventure Co.** (209-795-9310; snacattack.com) 2293 CA 4, across from Meadowmont Center in Arnold.

✳ Seasonal Events

July: **Bear Valley Music Festival** (209-753-2574 or 800-458-1618; bear valleymusic.org) Bear Valley. The music plays the last week in July through the first week in August. Voted the best summer attraction several times over, this is the musical event not to miss. International soloists, full symphony orchestra, legendary entertainers, and unique opera stars have all been guests in years past.

YOSEMITE NATIONAL PARK

GUIDANCE When first arriving at Yosemite, head straight for the **Visitor Center** (209-372-0200; nps.gov) in Yosemite Village. The helpful volunteers will guide you towards the ideal itinerary for your trip and educate you on special events. There are three other Visitor Centers in the park that are open in summer only (See *Guidance* above); they make great pit stops to figure out hiking trails, learn about where the wildlife are most likely to be seen, and which waterfalls have a particularly heavy flow.

HELPFUL WEB SITES
Yosemitepark.com
Yosemite.com
Yarts.com
Yosemite.org

FEES To enter the park, you don't have to make a reservation (though you must reserve for lodging in the summer and holiday weekends), but you do need to pay a fee. There is a $20 vehicle fee, a $10 individual fee (for people entering on bike, bus, or foot), or a year pass for $40. A lifetime senior pass costs 10 bucks, while a lifetime pass for the disabled is free.

Note that food in the park is very overpriced, and there are no gas stations in the valley. Fill up early and expect to get reamed at the pump. The few stations around are located in Wawona, Crane Flat, and seasonally at Tuolumne Meadows.

UP CLOSE WITH NATURE IN YOSEMITE.

TOURS If the idea of negotiating the park on your own is daunting, a number of tour companies are willing to help you out. My favorite, and the cheapest, is **Yosemite Bug Tours** (866-826-7108; yosemitebugbus.com). They offer camping, backcountry exploring, and plenty of information about the High Sierra or the Valley floor. If camping isn't your game, they can also arrange for you to stay in a cabin. **Yosemite Mountaineering School and Guide Service** (209-372-8344 or 209-372-84335) takes adventurers on overnight backpacking trips and guided day hikes.

There are also a number of **guided ranger hikes** (209-372-4386). You'll either take an enclosed motor coach or an open-air tram through the valley floor, Glacier Point, the eight-hour Grand Tour (which gets you the whole shebang), the Big Trees tram tour, or the Tuolumne Meadows and Hikers bus. Tours range from $16–62 for adults, with half-priced kids' and discount senior prices.

✳ To See

Ansel Adams Gallery (anseladams.com) Yosemite Village, shuttle stops #5 and 9. Open 9–6 daily. After a trip into the Visitor Center, pop in and view some prints of Ansel Adams's work. Adams arrived in Yosemite in 1916, when he was 14, and snapped a photo of Half Dome that would remain one of his favorites. He lived most of his life in the park, and today his family runs the gallery and leads photography walks three days a week. You can also pre-register to view some of Adams's original photos. Free.

VISTAS THAT WILL BLOW YOUR MIND

Every time I enter Yosemite, I catch my breath and marvel in nature's bounty. Honestly, there are no unattractive spots in the valley. But if I had to send you somewhere to find those postcard pictures to take home to your friends and brag about your trip, here are my favorite places to commune with nature.

Glacier Point—you can drive here in summer or hike in via the Four Mile Trail.

Tunnel View—east end of Wawona Tunnel off CA 41.

Olmsted Point—off Tioga Road, open in summer.

O'Shaughnessy Dam—off Big Oak Flat Road at Hetch Hetchy Reservoir.

Half Dome—okay, you have to do the toughest hike ever to get up here, but the brave deserve a reward.

El Capitan Meadow—in Yosemite Valley, along Northside Drive, make this your last stop before driving out of the valley.

Yosemite Lodge—sit outside and have a drink while looking up at Yosemite Falls.

Sentinel Dome—you need to hike it to fully appreciate all that Yosemite has to offer.

VIEWS LIKE THIS MAKE YOU CATCH YOUR BREATH.

Nature Center at Happy Isles Shuttle stop #16. Open 9:30–5 daily. Besides having a wonderful trail surrounding the center, kids love the tactile and auditory exhibits, as well as the interesting display of the animals you'll find in the park. Afterwards, take a stroll through the area.

Pioneer Yosemite History Center (Yosemite.ca.us) In Wawona, about 4 miles from the park's south entrance along the Wawona Road. Come see what Yosemite used to look like with a covered bridge, cabins, and a real blacksmith shop. Each building represents a different era of Yosemite's history. You can also take a stage-coach ride around the area, or ride horses (see *To Do*).

Yosemite Museum Yosemite Village, shuttle stops #5 and 9. Open 9–5 daily. Take a walk through the Indian Cultural Exhibit and learn about the Miwok and Paiute Indians from the mid-1800s to today. You'll also want to poke into the Museum Gallery (open 10 AM–12 and 1 PM–4 PM daily), which hosts a number of rotating exhibits, from the history of rock climbing in the region, to art inspired by the land. Afterwards head outside to the **Indian Village of Ahwahnee** to glimpse a traditional Ahwahneechee village—kids especially like the teepees.

Yosemite Valley Visitor Center and Bookstore Yosemite Village, shuttle stops #5 and 9. A visit to Yosemite would not be complete without a stop at the visitor center to view an interesting exhibit detailing how Yosemite was formed. Plus, the 23-minute film *Spirit of Yosemite* plays every half hour, and is quite good.

✳ To Do

ART CLASSES AND PHOTOGRAPHY TOURS **Ansel Adams Gallery** See *To See*.

Yosemite Art and Education Center (209-372-1442) Southwest of the Village Store. Open spring to fall. If you feel a bit of inner Georgia O'Keefe dying to get out, head here to let the artist in you shine. This wonderful center/gallery not only showcases art and art supplies, but also leads outdoor art classes for free.

BACKPACKING It might surprise you to learn that 95 percent of the park is designated wilderness. To explore the rich forests surrounding the valley, start with a visit to a wilderness center or a visitor center to get trail maps, as well as a permit if you plan to camp (209-372-0200). With over 750 miles of trails in the **Yosemite Wilderness**, you'll want to plan your trip well in advance. You can start your journey from Tioga Road, Tuolumne Meadow, Yosemite Valley, Wawona, or Hetch Hetchy areas. Trails of note include the John Muir Trail, Panorama Trail, Sunrise Lakes, Pacific Crest Trail, and White Wolf.

The most popular campground in the wilderness is the hike-in **Little Yosemite Valley,** which is frequented by folks climbing Half Dome. People who want a bed should look into the **High Sierra Camps,** which offer canvas cabins with blankets, but no linens, and breakfast and dinner. Other places to pitch a tent include **Yosemite Creek Campground** and **Sunrise High Sierra Camp**.

If you plan to backpack in the wilderness, you need a bear canister. Bears live in Yosemite and though they do not want to eat you, they do want your food. Take all precautions and pack everything out with you, including your toilet paper.

CYCLING Besides trekking out to the edges of the park, one of the best ways to explore the area is by bike. In the valley there are 12 miles of paved paths, and it is illegal for you to mountain bike in the park or surrounding wilderness—but just outside the park, get ready to hit the trails of Stanislaus and Sierra National Forests.

If you forgot your bike, you can rent one (and gear) at the **Curry Village Recreation Center** (209-372-8319) or **Yosemite Lodge at the Falls** (209-379-1208).

FAMILY FUN A number of activities take place each day to entertain the little guys. Check the park newspaper for specific schedules for the **Old Fashioned Campfires,** the 90-minute **Night Prowl, the Starry Skies over Yosemite and Wawona** (fee), **Junior Ranger, Little Cubs, Yosemite Institute** field science classes (209-379-9511), **Wee Wild Ones** storytime, **LeConte Memorial Lodge's** walks for kids, and **Children's Storytime and Theater**. Also see *Winter Sports* and *Rafting and Kayaking*.

FISHING There are 58 streams spread for 770 miles, offering anglers plenty of opportunity to cast for trout from April through November. The best spot to try your skills is the **Merced River**. Trout are plentiful in the **Tuolumne River** near Hetch Hetchy.

You'll need to get a license, which you can purchase at the **Sport Shop** (Yosemite Village), **Wawona Gift Shop** (CA 41), and **Tuolumne Meadows Store** (CA 120 East). For gear, head to the **Yosemite Village Sport Shop**.

GOLF Wawona Golf Course (209-375-6572) Open spring to fall, call for hours. One of the few organic golf courses in the United States, this nearly century-old course was the first regulation place to tee off in the Sierra. It is a great place to play for all levels, as well as just to space out on the views. $18.50–29.50.

HIKING AND WALKING There are a few thousand hiking trails in Yosemite National Park; aside from these listed, you should probably visit the Visitor Center

BEARS AND OTHER CRITTERS

Black bears, which are actually brown, live in the park year-round. In fact, they are so plentiful that the last time I stayed at Curry Village I was told to take my son's car seat out of the car, because bears now know that a car seat equals spilled goldfish crackers and Pirate's Booty. Even more, we were told that we could have no lotions, crumbs, or sweet-smelling gear of any sort in the car or the truck, and would be fined if we didn't abide by these rules. We had to keep everything that might attract bears (lip balm, shampoo, snacks) in a bear locker outside of our tent, and even with all the precautions a bear walked right through the property, creating quite the scene at 5AM.

ONE OF THE GENTLER CRITTERS YOU'LL FIND IN THE PARK.

Aside from these precautions, you should also know what to do if you see one of these big guys. First off, don't panic. The old adage, they are more scared of you, rings true. Our people have hunted their kind for centuries. However, we all know that when we get scared we do silly things. So in order to avoid a run in, when I am hiking, I tend to sing or talk loudly. My singing voice often ruins the solace of nature, but it lets bears know we are coming. If a bear sees you and doesn't run, make yourself look big and talk louder. Never come between a mama and her cub. And never get too close. They're cute, but they can be deadly—how would you like to be sat on by a guy that needs 20,000 calories to survive?

Though it is rare to see them, mountain lions also live in the park. If you see one, raise your arms to look bigger and back away slowly; pick up your kids and face the lion. If it starts to become aggressive, throw sticks and stones, shout, and act as scary as you can.

Yosemite is home to so much wildlife, yet you'd think that with all the people you'd never see it. Not the case. Last time I hiked up Vernal Falls, I saw a rattlesnake. I've seen bears, deer, rabbits, and birds. Keep your eyes open and consider yourself lucky when you see an animal in its habitat, but don't forget you are in the animal's house.

HIGHLIGHTS AND MUST-SEE SITES

1. The view from Glacier Point (or hike there from Four Mile Trail).
2. Tunnel View is the ideal picture spot.
3. The Vernal Falls hike is my favorite workout without breaking too much of a sweat—though maybe it is because the mist from the falls keeps me cool.
4. You don't have to ascend to the top of Yosemite Falls to fully appreciate it, but it helps.
5. Once in your life (if you can), hike Half Dome.
6. Walk amidst the giants at the Mariposa Grove of Giant Sequoias (or if you don't like crowds, head to the Merced or Tuolumne groves).
7. Explore the overlooked Hetch Hetchy Reservoir area and its waterfalls, lakes, and rivers.
8. Hike Tuolumne Meadows to an alpine lake, or to view wildflowers.
9. Laze the day away at Tenaya Lake.
10. Drive the Tioga Pass, stopping often to soak in the views.

or yosemitehikes.com. In general, if you have a stroller or wheelchair, or have limited mobility, you can attempt the trails listed in Short Easy Strolls. Otherwise, unless you parents have a sturdy baby carrier, or Aunt Suzie really has the urge for a 1000-foot gain in elevation, I'd leave anyone who is remotely out of shape to eat pizza at Curry Village or take the tram around the valley floor.

Most trails are best in the early morning hours, before the streams of visitors crowd the paths and the late afternoon thunderstorms arrive. In addition to those listed here, adventurers might want to check out tacking on trips from the Yosemite Valley to Olmsted Point, North Dome, Lukens Lake, or Porcupine Creek. You might also want to spend some time exploring the region around Hetch Hetchy, where you'll find Lake Eleanor, fishing in the Tuolumne River, and the Merced Grove of sequoias.

Short Easy Strolls

Bridalveil Falls (Bridalveil Fall Parking Area, one of the first stops you encounter from the west once you hit the Valley floor). This 0.5-mile gentle trail (with a little ascent) takes you to a lovely spot to view the skinny stream of a waterfall that drops dramatically down the face of a granite cliff.

Lower Yosemite Falls (Yosemite Valley, Shuttle stop #6) Mostly flat and very crowded, I've seen octogenarians with walkers meander down the mile of path to the falls. I recommend the loop trail, but start on the western trail for more dramatic views of the upper and lower portions of the 2,425-foot waterfall.

Mariposa Grove See *Highlights and Must-See Sites.*

Mirror Lake (Yosemite Valley, Shuttle Stop #17). This 2-mile round-trip paved path is ideal for folks wanting something a little longer, but not strenuous. Here you'll wander through the forest, passing views of the granite peaks all around, and finally arrive at the lake, which mirrors the pristine landscape. On the last visit here, I was a few feet from a deer and saw a bear just off the trail.

YOSEMITE FALLS.

Soda Springs (Lembert Dome parking area, in Tuolumne Meadows area) Depending on how far you walk, this can be a very simple stroll into these expansive meadows, which are usually filled with wildflowers through late spring.

Tenaya Lake (Off Tioga Road) You can come sunbathe here, or hikers will want to take the 2.5-mile loop around Yosemite's Audrey Hepburn of lakes. Get ready, this will be your screensaver for months to come.

Tuolumne Grove of Giant Sequoias (Off Tioga Road, look for the Tuolumne Grove parking lot). With fewer visitors than the Mariposa Grove, this 2.5-mile loop allows you to walk through sequoia tunnels and view the massive trees.

Trails to Leave the Stroller At Home

Cathedral Lakes (Off Tioga Road, near the west end of Tuolumne Meadows). Part of the famed John Muir Trail as well as the Pacific Crest trail, you (and many others before you) pass scenic vistas (I know, aren't they all?) leading you to Lower Cathedral Lake, where I like to picnic.

Gaylor Lakes (Off Tioga Road, just inside the eastern gate of the park). Okay, it is far and sure, you might be saying, "Where?" This overlooked hike is well worth a day of exploring when you are done with the diva sites and want the quiet sophistication of sweeping meadows, five lakes, and the mountains hugging Tuolumne Meadows. Call it the Jennifer Connelly of Yosemite—the gorgeous hike that is on most people's top 10 list, even though it doesn't have the assets of other superstars.

Mariposa Grove of Giant Sequoias (2 miles from Yosemite's south entrance—you can park at the Wawona Hotel and catch the shuttle from there, if the parking lot is full). I was tempted to put this hike in the easy strolls, but I felt you wouldn't really get the most out of it if you just took the 2.2-mile loop in the lower grove. Sure, that is a great way for your lazy uncle to see Yosemite's largest sequoia grove, but to escape the masses of people and really enter nature, you might consider taking the lower loop and the upper loop (6-mile round trip). You can also take the tram tour if little Timmy really wants to see the upper loop. Don't miss the Grizzly Giant, which is 27 feet in diameter and 2000 years old.

Sentinel Dome (Off Glacier Point Road). People hike this 2.2-mile round-trip trek to the dome for two reasons: views (of the valley, Mt. Diablo, El Capitan, Yosemite Falls, Nevada Falls, and Half Dome), and to photograph the Jeffrey pine that Ansel Adams immortalized in his 1940 photo. Bummer is that the tree fell in 2003, after drying up in 1977. When the road opens in spring, there is often snow still covering the trail. Also note that you don't want the kids running around near the peak, it drops dramatically and can be very slippery.

Vernal Falls (Happy Isles Shuttle Stop #16) I have seen my share of out-of-shape folks trucking up the mountain just to get to the footbridge of the falls (stop here if you are tired, the rest of the trek is even more strenuous). This is one of the most popular hiking spots—but completely worth it, especially if you make it to the top to get misted by the falls, view the Emerald Pool (3 miles round-trip), or even head all the way to Nevada Falls (7 miles round-trip).

Wapama Falls Head to Hetch Hetchy on Big Oak Flat Road and park near the O'Shaughnessy Dam (the second trailhead parking lot has bathrooms, but makes your hike 0.25 mile longer). Hetchy Hetchy is not just the water source for San Francisco, but also a favorite serene spot of John Muir (pre-reservoir). But visitors to Yosemite often overlook the area, which is a shame. The 5.5-mile round-trip Wapama Falls trail is one of the least-crowded waterfall trails in the region. Expect to get misted if you get too close.

Trails for Kamikazes

Four Mile Trail to Glacier Point Either start the trail at Southside Drive in the Valley, or at Glacier Point. A deceiving name, the Four Mile Trail is only 4 miles if you go one way, but you have to get back. Lucky you (as long as you have friends with another car, or 20 bucks to take the Glacier Point bus from Yosemite Lodge—but you need to book your tickets at least a day in advance; call 209-372-1240), you only need to hike this lovely trail one way. I call this trail the best of Yosemite because you climb from the valley floor over the Swinging Bridge to Glacier Point—if you are going one way, decide if you want to trek up or down. The best time to hike this trail is spring, when wildflowers and Yosemite Falls show off. You also get to see El Capitan, Cathedral Rocks, Sentinel Rock, Tenaya Canyon, Half Dome, Clouds Rest, the Royal Arches, and North Dome—I told you it was a winner.

KIDS PLAYING ALONG THE MIST TRAIL.

Top of Half Dome (Happy Isles shuttle stop #16) Adventure junkies who think an Ironman is a breeze will want to attempt Yosemite's most intense hike: 14.2 miles round-trip, with a gain of 4,800 feet. You'll start by ascending the Mist Trail, watching the masses huff and puff past Vernal Falls and Emerald Pool, then the valley starts to open and you'll be rewarded with unsurpassed views as you start to huff yourself. But that's not all. In summer

RELAXING ON THE WAY DOWN THE TRAIL TO HALF DOME.

you need to wait in line to climb the nail-biting cable that sends more than its fair share of folks heading back down the mountain—wait until you see it—but once you reach the top, you'll know the shaky legs are worth it. There is no other view in the valley quite so spectacular. Bring food and water. *Do not* even think about coming up here if there are thunderclouds on the horizon or if there is any threat of a storm. Bottom line, this is a dangerous hike—more than 20 people have died on Half Dome itself (times that number by three if you count deaths on the trail itself), so don't even try it unless you are in very good shape. The hike-in Little Yosemite Valley Campground gets you 4.5 miles up the mountain, so you can reach the cables earlier than the lucky folks who stayed at the Ahwahnee.

Top of Upper Yosemite Falls (Camp 4, near shuttle stop #7) This 7.2-mile round-trip trek has you gaining 2,700 feet in elevation in a very short time. Bottom line is that if you plan to hike up here, all you had better have on your schedule is some pasta, a beer, and bed. This is one of the only stops where you can view all of Yosemite Falls from above. Go in early spring when the water rushes past, spraying you with much-needed mist after your intense workout.

HORSEBACK RIDING Many people head out to explore the innards of Yosemite National Park (and the wilderness) by horseback. You'll need to make a reservation for the ride and be at least seven years old and under 225 pounds. There are three stables in the park, offering different types of rides. For all reservations, call 209-372-4FUN. Two-hour rides will cost you $53; half-day rides run $69, and full-day rides are $96.

Tuolumne Meadows Stable One of my favorite spots, either take two-hour ride deep into Tuolumne Meadows to view lakes and the Cathedral Range, a half-day ride to Twin Bridges, or an all-day 18-mile ride to Water Wheel Falls.

Yosemite Valley Stable Simple and perfect for families, choose between the two-hour Mirror Lake ride and the half-day ride, which offers views of Vernal and Nevada Falls. Healthy adventurers go for the all-day ride past Quarter Dome (you should be in good shape for this one).

Wawona Stables Either head down the historic wagon road for a two-hour ride or take the half-day climb to Chilanualna Falls.

ROCK CLIMBING One of the world's best climbing areas, the granite walls of Yosemite Valley and Tuolumne Meadows beg to be climbed. With many people coming to climb each summer, the effect of humans on the rocks is becoming evident. The National Park Service has set up a number of rules for climbers to follow, so you should check with the Yosemite Valley newsletter on current dos and don'ts. You don't need a wilderness permit to camp on a wall, except for camping on the base of Half Dome. The biggest walls to climb include Half Dome and El Capitan. For information, gear, and guide service for your climbing needs, contact **Yosemite Mountaineering School** (209-372-8344; yosemitepark.com).

RIVER RAFTING AND KAYAKING Rafting on the Wild and Scenic Merced River is a treat. Imagine paddling past Half Dome and Yosemite Falls, taking a dip in the waters, and passing a deer grazing in a meadow. Each year the rafting season changes depending on the water levels, though you can usually count on water from the end of May through the end of July.

Guided Rafting Trips and Rentals

Curry Village Recreation Center (209-372-4FUN) You can rent a six-person raft for $20.50 for adults and $13.50 for kids under 12 (no children under 50 pounds can ride). As of press time, the park was only allowing paddlers to take a three-mile journey.

Zephyr Whitewater Expeditions (209-532-6249; zrafting.com) Take a rafting trip down the Merced River in Yosemite. Trips range from half-day to full-day trips to two-day overnighters. This is an excellent way to view Yosemite from another perspective. $100–270 per person.

SWIMMING I like to swim in Tenaya Lake, but you can also take a dip in the chilly Merced and Tuolumne Rivers. Just outside the park (near Hetch Hetchy), you can buy a day pass at Camp Mather to swim in their little lake, or just after the San Jose Family Camp off CA 120, cross the bridge, turn left down a dirt road, and down the hill there is a popular swimming hole.

WINTER SPORTS I'll tell you a secret: Yosemite is a blast in winter. Sure, you can't swim in the rivers, but they are pretty cold in summer anyway. But when the snow covers the meadows, there is nothing as dramatic. The waterfalls still flow and the weather is mild in the valley. Instead of hiking, you can snowshoe or ski. And rooms are super cheap.

You also might inquire about the guided **Glacier Point Hut Trips** ($192–288) for one or two nights, or the self-guided treks ($110). Call for details, as reservations are required (209-372-8444).

Badger Pass Ski Area (yosemitepark.com) One hour from Yosemite Valley off CA 41, turn on Badger Pass Road. Open in winter from 9–4 daily. If you are staying at Curry Village, Yosemite Lodge, or the Ahwahnee, take the shuttle to Badger Pass. Imagine braving the slopes with unsurpassed views, sending the kids to tube down the sliding slopes, letting crazy Cousin Joe head off to cross-country ski on

the 350 miles of trails winding through the park, while you sip hot cocoa on the
deck. This is the ideal place for little Maceo to learn some downhill skills, as 85
percent of the slopes here are for beginners and intermediate skiers and boarders.
And if you want a real treat, find out about either the two-hour guided or the guided full-moon snowshoe walks. They also offer ski lessons and rentals. Lift tickets:
$28–38 adults; $22–32 kids; children under 6 free.

Curry Village Ice Skating Rink ((209-372-4FUN) Yosemite Valley, Shuttle Stop
#21. Open from November through April from 8:30 AM–9:30 PM—with breaks
between sessions. There probably isn't an ice rink as beautiful as this—skate in the
shadow of Half Dome and Glacier Point. $8 adults; $6 kids; $3 skate rentals.

✳ Lodging

Reservations for all of Yosemite lodgings are available 366 days in advance
of your visit, and you can reserve
campgrounds up to five months in
advance. Hotels, campgrounds, and
inns are generally sold out for spring
and summer. However, call 10 days
prior to your trip because people have
10 days to cancel for a refund. Openings tend to occur then. For all hotels
and resorts listed below contact **DNC
Parks and Resorts at Yosemite**
(559-252-4848; yosemitepark.com).
For campground reservations call 800-
436-7275 or 877-444-6777 or visit
Recreation.gov.

✦ ♿ "🍴" ◯ **The Ahwahnee** Ahwahnee Road, north of Northside Drive.
Near the entrance to the Dining Room
a sign boasts that (and I am paraphras-
ing) you need to be on good behavior
to be in the hotel. If walking into this
1927 Art Deco, Native American, Arts
and Crafts mishmash of architecture
and design makes you want to get all
goofy, you probably should head to
Curry Village. The plushest hotel in
the park, the Ahwahnee attracts a royal
following, complete with nouveau
riche surfing the net by the massive
stone fireplace in the great lounge. If
you are on a budget, consider staying
in one of the cottage rooms that share
a bath. Fans of classic pianos should
peek at the black Steinway (rumored
to have been played by Ansel Adams),

the mahogany Steinway, and the
Mason and Hamlin pianos. Amenities:
123 rooms, cottages, and suites, fabulous Dining Room (see *Dining Out*),
pool, tennis court, concierge, and room
service. $$$$.

✦ ♿ 🍸 ◯ **Curry Village** Yosemite
Valley, the southern edge of Southside
Drive. Since 1899, when the Curry
family decided to offer a bed on the
valley floor at a modest price, the
masses have arrived to capitalize on
just that. Don't come here for room
service or shoe shines, rather this is the

THE AHWAHNEE HOTEL.

spot for a large family traveling together, so the kids can sleep in a canvas cabin (heated or not), and Grandma and Grandpa can sleep in a traditional room. In summer Curry Village feels like a grown-up summer camp, complete with live entertainment at night, rousing campfire songs, streams of people lining up for food, army-like squeaky beds, and inevitably some dude screaming "Bear!" at 5 AM. If you want solitude, come in winter. Amenities: 628 rooms, cabins, tent cabins, shared baths, three restaurants, pub, entertainment, raft rentals, bike rentals, general store, pool, sport shop, and ice rink. Note that at press time, Curry Village was renovating the property; there might not be as many accommodations as are listed above. $–$$.

₁ **Evergreen Lodge** (209-379-2606; evergreenlodge.com) Off CA 120, turn on Evergreen Road. Just outside the gate of Yosemite, near Hetch Hetchy, these woodsy cabins offer families and friends an attractive option minutes from the park, but far from the crowds. Cabins range from simple budget rooms to two-bedroom family accommodations—though none have kitchens—while there are also campsites, a restaurant/tavern, and general store. This is an ideal spot for returning Yosemite visitors who want to spend time fishing in Tuolumne River and exploring the Hetch Hetchy area. $–$$$.

High Sierra Camps See *Backpacking*.

& **Housekeeping Camp** Southside Drive, west of Curry Village. Part refugee camp, part Meatballs, here you'll find 266 three-sided canvas cabins (with a curtain for the fourth wall), grills and linens for rent, beds, and a shared toilet/shower facility. What makes this such a steal is the location on the valley floor and along the river,

offering plentiful swimming opportunities, beds for six people, and a chance to commune with nature without pitching your own tent. Get a cabin by the river; it is quieter. $ (they raise the price $10–15 per year, so by 2010, they could be $$).

& **Tuolomne Meadows Lodge** Tioga Road, Tuolumne Meadows. Open in summer only, these tent cabins offer guests the experience of staying far from the hullabaloo of the valley, and an early start up to the High Sierra Camps. You get one of 69 A-frame tents with a bed and no electricity, though they provide candles for lighting, shared bath, breakfast, and dinner (fee). $.

& & **Wawona Hotel** CA 41, Wawona. Lofty, family-friendly, and just far enough from the masses to feel remote, staying here gets you 104 simple rooms (some share a bath) decorated with period Victorian furniture, a restaurant, no TV or phones, Saturday night BBQs in summer, golf course, pool, tennis court, horse stables, and board games. This is ideal for people wanting to ski Badger Pass or explore the Mariposa Grove. $$–$$$.

& **White Wolf Lodge** Tioga Road, between Crane Flat and Tuolumne Meadows. Open in summer, these 24 tent cabins (and 4 regular cabins) offer high-country solitude to explore meadows, lakes, and trails that often are overlooked by Yosemite visitors. Don't expect much and you'll be pleasantly surprised: There is a dining room, no electricity in tent cabins, limited electricity and bathrooms in regular cabins. $–$$.

& & ₁ ☾ **Yosemite Lodge at the Falls** Yosemite Village, Northside Drive. Besides the stream of visitors in the cafeteria, the central location of this lodge can't be beat. Views of Yosemite Falls and simple motel-like

rooms make this a good choice for families and folks on a budget who don't want to camp. If you can spring for it, go for a lodge room, which has a deck. Amenities: 226 lodge rooms, 19 regular rooms, and 4 family rooms, cafeteria, restaurant, lounge, and pool. $$–$$$.

CAMPGROUNDS You'll find over 2000 places to pitch a tent throughout the park, though in summer most of the sites actually fill up. For sites in front-country, you need to make a reservation well in advance for summer (they accept them 5 months in advance) or come early for non-reservation sites. Backcountry campgrounds require a permit, and since they only allow a certain number of campers at a time in wilderness, you'll want to arrange a permit as early as possible to allow your adventure to be in the outdoors rather than with bureaucracy. If you are like me and have an aversion to making reservations, you can often find first-come, first-served sites in the Sierra and Stanislaus National Forests (see *Sierra Foothills* and *Ebbetts Pass to Sonora Pass* sections). RV hookups can be found in some campsites. Bay Area locals might want to arrange to stay in **Camp Mather** (San Francisco residents), **Berkeley Family Camp**, and **San Jose Family Camp**.

Yosemite Valley

Camp 4 Base of Yosemite Falls trail. The only valley floor site available on a first-come, first-served basis, you need to be an early riser (or have superhero-sized luck) to score a spot here. No RVs or trailers allowed. Open year-round. $5 per person.

Housekeeping Camp See *Lodging*.

❀ **Lower Pines** East end of Yosemite Valley. On the Merced River, you'll find a packed campground with great proximity to the Mist Trail. This is ideal for folks wanting to hike Half

Dome. Reserve early, this is a popular one. Open April through November. RVs up to 40 feet allowed. $20.

❀ **North Pines** Near Curry Village. Very busy, probably because of its close proximity to trails and the river, with 81 sites, you should reserve early. Open March through October. RVs up to 40 feet allowed. $20.

❀ **Upper Pines** Near Curry Village. With 238 sites, this year-round campsite has folks packed like matchsticks. If you want quiet, this is not the place to be; but if you want to roll out of your sleeping bag and head up a trail, set up camp here. RVs up to 35 feet allowed. $20.

South of the Valley

❀ **Bridalveil Creek** Glacier Point Road. This high-elevation site is open from July through September. Cons of the campground include a far drive to the valley attractions and chilly nights. RVs up to 35 feet allowed. $14.

❀ **Wawona** CA 41, near Wawona. If you plan to explore the southern edge of the park, this is an ideal place, with 93 spacious sites open year-round. Though you have to drive an hour to get to the valley, you are close to Badger Pass. Open year-round. RVs up to 35 feet allowed. $20.

North of the Valley

❀ **Crane Flat** Off CA 120, just past Big Oak Flat entrance. Right when you enter the park, you'll find this mellow campsite away from the crowds, but popular with in-the-know travelers. You'll find 166 sites open in summer only, close to a sequoia grove and unexplored trails. Reservations are essential. RVs up to 35 feet allowed. $20.

❀ **Hodgdon Meadow** CA 120, close to Big Oak Flat entrance. Return visitors often camp here so they can feel like they are in nature rather than hearing cars circle the Valley all night. Open year-round. RVs up to 35 feet allowed. $14–20.

Porcupine Flat CA 120, west of Tuolumne Meadows. High-country camping in primitive sites (there's no water), you'll find 52 sites (tents and RVs up to 24 feet) open in summer only. First-come, first-served. $10.

Tamarack Flat Tioga Road, close to the Big Oak Flat entrance. Open in summer only and not suitable for large RVs, this primitive site offers 52 sites under a canopy of pines. $10.

🐾 **Tuolumne Meadows** CA 120, just south of the meadow. When I imagine camping in Yosemite, I think of these 304 sites, which offer expansive views far from the Valley insanity. Guests are allowed to use the showers at Tuolumne Meadows Lodge at certain times. First-come, first-served, and some reservation sites are available July through September. RVs allowed up to 35 feet. $20.

🐾 **White Wolf** Tioga Road, 15 miles from Big Oak Flat entrance. These 74 sites in the high country are sought after, so you'll need to get up early to get one of the first-come, first-served spots to pitch your tent. RVs allowed up to 27 feet. Open from July through September. $14.

🐾 **Yosemite Creek** Off Tioga Road about 30 miles past the Big Oak Flat entrance. High-country camping in a primitive setting, these 40 sites are available July through September. To get here you need to drive 5 miles down a rough road. No RVs allowed. No water. $10.

✳ Where to Eat

DINING OUT 🍷 ♿ ⛾ **Ahwahnee Hotel Dining Room** (209-372-1489) Ahwahnee Hotel, Ahwahnee Road. Open from 7 AM–10:30, 11:30–3 and

5:30–9 daily, and for brunch on Sunday from 7 AM–3 PM. The ultimate Sunday brunch complete with ice sculptures, oysters, an omelet bar, and views of the valley, eating in this dining room at least once is a must. Dinner favors rustic elegance, with organic produce and meaty dishes like prime rib, served on china beneath a 34-foot ceiling with candelabra chandeliers. Men must wear a collared shirt and pants for dinner. Reservations required. $$$–$$$$.

🍷 ♿ **Wawona Hotel Dining Room** (209-375-1425) Wawona Hotel, CA 41, Wawona. Open for breakfast, lunch, and dinner daily, and Sunday brunch from April through Thanksgiving. If you want some down-home cooking served in a Victorian room while the sun sets over the trees, this restaurant has your name on it. I like the Saturday lawn BBQs in summer. Before dinner, make sure to stop by and hear pianist Tom Bopp play his vintage Yosemite tunes. Reservations recommended for dinner. Men must wear a jacket for dinner. $$–$$$.

🍷 ♿ ⛾ **Yosemite Lodge Mountain Room** (209-372-1281) Yosemite Lodge, Northside Drive. Open for dinner nightly from 5:30–9:30. If you haven't had your fill of gazing up at the Yosemite Falls, head to this restaurant to munch on organic salads and sustainable meat and seafood, while staring at the U.S.'s highest waterfall. Go for the trout; it's local. Reservations accepted for parties of eight or more. $$–$$$.

EATING OUT Besides the restaurants listed below, you will find a couple of other places to eat in the valley. At times it isn't how good the food is, but rather what you can stuff into your mouth to avoid passing out. If you need some sustenance along Tioga Road, stop at the **White Wolf Lodge**

(breakfast, dinner, and to-go lunches) and the **Tuolumne Meadows Grill** (it has burgers and hot dogs). You can also find snacks at the **Glacier Point Snack Stand,** the **Happy Isles Snack Stand, Wawona Golf Shop Snack Stand,** and the **Sliders Grab and Go** at Badger Pass. The **Curry Village Grocery Store, Yosemite Lodge Grocery Store, Housekeeping Camp Grocery, Tuolumne Meadows Store, Crane Flat Camp Store,** and **White Wolf Camp Store** will also settle the rumble in your belly.

Curry Village Coffee Corner
Yosemite Valley, Curry Village. Open 6 AM–10 PM daily. Not the best coffee in the world, but perfect before a hike. You can also get ice cream and pastries here.

Curry Village Pizza Parlor
Yosemite Valley, Curry Village. Open 12–10 daily. This pizza counter has lines of up to 50 people at a time on summer weekends. Go before you are starving and have a friend wait in line at the pub for the beer. After a long day of hiking, there is nothing like sitting at the picnic tables with the granite peaks around you and going off on some pepperoni pizza and microbrews—well, once you add ice cream to that equation (for that, head inside). $$.

Dengan's Deli Yosemite Village. Open 7 AM–5 PM. Attached to **Dengan's Loft,** this is the best spot in the valley to nab gourmet sandwiches and goods to take with you for a picnic. $.

Food Court at Yosemite Lodge
Yosemite Valley, Yosemite Lodge at the Falls. Open 6:30 AM– 2 PM and 5 PM–8:30 PM. If you haven't had your fill of waiting in line yet, head to this surprisingly good food court for pasta, barbeque, sandwiches, coffee and more. $–$$.

Curry Pavillion Buffet Curry Village. Open 7 AM–10 AM and 5:30 PM–8 PM from March through October. Better than dorm food, but still kind of a racket. You know the deal—buffet scrambled eggs and sausages for breakfast, and a meat and potatoes dinner. Lines can get long, so go early. $–$$.

Tuolumne Meadows Lodge Dining Room (209-372-8413) Tuolumne Meadows Lodge, Tioga Road. Open for breakfast and dinner in summer only. Make a reservation to dine beneath a canvas tent? You bet. This family-style dining hall serves food fit for the American appetite. $$–$$$.

✳ Entertainment

In summer you will find a variety of shows, campfires, performances, and events. Check the valley newspaper for listings.

The Ahwahnee Bar Ahwahnee Hotel, Ahwahnee Road. Open 11 AM–11 PM. You probably won't find many people drinking Bud Light here, but this is a civilized place for a nightcap or pre-dinner adult beverage.

Curry Village Amphitheater Curry Village. Last time I was here the first nightly performance was interactive and great for kids, while the singer and film that came later were a wee bit loud for my taste.

Curry Village Bar Curry Village. Less like a bar than a beer stand with five stools. Good microbrews make people line up for 30 minutes for a brew.

Mountain Room Lounge Yosemite Lodge. Open 4:30–11 Monday through Friday and 12–11 on weekends. A pint and a view of Yosemite Falls anyone? Okay, well how about a TV, broadcasting sporting events?

Yosemite Lodge Amphitheater
Yosemite Lodge. Check listings for the
nightly event, which could be anything
from a play to a film to an opera.

Yosemite Theater—LIVE Valley Visitor Center Theater, Yosemite Village,
shuttle stops #5 and #9. When you
arrive and get your visitor guide, flip
through and find information on the
current play being performed. Tickets
cost $8 adults and $4 kids.

✳ Selective Shopping

Most of us don't come to Yosemite to
shop, but if you need a rainy-day
event, you'll surely want to breeze
through the super pricey **Ahwahnee
Gift Shop** at the Ahwahnee Hotel.
And for your adventure gear, head to
the **Valley Wilderness Center**
(Yosemite Village) to find bear canis-
ters, wilderness permits, and more.

✳ Seasonal Events

Events are planned daily, often making
you feel like you are aboard a ship with
a cruise director gone mad. Below are
a few events you'll want to plan your
trip around.

January: **Chef's Holiday** (yosemite
park.com) The Ahwahnee Hotel. For
the past 24 years, the Ahwahnee has
welcomed famed chefs who participate
in a three-day fiesta of cooking demonstrations, kitchen tours, and a five-
course gala dinner. Chefs in 2009
included Charles Phan, Traci Des
Jardins, Nancy Silverton, Douglas
Keane, and Gavin Kaysen. Book early.

April: **Earth Day** (yosemitepark.com)
For the weekend of Earth Day expect
to see Yosemite roll out the red carpet
and honor the planet that created such
an awesome landscape. Gather for
nature walks, food tasting, stories,
crafts, films, and more.

November: **Vintner's Holidays**
(yosemitepark.com) Ahwahnee Hotel.
Enjoy wine tasting seminars and a five-
course gala dinner paired with wine,
by famed winemakers like Robert
Mondavi, Plumpjack, Grgich Hills, and
Merry Edwards.

December: **Bracebridge Dinner**
(yosemitepark.com) Ahwahnee Hotel.
The historic hotel turns into a Dickens
novel, but with more food. Adapted
from Washington Irving's *Sketch Book*
of a Christmas Day, the Ahwahnee
Dining Room transforms into a winter
wonderland, and diners are treated to
a feast prepared by Chef Terry Shee-
han. Carolers, bells, and snow accompany your meal. It's super pricey and
sells out way in advance.

YOSEMITE SIERRA—
FISH CAMP TO OAKHURST

Officially Northern California doesn't actually include Yosemite or the towns south
of the park as part of its domain, but since we Nor Cal-ers like to claim Yosemite
as one of our favorite destinations, I decided to include it and a few of my favorite
towns to the south. Ideally, for the next edition of the book I will be able to
include Mammoth Mountain, Sequoia National Park, and even Kings Canyon,
even though they too aren't in Northern California. But for now, look at this section as a bonus—a free gift from me to you.

When deciding on a border, it was purely arbitrary—where could you comfortably drive back to San Francisco in a day without losing your mind? Where would you most like to stay in the Yosemite area? In asking myself these questions, I made Oakhurst the southeastern border for the book. If you are headed south and really want to pass through Coarsegold (to gold pan), North Fork (to visit the exact center of California), Madera (to taste wine), Merced and Fresno (hmmm), there are Visitor Centers to assist you in trip planning. I find the towns to the north—Oakhurst, Fish Camp, Ahwahnee, and Bass Lake to be the best places to stay, especially if you want to explore Yosemite Park, Bass Lake, Ansel Adams Wilderness, Mariposa, and the Sierra National Forest.

✳ To See

Fresno Flats Historical Park (559-683-6570; fresnoflatsmuseum.org) Road 427, School Road, Oakhurst. Open from dawn to dusk from March through December. Take a self-guided tour of the old cabins and jail, restored 19th-century homes, and the one-room schoolhouse. The fall Heritage Days Celebration is a kick—if you like to see people dress up and pretend they live in 1872. Guided tours of the park head out at 10 and 2 daily.

✐ **Golden Chain Theatre** (559-683-7112; goldenchaintheatre.org) 42130 CA 41, Oakhurst. After a visit to the Wawona Historical trail or the Fresno Flats park, culminate your night with a trip to this movie house. Here you boo the villain, munch on free popcorn, and watch either comedies or mystery films from another time. $12 adults and $6 kids (3–12); free for children under 3 who share a parent's seat.

King Vintage Museum (559-658-6999; kingvintagemuseum.org) 49269 Golden Oak Drive #100, Oakhurst. Open Wednesday through Sunday at least 1–4, call for seasonal hours. Ladies, do you hear the change clinking in your bag? Well unfortunately a visit to this vintage clothing museum won't allow you to walk away with a new paper crepe dress, but it will get you inspired to shop for some vintage steals. $2 donation.

Wassama Round House State Historic Park (559-822-2332; parks.ca.gov) Off CA 49, take Road 628, Ahwahnee. This was the last active ceremonial gathering place for local Indians. The third Saturday of October features music, dancing, and basket-weaving demonstrations. This is more a historic site than a place to go out of your way to see.

✳ To Do

CYCLING Serious mountain bikers head to the Bass Lake Recreation Area to brave the **Goat Mountain Lookout**.

FAMILY FUN ✐ **Yosemite Mountain Sugar Pine Railroad** (559-683-7273; ymsprr.com) 56001 CA 41, Fish Camp. Going 4 miles into the forest on a steam engine transports you back in time, when trains carted massive logs and everything was slower. Kids will love the daily trips and parents will enjoy the moonlight special. Steam train fees: $17.50 adults and $8.75 kids 3–12 (under 3 are free). Moonlight specials: $46 adults and half price for kids.

✐ **Yosemite Trails Pack Station** (559-683-7611; yosemitetrails.com) 7910 Jackson Road, Fish Camp. Quite possibly the best outfitter to lead you on a ride in southern Yosemite. They offer one-hour to half-day horseback riding trips through the sequoia forest, winter sleigh rides, and the rip-roaring Chuckwagon Jamboree, complete with an all-you-can-eat BBQ, and a campfire to roast S'mores. Kids must be seven or older to go on a trail ride, but they offer kiddie rides at the stables for the little guys to have their first horseback riding experience and the adults to snap photos. The two-hour Chuckwagon Jamboree costs $52 for adults and $32 for kids 3–12. Sleigh rides and trail rides range from $25–140 for adults.

FISHING Anglers have plenty of opportunities to catch some dinner. Trout, bass, and catfish are plentiful in the region. Fishing spots not to miss include **Bass Lake** and **Mammoth Pool.** Farther south head to **Eastman Lake, Hensley Lake,** and **Manzanita Lake.** For gear and licenses, head to the marina at Bass Lake.

GOLF **River Creek Golf Course** (559-683-5600; Rivercreekgolfcourse.com) 41709 Road 600, Ahwahnee. Cheap greens fees in the forest make this an attractive option if you are done with hiking. $18.

SCENIC DRIVES **Sierra Vista Scenic Byway** (559-877-2218) From CA 41 in Oakhurst, head east on CA 81 to explore 100 miles of beautiful scenery. Part of the road is unpaved so make sure you have a strong vehicle. This byway follows ridges and meadows through North Fork, Oakhurst, and Bass Lake, past the center of California, Redinger Overlook, Jesse Ross Historic Cabin, Mile High Vista, Jackass Rock, Arch Rock, Mammoth Pool, Clover Meadow, Globe Rock, Beasore Meadows, Cold Springs Summit, Fresno Dome, Kelty Meadow, and Nelder Grove of giant sequoias. Consider it the "best of" tour of the region. But make sure to check for weather conditions, since the road closes at the first threat of snow.

WATER SPORTS To rent kayaks, boats, Jet Skis, and more, contact **Bass Lake Boat Rentals and Water Sports** (559-642-3200 or 800-585-9283; basslakeboat rentals.com) at the Pines Resort on Bass Lake. They also take people on guided fishing excursions.

✳ Green Spaces

Ansel Adams Wilderness See *Sierra National Forest.*

Bass Lake Recreation Area (559-297-0706; fs.fed.us) Off CA 41, 3 miles north of Oakhurst, take the Road 22 turnoff. Probably the major reason people don't stay in Yosemite Park (well, that and packed lodging), Bass Lake is a High Sierra gem. Popular with boaters, swimmers, sunbathers, hikers, mountain bikers, and anglers, a visit (or weeklong stay) is a must. Boaters need to register at the Sheriff's Station at the north shore of this 5-mile lake, then you can launch your boat for free at Wilson's Boat Launch. There is also a handicap-accessible launch. You can rent boats at many of the resorts and marinas around the lake, as well. Swimmers head to Falls Beach. Hikers take the Mono Interpretive trail or the Goat Mountain lookout (bikers will like this intense ride, too). Anglers are in for a treat, with 16 species of fish living in the lake. There are five campgrounds around the lake, including the handicap-accessible Lupine/Cedar Bluff, Spring Cove, and Recreation Point. Only Recreation Point (113 sites) has showers and RV hookups, while the others have flush toilets but no showers ($14–20; reservations.gov).

Nelder Grove of Giant Sequoias

Nelder Grove is off Road 632, also known as Sky Ranch Road, 4 miles north of the intersection of CA 41 and CA 49 in Oakhurst. One of the least-crowded sequoia groves in the region is particularly beautiful in spring when the dogwoods are in bloom, or if you can get in, during winter when snow blankets the trees. You'll find a short trail through the trees. There are six free campsites in this grove, from May through October.

Sierra National Forest (559-297-0706 or 877-2218; fs.fed.us) Bass Lake Ranger District. The most popular area of the forest is Bass Lake (see above), but there are a number of other places to explore where you'll have privacy and some High Sierra grandeur. Anglers and boaters head to Mammoth Pool (closed May 1 through June 16 for deer migration) or June Lake. Hikers and fishermen will also want to explore the region around Beasore Road, which offers a wealth of

A RIVER RUSHING THROUGH THE SIERRA NATIONAL FOREST.

fishing in streams, hiking through meadows, and campgrounds. Clover Meadow region (off Sierra Vista Scenic Byway) offers the ideal starting point to backpack in the **Ansel Adams Wilderness** (free permits required for overnight visits—contact the ranger station)—head for the Rush Creek Trail. Campgrounds are plentiful but primitive. You'll find toilets, but no showers or RV hookups at Beasore Road's Upper Chiquito campground (20 sites; fee) and Clover Meadow's Granite Creek campground (20 sites; free). Locals swear this is the finest national forest in the country. Maybe it is the pristine streams, alpine lakes, and plentiful trout; maybe it is the redwoods and dogwoods, the wildflowers in spring and the autumn show in October. Whatever the case, make some time to explore the area, but head to the ranger station first to get a good hiking map.

✳ Lodging

HOTELS AND RESORTS &

Chateau du Sureau (559-683-6860; chateausureau.com) 48688 Victoria Lane, Oakhurst. The finest hotel in the Sierra Nevada Mountains; this is a Cinderella palace if I ever saw one. Birds chirp you awake; chambermaids dressed in black with white aprons greet you; the stone turrets, balconies (they just make me want to recite Shakespeare), canopy beds, and French country decor all will tempt you to give up your day-job and move in. Amenities: 10 rooms and suites, two-bedroom villa, amazing restaurant, spa, fireplace in most rooms, Jacuzzi tub in some rooms, pool, bocce court, life-sized chess set, no TVs, tea and refreshments delivered to your room. $$$$.

✄ ৬ 🐾 ⊙ "†" **The Pines Resort** (559-642-3121; Basslake.com) 54432 Road 432, Bass Lake. If I were staying at Bass Lake and didn't want to camp, I'd head here. Choose between 84 chalets, 20 waterfront suites, or a two-bedroom house, all decorated carefully to reflect the colors of the lake and the pines. This is a simple spot to bring the kids. Amenities: swimming pool, hot tub, spa services, restaurant, bar, water sports rentals, and beach access. $$–$$$$.

✄ ৬ ⊙ "†" **Tenaya Lodge** (559-683-6555 or 877-635-5807; tenayalodge .com) 1122 CA 41, Fish Camp. This is the ideal resort for families and people who want full-service amenities, close to, but not inside Yosemite National Park. The 244 rooms combine elegant touches like fireplaces and leather chairs with elements of nature, views, a restaurant, spa, pool, lounge, and business center. Come in winter and be dazzled by nature. $$–$$$$.

✄ ৬ **Yosemite Bug Resort** (209-966-6666; Yosemitebug.com) 6979 CA 140, Midpines. A wealth of lodging opportunities, this "resort" is more like a hostel, offering tours, spa, trails, swimming, food, and a variety of lodging options. A great idea for families on a budget and single travelers wanting to meet their match; stay in either a private room (with or without bath), tent cabin, or bunk. $–$$.

INNS AND B&BS ✄ 🐾 **Apple Blossom Inn** (559-642-2001 or 888-687-4281; appleblossombb.com) 44606 Silver Spur Trail, Ahwahnee. If my childhood dollhouse came to life, this is what it would look like. Three small rooms, packed with antiques and floral-printed furniture, give way to close access to the park, and one of the best breakfasts around. Super-sweet owner Candy Apple is one of the best

resources for getting to know the region. $$.

✄ ৬ **Narrow Gauge Inn** (559-683-7720 or 888-644-9050; narrowgauge inn.com) 48571 CA 41, Fish Camp. If John Muir and Granny Smith had an affair, this inn could be their offspring. It has 26 wood-paneled rooms, floral-print bedspreads, antique lights, and a woodsy outdoor space that never lets you forget where you are. The restaurant will make you glad you stayed here. $–$$.

✄ ৬ "†" **Queen's Inn by the River** (559-683-4334; queensinn.com) 41139 CA 41, Oakhurst. These nine newly renovated rooms have brought Yosemite lodging options up a notch. Urbanites who want rustic days of hiking but want to sleep in a sleek room more akin to Silicon Valley than the Sierra, head here. Though it looks like a motel from the outside, don't be fooled, you'll find continental breakfast, wine bar, private patio, flat-screen TVs, local art, and some rooms have fireplace or Jacuzzi tub. $$.

⊙ **Tin Lizzie Inn B&B and Model T** (559-641-7731; tinlizzieinn.com) 7730 Laurel Way, Fish Camp. I would send my parents here for an anniversary weekend. Inside and out, this three-room Victorian mansion offers guests the royal treatment, and the finest amenities from full breakfast to flat-screen TVs. The huge Tin Lizzie Suite has heated bathroom floors (a rarity in the High Sierra), a claw-foot tub, and a kingly bed. The Lady Suite is a bit more masculine, with wood floors and a parlor. The cottage makes a lovely respite from the world. Rates are pricey compared to other inns in the area, but if you want to go really big, you can pair a Model T or Model A tour with your room for an extra $350. $$$–$$$$.

VACATION RENTALS ⚓ **Owl's Nest Lodging** (559-683-3484; owls nestlodging.com) 1237 CA 41, Fish Camp. Quite the deal, these two vacation rentals deliver on incorporating the rustic surroundings with comfortable cabins. The Ponderosa Cabin is ideal for families, with a kitchen and an outdoor patio with a BBQ. The Tamarack Guest Suite makes a great woodsy getaway for someone wanting to be alone with nature, or a couple. $$; open May through September; fee for every person more than two (and up to seven) in the Ponderosa Cabin.

✳ Where to Eat

DINING OUT ⚓ ♿ ♟ **Ducey's on the Lake** (559-642-3121; basslake .com/duceys) The Pines Resort, 54432 Road 432, Bass Lake. Open for breakfast and dinner daily (for lunch head to the **Lakeside Grill**). Lakeside dining doesn't get much more beautiful. I prefer breakfast to dinner here, but if you happen to be around here, you won't go wrong with a plate of pasta and dessert. Reservations recommended for dinner. $$–$$$$.

♿ ♟ **Erna's Elderberry House** (559-683-6860; chateausureau.com) 48688 Victoria Lane, Oakhurst. Open for dinner and Sunday brunch. One of the 10 best restaurants in Northern California, even if you can't afford a night at the Chateau du Sureau, if you are in the region for a special occasion (or are a foodie), suck it up and make a reservation to dine in this classic dining room. Menus change daily, depending on the whim of Chef Karsten Hart. Examples of his style include a pan-seared halibut with hibiscus powder, mung beans, bok choy, water chestnuts, and sweet basil or a wiener schnitzel-organic chicken. The tasting menu is the way to go—though it costs $95 per person. Reservations required. $$$$.

♿ ♟ **Narrow Gauge Inn Dining Hall and Buffalo Bar** (559-683-7720; narrowgaugeinn.com) 48571 CA 41, Fish Camp. Open for dinner Wednesday through Sunday; closed in winter. Enchanting views coupled with good Alpine cuisine make this a wonderful dining choice. Either sit inside by the stone fireplace or out on the deck overlooking the gardens. This is the spot to get that prime rib, elk, or rainbow trout. Vegetarians will be stuck with greens or pasta. Reservations recommended. $$–$$$$.

EATING OUT ⚓ ♿ **Crab Cakes Restaurant** (559-641-7667; crabcakes -sweetdreams.com) 40278 Stagecoach Road, Oakhurst. Open Monday through Saturday from 11:30–8 (until 9 on Friday and Saturday). This is one of the best restaurants to bring the kids, to sit either on the trellised patio or inside the country-style dining room. Their kids' menu is the star (though their seafood, pasta, and fish and chips aren't so bad either), with the "Little Skippers" getting one of seven entrees with green beans, fries, and a drink. $–$$$.

⚓ ♿ **Todd's Cookhouse BBQ** (559-642-4900; Toddscookhousebbq.com) CA 41, across from Days Inn, Oakhurst. Open daily for lunch and dinner. Sometimes you just want some barbeque after a day of swimming or hiking. You are in luck. After winning a Kraft Foods competition for his sauce, Todd opened up shop here to serve the hordes of hungry post-Yosemite trekkers. Cheap and good, you can get everything from brisket sandwiches to a smoked chicken-breast plate accompanied by chili and cole slaw. $.

Yosemite Roasting Co. (559-683-8815; yosemitecoffee.com) 40879 CA 41, Oakhurst. Open daily, call for seasonal hours. Besides being the best coffee shop in the area, they also serve pastries, evening appetizers, beer, and wine. At night they offer live music.

✳ Entertainment

☡ **Ducey's by the Lake** See *Dining Out.*

Golden Chain Theatre See *To See.*

☡ **Narrow Gauge Inn Buffalo Bar** See *Dining Out.*

☡ **Yosemite Roasting Company** See *Eating Out.*

Yosemite Trails Pack Station See *To Do.*

✳ Selective Shopping

Along CA 41 in Oakhurst you'll find a number of galleries to explore.

✳ Seasonal Events

February: **Fresno Flats Ragtime and Vintage Music Festival** (559-683-6570) Oakhurst. Come hear music for three days in the historical park.

May: **Jazz on the Lake** (basslake.com) Bass Lake. For 15 weeks, you can listen to jazz on Friday nights by the pool at the Pines.

Antique Peddlers Fair (559-683-7766) Over Memorial Day weekend, come to Oakhurst to score on some serious antiques.

October: **Grizzly Century** (grizzlycentury.org) Every October in North Fork—this is the best Century ride in the state.

Sierra Art Trails (sierraarttrails.org) Throughout Madera and Mariposa Counties in mid-October, you can tour artists' studios and take home a piece of the High Sierra.

THE EASTERN SIERRA

✳ To See and Do

&. ♪ **Bodie State Historic Park** (760-647-6445; bridgeportbodie.org) CA 270, 7 miles south of Bridgeport off US 395. Drive 13 miles east to Bodie. The last 3 miles are unpaved. The visitor center is open in summer from 9–6, and the park is open (in summer) from 8 AM–7 PM (the rest of the year until 4). In 1881, the town of Bodie, boasting almost 10,000 people and over 60 dance halls and saloons, was so lawless, a Reverend called it a "sea of sin . . ." However, by 1882, the mines were becoming depleted, and after a major fire in 1892 and another in 1932 destroyed most of the town, it became a ghost town. There is a great map at the Visitor Center, where you can learn about the historic buildings. Bring food and water; there is nothing here. $3 adults; children (16 and under) $1.

Mono County Museum (760-932-7004; monocomuseum.org) Emigrant Street, Bridgeport. Open Monday through Saturday 10 AM–4 PM, Sunday 12–4 PM, from Memorial Day weekend through September 30. Located in the former Bridgeport Elementary Schoolhouse built in 1880, you'll find Paiute baskets, area artifacts, mining and farming equipment. Adults $2, Children 6–12: $1.

Mono Basin National Forest Scenic Area Visitor Center (760-873-2498; fs.fed.us) US 395. Open 9–4:30 daily. If the dizzying array of outdoor activities overwhelm, stop by this helpful visitor center. The ranger can help guide you toward hikes and campgrounds, plus they offer guided hikes of Mono Lake's South Tufa area, a film depicting the geology of the region, and interactive natural history exhibits.

Tioga Lodge Boat Tours See *Lodging.*

✴ Green Spaces

Humboldt Toiyabe National Forest (760-932-7070; fs.fed.us). Places to put on your itinerary include Walker River Canyon, Topaz Lake, Little Antelope Valley, Llewelyn Falls, West Walker River (for fishing), Twin Lakes, Travertine, and Buckeye Hot Springs (both natural and free—see *Scenic Drives* for directions), Sawtooth Ridge, Green Creek, Conway Summit, Bridgeport Reservoir, Virginia Lakes, and the Hoover and Ansel Adams Wilderness. Campgrounds of note include Lundy Canyon (where you can fish for trout, see wildflowers, autumn colors, and boat), Twin Lakes's four campgrounds (Crags, Lower Twin Lakes, Paha, and Robinson Cove), Green Creek Campground, and Virginia Lakes. For detailed information, hiking maps, wilderness permits, and all your questions answered, contact the ranger station or visit the **Mono Basin National Forest Scenic Area Visitor Center** (760-873-2498; fs.fed.us) US 395, Mono Lake.

Mono Basin National Forest Scenic Area (760-873-2498; fs.fed.us) US 395, Mono Lake. If California had its own Dead Sea (without the religious significance, but surely containing the restorative powers of salt, endurance, and rejuvenation)

SCENIC DRIVES

Calling the roads in this region scenic is quite the understatement. You'll pass everything from arid high-country desert to limestone formations in Mono Lake to seas of pines and dogwoods. Below are routes that will impress even the stodgiest of travelers. Do not attempt them in winter, when dirt roads turn to muddy mush.

US 395 from Topaz Lake to Bridgeport You'll probably get here from CA 89 in Markleeville, so head north on US 395 to view Topaz Lake to fish for trout, then turn around and drive south on US 395. If you want an off-road adventure, before you reach the artist community of Walker, turn off on Mill Canyon Road for 6.4 miles, where you might want to walk down to Mill Creek to explore Little Antelope Valley, see the trout (but you can't fish here), and smell the vanilla-scented Jeffrey pine. Once you get back to the car, turn around and drive back to US 395, make a stop at West Walker River to fish or relax by the shores. Afterwards, turn right at Twin Lakes Road and then right on Buckeye to the **Buckeye Hot Springs** (760-932-7070; free).

US 395 from Bridgeport to Lee Vining Start your day with a dip in **Travertine Hot Springs** (760-872-5000). Your next stop is the ghost town of **Bodie** (you'll see the signs). After exploring the town, drive south on US 395, passing Mono Lake to eat at the Lee Vining Mobil Station's **Whoa Nellie Deli**. The next day you can fully explore the lake.

John Hickok

THE LIMESTONE SPIRES AT MONO LAKE.

it would be Mono Lake. It seems over time everyone has wanted a piece of this salty lake—from oil drillers on the two nascent islands, black **Negit** or white **Paoha**; to nesting seagulls (85 percent of all seagulls in California come to nest on Negit Island); to the Indians who survived on the lake's fly larvae and shrimp; to more recently, the city of Los Angeles's Department of Water and Power, which built aqueducts to cart Mono Lake water to the desert of L.A. (from which a long, dramatic fight ensued—ask a local about it, they love to talk story about those Hollywood folks).

What makes Mono Lake so unique is its outstanding age—at least 700,000 years old—making it one of the oldest continuously existing lakes on the continent. Mono Lake covers 66 square miles, a mere fraction of its previous magnitude, for it once was over 60 times greater, while being fed by glaciers during the last Ice Age. There are streams that flow into Mono Lake, yet there are no outlets, leaving the lake naturally salty and alkaline.

Another point of interest, the lake is surrounded by volcanoes, both new and old. In fact, two of the islands in the lake are volcanic domes. Geologically, the lake is also unique because of the tufa towers, made from calcium carbonate from underwater springs, and some now reach over 30 feet high.

After a stop at the Visitor Center, head to the **Mono Lake Tufa State Reserve** ($3) for the best up close views of these limestone pieces of art. You might also want to explore the **Panum Crater**, **Mono Craters**, and **Navy Beach**. Afterwards, head to **June Lake** to hike the **Parker Lake** trail for spectacular views of the lake; the trail is 14 miles round-trip, or if you and your party have two cars, you can park the second one at Silver Creek.

❋ Lodging

Aside from a number of campgrounds listed in *Green Spaces*, if you want a more rustic experience with a bed, contact **Twin Lakes Resort** (twinlake resort.com), **Doc and Al's** (760-932-7051), and **Lundy Lake Resort** (626-309-0415).

✎ ♿ **Bridgeport Inn** (760-932-7380; thebridgeportinn.com) US 395, Bridgeport. From March through November, you can experience 1877 in this restored inn in the heart of Bridgeport. Rooms look much the same as when Mark Twain visited, though today you have a choice of 6 hotel (decorated with period antiques), 12 motel (the same type of bedspreads you'd see at a Ramada) or a couple economy (which means you share a bathroom) rooms; or families will appreciate the cottage (complete with a full kitchen). The restaurant here is a nice touch. $–$$$.

✎ **Hunewill Guest Ranch** (760-932-7710; hunewillranch.com) Bridgeport. Founded in 1861 by Napoleon Bona-parte Hunewill, this family-operated guest ranch has been offering a tamer *City Slickers* experience ever since. Stay in an authentic cabin, go on a cat-tle drive (if you sign up for it in advance), ride horses for days, sing songs around a campfire at night, dance, and eat three hearty meals. If this doesn't sound like too much work, give them a call in summer. $$; kids rates are less, but there is a fee for everyone in your party, even the babes; rates do not include tax.

✎ **Tioga Lodge** (760-647-6423; tioga lodgeatmonolake.com) 54411 US 395, Lee Vining. Open from May through September. The new owners of this one-time tollbooth are attempting to lure eco-friendly travelers into the country cottages with an organic restaurant and country charm. The

four cabins offer views of Mono Lake, and the owners arrange boat tours on the lake. $–$$.

✎ "❦" ❋ **Virginia Creek Settlement** (760-932-7780; virginiacrksettlement .com) US 395, 5 miles south of Bridge-port. John Wayne stayed here. There's even a tribute to the Duke in the room he slept in. If that doesn't attract you, then consider the seven basic, but sweet, rooms are some of the best deals in the region. That, coupled with dinner at the restaurant, and you'll be set for the night. They also offer a campground, camptown wagons, and housekeeping cabins—though you have to pay for a shower if you aren't in a room. $–$$.

❋ Where to Eat

✎ ♿ ♟ **Bridgeport Inn** (760-932-7380; thebridgeportinn.com) US 395, Bridgeport. Open March through November for breakfast, lunch, and dinner (closed Wednesday). I have two words for you: Prime Rib. That's why Calaveras County folks haul them-selves over Ebbetts Pass. Everything else on the menu is as you would expect from a historic inn—egg dishes and griddle fare, salads and sandwich-es, rich desserts and a fun bar. $–$$$.

✎ **Hammond Station Restaurant** (760-647-6423; tiogalodgeatmonolake .com) Tioga Lodge, 54411 US 395, Lee Vining. Open from May through September for breakfast, to-go lunch-es, and dinner. Still trying to define itself, this restaurant offers everything from Hawaiian-bread French toast, to ginger-spiced veggie pasta, to shrimp with a Basque chorizo, to pork tamales. $–$$$.

✎ ♿ **Lee Vining Mobil Station/The Whoa Nelli Deli** (760-872-1088) CA 120 and US 395, Lee Vining. Open through late October. A bit of a novelty in these parts. Walk into a gas station to be served fish tacos, lobster *taquitos*, smoked trout bagel, and gourmet pizza. $–$$.

♂ ♿ **Nicely's** (760-647-6477) US 395, Lee Vining. Open for breakfast, lunch, and dinner (closed Tuesday through Wednesday in winter). It's always fun to peek inside a small-town diner and see what the folks are really all about. If you like to see Old Stan at the counter chatting up Bessie Lou as she pours more coffee, or are in the mood for some old-fashioned American fare, Nicely's is the place for you. $.

♂ "♟" 🍴 **Virginia Creek Settlement** (760-932-7780; virginiacrksettlement .com) US 395, 5 miles south of Bridgeport. Open Tuesday through Sunday in summer and Wednesday through Saturday in spring and fall. Quite the mountain lodge, this restaurant serves breakfast and dinner. Italian American fare includes pizza and pasta in a wonderful family-friendly dinner house. $–$$.

The Shasta
Cascade

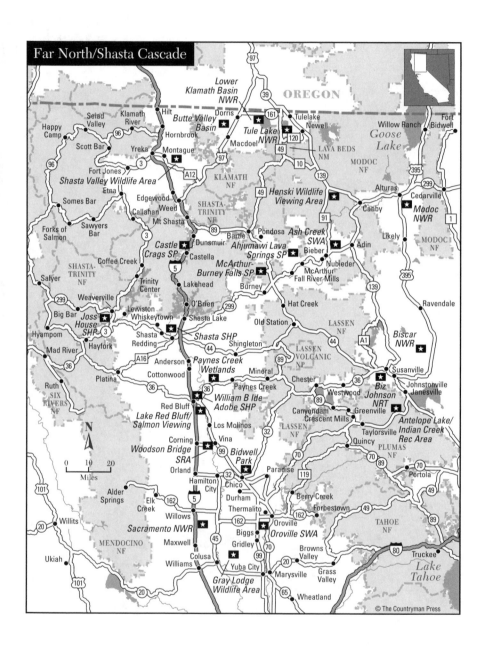

Far North/Shasta Cascade

© The Countryman Press

INTRODUCTION

A sea of green trees, rolling off volcanic peaks, dotted with sapphire lakes, and hidden obsidian lava tubs and mountains, the Shasta Cascade has been dubbed a wonderland for all the right reasons. Created by volcanoes that were still erupting 3000 years ago, this land is both nascent and wise. Indian tribes, spiritual seekers, and outdoor adventurers flock to the area to explore the rich landscape. But don't expect to soak it all in during one trip—visitors return year after year and still can't claim to have seen it all.

From the south, don't expect much besides agricultural fields and dust. But if you look a little closer, the small towns have an authenticity about them that you won't find elsewhere. The most prominent towns of the area are **Red Bluff** and **Chico**. Bisected by the Sacramento River, Red Bluff, though not exactly idyllic, is a gentle respite from the dust that accompanies your trip up I-5. Here the Wild West meets old Victorian architecture. Gold mines sprung up in the 1800s, and you can bet there were some fireworks between the hoity-toity rich folks and the cowboys. Today the town is pretty tame, save when the rodeo and boat drag racers pay a visit. Antiques and plenty of outdoor activities will keep you busy for at least a day or two. Save time for my favorite spot: the college town of Chico. Dubbed one of the most artsy small towns in America, you'll want to explore the vast public art, lovely galleries and shops, and the expansive **Bidwell Park**, named for the founder of the area.

Farther up Interstate 5 gets you to the largest city in the area, **Redding**, which used to be known as Poverty Flats. Today, the city is slowly beginning to grow up to welcome the hordes of visitors passing through. Sure, you still have your butt-slapping, truck-driving yeehaw types of boys, but the newly constructed **Sundial Bridge** and the renovated **Cascade Theater** allows the art lovers who graduated from Chico State to find more than burgers and shooting ranges.

Most visitors pass through Redding on their way to explore **Lassen Volcanic National Park** and the **Trinity Alps**, choosing instead to stay in one of the idyllic mountain towns of **Dunsmuir, Mt. Shasta,** and even the historic town of **Weed**. These spiritual centers attract hippies, yogis, and adventurers looking to tap into the wisdom they see emanating from the Cascade Mountains second highest peak, **Mt. Shasta**. Farther north, you'll find the historic gold rush and logging town of Yreka (pronounced "WHY-reka"), which makes a good jumping-off point to explore the **Klamath River and Basin, Marble Mountain Wilderness,** and **Lava Beds National Monument**.

The Eastern Mountains give space and good old country living a new name. Strangers wave, kids play in streams, and the seasons and the land dictate your every move. A trip to this eastern part of the region, inhabited by Indians and country folk, will truly give you an idea of the power of the area. **Modoc County** welcomes more migrating birds than anywhere else in California, who rest on the many lakes dotting the high-desert mountains. To the south of these mountains, **Lassen, Sierra,** and **Chester/Lake Almanor** Counties, is where the Sierra meets the Cascades, and you'll find empty wilderness, wildlife unlike any you have ever experienced, lakes and streams packed with fish, and historic towns lining the byways.

GUIDANCE **California Welcome Center** (530-365-1180; shastacascade.org) 1699 CA 273, Anderson. This is a great place to get up-to-date information about the Shasta area and the entire state.

Alturas Chamber of Commerce (530-233-4434; alturaschamber.org) 522 S. Main Street, Alturas.

Butte County Cultural Tourism (530-228-2860; experiencebuttecounty.com) 805 Whispering Winds Lane, Chico.

Chester/Lake Almanor Chamber (530-258-2426; chster-lakealmanor.com) 529 Main Street, Chester.

MUSTS FOR FIRST-TIME VISITORS
1. Explore Lassen Volcanic National Park.
2. Swim in Lake Siskiyou.
3. Walk through the caves at Lava Beds National Monument.
4. See the Sundial Bridge.
5. Spend a day in Chico's Bidwell Park.
6. Drive up to Mt. Shasta.
7. Fly-fish in Hat Creek.
8. Soak in Wilbur Hot Springs.
9. Hike or fish in Lassen National Forest.
10. See Burney Falls.

MUSTS FOR REPEAT VISITORS
1. Raft the Klamath River.
2. Visit the Klamath Basin to view the bird migration.
3. Explore the Trinity Alps.
4. Kayak Whiskeytown Lake.
5. Eat lunch at Mt. Shasta City's Lily's Restaurant.
6. Have a beer at Chico's Sierra Nevada Brewing Co.
7. Boat in Lake Almanor.
8. Ride the McCloud Dinner train.
9. Explore Quincy.
10. Ride a horse through the Plumas National Forest.

Mt. Shasta Chamber and Visitor Bureau (800-926-4865; mtshastachamber
.com) 300 Pine Street, Mt. Shasta.

Plumas County Visitor Bureau (530-283-6345; plumascounty.org) 550 Crescent
Street, Quincy.

Redding CVB (530-225-4100; visitredding.com) 777 Auditorium Road, Redding.

Shasta Cascade Wonderland Association (877-SHASTA4U; shastacascade.com)
1699 CA 273, Anderson.

Trinity County Chamber (530-623-6101; trinitycounty.com) 215 Main Street,
Weaverville.

HELPFUL WEB SITES
Weedchamber.com
Visitsiskiyou.com
Easternplumaschamber.com

GETTING THERE *By air:* **Chico Municipal Airport** welcomes flights on United Skywest (united.com) from San Francisco.

Redding Municipal Airport (530-224-4321) has flights to San Francisco on
United's Skywest (united.com), and Horizon Air (horizon.com) runs to L.A., Port-
land, and Eureka. For rental cars, Avis (avis.com), Budget (budget.com), and
Enterprise (enterprise.com) have offices at the airport.

By bus: **Greyhound** (greyhound.com) serves the area with stations in Chico (450
Orange Street), Redding (Butte and Pine Streets), Weed (628 S. Weed Boulevard),
Alturas (111 W. North Street), and Susanville (2900 Main Street).

By car: I-5 travels the distance of the region from north to south. Many of the
towns are accessible by this freeway or from highways that connect to it. For example, in the valley, to get to Chico (which is 30 miles off I-5) you'll need to take CA
32 east. I-5 also takes you directly to Redding, Dunsmuir, Mt. Shasta City, and
Weed.

For eastern mountain towns, see *Scenic Drives* sections in the areas you wish to
visit. Major byways leading through the eastern towns include CA 89 (McCloud to
Lake Tahoe area), CA 44 (Susanville to Redding), CA 70 (Oroville to Quincy), CA
99 (from Sacramento to Chico), and US 395 (Oregon through the southeastern
Sierra Mountains).

By train: **Amtrak** (Amtrak.com) arrives in Chico (450 Orange Street), Oroville
(Grand Avenue and CA 70), and Dunsmuir (Dunsmuir Railroad Depot).

GETTING AROUND *By bus:* To get around Chico, Oroville, and Butte County
by bus, take the **B-Line** for $1–1.25 per ride. In Redding, **RABA** (530-241-2877)
serves the community.

By car: You really need a car to fully explore the area. It is helpful to know that
most numbered highways are really two-lane roads that can be slow (and often
close in winter).

It takes a while to get anywhere, considering that Chico is 41 miles from Red
Bluff, which is 32 miles from Redding, and about an hour from Lassen National
Park. From Redding, you can get to Dunsmuir, McCloud, and Mt. Shasta City in

about an hour. And from there, it takes 90 minutes to get to Lava Beds National Park.

MEDICAL EMERGENCIES **Enloe Medical Center** (530-332-7300) 1531 Esplanade, Chico. **Redding Medical Center** (530-244-5400; shastaregional.com) 1100 Butte Street, Redding. **Mercy Medical Center** (530-926-6111) 914 Pine Street, Mt. Shasta City.

WEATHER If you don't like your summer hot and your winter cold, this is not the place for you. Summer temperatures scorch the area, reaching well over 100 degrees Fahrenheit, while winter brings on quite a chill (dropping at times to 5 degrees Fahrenheit at Mt. Shasta City). Even in October, you might see snow as you drive I-5 past Mt. Shasta City.

THE VALLEY

WILLIAMS, BUTTE, TEHAMA, AND SUTTER COUNTIES

✳ To See

Bidwell Mansion State Historic Park (530-895-6144) 525 Esplanade, Chico. Open Wednesday through Friday 12–4, and Saturday and Sunday 10 AM–4 PM. John Bidwell was one of California's most influential men. And, during his time, one of the richest. In 1860, he bought 28,000 acres in Chico and started the town. Tour the mansion and see what his life was like. $2–4.

Chico Museum (530-892-4336) 141 Salem Street, Chico. Open Wednesday through Sunday 12–4. A variety of exhibits focus on Chico's history. A visit here includes artifacts from the Chinese Taoist Temple in town. Free.

Kelly Griggs House Museum (530-527-1129) 311 Washington Street, Red Bluff. Open Thursday through Sunday 1-4. This Victorian house has been refurbished to represent a lost era. Victorian-dressed mannequins hang out around antique furniture, making you wonder how they survived in all this heat. Free.

🖉 ᕒ **Sacramento River Discovery Center** (530-527-1196) 1000 Sale Lane, Red Bluff. Open Tuesday through Saturday 11–4. Learn about watershed exhibits, tour a native plant garden, and enjoy a cool spot to bring the kids.

CHINESE INFLUENCE IN THE VALLEY

Though Marysville was named after a 15-year-old survivor of the Donner Party, and has been a city since the 1850s, in its historic western-style downtown, you'll find a Chinese influence. The **Northern California Chinese History Museum** and the **Bok Kai Temple** are both located in downtown Marysville (around 1st Street). The Bok Kai Temple is a sight, and an irony. Built to honor the Chinese god of water, sometime around the turn of the 21st century, the temple was about to crumble under the force of heavy rain. With help from the local and national Chinese community, the temple was rebuilt.

CHICO—THE ART CAPITAL OF THE NORTH STATE

You drive past fields of olive trees, golden hills, and cows. You never imagine that a small town out in the middle of nowhere would have an arts community that rivals some major cities. Well Chico does. In fact, there are so many galleries to explore you could spend an entire day strolling in and out of them. The best time to do so is the First Saturday, when all galleries stay open from 4–8 and welcome visitors. Favorites include **1079 Gallery** (1078 Broadway Street), **Avenue 9 Gallery** (180 E. 9th Avenue), and **Crux** (1421 Park Avenue).

But if you can't make it on a Saturday, there is plenty of public art scattered around town, including **Our Hands** (Municipal Center Bldg), **Dancing Trout** (411 Main), **The Trees** (Salem Street between 2nd and W. 3rd Streets), and **Salem Street Art Walls** (Salem Street, between 3rd and 4th Streets).

OUR HANDS, CHICO

William B. Ide State Historic Park (530-529-8599; parks.ca.gov) Adobe Road, Red Bluff. If the gold rush times make you pine for another era of gunfights, the American Dream, and a dusty search, here you can see what it was like in this old 1850s mining town. William B. Ide was the one and only president of the California Republic, so when you enter his adobe, you can play out what might have been if California had stayed its own country. $5.

🦤 ⅙ **National Yoyo Museum** (530-893-1414; nationalyoyo.org) 320 Broadway, Chico. Open Monday through Saturday 10 AM–6 PM and Sunday 12–5 PM. Yoyo fans will appreciate the collection of these fun toys from the 1920s through 1950s, including the largest yoyo in the world. Free.

✳ To Do

CYCLING Mountain bikers and cyclists will find plenty to keep them busy in the area. In Chico, the most popular trail is on **Bidwell Park's** Annie Bidwell Trail, which is a moderate 4.7-mile loop in a quiet section of Upper Bidwell. Other popular spots to bike are the **Sacramento River Bend Recreational Area** and **Black Butte Lake.**

Bike Rentals
Campus Bicycles (530-345-2081) 330 Main Street, Chico. This great bike store rents all the gear you need for a day of exploring Bidwell Park. $20 half day and $35 full day.

FARM TOURS California Olive Ranch (530-846-8000; californiaolive ranch.com) 2675 Lobe Tree Road, Oroville. Open May through September. Friday tours are at 9:30, 10:30, and 11:30. Oroville is known for being the olive capital of California; come visit the largest of the growers, with over a million trees. You can see how the fruit goes from the tree into the olive oil bottle, and taste some, too.

Chaffin Family Orchards (530-533-8239; chaffinfamilyorchards.com) 606 Cool Canyon Road, Oroville, Open during daylight hours. Organic and biodynamic farm techniques help this family of farmers grow a slew of products from fruit to olive oil, meats, and eggs.

Grey Fox Vineyards (530-589-3920; greyfox.net) 90 Grey Fox Lane, Oroville. Open weekends from 12–5. Big reds grow well out here in the valley, so fans of Syrah, Zinfandel, and Barbera will be pleased.

TAKE A BREAK AFTER CYCLING IN BIDWELL PARK.

LaRocca Vineyards (530-899-WINE; laroccavineyards.com) CA 32 E. and Nopel, Forest Ranch. Open Friday 1:30–6, Saturday and Sunday 12–6. For over 25 years, this organic winery has produced award-winning blends.

Lodestar Olive Oil (530-534-6548; lodestarfarms.com) 3719 Foothill Boulevard, Oroville. Open Friday and Saturday 12–5; if you are around on other days, call for an appointment. For over 15 years, this family farm has grown olives and pressed them into oil. At the tasting room, you can learn how it's done.

Long Creek Winery (530-589-3415; longcreekwinery.com) 233 Ward Road, Oroville. Open by appointment only. My first memory of wine tasting goes back to being in some winemaker's barn, tasting Cabernet from the barrel. Here you'll experience that same intimacy.

Pedrozo Dairy and Cheese Company (530-680-4041; realfarmsteadcheese .com) 7713 Road 24, Orland. Open by appointment. If your kids like cheese as much as mine, you'll want to take a trip out here to show them all the work that goes into making cheese. They'll also like the farm animals.

FARMERS' MARKETS Chico Farmers' Market 2nd and Wall, Downtown Chico. Saturday from 7:30–1 you'll find all the local growers and most locals, picking through local fruits and veggies.

Downtown Chico Business Association Farmers' Market Broadway and 3rd Street, Chico. April through September, head downtown on Thursday from 5:30–9.

FISHING Also see *Green Spaces*.

Northstate Outdoors (530-209-3996; northstateoutdoors.com) 2150 Main Street, Red Bluff.

CALIFORNIA AGRICULTURE PIONEERS— JOHN BIDWELL AND FREDA EHMANN

With the food renaissance occurring, folks not only want to know where their food comes from, but also how it got to be there. Both Bidwell and Ehmann helped put California land (and the growers) on the map.

In 1841, 22-year-old John Bidwell arrived in Chico, and what a splash this young man made. Not only did he fight in the Bear Flag Revolt and the Mexican War, help recapture Los Angeles, found Chico, serve in Congress, and find the first gold in Oroville, he was also a major player in the agricultural world. We can thank him for bringing almonds, walnuts, and peaches to California.

After losing her husband and money, Freda Ehmann turned to the only possession she had: a 20-acre olive orchard. She went out on the road to pitch her fruit, and before long had a number of major contracts for olives around the world. Today she is credited with creating the multi-million olive industry right here in Oroville.

Salmon King Lodge of Red Bluff (530-528-8727; salmonkinglodge.com) 19095
Bonita Road, Red Bluff. Here you can arrange for a guided fishing trip on one of
the rivers or lakes in the area, then relax in the lodge and talk story over your catch.

GOLF Bidwell Park Municipal Golf Course (530-891-8417; bidwellpark
.americangolf.com/) 3199 Golf Course Road. Located in Upper Bidwell Park, this
lovely course allows you to feel immersed in nature. $16–19.

Sevillano Links Golf Course (530-528-4600; sevillanolinks.com) 2657 Barham
Avenue. This is the only John Daly course on the West Coast. $30–60.

HOT SPRINGS Sierra Hot Springs See *Sierra Foothills.*

Wilbur Hot Springs Resort (530-473-2306; wilburhotsprings.com) 3375 Wilbur
Springs Road, Williams. Located in the coastal range foothills of Colusa County,
between Williams and Clearlake, this hot springs resort and spa offers rustic relaxation in a peaceful setting. Most people choose to enjoy the hot springs in the buff.
Day use: $45 adults; $20 children 4–12.

WATER SPORTS Bidwell Canyon Marina (530-589-3165; funtime-fulltime
.com) 801 Bidwell Canyon Road, Oroville. Rent all types of water sports equipment, including houseboats, fishing and ski boats, and kayaks.

Lake Oroville Marina (530-877-2414; lakeorovillemarina.com) 3428 Pentz Road,
Paradise. Here's another spot to rent all types of water sports equipment.

✴ Green Spaces

Bidwell Park (530-891-4671; bidwellpark.org) Manzanita Avenue, Chico. One of
the biggest municipals parks in the nation, at an impressive 3,670 acres, Bidwell
will keep the entire family entertained. Upper Bidwell (west of Manzanita Avenue)
is hilly and great for mountain biking and hiking, while Lower Bidwell (east of
Manzanita) is flat. Picnickers congregate in Lower Bidwell, as do folks looking to
cool off in summer at Sycamore Pool, a gigantic concrete pool built into the creek.
In Upper Bidwell there are also swim-
ming holes along Big Chico Creek.
There is a golf course here as well (see
Golf). Some of my favorite trails
include the North Rim Trail, Upper
Trail, Yahi Trail, and Wildwood Trail.
For wildflower viewing, head to
Horseshoe Lake in spring.

BIDWELL PARK POOL.

Black Butte Lake (530-865-4781;
spk.usace.army.mil) Go 8 miles west of
Orland and Interstate 5 on Newville
Road. The waters are warm, the fish
are biting, and it seems that not many
people know about this lovely lake.
Fishermen can hook bass. Hikers and
bikers will find miles of trails to
explore. You can camp here as well. $4
for day use and $15 overnight.

Gray Lodge Wildlife Area (530-846-7505) Pennington and Almond Orchard Roads, Gridley. This is a prime spot for bird-watching along the Pacific Flyway. Come in November through January to see the majority of birds. There are a number of species of geese and hawks. $2.50.

Lake Oroville (800-255-5561; parks.ca.gov) Oroville Dam Boulevard, Oroville. This is the tallest earth-filled dam: over 770 feet tall and 7,000 feet long. For most of us, a trip to this lake would not be complete without engaging in some type of water sports activity, and here you can do it all: houseboat, water-ski, swim, wakeboard, fish for bass, boat, or Jet Ski. Hikers will delight in the trails, especially in spring when wildflowers are in full bloom. The best part of this lake is the floating campsites, where you actually pitch your tent on a floating platform. $4.

Lassen National Park See *Redding and Vicinity.*

Oroville State Wildlife Area (530-538-2236) Bird-watchers and fishermen love this 11,000-acre green space. From February through June, bird-watchers should come visit the egret and heron rookery lining the Feather River. More than 177 species of birds call this area home. Free.

Plumas National Forest See *Eastern Mountains.*

Sacramento River (530-224-2100; blm.gov) This massive waterway feeds into Lake Shasta and provides plenty of water fun for all ages. You can fish, swim, boat, camp, hike, and see plenty of nature. A popular spot to visit is the **Sacramento River Bend Recreational Area**, where you can learn about the riparian habitat, explore the Pane's Creek wetlands, see birds travel along the Pacific Flyway, hike the Lake Plateau and Yana Trail, mountain bike, or camp.

Sutter Buttes Mountain Range (530-671-6116; Middlemountain.org) Yuba City. Most of the land in this "smallest mountain range in the world" is privately owned, so if you want to get up on those mountains, you'll have to take a guided trek. The mountain range is a mere 10 miles in diameter. On your hike, you'll pass through oak forests, ravines, and small creeks, hopefully passing foxes, deer, bobcats, and birds galore. $35 for guided hikes.

Table Mountain Wildflowers (530-891-5556) Cherokee Road, 20 minutes from downtown Oroville. From March through April you will want to check out the sea of wildflowers in bloom at this mountain. California poppies, daisies, and lupine show off their colors in a dramatic way.

Woodson Bridge State Recreation Area (530-839-2112; parks.ca.gov) Just 6 miles east of I-5, Corning. Along the Sacramento River in this SRA, there are plenty of swimming holes, wildlife viewing areas (including yellow-billed cuckoos and bald eagles), hiking, fishing, and camping opportunities.

✳ Lodging

Williams

♂ ♿ **Wilbur Hot Springs Resort** (530-473-2306; wilburhotsprings.com) 3375 Wilbur Springs Road. The ultimate getaway up in the coastal range, this hot springs resort is for those looking to commune with nature and soak those muscles. Apartments and rooms lean more towards rustic than classic, though the wood panels are nice touches. Those of you looking for a Palm Desert-like resort need to look elsewhere, here you will share bathrooms, cook for yourself, and see more naked people in one place than you probably have ever laid eyes on before. You can also camp here. $–$$$.

Oroville

A Riverside B&B (530-533-1413; riversidebandb.com) 45 Cabana Drive, Oroville. Wood panels, bed curtains, floral bedspreads, and rustic charm make this B&B a nice choice for people who want to spend time at Lake Oroville and the Feather River. Country-style rooms match the down-home friendly vibe. Amenities: 9 rooms, full breakfast, river access, some rooms have skylights, Jacuzzi tubs, and wood-burning fireplaces. $–$$.

Chico

◢ ♿ ⛾ **Hotel Diamond** (530-893-3100; hoteldiamondchico.com) 220 4th Street, Chico. Since 1904, this building has been a centerpiece of Chico. Classic rooms offer people with discerning taste granite countertops, hand-carved woodwork, fireplaces, and plush linens. During graduation weekend, book early, as this is the top choice for visiting parents. Amenities: 43 rooms and suites, continental breakfast, gym, AC, room service, parking, restaurant, live jazz on weekends, concierge, free local calls. $$–$$$$.

⛾ **Grateful Bed** (530-342-2464; the-gratefulbed.net) 1462 Arcadian Avenue, Chico. Besides having one of the better B&B names in Northern California, this homey lodging option is the epitome of the word quaint. Choose between four rooms with an iron bed or exposed brick, a claw-foot tub or bay windows. All come with candlelit breakfast and air conditioning. $$.

Paradise

⊗ **Chapelle de L'Artiste** (530-228-0941; chapelldelartiste.com) 215 Wayland Road, Paradise. A barn, a chapel, a wagon wheel, paintings, and landscaped gardens are just some of the personality traits of this B&B and

retreat center. Though the décor in rooms is slightly over the top, you know Melissa and Cliff pay attention to detail. Amenities: 3 rooms, breakfast, pool and spa, BBQ, kitchen. $$$–$$$$.

CAMPING See *Green Spaces*.

✳ Where to Eat
DINING OUT

Chico

⛾ **Crush 201** (530-342-7000) 201 Broadway, Chico. Open for dinner nightly. This new eatery brings urban dining to the country. Exposed beams, big booths, and a waterfall careening down a large sheet of glass complement the extensive wine list, making you want to hang out for hours. Since service can be slow, go with a group. Stick to brick-oven pizza. Reservations recommended. $$–$$$.

⛾ **Monk's Wine Lounge and Bistro** (530-343-3408) 128 W. 2nd Street, Chico. See *Entertainment*.

◢ ♿ ⛾ **RawBar** (530-897-0626; rawbarchico.com) 346 Broadway, Chico. Open for lunch and dinner Monday through Saturday. More hip than hype, this fusion sushi joint offers both traditional takes on sushi and a mishmash of foods from the entire Asian continent. Can't decide between spicy tuna and naan, here you can have both. Small plates and sushi: $–$$.

♿ ⛾ **Red Tavern** (530-894-3463; redtavern.com) 1250 Esplanade, Chico. Open for dinner Monday through Saturday. Though this is the finest restaurant in the entire area, you can still play a game of bocce ball between courses. Specializing in local produce and seasonal dishes, menu items change nightly, while the California wine list stays the same. $$–$$$.

◢ ♿ ⛾ **Sierra Nevada Taproom and Restaurant** (530-345-2739; sierra nevada.com) 1075 E. 20th Street, Chico. Open for lunch and dinner Tuesday through Sunday. I know what you are thinking: a taproom as fine dining? Sierra Nevada takes both its beer and its food seriously, serving wonderful microbrews and sustainable cuisine. Not only do they use a similar grain for their beers and signature gourmet brick-oven pizzas (burning only local almond wood), but they also grow their own hops and veggies. $$.

&. **Spice Creek Café and Gallery** (530-891-9951) 230 W. 3rd Street, Chico. Open for dinner Wednesday through Saturday. You can imagine the chefs of this artsy gallery/restaurant puttering through the farmers' markets just trying to find the right ingredients for their lasagna. Dining here is a must. Dishes are both delicate and bold. Save room for dessert. Reservations recommended. $$$.

EATING OUT

Williams

&. ⦿ Y **Granzellas** (530-473-5583; granzellas.com) 451 6th Street, Williams. Open for breakfast, lunch, and dinner daily. In 2007, Granzellas burned to the ground, and fans of this institution along the I-5 corridor thought they had lost a friend. Rebuilt to new heights to include a sports bar, a deli with plenty of gourmet groceries, and a full-service restaurant, Granzella's doesn't disappoint. You probably would rather stick to the deli, where you can get Thanksgiving Coffee, gelato, cheese, great focaccia, wine, an amazing beer selection, and sandwiches. The restaurant serves everything from Belgian waffles to garlic-herb chicken pizza. This is a great stop for folks headed out to **Wilbur Hot Springs**. Deli: $. Restaurant: $–$$.

Yuba City and Marysville

⦿ &. **Brick Coffee House Café** (530-743-5283; brickcoffeehouse.com) 316 D Street, Marysville. Open 6–6 Monday through Friday, 6:30–5 on Saturday, and 7:30–4 on Sunday. Live music, food, and decent coffee make this a good choice in Marysville. Menu items include veggie bagels, salads, and biscuits and gravy. $

Sunflower Natural Foods (530-671-9511) 726 Sutter Street. Open daily. This natural foods store, bakery, and deli is quite the surprise in the area. Their veggie burgers are decent. $.

⦿ &. **Taste of India** (530-751-5156) 1456 Bridge Street. Open Monday through Friday 9–6. Yuba City has one of the highest populations of Indian families in Northern California. Don't be put off that this Indian eatery sits behind a gas station off CA 99. This surprisingly decent restaurant shouldn't disappoint. $.

Oroville

⦿ &. **Checkers** (530-538-2007) 109 Table Mountain Boulevard, Oroville. Open for lunch Monday through Friday and dinner Thursday and Friday. Local youths show their stuff at this training school, where you can get organic seasonal dishes, including house-made pasta, meat, and good chicken. $.

Chico

⦿ &. **Caffe Ricci** (530-343-2167) 3269 Esplanade, Suite 155, Chico. Open 6–2 Monday through Friday, 7–12 Saturday. Simple sandwiches and pastries accent the fine coffee served at this local institution, I like to come here for breakfast before a stroll through Bidwell Park. $.

Chico Natural Foods (530-891-1713; chiconatural.com) 818 Main Street, Chico. Open 7:30 AM–10 PM daily. North of here, you'll be hard-pressed to find natural food stores, let alone a co-op, so if you plan to camp (or have your own kitchen) you might want to stop here before heading farther north.

☄ ✦ **Chronic Tacos** (530-895-8226; chronictacoschico.com) 119 W. 2nd Street, Chico. Open at least 9–9 daily. Sure, some might complain that this is gringo Mexican fare, but the food is good (especially the tostada bowls and tacos), the staff is friendly, and meat-eaters and veggie folks have much to enjoy in the same place. $.

Empire Coffee (530-566-4008) 434 Orange Street, Chico. Open from 6–10 daily. Coffee brewed up in an old train car makes a visit here a must. The beans are organic, the service is friendly, and the environment is quite unique.

☄ ✦ ✦ **Madison Bear Garden** (530-891-1639) 316 W. 2nd Street, Chico. Open for food daily from 11–10, bar open late. During the day, families populate the beer garden and the indoor tribute to things past—check out the old car hanging from the ceiling, the big ole bar, and the memorabilia on the walls. This is the spot for burgers, burgers, and more burgers. At night, college students take over, dancing, drinking, and singing karaoke. $.

☄ ✦ **Morning Thunder Café** (530-342-9717) 352 Vallombrosa Avenue, Chico. Open for breakfast and lunch daily. Students and local Chicoites head to this retro diner to cure their hangovers with big omelets, pancakes, and views of Bidwell Park. Cash only. $.

Naked Lounge (530-895-0676) 118 W. 2nd Street, Chico. Open until midnight daily. The ideal coffeehouse vibe: The smell of burnt beans, loud music, funky art, and hipper than hip folks surfing their laptops. The coffee is the best in town; there is a small selection of pastries. And it is open late.

Shubert's Ice Cream and Candy (530-342-7263; shuberts.com) 178 E. 7th Street, Chico. Open 9:30–10 Monday through Friday, and 11–10 on weekends. Family-owned and operated since 1938, you won't find ice cream much better than this.

☄ ✦ **Upper Crust Bakery Café** (530-895-3866) 130 Main Street, Chico. For years, I have drooled over the pastries and baked goods at this popular café. Lunchtime it gets packed, with students eating salads and sandwiches, sipping coffee, and savoring sweet treats. $.

✳ Entertainment

Oroville
Feather Falls Casino (featherfallscasino.com) 3 Alverda Drive, Oroville. Live music and slots, Bloody Marys and soda water, it ain't Vegas but it is as close as you'll get in these parts.

Chico
In downtown Chico, there are over 40 watering holes, making Chico the place to be at night. The best spot to find out about local happenings, including live shows and new bars, is the **Chico News and Review** (newsreview.com). Below is a small list of places to visit at night.

✦ **33 Steaks, Booze and Jazz** (530-893-1903) 305 Main Street, Chico. Closed Monday. Local jazz bands perform here, while patrons sip cocktails and grub on steak—as the name implies.

Blue Room Theater (530-895-3749; blueroomtheater.com) 139 1st Street, Chico. A local theater company, yet the shows are surprisingly good.

✦ **Crazy Horse Saloon** (530-342-7299) 303 Main Street, Chico. Closed Sunday and Monday. Even if you don't like country music, a visit to see the only mechanical bull in Northern California is an entertaining sight.

Ⴘ **Crush 201** See *Dining Out.*

El Rey Theater 230 W. 2nd Street, Chico. This renovated old theater is an intimate place to see touring musicians.

Ⴘ **Joe's Bar** (530-894-3612) 749 W. 5th Street, Chico. If you want a hole-in-the-wall bar with wood chips on the floor and a lot of people, Joe's is the place for you.

Ⴘ **Madison Bear Garden** See *Eating Out.*

Ⴘ **Monk's Wine Lounge and Bistro** (530-343-3408) 128 W. 2nd Street, Chico. Over 100 wines available, and more than 50 by the glass, this sophisticated downtown wine bar caters to grad students. They also serve food.

Senator Theater 517 Main Street, Chico. For major rock stars and musicians, the classic Senator Theater is the place to be. Recently big names such as Modest Mouse, and the Deftones, have played here, making this the main place to hear live music in the north state.

＊ Selective Shopping

Downtown Chico offers the best shopping in the area along Main Street between 1st and 4th Streets. Some shops to check out include **The Bookstore** (118 Main Street), **Expeditions** (228 Main Street), **Lulu's Fashion Lounge** (212 Main Street), **Made in Chico** (232 Main Street), and **Zucchini & Vine** (2nd and Main Street).

＊ Seasonal Events

Ongoing: **Chico Performances** (chico performances.com). Throughout the school year international performers, authors, musicians, and dancers come to Chico. Here you may see the Peking Acrobats or the 25th Annual Putnam County Spelling Bee.

April: **Red Bluff Round-up Rodeo** (redbluffroundup.com). A week of

events to celebrate the foremost event to grace this small town. It has been going strong for almost 90 years.

May: **Paradise Chocolate Festival** (530-899-0335) 6626 Skyway, Paradise. Three days over everything chocolate might sound like heaven to some of us.

Concerts in the Park (530-345-6500) Chico City Plaza. From May through September come hear live music in the square on Friday from 7–8:30 and Saturday from 6:30–9.

June: **Shakespeare in the Park** (ensembletheaterofchico.com) Bidwell Park. For over 20 years the Ensemble Theater of Chico has been offering pay-what-you-can shows in the park under the stars. Shows happen all summer.

Chico Microbrew Festival (sibidwell .rancho.org). Live music and micro-beers to welcome summer, you don't have to twist my arm.

July: **Fourth of July** Every town in the area celebrates this major holiday—Chico has a party in Bidwell Park during the day, Paradise has a parade and bluegrass festival, and Oroville hoists up fireworks over the lake.

August: **Butte County Fair** (butte countyfair.org). A full-blown carnival with food, games, and even a rodeo. Doesn't get more country than this.

September: **Taste of Chico** (down townchico.com). Throughout downtown Chico vendors open their doors to let you taste their goodies, music plays in the streets, and over 80 restaurants and wineries show up to help make you full.

October: **Artoberfest** (artoberfest .org). For the month of October, 130 art exhibits, performances, special events, lectures, and films fill the calendar of the small town of Chico. Big-name performers show up and major players in the art world showcase their work.

REDDING AND VICINITY

✳ To See

Shasta State Historic Park CA 299, west of Redding. A small, historic town, Shasta was the original county seat. Today you can view how buildings used to be in the 1850s, when people came from all over the country to pan for gold. Free.

Sundial Bridge Off Auditorium Drive, Redding. Designed by Spanish architect Santiago Calatrava, this glass and steel bridge initially peeved locals. Now, hundreds of people walk across it during the day to get between the Turtle Bay campuses, and at night to stroll along the illuminated structure with their sweetheart. Amazingly, on June 21, the summer solstice, the Sundial Bridge accurately tells the time. It's quite the architectural sight to behold. Free.

✤ ♿ **Turtle Bay Exploration Park** (800-TURTLEBAY; turtlebay.org) 800 Auditorium Drive, Redding. Open 10 AM–5 PM daily (winter hours may be shorter, call for details). A stop to visit this massive park is a must when passing through the area. This is Redding's grand dame of tourist destinations (and some claim, the only one in town), boasting a kids' play area called Paul Bunyan's Forest Camp

THE SUNDIAL BRIDGE.

(complete with an eagle, a hawk, and a fox); a natural science museum with rotating and permanent exhibits about watersheds, the Sacramento River, and local fish; an arboretum and botanical garden (that can be very dry in summer); a large butterfly house; a tropical bird house; and the Sundial Bridge. Plus, from here you can access the Sacramento River Trail. There is a small café serving sandwiches and coffee. $13 adults; $9 youth and seniors. Gardens: $7 adults; $5 youth.

Weaverville Joss House State Historic Park (530-623-5284; parks.ca.gov). CA 299, Weaverville, 50 miles east of Redding. Open Wednesday through Sunday 10 AM–5 PM. The oldest continuously used Chinese temple in California, the Weaverville Joss House is a sight. Built in 1874 as a Taoist center of worship, today you can view Chinese artifacts from the gold rush era. Come see the Lion Dance if you are here in January or February (it coincides with Chinese New Year). Small fee.

✱ To Do

BOAT CRUISES ✍ ☖ **Shasta Lake Dinner Cruise** (530-238-2341; shastalake dinnercruise.com) 20359 Shasta Caverns Boulevard, O'Brien. From May through Labor Day, cruises go out on Friday and Saturday evenings at 6 PM. You'll get to cruise on Lake Shasta and enjoy a multi-course meal. Children's menus are available. $60 adults; $30 kids.

FAMILY FUN ✍ **Lake Shasta Caverns** (800-795-CAVE; lakeshastacaverns.com) 15 miles north of Redding, 20359 Shasta Caverns Road, Lakehead. First, you'll boat across the lake, then take a bus to the top of the forest, finally you arrive at the caverns. Prepare for a visual feast. You can tour eight rooms of limestone formations, including miniature waterfalls, columns, and what look like multicolored drapes. $20 adults; $12 children.

✍ **Waterworks Park** (530-246-9550; waterworkspark.com) 151 N. Boulder Drive, Redding. Open Memorial Day through Labor Day, Monday through Saturday 10 AM–6 PM and Sunday 12–4 PM. This massive water park gets packed during hot days. You'll wait in line to ride down a huge waterslide, and then try to avoid the person coming down after you. $19 adults; $15 kids.

FISHING This area is prime real estate for catching trout and bass, fly-fishing or spin fishing. The best fishing spots around Redding include **Bonnyview Boat Ramp** (3855 S. Bonnyview Road), **Caldwell Boat Ramp** (56 Quartz Hill Road), and **Posse Grounds Boat Ramp** (715 Auditorium Drive). You can also fish along the Sacramento River (to the south and north), in Whiskeytown Lake, Lake Shasta, and Lake Britton; or in Lassen Volcanic National Park and Hat Creek (which is known to have the best trout fly-fishing in the country). Get fishing gear at **Strictly Fishin'** (530-241-4665) and **Western Bait Farm** (530-245-0270).

The following companies lead fishing trips:

Fly Shop (800-669-FISH; flyshop.com) For over 30 years this outfit has guided folks to that big catch on a fly-fishing adventure. Trips go to the Sacramento and Feather Rivers, McCloud, Fall River, Pit River, Yuba River, and the surrounding lakes. $360 for two people.

Mark Clarke's Guide Service (530-945-3267; marksguidessportfishing.com) Mark and his crew will take you out to the Sacramento River, Shasta Lake, or Whiskeytown Lake to hook trout, salmon, stripers, shad, and more. $125–250.

GOLF **Churn Creek Golf Course** (530-222-6353) 7335 Churn Creek Road, Redding. This 9-hole course might not be the hardest course you'll ever tee off in, but it might be one of the cheapest. $20.

Gold Hills Golf Club (530-246-7867; goldhillsgolf.com) 1950 Gold Hills Drive, Redding. Tee off in this par 71 course with spectacular views of Mt. Shasta in the distance. $35–60.

KAYAKING AND RAFTING Kayaking is one of the best ways to enjoy the plentiful rivers and lakes in the area. Some favorite spots to paddle include the Sacramento River, Whiskeytown Lake, and Lake Shasta. You can rent kayaks at **H20 Adventures** (530-241-4530; raftredding.com). If you prefer to raft downstream, rentals can be found at **North Country** (530-244-4281) Bonnyview Boat Ramp, by appointment. The rangers at **Whiskeytown National Recreation Area** offer free guided kayak tours of the lake in summer (see *Green Spaces*). For information about rentals in Lake Shasta, see Sidebar—*Lake Shasta Houseboat Rentals*. You can also rent kayaks and canoes at **McArthur-Burney State Park** marina.

SCENIC DRIVES **Volcanic Legacy Scenic Byway—All American Road** CA 89, from Lassen Volcanic National Park to the Burney area. This scenic byway stretches from Lake Almanor to Oregon. On this part, you can explore Lassen Volcanic National Park, passing Lassen Peak, and Manzanita and Summit Lakes. Outside of the park, you'll pass through **Old Station**, which traces its roots back to the Emigrant Trail, and was a stagecoach stop in the 1800s. Stop by **Subway Cave** (see *Green Spaces*) and fill up on gas (though it is almost a dollar more than everywhere else in the area). Next up is the small town of **Hat Creek**, which boasts the best trout fly-fishing in the country. Keep driving north and you will find the small communities of **Burney** and **Fall River Mills**, which offer plenty of food and services for the weary traveler and are the gateway to the **McArthur-Burney State Park**. Headed back on CA 299, you can get to **Redding**. The entire drive takes at least four hours and is about 70 miles.

WHISKEYTOWN STATE PARK.

✳ Green Spaces

Ahjumawi Lava Springs State Park See *Eastern Mountains.*

Battle Creek Wildlife Area (530-225-2317; fws.gov) Coleman Fish Hatchery Road, east of Cottonwood. At this riparian forest, you can see a variety of birds, hike through fields of oak trees, pass spawning salmon and steelhead, see bald eagles, and visit the **Coleman Fish Hatchery**. Free.

Caldwell Park Quartz Hill Road, Redding. This family-friendly park along the Sacramento River allows access to the Sacramento River Trail as well as being the home to the Redding Aquatic Park. This area has a fun pool (open in summer), a volleyball court, and more. Plus, you can get your boat in the water to fish.

Castle Crags State Park (530-235-2684 or 800-444-7275; parks.ca.gov or reserveamerica.com) Off I-5, 35 miles north of Redding to Castle Crags/Castella exit. So many people know about big old Mt. Shasta that they pass up this wonderful state park. What a shame. The 6,000-foot glacier-polished crags offer a dramatic backdrop while you fish, swim, and hike the area. Besides accessing the Pacific Crest Trail, you might also want to hike many of the 28 miles of trails, including the 5.5-mile Crags Trail. There are 76 developed campsites, as well as RV sites. Reserve early. $6 day use; $20 camping.

Lake Britton See *McArthur-Burney State Park.*

Lake Shasta (530-275-4463; shastalake.com) Off I-5, north of Redding. This is the most popular recreation lake in the state. Its 370 miles of shoreline make this the ideal place to find a private nook and hang out for the day—or a week. Houseboating reigns supreme, with bass and trout fishing, and recreational boating close behind. The lake is also home to Shasta Dam, the second largest dam in the U.S., which creates the largest manmade waterfall in the world. You can tour the dam for free (there are six tours daily, call for the schedule). The area happens to also be one of the largest nesting sites for bald eagles—because of this, a few campsites are closed from January through August. For houseboat rental information, see *Houseboat Rentals in Lake Shasta.*

Lassen National Forest (530-336-5521; fs.fed.us) From CA 89 east and stretching south to Lake Almanor and east to Susanville. Check out the Subway Cave (CA 89, between Old Station and Hat Creek; open in summer only), where you walk through a 0.33-mile lava cave that has the constant temperature of 46 degrees Fahrenheit (a welcome temperature after the scorching summer temperatures outside). Bring a flashlight and a jacket. Popular hiking trails include the **Pacific Crest Trail**, the 12-mile **Spencer Meadows** (north of Lassen Volcanic National Park), the **Spattercone Crest** trail (near Old Station), and around **1000 Lakes Wilderness**. In the Hat Creek area, there are nine areas to camp (all but Dusty are open in summer only). They are fairly primitive, with the lakeside Dusty being one of the better ones. You'll need to make reservations in advance and bring plenty of drinking water. Camping: $20.

Lassen Volcanic National Park (530-595-4444; nps.gov/lavo) From Redding, take CA 44 east for 48 miles. From Red Bluff, take CA 36 east. It takes about an hour to get to the park from I-5, but it is well worth your time. Relatively empty, with some of the most unusual scenery in the state, this National Park boasts four types of geothermal features including steam vents, fumaroles, hot springs, and mudpots. Set up camp at **Manzanita** and **Summit Lakes**, so that you can have

BUBBLING MUD POOLS SPARKLE AQUAMARINE AT LASSEN VOLCANIC STATE PARK.

time to explore. Or you can get a room at **Drakesbad Guest Ranch** (see *Eastern Mountains*). If you only have one day, head straight to Bumpass Hell to hike the 3-mile loop down to the boiling mud pools and sapphire water pools (in 1864 explorer Kendall Bumpass was wandering around the area, slipped through the thin crust and burned his leg so severely it had to be amputated—hence the name). Then cool off with a swim in Summit or Manzanita Lakes. The daring might want to hike Lassen Peak (10,457 feet). Another popular (though still rather tame) trail is the **Kings Creek Falls** (1.5-mile loop), which is covered with lilies and fir trees, deer and waterfalls. In summer, head to the **Manzanita Lake camper store** to stock up on goods and try out their soft-serve ice cream (there is another seasonal café open, but the selection is very limited). If you prefer not to hike, but want to see the sights, pick up the road trail guide from the ranger station. Another highlight is the **Loomis Museum**, which gives you a full history of the land and the Indian people who once inhabited this spectacular region. In winter, cross-country skiing and snowshoeing are exceptional. $10 for seven-day pass.

McArthur-Burney Falls Memorial State Park (530-335-2777; parks.ca.gov or reserveamerica.com) CA 299, 11 miles northeast of Burney. A trip to Burney Falls is a must. At first glance, the curtain of water dropping a half-mile into a river takes your breath away. At second glance, you're smitten. One hundred million gallons of water travels from above every single day! Here you'll see ribbons of water dancing down verdant lava rock and two gushing falls that steal the show. Walk the **Falls Loop** trail (just over a mile) down to the base of the falls (where temperatures seem to drop 40 degrees as the mist from the falls bathe you), then along the river and up over the falls. Afterwards, cool off with a dip in **Lake Britton** (or kayak, boat, or fish for trout), then camp out in a tent or one of their small housekeeping cabins (118 sites). During summer nights, rangers give astronomy talks by the lake. $6 day use; $20 camping.

McConnell Arboretum and Gardens See *Turtle Bay Exploration Park*.

Sacramento River Trail (visitredding.org) This 9-mile paved path follows the Sacramento River to the Sundial Bridge and is a fantastic place to walk, run, bike,

TRINITY ALPS—A WILD WILD WILDERNESS

Tourists are primarily concerned with the big sites this far north—redwood trees, Mt. Shasta, Lake Tahoe, Lassen Volcanic National Park—so that many of them never get to fully explore the rich forests that cut through the middle of the North State. Below are some highlights; if you make it up here, you are sure to be wowed.

Sites listed from south to north.

Ruth Lake (707-574-6332; ruthlakecsd.org) 12220 Mad River Road, Mad River. Off CA 36 in the Six Rivers National Forest. You'll be surprised if you arrive in summer to find so many people on the lake, but off-season the whole area will be yours. Head straight to **Ruth Lake Marina** (707-574-6194) for food, fuel, gear, and fishing info. You'll probably want to set up camp at one of the sites leading up to the lake (Hobart Creek, Fir Cove, Ruth Recreation Area, or Bailey Canyon), they take advantage of the expansive blue water surrounded by emerald trees. The only restaurants in the area are the Blue Moon Café in Ruth and the restaurant at The Journey's End (707-574-6441), so bring lots of food. The Journey's End also rents out cabins.

Trinity River This river stretches the length of the entire county, offering fantastic fishing, swimming holes, and white-water rafting. For rafting information, contact **Trinity River Rafting** (530-623-3033; trinityriverrafting.com).

Trinity Lake (530-286-2666) CA 3, 20 miles north of Weaverville. California's second largest reservoir offers 145 miles of forested shoreline and views galore. The Trinity Alps spike their granite spears in all directions for swimmers, boaters, fishers, and sunbathers to stare at. You can camp at a number of developed or primitive sites along the lake, fish for trout, salmon, and catfish, and try to spot nesting bald eagles. If you want to rent a houseboat, contact **Trinity Lake Resort** (trinitylakeresort.com)—they also offer lodging options if you want to hang out for a while. $5.

Trinity Alps Wilderness (530-623-2121; r5.fs.fed.us) Accessible off CA 3 from Weaverville, Trinity Center, and Coffee Creek. You need to get a free permit from the Forest Service to enter the Alps. Trails, granite peaks, blue water, and plenty of snow characterizes this wilderness. To fully explore the Alps, you need plenty of time and a strong back, because you have to hike them. Get a good trail map from the Ranger Station and head in from Coffee Creek.

Trinity River Byway CA 299 from Redding west to Willow Creek. This is both Big Foot country and an outdoor lovers' paradise. But even if you don't want to get out of the car, you can explore this rich landscape. As you head out of Redding, you pass the Whiskeytown National Recreation Area. You'll keep going to Weaverville, a gold rush town, which is now the county seat.

Farther on, you'll cross the wild Trinity River, where rafters come to battle from all over the world. As you continue, passing spiky trees and dark forests, you enter Willow Creek—Bigfoot country (see *Redwood Coast*).

State of Jefferson Scenic Byway CA 96 from Happy Camp to Yreka. In the early 1940s, progressive activists in the area tried to do what people in Northern California have been dreaming about ever since—create their own state (the fervor has been rekindled lately). They wanted to call attention to the need for good roads in the area, and today you can traverse this famed byway and see why it is important to be able to drive through this lovely wonderland. This area has a rich mining history, and you'll pass through small mining towns along the Klamath River, and plenty of agricultural land.

Lodging

Coffee Creek Chalet (530-266-3235; coffeecreekchalet.com) Star Route 2, Trinity Center. This vacation rental is perfect for a family or a small group of friends wanting to shack up. Surrounded by nature in a comfortable house with all the amenities you need—kitchen, DVD, wood-burning stove, hammock, and comfy beds. Rates: $$; week minimum stay in summer.

Lewiston Hotel (800-286-4441; lewistonhotel.net) Deadwood Road, Lewiston. Travel back in time to when luxury meant a bed with rich wood panels, red linens, and a reasonably quiet sleep. Rooms share a bathroom—as was custom in the 1800s. $.

Trinity Canyon Lodge (530-623-6318; trinitycanyonlodge.com) 27025 CA 299 W., Junction City. This Trinity River lodge offers nine cabins with kitchens, and motel rooms, plus places to camp and park your RV. Everything is rustic and simple, but if you prefer a bed to the stars, you won't find much better. Rates: $—$$.

Trinity Mountain Meadow Resort (530-462-4677; mountainmeadowresort.com) Star Route 2, Trinity Center. Open in July and August only. Cute rustic cabins in a forest are the perfect retreat for families, complete with that summer-camp feel of bunk beds, trees, and wood-paneled walls. Amenities: 10 cabins, solar-heated pool, childcare, three meals (including an adult gourmet dinner where the kids are entertained), games, books, and arts and crafts. $$; week stays in summer; cash only.

Campgrounds

Basically all you'll find in these parts are places to pitch a tent. In the Weaverville area, you can camp at East Weaver campground ($11). Around Lewiston Lake, Tunnel Rock ($7), and Ackerman ($7—13) are the only sites open all year.

You can also pitch a tent around Trinity Lake. The **KOA** campground (530-

266-3337) is just off CA 3. Other sites include Tannery ($17), Bridge Camp ($12), Jackass Springs (free), and Clark Springs ($12)—for all of these contact reservations.gov.

Other spots include Eagle Creek ($10), Trinity River ($10), and Big Flat (free). For more information, contact the Trinity County Chamber (trinity county.com).

Where to Eat

ϒ **La Grange Café** (530-623-5325) 226 Main Street, Weaverville. Open 11—9 daily (call to make sure as seasonal hours may change). This restaurant retains the historic air of town, while serving up fine wine and pretty good food. They smoke their own pork, so if you are into that kind of thing, that is the way to go. Chicken enchiladas, buffalo ragout, and banana cream pie are all worthy options. $$—$$$.

and access the river. You can get to the trail along Hilltop Drive, Caldwell Park, and the bridge.

Shasta Trinity National Forest See *Castle Crags State Park.*

Turtle Bay Exploration Park See *To See.*

Whiskeytown National Recreation Area (530-246-1225; nps.gov) CA 299, 7 miles west of Redding. The superstar of the area is the massive **Whiskeytown Lake**, where you can hike to waterfalls and down to the lake, fish for trout, mountain bike, camp, swim (with a visibility of 15 feet underwater), and even take a free guided kayak tour of the lake (call for reservations). The best beach for picnicking and swimming is **Brandy Creek Beach**. Hikers will enjoy heading up to Brandy Creek Falls, Boulder Creek Falls, and Crystal Creek Falls. $5 per vehicle, camp for $10.

✳ Lodging

HOTELS ♂ ♿ ϒ **Gaia Anderson Hotel** (530-365-7077) 2900 Alexander Avenue, Anderson. At this green inn, everything is both simple and extravagant, from the fluffy duvet covers, to the landscaped rock garden in the center of circular buildings, to the Swan Lake and the saline pool. At press time, they were working on opening an organic steakhouse, which will be a good selling point, as their continental breakfast falls short of expectation. The 122 rooms also have access to the spa. $—$$.

Burney and Vicinity
Clearwater Lodge (530-5005; clearwaterlodge.com) 24500 Pit One Powerhouse Road, Fall River Mills. A historic Arts and Crafts-movement lodge that once used to be the headquarters for the powerhouse nearby, now it mostly caters to fly-fishers. With lava rock and fir walls, you really feel like you are in the mountains. You can stay in the lodge (which is decorated with the touch of a lady), the shared bathroom Annex, or in the individual cottages. All offer an elegance and style you won't find in many places around here.

Amenities: 16 rooms and cottages, meals, golf, fishing guides, horseback riding, fly shop. $$–$$$; all rooms include three generous meals.

✦ ⑪ **Green Gables Motel and Suites** (530-335-2264) 37385 Main Street, Burney. In summer, the hanging flowerpots and an alpine paint job allow this motel to stand out from its roadside motel peers. Inside, rooms are simple, with wooden furniture and white walls. Suites are the way to go, since you get a kitchenette and a Jacuzzi tub. All 22 rooms include a spare continental breakfast. $–$$.

INNS AND BED & BREAKFASTS

Redding

Bridgehouse B&B (530-247-7177; reddingbridgehouse.com) 1455 Riverside Drive, Redding. Staying in a room here is like getting a history lesson on the area. Rooms are named after prominent bridges—Sundial, Diestelhorst, Dog Creek, Market Street—and are decorated with the same attention to foundation as the bridges themselves. Modern amenities like flatscreen TVs, breakfast, and massage tubs grace most rooms. $$.

Lake Shasta

✦ ♿ ⑪ **O'Brien Mountain Inn B&B** (530-238-8026 or 888-799-8026; obrienmountaininn.com) 18026 O'Brien Inlet Road, O'Brien. Stepping into this casual B&B near Lake Shasta feels more like coming into someone's home than a hotel. You get plenty of privacy in the theme-decorated rooms, with an attention to detail you won't often find in the area—think fresh flowers, plush towels, pastel walls and comforters, and big tubs. Amenities: 8 rooms and suites, breakfast delivered to your door, wine and chocolates on arrival, Jacuzzi, some rooms with kitchenette. $$–$$$$.

Shingletown

Weston House B&B (530-474-3738; westonhouse.com) Red Rock Road, Shingletown. Decorated to evoke a feeling of going back in time, the Victorian-style interior of the rooms complement the rustic exterior. Vaulted ceilings and private entrances allow you to feel you have your own hideaway in the mountains. Four rooms include full breakfast and access to the pool. $$–$$$.

VACATION RENTALS

Lake Shasta Area

✦ **Sugarloaf Cottages** (530-238-2448; shastacabins.com) 19667 Lakeshore Drive, Lakehead. One- to three-bedroom cottages lining the lake with full kitchens, BBQs, and small patio areas make this a perfect spot for families that don't want to camp or rent a houseboat. Cabins are pretty basic, but you'll be outside for most of the time. Rates: $$–$$$$; weekly rentals only.

✦ **Tsasdi Resort** (530-238-2575; tsasdiresort.com) 19990 Lakeshore Drive, Lakehead. A bit more private than the other cabin rentals in the area, this resort allows you at least a deck facing Lake Shasta. This is a fine place for families or romance (if you call a summer beerfest at Lake Shasta romantic). Wood-paneled, with full kitchens, pool, lake access, and a wood-burning fireplace, these one-to three-bedroom cabins are the best option around. $$–$$$; you must stay a week in summer.

CAMPING For other camping information, see *Green Spaces*.

Lake Shasta (877-444-6777; reserveamerica.com) There are 17 campgrounds surrounding Lake Shasta, including a yurt site ($45). Most of the sites are open year-round and all of them are located on the lakeshore.

LAKE SHASTA HOUSEBOAT RENTALS

People like to brag that Lake Shasta is the number-one houseboat capital of the U.S., and even if the statistics aren't quite true, you want to reserve your boat in advance. Summer months are packed. Below is a list of places that rent houseboats and often have a number of other services for your stay at the lake.

Antlers Resort (530-238-2553; shastalakevacations.com) Antlers Road, Lake Shasta. This outfit rents houseboats (including ones with hot tubs), ski and fishing boats, kayaks, canoes, and tubes; plus they have a store and fuel.

Jones Valley Resort (530-275-7950; houseboats.com) Dry Creek and Jones Valley Roads, Lake Shasta. If luxury is your thing, check out their triple-deck boat. Otherwise, you can rent regular houseboats, fishing, and ski boats. Other highlights of this resort area include a huge floating store, a party boat with a slide, fuel, and a new floating recreation center.

Silverthorn Resort (530-275-1571) On the Pit River Arm of the lake, off Dry Creek Road and Bear Mountain Road. One of the main "resorts" with a restaurant, this outfit also rents out luxurious boats. There is a store, fuel, and a gift shop.

Sugarloaf Resort (530-275-7950) On Sacramento River Arm of the lake at Lakeshore Drive, 5 miles south of I-5. Open in summer only, this spot rents out water sports equipment from houseboats to kayaks. They have a massive store, fuel, and free dock parking for their guests.

Gregory Creek and Ski Island are popular choices, but they close from January through August to protect nesting bald eagles. $8—30.

✳ Where to Eat

DINING OUT

Redding

& Ÿ **Maritime Seafood and Grill** (530-229-0700) 1600 California Street, Redding. Open Monday through Saturday 11:30–9. A bit too pricey, but decent for seafood, the Maritime Grill is quite the mainstay in Redding. Dine by a classical piano in a white dining room, on the likes of orange roughy, and save room for raspberry or choco-

late cakes. Reservations recommended. $$—$$$.

& Ÿ **Market Street Steakhouse** (530-241-1777) 1777 Market Street, Redding. Open 11–10 weekdays (until 11 on Friday), 4–10 weekends (until 11 on Saturday). Folks around here know how to grill up a steak. Here they like it with a salad and a side of sauce, but they serve it up in a semi-classy environment. $$–$$$.

✍ & Ÿ **Moonstone Bistro** (530-241-3663; moonstonebistro.com) 3425 Placer Street, Redding. Open daily for lunch, dinner, and Sunday brunch. Redding's only local, seasonal produce restaurant serves up California cuisine, like a BLT with arugula instead of lettuce. Though the restaurant has to cater to the crowd of beer drinkers who live in the area, it still manages to serve up herbed fries, fresh seafood, wine, and soju Bloody Marys. $$—$$$.

& Y **Rivers Restaurant** (530-223-5606; riversrestaurant.net) 202 Hemsted Drive, Redding. Open for lunch Monday through Friday, and dinner daily. On the outside the restaurant looks like a car dealership. Big, sleek silver walls and a lofty entrance already say that this place is trying really hard. Here's the deal, if you want very creative (probably a little too much so) cuisine, with a lovely river view, Rivers is calling your name. The chef does classic dishes much better than the unusual ones, so go for the Kobe burger, steaks, or salads. Vegetarians eat elsewhere. Reservations recommended. Entrees: $$–$$$.

Burney and Fall River Mills

✂ & Y **Angelina's** (530-335-4184; angelinasrexclub.com) 37143 Main Street, Burney. Open for dinner nightly. This new addition to the Burney dining scene makes locals happy. Here you get big portions of pasta, steak, and chicken served on white tablecloths, prepared by a friendly family. Prices are a bit steep for the area, but it's about as good as it gets around here. $$–$$$.

EATING OUT

Redding and Vicinity

✂ & **Buz's Crab Stand** (530-243-2120; buzscrab.com) 2159 East Street, Redding. Open 11–9 daily. Fried seafood, shellfish, and potatoes bring locals to this nautical-themed restaurant. For 30 years, families and friends have come to fill up on tacos, salads, charbroiled seafood, and fish and chips. $–$$$.

The Elegant Bean (530-347-9669) Holiday Shopping Center, Cottonwood. Cute, in a strip mall kind of way, this coffee shop/gift shop is all you'll find between Williams and Redding. They also serve ice cream and smoothies.

✂ & **Gironda's Restaurant** (530-224-7663; girondas.com) 1100 Center Street, Redding. Open 11–9 weekdays (until 10 on Friday), and 4:30–9 weekends (until 10 on Saturday). Bistro seating at wooden tables with burnt yellow walls, and friendly service. If you are daring, try the fried ravioli, or stick with traditional favorites like artichoke dip, veal marsala, and eggplant Parmesan. $$–$$$.

✂ & **Oldtown Eatery** (530-347-4499) 20828 Front Street, Cottonwood. Open for breakfast and lunch daily. This historical eatery attracts mostly the seniors living in the surrounding area. Maybe they like the hordes of memorabilia hanging from the walls, the friendly servers, and the egg fare. My family likes their pancakes. Note that if you pay with credit card, you'll have to pay an extra buck. $.

✂ & **Yak's Coffee Shop** (530-223-9999) 3274 Bechelli Lane, Redding. Open daily. All the profits go to a local church. This coffee shop is a gathering place for students, artists, and other coffee drinkers (the lattes leave much to be desired). Muffins and granola are quite good for breakfast. Lunches rely on paninis, quiches, and quesadillas. $.

Lake Shasta

✂ & Y **Tail O' the Whale** (530-275-3021; sevencrown.com) 10300 Bridge Bay Road, Redding. Open for breakfast, lunch, and dinner daily. Casual dining with lake views, you'll get all the traditional American fare you'd expect—eggs, French toast, steak, and sandwiches, to be exact. $–$$.

Burney and Fall River Mills

Gepetto Pizza (530-335-3789; gepetto sburney.com) 37227 Main Street, Burney. Open for lunch and dinner daily. Packed almost nightly, this local pizza parlor brings out everyone looking to grub after a long day of being outdoors. $–$$.

Ⓨ **Mayfly Pub and Deli** (530-336-1033) Fall River Mills. See *Entertainment*.

Mt. Burney Coffee Company (530-335-5282) 37155 Main Street, Burney. Open daily. The only place to get a latte in the area, this coffee shack serves decent Joe and lots of it.

Taqueria La Fogata (530-335-3338) 37063 CA 299, Burney. Open for lunch and dinner daily. Red vinyl chairs, plastic tablecloths, pictures of Mexico, and music characterize this family-owned Burney find. Heaping portions of tacos, quesadillas (with so much cheese it is impossible to finish), and burritos for a pittance, make this place easy to recommend. The salsa and guacamole are yummy. $.

✳ Entertainment

Redding

Cascade Theater (530-243-8877; cascadetheater.org) 1733 Market Street, Redding. After a long renovation, this historic theater is back in the game of presenting live theater and musical performances.

Ⓨ **Club 151** (530-222-1300) 2611 Bechelli Lane, Redding. For a town that brags about parties at the Senior Center, this DJ club might start to look like a good option.

Ⓨ **Vintners Cellar** (530-222-9463) 1700 California Street, Redding. If you want a wine bar that also serves small plates of food, Vintners Cellars might not give you the Napa attitude or style, but it will do the trick.

Lake Shasta

North Star Craft Brewery (530-275-2739) 3501 Iron Court, Lake Shasta. Live music by local bands, and beer, call out to sunburned lake lovers.

Fall River Mills

Ⓨ **Mayfly Pub and Deli** (530-336-1033) 43100 E. CA 299, Fall River Mills. More sports bar than anything else, you can come here to relax after a long day of hiking or fishing.

✳ Selective Shopping

To be frank, your shopping needs are better met elsewhere. Most shops you'll find in the area are the same old ones you see everywhere else.

✳ Seasonal Events

June: **Marketfest** (530-243-7773; vivadowntown.org) Library Park, Downtown Redding. Thursdays from 4:30–8:30, downtown wakes up for a farmers' market and live music. Through September.

July: **Freedom Festival** (530-225-4095) Redding Convention Center Grounds. On the Fourth of July hordes of people come out to watch fireworks.

September: **Blues by the River** (530-225-9926; shastablues.com) Lake Redding Park. Along the banks of the Sacramento, blues musicians sing their hearts out.

MT. SHASTA AND VICINITY

✳ To See

Living Memorial Sculpture Gardens (weedlmsg.org) Northwest slope of Mt. Shasta, off US 97, Weed. The 11 sculptures by Dennis Smith honor those who have been lost to war. You can drive it, but it is better to walk this magnificent site of metal humans in the shadow of such a magical mountain. Free.

Mt. Shasta Fish Hatchery See *Sisson Museum.*

Siskiyou County Museum (530-842-3836) 910 S. Main Street, Yreka. Open Tuesday through Friday 9–5 and Saturday 9–4. Learn about Native Americans and the early pioneers in the area, plus about the Chinese history in the region, mining, and logging trades. Free.

Sisson Museum (530-926-5508; sissonmuseum.org) 1 N. Old Stage Coach Road, Mt. Shasta. Open daily in summer from 10 AM–4 PM and in winter from 1 PM–4 PM. Fish Hatchery open from 8 AM–sundown. The city used to be called Sisson until 1924, and this 1906 building honors the past with self-guided tours of the museum. Learn about caves, fishing, railroad, and local water. Free.

Tulelake Butte Valley Museum of Local History (530-667-5312; tvbfair.com) 800 Main Street, Tulelake. Open at least 9–5 daily. Come view exhibits on volcanoes, Indian culture, wars, and industry in the area. You can see barracks and a guard tower. $3 adults; $1 children 6–12.

Weed Historic Lumber Town Museum (530-938-0550; snowcrest.net) 303 Gilman Avenue, Weed. Open Memorial Day through Labor Day from 10 AM–5 PM. If you are here during the off-season, call to set up an appointment. Artifacts from logging and milling in the area allow visitors to understand the history of Weed.

Yreka Sculptures Around the historic mining town of Yreka, you will find a number of sculptures by local artist Ralph Starritt. Made of metal to represent the mining history, check out the gold panner at the central freeway exit, the fire hall statue, the Native American statue, and the "Moodonna." Free.

✳ To Do

CYCLING Mountain bikers will adore the plentiful trails to explore the rugged terrain of this region. Favorite spots to pedal include Mt. Shasta, Gazelle Mountain (Yreka), Mt. Shasta Board and Ski Park, and around the many lakes. For more information, contact **Mt. Shasta Visitor Bureau** (See *Guidance*).

Rentals

The Fifth Season (530-926-3606; thefifthseason.com) 300 N. Mt. Shasta Boulevard, Mt. Shasta City. You can rent bikes for about $25–50 per day.

FISHING **McCloud** and **Sacramento Rivers** are the highlights for anglers here. Lesser known spots include Siskiyou, Castle, Grey Lakes, Cedar, Helen, Picayune, Tamarack, Toad, Porcupine, Kangaroo, Little Crater, and Dobkin Lakes. Marble Mountain Wilderness also has a number of wonderful fishing lakes. **Klamath River** is the spot for steelhead salmon. For fishing guides, contact **Riverbend Adventures** (530-778-3540) or **Trinity River Adventures** (530-623-4179).

GOLF **Lake Shastina Golf Resort** (530-938-3201) 5925 Country Club Drive, Weed. This Robert Trent Jones Jr. designed course is dubbed the "Magnificent Monster." $49–69.

McCloud Golf Club (530-964-2535) 1001 Squaw Valley Road, McCloud. Built in 1923, this course offers lovely views of Mt. Shasta. $32–36

Mount Shasta Resort Golf Course (530-926-3052; mountshastaresort.com) Mount Shasta Resort, 1000 Siskiyou Lake Boulevard, Mt. Shasta City. Views galore make these greens a must experience in the area. $10–55

HORSEBACK RIDING ✤ **Rockin' Maddy Ranch** (530-340-2100; rockinmaddy ranch.com) 11921 Cram Gulch Road, Yreka. These guides take folks out to ride Mt. Shasta and Lake Siskiyou. Trips last between one and two hours. $45–85.

OTHER ADVENTURES **Shasta Mountain Guides** See *Mt. Shasta.*

Shasta Valley Balloons (530-926-3612; hot-airballoons.com) 316 Pony Trail, Mt. Shasta. Float in the air at sunrise and take in the exquisite sight of Mt. Shasta, Mt. Eddy, and the forest below. Flights last an hour, but allow four hours for the whole deal, including post-flight champagne. $200 per person.

SCENIC DRIVES **Barrel Springs Back Country Byway** CA 299 east to CA 17 north to CA 201 east and south. Explore the northeast of California in the Warner Mountains, where Wild West takes on a whole new meaning. You'll travel through Cedarville, Fort Bidwell, and past open desert, which is actually a prehistoric lake called Lake Surprise.

Modoc Volcanic Scenic Byway CA 89 to CA 15 (north) to CA 49 (north). At 120 miles, this trip is best in summer and takes four to five hours. Starting in McCloud, you will pass through this small historic logging town and be able to view the three waterfalls that make up McCloud River Falls. Travel north towards **Medicine Lake Highlands**, the highest volcano in the region. Stop to fish or swim in Medicine Lake, then go explore Lava Beds National Monument. Finally, you will reach the spacious Tulelake National Wildlife Refuge, where flocks of birds pass on their migration. Some of the road is gravel, so it is best with a four-wheel-drive.

Mt. Shasta Drive Take Everitt Memorial Highway up to the 8,000 foot level of the mountain. Along the way, you'll have splendid views of the sea of trees, Mt. Eddy, and of course the magnificent Mt. Shasta.

Volcanic Legacy Scenic Byway From McCloud to Tulelake, take US 97 north to CA 161 east and then onto CA 49 south, where you can loop back to McCloud.

MT. SHASTA.

The trip takes two to four hours and is about 100 miles. Starting in the historic town of McCloud, pass Mt. Shasta City and Weed. You'll see Grass Lake and Deer Mountain, and of course you can't miss the massive Mt. Shasta. Look for birds as you drive north to Dorris, home to the tallest flagpole in the West, and especially as you enter the Klamath River and Tule Lake National Wildlife Refuges. Here, 75 percent of the birds that migrate across the West Coast stop here. Tulelake housed the majority of the internment camps during WWII, and now is the gateway to a lovely lake and Lava Beds National Monument.

SPAS AND HOT SPRINGS **Mount Shasta Resort Day Spa** See *Lodging*.

Stewart Mineral Springs (530-938-2222; stewartmineralsprings.com) Stewart Springs Road, off I-5, north of Weed. These mineral springs have been healing those in need for centuries. Choose to soak in the bathhouse, get a massage, or just relax on the deck. The views, the ambiance, and the quiet will help with whatever ails you. There is also a sweat lodge on the property, which gets cranked up on most Saturdays. You can camp here or stay in a room or a teepee (see *Lodging*). You'll pay $25 for mineral baths, $30 for teepees, up to $300 for a house. In summer there is a restaurant on the property and in winter they offer serious deals for lodging.

TRAIN RIDES ✏ **Blue Goose Steam Train** (800-973-5277; yrekawesternrr .com) 300 E. Miner Street, Yreka. Summer only. The 1920s-era steam train takes you through the Shasta Valley and you will stop in a park for a picnic lunch. Choose between a seat in the caboose, in the coach, a Locomotive Cab Ride, or the Great Northern Car. $20–50 adults; $12–50 kids.

TAKE A TRAIN FROM HISTORIC MCCLOUD.

McCloud Open Air Excursion Train (800-733-2141; shastasunset.com/excursion) Downtown McCloud. Ride through the forest of Mt. Shasta for an hour on diesel locomotives. Trips go out Friday (in July through August) and Saturday (June through September) at 3:45. $12 adults; $8 children under 12.

Shasta Sunset Dinner Train (800-733-2141; shastasunset.com) McCloud Depot, McCloud. Sit down to a four-course meal on a 1916 train, complete with fine china and white linens. You will travel along the base of Mt. Shasta to Mt. Shasta City in three hours. Occasionally they offer a murder-mystery trip on Thursday nights. Dress code preferred. Dinner options change by the month, but expect items like Beef Wellington, Port Schnitzel, Oyster Stuffed Chicken, and Baked Salmon. Vegetarians will go hungry. $100 per person, excluding gratuity.

WATER SPORTS

Rafting and Kayaking

Living Waters Recreation (530-926-5446; livingwatersrec.com) Mt. Shasta. Raft down the Klamath River, Sacramento, or Trinity Rivers on an inflatable kayak. You can choose between Class I to Class III rapids. In most trips, lunch is included, and you can rent a tent for longer excursions. For rapids of Class III and above, children must be over the age of 7.

River Dancers Rafting and Kayaking (530-926-3517; riverdancers.com) This group offers both guided trips on the Sacramento, Trinity, Klamath, and Scott Rivers, and yoga trips. Families are welcome on lower grade rapids. Trips are one to seven days, on Class 2 to 5 rapids.

WINTER SPORTS To rent ski and snowboard equipment, contact **Sportsmen's Den** (530-926-2295; mtshastasports.com) 402 N. Mt. Shasta Boulevard, Mt. Shasta City. For snowmobile rentals, contact the **Fun Factory** (530-926-7070; funfactory rentals.com) Deer Mountain Snowmobile Park, US 97.

Deer Mountain Snowmobile Park US 97. After you rent your snowmobile, head out on the 28 miles of trails at this fun park. Fun Factory (see above) offers guided trail rides or you can go at it on your own.

❧ **Dog Sled Express** (530-340-3647; dogsledexpress.com) Take Ski Park Highway off CA 89 east of Mt. Shasta City. Open December through March. If you ever wanted to try out dog sledding, this professional canine group will hook you up. Rides last about an hour and you should dress in layers (no jeans or tennis shoes, though). Children are welcome (not infants) but must be with a clear-headed adult. $100–160 adults; $35 children.

❧ **Mt. Shasta Board and Ski Park** (530-926-8610; skipark.com) Open 9–9 Wednesday through Saturday and 9–4 Sunday through Tuesday, from December through April. Ride for a full or half day at this mountain park. Locals like the night skiing at this 425-acre mountain. Boarders will appreciate the half-pipe and newbies have a whole beginner park to stumble down. Here you will also find a Nordic cross-country center chock-full of backcountry trails. $16–45 adults; $3–26 kids and seniors.

✦ **Siskiyou Ice Rink** (530-926-2494) Shastice Park, Mt. Shasta City. This huge ice rink opens in winter. It is outdoors and gets cold.

✳ Green Spaces

NATIONAL AND STATE PARKS/WILDERNESS AREAS For more specific (and timely) information about hiking trails, campsite openings, and fees contact the local ranger stations in Mt. Shasta (530-926-4511) or in Yreka (530-842-6131).

Ash Creek Wildlife Area See *Klamath Basin.*

Castle Crags State Park See *Redding and Vicinity.*

Klamath Basin National Wildlife Refuge (530-667-2231; klamathnwr.og) 4009 Hill Road, Tulelake. Open during daylight hours. Bring warm, water-resistant clothes and shoes. Both bird-watchers and hunters face off in these six refuge areas to get a glimpse of the 75 percent of Pacific Flyway birds that migrate past here each year. In California the main areas to explore are the Lower Klamath, Clear Lake, Tule Lake, and (though it isn't officially in this refuge) the Ash Creek Wildlife areas. The encyclopedia of birds you'll spot here—bald eagles, swans, geese, ducks, falcons, owls, and more—are too numerous to list. Go to the visitor center to find out what birds are currently in the area. They also have a nice historical exhibit of wildlife in the region.

Klamath National Forest (530-842-6131; fs.fed.us) Ranger Station, 1312 Fairlane Road, Yreka. This massive national forest spreads across the northernmost

OTTER BAY LODGE KAYAK SCHOOL

(530-462-4772; otterbar.com) 14026 Salmon River Road, Forks of Salmon. This kayak school gets a lot of press for being one of the best in the country. Not only are the classes meant to make you into a real kayaker, but also the grounds and the lodge are top-notch. Nestled in the Klamath National Forest between the Trinity Alps and Marble Mountain Wilderness, on the Salmon River, this lodge has a good concept. A lodge that sleeps 14, but feels intimate, with fine linens and gourmet meals, a private deck, outdoor hot tub, and intense kayak classes.

Classes are held in summer and split into a number of levels. The beginner takes a week to master the kayak and the river, culminating with a run down the Klamath. The Intermediate and Advanced classes are for people who have done a good deal of kayaking, but want to freshen up their skills or go further than they might on their own. A week's lodging, meals, and classes, including gear, will cost between $1900–2200. There are also much-deserved massage services.

part of California and into Oregon and comprises five wilderness areas: **Marble Mountain**, **Russian**, **Trinity Alps**, **Oregon's Red Buttes**, and **Siskiyou**. As you might imagine, outdoor enthusiasts will have plenty to do here. The Marble Mountain Wilderness is the largest wild area north of the Trinity Alps and offers 50 lakes, miles of trails, and plenty of space for backpackers to hide out. To explore here, you need to acquire a permit from the Yreka ranger station, where you can also get information on trails. The Pacific Crest Trail cuts through the area. The smaller Russian Wilderness is southeast of Marble Mountain and allows climbers and hikers to explore granite peaks ranging from 5000 to 8000 feet.

Lava Beds National Monument (530-667-2282; nps.gov) From I-5, take US 97 north to CA 161 east towards Tulelake; the park is 30 miles south, off CA 49. You can also get here from McCloud via the winding, gravel CA 49. Either way you drive, allow about two hours from the Mt. Shasta area, and fill up your tank before leaving. Bring plenty of food and water as well. Make sure to wear hard-soled shoes and pack warm clothes, no matter the season. The Visitor Center is open from 8–5 daily. Geology aficionados will appreciate the cinder cones, spatter cones, stratovolcanoes, and tubes (there are more lava tube caves here than anywhere else in North America—435 at last count). Places to explore include **Mushpot Cave, Valentine Cave, Labyrinth, Golden Dome, Schonchin Butte**, and the **Balcony Caves**. In winter, rangers lead tours of the Crystal Ice Cave. Those interested in the historical aspects of the area come to see the Modoc war sites— where a 30-year war between the Modocs and the U.S. Army took place. The major battle started in 1872 and lasted a year, as the Indians held off the U.S. Army forces for five months, way longer than anyone ever imagined they could. You can visit the sites of the Thomas Wright Battle, Gillem's Camp, and Captain Jack's Stronghold. You can camp at Indian Well (43 sites; $10) year-round. $10 for seven days.

Mt. Shasta Wilderness (530-926-4511; fs.ed.us) Up Everitt Road, just outside of Mt. Shasta City. The highlight of this wild area is the 14,179-foot stratovolcano, Mt. Shasta, the second highest peak in the Cascade Range and the fifth highest peak in California. Unconnected to any other mountain, it rises boisterously from the ground creating quite the sight. Hiking to the summit is intense and tough for most of us. I set out to do it and only made it about a mile—the air, the altitude, and the conditions made me turn back before it was respectable to do so. However, I wasn't prepared. Spring and early summer is the ideal time to reach the peak because the packed snow makes for better footing. It takes one to three days to reach the summit, and you must pay a permit fee at the ranger station (Bunny Flat). Shastaavalanche.org offers tips for first-time climbers (such as, begin your summit between 2–6 AM; know that thunderstorms strike in the afternoon). No matter what, take the **Bunny Flat trail** (which I recommend for people wanting a beautiful hike without even thinking of reaching the summit, as well)—this is the only spot with toilets before you head up. Along the trail, you can camp at Helen Lake. Other trails to explore from Everitt Road include **Panther Meadow, Sand Flat, Old Ski Bowl**. If you want a guided climb up the mountain, contact **Shasta Mountain Guides** (530-926-3117; shastaguides.com).

Six Rivers National Forest See *Redwood Coast*.

Trinity Alps Wilderness See *Trinity County*.

Tulelake National Wildlife Preserve See *Klamath Basin*.

Castle Lake Take Lake Street in Mt. Shasta City to Old Stage Coach Road (left), veer right into W. A. Barr Road and turn left on Castle Lake Road. The lake is 7 miles farther. In autumn, when the trees change colors and reflect off the water, there is no grander sight. More of a research lake than a tourist stop, locals love to bring their families here and take a dip in the cool waters. Camp for free in one of the six campsites (first-come, first-served).

Lake McCloud (fs.fed.us) From McCloud, take Squaw Valley Road south for 16 miles. This chilly lake is a fishermen's favorite, especially fly-fishermen. You can boat, camp at **Ah-Di-Na** campground (16 sites, $8; first-come, first-served). and hike the area.

Lake Shastina (lakeshastina.com) From Weed, go north on US 97, left on Big Springs Road, left on Jackson Ranch Road, and left on Dwinnell Way. Built as an irrigation project, now this lake is home to a famous golf course, a campground, a boat ramp, and is an active summer swimming area.

Lake Siskiyou (lakesis.com) From Mt. Shasta City, take Lake Street and follow the signs. A local gem in summer, this lake offers prime viewing of Mt. Shasta and plenty of swimming and fishing opportunities. The rock-sand beaches are kid-friendly and (at the Lake Siskiyou Resort) you can find boat rentals, kayaks, canoes, paddleboats, and a café. You can also hike or mountain bike around the lake. Day use: $1. Camping: $3.

Medicine Lake (530-667-2246; fs.fed.us) CA 89 from McCloud to Forest Road 15, turn onto Forest Road 49 and drive 25 miles. Road closes seasonally, but if you can get to this sacred Native American lake, you are in for an experience. Though there are no known outlets, the water stays pure. While here, explore the black obsidian Glass Mountain. You can camp, boat, and fish. Campgrounds are open in summer only and include Medicine Lake, Headquarters, and Hemlock.

RIVERS **McCloud River** Off CA 89 near McCloud. Many people never see this river; it cuts through basalt rock in the mountains east of I-5 and beckons anglers, rafters, and people looking for swimming holes. Complete with waterfalls and great hikes, if you get the chance to explore the many faces of the McCloud, you will be impressed.

Sacramento River Access the river through Prospect Avenue in Mt. Shasta City, Dunsmuir City, and Castle Crags. People come from all over the world to fish and raft this snaking waterway. Stretching the length of Northern California, on hot days you'll just have to jump in. In Dunsmuir, you can swim at the **Cantara Hole** and **Dog Creek**. To get directions for swimming holes, visit Dunsmuir.com/visitor/swimholes.

WATERFALLS **Hedge Creek Falls** Off I-5, north Dunsmuir exit, accessible by a five-minute hike from the west side of the off-ramp. You can walk behind this waterfall into a natural lava cave. It is an easy hike, one that will be fine for the little kids in the group.

McCloud River Falls CA 89 to Fowlers Campground, 5.5 miles east of McCloud. Drive to the Lower McCloud River picnic area. You'll take a mellow 20 minute stroll to see the lower, middle, and upper falls.

Mossbrae Falls On Dunsmuir Avenue, drive north from town to Scarlett Way (look for the arch that reads Shasta Retreat). Park on the left side of the bridge

Edward Broitman

SWIM IN THE SHADOW OF MT. SHASTA AT LAKE SISKIYOU.

and follow the train tracks north for a mile (be very careful because trains still use these tracks and often there is nowhere for you to get out of the way). When you get to a bridge, follow the trail to the right through the trees. These dramatic falls are only 50 feet high, but being 150 feet wide and cascading over emerald mossy rock makes them quite the visual feast.

☀ Lodging

HOTELS AND RESORTS You'll find a number of motels and motor inns in Mt. Shasta City, the finest being **Best Western Tree House Inn** (bestwest ern.com). Otherwise, the majority of hotels and resorts are decidedly rustic, ideal for families and adventure-sport addicts.

🍃 ☀ ❝₁❞ **Klamath River Resort Inn** (530-493-2735; klamathriverresort inn.com) 61700 CA 96, Happy Camp. On the edge of the Marble Mountain Wilderness and the Oregon border, this family-friendly resort offers more than accommodations. They take you out on paddling, hiking, fishing, and kayaking trips (for a fee). Though cabins are rustic, you get a kitchen, BBQ pit, and spa services. $.

🍃 ♿ **Marble Mountain Ranch** (800-552-6284; marblemountainranch.com) 92520 CA 96, Somes Bar. Dubbing itself a dude ranch, this is one of the most family-friendly accommodations around. During summer the ranch offers an all-inclusive vacation, complete with cabins, meals, pool, kayaking, arts and crafts classes, fishing, zip lines, and cheap childcare. The rest of the year, you can rent a cabin and create your own itinerary. The cabins look more like Paul Bunyan than *Queer Eye for the Straight Guy.* Summer: $$$ adults; $$ kids; five-night minimum stay. The rest of the year for just a cabin rental: $$–$$$; dinner $$$.

🍃 ♿ ❦ **Mount Shasta Resort** (530-926-3030; mountshastaresort.com) 1000 Siskiyou Lake Boulevard, Mt. Shasta. Mostly catering to golfers, this lodge offers reasonably priced accommodation with views of Mount Shasta that are unsurpassed. You can get a room, a one- or two-bedroom chalet, and plenty of online deals that include golf. Amenities: 30 rooms and chalets, lake access, Highland House Restaurant, kitchen and Jacuzzi in some rooms, day spa, lounge, tennis courts. $$–$$$.

✍ ♿ **Railroad Park** (530-235-4440;
rrpark.com) 100 Railroad Park Drive,
Dunsmuir. In the shadow of Castle
Crags peaks, these restored classic train
cars offer a unique night of rest. Here
you will also find RV hook ups and tent
sites, a pool, restaurant and bar, but the
draw is the trains. As you might imagine, rooms can be a little narrow. $.

INNS AND B&BS ♿ ⊙ **McCloud
Hotel** (800-964-2823; mccloudhotel
.com) 408 Main Street, McCloud.
Sometimes you just know a place has
class. This country-style inn offers 16
large rooms decorated with farmhouse
sensibilities (think bed runners, poster
beds, floral curtains and blankets),
breakfast, and wine reception. $$–$$$.

Shasta Mount Inn (530-926-1810;
shastamountinn.com) 203 Birch Street,
Mt. Shasta City. Getting to say you
slept in a 1904 Victorian farmhouse
isn't the only perk you enjoy when you
spend a night in this B&B. Simple
touches dot the landscape of this
accommodation, from fresh flowers to
the views of Mt. Shasta framed in the
window, from Tempur-Pedic mattress-
es to yummy breakfasts. Some rooms
have kitchenettes. $$.

✳ Where to Eat

DINING OUT

Dunsmuir

♿ **Café Maddalena** (530-235-2725;
cafemaddelena.com) 5801 Sacramento
Avenue. Open for dinner March
through December on Thursday
through Sunday. The chef from Trinity
Café opened his own bistro in the artsy
town of Dunsmuir and it quickly
became a local favorite. Menu items
change with the seasons, but tend to
be heavy on French-inspired meat and
Mediterranean-flavored pasta dishes,
with a veggie item thrown in for good
measure. Reservations recommended.
$–$$$.

Mt. Shasta

Trinity Café (530-926-6200) 622 N.
Mt. Shasta Boulevard. Open for dinner
Tuesday through Saturday. This small
and seemingly uptight bistro serves
fresh Cal cuisine in an upscale alpine
setting. The new owners are trying to
work out the kinks of the changing
menu. If you go, get the locally caught
salmon or trout. Reservations recommended. $$–$$$.

EATING OUT

Dunsmuir

✍ ♿ 🐾 **Brown Trout Café and
Gallery** (530-235-0754; browntrout
gallery.com) 5841 Sacramento Avenue.
Open Monday through Saturday 7–5
and Sunday 8–5. In winter they close at
3. Locals congregate here for coffee,
pastries, sandwiches, and breakfast fare
for cheap. Surrounded by local art and
occasionally live music, with dogs chill-
ing on the floor, you'll get a feel for what
makes this little town so darn cute. $.

✍ ♿ **Cornerstone** (530-235-4677)
5759 Dunsmuir Avenue. Open for
breakfast and lunch daily. The first
time I entered this small bakery café, I
expected a grease-slathered plate of
bacon and eggs. Was I mistaken! This
wonderful country diner serves some
of the best egg dishes (a triple-cream
Brie omelet anyone?), huevos
rancheros, smoked salmon bagels, and
muffins around. There is a small outdoor patio too. $.

✍ ♿ 🍸 **Sengthong Phelps** (530-235-
4770) 5855 Dunsmuir Avenue. Open
for lunch and dinner, call for seasonal
hours. Specializing in something you
don't find much of around here, Sengthong Phelps serves Thai, Laotian,
and Vietnamese food in an almost hip
spot. If you are from San Francisco or
an Asian country, you might not *love*
the offerings, but it's a change from the
burgers and fries that populate the
region. $–$$.

McCloud

♂ ᯓ **White Mountain Fountain Café** (530-964-2005) 241 Main Street. Open 7–3 daily. Chances are if you are in this area, you'll have to pop in to this old soda fountain/ice cream shop for breakfast, lunch, or a sweet treat. And you'll be happy you did. If you don't want to sit at a booth, the antique stools lining the counter are packed with locals chatting up the kind servers. Go for pancakes or French toast. $.

Mt. Shasta

Berryvale Grocery and Café (530-926-3535; berryvale.com) 305 S. Mt. Shasta Boulevard. Open 8:30 AM–7:30 PM Monday through Saturday and 10 AM–6 PM Sunday. If you don't might forking over big bucks for fresh produce and natural foods, head over here to stock up on groceries (especially if you are headed to Lassen or Lava Beds) and taste some of the great deli offerings, like salads and smoothies. $.

Ƴ **Billy Goats Tavern** See *Entertainment*.

♂ ᯓ **Lily's** (530-926-3372; lilysrestaurant.com) 1013 S. Mt. Shasta Boulevard. Open 7 AM–10 PM daily in summer and 8 AM–8:30 PM in winter. This country café will lure you back more than once, while you stay in Mt. Shasta. Breakfast dishes include Latin-flavored omelets and healthy griddle fare. Lunch and dinner offers a wealth of choices with everything from prime rib to house-made walnut-lentil veggie burgers. This local favorite is packed most days. $–$$$.

♂ ᯓ **Seven Suns Coffee and Cafe** (530-926-9701) 1011 S. Mt. Shasta Boulevard. Open from 6 AM daily. Sure, it might not be Ritual Coffee Roasters (see *San Francisco*), but this stone cottage allows for a coffeehouse vibe without the pretentious attitude. Bagels, muffins, sandwiches, and

loose-leaf teas round out the menu. On nice days, I like to sit on the patio and stare at the mountain. $.

♂ ᯓ Ƴ **Vivify** (530-926-1345) 531 Chestnut Street Open for dinner daily in summer, and for lunch and dinner Wednesday through Sunday in winter. Yogis, hippies, health-food nuts, and people who appreciate creatively crafted Japanese organic sushi and small plates head to this small house with views of the mountain from the spacious outdoor garden and deck. Though the menu changes, favorites include the Vivify Roll, fried tofu konbudashi, crunch sushi, and the wheat-free chocolate cake. They have a lovely selection of organic sake and wine as well. The owners used to run San Francisco's Kabuto restaurant. $–$$.

Weed

♂ ᯓ **Hi Low Café** (530-938-2904) 88 S. Weed Boulevard. Open 6 AM–10 PM daily. For a taste of historic Weed country-style living, head to the Hi Low Café for breakfast. Their pies are worth a try as well. $.

Yreka

♂ ᯓ **Nature's Kitchen** (530-842-1136) 412 S. Main Street. Open for breakfast and lunch daily in summer. Though this organic bakery and café might not be the best food you ever had, it is probably the best pit stop before Oregon. Sandwiches and pancakes are the way to go. $.

✳ Entertainment

Dunsmuir

Ƴ **Sengthong's Blue Sky Room** See *Eating Out*.

Mt. Shasta

Ƴ **Billy Goats Tavern** (530-926-0209; billygoatstavern.com) 107 Chestnut Street. Open daily for lunch, dinner, and brews. In summer, misters blanket the lively patio, as tired hikers and rafters sip one of 100 microbrews and chow on burgers and fries.

Weed
Y **Mt. Shasta Brewery** (530-938-2394; mtshastabrewingcompany.com) 360 College Avenue. Open at 2. You can taste beer and tour the facilities.

Yreka
Y **Rex Club** (530-842-2659) 111 S. Main Street This Yreka watering hole attracts locals and weary travelers.

✴ Selective Shopping

Along Sacramento Avenue in Dunsmuir, there are a number of sweet galleries and shops to explore. Favorites include the **Brown Trout Gallery and Café** (brown-trout gallery.com), **Ruddle Cottage** (ruddlecottage.net), and the **Window Box Nursery** (snowcrest.net).

Book lovers will enjoy searching the shelves in McCloud's wonderful **McCloud Book Gallery** on Main Street, which offers new and used books. In Mt. Shasta City, a walk along Mt. Shasta Boulevard will take you past some wonderful bookstores, including **Village Books** (a great selection of new and used titles), **Language Quest** (a wonderful travel book store), and **Golden Bough Books** (quite the mainstay around here, specializing in spiritual titles and aura readings). Also, pop into **Velvet Elephant**, which offers a nice selection of fair-trade gifts.

✴ Seasonal Events

May: **McCloud Mushroom, Music, and Wine Faire** (530-964-2431) Main Street, McCloud. As you might imagine, this tribute to this trio of delicacies is a treat. Ride the Dinner Train, try out mushroom feasts, and indulge in a down-home BBQ.

June: **Dunsmuir Railroad Days** (800-DUNSMUIR) Historic train cars are carted all the way to this historic trail depot for a parade and party.

McCloud Flea Market (530-964-3113) McCloud. The largest flea market in the region, head here for some amazing (and mind-blowing) finds.

Yreka Gold Rush Days Downtown Yreka. Celebrate Yreka's birthday with gold panning, music, a chili cook-off, a train robbery, and more.

July: **Mt. Shasta Fourth of July Celebration** (530-926-6004) Downtown Shasta and Lake Siskiyou. Fireworks over the lake, a parade, food, and entertainment throughout downtown, this three-day event milks this holiday for all it's worth.

ShastaYama Music Festival Shastice Park, Mt. Shasta City. Taiko drummers from around the world join master drummers in a day-long concert.

August: **McCloud Heritage Days** (530-964-3113) Downtown McCloud. Music, trains, demonstrations, cars, antique tractors, basically everything but the toilet is brought out to the center of town to celebrate McCloud's history.

September: **Dunsmuir Artwalk** Downtown Dunsmuir. Artists and galleries open their doors to show off their work before the cold winter makes them hibernate.

October: **Mt. Shasta International Film Festival** (530-926-4537) Mt. Shasta Cinema, Mt. Shasta and College of Siskiyou, Weed. For three days film buffs see movies before everyone else, at three locations throughout the region.

December: **Cal-Ore Chariot Club** Macdoel Downs, Macdoel. From December through March, come see chariot races on Sundays at 1 PM.

THE EASTERN MOUNTAINS

* To See

Regions listed from north to south.

Modoc County

Modoc County Historical Museum (530-233-6328) 600 S. Main Street, Alturas. Open May through October, Tuesday through Saturday 10 AM–4 PM. Learn about Indian history in this wild region, as well as exploring an old steam train.

Plumas and North Sierra Counties

Chester/Lake Almanor Museum (530-258-2742) 200 1st Avenue, Chester. Open Monday through Saturday, call for seasonal hours. Take a peek inside this library and museum to see photos and artifacts from pioneers and Maidu Indians.

Plumas-Eureka State Park (530-836-2380 or 877-444-PARK; parks.ca.gov) 310 Johnsville Road, Blairsden. The museum is open daily from 9–4 in summer. Part restoration of an old gold-mining town, part great hiking, camping, and fishing spot, this area offers much for the traveler. A bit of history, a bit of adventure. Start by visiting the stamp mill in the heart of the park. Fishermen head to Jamison Creek, where you can also camp and hike a lovely trail. You need to reserve campsites in advance ($20).

Western Pacific Railroad Museum (530-832-4532; wplives.org) 700 Western Pacific Road, Portola. Open April through October 10 AM–5 PM. Tour this railroad museum and understand why railroads were such a necessary part of Northern California's development and growth. Caboose train rides $5 per person or $12 for a family.

* To Do

Modoc County

Cedar Pass Ski Area (530-233-3323; cedarpasssnowpark.com) Off CA 299, Alturas. Open 10 AM–4 PM Saturday, Sunday, and holidays when there is adequate snow. This small ski area offers daylong lift tickets and rentals of ski equipment. There is a Nordic area for cross-country skiers as well. $5–15 adults; $5–12 kids.

Plumas and North Sierra Counties

Bodfish Bicycles (530-258-2338; bodfishbicycles.com) 149 Main Street, Chester. Open at least 10 AM–5 PM Tuesday through Saturday. Here you can rent bikes,

SCENIC DRIVES

Fandango Pass From McCloud, take CA 89 east towards Medicine Lake (CA 15). You'll pass over the Fandango Pass to CA 48, where you can access Goose Lake. Get a detailed map from a ranger station, since these roads are not maintained well. Your trip can take one to three days, so bring lots of food and fill up before leaving McCloud.

Feather River Scenic Byway From Graeagle, off CA 70, take La Porte Road. Here you will wind along the Feather River and pass the 1890 Nelson Creek Pedestrian Bridge. Pass the ghost camp of Onion Valley and continue until you reach Little Grass Valley Reservoir, where you can swim and camp. Afterwards, head to La Porte, an old gold rush town, where you can stay and eat. From here, either drive towards Oroville or back to Graeagle (County Road 900) where you pass McRae Meadows, fishing and swimming holes, and into Plumas-Eureka State Park. There are limited services along the route, mainly in Quincy and Graeagle/Portola.

kayaks, and canoes, plus get information about biking trails in the nearby Plumas-Eureka State Park.

Graeagle Meadows Golf Course (530-836-2323;) CA 89, Graeagle. Here you'll find a championship course where you can golf for reasonable prices. $20–55.

Lake Almanor Country Club Golf Course (530-259-2868) 951 Clifford Drive, Lake Almanor. A nice nine-hole course near Lake Almanor offers par 35 greens. $64.

Majors Outpost (530-251-7512; majorsoutpost.com) Plumas Pines Resort, off CA 89 by Lake Almanor's west shore. This outfit rents boats, Jet Skis, and snowmobiles. And they offer tours.

Reid Horse and Cattle (530-836-0430; reidhorse.com) Graeagle. Reid takes folks out on guided trail rides that last for one to two hours, or full-on pack tours. Call for current prices.

Stover Mountain Ski Area (530-258-3987) Off CA 36, Chester. When the snow pack calls out to locals, this small ski and snowboard park opens up and allows access to the slopes. Though not much of a destination (because it so often closes at odd hours), you'll want to call in advance to check if they are open. There are no rentals or services here, except a rope tow. $15.

✳ Green Spaces

Modoc County

Goose Lake See **Modoc National Forest** below.

Klamath Basin Refuges See *Mt. Shasta and Vicinity.*

Lava Beds National Monument See *Mt. Shasta and Vicinity.*

Modoc National Forest (530-233-5811; fs.fed.us) Ranger Station, 800 W 12th Street, Alturas. Highlights include the **South Warner Wilderness**, **Medicine Lake, Tulelake, Clear Lake,** and **Goose Lake**, which straddles the California/Oregon border. Goose Lake, a large alkaline lake, is a fun spot to kayak and swim. Often there is not enough water to fully enjoy the shallow lake (which is why you can't fish here). **South Warner Wilderness** offers hikers more than enough trails to explore. The daring will want to conquer the **Summit trail**, a 22-mile meadow that leads through alpine lakes and creeks. If you want to really go big, you can loop from Pepperdine to Patterson using the east side of the trail system, which will take you seven days and cover 50 miles. Most campsites close for winter (with Reservoirs F and C, and Big Sage being the exceptions). With 28 developed campgrounds, you'll have plenty of options in summer. **Medicine Lake** sites are lovely (see Mt. Shasta and Vicinity), as are **Ash Creek, Mill Creek Falls,** and **Blue Lake** (you can boat here as well). Anglers will be in heaven here with plentiful bass, catfish, and trout swimming in three parts of the Pit River, 12 lakes, 13 reservoirs, and over 35 streams. Mountain bikers will love the **Devil's Garden Route, Woodland Jurassic Ride**, and **Likely Mountain Challenge**.

Modoc National Wildlife Refuge (530-233-3572; modoc.fws.gov) Go 3 miles southeast of Alturas. Spread over 7000 acres of forest and marshes, this is a prime spot for wildlife viewing. At least 240 bird species pass through the area in spring and fall; tons of mammals and reptiles call this area home as well. Bring binoculars and closed-toed shoes to fully explore the area, and hopefully see cranes, swans, woodpeckers, geese, ducks, and even antelope. You can fish here as well. Hunters love this spot, so keep an eye out.

South Warner Wilderness See **Modoc National Forest**.

Lassen County

Ahjumawi Lava Springs State Park (530-335-2777; parks.ca.gov) The park can only be reached by boat (launch at Big Lake). From CA 299 drive north on Main Street down the dirt road. You need to do some research before heading out here. First and foremost, if you don't have a boat, call the park to inquire about renting one. Next, know that this is a rugged wilderness, covered in a mere 3000-year old lava flow (not too long ago by geologist standards), with streams, lakes and islets, lava cracks, tubes and craters. If you want to hike here, the best trails are Crystal Springs and Spatter Cone Loop.

Ishi Wilderness (530-257-2151; fs.ed.us) Ranger station, 2550 Riverside Drive, Susanville. About 20 miles east of Red Bluff you'll find the start of this 41,000-acre wilderness. Here you'll find everything from riparian forests and chaparral to caves and lava tubes. This wilderness honors the Yahi Indian tribe that was wiped out by white settlers, leaving all but one Ishi (which means man in Yahi). In winter, you will probably see Tehama deer. Fishermen head to Deer and Mill Creeks. Hikers explore the Racheria Trail, Mill Creek, Table Mountain, Lassen, Moak, Deer Creek, and Devils Den.

Lassen National Forest See *Redding and Vicinity*.

Lassen Volcanic National Park See *Redding and Vicinity*.

McArthur-Burney State Park See *Redding and Vicinity*.

Plumas and North Sierra Counties

Eagle Lake (530-257-2151; fs.fed.us) Northwest of Susanville. At the second largest natural lake in California, hike the **Bizz Johnson National Recreation Trail** (530-257-0456), starting from the old Railroad Depot in Susanville and going

25.4 miles to Mason Station. There are a number of developed campgrounds, which are open in summer only—**Aspen Grove, Bogard, Crater Lake** (handicapped accessible), **Eagle**, and the RV/tent area, which was recently renovated, **Merrill** (recreation.gov).

Frazier Falls CA 89, 1 mile south of Graeagle, go west on Gold Lake Highway and drive almost 2 miles until you see the sign for the falls; turn left and drive 4 miles to the trailhead parking lot. Walk a mile down to this 176-foot falls. Go before June to get the best water flow. The trail is paved and handicap accessible.

Lake Almanor (530-258-2141; fs.fed.us) Off CA 36 and CA 89. Its 53 miles of shoreline attracts campers, hikers, boaters, swimmers, and of course anglers. There are loads of marinas equipped with rentals and fuel, food and drink to keep you entertained for a week on a boat. Anglers will find plenty of trout and salmon year-round. Hikers and bikers share the **Almanor Recreation Trail**. Camp at **Northshore, Lake Almanor, Lassen View Resort** (one of the classic fishing resorts), and **Almanor** (reserveusa.com).

Plumas-Eureka State Park (530-836-2380 or 877-444-PARK; parks.ca.gov) 310 Johnsville Road, Blairsden. See *To See.*

Plumas National Forest (877-444-6777; fs.fed.us) Access off CA 89 in Quincy and CA 70 near Feather River. The main areas in the forest are **Lakes Basin, Feather River, Beckwourth,** and **Mt. Hough.** In the north, you'll find **Bucks Wilderness**, for which you need a permit (and an extra dash of roughness that requires you to be mountain-wise). For the following trails, contact the ranger station nearest the trail to get a map. Around Beckwourth's Lakes Basin in the southeast, hike the **Bear Lakes Loop** or **Jamison Creek Trail** (which connects to the Pacific Crest Trail), or around Frenchman Lake, the **Big Cove** and **Spring Creek Connectors** bring together campgrounds and lakes. Around the Feather River area, hike **Bald Mountain, Feather Falls, Hartman Bar**, or the **Pacific Crest Trail**. Finally, around Mt. Hough, the **Ben Lomond, Indian Springs, McCarthy Bar, Lost Cabin Springs**, and **Antelope Lake Nature Trails** all are accessible from the Quincy area. There are over 459 miles of snowmobile trails in the forest (see *Majors Outpost*). Campsites are plentiful, ranging from the RV/tent sites like **North Fork,** by the Feather River, to **Snake Lake** a free, first-come, first-served primitive site near Quincy. Other sites to find include **Silver Lake, Sundew Camp, Hallsted, Mill Creek, Lower Bucks, Grizzly Creek, Haskins Valley, Little North Fork, Horse Camp, Wyandotte, Red Feather Camp, Lakes Basin**, and **Snag Lake**. Campsite fees range between $0–20.

✳ Lodging

Modoc County

Mill Creek Lodge B&B (530-233-4934; millcreeklodge.com) This country inn won't win awards for the finest in interior design, but it does have a certain country charm lacking in other parts of the North State. Sure, you share a bathroom, and one of the rooms has a denim duvet, but the wood-paneled interiors scream country, and that's why you are here. Its two rooms include breakfast, and dinner can be arranged. $.

✐ ⚹ **Surprise Valley Hot Springs** (530-279-2040; surprisevalleyhot springs.com) CA 299, 5 miles east of Cedarville. Country décor—think teddy bears, wood panels, floral duvets, and doilies—meets luxury, with your own private hot-springs tub outside. This is the kind of spot where you don't want to do anything but soak and read that book you've been longing to finish. If you can afford the deluxe or villa suites, it is well worth the splurge for kitchens. $$–$$$.

Lassen County

❧ **Drakesbad Guest Ranch** (530-529-1512; drakesbad.com) Lassen Volcanic National Park, Warner Valley Road, Chester. Open in summer only. If you really want a bed in Lassen Volcanic National Park, this is your only option. This ranch gives new meaning to the word rustic, since most rooms don't even have electricity. In true ranch style, your lodging fee covers all meals; entrance to the park and horseback riding are extra. Choose between cabins, rooms, and bungalows. $$–$$$.

❧ 🐾 **Roseberry House** (530-257-5675; roseberryhouse.com) 609 North Street, Susanville. This historic 1902 house is the only B&B in the area. Expect period antiques, complete with shades of pink, deep oak beds, armoires, and breakfast. $.

Plumas County

❧ **Bidwell House** (530-258-2338; bidwellhouse.com) 1 Main Street, Chester. Built in 1901 to be John Bidwell's country home, now this is one of the nicest B&Bs in the region. Feel like you are actually on vacation, with views of Lake Almanor as you swing on the porch swing, drinking organic coffee, waiting for your delicious breakfast. Rooms combine antiques with a bit of romance. Imagine four-poster beds, pillow-top beds, and Jacuzzi tubs. $–$$.

Feather Bed Inn (530-283-0102 or 800-696-8624; featherbedinn.com) 524 Jackson Street, Quincy. Built in 1893 by the Hutchinson family, this small B&B offers a traditional night stay in the heart of Quincy. The breakfasts far outshine the rooms, which is reason enough to stay here in my book. Beds are comfy and the claw-foot tubs divine. $$.

CAMPGROUNDS The majority of campgrounds are listed under *Green Spaces.* There are a number of types of sites to negotiate through. If you plan to backcountry camp, you'll need to acquire a permit from the national forest you are entering, by contacting the closest ranger station to your entrance site. For state park camping, contact (reserveamerica.com) for a comprehensive list of sites—though my favorites are listed above.

In addition to those listed above, PG&E hosts a couple sites around **Lake Almanor**, which are first-come, first-served, and provide piped water, rest rooms, garbage collection, fire grills, tables, benches, and tent spaces. Call 916-386-5164 or 530-284-1785, or visit PGE.com/aboutus/facilities/properties/recreationareas for more information. The Forest Service also sponsors campgrounds around Lake Almanor (Almanor Ranger District, 530-258-2141; fs.fed.us/r5/lassen). They charge fees for the campgrounds that have developed water systems, maintained rest rooms, and garbage collection. Campgrounds identified as self service charge no fees, and you must pack out your own garbage. Campfire permits are required for primitive camping, visit Almanor Ranger office for those.

PG&E Sites

Cool Springs East shore of Butt Valley Reservoir. This site has 30 tent/RV sites and it is okay to bring Fido.

Rocky Point Campground West shore, north of Canyon Dam, entrance on east side of CA 89. Here you will find 100 tent/RV sites, piped water, dump station, and a safe place to bring your furry friends.

Forest Service Sites

Almanor West shore of Lake Almanor, CA 89, 7 miles south of CA 36. There are 103 tent/RV sites, a beach, boat ramp, picnic area, piped water, and you can bring your pets.

Echo Lake Northeast of Chester on County Road 10. There are five self-service tent sites.

✳ Where to Eat

EATING OUT

Modoc County

✂ ♿ **Antonio's Cucina Italiana** (530-233-5600) 220 S. Main Street, Alturas. Open at least 11–9 daily. Head here for big portions of pizza, pasta, sandwiches, and salads. After you finish your pizza, they bring you honey to dip the crust in. Reservations recommended. $–$$.

The Brass Rail (530-233-2906) CA 299, Alturas. Open for dinner. For 30 years, this family has been serving Basque specialties in this massive dining room. Lamb tends to be the winner. Come hungry. $–$$.

The Country Hearth (530-279-2280) Main Street, Cedarville. Open for breakfast, lunch, and dinner daily. Big country-style portions of pastries, meat, and burgers make this a local favorite. Dinners are accompanied by classical music and candlelight. $–$$.

Plumas and North Sierra Counties

✂ ♿ ♈ **Longboards Bar and Grill** (530-836-1305; plumaspinesgolf.com) Plumas Pines Golf Resort, 402 Poplar Valley Road, Graeagle. Open for breakfast, lunch, and dinner. Italian fare with views of both the golf course and the forested mountains bring locals and tourists out for risotto with Gorgonzola, rack of lamb, and elk with polenta and raspberry demi-glaze. The stone wall and fireplace add a lodge-like ambiance, especially in winter. Reservations recommended for dinner. Breakfast and lunch: $–$$. Dinner: $$–$$$$.

♿ **Moon's Restaurant** (530-283-0765) 497 Lawrence, Quincy. Open for dinner, call for seasonal hours. Locals love this casual, yet elegant eatery, where you can get a slew of California cuisine. Popular items include Mushrooms St. Thomas and Steak Diane. I go for the pizza. Reservations recommended. $$$–$$$$.

✂ ♿ **Morning Thunder Café** (530-283-0765) 557 Lawrence, Quincy. Open for breakfast and lunch daily. Quite the bohemian espresso joint here in the Lost Sierras. Fluffy wheat pancakes, burgers, and salads bring out the lumberjacks and hippies. $.

✂ ♿ ♈ **Pangaea Pub** (530-283-0426; pangaeapub.com) 461 Main Street, Quincy. Open 11–9 Monday through Friday. Vegetarians head here for enlightened organic fare like tempeh burritos, smoothies, and sushi. Everyone else comes for the live music, art gallery, coffee, and altogether hip mountain vibe. The aunt and her niece who own this café go out of their way to deliver farm-fresh food in a casual, unpretentious environment. $–$$.

✂ ♿ ♈ **Peninsula Grill** (530-596-3538; gambonispeninsulagrill.com) 401 Peninsula Drive, Lake Almanor. Open Monday through Saturday 5–9 in summer and Tuesday through Saturday 5–9 the rest of the year. Locals come on Wednesday for sushi night in the off-season. No matter when you come, this is probably the best restaurant in the area. Enjoy everything from tuna rolls to baby back ribs. Reservations recommended. $$.

✴ Entertainment

Ⓨ **Longboards Bar and Grill** See *Eating Out.*

Ⓨ **Pangaea Pub** See *Eating Out.*

Ⓨ **Peninsula Grill** See *Eating Out.*

✴ Selective Shopping

Antiques abound in the eastern mountains, with finds ranging from the 1880s to the 1950s. Explore Main Street in Chester for the majority of shops (often located in historic buildings). If you follow the **Beckwourth Trail** (CA 70), you'll pass through the historic towns of Beckwourth. Portola, Blairsden, Graeagle, and Quincy, where you can score some great finds.

In Chester the **B&B Booksellers** on Main Street makes a good stop to find another book; and in Quincy, check out **Epilog Books** on Main for new and used titles, and **Quincy Natural Foods** for some spiritual reads.

✴ Seasonal Events

July: **High Sierra Music Festival** (highsierramusic.com) Quincy. For three days music, camping, dancing, yoga, games, and arts come together in the mountains to celebrate the summer. Major musicians like Bob Weir, Built to Spill, and Michael Franti have played this event. Book your tickets and accommodations early—it is a popular festival.

Fandango Days Celebration (530-233-4434) Alturas turns into a big western party the first weekend in July to celebrate its heritage with a parade, music, and a car show.

Lassen County Fair (530-257-4104) Susanville. Rides, food, music, and parades characterize this old western fair.

August: **The Last Frontier Fair** (530-279-2315) Cedarville. Head here for a real rodeo, country food, and live music.

Plumas Sierra County Fair (530-283-6272) Quincy. If you have never seen a livestock auction or tried a deep-fried Twinkie, you might want to do it here.

September: **Alturas Balloon Fest and Migratory Bird Festival** (530-233-4434) Alturas celebrates the aerial wonders of birds and balloons.

INDEX